P9-CJJ-857

DATE DUE

OC 15 '96			
JY 27 99			
AO 5 99			

DEMCO 38-296

Writing Ground Zero

WRITING GROUND

*Japanese Literature
and the
Atomic Bomb*

John Whittier Treat

The University of Chicago Press
Chicago & London

Riverside Community College
Library
4800 Magnolia Avenue
Riverside, California 92506

DEC   '95

PL 726.82 .H52 T74 1995

Treat, John Whittier.

Writing ground zero

John Whittier Treat is associate professor of Japanese at the University of Washington. He is the author of *Pools of Water, Pillars of Fire: The Literature of Ibuse Masuji*.

The University of Chicago Press, Chicago 60637
The University of Chicago Press, Ltd., London
© 1995 by The University of Chicago
All rights reserved. Published 1995
Printed in the United States of America
04 03 02 01 00 99 98 97 96 95   5 4 3 2 1

ISBN (cloth): 0-226-81177-8

Published with the generous assistance of The Japan Foundation.

Library of Congress Cataloging-in-Publication Data

Treat, John Whittier.
　　Writing ground zero : Japanese literature and the atomic bomb / John Whittier Treat.
　　　　p.　　cm.
　　Includes bibliographical references and index.
　　ISBN 0-226-81177-8
　　1. Japanese literature—20th century—History and criticism.　2. Hiroshima-shi (Japan)—History—Bombardment, 1945—Literature and the bombardment.　3. Nagasaki-shi (Japan)—History—Bombardment, 1945—Literature and the bombardment.　I. Title.
　　PL726.82.H52T74　1995
　　895.6'09358—dc20　　　　　　　　　　　94-18403
　　　　　　　　　　　　　　　　　　　　　　CIP

♾ The paper used in this publication meets the minimum requirements of the American National Standard for Information Sciences—Permanence of Paper for Printed Library Materials, ANSI Z39.48-1984.

Calligraphy on title page: The Sino-Japanese character *gen* includes among its meanings that of "original," as in the word *genten*, "starting point" or "genesis." In the related sense of "indivisible," however, it is also found in the newer compound *genshi*, "atomic": for both nuclear scientist and postnuclear poet, it is the writing of ground zero.

In memory of my friends who have not survived.

Contents

Preface   ix

A Note on the Illustrations   xix

Introduction   1

One

1   Atrocity into Words   25

2   Genre and Post-Hiroshima Representation   45

3   The Three Debates   83

Two

4   Hara Tamiki and the Documentary Fallacy   125

5   Poetry Against Itself   155

6   Ōta Yōko and the Place of the Narrator   199

7   Ōe Kenzaburō: Humanism and Hiroshima   229

8   Ibuse Masuji: Nature, Nostalgia, Memory   261

9   Nagasaki and the Human Future   301

10   The Atomic, the Nuclear, and the Total: Oda Makoto   351

11   Concluding Remarks: And Then   397

Notes   403

References   447

Index   475

Preface

Japanese present at the nuclear bombing of Hiroshima or Nagasaki and who subsequently wrote of their experience commonly preface their accounts with a historical qualification. Each tells us, as if that place both permits and curbs the words to follow, where he was on the morning of August 6 or 9, 1945. This "where" is expressed in a measure of how far from, or close to, ground zero the writer stood or sat or slept. "Two kilometers" for one survivor, "two and a quarter" for another; and as one atomic-bomb writer recalls of his middle school class, "the difference of one's place in line was also a difference in the effects of the radiation."[1]

The distinction of less than a few feet is a detail the significance of which many of us who were not there may easily fail to note. In fact, it is of literally vital significance, for as with Dante's circles, to be in one rather than another can mean the difference of which of the fires we are to endure. The hell of Hiroshima, says a character in Takahashi Kazumi's novel *The Melancholy Faction*

(Yūutsu naru tōha, 1965), was a different kind of hell. No sin condemns one to languish there, only the collective mistake of having lived next door to each other.[2] Yet just whose door was next to whose mattered mortally. As one report noted in an antiseptic technical idiom, "The severity of early stage atomic bomb injury was roughly in inverse proportion to the distance between the site of exposure and the hypocenter."[3] Norman Cousins once said more tersely and thus more memorably of Nagasaki, a city whose hills concentrated the bomb's power in some neighborhoods while sparing others, "today all life is reckoned according to the side of the mountain you were on when the bomb fell."[4]

The geographical difference that determined living from dying is also a difference that determines meaning. First, there is meaning in language, as greater distance from the silent epicenter parallels the greater ease with which the victim of nuclear war can speak of the fact of that day; and second, there is meaning in the multitude of other ways the survivor of atrocity may seek to reconcile experience, memory, guilt, and rage with—and against—those inherited cultural systems of mediation incongruent with such lived reality. As an American army general who observed the Alamogordo test of the first atomic bomb from the safety of a bunker noted, "Words are inadequate tools. . . . It had to be witnessed to be realized."[5]

My own standpoint is safer still. I am not a *hibakusha*, or "bomb victim," of either Hiroshima or Nagasaki. I am not a Japanese, nor was I even alive at the time of the Second World War. But it is impossible for me to approach the topic of the atomic bombings entirely innocent of a cultural and historical, if not literally personal, involvement. As long as I or anyone else identifies my work as that of an American, my position is conditioned by and implicated in the distinctly American and unprecedented use of nuclear weaponry. But there is another reason why none of our readings, interpretations, and arguments about atomic-bomb literature cannot ever be conducted from a point of view free of profound risk. I take the term hibakusha to have two common meanings within the context of Japanese writings on Hiroshima and Nagasaki. First, of course, it refers to anyone who was physically present in either of the cities when they were bombed, or shortly thereafter. But it also refers to all those who relate to Hiroshima and Nagasaki on account of birth (as the child of a hibakusha, for example, or as an absent native of either city), family, nationality, or other contingent affinity. As more than one observer of the cynical truth has pointed out, all Japanese were potential hibakusha since any city—as long as it was a Japanese city—could have been targeted.[6]

Although it may be suspect for an American to do so, I propose that this concept of the potential hibakusha now has to extend to everyone alive today in any region of the planet targeted by warhead-carrying missiles, or, in our newly fragmented post-Cold War world, any region contested by any of the rapidly expanding "nuclear club" of nations. This is in effect to say all of us, although unlike the survivors of Hiroshima and Nagasaki, who had no credible warning, we have been "prepared" for what lies ahead. I am part of the American generation that rehearsed its dive beneath classroom desks at the wail of the siren. In October 1962 I was taken out of school by a mother who did not want to be left alone with her children while her husband took his annual hunting trip: all of us went together to the far reaches of northern Maine, where perhaps we would have survived had Kennedy wagered wrong. Back home, there were those shelves of dusty canned goods in the basement, as I am sure were stockpiled (a word whose comforting resonance was owed its Cold War usage) by millions of other suburban, middle-class families.

Today, every reader of this book inhabits a time when old countries with newly acquired nuclear capabilities hint of their resolve to use them, and when new countries with older ones diplomatically trade their neighbors' fate for their own economic needs; when Japan, of all nations, now threatens to renounce the Nuclear Nonproliferation Treaty. You and I are surely "survivors" in the sense that we are living while most of 1945 Hiroshima and Nagasaki is not, but we are only *provisionally* alive until that day when nuclear disarmament is a fact of life rather than a cover for a high-technology rearmament, and thus until the deep sense of contingency which currently informs our cultures is replaced with assurances of a future. It is in this sense, the post-August 6th sense, that my and our standpoint is actually less secure than that American general's was in July 1945.[7]

I write cautiously and uncomfortably as an American, as a citizen of the first and to date only nation to execute what an international science enabled: nuclear war. This means I cannot move through Japan or interpret its literature without associating my national identity historically with this wilful violence. I recognize that this association produces both a guilt and a responsibility, and I hope that nowhere in this study have I forsaken either, or here announced such hopes with insincere humility. But I do mean this project to be anything but objective: it is from the start a simultaneous study of a historical subject and a personal subjectivity, the latter of which I am sure most of my readers will have to explore for themselves before what I say will make its most radical sense.

I can illustrate my point here by sharing an anecdote. It is common in prefaces such as this to acknowledge everyone who has been of assistance in the research, and eventually I will do so. But first I must state that my attempts to speak with literary scholars, Japanese and otherwise, on the topic of the atomic bombings were met on occasion with passive or even militant resistance. I sometimes had the impression I was reviving some issue that has long

lain dormant, a question better ignored than addressed in all its current implications. I have been told that atomic-bomb writers are not representative of
postwar Japanese people in general, who are reputed to be "grateful that the
war ended," as if such honest and entirely plausible emotions preclude sympathy for, or even interest in, those Hiroshima and Nagasaki writers who may
wish to express something other than thanks.[8] Americans of the generation
that participated in the postwar occupation of Japan have told me, despite
never having read any atomic-bomb literature, that it is surely "garbage" full of
anti-American invective. Of course these are not everyone's reactions, but they
are frequent enough that I raise the issue here of just how far any of us can
proceed with a study of atomic-bomb literature before the unresolved and even
unspoken issues of history overwhelm how we will choose to interpret and
thus commit to a specific historical understanding. At what point, in other
words, does our own point of view, be it that of a postwar Japanese or American, preclude the possibility of our reading not so much intelligently as honestly, without foreclosing all the historical and ethical implications of the
genre?

I am not sure of the answer, or at least of how much I dare to make of my
intuition that those implications are quite fundamental ones. But I would like
to think that I have come to be somewhat sensitive to the issues of academic
work and its real-world consequences. It is one thing to claim, as I occasionally
will, that Hiroshima and Nagasaki are names that represent both events that
split human history into halves—the first in which our survival as a species had
nothing to do with our will to survive, and a second in which that is *all* it has
to do with—and events that signify a continuum of that same human history,
a history progressively knowledgeable of and "rational" in its will to end itself.
Again, it is one thing to claim that this contradiction is what most accurately
if problematically characterizes atomic-bomb literature. It is, however, quite
another thing to allow such interpretations to release us from the still cogent
obligation to address just what it is that makes Hiroshima and Nagasaki events
of which we are both the victims and perpetrators. Consequently, I state now
at the outset that I do not intend to convert such loaded words as "suffering"
or such newly weighty academic key words as "marginality" into a basis for my
own claims to any privileged insight. Rather my intent, if there is any beyond
the desire to introduce an important history of both a controversial "nuclear"
literary practice and its often even more controversial authors to English-
reading audiences, is to intervene in the practice of criticism whenever it turns
the traces of our barbarity into, as Murray Krieger has defined the work of
theory, "words about words about words."

Edward Said, a critic who has long and admirably sought to navigate safely
between the Scylla of criticism as blindly abstruse and the Charybdis of criticism as clumsily reductive has described his own working assumptions thus:

My position is that texts are worldly, to some degree they are events, and, even when they appear to deny it, they are nonetheless a part of the social world, human life, and of course the historical moments in which they are located and interpreted. . . . The realities of power and authority . . . are the realities that make texts possible, that deliver them to their readers, that solicit the attention of critics.[9]

There are of course ample grounds on which to contest Said's, and my own, belief in the pre-discursivity of a "social world" or even a "human life," but the critique against which I wish to offer a pre-emptive defense is implied in the first question that may naturally pose itself at this juncture: why *literary* texts at all, if we are in such danger of reifying a horrible history, be it that of Said's colonialism or my nuclearism, into conveniently acculturated and packaged "interpretations"? Why not leave the project of detailing and propagating the history of the atomic bombings in Japan to, quite properly, the historians? Or better still, the scientists? Especially in light of my provocative step of denying these literary texts any special, i.e., exclusively "literary," status?

There are at least two apologies for this, apart from the important fact that it is writers of stories, and not of studies, upon whom hibakusha themselves have most relied in order to comprehend what happened. First I would assert, along lines frequently heard today, that the speech-act of describing a text as "literary" is always a self-reflexive gesture, i.e., something which in its taxonomical exercise codifies us as much as we it. If, for example, we dismiss "atomic-bomb literature" as oxymoronic because we believe that literature must take as its object more "universal" themes, we indicate our "naming" selves as what produces, ironically, the oxymoronic contradiction, not the two terms "atomic-bomb" and "literature" themselves. The study of atomic-bomb literature, unlike a study of the atomic bomb, is an inquiry into the interpretative processes of the human subject in culture maneuvering against one monumental, irrefutably objective fact: that policide, now perhaps genocide or even, as philosopher Berel Lang and historian Michael Geyer put it, "omnicide," is a standard military and political threat.[10] I believe that the interpretation of *events* and interpretation of *texts* are intertwined; if "understanding Hiroshima" must mean to us non-hibakusha understanding the narratives of Hiroshima, then we stand most squarely and precisely where literary studies today make their most cogent and potentially explanatory contribution not just to human knowledge but to human accountability. Japanese critic Kuroko Kazuo has argued the Hiroshima version of Said's literary "worldliness":

To think about "atomic-bomb literature" is to be made acutely aware that "literature" proceeds with the world not as its telos but as its fundamental condition. That is to say, insofar as "language" locates its basis in actuality, however much it may be "fictionalized" a literary work performs its own role in the actual world. The very existence of an atomic-bomb fiction leaves us with no alternative but to recognize this.[11]

In quite another context Jonathan Culler has claimed that "contemporary work in literary criticism seems to reach its greatest intensity when dealing with a theoretically defined problem that explores the relationship between the literary and the non-literary."[12] But for many of the survivor-writers of Hiroshima and Nagasaki, the problem is not exhausted after we consider the formal or aesthetic issues of where the literary and non-literary meet to clash in language, but lingers on to ask what themes in language can be accommodated into human community as literary, opposed to those that cannot. "Thematic criticism" may be a term which sounds hopelessly old or, worse, schoolish; but what stands to be recuperated here is theme as agenda, agenda for human energy, imagination, work, and mission.

Although it is clear from the language I am using here that I want atomic-bomb literary criticism to remain as engaged, and morally and politically enabling, as atomic-bomb literature itself, one question I will refrain from asking is whether any one work is "good," or at least good in the belletristic way we may believe we can intuit. While of course some works of atomic-bomb literature are more polished, clever, or generally affective than others, none of those qualities carries quite the sense of moral approbation as does "good." Critic Hasegawa Ken once ruled it a "well-known truth that only a good life can produce good literature," but we should not be prepared to dismiss writing by atomic-bomb survivors simply because we are unwilling to substitute our own lives for theirs.[13] Moreover, I want to refrain from making the phrase "atomic-bomb literature" any more possibly oxymoronic by speaking of "good atomic-bomb literature," and thus indulge a pleasure at its existence. I want to replace such valuative criticism with ones that might lead to more mindful readings of ourselves as citizens in the postmodern, post-Hiroshima world. If it seems that I am making preposterously ambitious claims for the chapters that follow, I hope the reader will credit these claims less to immodesty on my part than to a sincere desire to make these stories, poems, and novels perform the work I unapologetically believe their authors intended for them.

The second defense I wish to make for a study of atomic-bomb literature hinges not on how we may now define literature, but how literature itself leads us to another term with a controversial referent: history. I will state now that I do not believe that literature and historiographic writing have equally fragile claims on referential truth. Otherwise, why would so many works of atomic-bomb literature—the testimonial memoir, the documentary poem, the diary-novel—aspire, even if only rhetorically, to "historical" modes of representation over the more imaginatively conceived "literary" modes? The power that a work of atomic-bomb literature holds over us, as opposed to a work of atomic-bomb "science-fiction," that genre of American writing so oddly popular despite our striking lack of a real-life atomic-bomb literature, is that we know that Hiroshima and Nagasaki happened; that atomic-bomb literature is literal, objective, and referential in just those ways that modern historiography aims to be. This is a "knowledge" which has also complicated the reception of atomic-bomb literature as "literature," precisely because—to begin with—it is so unimaginable in an age where imagination is crucial to our sense of what constitutes the literary. But the works discussed here are works that reveal at every moment the choice of a style, a word, a language that betrays the leap the imagination some survivor-writer made on our behalf. Writing we read with an awareness of such generous imagination permits an empathy, an "intersubjectivity" that produces an individual agency we find enabling. We read these subjective forms that to varying degrees insist upon their objective statuses because it is there, in the working of the creative imagination so frequently repressed in the rhetoric of atomic-bomb literature, that we can discern not how the "facts" of the bombings will be transmitted from hibakusha to non-hibakusha, from the wartime generation to the postwar generation, but how the individual and collective imagining of the events circumscribed within those facts will give them their credibility, and necessary terror. There is, after all, included within the moral dimensions of the atrocities a conceptual mapping of those same dimensions alongside historical experience.

We study atomic-bomb literature, in other words, not so much to "know" what physically happened in Hiroshima and Nagasaki—the publications of the United States Strategic Bombing Survey will tell you that much—as to give us the psychological means to act aware of that knowledge. And to act is always the implicit appeal of a literature only possible because of modern atrocity, even if that appeal has gone so often unheeded. Hiroshima poet, critic, and political activist Kurihara Sadako—made a hibakusha four kilometers from ground zero—has asked, "Just how has the idea that writers write in the privacy of their studies come to make literature something empty, and without a sense of the real?"[14] The rhetoric of her own question points to exactly the questions that atomic-bomb literature, and this study of that literature, pose for our theories of what we are capable of writing and of what such writing is itself capable.

My work on this project has been aided by financial support from the Japan Foundation, the Northeast Asia Council of the Association of Asian Studies, the Graduate Research Fund of the University of Washington, and the Japan Endowment of the University of Washington. I am indebted to the late Ikeda Tadashi of Aoyama Gakuin University for his hospitality while I was a visiting scholar at his institution. His student Suzuki Kazuko's enthusiasm for novelist

Fukunaga Takehiko led me to read him more carefully than I might have otherwise; similarly, so did that of my own student, Davinder Bhowmik, for Hayashi
Kyōko's writings. I am grateful to writers Itō Mariko, Kurihara Sadako, Ozu
Kunsō, and the staff of the *Chūgoku shimbun* newspaper for their hospitality
while I was in Hiroshima; and to the other bomb survivors and activists who
made me welcome there. Peter Schwenger, whose own work on the nuclear
sublime in literature has been an inspiration to me,[15] read this book while it was
still a manuscript, as did another, but unidentified, reader for the University of
Chicago Press. Alan G. Thomas of the University of Chicago Press encouraged
me from the time I first made his acquaintance, and I thank him for that as well
as for his guidance as an editor. Richard Allen, as copyeditor, both improved
my writing and clarified my thinking.

The reader I have had to take most seriously, however, is Alan Tansman.
As a scholar of modern Japanese literature who is also a Jew, Alan reacted to
many assertions quoted in or made by this book with a mixture of empathy
and anger that sometimes confirmed but sometimes challenged their truthful-
ness. He also recognized, quite correctly, that my own identification with some
of the writers I discuss precludes possible ways out of the literary and ethical
problems I insist this genre poses. I am grateful for Alan's honesty, which I
know could not have been easy; but I also want to say to him that any solution
to the problem of culture in the nuclear age must depend on its own set of
impassioned sympathies.

I am not the first academic or critic to approach the subject of Japanese
atomic-bomb literature, and I want to acknowledge those whose work precedes, informs, and provokes my own. In Japan Kurihara Sadako, the late Nagaoka Hiroyoshi, and Ōe Kenzaburō persistently kept the issues raised by hibakusha writings before the reading public; Kuroko Kazuo, with whom I all
too recently began to collaborate, today continues to press the logic of those
same issues to new conclusions for modern history, contemporary literary studies, and international anti-nuclear activism. In the United States Robert Jay
Lifton's pioneering *Death in Life: The Survivors of Hiroshima,* and *Japanese A-Bomb
Literature: An Annotated Bibliography* compiled by Wayne P. Lammers and Osamu
Masaoka, argued that those same writings were worth reading by the English-
speaking public. Indeed, a book such as this would be of much less use without
the growing number of English translations of Japanese atomic-bomb literature. Readers will find easily obtained translations of many of the works of
poetry, fiction, and drama to which I refer cited in the bibliography.

My most personal debt is to Douglas Allen Lind, who made the depressing
decade in which I conducted this depressing research not just bearable but in
fact happy beyond all expectation.

Finally I express my special gratitude to Elie Wiesel, whose faculty seminar
on the Book of Job at the Whitney Humanities Center at Yale in 1982 lent the

initial insight that occasioned this project. In a lesson as true of Japanese atomic-bomb literature as of the writings of inappropriate violence anywhere, Wiesel taught that Job's torment has an illogic that is purposefully inexplicable. To Bildad's assertion that God would neither reject the upright nor "grasp the hand of evildoers" (8:20), Job replied, " 'Tis all the same. Therefore I say, 'Guiltless as well as wicked he destroys' " (9:22).[16] A god who does not distinguish between his own judgments, like a war that no one can survive, is at root unfathomable. Yet this failure to comprehend indicates no careless flaw within the text. It is indeed that work's very nature, and for a precious reason to which we must tightly cling: as Elie Wiesel said in New Haven while surely thinking of a town in Poland, should our records of suffering ever become wholly familiar to us, they will make sense of what we must let remain senseless.

A Note on the Illustrations

While this study is concerned specifically with Japanese literary responses to Hiroshima and Nagasaki, a few examples of drawings, paintings, prints, sculpture, photographs (including a film still), and a page from a comic book have been added in order to suggest, if only minimally, the variety of responses in visual media as well. As in the case of literature, much of this art (including that featured on this book's cover) is the legacy of amateur as well as professional artists, and it may be important to keep in mind that the technical naivete of much of that art is testimony to the terror that one can imagine inspired it. For a comprehensive survey of atomic-bomb art and photography in Japan, see the six-volume *Hiroshima and Nagasaki: The Atomic Bombings as Seen through Photographs and Artwork* (Hiroshima Nagasaki gembaku shashin kaiga shūsei, 1993) edited by Ienaga Saburō, Odagiri Hideo, and Kuroko Kazuo.

Part Two of this book opens with aerial photographs of Hiroshima and Nagasaki taken shortly after the bombings. The locations of where the best-known survivor-writers were on the mornings of August 6th and 9th are indicated for the reader's reference, as well as out of my own appreciation for how fateful our positions can be, and how decisive the bearings of a viewpoint always are for the history one is consigned to tell.

It was not dying: everybody died

Randall Jarrell, "Losses"

Introduction

Since the destruction of two cities through the use of nuclear weapons in August 1945, some of us have the memory—and the rest of us, our imagination of that memory—of how the world may end. To "remember" the future may seem a contradiction, but of course it is always the past that governs the terms of our anterior historical speculation. What is different now, in the late twentieth century, is that we possess a past which implies a potential and even probable end to human history itself. The atomic bombs that leveled Hiroshima and Nagasaki were the distant forebears of the bombs that now hold civilian populations hostage throughout the northern hemisphere, fully three-quarters of humanity; and the Third World is acquiring the same capacity for collective suicide. Scientists' warnings of a nuclear winter following an exchange of missiles, if accurate, mean that no one, no matter how unaligned his politics or deep his shelter, will survive.

This is a reality of contemporary life to which most of us are oddly accus-

1

tomed, even indifferent. Nuclear annihilation, much on the order of an earth-quake, is a calamity we intellectually regard as possible but emotionally refuse to believe in. As a character in Iida Momo's Hiroshima novel *An American Hero* (Amerika no eiyū, 1965) observes, human beings can get used to anything: the dead in Hiroshima and Nagasaki numbered in "six figures," but "now we talk in terms of 'ten.'"[1] State strategists still argue with Orwellian logic that the exis-tence of nuclear weapons in fact guarantees they will never be used. Here is a risky bet on which to stake the future, as Europeans who survived the Second World War point out. "Now mankind as a whole can be wiped out by men," wrote Karl Jaspers. "It has not merely become possible for this to happen; on purely rational reflection it is probable that it will happen."[2] When Nobel lau-reate Czeslaw Milosz wrote with equally dark insight that "if something exists in one place, it will exist everywhere,"[3] his "it" referred to totalitarianism; to the survivors of the world's first two atomic attacks, the antecedent might be instead that instant of power that destroyed two cities and, to borrow the words of fellow European Albert Einstein, "our former ways of thinking."[4] Hi-roshima and Nagasaki were in this sense the first two targets in a nuclear war which has yet to be decisively resolved, and our present survival depends upon that irresolution. The welcome end to the Cold War has not meant a renuncia-tion of the deadly technology it spawned—as Margaret Thatcher put it, "nu-clear weapons can't be uninvented"[5]—but instead only a splintered posthege-monic political world in which nations whose new names we can hardly spell also possess it, or soon will.[6]

It is the survivors of these original targets who have the memory of a likely future in which all human experience concludes, and it is the writers among them who have supplied us with the metaphors we require to imaginatively join them. Japanese writers alone have commenced the writing of what would be, should Jaspers or Milosz prove prophetic, the final theme of literature— "final" because it is a theme beyond which there are none, if only because there will be no more readers. At the same time atomic-bomb literature, begun in the last days of the Second World War, can never come to a conclusion since no one will outlast nuclear war long enough to describe it.

As befits the final theme of writing, however, atomic-bomb literature nonetheless describes itself within a closure. It leads to no sequels. (Martin Amis punned in the introduction to his own collection of nuclear fiction: "The A-bomb is a Z-bomb.")[7] Its characters—one only very occasionally says "he-roes"—who are miraculously alive past the first paragraph do not have lives that continue beyond the last page; the last page is truly the last. The "final theme" is an idea that objects to the notion of "theme" altogether, implying as it does a plurality of other stories when in fact there will be, once the missile exchange begins, only one. Or, as is perhaps more likely, none at all.

One survivor of Hiroshima, Sugimoto Naojirō, later recalled that "it offered a dark view that made one think of the end of the world."[8] The realization of what Hiroshima inaugurated did not solely come, however, from surveying the damage afterwards. Tokyo, Osaka, and Nagoya had been effectively destroyed by conventional bombing, so much so that Secretary of War Henry Stimson had worried that there not might be any target worth using the atomic-bomb on once it was perfected.[9] Rather, that realization involved a dumbfounded amazement over how the damage could have been so unexpected in its delivery, so brief in duration, so inexplicable in its power. Effects overwhelmed causes, eclipsed comprehension, handicapped meaning. Testimonies offered by ordinary victims, as well as by the professional writers who are the principal subject of this study, commonly ponder the same questions. Can the causes—the "reasons"—be traced? Understanding achieved? Value restored? If so, to what end? Witnessing a nuclear attack is already an "end," and some of us have witnessed one. The literature that is the final theme of literature is one which, in the fashion of Sisyphus, struggles in vain to succeed—to overcome the contradictions implicit in a form of writing that would give a beginning, middle, and conclusion to events defying such narrative domestication.

But like Sisyphus, Hiroshima and Nagasaki writers have not desisted in the attempt. For half a century now these writers have experimented, spurred by an urgency often born of fading health as well as memory, with ways of telling us and themselves what happened in August 1945. Nearly all these writers have been Japanese, and their works directed towards a Japanese audience. Atomic-bomb literature—as opposed to "nuclear literature," the literature of a world harassed by inestimable megatonnage—remains a Japanese preserve. The Chernobyls of the world will presumably inspire their own books. But *gembaku*, or "atomic bomb," means more to the Japanese than just Hiroshima and Nagasaki. It means, for example, President Harry Truman's threat made at a press conference on November 30, 1950 to use nuclear weapons on the neighboring Korean peninsula; it means the death of Japanese fisherman Kuboyama Aikichi, widely believed to have been due to the radioactive fallout from an American test of a hydrogen device in the Bikini atoll on March 1, 1954;[10] it means the rumored illegal presence of nuclear weapons on Japanese soil. In other words, atomic-bomb literature is already a literature of the nuclear age.

Nowhere is this truer than in Japan. As recently as 1985, it was claimed that in Hiroshima one out of every seven people is a hibakusha; one of every six in Nagasaki. One of every three hundred Japanese nationwide is believed to be a hibakusha, and numbers of victims are to be found in South Korea and the United States.[11] This means not only that Japanese are historically more sensitive to nuclear issues than the rest of the world—an obvious point—but also that perhaps less obviously they have been the most astute observers of how contemporary thought must be revised in light of the ability we now possess to eliminate ourselves. Ōe Kenzaburō, one of the principal architects of the theory of post-Hiroshima civilization, has written—perhaps parochially, perhaps not—that he believes it is the Japanese who, after the unprecedented events of Hiroshima and Nagasaki, have had to reflect most on the possibility that the human species may not last into the next century.[12] This is a reflection that illuminates and questions the premises upon which culture is organized, just as the news that one is terminally ill causes an individual to regard his life with both a clarity and irony heretofore unknown. The results of such intellectualization by Japanese has not yet been recognized as parallel to other discourses of "discontinuity" that have arisen elsewhere in the world as the consequence of twentieth-century history. The literature of the Nazi camps was from its inception international because the camps themselves were. Survivors' accounts of the Holocaust eventually appeared in all the languages of Europe. Moreover, there has never been a Japanese counterpart to Anne Frank's diary, a work disseminated among school children the world over, including Japan. Instead, the Japanese experience of, and the varied responses to, their own catastrophes in Hiroshima and Nagasaki have not, by and large, been disseminated outside of their own language and geography.

Naturally, the radical impact of the use of nuclear weapons on human history has not gone unnoticed by non-Japanese. From scientists such as Einstein, who gravely noted on national television the day plans were announced to manufacture hydrogen bombs that "annihilation of any life on earth has been brought within the range of technical possibilities," through writers such as Sartre and Brecht and finally to contemporary philosophers as different as Günter Anders and Jacques Derrida,[13] important voices in the West have understood how the last premises of the world have had to be reexamined. Perhaps it was more easily intuited in the West, where those possessed of a critical awareness had long been struggling with the breakdown of modernity and its certainties. Japan, so committed since the mid-nineteenth century to an Enlightenment faith in science and its promised progress, found itself betrayed by the use of nuclear weapons in a way that Western thinkers, already made cynical by one world war, may not have been. Nonetheless, it is in Japan where that same breakdown has been most persistently pondered by writers whose lives have been its literal cost; it is in Japan, where the experience of modernity is of more recent vintage and perhaps of less defining moment, that the lessons of that breakdown have been more easily heeded.

There has always been a tension—sometimes explicit, sometimes ambiguous—in both the original and critical literature of the atomic bomb between the uniqueness of Hiroshima and Nagasaki, on the one hand, and, on the other, their connection with the ethical and technological rationalism that made the bombings possible. This tension surfaces, for instance, in any attempt to describe the atrocities in Europe and those in Japan in the same language, or indeed with the question of whether to treat the latter as an atrocity in the first place. It is not simply an issue of the scale of the violence. The physical damage in the two cities is widely and accurately known. From early on it was quantified, measured, and given a price tag. The extent of the human damage, particularly in light of the delayed and subtle effects of exposure to radiation, has never been determined with equal accuracy, however. Those wishing to minimize it have claimed as few as 200,000 total casualties; those who would exaggerate say a half-million or more. By August 1992, 176,964 names had been carved into the granite cenotaph commemorating Hiroshima's dead, but that figure can only account for those victims whose bodies survived and whose identities were known. According to the July 25, 1952 issue of Hiroshima's daily newspaper, the *Chūgoku shimbun*, the total population within the city on August 6th was somewhere around 440,000; the paper goes on to report that bomb-related deaths had, by 1950, reached 282,000.[14] Figures for Nagasaki list 73,884—out of a population estimated at 270,000—dead by the end of 1945,[15] and 140,000 by 1950.[16]

It is important to remember that those figures—in any case always well over half the populations of both cities—date from before the onslaught of deaths from cancer, principally leukemia, among the fatally irradiated survivors. What sort of bomb, or any weapon, had ever had such an insidious, attenuated, lethal toll? One report of the damage (compiled in 1955, by which time rising cancer rates among hibakusha were being documented) answers:

> The atomic bomb instantly produced a temperature upwards of one half-million degrees. One ten-thousandth of a second later, a fireball with a radius of seventeen meters burned at a temperature of three hundred thousand degrees. At the same time this extraordinary fireball created in the atmosphere an intense shock wave resulting in unprecedented destructive power. The heat from the ball itself wantonly ignited both human beings and buildings. . . . In addition the Hiroshima atomic bomb produced tertiary, and its most terrible, destruction through radiation.[17]

Statistics, even those available today, do not describe the damage with any greater finality than earlier ones. The aftereffects of nuclear war continue to surprise. The power of this weapon to exert itself over time, and into generations not even born at the time of the war, has had a thorough impact on the cultures of the cities where it was used. As a result of the initial damage then compounded by persistent aftereffects, all of Hiroshima and much of Nagasaki (whose topography, abetted with a slightly inaccurate targeting, spared many parts of the city) were eliminated not only as collections of "human beings and buildings" but as communities, as functioning social entities. The comparison is clear, for example, with the fire bombing of Tokyo on March 10, 1945. Though over three hundred B-29s dropped more than 1,700 tons of incendiary bombs, and though this assault resulted in the conflagration of forty percent of the capital, the deaths of one hundred thousand, and the rendering homeless of another million,[18] Tokyo remained largely spared. Only nine percent of its population was killed, as compared to fifty-nine percent in Hiroshima.[19] Once the bombing was over, fires extinguished, and the population traumatized, the intended damage was done. It was finite and imaginable and finally within the generally accepted limits of war. Hiroshima and Nagasaki were different. "Only the color of the sea," reads the first line of one Hiroshima memoir, "remained unchanged."[20] As Brigadier General Thomas F. Farrell, commander of the first U.S. Army investigating team to enter Hiroshima, remarked, "This isn't a bomb at all. The word 'bomb' carries with it a completely inaccurate picture of what this thing does."[21] Writer Toyoshima Yoshio noted in 1949:

> Some one hundred and twenty Japanese cities suffered heavy damage from air raids, but all with the exception of Hiroshima and Nagasaki were bombed with conventional and incendiary weapons. Regardless of how intensively or heavily these cities were bombarded, direct damage was limited in area and resultant fires took some time to spread. Yet the atomic bomb, with a single blast in a single moment, turned broad expanses into ruins.[22]

The Nagasaki writer Kawakami Sōkun, who lost his mother and his two sisters in the bombing, describes in his 1956 story "The Survivors" (Seizonsha) just what Toyoshima's contrast of a "single blast in a single moment" with the "broad expanses" it wrought meant for those there to witness it:

> Everyone had thought it was his own home, his own company, his own school, his own factory that had sustained a direct hit. When they had picked themselves up to crawl out of the clouds of dust and debris, in the dim light they learned that everything had been destroyed for as far as their eyes could see. . . . In the days that followed until they were told that this had been an atomic bomb, their experiences would teach them that an event so massive that it is impossible to grasp either its source or its power can indeed occur at any time. The many logical explanations they would later hear could not completely wipe out this insight. This is why those areas subjected to an atomic attack are able to insist upon their difference from places that suffered any other kind of air raid. (195)

It is finally not the scale of the damage in Hiroshima and Nagasaki that has made it difficult, or easy, to acknowledge them as atrocities.[23] It is, first, how seemingly spontaneous such damage can appear—and thus how easily beyond imagination—and, second and much later, it is the debate over whether such violence as this was "appropriate" or not. It was, apologists argue, licensed in the typical conduct of a war by one sovereign state against another—as if Germany's drive to sweep Europe clean of Jews is disallowable only because the Jews did not constitute a political nation. This question of "appropriateness" is argued in other ways, too. The bombings of Hiroshima and Nagasaki were justified, say some, because that specific level of violence was needed to end the war. What, one wonders, would have been "too much" violence to end the war? But even accepting the terms of this argument leads to the conclusion that the violence visited upon these cities was wanton, gratuitous, and thus atrocious. When Tokyo was bombed in March 1945, the case might have been made that Japan was still a potent enemy of the United States, and that Tokyo was the nerve center of its war machine. By August, however, the war was over and responsible leaders in both nations knew it. In its 1946 report "The Political Target Under Assault," the United States Strategic Bombing Survey concluded:

> Based on a detailed investigation of all the facts and supported by the testimony of the surviving Japanese leaders involved, it is the Survey's opinion that certainly prior to 31 December 1945, and in all probability prior to 1 November 1945, Japan would have surrendered even if the atomic bombs had not been dropped, even if Russia had not entered the war, and even if no invasion had been planned or contemplated.[24]

The much touted planned invasion of the Japanese home islands was never authorized beyond the planning stage, for by the summer of 1945 it was apparently not necessary. The dropping of the bomb was done for other than military reasons. Admiral William D. Leahy stated that "it is my opinion that the use of this barbarous weapon at Hiroshima and Nagasaki was of no material assistance in our war against Japan,"[25] and it is in light of such authoritative statements that revisionist historian Gar Alperovitz was able to conclude that the bomb was a "weapon of terror. . . . The only important question was how the bomb could be used . . . with the greatest psychological effect."[26] That effect, of course, was not intended solely for the Japanese, but for the world.

The atomic bombings were acts of mass and, according to some standards of international law, illegal violence. At the same time they were acts of official, state-sponsored terrorism propelled by the twin momenta of government bureaucracy and scientific curiosity. Dropping the bomb on Hiroshima was, according to Major General Leslie R. Groves, "basically a decision not to upset the existing plans."[27] The damage, given its scale and authority, destroyed more than lives and structures. It destroyed social organization, and with it much of what is used to define ourselves as human. The writer Nakano Kōji, attending a writers' conference in Europe as recently as 1982, recalls discussing the atomic bombings with his Western colleagues. Many, he was surprised to find, imagined the atomic bombs as merely bigger than other bombs: few really realized how qualitatively different the effects of nuclear weapons are. Nakano writes:

"No one knows as well as the Japanese that the impact of the atomic bomb was not just on human flesh, but that it had a profound effect on the soul of every survivor, however long he may provisionally survive."[28]

Personal lives, families, neighborhood affiliations—all were lost in cities attacked throughout the world in the Second World War. But in Hiroshima and Nagasaki, as in Europe's Jewish and Romany communities, the basic human ties between people were eliminated along with the economic fabric of the communities they inhabited. Hiroshima and Nagasaki demonstrated that the development of the atomic bomb could result in the effective liquidation of human beings living in integrated societies. As one group of Japanese researchers has written:

> A-bomb damage, then, is so complex and extensive that it cannot be reduced to any single characteristic or problem. It must be seen overall, as an interrelated array—massive physical and human loss, social disintegration, and psychological and spiritual shock—that affects all life and society. . . . Only then can one grasp the seriousness of its total impact on the biological systems that sustain life and health, on the social systems that enable people to live and work together, and on the mental functions that hold these two dimensions in integrated unity. The essence of atomic destruction lies in the totality of its impact on man and society and on all the systems that affect their mutual continuation.[29]

The terror of Hiroshima and Nagasaki lies not in the number of their dead. The fire bombings of Japan and Europe killed hundreds of thousands, too. What must now be accounted for in our definition of contemporary civilization is that the people of two cities were, and some still are, forced to live in a compromise state of both life and death at the same time; that that fate is a consequence of having barely survived a deliberate and methodical human plan to eliminate them; and that we today potentially face the same destiny. This has not necessary been understood any better by literary critics than by those of us in other professions. Frank Kermode, for instance, has flatly stated that it makes no difference if the apocalypse in literature is "nuclear bombs" or "armies in the sky."[30] Suga Hidemi, a prominent younger Japanese critic, has commented further that there is no difference between being killed by a nuclear weapon and dying in a traffic accident, an assertion nearly as calculatedly callous as that once told Cynthia Ozick by a fellow writer: "For me, the Holocaust and a corncob are the same."[31]

In all these cases, of course, there is all the difference. As long as any individual death is not the work of fellow individuals, or does not represent the end of an entire social organism, it cannot be an atrocity. What atrocity requires is scale, intention, and a ruthless logic; one of its best definitions occurs in remarks delivered by a hibakusha character in Takahashi's *The Melancholy Faction*:

> History couldn't care less. No matter what victims it claims as it moves forward, it keeps going ahead to cover its losses. Maybe that's the way it's got to be. But there's practically no distinction or rationality in who becomes a victim and who doesn't. Those that are going to be victims, become victims; and those that won't are merely lucky. No one can figure out why person A gets it between the eyes, or why person B is spared the same. (337)

In this, Hiroshima and Nagasaki starkly resemble other modern instances of mass murder. They most commonly recall, in a connection that must be made very carefully, the Nazi program for the extermination of various racial groups and subcultures. It has been common in writing on the Holocaust to add, perhaps for dramatic effect, "Hiroshima" to the litany of sites illustrating modern man's savage treatment of himself: the first atomic bombing, which like the death camps should be understood as a *model* for contemporary knowledge, is instead treated as *an optional example* of some other idea typically more colloquial and thus less unsettling (e.g., "man's inhumanity to man"). When Zygmunt Bauman observes that "if everything we know is like Auschwitz, then one can live with Auschwitz, and in many a case live reasonably well," he is warning us about the similes (including that "and" which connects Hiroshima to the names of our other modern crimes) we so casually employ.[32]

Still, the risks of conjunction should not deter us from contemplating history where it does present us with coincidences. The lists of both death camps and incinerated cities seem intended to establish the fact of a broad range of these instances and to indicate a universal complicity of mass state violence in the twentieth century. To an extent the inclusion of Hiroshima and Nagasaki among these acts is right and necessary. The words "Hiroshima" and "Auschwitz" (names that, as George Steiner says of "Holocaust," are "ritual, elevated, and therefore radically inappropriate"),[33] subsuming now as they do all other sites of mass murder, are terms that symbolize a reduction of history into two names no longer merely places but ideas, tropes of a new fact within the human condition: a condition compromised by our ability, in a matter of respective hours and seconds, to eliminate whole ghettos and cities of people.

As Robert Jay Lifton has noted, what Hiroshima and Auschwitz "share is their relationship to the contemporary technology of murder."[34] Berel Lang has convincingly shown that even if the genocide of the Jews and the potential omnicide of all the human race are not necessarily derived from the advances of science (though he does note that both Judeo-Christian thought and modern science are adept at explaining and justifying all "problematic events . . . whether as slight as a traffic accident or as large as a holocaust"), they do share a "material and conceptual connection."[35] The technology and science of which both of these men speak have been ones that Japanese, too, identify with ever greater alienation and dehumanization. Kurihara Sadako, in comparing Hiroshima to Auschwitz, has written that both represent the mechanized dehumanization of civilization: "Mankind stopped being mankind and completely became a machine."[36] Both Jews in Europe and Japanese in Hiroshima and Nagasaki were in some shared and significant sense technologically "processed" to death.[37] "His death," writes Hiroshima native Ishida Kōji of one boy in his story "Memory of a Cloud" (Kumo no kioku, 1959), "was extremely businesslike" (261). It is easier to kill people either by means of gas chambers—or even more so, with high aerial atomic bombings—precisely because of this alienated relationship between victim and victimizer, indeed between any one victim and any other. The alienation commenced long ago, perhaps as early as the guillotine ("that machine," as Foucault defines it, "for the production of rapid and discreet deaths"); but by August 1945, efficiency had increased exponentially along with the capacity for depersonalization. As the Hiroshima poet Ishihara Kichirō pointed out, what is truly terrifying about genocide is not that a great many people will die all at once, but that within dying there is no longer the possibility of an individual, private death—hence the pathetic and impossible plea of one novel's hibakusha for "a coffin, at the very least" for a dead relative about to be cast atop a mass pyre.[38] This is the ultimate demoralized result of the process of dehumanization now accepted as the tacit policy of governments.[39]

It is a process ethical as well as technological.[40] George Steiner ominously called Auschwitz the end product of a long "precise imagining," pointing not to so much our new scientific discoveries as to our desire, until recently checked by technological feebleness, to live in a world in which we and we alone exercise total power. Elie Wiesel in his book *One Generation After* argues that without Auschwitz "there would have been no Hiroshima . . . or attempts to dehumanize man by reducing him to a number, an object."[41] Japanese, too, have amply noted the threatening trend of "progress" culminating in the use of nuclear weapons. Ōta Yōko in her 1953 short story "Fireflies" (Hotaru) mentions the use of poison gas at Ypres within the context of her narrative of Hiroshima.[42] Writer and scholar of French literature Kamata Sadao, in one wide-ranging essay, looks at Hiroshima as the final outcome of a chain of events including Japanese atrocities in China and the Spanish Civil War as well as, inevitably, Auschwitz.[43]

Scientific advances seem only briefly to precede our ethical concessions to them. That the novelty, the efficiency, of the First World War machine gun so soon gave way to the atomic bomb points to how human society was both able to invent more powerful killing technologies and able to extend the moral as well as engineering limits to their use. Winston Churchill declared in the early 1950s, for example: "There is an immense gulf between the atomic and hydrogen bomb. . . . The atomic bomb, with all its terror, did not carry us outside the scope of human control or manageable events in thought or action, in peace or war. But . . . [with] the hydrogen bomb, the entire foundation of human affairs was revolutionized."[44]

Churchill's "immense gap" no longer exists; the terror of the hydrogen bomb's escalated potential for destruction has been naturalized and rendered "normal" for us. The pace of the secularization and abstraction of the relation of our technology to our imaginative uses of it has been accelerating for quite some time. The problem has been that science has long provided its own circular justification, and that is why it is not only ironic but unnerving to recall Truman's declaration of the atomic bomb as "the greatest achievement of organized science."

Even as early as the fall of 1945, when the full impact of what had happened could hardly have been gauged, Japanese writers were contemplating the changed relationship that would, after Hiroshima, obtain between science, ethics, and literature. Toyoshima Yoshio wrote in October of that year:

> The time has come for literature to engage science. Not to win a victory, but rather to assimilate in the name of man what science has wrought. The problem is not whether it actually can be assimilated or not. One can predict, given the present turn of events in the world, that there will be some people capable of comprehending what has happened. But what I wonder is whether those people will continue to be "human"; or whether, unable to survive as human, they will stumble into a tragic abyss.[45]

The issue for Toyoshima is one of literature's ability to prevent, or comply with, the shift in the terms of our humanity dictated by the "advances" of science which his own nation had most recently seen demonstrated. The effect was to produce among some Japanese thinkers a deep pessimism. In 1948, for instance, the prominent postwar writer Shiina Rinzō declared in Nietzschean fashion that any conception of science that does not now foresee its own potential to bring about the end of the world is nothing more than a "simple nihilism," that it is science's own refusal to acknowledge its authority which is now the "true nothingness."[46] Such remarks prefigure subsequent ones made by a number of Japanese writers to the effect that the myth of a benevolent science, so carefully nurtured in what seemed a necessary tandem with the equally benevolent notion of "modernity," is invalidated once one realizes that complex lethal devices and the apologies made for them now control how we live now and henceforth. As one Japanese writer points out, the myth of a science benignly linked with modernity had already collapsed by the time we realized that nuclear weapons control the human present and future.[47] In the past, as another argues, the intent of one person confronting another was relatively simple: to let him live or to kill him. But contemporary civilization has produced a way of thinking about murder which has nothing to do with one person taking individual aim at another. Rather, we can now kill each other much the same way we eliminate vermin with pesticides. It is in the nature of modern science to treat human beings "inhumanly," which means that the term "human" has been emptied of a heretofore most crucial distinction.[48] "We have no standard anymore for anything," wrote Elias Canetti, "ever since human life is no longer the standard."[49]

This exhaustion of human value signals a shift that has occurred in our ethical thinking. Many nations involved in the Second World War emerged with fundamentally changed presumptions of what is permissible behavior towards others. As Lawrence Langer, a literary historian of the Holocaust, charges, "The existence of the A-bomb and the concentration camp—supreme expressions of atrocity in our time—can eventually be traced back to the decisions of men."[50] In a related statement, Lewis Mumford observed perceptively that if the machine appears "to dominate life today, it is only because society is even more disrupted" now than previously.[51] The difference between the violence of war in former times and that of today, he wrote years before nuclear weapons would make his point trite, is the difference "between the ritual of the dance and the routine of the slaughter house."[52] The shift from shields and swords on the fields of Marathon to missiles hurled from space speaks not just to the direction of science but to the changed grip of the human hand which aims the weapon, a hand which is no longer unambiguously recognizable as "human." It is important to realize that while nuclear fission and fusion are products of science, nuclear weapons are a product of culture, and consequently implicated in all our cultural predispositions, assumptions, and crises. As Erich Kahler points out, what is of importance to us in contemplating the changes modern violence has wrought is the "dissolution of coherence and structure; not *inhumanity* which has existed all through history and constitutes part of the human form, but *ahumanity*, a phenomenon of rather recent date."[53]

To use a term such as "ahumanity" is to regard ourselves no differently from objects, equally reducible to fertilizer or tissue specimens. It means to regard ourselves without feelings or, more to the point, with a much lessened sense of responsibility. Hiroshima survivor Inokuchi Motosaburō noted that once he and others had witnessed the dying denied even drinking water, "for all the world we ceased trusting anyone but ourselves."[54] It is moreover to regard ourselves mechanically, or as a system. This is why the most radical impact of Auschwitz and Hiroshima, and of modern atrocity in general, lies in the fact that we have surrendered ourselves to the "logic" of modernity, which is to say to systems both technological and cultural—the distinction seems increasingly arbitrary—that we have created but for which no one person or even imaginable group of persons maintains some sense of ethical obligation. It may be comforting, and perhaps even strategically useful, to think of the Holocaust as a detour in the otherwise irreversible upward course of Western civilization and its imitators, and to dismiss Hiroshima as, like the monument in the city's Peace Park ambiguously notes, "a mistake never to be repeated." But the truth is that both events were reasonably consistent with the momentum of modern societies to rationalize their values and render their processes steadily more efficient. "From our point of view," admitted one who worked at Los Alamos, "the atomic bomb was not a discontinuity. We were just carrying on more of the same, only it was much cheaper. . . . We had already destroyed sixty-six [cities]; what's two more?"[55] Or as poet Brown Miller writes in "Sweet Blossoms Snow,"

> 135 days after
> Roosevelt's death
> analysis and justification
> were detonated over
> Hiroshima.[56]

Germany lost the war, so its Final Solution is now understood as a criminal "aberration" of Western civilization; but Hiroshima and Nagasaki, acts committed by the victor, "have passed into our culture as rational strategic actions."[57] The historian Richard Rubenstein has written in his book *The Cunning of History: The Holocaust and the American Future* that:

> We are sadly forced to conclude that we live in a world that is *functionally godless* and that human rights and dignity depend upon the power of one's community to grant or withhold them from its members.
>
> Thus, the Holocaust bears witness to *the advance of civilization*, I repeat, to the advance of civilization, to the point at which large scale massacre is no longer a crime and the state's sovereign powers are such that millions can be stripped of their rights and condemned to the world of the living dead. (91)

This "advance" of which Rubenstein speaks in relation to the political notion of the individual overlaps with the bureaucratic momentum leading to the bombings of Hiroshima and Nagasaki and finds a rhetorical counterpart in the "advance of science." Novelist Oda Makoto points out, in quoting from the memoirs of those officials who developed the first atomic bombs, that the Manhattan Project was such an immense undertaking that it assumed its own unstoppable momentum. It became an unquestioned imperative that at no point permitted questions as to its ultimate goal.[58] The modern technological state may be defined, in fact, as one in which we are bureaucratically organized to work on projects whose extent and final purposes remain unknown to most and ethically remote to all. The Manhattan Project involved 125,000 workers, but only a few dozen realized what was being produced, and for what end. "The terror of 'Hiroshima' and 'Nagasaki,' " writes Kuroko Kazuo, "is finally not the extent of the damage. It lies in having forced upon us the fate to both 'live' and 'die' beneath a man-made plan we know nothing of."[59] Unlike the Nazi camps, which did intend to eliminate all Jews, the destruction of two cities is no way planned the genocide of the entire Japanese people—though the means of that destruction made their genocide feasible. This is finally what Auschwitz and Hiroshima share most crucially in common. Both the death camps and the atomic bomb were products of an organic and bureaucratic undertaking that required the labor of thousands. The fact that, in the case of the Manhattan Project, that labor was uncoerced only makes it all the more "modern." Both Rubenstein and Oda pinpoint the real terror of the two atrocities (which they, though a Jew and a Japanese, were spared) as a terror that we all still face: the terror of the modern state now armed with fantastic power. It is the terror of the nuclear age. In this sense Hiroshima and the Holocaust partake of a shared lethal logic, an achievement of awesome efficiency, in an inarguably rational calculation that allows us to speak of them together in a single breath, as did Holocaust-survivor poet Nellie Sachs when she wrote the lines:

> O knife of evening red, flung into the throats
> where trees of sleep rear blood-licking from the ground,
> where time is shed
> from the skeletons in Hiroshima and Maidanek[60]

■

The atomic bombings and the Nazi atrocities differ in significant historical ways that have determined that their literatures would be different as well. The genocide of European Jewry was a long, literally tortuous and sadistic process that, although abetted by technology, culminated in ways of dying that still provided the victims with a knowledge, however unbelievable, of their assailants. The new kind of society that the labor and death camps of the Nazis represent—namely twentieth-century slavery, more ruthless and proficient than its predecessors—was also a variation on an older kind of society, a refinement of previous techniques, an extension of earlier impulses.[61] There is a historical "logic" to Europe's civilization in the extermination of the Jews (first forced conversion, then expulsion, finally massacre) and other disposable populations. Auschwitz may represent then the conclusive, inevitable ethical collapse of that civilization—or its final triumph. As we have been told, reading Goethe in the morning did not preclude barbarity in the afternoon. Sin, grace,

martyrdom, the soul, and even God—Judeo-Christian ideas that had so long
sustained the West's defining sense of itself—were rendered ironic to the point
of absurdity. Auschwitz was a reiteration of the well-known price with which
our modernity was purchased. "It is quite as modern to make guns as automo-
biles," writes one prominent historian of Japan, "and to organize concentration
camps as to organize schools which teach freedoms."[62]

Hiroshima, however, was the beginning of, as well as the end to, something. The war against the Jews was tragically part of Germany's entire rationale for conquering Europe, but Hiroshima and Nagasaki, bombed after Japan
was effectively defeated, lie outside the reason of the Second World War. Instead, they are first terms in the logic of World War III, though these terms
would have been inchoate, premature, and unrecognizable without the ever
enlarged moral and technological capacities pioneered by the Boer War, the
First World War, The Spanish Civil War, the Rape of Nanking, and the entire
tenure of Nazism. Survivor-writer Hayashi Kyōko has suggested, in fact, that
1945 be declared "Year One" of the "Atomic Age" and that the calendar now
ridiculously dated *anno Domini* be retired.[63] Hiroshima instantaneously altered
the world in ways that are doubtlessly permanent. A world dominated by
man—and that includes the world of Nazi genocide—was turned into one
dominated by science abstract beyond the comprehension of all but the spe-
cialists. There was no boot-clad executioner, rather only a brilliant flash and,
for some, a deafeningly loud noise. The degradation of human life in Auschwitz was still an perverse proof of human existence, if only because Nazi sa-
dism required fellow human beings to submit to its display of power. There
was no such proof in Hiroshima and Nagasaki. The intended audience was in
Tokyo and Moscow, not in the targets themselves. In the death camps individual human lives were rendered into pieces of common soap. Those lives, both
as slave labor and then as material, made some ghastly reference to economic
if not moral value. In Hiroshima and Nagasaki, however, individual lives were
rendered into useless residue. Nothing "productive" was ever required of the
victims. In a sense Hiroshima and Nagasaki were a grotesque performance—a
"dramatic finale," in the words of one historian[64]—put on for the benefit of
audiences in Tokyo and Moscow, as postmodern in its meaning as Nazi camps
were terrifyingly modern. Hiroshima and Nagasaki were the initiation of a
new phase of human history that we are still only beginning to inhabit, much
less comprehend.

In Hiroshima there could be no "resistance." The inspiring fight waged by
many hibakusha against the diseases that subsequently ravaged their health
should not be mistaken for a struggle against the evil responsible in the first
place. In the death camps there were occasions when people subverted direct
control through, for example, suicidal acts. Yet in Hiroshima, where there was
not only no time for such gestures but no knowledge or much less contact with

the victimizer, how could such existentialist acts even be contemplated? To survive, in hindsight, was perhaps resistance enough, for in Hiroshima as well as Auschwitz, no one was meant to. Gone with the idea of dignity is that of the hero: the dichotomy in the literature which has and will come out of the bombings is not between the heroic man and those who are not, but between those who live and those who do not. Studies of the Holocaust commonly interpret its events as embedded in a specifically Western history of philosophy, ethics, and technology. But Hiroshima, a Western event that occurred in the non-Western world, raises many more complicated questions for us. How, for example, are Western capabilities and rationales for destructive power to be understand in those cultures—all cultures—potentially targeted by that power?

Ōe Kenzaburō, himself a prominent theorist of the nuclear age, cites Jean-Paul Sartre as the first thinker to recognize how the advent of atomic weapons has changed civilization and with it the nature of the human imagination. Sartre, as Ōe indicates, awards great weight to the power we now possess to exterminate ourselves.[65] Auschwitz left some of its perpetrators intact, but the next nuclear war may not. The atomic bomb was for its time the product of the most advanced technology attained by the species. Science, its ethos long privileged in Western and Westernized cultures, and which had been expected to aid in, if not actually bring about, our liberation, became instead an abject lesson in how our discoveries can be turned against us. It is in this debilitating sense that Hiroshima and Nagasaki hibakusha feel themselves not simply the victims of a war, but even victims of the contradictions of civilization itself. As Hiroshima survivor Uchimura Yoshiko observed, "In the right hand, we have penicillin and streptomycin; in the left hand the atom bomb and the hydrogen bomb."[66]

What this means for the world today is that the use of atomic weapons marks a turning point in history that parallels and extends that signified by Auschwitz. Psycho-historian Robert Jay Lifton, whose work has sought to define the impact this shift has had on the human psyche, characterizes the new nuclear age this way: "Psychically speaking, a revolutionary situation exists. What is ironic to the point of absurdity, and still extremely difficult for us to absorb, is the fact that it is a *potentially terminal revolution*."[67] Such descriptions are neither exaggerated nor unique. Perhaps no one put it more succinctly, or in front of a larger audience, than when William Faulkner accepted his Nobel Prize with the words "There are no longer questions of the spirit. There is only the question: When will I be blown up?"[68]

This is the new actuality with which culture must cope: the imaginative and historical proximity of the final end. Ours is now a civilization largely devoid of the certainties to which earlier eras were accustomed, and this is precisely why literature and other cultural practices dependent upon those certainties are challenged. The survivors of Hiroshima and Nagasaki often if surprisingly harbor little of the rancor we might guiltily expect from them. Assaulted by light and sound and heat that seemed to come out of nowhere, how could they focus on what and whom produced, ordered, and executed such massive power in order to hate them? It is the conspicuous lack of conventional malice and vengeance that, in part, distinguishes the start of the nuclear age. It is an age not enjoined by emotions of epics, the stuff of storytelling from the beginning of our literacy, but rather one effectively voided of them. This is true of both those bombed and those who did the bombing. "It was beyond words," explained one Hiroshima hibakusha,[69] and a crew member of the *Enola Gay* was able to say a few hours after dropping the bomb over Hiroshima, "I knew the Japs were in for it, but I felt no particular emotion about it."[70]

What is as of yet unique about Hiroshima and Nagasaki is not the number of dead—240,000 Japanese died in the Allied conquest of Okinawa[71]—but that it has punctuated human history with a period. If everyone is killed when nuclear war breaks out again, there will be in Randall Jarrell's phrase no "dying: everybody died." This is more than rhetoric, and to realize it is to have one's thoughts and one's means of expressing them forcibly altered. Nuclear weapons, the product of a thousand years of human ingenuity, talent, and labor, question the basis for much that, since the rise of humanism, we preferred to think of as civilization, namely the belief in a communality among us that can serve as a basis for a humane literature. "The collapse of all familiar notions is, after all, the end of the world," wrote Nadezhda Mandelstam, and the end of what she speaks is also signaled by the seamlessly closed world of the hibakusha, a place where perhaps even more than in the Soviet gulag there were—are—no choices at any point.[72]

To take away familiarity is the theft of a great deal: action, language, belief. Günter Anders, for instance, has said that Hiroshima led him to abandon philosophy; the issue of simple human survival suddenly loomed larger before him.[73] To others similarly disaffected, literature too is undermined. It can seem hopelessly ironic, useless, or worse, even complicitous, when compared to the issues raised by the destruction of Hiroshima and Nagasaki. Stories of Russian aristocrats on trains, frustrated lovers in Ravenna, mysterious murders in Mayfair, or embittered Meiji period intellectuals suddenly seem not only irrelevant but somehow even fraudulent, if one believes collective human survival the paramount question for artists as well as politicians. For a moment at least, writers and readers are distracted from the recantation of normalcy to find their attentions so commanded by the unusual and the unprecedented that for many silence would appear the only unimpeachable response. Already one assumption of modern culture has to be considered a victim of Hiroshima and Nagasaki, and it is the same victim of Bergen-Belsen and Theresienstadt. "Normal men do not believe that everything is possible," wrote camp survivor David

Rousset. "Even if the evidence forces their intelligence to admit it, their muscles do not believe."[74] Now in Hiroshima as well as Auschwitz, in a time when we must acknowledge that we are capable of doing absolutely anything to one another, we must also acknowledge that the imaginative perimeters of literature have been so expanded as to make it difficult for anyone who would write to find one place to begin, or end, without repressing that knowledge. We cannot pretend that atrocity, in the words of George Steiner, "is irrelevant to the responsible life of the imagination. What man has inflicted on man, in very recent times, has affected the writer's primary material—the sum and *potential* of human behavior—and it presses on the brain with a new darkness."[75]

We use words such as "Hiroshima" and "Auschwitz" to mark that point after which these realizations are no longer unavoidable. But of course, the process of dismantling the heretofore set limits of human power, both technological and ethical, has been a long time coming. Immediate and like precedents to the violence of the Second World War were the Spanish Civil War—where men learned they could not fight machines—and the First World War, where mustard gas killed men invisibly. Murdered as well was the ritual nature of combat, as we were alienated from the hands of our assailants. Walter Benjamin, a Jew indirectly killed by modern terror as he fled for his life, reflected in 1936 on the altered terms in which human beings now occupy the world, and how those terms immediately and necessarily changed literature: "A generation that had gone to school on a horse-drawn streetcar now stood under the open sky in a countryside in which nothing remained unchanged but the clouds, and beneath these clouds, in a field of force of destructive torrents and explosions, was the tiny, fragile human body."[76]

Benjamin's "torrents and explosions" have been a long time in the making, and they are both figural and literal. They refer both to the escalating violence of war and to an equally swift cultural dislocation. One crisis faced by literature in the twentieth century but with roots in the nineteenth is the gap between what the world now shows itself to be and our minds' capacity to turn it into sense through their own conceptual and inventive capacities. This predicament for literature derives from a general cultural crisis, and it is one of which Japanese critics have been insightfully aware. Kuroko Kazuo, for instance, has argued that the nineteenth- and twentieth-century concept of humanism has, since Hiroshima, been supplanted by a "nuclear humanism," an observation which, if true, has clear repercussions for a modern literature still significantly anchored to the celebration of nostalgic and thus lost humanist values.[77] Novelist Ozaki Kazuo has more explicitly claimed that the brand of intellectualism identified with the West at the start of the modern period gave rise to an important shift in the way knowledge is regarded, taking mathematics as a model. Abstract science, which originally took its start from the study and example of human life, gradually took on a primary existence; the reverse side of which is that human life, once primary, has become secondary and subordinate.[78]

It is natural of course to expect the Japanese to be especially sensitive to this shift that has taken place. They too, while perhaps historically on the periphery of the West, have in recent times been made Western science's most dramatic sacrifice. No one has made this point more insistently and frequently that Ōe Kenzaburō:

> Blacks in America; Jews in Europe; the dead of Hiroshima and Nagasaki; there are masses of people whom cannot be compensated. It is not always the case that a day of judgment comes. In the case of Auschwitz, for instance, once Nazi Germany was defeated everything was mollified, written off. Then there is the bombing of Hiroshima; after the war all sorts of anti-bomb campaigns were held, but that has not meant that civilized people completely understand the guilty crime of the bombings. It has not proved inevitable that civilized people have balanced the barbarity within them and so let history go forward. Rather, they have never gauged the true barbarity; we have only gone so far, and inconclusively. I personally doubt whether there are any newly civilized people moving forward with such an understanding.[79]

For Ōe, Hiroshima and to a lesser extent Auschwitz mark a decisive turning point in the way we must define "civilized." Certainly, some Japanese intellectuals have indicated the changed terrain we all now inhabit. Writer Noma Hiroshi referred to a new, intense "human consciousness" that must necessarily come out of Hiroshima;[80] for poet Kurihara Sadako, Hiroshima is a mode of thought that transcends the fact of the weapons themselves and becomes the conscience of the world.[81]

Such changes in the way we now view the world charge literature with the considerable task of not only describing but understanding those changes. An "atomic-bomb literature" must document what happened in August 1945, and at the same time it must help us comprehend what it means to be living today in a nuclear age. The mission—missions—of atomic-bomb literature thus proceed at once in several and not always complementary directions. As literature, it struggles to function with recognized forms, within the confines of sanctioned genres and themes, which is to say within audiences' expectations of which and how stories are to be told. It adapts the genres, and with them invariably some of the content, of pre-Hiroshima writing. But atomic-bomb literature is obviously historical, and historical in a way that must somehow mark the discontinuity as well as continuity of history. As Abe Tomoji stated, literature has had to deal with epochal events before, but the problem of writing and nuclear weapons nonetheless marks a "rupture" (*rui o zesshite*) in culture that earlier cultural expressions faced with simply assimilating social and technological change did not.[82] It is not enough, Abe insists, that atomic-bomb literature profess a need for "peace." It needs, one might add, to note how the kinds of "peace" available to us have been permanently changed. In recent years Ōe has noted just how broad and vital the work of Japanese atomic-bomb writers has been in this regard. Addressing his responsibility as editor of an anthology of atomic-bomb fiction, Ōe writes:

> I have come to realize anew that the short stories included herein are not merely literary expressions, composed by looking back at the past, of what happened at Hiroshima and Nagasaki in the summer of 1945. They are also highly significant vehicles for thinking about the contemporary world over which hangs the awesome threat of vastly expanded nuclear arsenals. They are, that is, a means for stirring our imaginative powers to consider the fundamental conditions of human existence; they are relevant to the present and to our movement towards all tomorrows.[83]

What Ōe notes here, and others have elsewhere, is nothing either new or very controversial. Armed with the evidence of all sorts of crises, intellectuals have been proclaiming the end of the familiar world for quite some time. But as Ōe has said, few of us act differently in any informed way based on this easily articulated, but uneasily understood, pronouncement. We would be forced, were we to act sincerely, to deal with politics, ethics, history: in other words, with things that most of us prefer to refrain from contemplating too deeply. Many atomic-bomb authors are the difficult writers they seem because they could not be otherwise. We, in reading what they have written, encounter with resistance an evolving language, an expanded imagination, and perhaps a new mode of being: all things finally more complex than they are arguable. Toyoshima Yoshio, writing only weeks after the bombings, anticipated what lay ahead and understood what is still largely misunderstood even four decades later: "To trot out 'humanism' in the face of the atomic bomb is to talk nonsense. The new age, an age symbolized by the atomic bomb, includes wonders and possibilities beyond the imagination. I wonder what role the literature that explores this new age will conceive for itself?"[84]

Many answers to Toyoshima's question have been proposed. Literary historian Nagaoka Hiroyoshi has provisionally defined atomic-bomb literature, perhaps somewhat contradictorily, as writing that expresses both the evil of the bomb and the survival of human dignity.[85] Kokubo Hitoshi, in turn, takes the testimonial and documentary description in words of the blasts themselves as the initial phase of an atomic-bomb literature that goes on to explore the deep perplexities that all people living today have towards the concept of the modern.[86] Perhaps this view, too, is contradictory—a literature that describes an end must simultaneously be a beginning. The hibakusha writers themselves interestingly have had little to say on this matter . Perhaps recognizing such contradictions as inevitable, they have been discouraged from speaking too abstractly. One purpose of this present study is to show in more starkly analytical terms how varied but singularly paradoxical atomic-bomb literature is. It has changed over time from the testimonial accounts of survivors to the more imaginative fictionalizations of hibakusha culture and finally into a mainstream literature that articulates with its special perspective and concerns—in this "nuclear age"—just those anxieties inextricably tied up with the mythologies and ideologies of recent and not so recent times. Atomic-bomb literature has been censored and suppressed, and it has also been awarded Japan's greatest literary prizes. Much of it is out of print, but one Hiroshima novel discussed in a later chapter, Ibuse Masuji's *Black Rain* (Kuroi ame, 1966), was selected in a 1986 survey of Japanese intellectuals as the most important book written in the Japanese language since the end of the Second World War.[87] In other words atomic-bomb literature has been shunned and embraced, hidden and proclaimed. Such contradictions, I again suggest, are constitutive of this genre. How could it be otherwise? The use of nuclear weapons themselves in the pursuit, and now defense, of peace was the original contradiction.

Contradictions have not, however, deterred Japanese writers from reiterating and exploring them. The counterpart to Milan Kundera's words that "the struggle of man against power is the struggle of memory against forgetting"[88] are Ōe's words that it is always a struggle "to remember, to remember *against* forgetting."[89] How modern writers choose to struggle is as varied as the writers themselves. Some go back in time looking for the causes of the violence; some become propagandists for a literature avowedly political; some try to measure the change in consciousness effected in its victims; still others concentrate on how simply to live day to day.

Atomic-bomb writers—or more broadly, writers dealing with the issues of technology, power, and ethics raised by Hiroshima and Nagasaki—have fallen into what can perhaps be characterized as three post-nuclear "generations" roughly conceptual as well as chronological. For writers such as Ōta Yōko, Hara Tamiki, Shōda Shinoe, and Kurihara Sadako, their work is to convey the unconveyable, and thus they focus on the problems of mimesis and imagination. The next generation, the one that arose once the violence itself had been accepted as comprehendible fact, began to treat the bombings as a social or individual inner problem often touching on broader political or social issues. Examples of these writers are Hotta Yoshie, Iida Momo, Ōe, Ibuse, Sata Ineko, and the early Inoue Mitsuharu. The third generation, comprised of such figures as Abe Kōbō, Oda Makoto, and the latter Inoue, take the meaning of Hiroshima and Nagasaki to be our future as well as our past, a permanent imaginative state of threatened being. Theirs is writing often bordering upon philosophy, and here is the point where, perhaps, the Japanese come into their closest proximity with writing elsewhere: atomic-bomb literature is part of a world-wide phenomenon, namely that of culture reeling under the impact of twentieth-century violence.

Walter Benjamin, spared the literal sight of what was to befall Europe, wrote that "death is the sanction of everything the storyteller can tell. He has borrowed his authority from death."[90] To a point one is tempted to agree. Yes, we speak in order to survive. But something has changed since Benjamin wrote those words. It is no longer automatically true, as Hannah Arendt wrote, that "one man will always be left alive to tell the story."[91] The would-be storyteller of nuclear war will not be left alive long enough to borrow anything. We can no longer assume that the act of murder leaves the murderer alive. The stories that the atomic-bomb writers of Japan tell are of a world in which henceforth we can easily commit a global suicide that will leave no one behind. That is why to read these Japanese authors and poets is to read what is increasingly likely to be the ultimate, in the explosive sense of last, theme of literature.

One

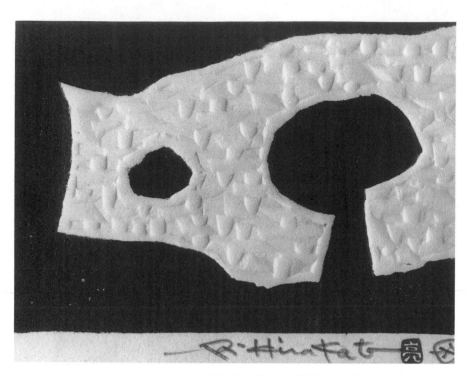

Hirakata Ryōzō, *To Speak*. (Hanasu koto, 1987)

When to write or not to write makes no difference,
then writing changes; it is the writing of the disaster.

Maurice Blanchot, *The Writing of the Disaster*

There are words that speak of a ruined Hiroshima.
And there are words that a ruined Hiroshima makes us speak.

Takenishi Hiroko, "Words that Hiroshima Makes Us Speak"

1

Atrocity into Words

We intuitively know that a discussion of atomic-bomb literature will be necessarily different from a discussion of, for example, detective stories. While both "atomic-bomb" and "detective" may be taxonomically useful terms for describing works that share a particular theme, Hiroshima and Nagasaki inspire a degree of care and even trepidation that other subjects do not. In Hiroshima and Nagasaki we are talking about the deaths of hundreds of thousands, a fact before which we understandably hesitate. Moreover, these are cities whose deaths we are apt to consider unique; we may think we lack the prerogative to speak of them. It has been debated widely whether the singularity of Hiroshima and Nagasaki affects our (referring to us non-hibakusha) ability or inability to understand and thus reflect upon those events. But it is inarguably true that hibakusha themselves have typically thought themselves proprietors of an experience wholly beyond the ken of others—and even themselves—to comprehend in its entirety. In her testimonial account of August 6th, Hashimoto Kunie described what she saw once she opened her eyes as "something so ghastly as to make incredible all that has been before": if Hashimoto herself is hardly able to believe her own experience, how are the rest of us to imagine that we can?[1]

Hibakusha who were or became professional writers, and who thus might be thought to have the talent to make the "incredible" available to us, similarly confess an emotional surplus that paradoxically paralyzed the expression of those emotions and that made ordinary communication impossible. Hiroshima poet Tōge Sankichi wrote in 1951:

> All people now know that nearly three hundred thousand were killed in Hiroshima by a single atomic bomb. In Nagasaki, more than one hundred thousand. But these are only the most general kinds of fact. The bigger the event, the less we are able to recognize that, no matter how many people may wail their laments, we will never come to terms with our truest feelings.[2]

Tōge speaks here of his failure to plumb the full depths of his own experience; when his fellow hibakusha poet Hara Tamiki wondered whether the meaning of the atomic bomb could be grasped by anyone whose own skin had not been seared by it, he made any understanding impossible for the rest of us.[3] Both Tōge and Hara jointly place Hiroshima beyond its assimilation by the culture that binds us together, victim and non-victim alike. A hibakusha character in Iida Momo's *An American Hero* insists that no one, be he a "doctor . . . or humanist, has any chance at all of entering in from the outside to empathize" with atomic-bomb survivors (388). Indeed, even among the victims themselves, there are often thought to be degrees of understanding determined by the extent of one's losses. The narrator of Hayashi Kyōko's short story "Friend" (Tomo yo, 1977), a woman who herself lost no relatives in the bombing of Nagasaki, guiltily realizes the gap that persists between her and a friend who had six members of her family die. This recurring theme of the historical, epistemological, or simply emotional isolation of atomic-bomb survivors most frequently takes the form of an insistence upon the incommunicability of what it meant to be in Hiroshima or Nagasaki, an insistence which challenges the feasibility and even possibility of what might subsequently be written of them. A character in Kurita Tōhei's story "A Bronze-colored Dark" (Seidōshoku no yami, 1979) has the following reaction to what he sees in Nagasaki:

> It was a tale from the land of the dead, impossible to believe. Were its extraordinariness to stir him to speak of it, he might not necessarily believe his own words; he would list bits and pieces of events, unconnected by any logical thread. He could speak of it for all time to come, and still not see it in its entirety. (280)

The purported inaccessibility of the experience of a nuclear bombing, its inconvertibility into a chain of words that might faithfully refer, represents a considerable technical and even ethical hurdle for those writers who profess it. Hachiya Michihiko wrote in his *Hiroshima Diary* (Hiroshima nikki, 1955) that "outsiders could not grasp the fact that they were witnessing the exodus of a people who walked in the realm of dreams."[4] Outsiders have, in fact, agreed. When Mary McCarthy stated in 1946 that Hiroshima had already become "a kind of hole in human history,"[5] she was pointing out a blank, a skipped page in the narrative of history on which Hiroshima should be inscribed but is not. McCarthy acknowledged the result of what Hiroshima poet Tokunō Kōichi called his "doubts over whether . . . the reality of that day . . . can be communicated by literature to third persons. . . . No matter how much one writes, one is left with the feeling there is more to say."[6] How is the hibakusha writer to share his experience with those not hibakusha? "It was a primal event that denies all but other hibakusha its vicarious experience," wrote Hiroshima author Fumizawa Takaichi.[7]

The difficulty these preemptive observations point to is the exaggerated breach between audiences and authors now separated by historical experience. The problem seems not, as is common in modern literature, that between a writer and the world from which he is alienated, but rather that between a writer involuntarily initiated into a world about whose dimensions we, the audience, can only speculate. Philosophy has long asked how can language represent reality, but our poor answers over the centuries have seldom seemed so inadequate as in the present one, when the violence that has segregated some of our lives—our deaths—from those of the majority has been so incalculable. Primo Levi noted that in Auschwitz the prisoners became aware that "our language lacked words to express this offense, the demolition of a man."[8] Levi's understanding of the limits of languages was echoed in Japan. One Hiroshima survivor, Kijima Katsumi, recalls that he thought to himself "Oh, look, there's another enemy plane coming" just as the *Enola Gay* passed directly overhead; then, remembering what happened seconds later, he states, "Thereafter there were no more words."[9]

No more words: language, its reliability already devalued by philosophy, has become almost criminally suspect in the wake of world wars. It has even collaborated in our collective victimhood. "Speaking always involves a treason," noted Albert Camus, and Japanese survivors of Camus' same war sometimes arrive at the same conclusion as they attempt to describe Hiroshima and Nagasaki.[10] "What words can we now use," mused writer Takenishi Hiroko in an essay on the potential of language after August 6th. "What words can we now use, and to what ends? Even: what *are* words?"[11] Another writer, Ozaki Shirō, has contemplated just these same questions in ways that emphasize the differences between what a hibakusha says and what we may hear:

One has so many things to say, but speaking always feels like a lie. In speaking one hopes to more or less approach truth, yet it is difficult to attest to that truth on paper. Speaking is supposed to establish knowledge with its subtle nuances of vocal tones and facial gestures. "To speak is to understand," but what one really understands is that we do not mean to speak with the limited words we write.[12]

Writing may seem impossibly far from speech, not only far from memory but from the authentic act of witness that accompanies the hibakusha's testimony. But to set up such obstacles to writing provides, oddly, a kind of consolation. Should language stop "failing" us, and somehow succeed in communicating "what" happened, then what? Suddenly the atrocity would be no longer original but available to us in infinite retellings. It would continue to "exist" and thus menace us. When someone argues that a literature of atrocity is a priori impossible because words do not, will not, suffice, that person is also insisting that he steadfastly refuses to cooperate with any such attempt and means for that stubborn insistence to suffice as its own message. To do otherwise, it is feared, would be in the renewal of memory a recognition—perhaps even a legitimation—of the experience thus recalled.

This is undoubtedly why all the voices protesting the efficacy of language in expressing Hiroshima and Nagasaki belong to the hibakusha and to those who identify with their fate. It is they, after all, who must fear that if a literature composed of such language were possible, the intimate links between themselves and the bombings would be severed and their existences violated even further. It is one of the hallmarks of atomic-bomb literature—indeed, lest this be mistaken as a peculiarly "Japanese" trait, of Holocaust literature, too—that it depends to an uncommon degree on implication and insinuation. It is in the words of Lawrence Langer "a literature of innuendo," "as if the author were conspiring with his readers to recapture an atmosphere of insane misery which they somehow shared, without wishing to name or describe it in detail."[13]

Ironically, however, it is only through their writings that most of us know of the hibakusha writer's difficulties. They *do* write: as Richard Poirer has noted, "to write at all is to salvage, however reluctantly, some part of the existent humanity . . . even if your writing is an invitation to reject and disperse it."[14] In other words, one's very attempt to tell of Hiroshima in language is one mark of a surviving faith in the connection of the past with the present. To doubt such connection might be interpreted as a rhetorical performance. Berel Lang has noted that "the description of an event as incomprehensible or inexplicable is often itself a figure of speech; the aporia, an extreme instance of hyperbole, asserts just this—that words cannot convey or encompass a given subject."[15] But presumably there were survivors who, discouraged by the violence they experienced, chose *not* to write, and so are unknown to us and our theories of writing after Hiroshima. We are left to distill how Hiroshima and Nagasaki are represented from the practice of those who did, and do, commit to the project of telling.

Seldom, however, does such commitment proceed without the frequent qualification of the struggle to which it condemns the writer. Ōta Yōko, for example, wrote: "From start to finish I think of literature as a burdensome struggle. Because I continue to write of the atomic bombing, I continue to be exhausted from my hand-to-hand combat with it."[16] Hara Tamiki expressed astonishment—"It seems to extraordinary to me"—at his ability to write of the things he did.[17] How were these writers able to summon the energy and resolve to write? Nagasaki writer Gotō Minako provides one answer:

> Why write? This is a question I hurl at myself over and over again when, late at night, I pick up my pen and face blank paper. The more this question is stifled by the very weight of writing, the more loudly it resounds within me. For me writing means reopening the "grave" I have tried to cover for good. To reach into what lies at the base of consciousness, to retrieve it and turn it into words, is painfully difficult to endure. Writing becomes distasteful, and I find myself wishing to begin living with these memories of the past interred. Yet I am urged to go on by another voice; out of my own experiences I still write of Nagasaki and its people since the atomic bombing.[18]

Gotō admits to the dilemma of many hibakusha writers. Does one abandon the past—and perhaps risk living in a ersatz present—or remain obsessed, and thus equally compromised, by it? Perhaps Nazi camp survivors are the only other group of modern writers so uniformly and so severely restricted by the same material of which they would tell. It is as if the paper they face is their enemy as well as ally, something to be feared as the bitter return to the site of their suffering as well as a recuperative means for collecting, organizing, and passing on the lessons of that suffering. In writing one inevitably faces choices: where to begin, whose voice to borrow or invent, which particulars to include and which to exclude; where to end even where there is no end. In writing one faces the challenge of converting into narrative, drama, or lyric some things and not others. For a hibakusha writer, already and uncannily estranged by his fate in simply surviving, such a challenge can overwhelm that writer and render words irretrievably ironic. Ōe Kenzaburō has written that literature by hibakusha writers "must commence with the question whether their experiences of yesterday's evil, their tragic, unredeemable experiences, can—and if so, how—be converted into something of value."[19] But, as Ōe knows, many such writers will not concur in the premises of value after Hiroshima and Nagasaki. For them, what they write is no longer so much "literature" as it is merely "words," and even words emptied of such liberal hopes if not of meaning itself. Atomic-bomb literature is already diminished before it starts, but in ways that say much. The silences, the oft-noted lacks and gaps in atomic-bomb writing, may be precisely where the genre "speaks" to us the most. "It is so short and jumbled and jangled," explains Kurt Vonnegut in *Slaughterhouse Five*, "because there is nothing intelligent to say about a massacre. Everybody is supposed to be dead, to never say anything or want anything ever again" (17).

The most creatively ambitious hibakusha writers have insisted that they must fill these unspeakable spaces with new words or even a new language. In part, some of them have. But what has more commonly happened is that older idioms have been put to new and richly ironic purposes. Readers of modern literature, in response, have grown accustomed to watching for such purposes. We read, in other words, at the edge of our epistemological, aesthetic, and even emotional borders, always ready for the unfamiliar as well as the familiar. We are warily prepared for experiences on the page less welcome than they are unfortunately real. But these are difficulties we non-hibakusha easily learn to live with, whereas for the writers themselves they are issues that lead them to doubt the civilization the rest of us reflexively rely upon to sanction our readings, and their significance.

■

The issue for many early atomic-bomb writers was how to begin to express their material experiences as a shattering of what once was immaterial language. Language, if necessarily something we share, can only represent its own discontinuity by ceasing to "mean" and thus ironically by "meaning" precisely that. Historians of Holocaust literature often make the point that the Hebrew textual tradition provided some survivor-writers with a tradition of cataclysmic narratives which could be drawn upon to place Nazi genocide within the context of Jewish suffering throughout history. Similarly, Paul Fussell points out how English soldiers in the First World War could translate their experiences in French trenches into the terms of their cultural inheritance, including, he notes, Bunyan's *Pilgrim's Progress*.[20] It is harder to imagine any such precedents that might have governed Japanese responses in atomic-bomb literature. Where they do exist, they are largely drawn from the visual arts, such as the not infrequent references to medieval Buddhist scroll paintings of hell as analogies for the fires of Hiroshima and Nagasaki.[21] In fact, when seeking the words to express what they wish to say, it is nearly rote for atomic-bomb writers to tell us they despair of ever finding those words. "Just once before he died," writes Kurita Tōhei of his narrator in "A Bronze-colored Dark," "he wanted to leave Nagasaki, breath clean air, and know once more the exhilaration of 'language' " (285).

Such laments are not new, of course, or peculiarly Japanese. In the West the collision between events and words has been noted despairingly since the Greeks; more recently—just at the time, in fact, when hibakusha were exploring in their own ways how to write in the face of this lesson—Roland Barthes declared that "language functions negatively, as the initial limit of the possible."[22] But inevitably language wins out, if only because words last longer than any one human memory. "By covenant or violence," as Michel Foucault put it, words and their untrustworthy meanings are imposed upon us. The problem is less one of any essential "nature" of language than of the figural powers of our literary discourses and what their relationships are with our cultures. The question—whether language can communicate what is essential about violence—is easily misstated. Obviously, language is a historical and social medium, and through consensus we make it mean: not as freely, certainly, as E. D. Hirsch would have it when he says that "verbal meaning is whatever someone has willed to convey by a particular sequence of linguistic signs and which can be conveyed (shared) by means of those linguistic signs,"[23] but perhaps more along those lines suggested once again by Barthes, who more subtly understands that language is "both a boundary and a perspective."[24] He acknowledges that language, like Marx's "history," is something over which we are capable of exercising will, even if the conditions in which we do so are not of our own making. Perhaps the same point is made, with even more subtle an understanding, by Takenishi Hiroko in those lines that stand as an epigraph to this chapter: "There are words that speak of a ruined Hiroshima. And there are words that a ruined Hiroshima makes us speak."[25]

In fact the real issue at stake may be whether one ought to recognize that we are prepared to let the properly trained human imagination deal with such violence as a representation, which is to say at second hand. This involves psychology, but it also involves the ethics of culture, and it is consequently a problem as important for the reader as for the writer. Philosophy, especially in the twentieth century, has inextricably linked itself with the problems of linguistic representation and specifically with the repercussions of the corollary that our notions of reality are tied to the means through which we speak of them. Such assumptions of the relation of reality to language raise fundamental problems for writers of atrocity, however. "Reality," if the experience of nuclear war, is something which exists prior to language—the victims' language—and is not originally contingent upon it. Indeed, the perennial quandary is not that reality is an illusion of words, but that words can do no more than make reality illusionary. Perhaps for both atomic-bomb writers and philosophers language is something not to be naively trusted, or something which refers as much to itself as to what it purportedly refers. But the specific histories leading both bomb victims and Western intellectuals to such conclusions are opposite: atomic-bomb writers, unwilling skeptics, insist that there *is* something that might be signified with unassailable confidence, if only they could. In Fukunaga Takehiko's novel *The Island of Death* (Shi no shima, 1971), for example, a hibakusha painter is continually frustrated in her attempts to depict on canvas a reality she calls "scattered, dead fragments" (1:453). But she does not stop painting.

Those attempts, already compromised by self-doubt, must proceed through an appeal to the reader based on some notion of inherited cultural norms. Critics have noted, even amidst the centrifugal forces of modern times emphasizing the ruptures in intelligibility, how unworkable any idea of an *original* practice of writing would be. "A painting or a poem without any vestiges of lived forms would be unintelligible, i.e., nothing" according to Ortega y Gasset.[26] Harold Bloom asks just as flatly: "What happens if one tries to teach or to think, or even to read, without the sense of a tradition? Why nothing at all happens, just nothing."[27] Naturally, it is misleading to believe we even have a choice. The quest of atomic-bomb writers to initiate us into their experiences necessarily implicates them in the history of our figures and the trained imagination they are meant to stimulate. Wayne Booth points out that "the author cannot choose whether to use rhetorical heightening. His only choice is of the kind he will use."[28] And in fact such choices may not be in the hands of the author at all, but in the language which speaks through us: as Roland Barthes put it, "To describe the event implies that the event has been written."[29]

The tropes of atomic-bomb literature, be they the choices of writers or the dictates of writing itself, are many. They range from eight year-old Maeda Masahiro's familiar simile of "white jade" for the Hiroshima explosion to avant-garde playwright Satō Makoto's metaphor of a "falling star" for the same.[30] Neither phrase, the former by a hibakusha seeking something for us to recognize, the latter by a non-hibakusha who would make Hiroshima something abstract and outside of human history, defines the bombing for us. Rather, such language merely augments the vocabulary we, as readers, will rely upon to create an imaginative and literary matter about the bomb, some of which limits its meaning and some of which defers it. When Maurice Blanchot defined disaster as "that which does not have the ultimate for a limit: it bears the ultimate away in the disaster,"[31] he was attempting to fix that word as something ultimately unfixable, a synecdoche of the open-endedness many writers of atrocity have wanted to establish in their works.

What atomic-bomb writers are finally asking for is not our recognition of the impossibility of a specifically Hiroshima and Nagasaki "language," but rather our cooperation in a special relationship between author, reader, and work against the backdrop of history. The atomic-bomb writer resorts to analogies to explain his experience to us, but such techniques translate, domesticate, that experience and make it less threatening as it is better "known." Yet by retrieving or inventing symbols for Hiroshima and Nagasaki we risk unleashing those symbols to act autonomously, to generate thematically spurious readings and interpretations. Fearful of this potential for distortion, the cooperation atomic-bomb writers ask of us is a kind of ethical restraint, a sort of respectful restraint from naively "understanding" what we read.

Language, Aristotle insists in the *Poetics* (1458a), is always imitative of reality but is either "proper" or "strange." "By a current or proper word, I mean one in general use among a people; by a strange word, one which is in use in another country." But just as Aristotle did not imagine that language could be both intelligible and unintelligible, neither could he have anticipated that a group of twentieth-century writers would struggle to keep—or make—language be precisely both those things. This is also the question atomic-bomb writers ask, and similarly do not always respond to. Some take desperate pains to keep what they remember untranslatable, lest it be lost or hopelessly changed; or perhaps worst, judged. What atomic-bomb writers most vitally wish to keep their own is the right to measure, explain, and evaluate the violence. "The atomic bombing was a unique experience. Others are utterly incapable of comprehending it," lectures an exasperated hibakusha character to a non-hibakusha one in Fukunaga's *Island of Death*. "It's of a completely different dimension than ordinary suffering or anguish. It's a different perception of reality, I'm telling you. A perception not your own" (289).

The analogues to which atomic-bomb writers must nonetheless inevitably turn are required, perhaps impossibly, to apprise non-hibakusha without simultaneously allowing us to judge what we learn, such as concluding it was "this" and thus presumably no "worse." The rhetoric of atomic-bomb literature is charged with changing the being of the reader—in fact, in the most extreme examples, to do so by inflicting a kind of damage on us—without conversely enabling the reader to alter the historical experience by subjectively interpreting it, or even fully comprehending it. "Understanding completely," warned Bruno Bettelheim, "comes close to forgiving."[32] But to have it both ways is, again, impossible: no text is safe from interpretation, fixed or free from the exercise of the reader's own prerogative. Once the pages leave the writer's hands, they become subject to an infinite number of readings and potential "misreadings"—to wit, the reaction of one American college student after reading a documentary account of Hiroshima: "Gee that was a neat story. Is it true?"[33]

A battle rages between the hibakusha writer who seeks to establish his experience as original and unique by declaring the language of its narration off-limits to the processes of reading, and the reader who comes to that account with an insistence on constructing meaning and, beyond that, significance, as he would from other literature. This struggle is particularly pronounced within the confines of atomic-bomb literature, and in a question whose answer lies within the larger confrontation between the rigors of historical writing and the play of imagination. It is this and the dialectic of the two

that makes the genre so difficult to accommodate within the categories of traditional literary criticism. The relationship between uniqueness and compara-
bility—between "history" and "literature," in other words—is the problem of
transferential relationships between knowledge and its object. Hiroshima and
Nagasaki may be unique in the manner that certain subjects have lived relationships with atrocity, but they are also comparable in how such relationships are
to be understood.

In the narrowest sense a strictly "historical" atomic-bomb literature is the
accumulation of fact, of details, within the formats of first-person accounts and
scientific reports. But beyond the simple massing and enumeration of facts lies
a quality of factuality. Beyond what is literally true lies what could have been
true, which is to say the more recognizably "literary" products of a fact-gov-
erned imagination. This may be what Toyoshima Yoshio had in mind when,
only weeks after the bombing, he insisted that literature must be "truth" (*shin-
jitsu*), but that truth is not equivalent to "fact" (*jijitsu*).[34] Early atomic-bomb
prose—where we would most expect to find "facts"—was indeed predominantly spare, unadorned, limited in its uses of metaphors. But indeed, it was
just such restraint of "bare" reporting which now gives rise to an uncanny irony
when we read. "August sixth. Clear skies. Very hot": the simple heading of a
diary entry speaks volumes. Distilled, terse prose is a style that both reports the
horror and suffers itself from it. Facts are so poignant that they easily become
symbolic, since abruptness produces exactly the kind of semantic compression
associated with symbols.

The forced objectivity of atomic-bomb writers attempting to restrict
themselves to the "facts" can, with no small irony, achieve the opposite of the
intended result. The very absence of overt subjectivity reminds us only all
the more that a human memory is there, however successfully repressed. In the
1950 preface to her novel *City of Corpses* (Shikabane no machi, 1948), Ōta Yōko
doubted that any writer could write about Hiroshima in a neutral fashion, yet
that is precisely what she attempted to do anyway.[35] The problem lies first in
establishing what is a "fact," and next in determining if there is a relationship
between it and the "truth" of the experience one would hope to convey. These
issues are not, as already pointed out, particular to atomic-bomb literature.
They have long been the concern of modern writing, especially the novel,
which looks to both fact—historical, social, etc.—and to the intuition of the
imagination. In what critic Frank Kermode calls "the dissonance between paradigmatic form and contingent reality," modern history with its fantastic technological and ethical transformations constantly isolates form, renders it specific and particular and therefore uselessly static.[36] This gives those of us who
inhabit modern times cause to reflect upon the way "fact" governs how we
write and read. What Edward Said calls "worldliness"—the historical context

and import of books beyond their internal relations—is of course found on every page of atomic-bomb literature, dominated as it is by one immense and powerful historical fact.[37] Reports of those facts are available in many places. Much modern writing commonly attempts to "totalize" truth, although this may indeed be truth that is often thought of as so inexplicable as to defy any description more comprehensive than a blank enumeration of its "facts." As critic Kuroko Kazuo notes, "Together with the immense problem of how reportage or documentary literature is to communicate 'fact,' also at issue is how to manage the distance existing between the writer and his object and his way of thinking—his ideology and philosophy—as he grasps at that object."[38]

■

The link between the object—Hiroshima and Nagasaki—and the writer lies in acknowledging and exploiting what, at least in its modern conception, is an indispensable presence in literature: imagination. Imagination (*sōzōryoku*) figures especially and crucially in atomic-bomb literature because such literature is a quest not so much for moral certainties as it is for the reliving of the experience, an imaginative recreation for both the victim writer and the nonvictim reader. Consequently, writings about the atomic bombings have two themes— the violence itself, and the act of writing about that violence—and the reader compares both themes in evaluating, or even believing, either. The imagination is the necessary link between these two themes. Imagination may be the only way to close the distance between the compassion we bring to our reading and the universe of the atomic-bomb author's unsentimental pain, at least as long as, in the words of Terrence Des Pres, "the division between unearned luck and unearned disaster remains a structure of our common world."[39]

This is actually the more optimistic view, the one that maintains such chasms can be bridged. Once again the line is drawn between those who identify with the atrocity and those who alternately side with the promises literature has habitually made. Kurihara Sadako, who despite her steady output of prose and poetry critically aligns herself with the pessimism of the former position, has asked rhetorically whether or not "the power of imagination in Hiroshima doesn't remain lost."[40] Yet fellow critic Konaka Yōtarō argues for the survival of just that power:

At the same time that the question of whether human sentiment can be communicated to another is the fundamental dilemma for writers, this question also involves the fundamental concept of humanity for all of us. Of course I, who unlike Ōta Yōko was not there to suffer the sight of the dead, cannot understand more than one ten-thousandth of her experience. Still, somehow that suffering is conveyed. Should it be entirely impossible to share experience, we human beings would never have been able to create what we know as culture.[41]

Konaka, a non-hibakusha, professes a stubborn faith in "what we know as culture." That "what" is something that has meaningfully survived Hiroshima in ways that victim Ōta Yōko, for example, would likely and indeed did deny. For Konaka, imagination is just that which survives. It serves to make words—even words of annihilation—stand for a truth that, for hibakusha writers, may be so literal as to immobilize our capacity for empathy. "Imagination" in atomic-bomb literature must be defined very carefully, with not only its powers but its limits noted. At issue is whether it allows us to move towards August 6th and 9th, or takes us ever further away.

There are at least two approaches to this issue. If we are Aristotelian, we hold that poetic truth is superior to the historical because the imagination is the faculty that idealizes and thus perfects. If Kantian, then we accept the imagination as a necessary and intentional premise of how a subjective consciousness perceives phenomena and thus gains understanding. In other words, do we acknowledge that our modern, i.e., post-Romantic view of literature (a view as Japanese as Western) derives from this philosophical history, that we do indeed regularly assume that "knowledge" is linked, through some personal and creative process, to "imagination"? If so, then imagination becomes a viable alternative to history, and literature thereby is entitled to tell us, perhaps in lieu of all facts, what Hiroshima and Nagasaki "were." "If one supposes that writing is impossible without experience," wonders the aspiring, non-hibakusha writer in *Island of Death*, "then how am I to write of the atomic bombing? . . . What matters is not the experience *per se*, but through the exercise of a will extending and focusing a power of imagination that can infer analogy from experience" (2:277).

But if this modern conceptualization of the imagination is the license of our ambition to pursue the unprecedented encounter of our individual consciousness with atrocity, then "imagining" Hiroshima risks our being repelled by the result. Such concerns can lead to the second of the two approaches, one which is linked to another powerful inclination in modern thought, particularly as it has been received in Japan. That inclination is to conceive of the imagination as intrinsically false because it more fictionalizes than elaborates the real. Many critics have taken great care to distinguish between "imagination" as a kind of intuited perception and "fantasy" as pure conjecture. Frank Kermode, for example, states that "the truly imaginative novelist has an unshakable 'respect for the contingent'; without it he sinks into fantasy, which is a way of deforming reality."[42] The most extreme of such a position leads to Wallace Stevens's very twentieth-century claim: "In the presence of extraordinary actuality, consciousness takes the place of imagination."[43] In other words, the modern Western philosophical and aesthetic tradition that maintains the primacy of the imagination as the fundamental faculty of art is challenged by lived experience which is itself so bizarrely unreal as to displace any need for such a faculty. Yet at the same time, it precludes the transfer—as in a work of literature—of the memory of that experience to anyone seeking it second hand. "If it is a novel, it is not about Auschwitz," has said Elie Wiesel, "and if it is about Auschwitz, it is not a novel."[44]

In fact, the role of imagination in Japanese atomic-bomb literature, as in Holocaust literature, has been both to facilitate figural representation and to obstruct it. Imagination appears simultaneously necessary to, and corrupting of, atomic-bomb literature. This is perhaps guaranteed whenever we feel inspired to "write" of "history," whether we think our approach literal or free. But for atomic-bomb literature such contradictions are especially vivid to readers because of its tendency to engender reactions of monstrous fantasy ("Can this really have happened?") *and* of confident insights into real experience in ways that leave the reader not sure whether he has read something actual or feigned. Here is where imagination in atomic-bomb literature must negotiate on our behalf. What is so crucially at stake is not the resolution of artistic issues but rather the tentative, indefinite tension between our naive belief in history as concrete and the individual imagination as creative.

The mediating role of the imagination in atomic-bomb literature takes many forms, as we shall see in the chapters that follow. For some of the writers discussed in this study, such as Ōe Kenzaburō, that role is teleologically political:

> We have no choice but to use daily our powers of imagination in considering just how catastrophic nuclear war is. That is first and foremost. Moreover, the Japanese are a people who have already, and twice, experienced nuclear war. . . . I believe that the fact that the Japanese concretely recall the tragedy of nuclear war should be of service for all the people of the world in imagining what the tragedy of future nuclear wars would be.[45]

The result of this, however, is less straightforward than Ōe would have it. The uneasy status of the imaginative response to Hiroshima and Nagasaki means that the genres of atomic-bomb literature range widely from the highly imaginative to the painfully literal. What that literature has no control over is the reader's exercise of his imagination in reading these works, and this potentially leads to more contradictions. "The free imagination makes endless plots on reality," Kermode has written, and it "makes endless plots on reality, attempts to make our proportionals convenient for our equations in everything; our common sense makes us see that without paradox and contradiction our parables will be too simple for a complex poverty, too consolatory to console."[46] Hayashi Kyōko, a Nagasaki hibakusha writer noted and specifically faulted for novels that fail to "console" precisely because of their inscrutable resort to "paradox," tersely described the bombing of Hiroshima as "a contradiction perpetrated by human beings upon human beings."[47]

In the hands of survivors who are not professional writers, the effect of such contradiction is typically expressed as the "confusion" commonly remarked upon in the testimonial accounts collected from Hiroshima and Nagasaki. Yaguchi Hisayo, a schoolgirl in Hiroshima at the time of the bombing, later recalled: "The more we heard and saw, the more astounded we were. No sign of the past remained. I know that it is a natural phenomenon for things to change with the passing of time. However, these changes which seemed to transcend the element of time simply left me with a feeling of bewilderment and disbelief."[48] The experience of violence on such a scale is, insofar as it is an experience of "extremity," means that the line between the real and unreal, the canny and the uncanny, risks being obscured if not dissolved altogether. All the years of his life prior to the bombing, wrote fellow Hiroshima survivor Yamamoto Yasuo, subsequently "amounted to no more than an all-too-fleeting phantasm."[49]

It should not be unexpected, then, that the writings inspired by these experiences would reflect thematically and even formally that fundamentally discontinuous quality of "bewilderment." To nonvictims, such reflections may look nonsensical or even absurd. When Robert Jay Lifton notes on the basis of his clinical evidence that "the ultimate counterfeit element for *hibakusha* is life itself,"[50] he reiterates what Elie Wiesel, in *The Gates of the Forest*, intuited: "To live is to betray the dead."[51] Perhaps for such survivors, the bombings—or the death camps—are both real and unreal. Perhaps, in retrospect, they both happened and did not happen. In her story "In the Darkness" (Mumyō, 1978), Hayashi Kyōko notes that Nagasaki's annual commemorative ceremonies take place "on a day dedicated to something we should not forget, as well as to something we wish to forget completely."[52] Hayashi's quandary is personal and resistant to resolution. It is the basis for all sorts of parallel doubting, confusion, and contradiction found throughout the intellectual and literary writings that have come out of Hiroshima and Nagasaki.

One such contradiction frequently encountered even today is the one posed by the twin convictions that literature, as "art," is ethically good and thus incapable of handling an "ethically bad" theme such as an atomic bombing without converting it into that good. Takahashi Shinji, a historian of modern European thought, considers Hiroshima and Nagasaki "an entirely new problem for ethics" that constitutes a fundamental critique of Western civilization, namely that its willingness to engage in policide undermines its touted commitment to post-Enlightenment humanist values.[53] Such a critique, should we agree with it, has to cast doubt on the confidence with which Saul Bellow asserts that "by assuming what it is that all men ought to be able to understand and agree upon, [the writer] creates a kind of humanity, a version of it composed of hopes and realities in proportions that vary as his degree of optimism."[54]

It is not that there are no optimistic atomic-bomb writers. Of course there are writers who indeed create a "kind of humanity" within their stories of individual courage. But such stories typically read as reactive, defensive moves, as if they are protests against an otherwise uniform view of the bombings as annihilating not only lives and property but the ethos of modern culture, and within that culture the construct of "Man" as the agent of progress. Novelist Sata Ineko, although rejecting as literature atomic-bomb writing singularly concerned with the violence of the attacks, does think it possible to discern something literary (*bungakusei*) in that violence's impact on human beings. There, Sata argues, is the narrow margin in which writers must work.[55] Critic and author Kokubo Hitoshi more cynically elaborates: "The atomic bomb can most certainly be an object for literature. The reason why is because it was made by 'Man' and made to explode above 'Man.' . . . The fact that the atomic bomb, which politics and science conspired to use in their betrayal of us human beings, can become an object for literature indeed starts from our very realization of that betrayal."[56] Literature remains literature because it is seen as a human enterprise. But importantly now, the word "human," like "Man," must be enclosed within quotation marks to denote how uneasily such terms signify. Literature, insofar as it narrates "Man," is as morally problematic as its announced, guilty, subject.

This inherent contradiction inevitably migrates from the indecisiveness of theme to the ironicized corruption of literary form. The most common explanation for this reaction of form to theme is a mechanistic one. Most Japanese theorists of atomic-bomb literature would concur with the Hegelian notion that defectiveness of form arises from defectiveness of content. Classical theories, sometimes both Western and Japanese, of the literary work locate the aesthetic pleasure of literature in the sublimity of the wholeness of form, so that when such "form" is present in a discourse of horrific violence, that pleasure/form is seen as antagonistic to the moral representation of that violence. Form, perfect form, is to be distrusted: a belief in the human instinct for form may make us think that the well-executed lyric or novel can restore coherence, through its own internal order, to even a disintegrating world. But we are no longer so sure. When the theme of the literary work is atrocity, we are less eager to have form transfigure or allegorize reality than we may be to have it "disfigured," made impossible to enjoy aesthetically or otherwise. Thus we look, even eagerly, for just such corrupted literary form—form that confirms our post-Hiroshima ironic understanding of the failure of modern times to be complete in any moral sense.

This is not of course an impulse limited to the Japanese reaction to the atomic bombings. It is part of the general movement in modern thought to undo its own assurance and claims to moral certitude. After Hegel, for example, that movement fashions itself as dialectic; after the world wars of the twentieth century, it is dialectic without synthesis. When Walter Benjamin wrote in 1937 that "there is no cultural document that is not at the same time a record of barbarism,"[57] he was proclaiming the irremovable presence of a terrible human history underlying all of culture's aestheticized discourses suppressing that same history. Tadeusz Borowski, a fellow European, would after his experiences in Auschwitz echo much the same conclusion about civilization with added assurance: it is built on the backs of slaves.[58] The impact of modern history, metonymically represented most forcefully in our discourses of the Second World War, is to make these insights not what informs literature but what has become its own contradicting, unraveling theme. The paradox of the literature of atrocity—namely that it is our modern reality that makes the genre possible, but at the same time it is a genre that works to make that reality acceptable to the imagination—results in a major frustration for our post-Hiroshima culture. Literary forms that had been respected before the Second World War either fail or are ironicized beyond immediate recognition afterwards. Each new assault upon our assumptions of how a life might be appropriately led upsets culture's formal capacity for acceptance. The struggle is focused within the project of the individual author, whose very choice of a form begins to account for his experience and consequent understanding of atrocity.

In a sense such choices are already programmed explanations, or at the very least the allocation of some kind of "meaning" to Hiroshima and Nagasaki. An atomic-bomb novel, for example, gives both the hibakusha writer and the non-hibakusha reader a key by which to respectively encode and decode the bombings. A genre sets up expectations for us that guide how the story is to be told. It is easy to see, however, why some hibakusha writers might resist such an imposed mapping of their stories. Perhaps for them, it is precisely in their defiance of such authoritative and reductive structures as the "novel" that they best express themselves artistically. Sidra DeKoven Ezrahi, in her study of Holocaust literature, has noted a similar resistance to conventional literary form among some Western writers:

> The writer who touches such events with his inheritance of words appears to be reaffirming if not the sanities then the forms of civilized existence. . . . There is a basic tension within the artistic enterprise between the instinctive revulsion against allowing the monstrous creatures to

emerge and the base sounds to be heard—as if by exposing them to the light of day the artist were somehow affirming or legitimating the deformities of man's nature—and the equally compelling instinct against repressing reality, against the amnesia that comes with concealment.[59]

Such struggles, while probably not so much "instinctive" as they are themselves culturally formulated, generate an ambivalence in many works of atomic-bomb literature as well as Holocaust literature seen, for example, in the negotiation of genre. Perhaps such struggles are especially violent in the Japanese context, where violence has historically been so limitedly, or at least so aesthetically, portrayed Perhaps significantly for twentieth-century writers, there is no equivalent of the *Iliad* that stands at the head of the Japanese literary tradition.

We are likely to approach texts generically identified as "A-bomb works" with a set of expectations more historiographic and less literary than we do others. These expectations can clash with others prompted by the overlapping, competing classification of such works as "novels," "poems" and "plays." For example, poet Miyoshi Tatsuji declared himself incapable of reading a collection of Hiroshima writings by child survivors. "The horrors told in this work are beyond words. There are no words of my own to add. We are commanded to a silence already beyond language."[60] The power noted by Miyoshi that excludes us from the ordinary engagement with literature comes from our terror before its close and weighty referents, the destruction of two metropolitan populations. Perhaps we feel powerless to appropriate or critique; perhaps we sense we readers have no such rights. As one critic, Takekoshi Yoshio, has flatly asserted, "There is no room to insert 'interpretation' or 'appreciation.'"[61] Or as Susan Sontag put it, interpretation can in some cultural contexts be "reactionary, impertinent, cowardly, stifling"; for some things, perhaps a nuclear attack, there is no need for interpretation for there is no need to explain.[62]

The fundamentally different and potentially radical way we read atomic-bomb literature has been pointedly noted by critic Nakajima Kenzō. Speaking of the most famous Japanese examples of atomic-bomb literature, he claimed that they

> are of a different species from other literary works. . . . The reason has to do with the situation in which they were written. This is not a question of artistic merit. Rather, the conditions that produce art are different here than in other works. . . . Is it not a characteristic of contemporary literature that we can no longer ignore the conditions that exist prior to literature, the conditions that allow the literary work to assume its shape? Indeed, it does not suffice to say that we "cannot ignore" such conditions: we must consider them paramount.[63]

What Nakajima acknowledges is the controlling presence of the historical event—one that inspires fear, awe, and guilt—in the production and reception of atomic-bomb literature's meaning as well as significance. Has a work in the history of Japanese literature ever had to overcome a reluctance to read it that is derived not from an inability to understand its contents, but rather from our purported notion that we already, in our imagination, understand it *too* well? That there is then little or no need to bombard that imagination with further, grotesque details? Details with which any modern person is presumably acquainted?

We think of a literary work's systems of meaning in terms of the diverse processes that operate between text and reader. Sometimes, if now less often, we include an author. But only very infrequently do we add anything as extratextual as "reality" or "the outside world" as a control on the work's production of meaning. But in the case of atomic-bomb literature, this often absent or suppressed context is overwhelmingly and devastatingly present. The "bombing" cannot be fiction: its vestiges are there in Hiroshima and Nagasaki to see. But of course it *is* a "fiction," a story for those of us who were not there, and a memory structured as a story for those who were. This ambivalence, this contradiction, of the status and value of the bombing as "reality" within the poem, the novel, or the play makes that "reality" problematic as well as literary, and it is a problematic often noted by writers as well as critics. The very act of *writing* the bomb is a willed participation *in* the bombing, and consequently it is an act approached with a trepidation bordering on terror. In October 1945 the novelist Unno Jūza discussed his coming to grips with the reality that something called an "atomic bomb" was used on Hiroshima: "When I think of how casually we use the words 'atomic bomb,' I interpret them as a phrase identifying whatever *that* was."[64] Unno finds the application of the two words "atomic" and "bomb" to signify "what" happened uncanny, strange, even alienating. How much more so, then, for a hibakusha writer such as Ōta Yōko, who told us that those same two words were ones she both had, and had not, to write.[65] Perhaps all memoirists of atrocious violence experience such feelings of radical estrangement, feelings that can so easily handicap writing; then again, perhaps for all of us writing has to be, as Barthes insisted, a "compromise between freedom and remembrance."[66] It is something to marvel, then, how so many—and not so few—have succeeded in repressing, or occasionally exploiting, those feelings (that memory) in order *to* write.

Such contrary impulses come from the fact that words on a page suddenly seem detached from assimilated experience to become part of something "other," something which the author no longer controls or perhaps will ever again completely recognize. Despite the destruction of which they speak, those portable words become something oddly affirmative, present, permanent. This runs directly counter to what many hibakusha believe to have been the most far-reaching consequences of the bombings. Kurihara Sadako, for example, has written that "all the literary arts created by the human race, all the bittersweet romances of men and women, all the babies sleeping in their cradles, all our species—all were destroyed in an instant by that evil energy."[67] Kurihara's "all" is not qualified. It includes the most social of our cultural inheritances, the very language in which we communicate, or perhaps now do not communicate. Atomic-bomb literature is riddled from the first of its words with a self-critical suspicion of its own worth, with a nagging doubt that it may somehow constitute a moral betrayal. Hiroshima and Nagasaki began as atrocities undergone involuntarily, without choice. To write of it is to be confronted with a chain of choices, such as whether to narrate, dramatize, or lyricize; whether to speak from one's own point of view or that of another; whether to speak *to* the victims or the nonvictims, or even the victimizers; and of course, what words to use to communicate, what words to use to *not* communicate. The resolution of any of these decisions is the first abrogation of—for some, the liberation from—the debilitating passivity imposed upon the victim-writer, a term which in itself combines both powerlessness and power. This is a process of self-realization that perhaps every atomic-bomb writer we read today has gone through, a process which doubtlessly results in the suppression of some truths of the bombings in order to promote others. "Critical and imaginative works are answers to questions posed by the situation in which they arose," wrote Kenneth Burke. "They are not merely answers, they are *strategic* answers, *stylized* answers."[68] It is a process, then, that entails both an engendering and a killing off; it is an acute understanding of what happens, albeit with far less at stake, in other literature as well. The literary work, far more consciously for these writers than others, is a manipulation, a compromise, a closed door as well as an open one. It is a work that knows well how slippery and often ironic the relationship can be between the thing and how it is signified. At the same time we readers note how we construct that signified in an active process of reception, if only because the signified is something which inspires such apprehension in us. Cornered by history, atomic-bomb writers have made choices that lead them variously to represent the bombings in ways disturbingly strange and familiar to us all at once.

Some write on pebbles: wishes for peace placed at the foot of the
Hiroshima memorial to Korean victims of the bombing.

Defectiveness of form arises from defectiveness of content.

Hegel, *The Philosophy of Fine Art*

2

Genre and Post-Hiroshima Representation

We are accustomed to thinking of literary genres—such as, in the West, lyric poetry, epic poetry, the novel, and the essay; or in Japan, *waka* (traditional thirty-one syllable lyric), *shi* (modern free verse), *shōsetsu* (fiction), and *hyōron* (criticism)—as primarily taxonomic devices, collections of "like forms." At the same time, however, we recognize their historicity. Novels or shōsetsu, for example, are thought of as those genres that in modernity have superseded others, as genres both formally and topically better suited to representing contemporary life and its problems than other forms of writing. Neither of these assumptions is to be discarded when discussing the genres in which atomic-bomb literature is written. In them, too, previous "forms" will be evident (if in some cases only through their conspicuous absence), as will strikingly new elaborations of those forms.

Any survey of atomic-bomb literature's genres additionally emphasizes the schemata of generic forms that are protean in how they negotiate their intelligibility to the reader. Genres are indicative of a particular productive relation to reality acting as a standard—more precisely, an expectation—to guide us in our reading. What we typically mean when we identify a genre is to pinpoint a possibility of meaning, a way of naturalizing a work and of assigning it a place within our categories of cultural representation: to tame, as it were, an experience by tailoring it to a familiar discourse, a discourse we privilege by deigning it "realistic," "aesthetic," or "affecting."

Or, as it turns out, none of those things, should the atomic-bomb writer's aim be to make strange or discontinuous our conventions of cultural representation. If any genre invites a particular form of communication, while precluding others, then the choice of any one genre in lieu of others is already a communication inscribed with the "meaning" of Hiroshima and Nagasaki. If the theme of a work is to play a role in determining the nature of that work's genre, then in theory there may be subjects finally intractable for *any* genre: and then that very failure serves us as a "representation." Any statement on representation, in other words, *is* a representation. Genre is an operation of confinement, privileging, and sometimes protest: but it always *means*.

Consequently, the atomic-bomb writer's determination of genre is not just an aesthetic selection but indeed a historical, epistemic, semiotic, and quite possibly political one, an exercise of choice charged with the weight of responsibility remarkable for its implications for our cultural givens. The "truth" of a historical or artistic representation resides in its effectiveness in supporting a position we can often identify as ideological. Many early discussions, both Japanese and American, of the bombings were conducted against the backdrop of a romantic "atomic energy utopianism." Hiroshima and Nagasaki are cited as "steps" in a process that may have produced terrible weapons but will also lead to a perfected technological society. Such discussions, now rarer but by no means extinct, are "redemptive narratives" that manage to justify nuclear energy's initial, unfortunate, military uses. The ideology informing this scientific utopianism resonates with that of industrial capitalism dating back to the eighteenth and nineteenth centuries, when each new alienating development in the workplace was accommodated with a promise of an augmented human freedom from toil and poverty. "Better living," we once were told, "through chemistry." Such leaps in logic are linked to the naturalization of the bombings into Japanese literary and nonliterary discourses, and beyond to the accommodation of new stories to genres variously capable of retelling them. The hibakusha writer has new experiences that for us must be translated into new expectations: expectations that both comply with and deviate from heretofore accepted modes of intelligibility, "intelligibility" defined as congruency with either the newer or older ideologies we often unreflectingly inhabit.

To some degree the Japanese writer has specifically Japanese problems when choosing a genre. One of the many ironies of atomic-bomb literature is that it is the Japanese who would have to deal, first, with the literary theme of nuclear war, since in various ways their high cultural traditions, when compared to those of the West—especially after the carnage of the First World War led to the articulation of a modern ironic idiom—were less equipped for the task. When Ortega y Gasset wrote with that carnage in mind that "The first consequence of the retreat of art upon itself is a ban on all pathos. Art laden with 'humanity' had become as weighty as life itself,"[1] it was Europe's experience of modern, technologically enabled atrocious warfare that made his words so appropriately ironic. The Japanese, whose modern wars have largely been fought in other peoples' countries, had not quite such an ironic idiom for their literature. But with the last years of the Second World War, Japanese writers' historical gap with their counterparts in Europe narrowed, and they faced the same difficult issues, including those of selecting genre, that many twentieth-century writers seeking an accommodation of terrific violence with aestheticizing cultural practices confronted. The rupture between the memory of experience and generic forms for both Holocaust and atomic-bomb writers may be so unbridgeable that some of the literary attempts to reconcile the two appear today awkward, trivial, or even nonsensical.

Western literature of atrocity and Japanese atomic-bomb literature both occupy all genres, which is to say they have sought the authority of each genre's diverse rhetorical potentials to represent violence, cruelty, and ethical havoc. At the same time the literature of atrocity both East and West has sought to describe, within respective rhetorical systems, systems of survival. There are many ways of looking at genres—each exerts its particular power over the reader, such as theater's tendency to involve (or alienate) us, poetry to enthrall us, fiction to engage us, and so on—but insofar as all genres represent Hiroshima and Nagasaki by choosing some representative or associative aspect of those cities, each genre dictates its representation of Hiroshima and Nagasaki as, broadly defined, a figure. Each trope moreover carries with it a foregrounding and an erasure of the totality of the bombings. A metaphoric approach, while it ambitiously aspires to mark the whole of the atrocity, simultaneously risks distraction through its substitution of one *thing* for another. The metonymical approach, where some associated part of the violence—most commonly one victim's testimony, or fate—while focusing on literal fact in ways metaphors do not, again risks distortion by implying a limit to the ultimate force of those isolated facts.

The first strategy to circumvent the pitfalls of rhetoric and figural structures is, most commonly, to be as literally "historical" as possible so as to preclude the corruptive effects of language. In fact, discursively restrained scientific and historiographic materials likely constitute the most voluminous category of writings on the atomic-bombs, a fact that points to the same valorization of the rational that was implicated in the production and deployment of nuclear weapons in the first place. The most widely disseminated example of a hyper-objectivized account of Hiroshima and Nagasaki, i.e., an account that works to expel sentiment and ethical evaluation from its enumeration of fact, is the massive *Hiroshima and Nagasaki: The Physical, Medical, and Social Effects of the Atomic Bombings* (Hiroshima-shi Nagasaki-shi no gembaku saigai, 1979). Collaboratively produced by a committee of Japanese scholars drawing upon several decades of scientific study, most of this work represents a collation of diverse disciplinary "truths" that in aggregate attempt to comprehend the "fact" of Hiroshima and Nagasaki without resort to arguable interpretation. To cite one of the less technical passages:

> Ultraviolet rays and near-ultraviolet rays were almost completely emitted within 15 milliseconds (time to temperature minimum in figure 2.4) after the explosion, and the total energy of ultraviolet rays and near-ultraviolet rays reaching the ground was extremely small. It can, therefore, be assumed that the heat rays causing thermal burns in human subjects were infrared rays emitted in vast amounts 0.2 to 3 seconds after the explosion.[2]

To term the victims of thermal burns "human subjects," rather than "human beings" or simply "humans," is to turn humanness into just one type of "subject" among others. It is difficult for the reader to associate himself with the targets being killed by "infrared rays emitted in vast amounts." The effect on the reader of such depersonalized narrative can easily be detached indifference, and may even preclude the possibility of reading with a sense of irony—and thus of the "real"—the import of such assembled facts, statistics, and charts. When the United States Strategic Bombing Survey of 1946 concluded of Hiroshima and Nagasaki that many "people undoubtedly died several times over, theoretically, since each was subjected to several injuries, any of which would have been fatal," it is both an easy thing—given the matter-of-fact tone of such wording—and an impossible one to continue reading any further, should we stop and consider the implications of what it means to die "several times over."[3]

Any of several things can happen to these sorts of highly "objectivized," historically and ethically disinterested narratives when transferred to disciplines granted license to interpret. In the face of so much raw data that must somehow be organized to "make sense," historians are forced, as Erich Auerbach noted of the David stories in the Old Testament, "to make concessions to the technique of legend."[4] This is to say the historian may present his data in the form of linked anecdotes, a method that produces both a story and the impression of comprehensiveness, i.e., a story beyond that which we are reading. John Hersey's *Hiroshima* is an example of this. Or conversely, we may intellectualize by abstracting from data, as in the "academic writing" represented by this study, and withdraw from the weighty import of such data by treating it with professional detachment, and thus remove ourselves from the literalness of the atomic-bomb experience. In the former approach, we gain a degree of readability but at the cost of precise historiography; in the latter, we may think we are precise, but that precision does not translate into the most compelling of understandings.

Testimonial literature is the earliest and still most voluminous genre of atomic-bomb literature. It is also the least professional, in the sense that it is generated for reasons other than those demanded by a career. "The will to bear witness," noted Terrence Des Pres, "is an involuntary reaction to extreme situations. Survivors do not so much decide to remember and record, as simply find themselves doing it, guided by the feeling that it *must* be done."[5] In large measure testimonial accounts are examples of the anecdotal, in fact metonymical, strategy used for the representation of Hiroshima and Nagasaki. In a Hayashi Kyōko story entitled simply "Document" (Kiroku, 1977), the narrator notes of her project in writing of the atomic-bomb death of a classmate that "it may be an obvious thing to say, but unless I record [*kiroku*] with care how she died, then her very life becomes something that was obscure."[6] By "recording" is meant testimony: the chronological narration of recalled experience from a single and unified first-person point of view wholly identifiable with the author, which is to say the testifying survivor. "In 1945 at that time," begins Doi Sadako's account, "my sister and I were working at the Munitions Authority."[7] "Standing at my picture window facing west," writes Kanaya Masako in hers, "I was idly gazing at the deep blue sky."[8] "I" (*watakushi*) so often commences these memoirs because both the genre and the experience converge upon that singular pronoun, charging it with both narrative and historical "authority." "At the time each of us believed that our house had received a direct hit," recalls Hiroshima hibakusha Sera Megumi, suggesting that the experience of the bombing as well as her account of it that followed placed "each" victim alone at its very center.[9]

But the eye-witness subject is itself a rhetorical position insofar as it argues for an inarguable right to experience that is construed as "remembered." When Hara Tamiki said that his method in the semi-testimonial work *Summer Flowers* (Natsu no hana, 1949) was "simple realism," he feigned an ignorance of literary artifice in order to gain, from us readers, credibility.[10] Yet such artifice is abundantly there even in its very denial. Despite the fact that most works by atomic-bomb victims are in no way conceived as "literary," beyond the obvious literary choice of a point of view there are also the domesticating—if nonetheless terrible—similes, metaphors, and ironies strategically embedded in even the most naive of descriptions. "As the tongues of fire spread," writes Iwamoto Hakuzō, a chauffeur by profession,

all the city became a sea of flames. . . . From time to time, from moment
to moment, the northerly wind would rage to turn the fires erupting from
windows into dragon-like tornadoes, snaking in circles to ignite everywhere the foliage about the shores of the pond. The smaller trees, from
their roots to their uppermost branches, were carried up to the heavens
only to plummet back down into the water.[11]

Even terms as frequently used in testimonial accounts to describe what
occurred on August 6th and 9th as *jigoku, abi,* and *kyōkan*—all terms for various
types of Buddhist "hells"—are examples of how the victim-writer seeks a historical and cultural context within which to express his memory. Hiroshima
hibakusha Kitayama Futaba, for instance, cited a mother's dedication to her
children—a sentiment that squares with the most conservative Japanese cultural assumptions—as the source of her determination to survive. "For the five
years that have passed since that day," she declared, "I have endured the shame
and ignominy of my ugly crippled body only for the sake of my poor children."[12] Indeed, where individual "memory" ends and participation in the signifying conventions of a language, discourse, or cultural tradition begins is not
easily ascertained. Memory itself is often what the social self has been cultivated to note and preserve, not what the experiential self recounts as any literal
sequence of events.

"Memory" is a term that, despite its privileged rhetorical tie to experience,
is routinely subjected to the same rearticulations and recontextualizations as
any narrative that circulates synchronically through a culture, or diachronically
through time. One of the most important collections of hibakusha testimonies
is *Surviving the Bomb: Atomic-bomb Victim Memoirs* (Gembaku ni ikite—gembaku
higaisha no shuki, 1953), compiled under the principal direction of Hiroshima
left-wing organizer and writer Yamashiro Tomoe. Its twenty-seven personal
accounts were not assembled as most such collections have been: rather than
advertise through the media for submissions, Yamashiro and her colleagues
decided to approach hibakusha less apt to promote their own accounts, or who
in fact were for physical or emotional reasons unable to compose them in the
first place. They visited hibakusha in their homes, transcribed oral histories,
and edited them around one common theme: the isolation and loneliness of
the most marginalized of the survivors. But this aggressive role played by the
editors made Yamashiro especially aware of her role in speaking *for* hibakusha
as they were, in theory, assisting the survivors to speak for themselves:

Our fundamental rule in aiding the hibakusha with their memoirs was
not to interject our own point of view. . . . Even when we provided aman-
uensis, we always remained faithful to the testifying survivor's intention.
Yet because we were so aware of hibakusha concerns and limitations, it

was as if we ourselves were speaking directly of the experience, and we found ourselves unable to write in the frankest of language.[13]

The testimonies in *Surviving the Bomb* are articulated twice: once by the victims themselves, and a second time by the editors who confuse their own position with that of those they mean to serve. Kamata Sadao, editor of the final volume in the massive series of survivor accounts entitled *Nagasaki Testimonies* (Nagasaki no shōgen, 1969–78), acknowledged a similar point when he noted that "Most atomic-bomb memoirs are one-time accounts. But through the collusion of the survivors and the editors, these stories remain in circulation to cross into new and unexplored territory."[14]

This territory is presumably what happens to testimonial accounts once they are edited, printed, and allowed to pass among readers with no direct knowledge of what is described. The tendency must surely, for even the most literal of survivor memoirs, inspire allegorical or symbolic readings, given the non-hibakusha's presumed lack of specific reference. In testimony particularly, the form which experience assumes is so personally and thus "reliably" conveyed that it can seem actually contrived lest the reader take care to understand how the words have come to his attention. Hibakusha themselves have remarked how "unreal" their own words seem to them, upon rereading, years later. The memoirist, the veteran of atrocious violence, is often estranged from that experience in ways that give the retelling a "distancing" that might resemble a consciously literary stance. Kitayama Futaba, in her testimony cited earlier, reflected that she "felt a dull pain that seemed to come from a pain originating in some far place not my own body."[15] This is an estrangement, however, that leads not to a wider comprehension of the range of the violence but indeed frequently to a willed blindness to its import. The survivor—and even more often, the interested non-hibakusha—may elect to move away from first-person testimony and toward the documentary narrated in the third person: a choice that seems to be the consequence of an acute awareness of just such an existential alienation.

■

In September 1945, novelist Toyoshima Yoshio noted that during the war everyone had been hoping for a truly "literary work." But what, Toyoshima countered, is such a work? What is now needed in the immediate wake of history, he argued, are "human documents" (*ningen kiroku*). With such words he invoked the power of the literal fact over not only the imagination but the individual.[16] Documentary writing is still writing focused on factuality, but the point of view is less fixed to a testifying first-person subject. Narration in documentary, and especially in documentary fiction, is fluid: in some instances it is omniscient, in others it is comprised of shifting first- or third-person perspectives. In one of the genre's best-known examples, Hachiya Michihiko, head of the Hiroshima Communications Hospital when the city was bombed, took careful notes of what transpired in his clinics—purposefully avoiding all unverifiable second-hand reports—over the next month and a half. These notes, rewritten, comprise the text of his *Hiroshima Diary*. But as in the case of testimony, no work of atomic-bomb literature with any point-of-view is merely "factual." From a purely formal perspective, there are properly speaking no facts at all, but instead only narrative elements that appear (or are made to appear) as such because the reader accepts them without the resistance of doubt. This is not to say that a statement such as "An atomic bomb was exploded over Hiroshima" is not in some inarguable, verifiable sense a fact. Rather, it is to note, additionally, that such statements are also positioned within narratives that make use of facts in ways better characterized as interpretive and rhetorical. Take, for example, this famous paragraph:

> Everything fell, and Miss Sasaki lost consciousness. The ceiling dropped suddenly and the wooden floor above collapsed in splinters and the people up there came down and the roof above them gave way; but principally and first of all, the bookcases right behind her swooped forward and the contents threw her down, with her left leg horribly twisted and breaking underneath her. There, in the tin factory, in the first moment of the atomic age, a human being was crushed by books.[17]

We are apt to read this as documentary description, though it could conceivably be the extremely sophisticated literary testimony of a first-person narrator who observed Miss Sasaki's death. What marks it as documentary is its terse but powerfully organized account of an incident narrated "objectively" from some exteriorized viewpoint. But in fact, that viewpoint is thoroughly integrated, interpretively and rhetorically, in key phrases of the paragraph. "Everything fell, and Miss Sasaki lost consciousness." This is a statement of fact perhaps, though unlike "An atomic bomb was exploded over Hiroshima" one probably unverifiable and conceivably even invented. Yet here is a "fact" that anthromorphizes August 6th in ways that make it a cultural property as well as a historical event. Sasaki, an individual "Miss," becomes a metonymy of the "everything" that "fell." And her tragedy, described both chronologically and ethically as "principally and first of all," is the devastatingly ironic fate of being "crushed by books": this is also potentially a fact, but it is certainly a trope of the bomb itself, as it makes "books" and nuclear fission the newly covalent signs of our advanced civilization.

Such use of metonymy, metaphor, and irony is only possible through the agency of an authorial point of view, in this instance that of the "documentary" author. On the one hand, we may believe all these things happened largely because the documentary narrative authority—the impersonal voice—presents them as facts. The strong impression of its certainty serves to buttress a particular explanation of events, of history, implicit in the choice of the documentary approach. On the other hand, for all we really know, this incident might be entirely invented—its author, John Hersey, was after all not actually present in Hiroshima. This indeterminacy, however, is accommodated without issue because the reader quickly grasps the important point of the anecdote: not that one person died—we already know that tens of thousands did—but someone who could have been ourselves, or our sister or daughter, died in a way that signified how all human life and history of achievement were changed by the events of that morning.

This paragraph is excerpted from probably the best known documentary work on either Hiroshima or Nagasaki. Though not written by a Japanese— John Hersey was a news correspondent when he published it in the *New Yorker* in 1946—that circumstance was in fact precisely what allowed it to be published in Japanese translation, in Japan, three years later.[18] The Occupation censors would not have allowed a Japanese the same liberty in sympathetically portraying the half-dozen Hiroshima hibakusha whom Hersey memorialized. *Hiroshima* had at least as powerful an impact in Japan as it did in the United States. Nagaoka Hiroyoshi, Japan's first and most widely read literary historian of Hiroshima and Nagasaki, has noted that it was Hersey's work, and not any by fellow Japanese, that first introduced him to what had occurred on August 6th.[19]

Hersey's method was to rely upon reports he gathered from hibakusha and present them, in narrative fashion, as a general account of the bombing. The impact on readers was apparently overwhelming precisely because Hersey's prose was so underwhelming. Taking care not to alienate readers only a year distant from the racial rhetoric of the Second World War by demanding sympathy for the victims as a group, Hersey wisely and cleverly deracinated his handful of victims by, first, making one of them a German Jesuit, and secondly but more effectively keeping his narrative focus on the details of lives so individual as to resemble the reader's own. One critic praised Hersey's approach in terms consistent with the favorable reception the book received from the majority of its readers:

> Hersey's language is always kept under rigid control—a plain, direct language that rarely reaches for rhetorical effect and remains subordinate to character and event. . . . The tone of the book is one of artful understatement—appropriate for the muted, uncomprehending suffering of the survivors, and appropriate for the reader; the tone allows him to experi-

ence, through a matter-of-fact language pitched carefully below the inherent level of the event, what otherwise might have been unendurable, overwhelming consciousness rather than heightening it.[20]

It can be argued, of course, that even if there is no rhetoric in *Hiroshima*—an assertion I hope to have already demonstrated to be inaccurate—the very suppression of rhetoric is itself rhetorical when the event described, here an atomic bombing, would seem to warrant at the very least some deserved measure of hyperbole. "Artful understatement" begins to look oxymoronic once one sees that Hersey's restraint of his subjective display of manipulative language may only serve to reassert it.

It is revealing, however, to note that *Hiroshima*, like Hersey's earlier *A Bell for Adano*, was modeled on Thornton Wilder's *The Bridge of San Luis Rey*, a wholly imaginative work which, like *Hiroshima*, leaves the reader oddly comforted by the inevitability, the appropriateness, of the deaths described. All three rely upon the similar rhetoric mechanisms: the power of impersonal narration to mimic historiographic narrative authority and the hallmark of documentary writing, deliberate understatement:

> Dr. Fujii sat down cross-legged in his underwear on the spotless matting of the porch, put on his glasses, and started reading the Osaka *Asahi*. He liked to read the Osaka news because his wife was there. He saw the flash. To him—faced away from the center and looking at his paper—it seemed a brilliant yellow. (15)

This hibakusha started his day as many of us might, and moreover does so in a way that demonstrates affection for his wife. We are there with him, in other words, and the oblique way in which he takes note of the blast—a light reflected on a page of paper—is again a trope of our own knowledge of the bombing via Hersey's linked anecdotes on the page not of Osaka's daily newspaper, but New York city's literary weekly.

Hiroshima undoubtedly had an important and salutory effect on its readers, especially those in America. It converted the Japanese—the "Miss" and the "Dr." and the "Rev."—into easily recognized human beings and repealed the degrading effects of earlier wartime propaganda. Hersey's project seems to have been to make Hiroshima familiar but also ideal. The lives of his subjects strike us on one hand as typically quotidian, but their moral characters are clearly, from the general American point of view, exemplary. Several of them, for instance, are Christian: an adherence statistically rare in Japan, but perhaps diplomatically useful for Hersey in the rehabilitation of the Japanese people after a decade of systematic vilification. There are many risks Hersey takes here, however. In addition to the narcissism such representation of hibakusha legitimates—that is to say, the victims are to be regarded sympathetically to the degree they resemble "us"—a related danger is the likely implication that the humanness of the victims was indeed contingent upon their leading a recognizably good life. Most of those present in Hiroshima on the 6th, of course, subsequently led no life at all. A reviewer for the *Times Literary Supplement* cited the work for its inauthenticity when he observed, "The living occupy all the foreground, and the mounds of the dead are only seen vaguely in the background."[21] Mary McCarthy, the critic who took the most pointed exception to Hersey's approach, attacked *Hiroshima* for similar reasons. "To recreate the Hiroshima bombing by interviewing survivors . . . was an insipid falsification of the truth of atomic warfare. To have done the atom bomb justice, Mr. Hersey would have had to interview the dead."[22]

There are other problems, however, not specific to Hersey's *Hiroshima* but in fact germane to much documentary writing on atrocity. Such writing raises its own set of obstacles even as it avoids testimony's tendency to restrict the focus of its description. These quandaries derive again from the exclusions that the inclusion of certain rhetorical strategies necessitate. The impersonal narration of documentary serves to remove the author from participation in its events, which may engender a kind of lack of moral participation in the implications of those same events. "The 'little people' of Hiroshima whose sufferings Hersey records in antiseptic *New Yorker* prose," wrote Dwight MacDonald, "might just as well be white mice, for all the pity, horror, or indignation the reader—or at least this reader—is made to feel for them."[23] The deliberate understatement used to create such distance, while avoiding the alienation of the reader that can conceivably arise from hyperbole, nonetheless chances giving rise to ironic effects that can license the counterproductive reaction of reading from a point of view safely removed from that of the hibakusha themselves. In a chapter whose very title—"Details Are Being Investigated"—guarantees we readers are to be in a position epistemically superior to the agents conducting such investigations, Hersey writes:

> Those victims who were able to worry at all about what happened . . . discussed it in more primitive, childish terms—gasoline sprinkled from an airplane, maybe, or some combustible gas, or a big cluster of incendiaries, or the work of parachutists; but even if they had known the truth, most of them were too busy or too weary or too badly hurt to care that they were the objects of the first great experiment in the use of atomic power. (65–66)

The premise of this passage's irony, namely that we today know "the truth," is of course subject to debate. We may, if scientifically literate, be familiar with how an atomic bomb functions; but that "truth" is distinctly abstract, and it might well strike a hibakusha rich in experiential "truth" as not true at all. Such writing may indeed work to undo the empathy between reader and hibakusha that Hersey's narrative strategies so carefully cultivate. This is not to argue, however, that Hersey should have done differently. In another of the many contradictions found throughout atomic-bomb literature, both Japanese and American, *Hiroshima*'s rhetorical inconsistencies reflect the same crisis the rhetoric was intended to convey in the first place. What choice, after all, did Hersey, or any other writer of documentary, have? One cannot interview the dead, and to invent such interviews is only to invite one charge of inauthenticity to take the place of another. Perhaps to write "documentary" is already to insert an epistemic distance between the writer and his subject that, besides allowing for an anesthetized and safe moral barrier, exposes the deficiencies of naturalistic writing, writing that pretends to make reality readily available. Both aesthetically and ethically, such writing is no longer capable of coping with the scale of modern violence. Hersey himself concludes much the same when he wrote that "the change was too sudden, from a busy city of two hundred and forty-five thousand that morning to a mere pattern of residue in the afternoon" (53). Too sudden, that is, to register, comprehend, or explain: the mere accumulation of facts can indeed disorient our capacity to respond to them, the same difficulty encountered with testimony but further compounded by the implausible construct of an omnipresent, omniscient point of view. Finally, what plagues equally the practice of testimonial and documentary atomic-bomb writing is both the devalued utility of fact within our twentieth-century stories and the simultaneous requirement of our twentieth-century history for comprehending some facts, at least those implicated in our very survival, with urgently exacting precision.

■

If facts—thus far understood as constructions in language that point outwardly to verifiable events and phenomena imbued with a privileged significance, and inwardly to their formal functions within the rhetorical systems of narrative—become meaningless in the face of sheer incredulity or multiplicity, then there is a genre that does not rely upon them. Or rather, there is a genre that easily surrenders the dogmatic view of facts as unyieldingly fixed and instead exploits the otherwise frustrating duality of a fact's centrifugal and centripetal semiotic nature. Such a genre is not rare, avant-garde, or experimental: indeed poetry may be the most voluminous of all atomic-bomb literatures. For reasons that no doubt have much to do with Japan's long tradition of popular (in the sense of amateur) as well as professional poem-making, hibakusha have composed poems that, even in the select examples eventually anthologized, number in the tens of thousands. The question arises why a practice of writing ordinarily considered of little use to the representation of history should have proved so attractive to the victims of Hiroshima and Nagasaki.

The poem, of course, enjoys a special renown among literary genres. In Japan as well as in the West, for most of cultural history to speak of literature was in effect to speak of poetry. Unlike prose, poetic language in various cultures and eras has pretended to a transcendental, immanent, or spiritual status that privileges that language with its own rhetorical authority. And in Japan, where poetry has long been predominantly lyrical, there is an oblique subjectivity posited in poetry that can resemble the testimonial potential of prose accounts. What is immediately salient about atomic-bomb poetry is how these features of poetry are preserved at the same time that its lines and language are infused with great numbers of "facts," and indeed much the same facts as one might discover in the testimonial and documentary texts of Hiroshima and Nagasaki. When Kurihara Sadako published *When One Says Hiroshima* (Hiroshima o iu toki, 1976), a collection of her Hiroshima verse, critic Kuno Osamu perceptively noted it was a work more properly termed a "poetic documentary" than a "poetic collection."[24]

It is perhaps the very tradition of poetry's inhospitality to fact, by which I mean historical representation, that makes Kurihara's and others' purposeful citation of Hiroshima and Nagasaki data—both personal and collective—so powerfully effective. "The concrete emphasis in poetic discourse that is, however, dislodged from any *particular* context," writes Berel Lang of Holocaust writing, "ramifies any specific historical point of reference designated in poetry."[25] At the same time, even where there are "facts" borrowed from memory, testimony, or documentary to be inserted into lyrical discourse, those facts become poetic themselves. What might be termed accurately, if awkwardly, as testimonial poetry—the largest category of atomic-bomb poetry—takes the witness's account, constructs it as verse and proceeds to "overdetermine" it in ways that encourage us to discern figures and symbols as well as phenomenal events. A Hiroshima professor of history, for example, wrote the following poem:

> Thinking a bomb must have fallen close to me
> I looked up.
> But it was a pillar of fire
> five kilometers ahead.[26]

This poem, aside from the single quasi-metaphor of "pillar of fire" (*hibashira*), is a straightforward and typical description of a literal experience, in no way different from a myriad other lines found in testimonial accounts. All that establishes it as a waka, the most common lyrical form in Japanese poetry, is that in the original Japanese, it presumably conforms to the standard of thirty-one syllables divisible into semantically viable lines of five, seven, five, seven, and seven syllables. But that suffices to shift the description into the realm of po-

etry, and thus into a mode in which we charge these otherwise "artless" words
with an authority, and a figural power, denied the prose it so closely duplicates.
Of course, such poetry and in particular its claim to *being* poetry are controversial: we are accustomed to dehistoricizing explicit references in poetry, making
a testimonial or documentary poetry all the more difficult to countenance.
What is at stake is the very relationship between what we readily accept as the
historical "event"—itself available to us only through a discursively organized
communication—and an experience that the hibakusha poets themselves
might well claim eludes articulation in language.

On the one hand atomic-bomb poetry, because it is poetry, is conceivably
the most explicitly "literary" of all atomic-bomb genres, while on the other
hand that same degree of literariness seems to disqualify it as atomic-bomb
literature because its relation to history is subordinated by that to language.
There has been a debate over whether, for instance, atomic-bomb poetry—
unlike testimonial or documentary atomic-bomb literature, which has never
justified its legitimacy on being imaginative "literature" *(bungaku)* per se—can
even be possible. Poet Yamada Kan asserts:

> The poverty of poetic expression after the August 9, 1945, atomic bomb-
> ing of Nagasaki, when compared to that city's rich tradition of poetry,
> makes one wonder what has happened. The subject of poetry has be-
> come greater than tragedy; the immense ruins that repudiate the tradi-
> tional rhythmic forms of waka and haiku, and the anxiety over death
> caused by the lingering effects of atomic-bomb disease, mean that the
> spirit of poetry is extinguished with only powerlessness left to it.[27]

There are, as I will argue later, perhaps special reasons why Nagasaki, more so
than Hiroshima, would see its production of poetry so stunned after the bombings. In any case, Yamada's point, while certainly valid, somewhat exaggerates
his native city's postwar dearth of poetic activity. But the passion of his words
echoes that of similar pessimistic assertions over the potential of literature in
the wake of mass violence, such as Adorno's famous, if eventually amended,
claim that poetry was impossible after Auschwitz.[28] In point of fact it is not so
much that there is a lack of atomic-bomb poetry. Rather, there is a changed
idiom in which that poetry writes itself, and a new inspiration to animate it.
Ōhara Miyao, a Hiroshima poet, argued in 1972:

> While the atomic bombing can never be anything considered "naturally"
> poetic, it is "natural" that residents of Hiroshima and Nagasaki would live
> their lives in an environment related to the bombings, just as city dwell-
> ers today find in their surroundings such new things as typewriters and
> stereos. It is also very "natural" that they would then create imaginative
> works out of that encounter. Consequently, should not "atomic-bomb

poetry" be permitted as a genre of the lyric, just as "romantic poetry," "religious poetry," "narrative poetry" and so on, are?[29]

Both Yamada and Ōhara have taken positions which, though contradictory, are common among both critics and practitioners of atomic-bomb poetry. That such poetry is both "unnatural" and "natural," something which seems so out of place in the ordinary world but so familiar to those who themselves lived through Hiroshima and Nagasaki, could have been an expected consequence of what nuclear war might produce. This gap between the local cultures of the two bombed cities and that of Japan—and the world—in general produces a poetry which, in large measure, has been produced and received with a disarming irony. Akiya Yutaka writes in his poem "Winter, the Assigned Theme" (Fuyu no shudai):

> What is this age to be called now?
> An age when all is only black?
> One word,
> one dream,
> one poem that is utterly gone.
> In my heart I feel like a soldier of silence.
> All you who speak so much,
> you call the illusions of this city "peace"?
> All that I believe in
> are the words within silence,
> words full of danger.[30]

Hiroshima and Nagasaki poets do write, despite the impulse to remain silent: the words they summon "are the words within silence," words that come not out of language but *into* it. The most interesting and demanding of these poets write with a sense of history peering over their shoulders, a history that forces them to see the difficulty of believing not in sure referents for their words, but in words for their sure referents: the bombings of August 6th and 9th. Such words may indeed be "full of danger." For poets of Hiroshima and Nagasaki, as perhaps for many modern poets, language is no longer an instrument of coherence, but a contrapuntal tool exploited to expose the slippage between language and its reality held to exist somewhere other than merely in tropes and meter. In this "concentrated" sense, atomic-bomb poetry exists at the center of the issue of the relationship between atrocity and human expression, which is to say atrocity and culture in general: "burnt lips" (tadareta kuchibiru), the recurring phrase in Hara Tamiki's poetry, for example, is literal and at the same time a metaphor for how the poet must speak: in pain, under duress, at best only in a soft murmur. That there is so much atomic-bomb poetry in Japan points to how such hurt may well be what the poet must finally speak.

■

The pain of the atomic-bomb poet, while "real" in ways we must be careful not to slight, is nonetheless a representation in language, and moreover a representation in language that—unless delivered in person, as in a public reading—is written and thus removed even further from the immediacy and authority of the testifying voice. This both restricts and frees the poem. The scripted nature of the poem opens it to interpretation. As a record of a historical experience, there may loom the risk of *mis*interpretation, but how is one to tell? Drama, by which I mean the modern representational stage, is also restricted and freed by its technology, yet in ways perhaps diametrically opposite that of poetry. On the one hand, the presence of speaking humans before an audience grants their speech a power and presence denied a text; but on the other, the imaginative participation of that audience is limited by such presence. This raises issues for a theater of atrocity, where presumably its theme cannot historically, practically, or ethically be reenacted, and where then the imagination must, as in poetry, be required to work with the dramatic "scene" tropically, be it as allegory, metaphor, or metonymy.

Ōhashi Kiichi, himself a noted atomic-bomb dramatist, has speculated on what the crucial differences might be between the prose literature of Hiroshima and Nagasaki and their theater:

> In literature the reader reads what is written; he forms an image in his mind created with the power of imagination. In the theater, however, the actor performs something before the spectator, and consequently does not have the assistance of the imagination. He communicates rather through the senses of sight, speech, and theatrical presence.[31]

Ōhashi cites imagination as the principal faculty in our ability to represent, and comprehend the representation of, Hiroshima and Nagasaki within literature. While more sophisticated theories certainly noted the role of imagination in the theater, Ōhashi exaggerates how modern mimetic drama works in order to establish what seems a crucial point. If a nuclear explosion cannot be presented literally on a stage before us, then like the battles for Troy in Shakespeare's *Troilus and Cressida* it must be displaced by and circumscribed with the more domesticable matters of its aftermath. In fact, there is no play, as there are many poems and stories, which mimetically depicts the actual bombings themselves. Ōhashi's banishment of imagination from the theater may be extreme, but certainly what faculty of imagination might intervene between stage and audience differs from that between reader and text. The "sense of presence" to which he refers curbs to some degree the associations we are apt to postulate between the immediacy of the play and the extent, historical or spatial, of its import.

It is this "sense of presence"—the fact that a live audience is watching live performers—that makes a theater of Hiroshima problematic. A nuclear explosion is not anticipated in the theories of either Aristotle or Zeami. How are actors to "act out" an atomic blast? Or be "there" on the mornings of August 6th and 9th? Moreover, how are we, the viewers, to countenance such violence even if it is "represented"? Imagination seems stimulated by the stage insofar as the acted allegory or the anecdote is taken metonymically by the audience as generally representative. But representative of the living: the very presence of live, speaking actors on the stage, even more so than that of survivor characters in a book, is already an exception, even a repudiation of the grotesque "whole" which is purportedly represented. When Berel Lang, for example, doubts the possibilities of representing the Final Solution within the confines of theater— "As drama does not have available the distancing device of authorial interven- tion, its action is characteristically motivated by the thought or will of individ- ual characters"[32]—that doubt arises from his understanding that modern geno- cide, Hiroshima and Nagasaki included, is an event whose causal chain is too abstracted and immense to be intimated easily in conversations between a few individual actors.

If a complex history, then, must necessarily be revised in order to make it amenable to dramatic representation, that revision is typically carried out through the process of retelling the story of Hiroshima and Nagasaki as either "comedy" or "tragedy." Comedy might at first seem an unlikely, even offensive, formula for a dramatist seeking a distilled, accurate truth of nuclear war. In the *Poetics*, Aristotle briefly describes comedy as dealing with everyday life in an amusing fashion, and with the aim of "representing men as worse . . . than in actual life." An atomic bomb, however, is hardly everyday or amusing, and its use—twice—leaves little room for the depiction of our moral character as baser than in fact. But if comedy, in contrast to tragedy, commences with a misfortune and concludes with a restoration of life "as it should be"—and this is as true of modern television programs as it is of Aristophanes—then comedy is not only a seductive but even irresistible formula for coping with what other- wise looms as profoundly threatening. In fact a great deal of atomic-bomb literature, not only drama, functions recuperatively as "comedy."

Despite its fantastic, nonrepresentational dramaturgy, playwright Satō Makoto's 1969 *Nezumi Kozō: The Rat* (Nezumi Kozō Jirokichi) is perhaps one of the best examples of how a comic atomic-bomb theater works. Its avant-garde idiom suggests a probable departure from the typically sentimental formula associated with more popular theatrical, film, or television representations.[33] At the same time, however, this avant-garde character makes its difficult to discuss the plot of *Nezumi*. Explained briefly, in a room decorated minimally as a cross between a communal bath and a Shinto shrine, a cast of five rats (*nezumi*) chase a "trans-historical" Lord of the Dawn (represented by a phallus-like prop meant apparently to signify Japanese emperors) and his Guardian through the "sewers." There are other characters as well—such as Heh-heh, So-so, and Bo-bo, Shinto mediums who are incarnations of "female genitalia, guides to hell, and cats." The atomic bomb figures in Satō's play as a mistaken falling star, the answer to the wishes of the rats. The climax of the action, according to the play's translator David Goodman, comes "at the point when the Nezumis' messianic élan is pulled out of its trajectory into the redundant orbit of Heh-heh, So-so, and Bo-bo."[34]

While much of the gleeful confusion of *Nezumi* may be attributed to the exuberant and perhaps self-indulgent excesses of late-1960s underground the-ater in Japan, it is precisely the awkward attempt to mythologize Hiroshima and Nagasaki by integrating them, again in the translator's words, "into the great pattern of human metahistory" (251) that renders the work less revolu-tionary than comic. As part of any "pattern," the destruction of two cities be-comes the validating demonstration of a law governing life "as it should be." Such a law inspires the playwright to view the bombings as events internally consistent historically. If Satō's view is that, as Goodman claims, the atomic bomb was dropped because "the Japanese wished it upon themselves" (262), then it is not only clear how a comedy of Hiroshima can lead to implications impossible to countenance, but also how, as George Steiner noted of Sylvia Plath's use of Holocaust imagery in poetry concerned with her relation to a deceased father, a "subtle larceny" is committed when a writer "appropriates an enormity of ready emotion to his own private design."[35]

If a Hiroshima comedy is inconceivable because the event itself cannot be reconciled with any private or public unity of experience, then it might be argued that a Hiroshima tragedy would, conversely, circumvent such a rewrit-ing of history. Certainly if, as Aristotle asserted, tragedy is the presentation of a serious and important action, arousing such emotions as pity and fear in order to purge those same emotions cathartically, then the atomic bombings would seem to qualify as suitable themes. If plays such as *Nezumi* are unworkable repre-sentations of atrocity because of their suspect displacement of tragedy, then perhaps tragedy is the strategy best suited for atomic-bomb drama, or at the very least the sort of theater we would expect to encounter the most frequently. The classical definition of tragedy, taken from Aristotle's *Poetics*, is that as the "imitation of an action that is serious, complete, and of a certain magnitude . . . through pity and fear effecting the proper purgation of these emotions." We might look for atomic-bomb tragedies among plays already "serious," and pos-sessing the "magnitude" to induce such a necessary, cathartic "purgation." "Tragedy," Camus wrote, "is not a solution," but it might still offer consider-able solace.[36]

In Hotta Kiyomi's 1955 *The Island* (Shima), Kurihara Manabu is a young Hiroshima hibakusha who, having fallen in love with a non-hibakusha, desires to marry her. Both his family and hers, however, oppose such a union on account of Manabu's uncertain health. When an acquaintance does die of atomic-bomb disease, the realization of their fears does indeed overwhelm their affection, and Manabu is resigned to his fate. Similarly, *The Elephant* (Zō), written by Betsuyaku Minoru and first performed in 1962, features as its central character a hibakusha, identified only as the "invalid," who is suffering from advanced atomic-bomb disease. Once he actively promoted himself as a victim, but now he is no more than a hospital patient forgotten by the public. As he nears death, he wants once more to display his keloid scars to strangers, but his nephew, also ill, tries to discourage him. At *The Elephant's* conclusion, the nephew delivers the play's key lines:

> Uncle, get this through your head. Listen. We mustn't do anything anymore. Not anything. To do something is the worst thing of all. No matter how hard it is, we've got to lie here patiently and keep our mouth shut. It's not because we're sick. That's not it. I don't say that. I'm no doctor. It's just that mustn't try to do things, that's all. We are incapable of doing anything except being persecuted, hated, and destroyed. We cannot even think about being loved. When we're not being murdered, hated, or tormented, we wait. There's nothing left for us but to wait. We rest quietly. (246)

Both plays are often considered tragedies (*higeki*); their hibakusha heroes consigned to destroyed lives they are powerless to affect, Manabu has been described as a "tragic hero," and Betsuyaku's nephew compared to Hamlet.[37] This is to confuse, however, the requirements of tragedy with the sentimentality of melodrama. Where is the requisite catharsis, the Aristotelian and distinctive effect of the tragic pleasure of "pity and fear"? Nowhere: either characters such as Manabu and the nephew are devoid of the essential flaw in their characters that must lead to a "tragic error in judgment," or, as David Goodman suggests in Manabu's instance, the tragic flaw lies in being a hibakusha. But the judgment that an audience must exercise in achieving its catharsis implies a kind of individual autonomy, an empowered subjectivity, which is invalidated or at least compromised by the mass and passive experience of modern atrocity. Indeed, it is hard to understand how any thorough victim can ever be rehabilitated as a tragic hero; and perhaps especially, this sort of hibakusha victim. When Frederick Hoffman wrote that "death as total surprise loses much of its tragic value," he identified one crucial characteristic of contemporary violence that steadfastly resists the formalization attempted in drama. This is of course also the reason why, in theater, the actual bombings themselves are never depicted on the stage. But more to the point, it is insurmountably difficult to write what Hoffman means by a "classic tragedy" about Hiroshima and Nagasaki. It would seem key to tragedy that the hero's death will, postmortem, mean something. There must be, again in Hoffman's words, "a clean view of the corpse."[38] In a sense it is a tragedy that has today precluded tragedy—if the greatest "tragedy" of the bombings was to have cast its victims out of any familiar terrain of human destiny and to have thrust them into an unknown and meaningless suffering, then we cannot call their fate conventionally "tragic" without making that suffering "known," "meaningful," and thus possibly ahistorical.

This is precisely what such works as *The Island* and *The Elephant* do in common, though one is cited as an example of "orthodox realism" and the other of Japan's "postmodern" theater. They become tragic only through repressing the uniqueness of Hiroshima and Nagasaki, which is to say those events' historicity. In *The Island*, for instance, Manabu's desperate fate is linked repeatedly with that of the historical figure and tragic epic hero Taira Kiyomori, who led his powerful clan to defeat in the twelfth-century civil wars. To connect rhetorically the destiny of Manabu the hibakusha with that of Kiyomori the fallen hero is to use metaphor, powerfully and deftly, to grant a bizarre kind of understanding and even sanction to what lies ahead for Manabu, namely his imminent death. The use of such a metaphoric strategy results in a dramatic work which, rather than demonstrating how the world has changed since and because of Hiroshima and Nagasaki, does just the opposite: it argues for a kind of changelessness, and a resignation, in the face of an essentially homogeneous Japanese "history" no more devastating now than in the twelfth century.

■

Other genres, however, have proved more hospitable for representing Hiroshima and Nagasaki in the context of a verifiably discontinuous, rather than mythically redundant, modern history. The imaginative literary genre often, if paradoxically, held to be the most faithful to the representation of the twentieth-century's ruptured history, as well as the most popular among readers, is the novel: or, as the Japanese more broadly term it, "fiction" (*shōsetsu*). It is upon this genre of atomic-bomb literature that subsequent chapters of this study will most often dwell, and consequently it will be that genre's especially stubborn, and indeed definitive, set of contradictions that animate critical debate. "Whoever pleads for the maintenance of this radically culpable and shabby culture," wrote Theodor Adorno with the post-1945 writer of fiction certainly in mind, "becomes its accomplice, while the man who says no to culture is directly furthering the barbarism which our culture showed itself to be."[39]

In addition to the ethical issue of writing at all after Auschwitz and Hiroshima, there is the formal hurdle of our investment in the novel as our most mimetic, and thus most narcissistic, practice of literary writing. Yet in Japan as elsewhere, the basic inclination of modern literary inquiry has been to make the difficulties of mimesis themselves a subject of mimesis, leading to a kind of stubborn self-doubt that already brackets the novel and discounts its worth to us as any reliable source of historiographic knowledge. This immanent ambivalence over the relationship of modern fiction to the possibility and validity of knowledge becomes disabling. Positions as opposite as Frederick Hoffman's—that "violent events fall outside factual representation"[40]—and Terrence Des Pres's—that those very events resist fictionalization, that "symbolic manipulations of consciousness no longer work"[41]—are positions that make for very different sorts of "novels" taking up the theme of atrocity. Like James Agee before him, Tanizaki Jun'ichirō gave up the attempt,[42] and novelist Takeda Taijun echoed Adorno when he argued that fiction is patently "impossible" after the bomb.[43]

Indeed, it is difficult, considering the fictional works of the modern canon, to imagine how Don Quixote, or Madame Bovary, or Anna Karenina, or any of Sōseki's antiheroes, would react to nuclear war. How they would *speak* of it, much less *live* it, in the orderly ways novels traditionally seem to structure themselves, is an important question for modern communities that rely on such fictions to represent themselves to themselves. What are we to make, after the events of the twentieth century, of Trollope's dictum that the novelist must first make himself "pleasant"? A "pleasant" hibakusha-writer, should one exist, might well be judged by readers to be insane. Yet an "unpleasant" one, true to Trollope's insight, could offend and thus lose the reader. How is the novelist both to make us identify with his victim-protagonists and at the same time spare us the consequences of that identification? How is the novelist to turn his "evidence" into our "narrative"? Is it perhaps inevitable that our non-hibakusha assumptions in reading will not make hibakusha texts sensible? Do we inevitably create "comfortable" novels out of ruinous experiences?

One possible way of coping with the questionable capacity of the modern novel to encompass Hiroshima or Auschwitz is to announce the death of the "novel" and proclaim the advent of something new and post-atrocity. When, for instance, Ortega y Gasset predicted long before the unprecedented events of mid-century that the modern novel, in effect "a vast but finite quarry," would not go on to render "ever new forms," he uncannily anticipated a world whose common occurrences could not, other than in the most ironic senses, be represented in bourgeois sitting rooms or first-class train compartments.[44] In fact, novels written today about the violence that divides this century usually qualify themselves as *different* sorts of novels, usually with some prefatory adjective: hence the "docu-novel," the "mythic novel," or even the "anti-novel," each an uneasy qualification that in some seemingly vital way amends or contradicts the means through which novels would conventionally represent "reality." What is at stake here is the definition and even the possibility of a common "humanity" whose presumption informs traditional understandings of the novel. The liberalism of traditional fiction is put to the test: how do we recognize as universal the scene we are presented? By the hibakusha writer's basic tendency to "tell" rather than "show"—so impatient are they that both their time and our powers of understanding are limited—atomic-bomb novels already discourage us from taking their contents as our own. But more to the point, if the basic convention of modern fiction is the expectation that we readers will therein construct a life which that fiction itself seems to propose, then the works of writers who insist on the particularity of their experience must be termed something other than "novels" or "shōsetsu."

But in fact all these issues are ones the novel has constantly faced in its history. The atomic bombings, like the death camps, are new "real" events for a new "realism" to encompass. Fiction has long had to confront the decay of what it seeks to preserve. The modern extended form of fiction, the novel, developed just as civilization, armed with an invigorated science, suddenly expanded to provide itself with an future limited only by our will to postpone collective suicide. A tradition of writing that had operated under the assumption it had inherited an order at once became something that would have to produce a new tradition bounded by that limit. In the words of Frank Kermode, this is an order "possibly attainable only after a critical process that might be called 'decreation.'"[45]

Decreation: the novel takes apart even as it builds up. For Kermode, examples would include Modernist and Existentialist literature, literature that plays with order instead of imitating it. But for Japanese atomic-bomb literature, the aesthetics of decreation are rivaled by the exigencies of destruction, an dis-order that still requires a mimetic art to make it culturally available, and thus real. Fukunaga Takehiko's *Island of Death,* a lengthy and rich novel whose complex manipulations of point-of-view and narrative time led fellow novelist Kaga Otohiko to term it the most avant-garde fiction produced in Japan since Natsume Sōseki's 1916 *Light and Dark* (Meian),[46] takes as its key theme the incommensurability of experience with representation. Motoko, a painter and also a Hiroshima hibakusha, is frustrated in her attempt to give form on canvas to something she only knows, or recalls, indistinctly. In the end Motoko destroys her paintings—as indeed she destroys her own life—in what is perhaps the ultimately mimetic gesture for an atomic-bomb victim who feels, as Motoko says of herself in the third person, impossibly empty, alienated, and lifeless:

She realized that she had already been utterly transformed into a separate existence no longer "woman," into something neuter neither male nor female. She had turned into a simple, single thing no longer human.

She knew all this because she could not believe that any act of will, or effort, or bravery would make her a woman or a human being again.[47]

Novels such as *Island of Death* display the very indetermination of human life even as they seem to determine it: this rhetorical aporia is very much the ironic lived experience of the victim-writer as well as perforce his literary strategy. The atomic bomb novel negotiates its form with its content, like all novels, but with special energies and a unique history. At stake is always the "realism" of the genre. Realism is a notion riddled with ideological premises—when Camus called it "an empty word (*Madame Bovary* and *The Possessed* are both realistic novels and they have nothing in common)" he was observing just how historically contingent it really is.[48] Realism, of course, is an idea that inspires especially loud controversy and debate, and not only within the circle of literary critics: if the charge of the novel is the pursuit of the real, it is a permanent quest, given that the "real" assumes such markedly different manifestations in different contexts and to different observers.[49]

The protean life of the "real," and thus the necessity for an equally fluid theoretical approach to its representation in atomic-bomb fiction, has been both an inspiration and frustration for Japanese atomic-bomb writers and critics. Hibakusha authors, for example, have regularly complained of the failure of language to be of use to them, post-Hiroshima. Yet it is that same perceived "failure" that is creatively challenged in so many of their works. Similarly, non-hibakusha intellectuals sensitive to the same slippage between the historical event and our discourse of the event have both despaired of, and been intellectually invigorated by, the implications of that slippage for literary practice. Odagiri Hideo, for example, wrote in an influential 1954 essay: "Conventional realism must move forward to meet with what [atomic weapons] now confront it. A new reality demands the development of new literary methods in order to grasp it. 'Realism' must make a quantum leap if it is to deal fully with the immense problems posed by the hydrogen bomb and its relation to it."[50]

For some writers, if only a few, this leap to a new realism has meant a move towards what may understandably look like "non-realism." The genre of Japanese atomic-bomb science fiction, represented most prominently by Takeda Taijun's 1951 *Button Number One* (Daiichi no botan), is an example of the attempt to be realistic, yet in ways not at complete odds with readers' notion of what appears presently "real." Set in the then distant year of 1990, an advanced and inhumanly rational science fully dominates private and national life but still requires crucial human collaboration: Suzuki, a man sentenced to die for assaulting the man who attempted to rape his sister, is pardoned in order to sit in front of a button ("Button Number One") whose function he is not told. Ordered to push the button one day, he becomes a national hero for destroying "the enemy of the species." Tortured by his conscience, he betrays a colleague who has begun to doubt the system they both serve: ironically, that colleague is killed by a member of a radical faction that opposes the tyranny of science. Published only a few years after Hiroshima and Nagasaki, *Button Number One* may reflect the public's widespread postwar apprehension over the ascendancy of a scientific technology undisciplined by humanism. To the degree that science fiction must be plausibly congruent with current expectations (including our apprehensions) of the future and at the same time cognitively estranged or disassociated from everyday life, it is a genre that, if unavailable to writers concerned with past events like Hiroshima or Nagasaki, nonetheless promises to negotiate the literally "real" and imaginatively "unreal" aspects of nuclear war.

But for most atomic-bomb writers, and certainly for those hibakusha writers singularly concerned with August 1945, the demand for a new realism has meant—and here the specificity of modern Japanese literary practice matters greatly—a renunciation of the tradition of the highly subjective and introspective I-novel *(shishōsetsu)* and in its stead a commitment to the pursuit in the novel of a more objectifiable historical, social milieu. This is not an original demand made of modern Japanese literature—atomic-bomb writers are certainly not the first Japanese to resist the excessively private purview of the I-novel and its progeny—but it is a demand especially pressed by atomic-bomb writers because, as Japanese literature has been aesthetically "psychologized," its potential as a tool of social critique is proportionately reduced. The resistance to the continued valorization of I-novel literature was waged with renewed and even urgent vigor by many writers in the wake of the Second World War, but none more than hibakusha writers writing out of their experiences in Hiroshima and Nagasaki. "Japanese literature . . . is a literature of defeat," complained Kurihara Sadako, speaking for many of her fellow Hiroshima authors and critics: "an I-novel literature full of evasion and complaint. There is no greater misfortune for literature in Japan than whenever the author must be sacrificed to this tradition."[51]

In the face of the ahistorical writing associated with the Japanese I-novel, the hibakusha response has often been to write testimonial or documentary novels, such as Ōta Yōko's *City of Corpses*, in which the narration is not exclusively concerned with the inner life of a first-person subject but instead places that subject in the midst of a world event. Although both responses, whether "testimonial" or "documentary," seek to replace the aestheticized world of the "artistic subject" with a larger world of atrocious fact, it is important to distinguish the quite different epistemologies associated with these two alternatives. It is a matter of the status of the narrator: whether, as in testimony, the first-person narrator will be allowed his urgency, authority, and centrality, or whether, as in documentary, that narrator is either an authorial fiction or, as is most often the case, absent entirely. With this choice comes the decision to represent Hiroshima and Nagasaki as individual "experiences" or historical "fact": it is a question of the relations that obtain between a literary form—a "genre"—and the gruesome details of a story that work against their own containment.

Those relations are, both in theory and practice, unfixed. Variously negotiated between writers and the words they use to authorize their representations of Hiroshima and Nagasaki, the awkward coupling of the hibakusha's words with his distrust of those words predicts a pattern of contradiction, tension, paradox, and above all irony that, more any than other characteristic, defines atomic-bomb literature. And, one could add, its significance as well. The undermining of so many determinants of modern culture—progress, civilization, the ethical, and even the cognitive subject itself—is in fact the potential subversion of modernity and its collateral cultural effects within literature. Adorno, for example, speaks of a man who, having escaped Auschwitz, was impatient with Samuel Beckett's comfortably disdainful absurdities—absurdities we associate with the modernism of this century. "The escapee is right in a fashion other than he thinks," observes Adorno:

> Beckett, and whoever else remained in control of himself, would have been broken in Auschwitz and probably forced to confront that front-line creed which the escapee clothed in the words "Trying to give men courage"—as if this were up to any structure of the mind; as if the intent to address men, to adjust to them, did not rob them of what is their due even if to the contrary.[52]

It is just this inevitable theft that both distinguishes atomic-bomb literature and accounts for its cultural blasphemy. As the issue of inhuman history, it must remake itself into an inhuman literature, a prospect that quite properly brings us to a full and impassable stop. There, at that precise point, should occur in the minds of writers and victims alike a question whose lack of an answer provides the very story a literature of atrocity might well tell.

■

In both the Japanese and Western philosophical traditions, the faculty of doubt has been repeatedly construed as the starting point of knowledge, knowledge as varied as that of the "self" to that of a "God." Doubt, be it Socratic, Cartesian, or that of Zen Patriarch Dōgen, introduces a cleavage—typically phrased as the philosopher's dialogic question—into an intellectual assumption previously unqueried. It is in this dialogue between the world and our interrogation of it—itself a philosophical "questioning"—that the doubts forcibly raised among human beings caught in this century's world wars may serve as the functional origin for new forms of knowledge: first as critique, and then as the restructured analyses of general cultural and social theory in the wake of modern violence.

The variety of doubt expressed by the survivors of atrocity—for a European Jew, whether God exists; for a Hiroshima or Nagasaki Japanese, perhaps whether anything will be allowed continued existence—is united by its common property of being read ironically, which means no sufficiently cogent answers have been proposed to the questions such doubt inspires. Of course, there is a kind of doubt which we would like to think provides ready answers *outside* the experience of the victims themselves. When the Joseph Mengele character in Rolf Hochhuth's play *The Deputy* says, "The truth is, Auschwitz refutes creator, creation, and the creature,"[53] he posits a "truth" that does away with everything, even that truth itself. Here is an irony which leads either to a basic ridicule of how we have imagined "reality," or to a sequestering of "Auschwitz" as a localized event having its own cloistered truth. Hochhuth puts these words in the mouth of one of the most notorious criminals of our time in order to universalize his point. Yet in practice we do continually "bracket," i.e., treat the contradictions raised by modern atrocity as particular and thus safely limited, truths. In a sense, what other choice have we had? To treat, as Hochhuth might have put it, *Dichtung* as *Wahrheit* would mean we take the worlds of the camp and of atomic-bomb survivors as *our* world, in the most literal of ways. That is an option which, while it should not be ruled out as perhaps the only way we will properly account for what we have done, hardly can be approached with much enthusiasm.

In fact we defy literal truth, only to put in its place imaginative truth. We, those of us who are "outside" the violence, are readers who resist. Resisting is itself a consequence of doubt, and it is therein that I would argue we can salvage our own forms of knowledge. When the symbolic systems heretofore provided us by modern culture to displace awareness of what is terrible fail us, we look for new symbols, and thereby initiate new cultural expressions. There is a kind of grotesque dialectic at work in writing, reading, and rewriting our accounts of atrocity. If the experience of "reading" "literature" is already a confrontation—that is to say, a moment when we readers are forced to recognize what our codes and moral expectations are—then we are in effect being interrogated and challenged by that writing. Those codes and expectations are always being renegotiated, and our routine habits of perception are silhouetted as indeed no more than "routine" and "habit."

All this seems especially true in the encounter with atomic-bomb literature. This may be understood as not so much a "failure" of our literature but an exaggerated instance of all modern reading, which is to say reading which is self-cannibalizing, or which proceeds by undermining itself. In a 1952 essay entitled "Before and After Reading" (Yomu made to yomioete to), Tokyo poet

Satō Hachirō describes the fear and trepidation with which a reader might approach a work of atomic-bomb literature, feelings linked with expectations that so condition the prospective reading they threaten to preclude it. Satō, who lost his younger brother in Hiroshima, describes what happened when he was sent an anthology of children's atomic-bomb poetry:

> I have always read books sent me the day they arrive, or at the latest by the evening of the following day. I have always thought that the po-
> lite thing to do.
> But this time I did not feel like picking it up. A good book, a famous book, a book which must be read at least once. . . . This book came to me, yet I put it away on the shelf. . . . Never before had I had the experi-
> ence of being gripped with the inability to take a book off the shelf. . . .
> I was frightened.[54]

Satō's terror is of course more acute than that of most readers, who pre-sumably did not lose family members in the bombings. But every sensitive reader, and perhaps especially the American reader, understandably hesitates before a work of atomic-bomb literature precisely for the same kind, if not degree, of fear over being directly confronted with one's own threatened pros-pects for living. This anecdote of submitting oneself to, while simultaneously rejecting, the work of atomic-bomb literature illustrates how one's tense expec-tations in reading such literature disclose the decisive and fixed milieu in which "writer," "reader," and "work" are historically situated. Awareness of this milieu moves us towards the prospect of a specific literary practice capable of repre-senting specifically nuclear violence.

How is such violence to be inferred and expressed? There is no single answer, but there is one, already described, to which writers most often turn, if for no other reason than atomic-bomb writers are also twentieth-century writers. If we take the Hiroshima or Nagasaki author to be one who goes to the scene of writing technically handicapped as well as thematically inspired— how are stories ever to tell *his* "story"?—because of what is our enlarged com-prehension of the human condition, then this writer experiences a *surplus* that might be accommodated through the work of modernist *irony*, itself privileged as a "realistic" technique. "Every war is ironic because every war is worse than expected," writes Paul Fussell of the First World War, and so "every war consti-tutes an irony of situation because its means are so melodramatically dispropor-tionate to its presumed ends."[55] But after the next world war, we can now say we live in a hyper-ironic age, a time where all manner of expectations, once exceeded, generates as surplus this overriding sense of incongruity. Kitayama Futaba, like other witnesses to August 6th, began her testimony with a descrip-tion of how beautiful her city was early that morning;[56] her "ironic revelation,"

Fussell would surely concede, is so total as to define, rather than simply characterize, her writing.

Ironic literature is the most modern, as well as modernist, of literatures. As Northrop Frye characterized it, ours is a literature in which we often look upon scenes of bondage, frustration, or absurdity; in ironic literature, the standard character is the one to whom things "are done to."[57] This is of course true of Greek and Roman classical ironic literature as well, but there irony is a mode of address and not the quality of an era. But now in the twentieth century, when "things are done to" the standard character they are done in such a way as to spill over, go beyond the story, and attach its irony to what initially enables not just the story but storytelling. Atrocity, its massive nature, is itself so ironic as to be destructively absurd, and it is thus literally disastrous for so many of our linguistic, philosophical, political, and cultural commonplaces.

Such irony does not necessarily or in fact produce original genres of writing. Rather, it infects all the ones we already have and threatens to break them down in irony's efforts to create, unsuccessfully, that impossible "new" genre that would encompass the scale of atrocity and the plethora of human responses to it. The atomic-bomb writer, faced with an overabundance of phenomena to tell us, is typically overwhelmed—the world after Hiroshima and Nagasaki seems consequently immense, boundless, incomprehensible. How to orient oneself within this indeterminacy, where to stand in order to speak—these are questions that are provisionally answered by ironicizing the poem, the play, the novel. By applying to Hiroshima and Nagasaki a paradigm of irony, the writer organizes, collates, and differentiates the past of the nuclear blast and the present of the recollective moment of writing. Modern understanding, if we take it to be predominantly ironic, resembles a figure of aporia in that it simultaneously builds and takes apart. But this is not just the rhetorical aporia of writing that tries to be something more than self-referential. It is a *lived* contradiction. Kuroko Kazuo has written: "Is our 'future' in fact open to us? Or is it closed? For us, forced to live under a 'nuclear civilization' unimaginably enlarged in the world's structural 'cold war' since August 6th and 9th in Hiroshima and Nagasaki, that question is the original aporia we are made to confront."[58]

It is such profound depth of doubt, this sense of a more or less imminent apocalypse, without salvation, that renders the "present" so indelibly ironic. The essentially paradoxical nature of a modern literary work both idealistic and realistic—paradoxical because the work both represents history and resists it—seems especially salient in atomic-bomb literature. The "necessary relation" that Frank Kermode sees between the fictions by which we order our world and the increasing complexity of what he, and many of us, take to be the "real" history of that world is a relationship expressed in increasingly detached, laconic, and most of all ironic terms.⁵⁹ In his testimonial account Inokuchi Motosaburō writes in such terms no less powerful for being so typical:

> F was sure when he spoke after burning his seventh corpse. "The potatoes in this field are gonna be real big ones. There's no fertilizer as good as human ashes."
>
> Y, lighting a cigarette with a still-smoldering piece of wood from a coffin, added "And cheap, too."⁶⁰

While human life may, as here, be reduced to a joke as well as to ashes, what escapes irony in atomic-bomb literature—at least in that by hibakusha writers—is what the resolute modernist Kermode encircles with cynical quotation marks: real history. When Karl Popper said that "any argument against realism which is based on modern atomic theory—on quantum mechanics—ought to be silenced by the memory of the reality of the events of Hiroshima and Nagasaki,"⁶¹ he was cautioning against the recurrent sophist and skeptical impulses of Western thought, and asserting with equal conviction the materiality of history, of the history that destroyed two cities not with rhetoric but with atomic weapons. Rather, where the doubt is—where post-Hiroshima knowledge begins—is in Popper's and the atomic-bomb writers' ironic speculation whether culture can comprehend this massive reality.

It is precisely at this point where the problematics of language intervene, and it does indeed become important to look at Hiroshima and Nagasaki as events constituted in our languages and discursive habits as well as in real time and space. At the beginning of her essay entitled "The Words Hiroshima Makes Us Say" (Hiroshima ga iwaseru kotoba, 1983), Takenishi Hiroko writes:

> There are words that speak of atomic-bombed Hiroshima.
>
> There are words that atomic-bombed Hiroshima makes me speak.
>
> This is not a distinction based on any theory. I know it intuitively. Perhaps I am mistaken in this. All I can say is that for the past twenty-five years it has remained for me a fact that has sometimes been stronger but never weaker.
>
> I am glad that there are words that speak of Hiroshima. One would be unable to live were there not such words that we mutually acknowledge. What sort of life in which we are to be more than simple wayfarers is possible for us without such words?
>
> But the words that Hiroshima makes me speak always lead me to an abyss of grief. My feelings when I stand at the edge of that abyss of both a cold gripping constriction inside me, and of something warmly oozing out of me at the very height of that constriction, are my proofs that such words exist.
>
> When I learned, when I felt, that words Hiroshima makes me speak

do exist, I felt that this Hiroshima was both "Hiroshima" and not "Hiroshima." I felt, and learned, them to be words that substituted for the names for limitless things and had a greater expansiveness. At times I am angry that the words that speak of Hiroshima are so very insufficient. Don't even I use those words to speak of things apart from Hiroshima? No doubt when I do, there are those whom I anger.

Does that mean I, so rebuked, can be tolerant of those words that speak of Hiroshima? No, it does not. This contradiction, this problem, this anger, this helplessness: I believe there can be no possibility of my deepening the knowledge of Hiroshima, no possibility of sharing it with others, without enduring my use of such things.[62]

Takenishi's quandary in and with language is the struggle between the author who uses words and the author who is used by them. "Perennial suffering," Adorno pointed out, "has as much right to expression as a tortured man has to scream."[63] But screams of the victim, like the words of the atomic-bomb writer, are only partially those of his own making. Takenishi is an author for whom her material is of such import and urgency that her own autonomy, her own prerogative in "writing," withers before the massiveness of experience, memory, History. Because such writers as Takenishi exist, our accounts of the "modern artist" must be amended to explain this loss of control; our accounts of literary history must add how contemporary times have reduced the notion of the individual to a banal statistic that always occurs in multiples of targeted millions. The lesson, an "intuitive" one for Takenishi and many other atomic-bomb writers, is that our forms of "modern" literature were short-lived and fragile, indeed: the product of a slim slice of history between the notion of the individual as free actor and the fact of individuals freely acted upon by the same political and technological ideologies that our social and political existence as "individuals" authorized. The question of the "subject" which so animates literary criticism today is not just a question of who speaks and who does not, but quite literally who survives and who does not.

■

There is a growing suspicion that the principal theoretical controversy in the literature of atrocity—namely whether mass violence can be represented or not—is a controversy only because modernism itself produces the "unrepresentable" as a corollary to its own ideological grounding and functions. Writer and critic Hanada Kiyoteru noted as early as 1955 that the "artistic method" of a mimetic atomic-bomb literature necessarily fails in both its overall structure and detailed descriptions.[64] The reason why may lie in the nature of the bombings themselves. If Hiroshima and Nagasaki are themselves events that are "original" in the sense that they are without meaning, that they were signature performances for Tokyo and Moscow audiences lacking local referents, then they are events that link the "modernist" logic of the Second World War with that of a Cold-War "nuclear sublime." They are events that, as Jean-François Lyotard claimed of Auschwitz, finished the project of modernity and thus should not be expected to inspire writings of epic scope.[65] They should look instead, as Alvin Rosenfeld said of Auschwitz literature, "to the shards and fragments that reveal, in their separateness and brokenness, the uncountable small tragedies that together add up to something larger than the tragic sense implies."[66]

It might be expected at this juncture that contemporary criticism would seize upon the "shards" and "fragments" of which Rosenfeld, and indeed many Japanese writers, speak and posit the possibility of a "postmodernist" atomic-bomb literature that might more accurately correspond with the similarly shattered lived experiences of atomic-bomb survivors. "The Mieko of today," wrote Hiroshima survivor Hara Mieko of herself in the third person, "is completely different from the Mieko of the past."[67] The fractured sense of self in the bomb victim whose psychological continuity is as ruptured as history's own suggests its narration in terms of the myriad little stories of a single life that now have replaced the larger stories of—for example—a "world war." Adorno seemed to have predicted that a literature of fractions rather than wholes was inevitable when he wrote: "Our metaphysical faculty is paralyzed because actual events have shattered the basis on which speculative metaphysical thought could be reconciled with experience."[68]

But in fact there are few, if indeed any, examples in either Holocaust or atomic-bomb literature unproblematically termed "postmodern." While one is often struck in reading personal testimonies of hibakusha by the personal, restricted, but highly detailed and intensive experiences of each survivor, and while each is indeed independent of each other and never takes into account the immense scale of the complete disaster, one never doubts that there is, somewhere if not within the sight of any one man or woman, an entire "Hiroshima" or "Nagasaki" that resists division into the pieces of any postmodern pastiche. If Michael Geyer is correct when he stated that we cannot write from a post-genocidal point of view since mass death is still with us as a "nuclear imaginary,"[69] then any attempt to create an atomic-bomb literature within an aesthetic or historical stage "beyond" the atomic bomb itself would be a literature about that aesthetic, or history, and not the bombings themselves.

There is a kind of writing that has emerged out of Hiroshima and Nagasaki, however, which has amended if not displaced modernism, and it is a kind of writing that Hayden White tentatively identified when he argued that atrocity is not unrepresentable, but rather requires a novel strategy of representation. Insisting that the anti-rhetorical thrust of Holocaust studies is wrong because it is based on an outmoded nineteenth-century Romantic concept of representation, White suggests we can represent the "new" by treating it as a "devoted" event: something whose "strangeness" both attracts and repels us. This strangeness, White claims, is a very twentieth-century "strangeness" that Marx and Hegel could not have anticipated, a strangeness produced by an impersonal civilization and which calls for its representation with the "middle voice"—a voice somewhere between the literal and the figural, somewhere between subjectivity and objectivity.[70] What White is seeking is a post-atrocity point of view that effaces neither itself nor its historical context, and yet stands apart from our rote representations of each, a narrative center that is both personal and social and which argues its difference from our own individual being and common experience.

It is difficult to imagine, perhaps, how exactly such a point of view might be achieved in practice. Other theorists, too, have posited alternatives to the now traditional modern "subject," that is to say the highly individualized and confidently knowledgeable character we are accustomed to in, for example, Europe's high-bourgeois narrative fiction. This subject is certainly split, if not eliminated, in a work such as Agawa Hiroyuki's 1947 "August Sixth" (Hachigatsu muika), in which the single testifying hibakusha point of view is divided among several characters. With the story organized in discreet sections subtitled "Father's Note," "Daughter's Story," "Son's Note," "Mother's Story" and "Father's Postscript," the central event of Hiroshima is told both individually and collectively at the same time. Unlike Kurosawa Akira's famous film "Rashōmon," these accounts are not incompatible, but are instead only multiple retellings of a common experience undergone and reconstituted "subjectively." What Agawa thereby avoids is making Hiroshima a story which, because testimonial writing must proceed so privately, loses its crucial historical import, and what he thereby preserves is the integrity provided by that same testimonial mode.

Writing under the pressures of concerns somewhat different from those of White, Marxist critic Fredric Jameson has argued for the exploration of a "collective subjectivity" that functions alongside what he calls the "old bourgeois ego" and "schizophrenic subject of our organization society today" in such genres as "certain forms of storytelling . . . [and] in testimonial literature."[71] While the project of writers such as Agawa Hiroyuki is not to displace an ideology, it does seem conceivable that atomic-bomb literature, certainly to the extent that it is testimonial or documentary, proposes the actual practice of such a collective subjectivity. The hibakusha writer must necessarily find his voice depersonalized because, while his experience is of course one that happen to "him," it is not a story—like those told in Japanese I-novels—that *belongs* to him: the narrating subject within atomic-bomb literature cannot control its relation to its world the way that a modernist or bourgeois "master subject" purportedly can. The reasons for this go back to the oft-noted inadequacy of a purely imaginary approach within atomic-bomb literature, where characters and their actions cannot be represented solely in terms of individuality and subjectivity without risking the representation of an atomic bombing as a mass, anonymous event. Kawakami Sōkun's story "The Survivors" is a brilliant study of just how anachronistic a sense of discrete individuality must be for the human being who has undergone mass violence. Through its two characters—Shōzō, a demobilized soldier who returns to Nagasaki after the 9th, and an unnamed young woman who was there for its destruction—"The Survivors" confronts its readers with an insight that has to challenge one important ontological premise of modern culture:

> Shōzō, who had not experienced the bombing, possessed a secure sense of himself as the center of the world, a sense that allowed him to think of himself as "unique." On the other hand it was precisely because the woman had long ago abandoned any such thoughts, that she could envy Shōzō and his luck. (198–99)

Atomic-bomb literature has been critically regarded in Japan with disdain, or at best suspicion, for just such insight. The broad collective nature of the subject risks subverting the old "bourgeois ego" (in Japanese parlance, *kindai jiga* 'modern self') so valorized in modern Japanese literary practice, while at the same time the survival of personal narration suggests it is still part of that practice. One of the more powerful—and, in its technical manipulation of point of view both personal and collective, successful—works of Japanese atomic-bomb literature is Takenishi Hiroko's 1963 short story, "The Rite" (Gishiki). At first it reads quite like much atomic-bomb literature. Governed from start to finish by a single third-person point of view—that of Aki, presumably a Hiroshima hibakusha, though neither Hiroshima nor the atomic bombing is explicitly referred to—"The Rite" tells the familiar story of a survivor permanently and psychically impaired when, as a child, she witnessed the annihilation of her city and the massacre of her schoolgirl friends. "Aki has never seen Kazue's dead body," Takenishi writes. "Nor Emiko's dead body. No, nor Ikuko's. Nor has she ever come across anyone else who has witnessed their end or verified the deaths of Junko or Kiyoko or Kazue or Yayoi" (183). Throughout both the narrative present of the story—a sleepless night throughout which Aki is plagued by the memories of her childhood and the current pain and damage they still inflict—and the flashbacks of her life adroitly used to give her suffering a plausible history, Aki seeks the "rite" that would let her long-dead friends rest.

"The Rite" is a story purposely full of other people's rites. The first is the emotional funeral of a Korean laborer Aki recalls from her early, pre-August 6th youth: "From the far off days of her childhood, long before Aki had ever expressed such things as the sickness or death of her own flesh and blood, that was a funeral that stayed like a weight on her mind" (171). Another is the somber funeral that she imagines for her friend Setsuko, now dying in hospital; after the ceremonies, she knows that "in the deserted place of mourning there will be no sign of life until the garbageman appears, his hand towel round his head. He will come from the doorway and approach the altar and begin to clear away the funeral wreaths" (180). And in tortuous counterpoint, there is the peaceful Saturday routine of a neighboring family which strikes Aki as a "fitting end to a fine summer's day" and makes her memory of another, but horrific, summer's day painfully present. She muses enviously about the elaborate embalming ritual that must have celebrated the death of an ancient Egyptian nobleman whose portrait she spots on the cover of a magazine:

> There without a doubt was a fitting way to start out on death's journey, with the dead well tended and watched over by the living. Thinking of that man who had left behind a part of his own flesh, and his people who had taken it into their keeping, in what was surely a most dignified and solemn ceremony, it seemed to Aki that there was a secure and reassuring way to die. (173)

Aki's inability to impose a closure on the lives, and stories, of her own life and the lives around her is traced to an inability to focus clearly on the object of her rage and anger, the object that is responsible for all that has happened: an object that, as an Aki guiltily ashamed of outliving her friends suspects, may be her own self.

Unable to return the love of a man who loves her, and unable to talk honestly about their lives with her fellow survivors, Aki doubts whether she is capable of making the distinctions others find necessary to lead normal existences. Existence itself is subjected to radical, even metaphysical, doubt. "Wherein lies the realness of things?" she wonders on one page, a question she answers on the next when she asks rhetorically, "can the senses grasp reality as well as she could with her consciousness, once she could cease to treat as an unreal thing the presence in it?" (195–96). "The Rite" is a work that astutely links the loss of one hibakusha's sense of participation in both the world around her and her own life with the crisis of history and even the modern "questioning of 'being'" that Takenishi, through her narrator, associates with mass violence's elimination of the possibility for recognizing, one by one, any individual's death: "The rite that should have been performed and never was, and my unassuaged thirst for it, I must recognize as the beginning of a questioning of 'being' that I must now develop" (195).

This questioning—an expression of just that doubt which potentially leads to knowledge—comes from the gap not only between Aki's survival and her friends' demise, but from her singular existence and her friend's undifferentiated nonexistence, which is to say their unmediated collective existence as unidentifiable bones and ashes, her friends "in the devastated schoolground . . . buried beneath in unglazed urns, indiscriminately gathered up with all those other deaths" (183). While narrator "Aki" is the point of view that organizes this story, the integrity of that subject is continually challenged by, first, a surplus of grotesque memory that threatens that subject's right to a "present," and second, her membership in a group—that of her dead classmates—who have lost all meaningful private being. It is here that we may posit the function of a "collective subject" generated not by a progressive ideology seeking to replace the "old bourgeois ego" but by an atrocity that renders every victim of it, including Aki, a composite point of view ironically articulated from the schoolyard mound of an unmarked "mass" grave. Aki's troubling insomnia, the waking that allows her to think and remember as an individual, would be remedied solely by sleep, a substitute death state in which unconsciousness would permit her to join the permanent, collective silence of her incinerated classmates.

A collective subject such as that which prospectively emerges in Takenishi's "The Rite," or indeed in many examples of atomic-bomb literature, is initially difficult to conceptualize because it reads as a contradiction or even an oxymoron. But, as I have suggested, so does an idea like "atomic-bomb literature" in the first place. What all such concepts ask of us is to accept a post-Hiroshima imperative to use culture, and with it its ideology of the self, to represent the antithesis of culture implicit in our use of total weapons on "populations" within which the "self" is an irrelevant, anachronistic word. The various difficulties suggested here in structuring a textual representation of Hiroshima or Nagasaki within the contours of any genre—testimonial, documentary, tragic, comic, poetic, or prosaic—are just those difficulties that, once addressed, become that representation.

It is possible to conclude at this point that the array of contradictions inevitably faced by an atomic-bomb writer are accommodated by recognizing that contradiction is to be preserved rather than reconciled. Finally there is no contradiction *to* contradiction, for there is no incompatibility between conceding the possibility of cultural meaning in a text and yet maintaining that no author is immune to the moral and literary dangers incurred when his subject is mass atrocity. As Berel Lang asked importantly of Holocaust writers, "The question remains to what extent writers are able to avoid these dangers, with the presumption that at best they will not escape entirely and that even insofar as they do the writings have to be read as a response to those dangers."[72] There is implicit in this question the insight that any work of such writers must necessarily "fail" in order to "succeed."

In Takahashi Kazumi's novel *The Melancholy Faction* the central character, a hibakusha by the name of Nishimura Kōichi, has long been at work on a book that would memorialize his friends who were killed in Hiroshima on August 6th. Likening his role to that of an archaeologist, Nishimura knows his book is important because, as he says, "Human memory is a fleeting thing" (199), but he cannot fathom why it is particularly his fate to be Hiroshima's chronicler:

> Unfortunately I cannot explain why I decided to undertake this project. . . . For most of humanity, one's own comfort is of more import than the restoration of dead people's dignity. And were such a restoration my real purpose, then a talent for idealizing would surely be more necessary than any faithful account of the facts. Moreover, were I blessed with any such brilliant talent, the lives of the dead would still not return. Yet, driven by an anger that I cannot explain but that nonetheless menaces me, I have chosen this path and now pursue this work. (58)

Like actual survivor writers such as Ōta Yōko, the fictional Nishimura's motives for writing are unclear even to himself. It is as if Hiroshima and its victims, rather than being the object of his efforts, write collectively through the living author in order to tell their own story. The inevitable confusion of who writes what for whom necessarily complicates both the shape Nishimura's work finally assumes and the themes that shape is intended to contain. "Describing the catastrophe as such was not Nishimura's purpose," writes Takahashi. "Yet at the end of his thirty-some epitaphs, he somehow had to put down onto paper the circumstances of their deaths, and the combination of silence and screams" (118). This "silence and screams," or in other words the enforced quiet of the dead and the unintelligible howling of the living that surround the very small place from which atomic-bomb writers strive to speak in words we can understand, provides the contradiction which has always compromised as well as produced atomic-bomb literature. As Nishimura explains at length to a friend who has criticized his book,

> There is not a single day when I do not ask myself, as I write and rewrite, why I wallow in the degradation of the dead and bring back what everyone only wants to forget. Of course, such abstractions as "the peace movement," "welfare assistance" and "medical care" are all available, even if there are not enough. The victims want it that way. But no one hopes for a revival of "that." Sure, movies are made about it. And novels are written, too. Most of the testimonies have been ignored, but some have been published. Peace demonstrations are held annually in this country's capital, and in the first city bombed, and in the second city bombed. On those occasions hymns sung by priests and nuns in black robes and white hoods are broadcast nationwide on radio and television. Along with the sad sounds of the memorial bell.
>
> But who in hell was it who filled in that deep chasm that had split wide open there in that terrible sight, a sight like an immense, porno-

graphic picture? They say there's been no paradise for mankind since Adam ate the forbidden fruit. But that's the talk of people who are alive. All survivors have been made spiritual vagrants by having seen "that." I'm a good example myself. I am one of the chosen, no thanks to the grace of God but to the malice of human beings. (120)

Nishimura, and with him those actual atomic-bomb writers whom he represents, is bitterly scornful of literature and its audience even as he continues to search for a publisher for his own book. He cannot abandon his project, nor can he trust in its worth. As Theodor Adorno remarked of writing after Auschwitz, "our feelings resist any claim of the positivity of existence as sanctimonious, as wronging the victims: they balk at squeezing any kind of sense, however bleached, out of the victims' fate."[73] But those feelings are still ones that demand description, either in the context of Adorno's Western philosophy now permanently deformed by atrocity or in Nishimura's personal epitaphs for his deceased Japanese friends. The task of the writer after Hiroshima and the Nazi genocide is his awkward accommodation to the impossibility of writing and not writing.[74] As we shall see in the next chapter, it is the task of the reader to acquiesce in that writer's crisis without censuring, and thus silencing further, him for his sketches of our collective barbarism.

Terao Tomofumi, *A Flash of Light, a Clap of Thunder*
(Senkō to bakufū, 1982)

Well, as soon as I mentioned the word "bomb"—the atomic bomb—even in that select circle [of high Administration officials]—it was sort of a shock. You didn't mention the bomb out loud; it was like mentioning Skull and Bones in polite society at Yale. It just wasn't done.

Assistant Secretary of War John J. McCloy

Words kill. At the beginning is always the word.

Elie Wiesel, *The Gates of the Forest*

3

The Three Debates

The first work of atomic-bomb writing may not be Japanese at all. Depending on how one wishes to think of origins, or define literature, that work might be Einstein's famous formula, Truman's executive order, or, as told in Iida Momo's *An American Hero*, the graffiti that the flight crew of the *Enola Gay* wrote on the Little Boy, their single payload: "To be or not to be, that is the question" (344). In novelist Iida's imagination if not historical fact, atomic-bomb literature begins on the smooth metal surface of the nuclear weapon itself. He suggests that the Little Boy was in fact its own murderous writing, and one that appropriately posed the fundamental rhetorical and existential question of the humanist culture it was about to challenge. "What" will be, or not be, is many things: the city of Hiroshima, of course, but additionally the very question of *being* in a nuclear age. This quote from Shakespeare recalls what Elie Wiesel, in one of his post-Holocaust novels, made the modern rewrite of Hamlet's dilemma. "The problem is not: to be or not to be. But rather: to be and not to be."[1] How, in other words, can we make sense of the contradictory condition into which mass-produced death has put our lives and our "being"?

The practice of atomic-bomb literature is, as I argued of its theory, an incommensurable record of contradiction. Another candidate for designation as the first instance of atomic-bomb literature is the initial media announcement made by the Japanese authorities on the destruction of Hiroshima, issued at 3:30 P.M. on August 7th:

> 1. On August 6th the city of Hiroshima sustained considerable damage [*sōtō no higai*] from a raid by a small number of enemy B29s.
> 2. The enemy's use in this raid of something resembling a new type of bomb is currently under detailed investigation.[2]

The first paragraph of this terse report contains an ironic contradiction: "a small number of planes" is held to have produced "considerable damage," an overstatement combined with an understatement, a sentence that can now only be read rhetorically as a hyperbole joined with a litotes. Set into motion is a "detailed investigation" of what was then only a simile ("something resembling") but would soon be understood as a historical event of very literal implications. From this beginning, the language which speaks Hiroshima and Nagasaki is uncanny, strange, wrong. The news release on August 7th had been based on the report of a single observer, Lieutenant General Arisue Seizō:

> I said the bomb was a special bomb, a type we had never known before. I had talked with a man who had been burnt by the bomb on only one side of his body. His other side had been in the shade. I advised Tokyo that in the event of a second attack the people should seek protection in the shade.[3]

"Protection in the shade," like "a small number of planes" or "considerable damage," is an ordinary phrase that, in light of what would soon be learned, made no ordinary sense. Everything one first reads of Hiroshima and Nagasaki is revealed to be incorrect somehow: either the number of bombs, their power, the extent of the damage, who survived and who did not, or who *will* survive and who will not. But at the same time everything one reads is truthful, if not exactly true, in terms of the pre-Hiroshima world—in which the terrible power of a single weapon could not have been comprehended—and in terms of the post-Hiroshima understanding of the fissure in human culture that created such nonsensical sense. The words, the poem, the story that are wrong but right, inaccurate but precise, misleading but insightful—such contradictions are the puzzles that have to serve as the definition of Japanese atomic-bomb literature. This inherently unstable paradigm of writing achieves meaning by refuting it, by resisting collaboration with a language treacherously intent upon signifying only past meanings.

This paradigm, however, was only one among many in postwar Japan, and a relatively marginal one at that. The oppositional stances both political and aesthetic taken by atomic-bomb literature writers resulted in a literary practice far from readily sanctioned within the varieties of postwar Japanese literature produced in, and supervised by, Tokyo and its literary-critical establishment. The late Nagaoka Hiroyoshi, Japan's foremost historian of atomic-bomb literature, recalled how in the late 1960s, when he began his research into the genre, it took more than half a year—and only by combing the second-hand bookstores—to find copies of Hara Tamiki's *Summer Flowers* and Ōta Yōko's *City of Corpses*, surely among the most widely disseminated, read, analyzed, and thus potentially canonical works of atomic-bomb literature by any hibakusha writers.[4] Nor, Nagaoka also noted, was there much to find even in the National Diet Library. Works by the survivors of Hiroshima and Nagasaki were out of print, uncatalogued, invisible; and even more so were any comprehensive historical or interpretive studies, which did not exist at all until Nagaoka published his own *History of Atomic-bomb Literature* (Gembaku bungaku shi) in 1973. The nearly thirty years that separated the origins of atomic-bomb literature and the first proper academic studies of the genre effectively meant that the critical process necessary for converting hibakusha writings into an institutionally recognized and valued literary category worth studying, preserving, and teaching simply did not take place until well after many of the first hibakusha writers were dead. In contrast, writes Kurihara Sadako,

> Soon after the end of the war works of poetry and fiction about Auschwitz were published in Europe. Poets such as Anthony Hecht, Paul Celan, Sylvia Plath, and Nelly Sachs appeared one after another, and the theme of the death camps has been widely debated as a subject for the literature of violence. But talk of Hiroshima and Nagasaki was suppressed by the Occupation's Press Code and their literature quarantined from the literary establishment. Alienated, trapped in a bitter struggle with an unfair set of literary norms, hibakusha poets have died of illness, committed suicide . . . and abandoned their work unfinished.[5]

In some sense the shadowy presence of atomic-bomb literature and the parallel critical activity one might reasonably expect it to have occasioned a quarter of a century after the bombings are themelves in retrospect the logical consequences of the equally marginal status of the historical violence. The bombings, it should be remembered, were not dropped on Tokyo (contrary to the commonly held belief—that after the March 10, 1945, fire bombings of Tokyo there was nothing left worth targeting—there was of course a good deal) but on "tangential targets" where national political authority, epitomized by the person of the emperor himself, did not reside—authority which, it was hoped, would be sufficiently demoralized by the demonstration of nuclear weapons to consider surrender. Consequently, from the point of view of Hiroshima and Nagasaki their very selection as targets was already a "marginalization," an "alienation," from both the moral and tactical point of view of those who dropped the bombs, and from that of their fellow Japanese countrymen, left alive, for whom the use of nuclear weapons was intended as a "demonstration."

The historical fact of Hiroshima and Nagasaki's dispensibility—their significance as the site for *performances* in which they were, so to speak, unwitting anonymous "extras"—is reproduced in the continuing negligence of cultural and historical discourses constructed around that fact. The comparison with Holocaust literature in the West is instructive. No one other than anti-Semites has questioned the right of Holocaust literature to exist, as indeed many Japanese critics have of atomic-bomb literature. While it has been chillingly suggested that within a few years "the accumulation of items concerning the Holocaust—books, films, poems, articles, stories—will equal or exceed the total number that have been produced about any other subject in human history," Japanese atomic-bomb literature has not yet attained even any generally acknowledged status as "literature."[6] Part of the reason for this derives from both the general aesthetic resistance of Japanese literature to narratives of violence, and the specific refusal of much so-called postwar Japanese literature to confront war at all. Prominent literary historian Okuno Takeo noted that literature after 1945 developed as if the Second World War had never happened.[7] Others have asked why, since modern Japanese history is itself so largely a record of wars with brief respites in between given to preparations for war, have writers produced so few memorable works about them.[8]

It is probably more correct to say that by "memorable" is meant canonical, i.e., works that are routinely circulated in the pedagogic, commercial, and critical loci of schools, bookstores, and scholarly journals.[9] Where examples of atomic-bomb literature have been mentioned in standard histories of postwar Japanese literature, it is mention in terms of an antagonistic, oppositional relationship with other literature taken as normative—terms which simultaneously restrict atomic-bomb literature to the margins and fix those "other" works in places nearer an implicit center. Kuroko Kazuo has written of how atomic-bomb writing's position outside the mainstream of Japanese literature is both the consequence of that mainstream's exclusionary practices and its own "fundamental critique":

> Atomic-bomb literature, while one element of postwar literature in general, is at the same time a literature that exists as a result of the fundamental critique it has conducted of the retrogressive tendencies produced in postwar society. In particular, literary works by writers who experienced the bombings take their readers back to what novelist Hotta Yoshie has

termed "the natural consequence of the human species." In the sense that it leads us back to the origin of such thought, atomic-bomb literature occupies a valuable position.[10]

This "valuable position" is, as such language suggests, an ambiguous one. What sort of value? And position *where*? Such questions soon lead to the issue of the ambivalence of the individual text, literary criticism, the institutionalization of a canon of consistently approbated "masterpieces," and the overdetermined relationships which culturally, socially, and ideologically link them. As in much of the modern West, the practice of literary canonization begun in late nineteenth-century Japan arose in tandem with the production of other national (more precisely "nation-building") discourses. If canonization in the West worked, and still works, as a metonymy for national "character" (a metonymy sensitive to contemporary social and political concerns), canonization in Japan was and is similarly deployed rhetorically as an important adjunct to the ideological precepts underlying the "modernization" of other Japanese institutions. From the late nineteenth century, when the idea of a Japanese literary canon (often termed a *taikei*, or "system") was translated into a set of pedagogic practices, it was unmistakably a political project meant to aid in the establishment, in the words of its early architects, of Japanese literature as one that "towers above Chinese and European literature."[11]

A century ago the assumption of those superintending the formation of a native canon was principally that of a "classical" tradition, i.e., poetry, diaries, and court romances of a "past" Japan that, it was argued somewhat tautologically, nonetheless encode the continuous aesthetic values of the Japanese "people" (*kokumin*). Modern Japanese literature—literature written and published from precisely those years when classical texts were undergoing this process of canonization—has not proven as easily assimilated into a standard syllabus as has—despite our own controversies—American literature. There are plural reasons for this, but one is that the Japanese cannot speak with assurance, or even speak at all, about a "canon" of specifically postwar Japanese literature. There persists a highly politicized confusion in Japan over what national "identity" is to be represented by a canon, and this confusion is produced in part by the Japanese defeat in the Second World War, a defeat in which the bombings of Hiroshima and Nagasaki are typically considered to have played a decisive role. Consequently the debate over which literary works are to be sanctioned, promoted, taught, and thus incorporated into the governing narratives and tropes of Japanese national identity is not carried out by arguing the larger, but related, issue of what should or should not be admitted to a "canon," but by arguing whether any given work qualifies, in fact, as *bungaku* 'literature' at all.

Bungaku is a very old term, a loanword from Chinese once best translated simply as "learning" and historically linked to Confucian dogma, scholarship, and moral instruction. Such associations are not entirely erased today. Understanding which writings earn the designation of bungaku involves a whole range of assumptions of what texts—what types of texts—are prefigured as part of a literary field. Through conferring such privilege, critics judge a work significant on aesthetic grounds surely implicated in prescriptions of social, ideological formations. But as we shall presently see, both those aesthetic grounds and the assumptions they subsume have been heatedly and inconclusively debated by postwar Japanese writers and critics for now nearly half a century. And most importantly for this particular study, this has been a debate in which the specific representations of Hiroshima and Nagasaki have played an illustrative and perhaps even essential part.

When the conservative literary critic Alistair Fowler ruled categorically that "any work that belongs to genre belongs in some sense to literature," he made explicit an axiom that operates in Japanese literary culture, too. He elucidates why even entertaining the possibility of an atomic-bomb "literature" is to revive important questions about the general structural nature of "literature" as an idea which can only produce meaning as long as there is something "not literature." To label a work as a "novel" or "poem" is to induct it into a system of literature and let it enjoy the cultural privilege to which literature—bungaku—is entitled. The first, and also last, battle line for those who wish for whatever reasons to deny atomic-bomb literature any special status is to deny it under any conditions the description as "literary."

These decisions are invariably valuative, interpretative, subjective, and thus open to the kind of "intuitive" judgment through which ideology routinely operates. When those decisions are exercised over texts that thematically represent violence—the violence of war—the valuative, interpretive, and subjective character of those decisions, and thus the existence of the underlying ideological assumptions, becomes particularly salient. "The reaction of literary critics to violence needs to be interpreted, first and foremost, as an ethical gesture performed with a human context," writes critic Tony Siebers, "and in this context literary and ethical problems cannot be separated, no matter how zealous the claim for the autonomy of literature."[12] The "literary and ethical problems" that invariably arise when critics, and writers, seek to explain, interpret, or evaluate works that describe violence, or are engendered within the context of violence, are problems that are naturally at odds with each other. It will be in the margins of those "odds," that narrow ledge on which hibakusha writers stand not only as impaired survivors of nuclear war but as frustrated cultural voices, that atomic-bomb literature will, by virtue of where it exists and where it is not allowed to exist, define how literature, in full and without significant regard to theme or genre, functions in post-Hiroshima Japan.

■

It is commonplace for literary historians to note the proliferation and diversity of Japanese literature in the postwar period, an imprecise span of time nonetheless generally understood as the first decade, 1945–55, of the post-Hiroshima era. Writer and critic Katō Shūichi, who was himself personally responsible for some part of this resurgence, describes these years as "vigorous," and American academic Donald Keene says they were "a period of extraordinary literary activity. . . . Publication flourished as rarely before in Japan."[13] Another scholar, Jay Rubin, calls "the literature that poured out after 1945 . . . an expressive explosion."[14] Such frenetic activity, however, was largely a Tokyo phenomenon. Despite that city's own massive destruction, recovery there was also the quickest. In Hiroshima and Nagasaki, perhaps more than in other Japanese cities, problems beside the artistic would have to come first. As a consequence of the war, Kurihara Sadako has written, "Hiroshima became an atomic waste land. For the survivors, struggling for food among rumors that ten million would die of starvation, thinking of culture or cultural activities was impossible."[15]

Any discussion of postwar Japanese literature has to proceed against this background of material deprivation, political uncertainty, and, in the case of Hiroshima and Nagasaki, widespread and untreatable disease.[16] Such conditions were, on the one hand, obstacles for writers and, on the other hand, the same conditions that would inspire, characterize, and distinguish their writings. Nagaoka Hiroyoshi among others noted that most atomic-bomb literature even today has been written by nonprofessional writers, evidence of the general urge to write despite the obstacles.[17]

Yamamoto Kenkichi, a critic generally unsympathetic to atomic-bomb writers, did state on one occasion that amid all the literary fanfare of the postwar period, it was perhaps only those who had experienced one of the atomic bombings who had their creative "feet" firmly planted on an unescapably "real" firmament.[18] This relationship between an undoubtable referent—an unquestionable *experience*—and literary creativity had long been a privileged one in Japanese literary criticism, but the specific nature of this "experience"—no longer that exclusively of the individuated subject, but instead that of a national collective target—would complicate and govern how atomic-bomb literature would develop and be critically received.

At the same time that the autonomy of Hiroshima and Nagasaki literary practice was handicapped by its relationship to Tokyo and the metropolitan culture, Japanese literary practice as a whole was concurrently subject to the restraints imposed by a foreign military occupation. On September 19, 1945,

General Headquarters of the Allied Occupation enacted a Press Code author-
izing the censorship of topics considered inimical to Occupation aims and policies, a censorship that in retrospect critic Etō Jun has attacked as an "invisible
war of attrition."[19] "At that time it was forbidden to speak of write even of the
fact that there was a censorship system in existence," Kurihara Sadako sardoni-
cally observed. "It was not permitted even to leave traces indicating that the
censors had deleted anything. All in the name of 'free speech.' "[20]

Among the topics of print and electronic communication deigned the
most sensitive, and thus subject to the most severe censorship, were the bombings of Hiroshima and Nagasaki: a fact not unrelated to American apprehensions, perhaps even sense of guilt, that the details of those events be widely
reported. Jay Rubin states:

> The Occupation's greatest fear of causing resentment or otherwise dis-
> turbing the public tranquility is manifested in their handling of refer-
> ences to the atomic bombing of Hiroshima and Nagasaki. So monstrous
> an accomplishment as the destruction of an entire city full of people with
> a single bomb was, of course, beyond hiding, and the Americans were
> willing to permit the publication of "objective," "scientific" news stories.
> "Editorial opinion," however, was another matter. Literary works on the
> bomb, which invariably included an element of "editorial opinion," were
> difficult to publish at first.[21]

This is not to say that there was no public discourse, other than the "scientific," on the bombings during the Occupation. In a few instances there were
simply oversights. Critic Mizuta Kuwajirō has suggested that Hara Tamiki's
1947 short story "Summer Flowers" escaped the censors because the journal in
which it appeared, *Mita bungaku* (Mita Literature), was of such limited circulation that it fell, so to speak, between the cracks.[22] In other instances there were
ways of speaking of the bombings in absurdly sentimental tones to which the
censors seemed quite indifferent, or were perhaps even pleased over. For instance in 1952, the year the Occupation came to its formal end, there was a
popular film entitled *Never Forget the Song of Nagasaki* (Nagasaki no uta wa wasureji) in which, incredibly, the hibakusha heroine falls in love with the American pilot of one of the planes that flew as part of the air raid on her city. Despite the fact that the director, Tasaka Tomotaka, was himself a Hiroshima
hibakusha, film historian Satō Tadao thought this picture would have been
better entitled *Let's Forget Our Hatred of the Bomb*. He termed it a "worthless sentimental work beyond any hope of repair."[23]

Such mawkishness was perhaps possible only because of the very conflicted reactions among Japanese, including intellectuals, to the bombings and
their political and historical contexts. America, the country both "conqueror"
and "liberator," elicited frequently and maybe even necessarily ambivalent re-

sponses from Japanese sensitive both to issues of democratic freedom and of national autonomy. One major contradiction evident throughout early atomic-bomb literature and its criticism is that Hiroshima and Nagasaki were "atrocities" that were nonetheless credited at the time with ending the war and the reign of Japanese militarism. Many Japanese have candidly admitted their sense of relief when the war ended, even if at the cost of two civilian cities—cities in which, it should be pointed out, none of these relieved voices were present. Marxist writer Nakano Shigeharu once reminisced about August 6, 1945, a day in which he was far from Hiroshima but nonetheless engaged, against his will, in a military project. His reaction at hearing on the bombing was to think that it was a "merciful deed."[24] In this anecdote, other versions of which are still commonly recounted in Japan today, the victims of Hiroshima and later Nagasaki were unfortunate, albeit necessary, sacrifices. As I was once myself admonished, "It is only the indignant intellectuals who think otherwise." But as in the case of Nakano Shigeharu, even the "intellectuals" were capable of rationalizing atrocity as an equitable price to "pay" for the cessation of the war.

This ambivalence in reactions to the bombings anticipates the variety of literary activities—some literary "responses," others not—that were apparent even in the targeted cities themselves. In Hiroshima the group of highly politicized writers—mostly local established poets—gathered about Kurihara Sadako, her husband Kurihara Tadaichi, and their early postwar journal *Chūgoku bunka* (Chūgoku Culture) had its equally insistent, antipolitical (but effectively reactionary) counterpart in the group of writers who published the journal *Kyōyū* (Hometown Friend).[25] *Kyōyū* managed in its three years of publication to not mention the atomic bombing in its featured fiction even once. Conversely, no issue of *Chūgoku bunka* ever failed to mention it. It is important to know that literary production in Hiroshima was varied, controversial, and contested, if only because the struggles of atomic-bomb writers to establish reputations nationally were rehearsed in struggles similarly arduous in the targeted cities themselves.

Americans all too commonly assume that the bombings of Hiroshima and Nagasaki occupy an important place among the themes of postwar Japanese literature. In part this assumption may have no relation to any specific acquaintance with that literature. It can arise from our compensatory if guilty expectation that the first victims of nuclear war would of course have repaid us, in literary kind, with their anger, indignation, and pain. But at the same time it is an assumption at which an avid reader of modern Japanese literature in English translation might quite reasonably arrive. Among the relatively few postwar Japanese novels available in the United States, one of the most widely read has been Ibuse Masuji's *Black Rain*, the story of a hibakusha family living in a small village several years after the bombing of Hiroshima yet who only now realize how inexorable the eventual toll of latent radiation disease can be. But in fact,

Black Rain is the only atomic-bomb novel even in Japan to have achieved what we may call a canonical status—a work always in print, frequently anthologized, taught in schools, probably translated into one or more Western languages, and most importantly subject to a continuously high level of critical or academic study and interpretation. Still, despite the fact that *Black Rain* meets all these qualifications, its claim to that status has never been free of controversy,[26] and the reasons why are not unrelated to the generally hostile reception accorded most literary works concerned with these epochal events.

In the almost fifty years that have passed since the end of the Second World War, the usual reluctance of critics in Japan to regard atomic-bomb writing seriously has, however, been punctuated by several brief and semipublic debates on the right and value of such writing to exist as its own legitimate genre or subgenre of literature (bungaku). These debates have always followed closely on the heels of political events focusing attention on the nature of U.S.-Japanese relations, such as the mass demonstrations provoked by the renewal of the joint U.S.-Japan Security Treaty in 1960.[27] Not only did those protests result in Prime Minister Kishi's resignation and President Eisenhower's cancellation of a planned state visit to Tokyo, but they prompted a widened discussion among critics and writers of the political contexts and responsibilities of literature whose themes included, on this rare occasion, the atomic bombings. It was in 1953, however, that the nominal return of sovereignty to the Japanese people with the end of the American Occupation the previous year brought the heretofore greatest, though still circumscribed, attention to atomic-bomb literature.

Eight years after the destruction of Hiroshima and Nagasaki, both the hibakusha who were creating what they claimed was a new genre and the literary critics who disparaged it agreed on little but this: representing nuclear war was still an experimental, tentative, and in part self-contradictory literary activity involving much more than such formal issues as style, character, or plot. If the main point of contention was whether these initial efforts could be called bungaku—an appellation used since the late nineteenth century as a convenient gloss for the Western term "literature" but made problematic by its inherited Confucian overtones—then the real issue was over the relationship of historical and social trends (as opposed to "purely" aesthetic ones) with the definition of bungaku. From the point of view of the conservators of the traditional canon, a canon comprised largely of works shunning social themes in favor of individual ones, Hiroshima and Nagasaki were inadmissible subjects for serious fiction. Yet from the point of view of many hibakusha writers, the reservation of bungaku for the concerns of modern, i.e., individualistic culture, would in the wake of the violence of the Second World War have to be rethought and expanded to include issues of collective survival. The first of the confrontations between these two positions in 1953 comprised one of the

more important reassessments of qualifications for membership in the canon—
for claiming status as "bungaku"—since the end of the war and the ensuing
upheaval over Japanese culture's relationship to its modern history.

In 1954 sympathetic critic Odagiri Hideo was able to cite, summarize, and
evaluate all existent major works of atomic-bomb literature in just over two
pages; in 1985, Nagaoka Hiroyoshi could do so in seven, including even Japanese translations of foreign works.[28] The reasons for this conspicuous poverty
in an otherwise frenetic literary culture are several—not the least of which is
that most of those who could have written of the bombings were killed by one
of them—and extend beyond the understandable timidity of writers faced with
a difficult theme. They also number the specific historical circumstances governing not only the freedom of expression accorded writers under a military
occupation, but the prospective reception of writings concerned with the implications of two recent atrocities. The critical establishment was still committed to an ideal concept of bungaku as an account of individual consciousness
inscribed within a detached bourgeois subject commonly equated with that of
the author himself or, on rare occasions, herself. No atomic-bomb writers, their
attentions riveted on more particular and certainly more public events, have
ever produced such canonically acceptable works of fiction.

Although Ōta Yōko's *City of Corpses* appeared in 1948 once an important
but possibly seditious chapter had been expunged, it was not Occupation censors but the book's Japanese publishers who had decided not to print the work
in its entirety: this after a full three years of refusing to publish any of it. Perhaps the publishers feared the authorities' reaction, but Ōta's biographer, Esashi
Akiko, argues that the novel was deemed "too real" a work, one that possessed
such "power to accuse that no one, however insensitive, would not rise in
rage."[29] Too real, presumably, for those of us not victims: the ill-ease with writing too powerfully visceral to be read without alienating audiences would work
as much against the establishment of an atomic-bomb literature as any explicit
control prompted by an occupying power. Indeed, when in 1953 Ōta was ostensibly free to speak out against whomever she wished, she reserved her most
acrimonious attacks not for Americans but for the Japanese literary establishment itself, the small and exclusive milieu of professional writers, critics, and
editors known collectively as the *bundan*.

The bundan (or rather bundans: Ōta speaks, for instance, of both the "central bundan" located in Tokyo, the center of national cultural production, and
the "Hiroshima bundan" comprised of local notables exerting the same authority over provincial activities, principally the publishing of small coterie journals) has existed since the late nineteenth century, when the expanding con-
sumption of print media incurred the same conservative and oligarchic
stewardship accorded other categories of developing capitalist production in a
rapidly industrializing Japan.[30] The members of this early bundan typically

shared similar class origins or aspirations, namely those of the middle and upper bourgeoisie. In her youth, from the time of her tutelage under the influential author and editor Kikuchi Kan to the end of the Second World War, Ōta was herself on the fringes of the Tokyo bundan. One of its principal responsibilities had been to protect the canon from infiltration by works viewed subversive to its identity as self-evident assemblage of "pure literature" (*jun-bungaku*), a later refinement of the simple term "bungaku." All bungaku is "literature," but jun-bungaku, the most highly prized of it, is literature dedicated to replaying the personal reflections of a narrator who, whether an "I," "he," or "she," is understood by the reader to be the author and thus to be absolutely authentic, unmediated, and real. As critic Masao Miyoshi has pointed out, the net effect was to replace "the pluralist 'real' world with a private universe."[31] Critics who favored the merits of jun-bungaku were, perhaps not surprisingly, antagonistic to atomic-bomb literature. "Pure literature" should, in their estimation, always be devoid of any sullying historical or social consciousness extending beyond that of a privileged and withdrawn bourgeois subject. Ōta's own prewar work, exemplified by the 1939 *Drifting Shores* (Ryūri no kishi), safely conformed to those rules for "pure literature" despite an implicit feminism that might have questioned at least the gender of that same subjectivity, if not its position in and towards history.

By the 1950s, however, the bundan as a recognizable society of only a few dozen writers and editors was long gone. The industry had outgrown such intimate control, and the institutions of Japanese society were realigning along new class lines. Rather, by 1953 Ōta's use of the term "bundan" served as a kind of convenient if not completely accurate shorthand not for an identifiable group but for a set of views now widely accepted by Japanese readers. Out of the hands of a few writers and into the assumptions of the public, what was now signified by the "bundan" exercised perhaps an even greater, certainly more subtle discipline over the stringent definition of "bungaku." When Donald Keene notes in his history of modern Japanese literature that "the bundan at times has been able not only to promote but to frustrate writers by denying them outlets for their works," he identifies both an earlier institutional authority and a later ideological "rule of taste" that dismissed, and infuriated, Ōta Yōko once she turned away from mainstream confessional fiction and towards historical narratives that raised issues anathema to the polite discourses of postwar Japan.[32] Those issues included not only American moral culpability for the destruction of two cities, and not only Japanese responsibility for the continuing degradation of hibakusha living in reduced health and wretched poverty, but the very commitment of Japanese literature since the nineteenth century to Western notions of "modernity," "progress," and even "the self," all concepts now made more or less ironic by that same Western civilization's use of weapons that can annihilate indiscriminately.

In 1953 atomic-bomb literature was generally regarded as a local literature restricted to the provinces, a minor literature concerned with a minor theme. For instance, when Japanese publishing houses in the 1950s began marketing a wide range of collected works for an economically resurgent middle class, none was compiled for atomic-bomb literature, nor did even the many general anthologies include atomic-bomb writers. The widespread perception among publishers was that such books would never sell, and a jinx settled over the genre. Nagaoka Hiroyoshi has noted that the phrase "atomic-bomb literature" is not included in any of the many, and otherwise eccentrically complete, literary encyclopedias available even today.[33] That absence is emblematic of the stubborn refusal to acknowledge atomic-bomb literature as literature. In the Japanese context, a work recognized as "literature" is already minimally canonized, or nearly so: therefore, that the taxonomical literary reference works that abound in Japan still refrain today from recognizing the phrase "atomic-bomb literature" is significant and indicative.

The claims of early atomic-bomb writers such as Ōta Yōko to have created a new "literature" were greeted with especially deep suspicions. For example Maekawa Noritaka, editor of *Kyōyū*, defended in October 1947 his journal's total exclusion of any fiction that touched on the bombings:

> What sort of literature are we left with when writers abandon humanity? . . . To write about a social context should not mean surrendering to that context. . . . "Social context" is no more than an illusory concept. . . . We must be careful not to be charmed by such phrases.[34]

"Social context" (*shakaisei*) is used here somewhat euphemistically to allude to a Hiroshima still laid waste and to the tenuous, reduced lives of the bomb's surviving women and men. It refers more generally, however, to all historical references in writing that might divert our attention from the crisis of an individual to the crisis of a society. In part Maekawa may be reacting to the prestige of Marxist writers in the immediate postwar period, and their largely unsuccessful attempt to make Japanese literature respond to issues of militarism and imperialism. But specifically he was reacting to charges that his journal's editorial policies were suppressing what was an obvious theme for Hiroshima writers whatever their political leanings: the city's destruction.

To cite a later example of such charges, Yamamoto Kenkichi, a critic originally from Nagasaki, noted with exasperation that *Hiroshima bungaku* (Hiroshima Literature) a much-heralded literary magazine launched in 1952 with the assistance of some of the writers associated the former *Kyōyū*, was "a magazine that could have been published anywhere," so oblivious was it to the theme of the atomic bombings.[35] Nor was the opposition to allowing atomic-bomb writers access to publication limited to the target cities themselves. In 1953 the Hiroshima writer Iwasaki Seiichirō traveled to a meeting of the P.E.N.

Club in Tokyo to request that prominent organization's assistance in publishing an anthology of atomic-bomb literature. Iwasaki recalls that at the time he was hopeful that the end of the American Occupation would now mean freer expression for and availability of Hiroshima and Nagasaki writing. To his surprise, however, an officer of the Club—Tateno Nobuyuki, formerly a left-wing writer—contemptuously dismissed the proposal with the rhetorical question, "What in hell is atomic-bomb literature!"[36]

■

Iwasaki's hopes that the P.E.N. Club would take a leading role in promoting worldwide a literature that would raise wartime issues were, in retrospect, perhaps naive. But it was in the year of his visit to Tokyo, with the direct control of publishing by political authorities largely in the past, that the struggle between the desire for a literature which would not only document but make imaginatively available Hiroshima and Nagasaki and the reactionary institutions seeking to contain, deflect, or even eliminate such a literature was made widely public. In early 1953 both sides directly addressed each other through the pages of Hiroshima's principal daily newspaper, the *Chūgoku shimbun*. Authors, critics, and ordinary citizens debated the status of the atomic bombing of their city as a proper theme for art, and whether such art should be recognized as bungaku or as something else.

Japan is not, of course, the only culture in which the representation of atrocious violence is controversial. In recent years American novelist Leslie Epstein has doubted the possibility of any Holocaust literature other than the most starkly testimonial. Death-camp fiction, claims Epstein, "instead of increasing our capacity to suffer and to bear the unbearable, diminishes our ability to see and to feel and to think."[37] Japanese cultural traditions, however, may pose special difficulties for atomic-bomb writers seeking to depict the violence to which they were subjected, except perhaps as, according to Nagaoka Hiroyoshi, "August 6th and 9th as days one mournfully prays for the repose of souls": "Even if it is comfortable for our [Japanese] cultural traditions to think of the atomic bombings in such terms, one must also say that our country's cultural traditions make it uncomfortable to inquire into the logical and scientific, or ethical and artistic, import of those same bombings."[38]

From the very inception of atomic-bomb literature there had been a covert contest between those who, like the P.E.N. Club's Tateno Nobuyuki, declaimed it as something which went far beyond that with which literature should concern itself, and others who would define it as writing that contemplates, in the words of writer Kokubo Hitoshi, something as large as "the relationship of man to all problems past, present, and future implicit in the existence of atomic bombs."[39] But what specifically set the stage for the first open debate on this and related issues was, along with the lifting of Occupation censorship in 1952, a short exchange between Ōta and one of her critics in the prominent Tokyo journal *Kindai bungaku* (Modern Literature) that summer.

Ōta initiated the exchange when she published her responses to a mailed survey she had recently received. The questions had to do with what sort of restraints she worked under as a writer, and what sort of literature she intended to pursue. Ōta went on, after stating that some part of her frustration as a writer stemmed from her own weaknesses and a self-imposed taciturnity under Allied censorship, to lambast her bundan critics and what she saw as their elitist literary prejudices. After confirming her dedication to creating an atomic-bomb literature, she singled out for special contempt some dismissive remarks made earlier by the writer Eguchi Kiyoshi. Eguchi had claimed in the pages of *Kindai bungaku* that atomic-bomb literature had exhausted itself, that it had run out of things to say. Somewhat condescendingly, he invited Ōta to return to her native Hiroshima and find something new to write about. It was with equal condescension, then, that Ōta invited Eguchi to go to Hiroshima himself and witness the degraded lives of hibakusha living in poverty and ill-health, if he truly believed there is nothing more for atomic-bomb literature to do. Raising the rhetorical decibels of the debate that soon followed, Ōta declared that her atomic-bomb literature would be literature that everyone can read and understand, and thus by implication a literature less inbred and aestheticized than that practiced by any establishment coterie.[40]

Sometime later Eguchi would answer Ōta's ridicule of him by insisting that she had misunderstood him. But by that time his feud with Ōta in a Tokyo journal of limited circulation had been superseded by the one in the Hiroshima paper *Chūgoku shimbun* which, if not directly ignited by Ōta's 1952 essay, certainly addressed the same issue of whether there can even be an atomic-bomb literature. From January until April of 1953, the paper's literary column featured the views of more than a dozen largely local writers, poets, critics, and readers on the legitimacy, worth, and future potential of what was fitfully emerging as Hiroshima's most important, certainly most controversial, genre of writing.

The opening essay was published on January 25 by a minor Hiroshima writer associated with the conservative "Fiction Study Group" (Shōsetsu Ben-kyō Kai), Shijō Miyoko. Her essay, entitled "On 'Atomic-bomb Literature'" ("Gembaku bungaku" ni tsuite), began with a declaration of her irritation with the phrase "atomic-bomb literature" itself. Shijō argued that unlike a legitimate term such as "naturalism," which describes an authentic "historical trend" in literature, so-called atomic-bomb literature was created "accidentally" and out of reflexive emotional responses that do not constitute a sufficient basis for art. Literature, Shijō insisted, is properly concerned with "more genuine and pure human problems," which is to say the problems of "life itself." She went on to ask rhetorically why, if atomic-bomb writers wish to write about death, can they not content themselves with "plane crashes and train wrecks?" Why the bombing again and again? Isn't it time, she asked rhetorically, that we graduate to more important themes? We all die anyway, Shijō argued, and the real themes for writers must remain "love, peace, and happiness." The bomb, she concluded, "is science. It is politics. But it is not art."[41]

Shijō's complaint, condensed, was that simply writing about the bombing did not automatically result in "literature." Her essay was a reaction to what was then called the "utilitarianism" of atomic-bomb writing, a term meant to compare poorly with the aestheticism of "pure literature." Shijō's position would later be characterized by Kurihara Sadako as "a complete denial of atomic-bomb literature," "a desperate defense against bringing the atomic bombing into literature."[42] Her arguments are both historical and aesthetic. Not only does she challenge any special status accorded modern atrocity ("why not plane crashes and train wrecks?"), but she insists on preserving "genuine literature" (another way of translating "jun-bungaku") for such "genuine problems" as "love, peace, and happiness," the problems of pre-Hiroshima fiction for which many survivors—Shijō among them—feel nostalgia. It is particularly interesting that she would choose to compare atomic-bomb literature unfavorably with the "legitimate" works produced by Japanese Naturalism. A phenomenon both like and unlike the European Naturalism from which it took its name, Japanese Naturalism and the intensely introspective bourgeois novel that evolved out of it established the ideal of modern Japanese fiction as the privatized discourse of personal, psychological reflection, and directed fiction away from wider social, political, and historical contexts. Iwasaki Seiichirō termed Shijō's position as one "founded on the conventional ideal of I-novel," and to that extent was thus no more than an "old-fashioned and emotional critique."[43] Shijō's spirited defense of "legitimate" writing sought, in the view of her antagonists, to reinforce that prohibtion.

Shijō was not alone in her attempt to maintain a clear distinction between what the bombing was—to be sure, Shijō never denied its power or importance—and what literature must be. On February 25 another contributor to the debate, a poet named Hirakushi Kenjirō, placed the bombing and literature in opposition when he argued there exists a "broad gap" between "thinking that takes the bomb as central and thinking that takes literature as central."[44] Hirakushi and Shijō shared a difficulty in reconciling the theme of the atomic bombing with those themes conventionally deemed literary by those critical and commercial forces producing the canon, forces collectively denoted in Ōta's use of the term "bundan."

This is not to say, however, that only those opposed to atomic-bomb literature cared to distinguish between writings on the bomb and all other writings. The position that the destruction of Hiroshima and Nagasaki cannot be tamed as a theme for literature, that it cannot be made to address the bourgeois formulations of "love, peace, and happiness," found supporters on all sides of the debate. On the one hand there were those who wished to insure the historical uniqueness of the atrocity by constructing a unique literary genre for it, while on the other there were also those who sought to dismiss that same genre, in a move ironically compatible, by exploiting that same difference as sufficient cause for the bomb's exclusion from the ken of literature. Often the argument seemed limited to whether literature should adapt itself to the changed land-scape of Hiroshima, and not whether the bomb is a radically different topic which a changed literature will accommodate and an unchanged literature will not. That, it is important to note, was an assertion with which apparently no participant in the debate would have taken issue: despite their differences, they were all citizens of the same leveled city.

The debate's most important questions were shaped in part from the par-ticular history of views on the relationship of imaginative fiction to authorial experience. In Japan the prevailing conviction in modern times has been that "pure literature" must document a certain kind of highly circumscribed autho-rial experience. This is not to say that bungaku must be documentary. Rather, what is insisted upon is the subjective mediation of reality by the lived experi-ence of the bourgeois author, a mediation that narrows the focus of modern Japanese fiction to the range of the individual consciousness. Not only too much obvious invention in fiction, then, but too much reference to the world beyond the direct supervision of that individual consciousness, as well, risks the charge of being "unliterary." This bias towards the subjectively individual-ized experience and against the collective has meant that an overt interest in history, especially in a genre as recently historical as atomic-bomb literature, is regarded as crudely unartistic. In 1950, for instance, critic Aono Suekichi demanded from Hiroshima and Nagasaki writers documents in lieu of litera-ture. His exact phrasing was "not a documentary literature but documents which are not literature."[45] This is another way of opposing not just the factual and the fanciful, but the massive, nonindividual experience of an atomic bomb-ing with the introspective aestheticized tradition of modern Japanese litera-ture. Consequently, writing concerned with the annihilation of a city's popula-tion—rendering its authors not so much epistemological "subjects" as strategically targeted "objects"—could not be considered literary, and none of its examples eligible for incorporation into the canon.

Partisans of atomic-bomb literature, working within this traditional char-acterization of the literary as the narration of a quarantined self-contemplation, experimented with a variety of tactics to open the canon up to their work. One way to include Hiroshima, and thereby grant that atrocity the broad cultural acknowledgement that such inclusion would signify, was to extend the defini-tive perimeters of "bungaku" so far that it encompasses all writing regardless of its relation to "fact" or "fiction." One might subsume atomic-bomb literature in what is deemed literary by arguing, as Ōta Yōko in fact did, that a work even as documentary as *City of Corpses* qualifies since it describes, in words Ōta used in her own defense, "the acts of men." This was an appeal to a tenuously extended humanism, and at the same time a political challenge. Will we, Ōta seems to be asking, recognize Hiroshima as a deliberate exercise of human authority as well as an achievement of science? But the implicit critique of power in Ōta's definition has been overlooked, even by her sympathetic critics, in favor of its attractive rationalization of the atomic bombing as just another human act.

A similar proposal, liberal in the sense that it not only pushed further the boundaries of the definition of the literary, but that it domesticated the atomic bomb by bringing it into the realm of the human, and thus the traditionally familiar, was advanced in the 1953 *Chūgoku shimbun* debate. On February 4 writer Kokubo Hitoshi joined the chorus of responses generated by Shijō's essay and argued that the atomic bomb was most certainly a fit theme for literature since it was a weapon created and used by men on other men. Kokubo, who of all the participants in the debate dealt most intimately with the theory of atomic-bomb literature, sought to explain the naturalistic, descriptive (and thus apparently "anti-literary") appearance of the genre because of its imperative to remain documentary. He went on to claim that atomic-bomb literature must proceed from the realization that the bomb—whose advent proved that "politics and science conspired to betray us human beings"—will henceforth be the central concern of writing, implying that such literature alone now preserves an unbetrayed morality, the humanism otherwise voided by the use of nuclear weapons on civilian populations.

Kokubo's argument that literature can retain its moral force after Hiroshima, that indeed that moral force is augmented by humanity's betrayal by "politics and science," becomes clear in the latter part of his essay when he argues that atomic-bomb literature, given the loss of our faith in mankind's ability to find happiness—we are unable now, Kokubo claimed, to "embrace anything other than visions of catastrophe"—has the obligation to be an "ambitious movement" dedicated to restoring "human life" and the "love of man." He thus ironically reproduces the logic of his opponent Shijō's insistence that literature deal with "life itself." Although Kokubo defines atomic-bomb literature as commencing with the descriptions of the blasts, he sees it naturally maturing into a "second stage" which will cause readers to "hold and reflect upon the deep doubts of modern times." In other words, atomic-bomb literature, after its predicted evolution from the depiction of unprecedented violence to the reiteration of long-standing intellectual uncertainties, will no longer *be* atomic-bomb literature. It will become thematically diffuse enough, and politically abstract enough, to join the ranks of those conventional Japanese works of fiction that also "reflect upon . . . deep doubts" held by their self-absorbed authors. "Mumbling that the atomic bombings are something far beyond the bounds of what literature to date had considered a proper theme, those writers stood on their grounds far removed from reality and began to write their insular works."[46]

Such charitable and well-intended defenses of atomic-bomb literature are popular, and no doubt effective, because they appeal to values typically associated within modern, i.e., post-Enlightenment, Western or Westernized, culture. However, these are values often repudiated by Japanese who, like Ōta, were actually subjected to the use of nuclear weapons. When one anonymous survivor stated of the atomic bomb that "such a weapon has the power to make everything into nothing," she or he could not have meant to except "human life" or the "love of man."[47] Kokubo's concept of a critically acceptable atomic-bomb literature, then, must itself suppress the radical nihilism that the bomb so frequently inspired among its victims. Defenders such as Kokubo have seen in the destruction of Hiroshima and Nagasaki the opportunity for literature to be, in the time-honored tradition of the Confucian didactic precept of "promote the good, castigate the evil" *(kanzen chōaku)*, to act as a cathartic agent insuring nothing so terrible happens again. Objecting to such a defense, however, is Ōta, who remained convinced that the use of the bombs had permanently damaged the bases on which such didacticism must be predicated. As a hibakusha, it was Ōta's steadfast conviction that mass atrocity has ridiculed not only the worth of the "individual life" but the literary ideology which takes that experience as sufficiently representative of modern society. This disillusionment seems limited to those atomic-bomb writers who were also hibakusha. Despite Kokubo's credentials as an important and supportive atomic-bomb writer, it is evident in his 1953 defense of the genre that he sees the purpose of atomic-bomb literature to be the return the world as it was before the arrival of nuclear weapons, a world that has not been fundamentally changed by them. Kokubo's position represents a deflection of the violence of the bombings, a deflection possible only if those bombings are seen as tragic yet singular events and not as the inevitable result of powerful historical forces. His generous argument nonetheless minimizes the radical import of the violence and alternatively substitutes the agreeable proposition that such literature ultimately serves a conservative social good. This argument is not, as was Shijō's, an assault on atomic-bomb literature but rather a subtle shift in the terms with which it was to be formulated.

This shift indicates how the 1953 debate on atomic-bomb literature simultaneously succeeded and failed to win it general cultural franchise. It may have recuperated the genre for Hiroshima writers, but did so perhaps at the cost of just how they were henceforth authorized to proceed. As Iwasaki Seiichirō pointed out, once the debate on atomic-bomb literature was deflected onto other themes, atomic-bomb literature was consequently marginalized:

For along time it has been repeatedly debated in Hiroshima just how one should confront the issue of the atomic bomb, just how one should write about it. The result, or rather within the process itself, the principal issue became diffuse, and turned into an issue over the conduct focusing on the realities of politics. It was very rare for any of these debates to deal with any specific work. It is not possible to hold that, as far as prose writing is concerned, the debates have been that productive.[48]

A similar shift occurs whenever it is argued that atomic-bomb literature will "transcend" or "outgrow" itself to become "genuine literature." Perhaps the best-known example of this seemingly progressive argument is found in liberal critic Odagiri Hideo's 1954 "The Problem of Atomic Energy and Literature" (Genshiryoku mondai to bungaku). While declaring that "the issue of the hydrogen bomb and literature marks a new dimension in the history of world literature," Odagiri goes on to claim that atomic-bomb literature is ultimately important because it is a "step" to a more "social" and more "human" literature: in other words a literature that, while descriptive of the bombings, becomes their historical antithesis.[49] This is an argument that posits an odd atomic-energy utopianism. It plots a historical future in which the same process that developed the bomb ("progress") will also lead to an improved society, thus somehow justifying, or at least compensating, the initial and unfortunate violence produced spuriously. The focus of atomic-bomb literature is shifted from a discussion of the details of, and responsibility for, two real historical events to a potential and therefore comfortably intangible future without actual victims and victimizers.

The perhaps irresistible impulse to replace the destruction of Hiroshima and Nagasaki with its thematic opposite—the *construction* of a society made better rather than worse by the use of the bomb—is as much a censure of the kind of atomic-bomb literature written by Ōta as was Shijō's blanket dismissal of all atomic-bomb literature, and has surely contributed to her continued banishment from the ranks of critically approved postwar writers. In her frustrated attempt to write a literature she defined as the expression of the total collapse of moral restraints, she could not countenance the one rationale of atomic-bomb literature that might have won her admission to the canon. Incapable of repressing her own memories of August 6th, and thus incapable of Kokubo's or Odagiri's brands of futurist optimism, Ōta continued to place the unalterable and historical *fact* of Hiroshima at the center of her works. As a result she remained on the periphery of Japanese literary and critical circles from 1945 until her death of bomb-related causes in 1963.

Ōta's views were occasionally seconded by others. For example, the danger of defending atomic-bomb literature on grounds which reaffirm the cultural and political history that produced the bomb was pointed out by author and critic Abe Tomoji in a 1955 essay entitled "The Atomic Bomb and Literature" (Gembaku to bungaku). After acknowledging that the bombings confront literature with problems unlike those of any other "new phenomenon," and that literature has an obligation to grapple with those problems, Abe rails against the insidious view of atomic-bomb literature as that which is built on "the love of peace." What is at stake, he argues, is the question of what will replace, in literature, the "old humanism" destroyed along with two cities; like Ōta, he has no answer.[30] But in 1953 no such radical perspectives were heard. Rather, the developing consensus of the participants in the *Chūgoku shimbun* debates was that, as poet Matsuhara Takahisa asserted, "Hiroshima could be a forceful, positive energy in literature."[51]

In early March of that year another local poet, Fukagawa Munetoshi, summarized what he saw as the two contending schools of thought that had asserted themselves during the two-month debate. He likened them to the two positions in another debate then underway in Hiroshima, namely the controversy over what should be done with the ruins of the Atomic Bomb Dome, the steel-reinforced concrete building left partially standing near the epicenter of the blast. Some residents of the city felt the ruins should be cleared and new buildings built, but others wanted them preserved as a memorial. Similarly, some critics of atomic-bomb literature felt the genre an inappropriate and even dire threat to their imagined future for literature, while others looked upon it, for better or worse, as a necessary and even enabling part of the future that they imagined. The basic issue of the debate, Fukagawa concludes, was not atomic-bomb literature or even Japanese literature at all, but rather "the way in which we live as human beings."[52] Such high stakes account for the exceptionally urgent and tense tone of the exchange, an exchange which has resurfaced sporadically in Japan over the decades that have passed since 1953.

■

In 1960 another public argument took place in what is referred to as "the second atomic-bomb literature debate." Like the first it was spontaneous, direct, and sparked by a calculatedly provocative essay published in Hiroshima's *Chūgoku shimbun*. Kurihara Sadako, whose reputation as a perspicacious critic of post-Hiroshima culture had only grown in the intervening eight years,[53] published a two-part piece entitled "On the Literature of Hiroshima" (Hiroshima no bungaku ni megutte) and subtitled "Auschwitz and Hiroshima" in the March 19 and 21 editions of the paper. She states that she had been angered to words by what she saw as the continuing suppression by the critical establishment of discussion on the utility and theory of atomic-bomb literature. Locally this establishment was represented by an organization of prominent writers and poets calling themselves the "Hiroshima Literature Society" (Hiroshima Bungaku Kai). Yet for a long time, Kurihara notes with evident disdain, this coterie had gone by the affected name "Hiroshima Literati Salon" (Hiroshima Bunjin Konwakai). Kurihara found it absurd and offensive that the reputation of literature in Hiroshima might rest in the hands of soi-disant "men of letters" passing judgment over the writings of bomb survivors who in fact often perceive the bomb as a total reputation of the remote, aestheticized culture which these arbiters of taste convened to advertise.

Kurihara is quite clear in her own dissenting views: the bomb wreaked havoc not only in the cities it leveled but in the literature which now must accommodate the fact that we are capable of doing anything to ourselves with no effective moral restraint and little compunction. No drawing-room dilettantes, Kurihara insisted, can put things back the way there were. She protested that the Society is not, despite its name, interested in promoting Hiroshima *atomic-bomb* literature. Instead they have organized to purge Hiroshima literature of the bomb altogether, or at least displace that theme for more "genuine" ones. In her essay Kurihara quotes various Society members as having made such comments as "the bomb is not an urgent problem," "I would rather write about ordinary everyday life," and "atomic-bomb literature is a psychological complex which obstructs the development of literature."[54] Kurihara interprets these opinions as being not merely obdurate but illustrative of the inability or unwillingness of many intellectuals to perceive what the word "Hiroshima," like "Auschwitz," has come to signify.

Kurihara believes that nuclear weapons pose as great a challenge to the premises of civilization as does the Nazi genocide of European Jewry because both atrocities signal the completion of the dehumanization of culture. When she writes that "mankind has stopped being human and become a machine," she echoes the thought of those postwar critics in the West who understand the lesson of the war to be the inescapable realization that efficiency has replaced ethics. Kurihara notes, however, that although atrocities both East and West have generated their own literatures, that of the death camps is far more plentiful than that of Hiroshima and Nagasaki. With no little frustration over the ground rules set for the practice of modern literature in Japan, Kurihara speculates why:

> European postwar literature could confront the fact of Auschwitz because throughout the Second World War there had existed, especially in the cultural tradition of France, a resistance movement borne of *humanité*. Japanese culture, however, with its dilettantish concern for elegant pursuits and the beauties of nature, has never known such *humanité*. Consequently there has been no soil for a literature of defiance to take root and grow, and postwar literature in Japan has continued, unchanged, to be dominated by quotidian, domestic, egocentric fiction. Perhaps noth-

ing can be done about this lack of a historical sense, a lack which means that atomic-bomb literature cannot be seen as anything other than a literature of pariahs. (261)

Unlike Holocaust literature, atomic-bomb literature is repressed as "non-literary" by a native ideology nonetheless akin to that which informs Western belletristic literary practices, an ideology articulated in aesthetic codes that privilege the decorative, lyrical, or psychological while eschewing historical, political, and broadly social concerns. Kurihara links the resistance of dominant tastes in Japan to the accommodation of the unpleasantries of mass death with the bundan's refusal to legitimate atomic-bomb literature. The Hiroshima Literature Society turned its collective back on its most obvious subject matter because it came to the theme of atrocity theoretically and methodologically empty-handed.

In the April 1, 1960 issue of *Chūgoku shimbun* Matsumoto Hiroshi—a critic, translator of Hemingway, and member of the Society—responded to Kurihara's charges. But in doing so he revealed himself to hold just that attitude towards the relationship of the bombing to literature which so exasperates survivor-writers who, like Kurihara, want that relationship to be literal, imperative, and primary. No one at our meetings ever said what she claims we did, insists Matsumoto; or rather, we did not mean those things quite the way in which she took them: "When I said that the problem of the atomic bomb should be thought of as a symbol, that is precisely what I meant. If in writing of the bomb we speak of nothing *but* the bomb, then our literature will do no more than a single documentary film could."[55] In another curious turn, Matsumoto argues here along lines similar to those of Kokubo Hitoshi in the first *Chūgoku shimbun* debate. Both are seeking a transcendence. Both would identify the bomb as a trope—minimizing its real and lethal actuality—which will then be superseded when it is incorporated within a greater, "genuine," theme. The atomic bomb is converted into a "symbol," a sign, something less than real: the concrete experience of the survivor-writers is displaced by a political or social "cause." To treat the destruction of Hiroshima and Nagasaki as a real event worthy of a literature all its own—to treat it as many hibakusha writers insist it must be—is to reduce it to "no more than a single documentary film," which, remembering the words of bundan writer Aono Suekichi, is to disqualify it as literature.

Matsumoto's views, as we have seen, were popular among many of the genre's defenders and detractors. On April 22 another participant in this second debate, Yoshimitsu Yoshio, baited atomic-bomb writers with an essay provocatively entitled "I Doubt We Can Expect an Atomic-bomb Literature" (Gembaku bungaku taibō ron o utagau). In it he states that the story of the bombings is old news, and since no one wants to read old news, an atomic-bomb literature would be a literature with no audience and thus no value or significance. Here the anti-atomic-bomb literature argument forsakes the high-cultural grounds of aesthetics and turns, uncharacteristically, to the unsubstantiated assertion of sheer unpopularity. Yoshimitsu scorns not only past attempts to create a literature of the bomb but future ones as well. Atomic-bomb literature can have no future of its own because it amounts to nothing more than a theme of conventional writing. Again, the genre disappears once it is reduced to a variation of other, and thoroughly domesticated, literatures.

A reader named Nakagawa Kunio brought the second *Chūgoku shimbun* debate to a close of April 29 when he attacked Yoshimitsu in an essay entitled "Towards an Atomic-bomb Literature of Possibility" (Kanōsei no gembaku bungaku o). Nakagawa, however, likewise pursues a line of argument which eventually diminishes the unique nature of the genre he defends. On the contrary, he says in response to Yoshimitsu, atomic-bomb literature does have a future because it is a theme that leads to other themes (themes not, he writes, so "miserable"), and he cites recent novels which used Hiroshima and Nagasaki as settings for treatment of such topics as racial discrimination and wartime responsibility. Nakagawa's reasoning is doubtlessly well-intended, but after all an atomic-bomb literature that takes us to utterly different problems is no longer atomic-bomb literature, any more than a murder mystery set at a women's college is necessary a feminist rather than detective novel. Once again, an apology for atomic-bomb literature makes its point by repudiating the bomb in favor of themes clearly established as "literary" long before August 1945.

What is particularly noteworthy about the second *Chūgoku shimbun* debate of 1960 is the participation of ordinary readers—not writers—such as Yoshimitsu and Nakagawa. That such Hiroshima citizens would be inspired to join in a debate initiated by professional writers such as Kurihara demonstrates the importance of the stakes involved in legislating the permissible boundaries of literary discourse over the atomic bombings. That such citizens would endorse the possibility of a larger social critique through the vehicle of atomic-bomb literature suggests the degree of passion with which the need for such critique was, and still is, apparently felt. All this points to the long-standing tension within the practice of Japanese literature between its interests in formal authenticity and thematic utility, a tension not yet resolved and which would again, repeatedly, erupt on whatever occasion the specific issue of the bombings or postwar nuclear terror becomes a public controversy.

■

In the late 1970s and early 1980s there were several other, often heated, exchanges over the quality and value of atomic-bomb literature and nuclear issues in general. While these discussions did not take place in quite the succinct form that they had earlier in the *Chūgoku shimbun*, they might still be thought of collectively as Japan's "third atomic-bomb literature debate." Despite the fact that this most recent exchange took place some thirty-five years after Hiroshima and Nagasaki, and thus took place in the hands of critics and writers almost all a generation removed from the bombings themselves, it seems significant that the issues involved were much the same as those discussed in the early 1950s and 1960s. It is further significant that these issues were not so much "revived" in a third debate as they were long-standing points of contention within literary and critical circles simply articulated in an exceptionally acerbic set of terms. What may have accounted for the raising of the rhetorical stakes over the problem of the relationship of writing to the social and the historical is the contemporary urge in Japan—and elsewhere too, given the passion with which the "Historians' Debate" (*Historikerstreit*) was pursued in both Germanies only a few years later—to "normalize" the events of the Second World War. This urge, which has its most recent expression in such acts as President Reagan's mission to Bitburg and the official Japanese campaign to rehabilitate such symbols of its imperial past as Yasukuni Shrine, found its high-cultural counterpart in the labors of younger Japanese critics exerted on the behalf of a self-consciously intellectual literary practice still, if weakly, menaced by interventions by a generation of older hibakusha writers accustomed to writing personally, emotionally, and often politically.

Since the death of Ōta Yōko in 1963, without a doubt the most widely read woman atomic-bomb writer has been Nagasaki native Hayashi Kyōko.[56] Like Ōta, and indeed like most of the first generation of atomic-bomb writers, Hayashi's work has been and continues to be largely testimonial and always autobiographical in nature. As a prolific writer, and moreover as one with a reputation as "the" Nagasaki—even "the" A-bomb—writer, Hayashi provided the same kind of prominent, easy target that Ōta herself once had.

In October 1978, a serious and uncharacteristically intemperate charge was leveled against Hayashi by one of Japan's most talented younger novelists, the late Nakagami Kenji. Participating in a round-table discussion entitled "Our View of Literature: Transcending the Idea of a Generation Gap" (*Warera no bungakuteki tachiba—sedai-ron o koete*) and featured in the widely read monthly journal *Bungakkai* (Literary World), Nakagami was prompted to make the following comments in response to Hayashi's then recently published short-story collection, *Cut Glass, Blown Glass* (*Giyaman—bīdoro*):

> It is ironic that the more one realizes that, among all Japanese fiction, there is none more poisonous than atomic-bomb literature, one also realizes that there is no more perfect fiction for those Japanese who wallow in the war. "This is how badly I was bombed," etc. But what really happened back then isn't in any of this fiction, is it. And that's why it can't

be literature. . . . In Hayashi Kyōko's *Cut Glass, Blown Glass* readers are easily moved to tears just because it's about hibakusha. This is fiction put together through tricks. And nothing could be better suited for those old folks who made the war and committed crimes and yet want to feign innocence and profess their regrets. (109–10)

Nakagami angrily gives vent here to the collective impatience of a number of younger critics who have reacted negatively to what they perceive as the indulgent, manipulative, and ultimately self-serving literature of a wartime "victimhood" exclusive both of the legacy of Japanese victimizing and of the cogent historical analysis of either. If Ōta Yōko was too plainly documentary for the tastes of an earlier generation of critics, then Hayashi was altogether too subjective for those of a later one. In light of the attempts in both mass and elite circles to rewrite modern Japanese history, or to forget it altogether, Nakagami's complaints seem inspired by a legitimate suspicion of the consequences, if not motives, of a literature that seems myopically and miserably focused upon the individual measure of suffering in the Second World War rather than its international origins and import. This is a literature with which Hayashi, a survivor-writer, has come to be identified but which Nakagami's postwar generation would, in another irony, prefer to subordinate to a more contemporary or basic agenda of political and historical issues. Yet if history is, as critic Kobayashi Hideo defined it, "in the end memory," then Hayashi's long-time project as the *kataribe*, or "ritual reciter," of her city and its fate has been little but the relentless reenactment of history, if not its redress: it is just in the very different meanings of this word as welded by Nakagami and Hayashi where lies their irreconcilable dissonance.

A little more than three years later, Nakagami and others noted in greater detail and even more blunt language their objections to Hayashi, her writings, and the tendency in fiction to replace, they feared, history with an egocentric sentimentality. In January 1982, Hayashi published in the literary monthly *Gunzō* (The Group) a piece entitled "Safe: 1981 A.D., 37 Atomic Age" (Buji— seireki senkyūhyaku hachijūichi-nen, gembaku sanjūshichi-nen), in which she recounts a trip taken the previous year to Hiroshima, Japan's other A-bomb city but to which she had not traveled before. Writing in the first person, Hayashi tells of going to Hiroshima with memories of her native Nagasaki fresh in her mind, revived by the recent death of her favorite high school teacher from bomb-related causes. As her plane approaches Hiroshima's airport, she is haunted by the delusion that she is aboard the *Enola Gay*. Once on the ground, however, Hayashi is struck by how beautifully rebuilt Hiroshima is, and then by other differences between this city and her own Nagasaki.

Most prominent of these differences is one that unexpectedly subtracts from Hayashi's confidence to report on Hiroshima. When she visits the Atomic

Dome memorial, she is humbled to discover, despite her presumption of the congruence of the experiences of Hiroshima and Nagasaki hibakusha, that August 6th belongs in fact to Hiroshima, and Hiroshima alone:

> Until today I had never regarded August 6th and the Atomic Dome with such poignant emotion. I had forgotten the Dome's existence until, walking through Peace Park, I recognized it towering above the verdant leaves of the laurel trees. "Forgotten" is not quite right: I had come here thinking that our commonality as hibakusha meant that August 6th belonged to all of us. But the Dome made such comradery utterly impossible. (41)

Hayashi's brief experience in Hiroshima thwarted her prior confidence in the assumption of all that the bombings, in their plural senses, had meant. But the visit also reaffirmed her knowledge of the continuing crisis produced by the advent of nulcear weapons and in the nuclear age they initiated. Despite her confession of doubt over the comprehensiveness of her own command of the "A-bomb experience," which might seem to qualify the seeming arrogance in Hayashi's earlier writing to which Nakagami had objected in 1978, at the same time Hayashi's realization of how the dimensions of Hiroshima's tragedy are not fully graspable even by a Nagasaki hibakusha also implies that an even greater and perhaps wholly unbridgeable gap separates the non-hibakusha from that experience altogether. It was perhaps that implication that inspired the renewed and even more pointed attack on Hayashi Kyōko soon thereafter. In a joint review of "Safe" by Nakagami and two other important younger critics, Karatani Kōjin and Kawamura Jirō, Nakagami launched into a diatribe whose rancor revealed evident signs of a long-standing complaint, not only with Hayashi Kyōko but with the theme of Hiroshima and Nagasaki in literature overall:

> I have never, even once, recognized as fiction anything that Hayashi has written. . . . Basically she believes that merely writing about atomic bombings achieves something literary, but . . . her work is neither essay nor fiction. . . . I felt her piece "Safe" somewhat pathetic when I read it— pathetic in that Hayashi should have thought that just writing so artlessly about the atomic bomb could be literature, or that she thought it could be publishable in a literary magazine. . . . If she thinks the atomic bomb automatically equals literature by making a text out of it, then I guess we've got to conclude that the A-bomb has finally shown us how literature is to be done, don't we?[57]

This sarcastic rejection of writing of the atomic bomb as literature echoes similar charges made against Ōta Yōko three decades earlier when, for example, Shijō Miyoko rejected the genre in toto on account of its disqualifying "utilitarianism." Just as Nakagami resisted the immediate equivalence of atomic-bomb discourse with what he meant to reserve for literature, generations of hostile critics before him similarly railed against the implication that the literary could ever the product of anything but talent and dedication to pure aesthetic form. The longevity of such critical reaction was demonstrated again when Kawamura confirmed Nakagami's dismissal of Hayashi. Since her first works, Kawamura observed,

> she wrote out of an absolute need to write of her experience, but that has come to be replaced in her works with a sense of "mission." In my view this sense of mission—the sense that this experience must not be allowed to fade from memory—is itself a manifestation of the fact that it *is* fading. (289)

Finally, in a phrase that would raise the rhetorical level of this verbal assault on Hayashi to new heights, Nakagami accused her of being what he called an "atomic fascist" for insisting that whatever she wrote—wrote of the bombing—was instantly literature. To this unanswerably damning political brand was added a psychoanalytical diagnosis when, in this same review, Nakagami and Karatani concurred that the nuclear issue had in fact become something of a "fetish" in literary circles (290). The use of such powerfully censorious language as "fascist" and "fetish" derives, at least in part, from the admittedly unswerving attention paid to the atomic bombings by their survivor-writers. Ōta Yōko, and then later Hayashi Kyōko, upset their critics on at least two scores: their single-minded dedication to a politically suspect theme, and their concomitant refusal to translate that dedication into a privileging of other, more ostensibly "human" and thus more "literary" issues.

But there are, as one could argue, material and historical differences between these survivor-writers and their non-hibakusha critics that should provide a context for, and perhaps thus disarm, these complaints. First of all, Hayashi, like Ōta before her, *is* a literal victim of nuclear war, and Nakagami is not. Secondly, she and other survivor-writers are victims of an event in human history of such moment that it might well be dominant in their writings: what looks hyperbolic to some may be mimetic to others. Even if Hayashi's work is to be judged "obsessive," it is certainly so in ways hardly at odds with what literature has taught us to expect from writers subjected to incessant personal crisis and struggle. In her 1979 essay "Wishing Life As It Should Be" (Shizen o kou) Hayashi wrote:

> My life has been one built on August 9th or, to put it another way, on my bomb-victim health booklet. Just what joy have I had in living? For one, I am in good health. There is a happiness I cannot hide the moment I see the words "nothing abnormal" written into my notebook. For another there is my son, who has grown up to be like any other normal

person. And there is my appreciation for a friend who, still struggling against August 9th, has survived to make it to fifty. My thoughts go back to August 9th. Over and over again, August 9th is a day which never should have been. Yet it is also a day that taught me the preciousness of life. (31)

There is clearly the potential in these experiences and emotions for whatever Nakagami and his fellow critics might mean by "literary"—stories here as real and human and important as any other. The implicit target of these attacks on Hayashi was not, however, in fact either Hayashi or her stories—it was the status and function of a term notoriously mercurial: history. Lévi-Strauss once quipped that calling something "historical" is tantamount to calling it a "thing-a-majig,"[58] and it does certainly seems that in lieu of concepts of the "real"— concepts that are so problematized as to be effectively useless—"history" now serves as that thing "out there" which, if only we could describe it, would provide us with the truth. But ironically if perhaps predictably, the demands of critics such as Nakagami in insisting upon the critical analysis of "history" from the works of Hayashi, are demands that strikingly resemble what Kurihara Sadako decades earlier had pointedly asked from those of her Hiroshima colleagues who had, in stark contrast to survivor-writers like Hayashi, steadfastly avoided the theme of the atomic bomb in their writings. History, in other words, apparently serves as the rhetorical sanction of whatever particular political or ideological position we—certainly Kurihara, Hayashi, or Nakagami— wish to assume.

In the early 1980s, the range of those positions was wide and their immediate consequences for Japanese intellectuals crucial. Those consequences account, in part, for the particular hysteria to which Hayashi's in fact rather innocuous essays gave rise. At the root of Nakagami Kenji's frustration over the theme of the nuclear lay something at stake that had been debated in intellectual circles since the last months of 1981. An attack on Hayashi in 1982— particularly an attack resorting to such words as "fascist" and "fetish"—had a widely publicized and public context that explains, if not justifies, the shrillness of her critics' remarks. The references to Hayashi's supposedly fascist insistence upon, her "fetish" for, nuclear themes echoes what was in fact a highly visible and controversial debate within both the literary establishment and the nation at large in 1981 and 1982.

This "within" began, as was to be later pointed out by many of its critics (the same critics who, not coincidentally, took Hayashi to task) with an impetus from the "outside." In November 1981, the West German writer Hans-Peter Brohl traveled to Japan to ask for Japanese support of the antinuclear appeal signed by over fifteen-hundred writers across Europe, an appeal prompted by the threat of a Europe about to be strewn with the medium-range nuclear missiles then being planned by the United States, the Soviet Union, and their allies. Writer Nakano Kōji, who would become the principal organizer behind the support that did indeed follow, was in the small audience that heard Brohl's appeal for help. He recalls that at the time the international nature of this antinuclear movement gave him, as a Japanese intellectual, a renewed sense of hope. After Brohl's talk, Nakano and some fifteen others reconvened in a nearby restaurant and laid the initial plans for what became the "Writers' Appeal Against the Dangers of Nuclear War" (Kaku-sensō no kiken o uttaeru bungakusha no seimei), a petition calling for immediate nuclear disarmament. It soon was signed by almost three hundred leading intellectuals and writers, including such senior figures in the literary establishment as Satomi Ton and Ibuse Masuji. Eventually, the number of signatories would swell to more than five hundred.[59] The impact of this appeal and the number of its signatories was not lost on either the public or the conservative, generally pro-American government, which it embarrassed. Despite the fact that Japanese literature had previously taken note of international antinuclear movements—*The Songs of Hiroshima* (Hiroshima no shi, 1955), an anthology of atomic-bomb poems compiled by Yoneda Eisaku, Ōhara Miyao, and others, was translated into English in the 1950s to express solidarity with those movements—Ōe Kenzaburō did not exaggerate when he said of the Writers' Appeal, "In the forty years since the end of the war, no other movement in Japan equalled this in the number of writers mobilized."[60]

The Writers' Appeal was announced to the public at a press conference held in Tokyo's Shimbashi Daiichi Hotel on January 20, 1982.[61] Its brief text read:

> There are at present sufficient nuclear weapons to slaughter all living things on the planet many times over. Should nuclear war ever occur, this means that the destruction will not be that of a single nation, region, or continent, but the entire globe. Nonetheless, fearsome announcements positing the possibility of a limited nuclear war using neutron bombs, new types of rockets, and cruise missiles have been made, and are now being put into effect.
>
> We oppose all such plans and actions. There can be no such thing as a limited nuclear war. Should such nuclear weapons ever be used, they would soon escalate into total nuclear war. It is all too clear that this would result in the annihilation of the entire world.
>
> In order that our species survive we here today call upon the world's leaders to transcend all national, racial, social, and ideological differences, and halt at once this new arms race and work instead for the abolition of nuclear weapons. At the same time we demand that the government of Japan strictly observe its Three Non-Nuclear Principles.

As writers from the country of Hiroshima and Nagasaki, we believe it is our obligation to the human race to dedicate all our energies to preventing a second, and final, nuclear war. We urge all the peoples of the world to work at once for peace. We will not abandon our goals, and will apply all our strengths to them.[62]

There is no reason to doubt the deep sincerity with which the hundreds of signatories to this document pledged their support, or certainly any reason to doubt the danger that the world did indeed face during the early 1980s from the threat of a new high-technology arms race. Typical of its supporters' sentiments were remarks made by Kinoshita Junji, Japan's most famous postwar playwright and no stranger to political controversy:

In the more than thirty years since the Second World War I believe that I have come to know a few things. When people speak today of their opposition to [nuclear] war, I feel that the pacifism I hold so dear is something now part of my very being. And so my willingness to sign the Writers' Appeal, too, comes from somewhere deep inside of me.[63]

It was precisely for such sentiments, doubtlessly sincere, seldom analytical, and often plaintive, that the Writers' Appeal was subjected to a broad, bitter, and unanticipated critique by other intellectuals too young to have lived through the Second World War but old enough to be familiar with what they considered the tired cant of their elders. There was of course a small crowd of voices on the left that indicted the Writers' Appeal for its hopeless liberalism and its studied cliches lacking any real potential to effect change. These critics complained that the language of the Writers' Appeal did not go far enough, that it did not come out four-square against the nuclear power industry, imperialism, war in general, and so on. Voices on the right, however, were louder and more numerous. Etō Jun, an immensely influential critic, wondered in print whether the Writers' Appeal had been financed by the Soviet Union, so much to that country's advantage were its demands.[64] Less paranoid but equally publicized was senior poet Ayukawa Nobuo's comparison in a wide-circulation popular weekly of Japan's antinuclear movement to the American and British communist parties' antiwar, and in hindsight ill-fated, position in the early days of the Second World War.[65]

But the most startling, and certainly astute, attacks on the Writers' Appeal came not from any conventional and entrenched ideological position, but from an eclectic circle of literary critics not easily typed in terms of their politics or ages. What did unite this group was a shared distaste for the lemming-like behavior of so many Japanese intellectuals, but particularly that of those associated with the Tokyo literary establishment.

The first of the attacks from these critics came only two weeks after the announcement of the Writers' Appeal. In the February 8, 1982 issue of a weekly

trade newspaper, Suga Hidemi—one of the most prominent younger critics—
argued that there were, in fact, many criticisms one could level against the
Writers' Appeal. As examples he cited its embarrassing sentimentality and its
failure to consider the problem of nuclear weapons in any wider context. These
two criticisms overlap somewhat with those that emanated from both the ideological left and right. But Suga's greatest complaint was one unique to his own
critical cohort of sophisticated critics:

> What is most frightening about this Appeal lies precisely in how
> its dynamic disallows any criticism of itself. The apparently subjective
> position of being "antinuclear" is in fact an extremely hackneyed thing
> to claim, as hackneyed as the very words "Hiroshima" and "Nagasaki"
> indicate. And because being "antinuclear" is such a cliche, "all the peoples
> of the world" "transcend[ing] all ideologies" have no choice but to ac-
> quiesce.
>
> But perhaps what we should call this subjectivity, this all too con-
> ventional subjectivity, is "fascism."[66]

This charge of "fascism" of course recalls the similar language used in the
attack on Hayashi Kyōko by Nakagami Kenji made only a few weeks earlier.
Both Hayashi's attempt to define her hibakusha experience as central and the
Writers' Appeal signatories' insistence upon the unanimity of their views on
nuclear disarmament are seen as totalitarian in their refusal to countenance
dissent. This refusal particularly distressed younger critics such as Suga because
of their heightened sensitivity to certain issues of rhetoric raised by recent
literary and political criticism. A month after calling Hayashi's writings fascist,
Nakagami Kenji would, in the middle of a work of fiction he was serializing in
the same magazine, use similar language in his equally vociferous dismissal of
the Writers' Appeal:

> There's another envelope on my desk. Sent by author Nakano Kōji, it
> contains a request for signatures to an appeal for the abolition of nuclear
> weapons. It disgusts me. I know some of its sponsors, and some are writ-
> ers whom I usually respect, but do they really think some document like
> this can eliminate nuclear weapons? It's just like the [wartime fascist] Im-
> perial Rule Assistance Association, the way everyone rushes like an ava-
> lanche to sign it. It's all nonsense, especially the way even someone like
> Murakami Ryū signs it as if he's some sort of official representative of the
> subculture. This proves that their literature is, after all, andropocentric
> [*ningenchūshinshugi*]. Unabashed humanism.[67]

It may be confusing to see charges of behavior akin to that of the wartime
state-sponsored fascist writers' organization linked to charges of "unabashed
humanism," but it is apparently just this notion of "andropocentrism" that Na-

kagami considers just as compulsory among writers today as allegiance to the ideology of the "Greater East Asia Co-Prosperity Sphere" had been a generation or two earlier. This label of andropocentrism—which some found wholly incomprehensible[68]—was used by a number of writers apparently to indict older critics for their smug and even intimidating use of a finally meaningless concept. Suga Hidemi, in his essay on the Writers' Appeal, assailed its signatories' "andropocentrism" for their implied resistance to scientific progress, as did Yoshimoto Takaaki (who used the variant term *ningen'yuishugi*, or "human chauvinism").[69] Just what may be objectionable in andropocentrism, or its synonym "unabashed humanism," may be its uncritical nature, or its sentimentality, or perhaps even its vanity. It is almost certainly, however, the uncomfortable resemblance that its insistence on the unquestionable consensus of world opinion shares with other, more dangerous, forms of "imperialism" that alarmed literary critics already made sensitive to any such rhetorical claims by the force of modern textual theories.

The antagonists' complaints were also importantly institutional. Yoshimoto, who despite his noted role as a progressive during the national debate over the U.S.-Japan Security Treaty in 1959 and 1960, was the most vociferous and sustained of the Writers' Appeal critics, finally had at the root of his varied objections what he rightly or wrongly perceived as the all too typically arrogant, intellectually and politically vapid and cynical slavishness of the literary establishment's fringe of has-beens, parvenus, and outright pretenders.[70] Such objections may or may not be valid for the internecine politics of Tokyo writers and critics, but they are objections that do not address the undeniably real issues nonetheless raised by the Writers' Appeal. Consequently, the foes of the Writers' Appeal repeat the arguments made by the conservative voices in the 1953 and 1960 debates, when the crisis of post-Hiroshima culture was deflected in directions considerably less germane than the issue of human survival.

The most reasoned, perceptive, and interesting critique of the Writers' Appeal also suffered from a similar distraction. Leading critic Karatani Kōjin, writing in the April 1982 issue of the monthly *Bungei* (Literary Arts), began by paraphrasing both Marx and Nietzsche to the effect that whenever universal statements are made, one should look not at what is being said, but rather at whom is saying them. Engels, Karatani continues, states that any class will attempt to exercise hegemony by universalizing its own perspective. That is precisely the nature of "ideology." Even the question—one asked, in effect, by the signatories to the Writers' Appeal—"How can we overcome ideology?" is thus ideological. This is why, Karatani suggests, Suga Hidemi saw a strain of fascism in the Writers' Appeal's remarks about "overcoming" national, social, philosophical, and ideological differences.[71] Who can oppose such pronouncements? They take on the dangerous attributes of an ideology masquerading as common sense. Yet Karatani himself is more troubled by exactly whom is making this Appeal. Who are these "writers" in the Writers' Appeal? What, Karatani skeptically asks in the Heideggerian spirit of a distrust of borrowed language and its slippery referents, do they presume to know about the European contexts from which came the call to organize in the first place? Karatani accuses the organizers of the same naivete charged by Yoshimoto, Etō, and others, but adds a poststructuralist twist when he asserts "there is neither literature not essentially political, nor any politics not essentially literary."[72] In conclusion Karatani darkly speculates whether the signatories could really be so naive— are they really free of the desire for power? Karatani wonders whether the twentieth-century signatories to the Writers' Appeal believe, as did the nineteenth-century Dostoyevsky, that: "With no nuclear war—no God—everything is permitted"—is that not what they are really saying?[73]

However telling Karatani's doubts, they do not address the incontrovertible fact that nuclear war is a distinct menace, and one that might reasonably command the attention of intellectuals, even if that attention is not at once efficacious, or even motivated by the most rigorous logic. That was, in fact, the retort made by some of the Writers' Appeal sympathizers to these insinuations by Suga, Nakagami, Yoshimoto, and Karatani. While some of the supporters of the Writers' Appeal did concede that their cause had, since it was indeed a fashionable one, attracted some less than fully sincere signatures,[74] for the most part writers associated with it defended their actions with an equally spirited offensive of their own. Kuroko Kazuo, for one, in answer to the question why this "anti-antinuclear movement" should have arisen among Japanese intellectuals, and why the attack focused specifically on Hayashi Kyōko, answered: "Even if they knew that they were blind to how they expressed the very nihilism endemic in contemporary society, their arrogance did not permit them to take note of how atomic-bomb literature has ceaselessly hammered away at that same nihilism which has ruled in the thirty-seven years since the end of the war."[75]

This "nihilism" to which Kuroko refers is the ethical opposite of the "andropocentrism" decried by the anti-Writers' Appeal faction. Its proof is evident in the remarks frequently made by younger critics and writers who claim that nuclear war is not truly the issue it is purported to be. Novelist and social commentator Tanaka Yasuo, for example, once stated on a radio program that he did "not feel any 'nuclear threat.' . . . It's no problem as far as I'm concerned since I can't believe that any bombs will be dropped in the coming decade."[76] To such indifference and contempt, others, and not just those who had lived through the Second World War, had a ready response. Hoshino Mitsunori stated that his generation born after the war can claim no moral superiority over older others, and moreover that his generation carries a special responsibility for the rearmament that had taken place since 1945. Younger critics like Kikuta Hitoshi, who claim that the war might just as well have never occurred as far as they are concerned, are, in Hoshino's view, simply wrong.[77]

The principal counterattack against those who denounced the Writers' Appeal targeted the perceived covert agenda of those critics. Many defenders of the Writers' Appeal purposely linked the criticisms of it with the long-standing legacy of assaults on both the older, institutionalized left in Japan and the cloistered literary establishment in general. Kuroko Kazuo, for example, suggested that Yoshimoto Takaaki's opposition to the Writers' Appeal was spurred by his well-known and oft-stated disgust for the insular nature of Japanese intellectual circles. "Fundamental to Yoshimoto's thinking," wrote Kuroko, "is that there are masses of people for whom politics have absolutely no relevance at all, and that any philosophy that does not take into account the existence of such people is pointless."[78] More specifically, intellectual historian and critic Matsumoto Ken'ichi explained: "Yoshimoto Takaaki's criticisms were carried out mentioning the names of [such established leftist intellectuals as] Nakano Kōji, Itō Narihiko, Odagiri Hideo, Ōe Kenzaburō, and Oda Makoto. . . . For whatever reasons, Yoshimoto opened a full-scale attack on the 'old left' that had reconvened within this 'antinuclear movement.'"[79]

Yoshimoto's complaint, if Matsumoto's characterization of it is apt, is not without its point. But that point has little if anything to do with the nuclear age or atomic-bomb literature. Obsessed by whom was bearing the message, critics of the Writers' Appeal failed to address the merits of that message itself. What was particularly irksome, however, to the supporters of the Writers' Appeal was the unusually widespread attention this intellectual falling-out received from the public, especially lowbrow, media. Kuroko Kazuo understandably and skeptically wondered how it was that Yoshimoto's anti-Writers' Appeal views were splashed across the pages of the popular weekly *Heibon Punch*, a magazine more generally noted for its reports on baseball players, show business gossip, and soft pornography.[80] Masuoka Toshikazu would observe some years later that the "anti-antinuclear" writers such as Etō, Yoshimoto, and Ayukawa "were protected by the mass media" and thus "exerted a definite influence" on public opinion and policy.[81]

The reason that these critics had such unusually open access to the media may be linked to the fact that their views overlapped with widely held assumptions on the proper relationship—more precisely, nonrelationship—of writers to explicitly political themes. This is the same belief in the exclusively aesthetic ken of the writer that worked against atomic-bomb writers and their works in the earlier two debates on atomic-bomb literature, first in 1953 and then in 1960. As Masuoka also pointed out, "Although the views [of the anti-Appeal faction] were diverse, in general they held that to speak out on the issue of nuclear weapons was to lose one's qualifications as a writer *[bungakusha shik-kaku]*."⁸² In fact, the critics of the Writers' Appeal were themselves unambiguously clear on just this point. Yoshimoto wrote in June of 1982 that:

> There cannot be any "atomic-bomb literature" or "Vietnam literature" or "untouchable caste *[buraku]* literature" or "literature of the physically-disabled." There is only literature *[bungaku]*. . . . Its themes are to be determined only by the "intensity" of the writer's concerns. If a writer does not select his theme out of a irrepressible concern, then that theme has no meaning whatsoever.⁸³

Just why Hiroshima and Nagasaki—or for that matter Vietnam, racial discrimination, or physical disability—cannot be of "irrepressible concern" to a writer is not explained, despite the extremely passionate nature of many literary works that take up just those themes. What Yoshimoto must have meant to do was reserve for the label of "literature" what he personally finds of intense interest, and argue their aesthetic "universality."

This rhetorical intimidation echoes the equally indignant and disparaging comments made previously by those antagonistic to what they saw as the limited, parochial, and finally "inartistic" nature of atomic-bomb literature. It was almost thirty years earlier that local Hiroshima poet Shijō Miyoko had opened the first public debate on the literary quality of atomic-bomb literature by declaring that true literature had to be reserved for "more genuine and human problems" than nuclear war. Hoshino Mitsunori, commenting on what was most at stake in this third and most recent atomic-bomb literature debate, made a point equally valid of the earlier two: "Finally the issue was one of the definition of 'literature.' What Yoshimoto wanted to say was, even if literature is theoretically capable of encompassing the world, in practice it never does—if one is convinced that literature can encompass the world, then isn't it already not literature?"⁸⁴

"Encompass" may be taken to mean, in a more critical idiom, "represent." For Yoshimoto Takaaki to believe that the real, in all its historical, ethical, and political respects, can be objectively represented is "already" to abandon the prized subjective point of view deemed by Yoshimoto and his cohort as essential to literary value. This raises once again the issue of a collective subjectivity produced in much atomic-bomb literature, and the collective agency articulated in the Writers' Appeal by the "we" that so annoyed its critics. The implicit threat is to the individual subject so passionately linked to the nature and mission of what is referred to as "modern Japanese literature": a post-Hiroshima, post-nuclear literature may necessarily be one in which the possibility, even probability, of omnicide so menaces our collective survival that only collective responses make practical, as well as literary, sense.

Three general areas of disagreement regularly dominate Japanese debates on atomic-bomb literature, and all involve controversies over the definition of literature, the character of the canon, and the unresolved political or historical issues for which those controversies serve as proxies. First, can descriptions of the bombings and their aftermath ever be termed "literature" in the same sense that term is used to approbate works that narrate our common, rather than unique, experiences? Second, should atomic-bomb literature remain realist, and thus mired in its own grotesqueness, or should it strive to be therapeutically and morally instructive, even if that means repressing some of the bombings' historical implications? Third, can writing that does not endeavor to describe the direct consequences of the bombings per se but only uses post atomic Hiroshima or Nagasaki as a gothic background for more conventional themes, also be "atomic-bomb literature" without trivializing the bombings themselves?

Looming behind these questions is the one doubt, the one pervasive ill-ease that animated the fury of the debate: how much will we allow atomic-bomb writing to redefine our ideas of what literature is, and does? Will the traditional critical consensus on bungaku as the representation of a highly circumscribed, individualized bourgeois consciousness be revised to allow a new tradition of writing intimately involved with global issues of human survival? Will we, in other words, allow literature to be actively political by merely being historical? Kurihara Sadako, who along with Ōe Kenzaburō has striven to bring works by atomic-bomb writers into the Japanese canon, noted the importance of these questions in one of her essays: "No one can deny that the development of atomic-bomb literature has lagged behind that of other writing since the war, but the issue is not one of literature. One might say that an uneasiness with the bombing itself becomes an uneasiness with its literary works, and that atomic-bomb literature thus exists as a distinct subset of literature."[85]

The bracketing of atomic-bomb literature as a "distinct subset" is, in Kurihara's estimation, the result of unresolved questions over Japan's legacy as the first nation to be attacked with nuclear weapons. This ambivalent repression of atomic-bomb literature implied by Kurihara's characterization of it as having an adjunct status within the larger institution of "all" literature—whether it is unique because it is feeble or particularly astute—provides critics such as Ōe and herself with a means for understanding more precisely what the identity of that institution is. When Abe Tomoji wrote that "the problem of literature and nuclear weapons . . . is not the same problem as wondering how to write skillfully about the beauties of nature or the passion between men and women," he noted the difference between a literature that deals with supposedly ahistorical themes and a literature that deals with historical ones; he also noted the difference, given the current crisis among the nuclear powers, between a irresponsible literature and a responsible one.[86]

Despite the increased attention paid atomic-bomb writers in the controversies of the early 1980s, all still remain marginal figures in the critical histories of Japanese literature since the war. Japanese writers in the 1980s, while enthusiastically outspoken on the issues of postmodernism and other emblems of their contemporaneity, continue to avoid precisely what some may have long, if erroneously, assumed to be one of the preeminent public issues of Japan's literature since 1945: the nuclear policide of Hiroshima and Nagasaki as a fundamental event in human history, a history whose future prospects have been and continue to be compromised by that event.

The Japanese canon has only recently begun to make room for Ōta Yōko, or for most survivor-writers of equal talent. Eliminated twice, once by fission weapons and once by a critical establishment often incapable of or unwilling to comprehend the depth of their postnuclear skepticism, their work remains only slightly more accounted for in Japan's literary histories than the use of those weapons themselves does among the themes of our own literature in the West.

Two

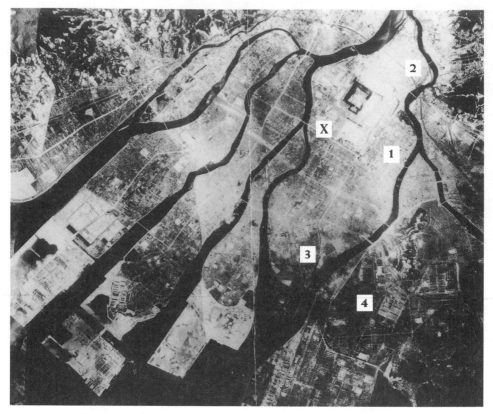

Hiroshima, August 13, 1945: Location of the writers on the 6th
  1 = Hara Tamiki
  2 = Ōta Yōko
  3 = Shōda Shinoe
  4 = Tōge Sankichi
  X = Ground Zero

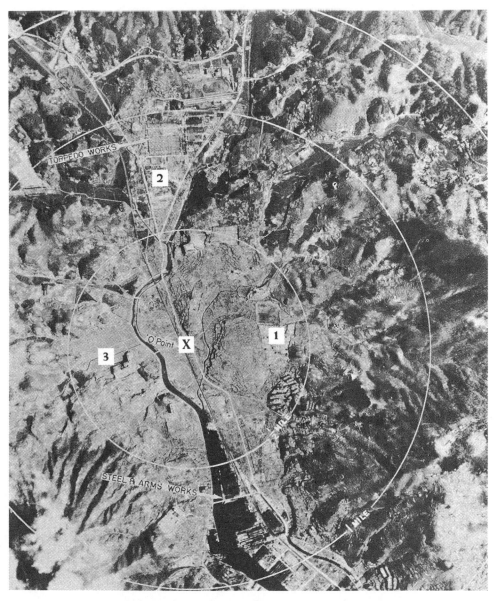

Nagasaki, August 12, 1945: Location of the writers on the 9th
  1 = Nagai Takashi
  2 = Hayashi Kyōko
  3 = Gotō Minako
  X = Ground Zero

Which world is natural? That which existed before,
or the world of war? Both are natural, if both
are within the realm of one's experience.

Czeslaw Milosz, *The Captive Mind*

4

Hara Tamiki and the Documentary Fallacy

Hara Tamiki was born in Hiroshima in 1905 and died in Tokyo on March 13, 1951, when he lay down on the busy railroad tracks between the Kichijōji and Nishi-Ogikubo stations. His death, although technically termed a suicide, has also been attributed to his presence in his native city on August 6 half a dozen years earlier. Fellow writer Ōta Yōko, for whom Hara's death was a disturbing reminder of her own tenuous grasp on life, proclaimed it no less a sure consequence of the attack on Hiroshima than the deaths that occurred during the initial blast.[1] Just before he died, Hara had heard on the radio that the United States was contemplating the use of nuclear weapons in Korea and, according to the folklore that now surrounds him, his anxiety as a hibakusha in the first use of fission bombs on human targets was so worsened by this prospect of a third use that he was driven to his grisly end. Like the deaths of so many of the first generation of atomic-bomb writers—Ōta's among them—Hara's seems in retrospect a delayed effect of, and one guaranteed by, the atrocity that few survived bodily and that even fewer survived psychologically intact.

Hara's career as a writer is now overshadowed by his last few years and by his preoccupation with the destruction of Hiroshima. His present reputation is built nearly entirely upon his literary responses to that destruction. Recent years have seen new editions of his work and generous praise offered him by some of Japan's most respected critics;[2] as interest in atomic-bomb literature rises so does Hara's status as the genre's first acknowledged pioneer. More than forty years after his death, he has been retrieved from the ranks of third-class prewar writers and installed as perhaps the foremost of that small corps of survivors who chronicled the incineration of their cities: some might say the incineration of their—our—civilization, for what Hara's postwar work continually reiterates with its relative successes and failures alike is the theme of a world wholly changed and potentially incapacitated by its newly exercised power to annihilate itself.

It is wrong, however, to sever Hara's early writing from his later. Even his juvenilia seems to foretell his future as a writer of calamities, and critic Honda Shūgo has proposed that in his atomic-bomb literature, Hara found his "destined theme" (*ummeiteki shudai*).[3] While the documentary quality in his early atomic-bomb writing is not typical of his work as a whole, its concern with the catastrophic is. Like that of many of his fellow atomic-bomb writers, Hara's disposition perhaps naturally inclined him to regard, and dwell within, the darker side of human existence with an insight more perceptive than most. The origins of this disposition are debatable.[4] As the son of a military supplier in a city important to both the army and navy—he was named "Tamiki," or "the people rejoice," to commemorate Japan's victory over Russia in 1905—his circumstances were, in the words of his critic Kokai Eiji, "financially affluent."[5] This same critic notes, however, that his youth was also a time of "Sturm und Drang," of impending doom.[6] Two losses affected him particularly: the death of his father from cancer in 1917, and the equally painful death the following year of his elder sister Tsuru, to whom he was especially close. There are more than a few references to these deaths in Hara's stories and essays,[7] and perhaps their frequency illuminates Hara's declaration in the 1935 story "Fog" (Kiri) that "man's greatest woe is the terror that is death" (19). Neither is it irrelevant to understanding his post-1945 work that as a youth Hara chose as his poet's pen name "Kiyū," an elegant Chinese word (Ch'i Yu) meaning "needless anxiety" and derived from an anecdote found in the classic Chinese text *Lieh Tzu* about the angst (*yu*) of a man from Ch'i who was convinced the world was near its end.[8] Adding to the young Hara's apprehensions about his own mortality was his failure, in the same year as Tsuru's death, to pass his middle school entrance exams, an event which again in the view of his later interpreters rendered him even more isolated and alone than the loss of either a father or beloved sister could have.[9]

Throughout his adolescence Hara was already, in temperament if not yet fact, a young poet of the twentieth century. Like Rilke, later to be his remote mentor, he remained socially introverted and emotionally handicapped. His classmates (in the school to which he eventually gained admission in 1919) thought him odd, while he saw himself as a denizen of the same nether world in which the antiheroes of his favorite nineteenth-century Russian novels dwelled. His life was prematurely a reflective one. He kept a journal beginning in his primary school days, and by his second or third year of middle school his interest in literature had matured into a commitment to become a professional writer.[10] At the age of nineteen, already well-versed not only in the works of such writers as Murō Saisei and Uno Kōji, but those of Verlaine, too, Hara entered the lower division at Keiō University and in the company of such classmates destined for literary prominence as Yamamoto Kenkichi and Chō Kōta tentatively joined the famously intense world of young literary hopefuls of Tokyo in the 1920s.

At this time Hara thought of himself as primarily a poet. Indeed, he never entirely abandoned poetry, and some today still consider him a far better poet than writer of fiction.[11] To be an ambitious poet in 1924 meant to experiment with various schools of Modernism and Symbolism which, though ultimately of European origins, in their Japanese incarnations fairly dominated the then most prominent circles of serious poets. Although Hara had come to Tokyo under the influence of his readings in the eighteenth-century poet Yoza Buson, he soon found himself intrigued with Dadaism and Surrealism (and with politically radical movements to the extent that he was cautioned by the police). His prewar reputation, though small, associated him with these avant-garde trends.

Yet as critic Terada Tōru has pointed out, it is difficult to place Hara's work in its entirety in the history of modern Japanese literature.[12] Katsumoto Seiichirō considered the prewar Hara Tamiki an Expressionist writer.[13] But all that can be said with any certainty about the whole of his career is that his work was consistently solicited by and published in the journals *Mita bungaku* and to a lesser extent *Gunzō*, both prestigious places for writers to appear. No one cites Hara as representative of any particular school of modern literature. This is true for perhaps any of several reasons. It is hard, first of all, to imagine that any writer who is noted for his descriptions of an unprecedented human catastrophe might be fit effortlessly into a long-standing tradition of more genteel themes. Nor is it a simple matter to dispose of an author whose work, no matter what his earlier themes, is as fundamentally bifurcated as that of the survivor writers of a nuclear holocaust. Terada's comments on Hara are echoed by those of other critics on other atomic-bomb writers. Perhaps this general ambiguity, then, reflects a general difficulty literary historians have had situating works that take up the theme of overwhelming violence because of the atypical forms such works can assume. Perhaps, too, the difficulty is nothing more than a hesitancy, as guardians of the canon resist admitting those authors' works that, because of their nihilistic inferences for writing itself, threaten the feasibility of more conventional literature.

Nonetheless, Hara's pre-1945 work, even if considered apart from what followed, still defies facile classification. This raises an issue independent of his later career as an "A-bomb writer" but germane to his particular generation: germane in ways that, in fact, might have had some impact on his approach to writing about Hiroshima. Hara came of age as a writer once he graduated from the English Literature Department of Keiō University in 1932, a rather inauspicious decade to embark upon such a career. Probably no one issue dominated the institution of literature in the 1930s more than *tenkō*, the political apostasy of the left, and the dissent it provoked among some intellectuals. Proletarian literature had collapsed under the combined weight of its own vapidity and state suppression; Modernist experimentation had grown dull; and novel-writing as a whole declined. Naturalism, by which I mean *shizenshugi*, the literary school with the greatest impact on modern Japanese literature, had as a movement atrophied long before, and the genre it inspired, the autobiographical *shishōsetsu*, did not enjoy its previous popularity.

None of this is to say, however, that Hara began writing fiction in a vacuum, or that he could even conceive of a story without recourse to some kind of narrative approach informed, in turn, by at least the implicit force of an idea. Literary schools can formally dissipate while their formal or aesthetic premises continue to exert influence in the guise of assimilated "approaches" to how events in a story should be ordered and related. For instance, Hara's earlier occasional foray into a fictional world of trees that talk certainly seems reminiscent of Surrealism and the playful distrust of certainties it represents, although like humor it is wholly absent from his post-Hiroshima work. Convincing is critic Nakahodo Masanori's insight that it was the predominant narrator who "sees" *(miru)* the world around him in Hara's prewar work that subsequently, with the substitution of a first-person "I" for the earlier "he," made it possible for him to document Hiroshima.[14]

Of the many diverse influences traversing Hara's work, however, the one most useful to him once he took up the theme of Hiroshima is precisely the one least obvious to us because it remains today so pervasive: the naturalistic, broadly defined as the depiction of people and events as phenomena, i.e., as manifestations rather than as origins. As Donald Keene has noted of Japanese literature and Norman Mailer of American, Naturalism (the philosophical theory behind the practice of naturalistic writing) is still an important force in literature today.[15] Its ideological thrust—the final secularization of the individual—had been present in both nineteenth-century European and early twentieth-century Japanese writing (where, secularization never having been an issue, the emphasis had been on the social demarcation of the individual). While this ideology lost its novelty, it survived to provide writers with highly attractive systems of rhetoric for constructing characters and plots in their work. Naturalism posited people as conditional, as products of heredity and environment; such a view invites novelistic writing, with its attention paid to both background and milieu. Naturalistic writing, even as it is practiced today, shares this view of human beings as contingent upon the world about them, even though that world is no longer easily explained solely in terms of Darwin or Freud.

For instance, in the two founding novels of Japanese Naturalism, Shimazaki Tōson's *The Broken Commandment* (Hakai, 1906) and Tayama Katai's *The Quilt* (Futon, 1907), the heroes are victimized, respectively, by the consequences of birth and a nearly uncontrollable libido. They exist as literary characters only insofar as they reflect the particular, and abstractable, forces that act upon them. The inner world of the person is determined by a mappable outer world. Moreover, a look at the history of Naturalism, in Japan as elsewhere, indicates that that inner world is increasingly constricted as the outer world—the world of the twentieth century—tends toward continuously greater violence.[16] Likewise, naturalistic writing, as it takes stock of the phenomena that constitute literary "character," has had to face the fact that those phenomena are more often than not related to the sudden proliferation and diversification of the ways men and women can be killed. Hara's heroes, conceived decades after those of *The Broken Commandment* and *The Quilt*, may no longer be examples of a smugly deterministic, mechanistic universe, but they are still subject to a menacing array of forces and still the passive inhabitants of a landscape rendered evermore inhospitable by technological "advances"—advances that would culminate in another atomic-bomb writer's insight that "the one thing for certain is that what caused these deaths was the raid of a B-29, was a war, was a gigantic explosive force that came from somewhere beyond. As a result, human beings lived their brief lives and were summarily crushed, burnt, and died."[17]

One of Hara's first short stories illustrates how this adversarial rhetoric of abstract forces channels the development of his characters and prepares the way for how he will describe the impact of a nuclear attack. In "Flames" (Honoo, 1935), Yasuo, a troubled adolescent, is under pressure to pass his middle school examinations when his distressed state is aggravated further by the imminent death of a favorite older sister. This is the sister who interested him in Christianity, and who convinced him that love can potentially change anything in the world. Yasuo is intrigued by this notion of an omnipotent love because he perceives in it a counterforce equal to those other forces fighting to control him, such as the pressure of societal expectations and the fear of death, but most of all the power of his awakening sexual drive. In the end, however, Christian love loses. His sister dies, school goes badly, and he is humiliated by an adult who discovers an erotic note he had sent a friend. Yasuo increasingly seems an observer watching a battle being waged within him; he begins to hallucinate and risks suffering a mental breakdown. "Flames" is a work in which a battery of conceptualized forces from both inside and outside—anxiety over his academic future, his shameful desire for the opposite sex, his encounter with the power of Christian belief, and most of all, mortality—align and conflict to portray an adolescent constricted by a dark world more powerful than himself:

> Yasuo was sitting in the small room where he studied. It was night, and the large drops of an unseasonably warm rain were striking the eaves of the house. When the wind blew, the sound of the rain grew wild. The wind, too, was warm for this time of year. Fresh out of the bath, Yasuo found himself in a trance as he listened to the rain, a rain much like that of spring though it was only February. He wondered if it might not make the plants in the garden come up. The rain lapped the leafless trees. No, the rain was talking to them. He forgot about his studies for the test as he listened to what the rain was saying. The blue wall before him shone like pieces of mica in the light of the lamp, just like stars in the sky. Oh please, God, let me pass this test. Damn it, gently, gently, he wanted to sing a song. Recently dogs had been copulating on the street corners. The dogs were making noises like flutes with their snouts. But if I grew wings I bet I could fly, gently, gently. I'd be an angel, wouldn't I? Angels all have the faces of women, and eyes just as in a dream. The sound of the rain grew more violent. (113)

As this anxious adolescent sits in his room, potent forces symbolized first by an unusual storm batter the outside of the house, forces that risk perverting nature. Through an association of ideas he fantasizes in fragmentary images that recall his other obsessions: sex, death, school. His hallucinations degenerate into chaotic nonsense; he collapses under the combined weight of his worries. This scene is not without its ironies for the readers of Hara's postwar atomic-bomb stories. The description of a person passive and helpless before forces he cannot wholly fathom will occur again, and as nonfiction. Though one must be careful not to minimize the unprecedented rupture of Hara's world that the atomic bombing was, one can still detect in a pre-Hiroshima work such as "Flames" a schema, a rhetorical appeal, that will serve him in ordering his narration of an experience that other, perhaps less-prepared, survivors found impossible to articulate. Although the circumstances of a troubled youth and those of an atomic attack are incomparable, Hara's designs for describing them might be viewed as similar, namely to subjugate human behavior, even identity, to exteriorized, objectified phenomena. This approach shares an important common ground with naturalistic writing: literary character exists beyond itself and yet within nature. This arena of possible explanations for events might be termed, in anticipation of Hara's post-1945 work, "proto-documentary" in the sense that the writing subject of "Flames" (Hara/Yasuo) notes and records the phenomena observable to him. It is important to recognize in a story as fantastic as "Flames" a kind of documentary amid the play of metaphors in order to also recognize, when one comes to later writing explicitly called documentary, the metaphors that then conversely obtain. Documentary writing is not naive: it takes its method from a prejudiced, value-laden view of reality, a view which in the very best traditions of the nineteenth century equates the interaction of quantifiable forces with the operation of the "natural world."

"Flames" is more conventionally understood as "documentary" insofar as it is roughly autobiographical. All of Yasuo's worries and apprehensions were, reportedly, Hara's own. In another coincidence, the greatest of those fears were of death. Whether it was the death of a sister or that of a city, mortality is found throughout Hara's writing as a powerful naturalistic force that curbs a great deal of behavior, that affects much in life even as it itself cannot be affected.[18] Hara's obsession with death awaits the atomic bombing of Hiroshima as an inevitable theme, and more importantly, his position vis-à-vis death anticipates his documentary approach. This is evident in his story "The Procession" (Gyōretsu, 1935), a work in which death is the only theme. Its central figure, another adolescent but this time named Fumihiko, happens upon a funeral procession. Whose, however, he does not know. Only after he catches sight of a wreath with his own name on it does he realize that it is he who has died. To an old woman near the end of the mourners' march he admits that he has often dreamt of a scene such as this, his own funeral. She suggests that perhaps he is dead only because he had already resigned himself to oblivion in those dreams. Will I disappear, he asks. Yes, of course, you will. Who am I now then? "You are an empty husk" (248). Finally, at the story's conclusion, Fumihiko walks on to watch his former self be cremated.

The victim of death in "The Procession" perceives death as an object and grants it a near-tangible presence. There is nothing spiritual, metaphysical, or irrational about it; it is both in nature and real. Freud, whose relationship with the idiom of naturalistic writing is profound, pointed out in one famous argument that no one can live through his own death, and that when we attempt to do so—in our dreams—we are in fact present only as spectators.[19] As the procession winds its way past him, a spectator is precisely what Fumihiko is: "The Procession" is the eyewitness account, the document of his own imagined death. Just why a person barely thirty would dwell on such a morbid theme is another irony that has inspired speculation. If we recall that Hara himself called "the terror that is death" "man's greatest woe," then the critic Nagata Hiroshi's view that Hara saw in death a kind of "revenge" against an exterior evil world that repeatedly violated him confirms the nature of death in Hara's works as the foremost of the abstracted metaphorical forces governing his literary characters.[20] It is not, therefore, only that death is an important theme in Hara's prewar work that will contribute to his ready success as one of the first atomic-bomb writers, but that his early handling of death as an overwhelmingly powerful and observable entity will coincide with the manner in which conventional documentary would seek to depict a nuclear attack.

Historical events both personal and international eventually brought the force of death experienced in 1935 at a distance into much closer proximity. After a brief and unhappy affair with a prostitute and an attempted suicide in 1932, Hara married Nagai Sadae, a Hiroshima native and sister of writer Sasaki Kiichi in 1933. For six years they lived in apparent happiness,[21] but then in 1939 Sadae's health began to fail. A long and moving series of brief prose works chronicles the course of his wife's illness and eventual death from pulmonary tuberculosis in September 1944.[22] Although Hara's literary production slowed while he looked after his ailing wife, her death, according to fellow author Itō Sei's rather morbid judgment, "made Hara a beautiful writer, one whose reputation would last."[23]

One of these works, "On the Brink of a Beautiful Death" (Utsukushiki shi no kishi ni, 1950), describes the last days leading up to Sadae's death. The story is constructed with the multiple interplay of powerful forces—often expressed in the vocabulary of light, wind, and temperature—swirling about the inner world of a dying wife into which the ultimate force, death, has already penetrated. Crazed wild things are said to force their way into their home, while Sadae dwells "within a world somehow possessed." This inner world takes on the attributes of Hara's bedridden spouse: immobile, passive, and the prey of a terrible maelstrom without. When narrator "he" (*kare*) ventures out of the house, he sees everything in terms of these forces destroying his domestic life. Grammatically passive and causative constructions abound in the Japanese; the train he takes to work is described as "the train that took him" (*kare o noseta densha*) rather than the more idiomatic "train that he took" (*kare no notta densha*). Bright rays of sunlight are often intruding into whatever room he passes. But the mortal impact of these menacing metaphors is focused on Sadae. She is "invaded" by a severe cough at night. Her pain is described as "violently attacking the whole of the house." As her condition deteriorates, Hara too is threatened endlessly "by the vision of death." When Sadae at last dies after a long and tortuous night with Hara at her side, the morning light and everyday noises outside their home are noted, as if to prefigure the unprecedented light and noise that will intrude upon Hara later. "On the Brink of a Beautiful Death" serves as a rhetorical model for the atomic-bomb literature to come. In both, the world seems split into two halves, the outer powerful world of danger and the inner world of human lives shaped, directed, and finally terminated by that danger. Hara's style in "On the Brink of a Beautiful Death" is often nearly poetic, but it shares with naturalistic writing a common calculus of cause and effect, of broadly determined consequences; with documentary it shares the chronological reiteration of facts; and with atomic-bomb literature it shares the topos of death.

The fantasy of death that animated an early work such as "The Procession" was replaced, after the actual death of Sadae, with unalterable reality. It was, once coupled with the destruction of Hiroshima the following year, a reality whose dimensions he would never fully measure, yet out of this consternation would come his best and most original writing. In his essay "Death, Love, and Loneliness" (Shi to ai to kodoku, 1949) Hara wrote that of all the tragedies encountered in his life, it was that of his wife's death that gave him his literature (540). In one of his works he had mused, "Were my wife to die before me, I would live only one year longer to leave behind a volume of beautiful, sad poetry,"[24] and in a letter to his brother-in-law Sasaki Kiichi appended to his very last story, "The Land of My Heart's Desire" (Shingan no kuni, 1951) he lamented that quite nearly all he wrote after Sadae's death was no more than a last testament (404). In some sense, of course, this Hiroshima survivor-writer's postwar work was necessarily testimony if not precisely and always a literal testament: as Kurihara Sadako noted, it was also Hara's writings that "best speak of postwar Japanese literature as an extraordinary discourse previously unknown anywhere in the world."[25] Yet that discourse is one that now seems eerily familiar. What finally makes Hara so compelling a writer, so representative of much twentieth-century literature, is the inescapable conclusion that his works track a descent into a new world where our mortality, now never remote, is manipulated by forces that neither the victim nor the survivor can ever hope to control or comprehend.

■

While the forces of death were pressing in on Hara Sadae, the Allies were, island by island, approaching Japan proper. Literary historian Nagaoka Hiroyoshi stated that Sadae's death gave Hara "a premonition of the destruction" that was soon to follow.[26] That destruction was less than a year away, but Hara hardly could have imagined it.

In January 1945, Hara closed down his and Sadae's house in the Tokyo suburbs and went to live with his older brother Nobuhide and his family in a central Hiroshima neighborhood. Tokyo was facing mounting attack from American bombers; Hiroshima, so far unscathed, was thought the safer city in which to wait out the end of the war. Nobuhide's home, however, was only slightly more than one kilometer from ground zero. According to official reports compiled later, everything within 2.8 kilometers was "completely destroyed";[27] according to fellow atomic-bomb writer Tōge Sankichi, everyone exposed within three kilometers "eventually died" of the bomb's effects.[28] Hara's survival was extraordinary.

He himself believed his life after 1945 an anomaly, and many of his generation thought the same of their own lives. Consequently, for those who did survive the initial attack, their atomic-bomb literature had to be a literature of record, of writing as journalistically faithful and free of rhetoric as possible. Ōta Yōko recalled, for instance, that as she worked on her first documentary-novel in the early autumn of 1945 she felt she was racing against the clock, struggling to finish her story before radiation sickness claimed her life as it had all those around her.[29] Hara was no more certain of his own choices. The unprecedented experience of living through an atomic explosion demanded it be described, preserved, and passed on. Hara felt this urge to put into words for others what had happened to him no less than the other survivors who were also professional writers. Hara alone however had the distinction of being the first in print, and he thus occupies a special place in the history of Japanese atomic-bomb literature.

Immediately after the bombing and his subsequent flight from the city, Hara briefly noted the events of August 6 in a few pages of telegraphic notes written in the stark *katakana* syllabary and without punctuation.[30] These notes were not published until Hara's collected works were issued in 1965 and only then under the miscellaneous category of "Odds and Ends" (*dampen*) and dryly entitled "Notes on the Atomic Destruction" (Gembaku saiji no nōto). Nonetheless, Nagaoka considers these bare and often cryptic sketches "the beginning of atomic-bomb literature," the first written records of a new era in human history.[31] They begin:

> August 6. Approximately 8:30
>
> Suddenly an air attack in one instant the entire city destroyed I am in the bathroom, while above my head there is the sound of an explosion something hits my head the next moment, blackness and noises
>
> When I look through the dim light, the house is already destroyed my things are scattered everywhere something stinks, my eye is bleeding I recognize Kyōko
>
> Because I am naked I look for clothes I find a jacket but no pants Tatsuno comes, his face smeared with blood he says that Esaki has been hurt

I pick up my emergency bag on the veranda outside the parlor We depart for Sakae bridge heading for Sentei Park, stepping over the maple that has fallen over in front of the house. (529)

"Notes on the Atomic Destruction" continues to list the most crucial of Hara's movements and the most unforgettable of his sights over the next few days. This list would provide Hara later with his material for a number of expanded, and in part fictionalized, stories about the bombing. None, however, ever quite matched the raw urgency and vividness of these first semi-articulated notes. Each subsequent elaboration would entail a distancing, a rhetoricization, of the original text. Each re-presentation would alter as well as accommodate the confusion of an atomic attack so well conveyed here.

It would take some time, however, before Hara was again in circumstances comfortable enough to permit the reflective writing of stories. After spending two days as a refugee on a Hiroshima military parade ground, he fled the city on August 8 with some of his surviving family and settled temporarily in the nearby village of Yawata. Although Hara is not said to have suffered from any specific symptoms of radiation sickness, he never enjoyed full health again. In part this must have been due to the near-universal conditions of malnutrition he and so many others suffered in the immediate postwar years. In fact, Hara is also well known for his descriptions of hunger during the Occupation;[32] one especially memorable story has Hara fantasizing about eating the paste he is using to repair his paper screens.[33]

In April 1946, Hara returned to Tokyo and became a student at Keiō once more, at first lodging with boyhood-friend Chō Kōta and later with a nephew in Nakano before moving into his own squalid apartment in the same neighborhood. His life, like that of many in Tokyo, was difficult, but he nonetheless managed to contribute regularly to Keiō's prestigious literary journal, *Mita bungaku.* In June 1947, he published his most important work of atomic-bomb literature and perhaps the most famous of any survivor's account: "Summer Flowers" (Natsu no hana), which is the middle third of a triptych formed with "Prelude to Annihilation" (Hametsu no jokyoku, 1949) and "From the Ruins" (Haikyo kara, 1947) and jointly published as a single volume in 1949 under the general title *Summer Flowers.*[34] Only this middle part, "Summer Flowers," is widely read any longer, however, and it was for this that Hara was awarded the first Minakami Prize in 1948. It occupies a special place in Hara's writing, as he says himself in "Death, Love, and Loneliness":

Amid the catastrophe of the atomic bombing, I was left alive. Since that time, both I and my writing have been violently dislocated by something. Even if I were to die, I still wanted to put down on paper all the graphic scenes I witnessed. I recorded my unique experiences in my se-

ries of works "Summer Flowers" "From the Ruins," and "Prelude to Annihilation." (540)

Hara's account here and elsewhere of his original inspiration for "Summer
Flowers" prefigures the shape it would assume as a narrative of atrocity. In "The
Bells of Nagasaki" (Nagasaki no kane, 1949), Hara tells that it was his troubled
state of mind on the day the war ended that "made him write" "Summer Flow-
ers," a choice of words that further suggests how deterministic and passive
Hara's view of himself in the world was:

> I learned the name of *that* on August 16. We had had no newspapers, but
> my nephew, who had joined us from the city, called it by the strange
> new word *genshi* [atomic]. What first flashed in my mind was the hom-
> onym *genshi* meaning "genesis" or "primitive." The expanse of squirming
> victims and swollen red corpses all fused together did somehow seem
> like the nightmare of some primitive new age. I wondered if the entire
> world might not suddenly slip into that bad dream.
>   However the war was already over by then. It was my sense that it
> really was over that made me write "Summer Flowers" so soon afterward.
> Confronting the immense scope of what had happened, I felt that all
> human energy and imagination had been quietly blown away. I planned
> to describe in detail the tragedy of what I personally experienced on
> August 6th as calmly as I could before it became distorted by time. (577)

The confusion caused by the very word used to label what destroyed Hiroshima underlines the confusion any survivor faced in attempting to describe
that destruction. Hara's response is to tell "calmly" and "in detail" what "he
personally experienced"; his urge is to document. In fact, "Summer Flowers"
has often been praised as an invaluable "record" (kiroku) of Hiroshima, perhaps
cued by Hara's own characterization of it as "the record of an unprecedented
personal experience."[35] Masuoka Toshikazu refers to it not as a work of fiction
but as an "atomic-bomb testimony."[36] Historian Richard Minear, the work's recent translator, calls it "the classic account of the atomic bombing of Hiroshima" and was presumably drawn to it for reasons of its documentary utility.[37]
Getting the "facts" "straight," with a minimum of interpretation, was the paramount concern of the first stage of atomic-bomb literature since those very
facts were themselves so unimaginable, so elusive.

"Documentary," or variously "documentary literature," "docu-novel," "documentary fiction," and so on, has grown as a genre of writing in the twentieth
century as current events have continued to exceed every normal expectation
of what men can allow themselves to do to each other. No one could have
imagined anything as inhuman, ahuman, as the Nazi program of genocide, or
as total and efficient as a nuclear device; now, however, the recreation of these

events entertain us on television. "Fact" has come to demand the same "suspension of disbelief" once required only by fiction. Documentary hopes to gain immediate and unmediated access to "truth," to dispense with style and proceed directly, urgently to substance. Unfortunately, that hope seems continually frustrated. Words, when robbed of their right to be words, leave nothing behind. How are we, the readers, to recognize the "reality" behind the victim's account without recourse to what obfuscates it, namely the translation of experience into signs? There is, no matter how eagerly a literature of atrocity demands comprehension, no reason to expect that the rhetorical action of language should efface itself simply because a particular theme is impatient with it. Indeed, perhaps just the opposite holds true. An atomic-bomb writer, desperate to make us believe what happened was real, is the Aristotelian orator at his most earnest, dedicated to convincing his judges with all the tropes at hand. Documentary techniques, while they differ in approach and thus confirm their arbitrary (in the sense that language, too, is "arbitrary") nature, are united in their appeal to rhetoric no less than that of any other variety of literary language.[38]

It is, in fact, the presence of rhetoric and not its absence that is conspicuous in the memoirs and first-person accounts that have come out of Hiroshima and Nagasaki. It was not just professional writers such as Hara, who might be expected to be self-consciously "literary" out of habit, who resort regularly to language that departs from the strictly denotative to connote, hopefully, an experience lacking ready analogues. One of the most important collections of Hiroshima testimonies, *Atomic-bomb Testimonies* (Gembaku taikenki, 1965), an anthology of brief memoirs of August 6th by children, housewives, businessmen, and other nonprofessional writers, demonstrates how recollection is inconceivable without elaboration. None of the anthology's testimonies opens more impressively literarily than that by a middle school teacher, Mutsu Katsutoshi:

> As others, startled by the brilliant moment of light and the explosion like that of distant thunder, raised their heads to gaze with eyes of awe at the beauty of a strange mushroom cloud silently billowing high in the far blue skies, in another small corner of Hiroshima I was a traveler wandering somewhere betwixt the land of the living and the land of the dead.[39]

Mutsu, in resorting to a number of images and in constructing a sentence with both tragic and ironic overtones, succeeds in involving his readers in a story nearly as mythical as it is historical; one will recall this account longer than most others in the same anthology. Nonetheless both the preface and the epilogue to *Atomic-bomb Testimonies* stress the documentary nature of the testimonies over the inventive, as no doubt would the authors—witnesses—themselves; and this despite the fact that the entire project of any "eye-witness" account must pivot upon the work of metonymy. The reason for this critical myopia lies in the particularly important relationship atomic-bomb literature must preserve with history, i.e., the myriad cacophony of facts that threaten continually to dissolve into unintelligible noise, into yet another conveniently distorted or even forgotten "incident." As Kuroko Kazuo has written in connection with Hara:

> The overwhelming accumulation of facts that disallow imagination compels the author to adopt a documentary approach devoid of inventive intentions. What is created by this kind of immense force is the atomic-bomb literature of such survivors as Hara Tamiki.[40]

Atomic-bomb literature and its architects are often troubled by the uneasy suspicion that a different logic rules in regard to "reality" when a survivor-writer crosses over from history or autobiography to imaginative truth. Their fear that fiction somehow must be subversive of truth is repeatedly manifested in the insistence of those who write memoirs that what they are writing is not, in fact, fiction, which is to say contrived or false. It is upon this insistence that Hara, in attempting to "record" Hiroshima, would base his authority. Beyond merely "telling," speech is perceived by many of the victims as inevitably suspect.

In other words, Hara's stated intent to pursue in "Summer Flowers" a factual style is a paradoxical quest for a language that excludes as much mitigating circumstance as possible—rhetoric being the most easily targeted circumstance. Elaboration, it is understandably feared, would dilute the isolated factuality of fact. Overtly literary language risks allowing the cultural implications to reestablish themselves in the work, to detain the reader from what is crucially important, to fix the focus apart from the actual historical violence.

This popular position of the first generation of atomic-bomb writers is largely untenable because they wish for a language free of extraneous associations and meanings. They are groping for an escape from interpretation. Of course, this escape would be desirable from the point of view of writers such as Hara who implicitly insist that a literature of "record" equals a literature of "fact," and that only "fact" can convey "truth." Every stage of this formula is uncertain, however. How are we to recognize a "fact" when we come across one? How are we to structure a documentary composed only of facts? And finally, how are we to understand that documentary as synonymous with truth? Each of these questions undermines the assurances of "documentary literature," a phrase which like its cousin "atomic-bomb literature" contains a puzzling contradiction. Literature is imaginative, documentary is literal; literature is the product of culture; the atomic bomb is its negation. The effort to distill in "Summer Flowers" the reality of Hiroshima "before it became distorted in time" ignores the fact that anything processed by memory is already fiction. Imagination and memory can be names for the same thing. The reader naturally expects a memoir to dramatize; we do not want every detail of Hara's experience, but only those that, when strung together convincingly (and here is where rhetoric reenters), cause us to "imagine" what Hara "remembers."

Each specific instance of documentary literature is subject to its own conventions and assumptions. Hara, although he strove in "Summer Flowers" to create a kind of work unparalleled in his oeuvre, falls back on his old techniques, techniques that always resembled, in an extended sense, the naturalistic, but when coupled with the desire to document especially recalled the subtle ideology of a determined mechanistic world. In the attempt to "measure" and "quantify" the destruction wrought by a nuclear weapon, Hara's memoir depicts his environment as the result of the causal relationship between his milieu and his fate, directing the reader away from Hara himself and toward the forces that batter him about. As we shall see, however, this force is one of ultimately incalculable violence and thus overwhelming, perilously threatening the fabric of his narrative. The rhetoric Hara so adroitly exploits will finally appear feeble and impotent in the face of atomic megatonnage, and that is ironically how "Summer Flowers" succeeds as both a work of literature and a history of atrocity.

■

According to Hara's brother-in-law, Sasaki Kiichi, "Summer Flowers" was originally entitled "Genshi bakudan," the full term in Japanese for "atomic bomb."[41] Hara evidently intended at first to make his memoir a definition of what the atomic bomb meant for him and his city.[42] Later, with the new title, Hara was already moving away from history and toward its transformation into metaphor. Brilliantly yellow, an explosion of color at the height of the summer heat, Hara's flowers portend the imagery of the bomb and ironically shift our attention to its inverse: life, beauty, nostalgia. The documentary nature of the memoir seems less than complete; there is already poetry in the title, and with it the suggestion that imagination will be indispensable for our reading of what follows.

The important postwar novelist Kaikō Takeshi once meditated on the complex relationship that obtained between Hara's ostensibly literary "Summer Flowers" and the earlier, fragmentary "facts" from which it was developed, "Notes on the Atomic Destruction." Of Hara Kaikō asked:

Is his "Notes" a falsehood, or is it the truth? Is "Summer Flowers" a lie, or the reality? Or are both works true? Which are we to believe? In the final analysis we must read with the understanding that anything expressed in words is fictional—though it is no easy matter to do so—and concur with Rabelais' simple yet perceptive words that one beautiful lie is better than any three truths.[43]

If indeed "Summer Flowers" is that one beautiful lie, its elegant brevity is one source of its aesthetic appeal. Only seventeen pages long, it is loosely structured into nine sections of varying length. Typically for a Hara work, it seems casually written, though that hardly could have been the case. It begins unsuspectingly and innocently with two brief paragraphs totaling only nine lines that relate an incident several days before the attack. As if simply resuming the story of Sadae's death told in "On the Brink of a Beautiful Death," Hara (who refers to himself throughout the memoir as "I") describes a visit to his wife's grave in her native city of Hiroshima. Although the first anniversary of her death was not technically until the fifteenth of August, Hara is not sure that the streets will still be safe by that time; everyone is expecting air raids. Thus, even though no other person could be seen walking about—everything was closed that day to conserve electricity—Hara puts some ceremonial incense in his pocket, buys a bouquet of yellow flowers ("They seemed so much like summer"), and sets off for the grave site.

Once there he performs a private ritual. Sprinkling the grave marker "exposed to the scorching sun" with water, he lays the flowers before it and stares intently for one moment. His parents, too, are interred here. He lights the incense, bows reverently, and takes a drink of water from a nearby well. He returns home, but the lingering scent of the incense permeates the fabric of his pants for the next two days; it is on the third day that Hiroshima is "attacked with the atomic bomb."

This opening chills the reader with irony, some of it conventional but some of it peculiar to the events of August 6th; it will seem an extravagant luxury to be buried at all, much less to have one's grave graced with flowers. The sadness of a widower visiting a cemetery is familiar to us, and we readily identify with Hara's grief. He has seduced us into caring about him. We are ready to follow his fate, a fate intimated by the "scorching sun." Particularly effective is the image of the fading incense; as it slowly dissipates, the world implied by peaceful graves draws to a conclusion and another one awaits. Somewhere in the cataclysm to come, the reader's initial attachment to one dead woman and the man who honors her will be obliterated by the total force of a nuclear explosion. So far, "Summer Flowers" is not a memoir; it is a romance at a point in time after which romances will seem impossible.

"I was saved because I was in the toilet." The second section of Hara's work begins with a dramatic irony that, while true, also serves to place the early morning events of August 6th within the most domestic of contexts. Hara extends the irony when he remembers, after arising at eight because his sleep had been interrupted twice by air raid warnings, how his sister Kyōko scolded him for staying in bed so late. The reader understands this family; the situation recalls many of our own lives. Any of us could be Hara as he ignores his sister's nagging and goes, pajama-clad, into the bathroom. It is the next instant, however, that will set Hara's life apart from our own.

"Uncertain . . . of how many seconds later," Hara is plunged into total darkness. He thinks he may have received a blow to the head, but he is clearly aware of nothing in the darkness except for "the sound of something like a storm crashing down." Crawling out into the open hallway, he hears his own screaming voice within the cacophony of noises as if he were observing himself from afar. Soon his vision and his other senses return, and before his eyes in the dim light looms his brother's damaged home.

He experiences a dizzying succession of rapid and vivid sensations. He knows he is still alive, but life seems no more real than "an unpleasant dream." He is angered by the "nuisance" all this will cause him. His own voice sounds like that of an entirely different person. As his eyesight grows clearer he feels as if he is on stage performing in a tragedy. Like Fumihiko in "The Procession" watching his own funeral, Hara stands apart from himself as a spectator treated to a horrible spectacle. "Certainly I've seen such things in the movies," he says to himself. Spots of blue break through the clouds of dust; have the walls of the house collapsed? Light is now pouring in from unexpected directions. He walks through the house in a confused daze.

In this section of "Summer Flowers" Hara's style is literal; he is attempting to catalogue the diverse and disorienting elements of his experience. His sentences are disconnected. At times they are abstract, at others concrete; they are all fragmentary. One notes, however, that there is much here not present in Hara's earlier "Notes on the Atomic Destruction," especially the description of himself as an actor on the stage. Hara is introducing into the narrative a consciously cultural and, more significantly, subjective implication, precisely the sort of comment that deflects the work from simple documentary toward introspective memoir. Like an actor, Hara is featured under the lights, cast as the tragic hero. Competing, however, with this tendency to make a story out of his experiences is their fundamental disarray. There is no orderly progression, as one might expect were it the description of an ordinary neighborhood fire, from smaller details such as the first whiff of smoke (and incomprehension) to the complete picture (and truth). Instead, the reader of "Summer Flowers" is left to navigate his way through images not easily assembleable into a whole. We cannot imagine the content of each successive sentence. Nothing of the sort has ever happened to us. However remotely, or unintentionally, the chaos of the atomic bombing is reflected in the awkwardness of its retelling, and at the cost of what usually makes a story "literary." Present in Hara's writing are both the desire to impose art on experience and the refusal of experience to submit to the order of that art.

Other accounts show that Hara's bewildering first moments were typical for the bomb's victims.[44] Everyone thought that a conventional bomb had exploded directly over them and that if they got away from the immediate vicinity all would be well. Hara, like thousands of others, thought only of flight.[45] Suddenly realizing that somehow his pajamas have been ripped off to leave him naked, he has his sister—herself a grotesque sight—find him a pair of underpants. Just as he puts them on, a stranger even more distraught than himself charges into the house insisting that he be allowed to use the telephone. He disappears as abruptly as he entered: Hara's memoir does not accommodate any conventional character development. Turning back to his preparations for flight, Hara takes stock of the house amid the "weird silence" that persisted after the bombing.[46] The building's frame had been laid bare by the destruction of its more fragile materials. Hara writes that "according to what I later learned," this house, sturdily built forty years earlier to the specifications of Hara's demanding father, remained standing even though all others in the vicinity had been knocked flat by the blast. This is the first of Hara's interlinear references to a "later" time after the bomb; taken together with the "earlier" time of his visit to Sadae's grave, the effect is to sandwich, and contrast, the very disorder of the bombing between an ordered past and future, thus drawing attention to the atypical dimensions of that single day that would henceforth bifurcate Hara's life.

As he searches for more clothes Hara's eye is caught by the jumbled disarray of his possessions. Books he had been reading are turned upside down and picture frames are scattered on the floor. Just then a man identified only as "K from the office" appears on the veranda. Injured, K urges Hara to take him with him when he flees. Hara notes that K, a fellow ordinarily more cheerful than himself, now seems nearly deranged. Like the books turned upside down, the world seems reversed, and Hara, still feeling as if he were at the very center of the turmoil, understands nothing.

Hara surveys the neighborhood from his veranda, but there is nothing to see other than devastated homes and a single steel-reinforced building left standing. Hara concludes his preparations by locating his previously packed bag of emergency provisions. He hurries when he notices a small fire starting in the warehouse next door. As he and K depart—the reader must wonder what has happened to Hara's sister, but it is typical of "Summer Flowers" that characters come and go with no explanation—he must step over a toppled maple tree:

> Since very long ago that big maple had stood in one corner of the garden. When I was a boy the tree had been important in my dreams. Since I

returned home this spring after a long absence, I had thought it somehow strange that even this tree could no longer evoke its former charm. What was even odder now, was that this place where I grew up could have lost its soft natural appeal and feel like some composition of cold inorganic matter. (53)

Hara is again isolating the unusual nature of his encounter with a nuclear explosion by shifting the focus of his narrative back to the nostalgic pre-bomb past represented metonymically by the "former charm" of the family maple. This past and the comfort it provided him in his youth contrast pointedly with the "composition of cold inorganic matter" of the world now surrounding him, a world in which trees have been snapped in half and entire neighborhoods flattened. The force of the bomb has "killed" the living world imaginatively as well as literally. With everything once alive now reduced to inert chemistry, Hara's universe is "natural" in ways unimagined by nineteenth-century promoters of a "scientific literature." Hara finds himself amid things without warmth or significance; as he stumbles out of his garden he discovers, as in the original Fall, an environment no longer cultivated for human ease, or even existence.

As Hara looks upon the tree, a single phrase keeps occurring to him: "The Fall of the House of Usher." This reference to Poe and his gothic tale reiterates Hara's utter powerlessness before forces he cannot comprehend.[47] His is the object of subjectless energies; what exploded, who is responsible and why, are questions that never arise in "Summer Flowers." They are irrelevant. Only the destroyed maple retains reality; only broken "things" seem meaningful. The metonymical trope of the fragment—here, the shattered trunk of a tree—overlaps with that of the eye-witness, Hara himself, also a "fragment" of some whole which he represents even if he lacks knowledge of its complete extent. Both such knowledge and ignorance are the outcome of a weapon that dislocates both recognition and reasoning. It is also the consequence of naturalistic description, a tradition that looks in all human events for the workings of schematic laws, the manifestations of abstract energy and matter. In Hiroshima on August 6th, the motionless earth and the swirling, glowing skies must have seemed to harbor little else.

At the same time, Hara's invocation of Poe's story reminds the reader of literature, of fiction and entertainment; Hara couples his own work with that of others, conjuring up out of English literature a canon of mysterious and tragic stories to which he adds his own. Our memory of "The Fall of the House of Usher" supplies irony here; we read literarily for at least one self-conscious moment. The effect is to render, temporarily, Hara's memoir opaque, no longer even a pretended direct view to Hiroshima but instead an imaginative re-creation of it. The ambiguity of Hara's style is itself disconcerting as it vacillates between what he *sees* and what he *interprets*—precisely the quandary in which a writer attempting to remember (for himself) and describe (for others) might well find himself.

The third section of "Summer Flowers" takes the reader from shortly after the explosion until noon. Hara abruptly switches the tense of his sentences from the past to the present, which Japanese convention ordinarily dictates for literary narrative but which additionally suggests here a shift from Hara's remembering his experiences to his reliving them. In any case, the change further detains the reader and gives him cause to consider, perhaps, the difficulty of recalling and retelling such an experience. Timing is important; tense is altered just at the moment when Hara and K make their way onto the streets. Amid the rubble they first encounter an injured woman crying out for help. A little further on another woman is, like a child, "crying that her house is burning." Neither of these women is dead yet, and none presents a scene the least suggestive of the scale of the catastrophe. Any type of bomb could have caused the damage Hara sees so far. "Summer Flowers" will slowly reveal the extent of the tragedy, and like any good writer Hara will use ironic suspense to keep the reader engaged. For instance, he next comes across a person who is insisting that all uninjured people help extinguish the neighborhood fires. This person, like Hara, as yet has no idea that this has been no limited attack. He is the sort of person whom Hara labels in "Prelude to Annihilation" a *kōkan robotto*, or "a well-meaning automaton," someone trained to react affirmatively but conventionally to even the most unprecedented calamities. Hara is resorting to a calculated measure of understatement when he introduces us first to such relatively robust victims so that our shock and revulsion will then be all the greater in the memory. As he warns us at the end of this section, "At this time I still knew hardly anything about the full extent of the air attack."

As Hara continues on foot, a careful reader might note that he is taking, in reverse, precisely the route he followed three days earlier in returning from Sadae's grave. The streets are no longer deserted, however. At the foot of a bridge spanning one of Hiroshima's then seven rivers they find other refugees like themselves, and Hara loses K (never to be mentioned again) in the crowd as he heads for what he hopes will be safety in the wooded grounds surrounding a shrine. When he arrives there he finds its trees as mutilated as those everywhere else. His suspicion that something truly extraordinary has occurred is strengthened when he spots the horribly disfigured face of a middle-aged woman: "This was the first time I had seen such a face. Yet later I would be forced to see, without number, even more terrible ones." Suddenly he encounters his eldest brother, who is incongruously holding on to a beer and who "looks to be all right." In any other story we might expect the narrator to rush to his brother's side and celebrate their unlikely reunion. Instead, Hara ignores his kin and reflects upon his own survival in terms most meaningful to those familiar with his prewar stories:

What had terrified me for so long, what had to happen, had in fact arrived. With a sense of relief I looked back on what I had lived through. I once thought that my chances in life were few, but now the fact I was alive, and its significance, suddenly struck me with full force. (54)

What had "terrified" Hara "for so long" does not find its ultimate antecedent in "Summer Flowers." This passage refers instead to the passive feelings of doom found in a pen name such as Kiyu and works such as "Flames," "The Procession," and "On the Brink of a Beautiful Death." His great relief is the realization that he had not met the fate he thought reserved for him. This "document" of Hiroshima is increasingly a sequel to Hara's earlier work and an elaboration of his own obsessions, and its dual nature as both historiography and confession accounts for some measure of its popular success; accurate enough to fascinate us, and literary enough to remain readable, "Summer Flowers" straddles the facts of Hiroshima while it labors to translate those facts into terms available to a nonvictim audience. To the extent that Hara thus seeks to explain, as well as describe, the events of August 1945, his work can begin to approach that of the historian, though that should not be cited as any demonstration of "Summer Flowers'" failure as literature. On the contrary, as Hayden White points out, it is precisely in such "literature of fact" that "the discourse of the historian and that of the imaginative writer overlap, resemble, or correspond with each other. Although historians and writers of fiction may be interested in different kinds of events, both the forms of their respective discourses and their aims in writing are often the same."[48]

Both Hara's discourse and its aim are elaborated in the fourth section of "Summer Flowers," which runs from noon until the middle of the night. Still in the shrine grounds, Hara watches as the fires on the opposite bank of the river intensify. He feels hot winds blowing overhead. Suddenly the sky darkens, and he is caught in a short but torrential downpour. Then just as suddenly he finds his eldest brother again, and, together with his younger sister who has reappeared and several neighborhood acquaintances, they speak of what happened that morning. As each describes his or her independent impressions of the bomb's power, each adds to the growing vocabulary of its violence. Shared, however, is their acknowledgement of the overwhelming authority of that violence ("Everyone thought the bomb . . . had hit his own house") and their inability to comprehend it ("They were struck dumb . . . when they looked about"). There is interestingly no curiosity about what caused the damage, only consternation at its extent. Unlike the early work of other atomic-bomb writers—Ōta Yōko, for instance—that of Hara Tamiki evidences no will to understand, no desire to master experience by comprehending it. Hara remains utterly passive before the experience, so much an object of the bomb's force that he does not even wonder about its origins. This is in keeping with the dynamics of Hara's earlier work, for what kills Sadae in "On the Brink of a Beautiful Death" is neither named nor explained: menacing force, be it disease or weapon, is anonymous and uncomprehended throughout Hara's writing.

Force is constant, as well. Even as the survivors discuss what has already happened, nearby a tornado "wrapped in a greenish glow as if from a painting of Hell" rips whole trees out of the ground and flings them high into the air. Fearful that encroaching fires now threaten the park itself, Hara and another of his brothers who has made it to safety set out to find a boat that can take the whole family to the other bank of the river. While walking upstream, Hara encounters for the first time what he calls "a crowd of people beyond description." These are victims who are alive but so terribly disfigured that even their genders are indiscernible. Two of them—their voices identify them as female—politely ask Hara to retrieve a cushion for them from under a nearby tree. This cushion however is in use by another moribund victim. The contrast between the women's appearance and the civility of their words, contrasting further with the moral import of their request, jolts the reader. Hara, too, finds it a scene altogether "more gruesome than pitiful." Hara's encounters from this point on in "Summer Flowers" will likewise defy standard responses and inspire only numbed irony; that is why, perhaps, the victims he finds are "people beyond description."

To be "beyond description" (*gengo ni zessuru;* literally, "cut off from language" or "beyond words"), a phrase not uncommon in atomic-bomb literature, establishes one set of limits that Hara's project in "Summer Flowers" will not exceed. One wishes to ask, whose words? Those of the crowd, or Hara's? Our own? The answer is not clear, and necessarily so. What is inaccessible is not any particular trope that could somehow convey all we wish to know, but rather the very idea of language. At a certain stage Hara has to tell us that his words can do no more. If language, then, cannot tell the whole story, perhaps not telling the whole story is part of the story. At times in "Summer Flowers" there figures prominently a silence brought about by the collapse of words to say anything meaningful. One example occurs after Hara and his brother find a raft to transport their family to the far side. Once there, Hara witnesses only more crowds of horribly hurt victims. In of them is a soldier who asks Hara to help him obtain a drink of water. On their way to the water the soldier sighs that it would have been better had he died. "I gloomily nodded in assent," writes Hara. "No words came forth. It was as if at that moment an unbearable resentment at what this senseless thing had done was bringing us together in silence" (58).

Their moment of mutual silence implies the failure of words to express just what they felt; in a sense this is the failure of anything to "mean" exactly as it did before the bomb. The challenge that the destruction of Hiroshima presents to Hara's ability to discern, synthesize, and relate his perceptions is fundamental. His endless view of corpses, for instance, makes the distinction between the living and the dead moot, and with it the premise of culture—of life *against* death—is called into serious question. Hara's anger at what he sees about him is not an anger directed against "the bomb" or "America," but rather a rage at the very fragile nature of what he had once so easily taken for granted. The only option left a survivor stranded in a burnt world is to retreat into either memory or illusion. Hara chooses the former. That night, while trying to rest within a slight hollow of the ground in the company of several injured school-girls, he is kept awake by the tortured cries of a young person nearby. What Hara thinks about, however, is how years ago he would come to this area of the city to fish or watch the trains pass over the steel bridge. "It was a place of peace now like a dream," remembers Hara, and so he is both able to console and distract himself. In lieu of "living" in post-bomb Hiroshima, Hara seeks the slumber of an idealized past.

The fifth section of the memoir briefly recalls Hara's activities on August 7th. He and five members of his surviving family make it to the vicinity of the Tōshōgū Shrine, now a crowded encampment, and they assemble a ramshackle shelter. Much of the day is spent in line for rations. All about them are seriously injured victims, some pathetically near death and others well enough to act selfishly in only their own interests. Hara dispassionately notes the pain and cruelty that have come to mark Hiroshima "society." "When I thought that I might have to spend another night here I felt strangely alone."

The sixth and seventh sections describe the following morning and afternoon. "With daylight came constant voices praying. In this place someone was always dying." The situation is not much better for the living. The succession of impressions that Hara records—air raid sirens, growing hunger, confusion, an endless view of the injured—are piled atop each other to form a seamless mass of unrelieved and depressing detail. Just as everyone, including Hara, seems on the verge of a collapse into a listless depression ("It was all too much, and everyone was so weak"), the eldest brother returns with a horse-drawn wagon to transport everyone to a safer refuge outside the city proper. With his younger sister and his other older brother and his family, he sets out for the village of Yawata on a route that takes them through the entire smoldering city. They are not long into their journey when they make a discovery.

> In a vacant lot near the West Parade Grounds, my second eldest brother caught a glimpse of a corpse wearing short yellow pants that he seemed to recall from somewhere. He got down from the wagon. My sister-in-law and I gathered with him around the body. The familiar yellow pants were tied with an unmistakable belt. The corpse was that of my nephew Fumihiko. Fluid oozed from an immense abscess on his shirtless chest. White teeth were faintly visible on the black burnt face. The fingers on

the outstretched hands were stiff and turned inward. The fingernails were held like claws. . . . My brother tore his son's fingernails off, took the belt as [another] memento, attached a name tag to the body, and departed. It was an encounter that brooked no tears. (63)

This is the first time in "Summer Flowers" that an individual corpse is described in detail. Fumihiko—a name with possible ironic connotations—is treated as an inanimate object, just as inert as the "cold inorganic matter" that Hara saw his childhood neighborhood become. The entire world, including dead family, had been reduced to immobile matter by the energy of a single moment, all emotion eliminated ("It was an encounter that brooked no tears") by the scale of the destruction. The factuality of the account is overwhelming, and the reader's own ability to comprehend the implications of such a description handicapped. What part of "Summer Flowers" is documentary now risks engendering a numbed indifference: how are we really to understand what such a reunion of father and son means? Hara, perhaps because he sensed he had exhausted the power of minutiae, suddenly shifts in the eighth section to a different narrative point of view:

Our wagon then headed in the direction of Kokutaiji Temple. Since we were going toward Koi, and passing over the Sumiyoshi Bridge, I was able to survey in a single glance nearly all the major ruins. Within the expanse of the silvery nothingness that stretched out beneath the intense sun, there were streets, there were rivers, there were bridges. And then, here and there, there were piles of swollen, red, and raw corpses. This was a new Hell, one brought about by a precise and elaborate means. All things human had been obliterated. What had once been, for example, the peaceful look on the face of someone dead was now replaced by something standard, and mechanical. (63)

Hara has abandoned his narrow and specific narration of the atrocity. He steps back to survey broadly—both geographically and philosophically—the greater impact of the bomb. From the vantage point of a high bridge, Hara sees the limitlessness of the violence and realizes its source, "a precise and elaborate means." Not once in "Summer Flowers" does the term "atomic bomb" occur. Rather, Hara refers here to what the bomb signifies, not what it is called. It is the product of exact and deliberate science, an "achievement" of physics and engineering, and the "new Hell" bodied forth is the logical consequence of the naturalistic world view, the nineteenth-century commitment to the ultimate triumph of that science coupled with the widened applications of modern violence. In these several sentences Hara has traced the history of recent times and predicted one likely outcome of writing governed by it. "All things human had been obliterated" "by a precise and elaborate" technology whose rationale once offered literature a powerful new way of perceiving man in the universe, leaving nothing behind but "something standard, and mechanical" to mark its victims. In this passage Hara has found new and astute similes for his dislocated and destroyed world, a world that seems as alienated and machine-like to him as it does to a molecular physicist. It is a world of people rendered inorganic, no longer comprehensible as creatures but instead reduced to "something . . . mechanical."

Hara himself, of course, is not immune to the power of the bomb to reify life. Part of "Summer Flowers" is the story of Hara's loss of his fundamental ability to connect and compare his impressions. He, too, has been made physically inert by the force of the explosion. In his essay "Nightmare" (Akumu, 1949?) Hara writes that "the darkest shadow cast by the power of the atom is that mankind does not seem to possess the ability to control it" (573). In the naturalistic universe, force has grown so total that men no longer dictate even the smallest part of it, and in "Summer Flowers" the reader accordingly finds that Hara has problems telling his story smoothly. After noting that the Asano Library (a metonymy for texts, words, meanings) has been converted into a receiving station for the dead, Hara writes that "it seems appropriate to jot down my impressions of the scene in katakana." Katakana, the Japanese syllabary used for transliterating foreign words and native slang, or for issuing official announcements, is unexpectedly found as the script for a poem. The appearance of a poem in the middle of a work of prose documentary leaps from the page with a sudden force of its own. The orthography is strange, and the poetic language stranger; it is as if discursive language has failed and Hara has turned to the most "literary," the most obviously rhetorical of genres to try to convey what has so far evaded expression. Hara's resort to katakana makes the poem's lines reverberate with an urgency and intensity beyond what its contents alone can achieve:

> Glittering pieces of debris and
> White burning embers
> In a vast expanse
> Of burnt and inflamed
> Red human corpses, their odd rhythms—
> All that was? Or all that could have been?
> Stripped of everything in a flash, the world is now
> The belly of a horse, the way it swells
> Beside a toppled streetcar
> And the stench of burning wires. (64)

The discontinuity between the world that was (before the bomb) and the one that is (after it) is mirrored by the purely emotional difficulty in reading this poem compounded by the additional problems of an unfamiliar script.

The bomb has precipitated a special crisis for Hara and his writing; no longer accessible to him denotatively or conventionally, he mediates upon the violence in obscure terms, as if he were purposefully withdrawing from the site of the destruction and the prose that envelops it. The reader's control of the text is disrupted by this sudden intrusion of the poem, and his or her assumption of what "kind" of writing "Summer Flowers" is—documentary, fiction, memoir, etc.—is further undermined. "All that was? Or all that could have been?" is a line that implies a radical doubt extending beyond Hiroshima to include the rules of reading, first and foremost the one that claims language is capable of self-identity, that what Hara puts into a sentence can be retrieved, intact, by his audience. This is the documentary fallacy: the reportage of facts is invariably caught up in the exercise of rhetoric, and perhaps luckily so, for without the seduction of the reader by language the reader will quite simply never believe what is on the page. And with rhetoric comes, of course, both point of view and subjective interpretation, regardless of how accurate—historical— the documentary author intends to be. Hayden White persuasively maintains that the presence of an interpretation is always accompanied by some set of ideological considerations, accompanied "aesthetically (in the choice of a narrative strategy), epistemologically (in the choice of an explanatory paradigm), and ethically (in the choice of a strategy by which the ideological implications of a given representation can be drawn for the comprehension of current social problems)."[49] While not all these ideological determinations appear in "Summer Flowers"—Hara hardly offers any "explanatory paradigm" for the nuclear explosion—it does seem clear that insofar as it is a work of storytelling it "naturalizes" the author's experiences much as ideology makes "common sense" out of the more typical structures of our everyday lives.

The ninth and final section of Hara's work offers a succinct illustration of the subtle power of his narrative. This section comprises its own independent and self-contained story: a story within a story. Its hero is called simply "N." At the instant of the blast, N was on a train traveling through a tunnel and thus escaped the initial force of the explosion. When he reached his destination in the suburbs, he heard what had happened and rushed back into the city. "Unable to wait for the city's fires to die down, he walked on and on atop the hot asphalt streets." He makes it to the girls' school where his wife taught, but nowhere among the bodies does he find her. Nor is she found at their home. He examines each and every corpse on the route between the house and the school, but none is his wife's. When he starts searching wildly in all directions, he comes across a dozen people who drowned in a water tank in trying to flee the fires; three people frozen in death as they attempted to climb a ladder along the river bank; a queue of people waiting for a bus who died standing up, their fingernails embedded in the shoulders of whomever stood before them. He sees an entire company of civilians mobilized to construct fire lines who were wiped out, and he sees "the soldiers' mountain of death" at the West Parade Grounds. But he does not see his wife.

N wanders through every camp and looks into every face. "Every face was the height of wretchedness, but none belonged to his wife." The story of N concludes like the myth of Sisyphus: "After three days and three nights of looking at the dead and injured and being sickened by them, N went back again to the girls' school where his wife was employed."

Few readers could remain unmoved by this story. We have no idea if it is literally true or not, but we certainly believe it truthful. It mentions neither Hara nor any of his family, and it has nothing to do with their survival. Rather, it is a poignant distillation, a figurative synecdoche, of the pathetic lengths to which tens of thousands likely went, a individual trope of what was a mass atrocity. It is precisely the narrative power channeled through the conceivably fictionalized tale of one survivor's futile efforts to find one corpse among many that makes the reader identify with N and vicariously feel his desperation. Its use of rhetoric accomplishes what the sheer statistics might not, namely the creation of a visceral reaction in us. The story of N marks the triumph of fiction over fact in "Summer Flowers" because no number of facts would ever have quite the same effect, and it contributes to the success of "Summer Flowers" as a whole over less cleverly executed documentary memoirs. Nietzsche once said we have art in order not to perish from the truth: for Hara, art was a means of representing a truth from which he quite literally nearly perished.

■

In his infamous journal of life in the Warsaw Ghetto, Chaim Kaplan wrote that "at times it seems to me I am in an alien land, entirely unknown to me."[50] Halfway around the world, and in a related but even more estranged simile, Hara Tamiki wrote that "I feel like a human being who has fallen to earth for the first time."[51] Perhaps Hara felt this way because, since the bombing, everything he encountered seemed radically alien to him; with his past no longer continuous with his present, there were no familiar landmarks to guide him. Even the death of his wife—an event, as we have seen, powerfully present in Hara's postwar writings—appeared different from the death of Hiroshima. In "Dreams and Life" (Yume to jinsei, 1949) Hara compares the death of Sadae with the "numberless dead" of their city. The latter remain unreal to him. His wife died "under a peaceful roof"; the others "are not 'deaths'" in quite the same way. Hara is distinguishing between the pre-atrocity and post-atrocity phenomenologies of death, each of which imbues the dead with different meanings; in the death of an individual such as Sadae there is the tragic loss of a single person, but in the death of an entire community without a chance to mourn there is the loss of everything.

In a work entitled "A Troubled Heart" (Mune no uzuki, 1949?), Hara tells of attending a beautiful production of *Romeo and Juliet* in a theater built amid the rubble of Hiroshima, and of being struck by the incongruity. That art can be created even in the midst of atrocity is certainly a paradox that many postwar writers, Hara included, must marvel at. Somehow, however, a performance of *Romeo and Juliet* in Hiroshima will always be different than one done elsewhere, for in what other city, except Nagasaki, could the death of two lovers inspire envy for an era when people could choose the time, place, and means of their demise? Or more importantly, when such deaths could have tragic meaning? In an essay on Hara, fellow atomic-bomb writer Hotta Yoshie argues:

> Needless to say, from that moment when the human world is no longer perceived as anything but "inorganic matter," literature utterly disintegrates. The abstract scientific and inorganic worldview symbolized by the nuclear bomb, together with our eschatology and consciousness of it, makes all literature impossible as artistic, religious, or philosophical forms in any traditional sense of those disciplines.[52]

Hotta's view is a radical one, and not completely accurate in its hyperbole. Literature does not "utterly disintegrate," but rather it is rendered peculiarly ironic by atrocity, put under the controlling trope of the twentieth century. "Summer Flowers" is, if read with attention to its persuasive turns, a work of modern literature, which is to say writing in which the imagination depends on the rhetorical nature of language to manifest itself as the reader's own experience, but it is also a work thoroughly informed—and overshadowed—by the ever-present potential for the end of human history demonstrated first in Hiroshima. The only reason, after all, that a work entitled "Summer Flowers" exists at all today is because America's earliest fission weaponry was not powerful enough to do all that was intended. That it should be, however imperfectly, a patchwork of first-person account, second-hand testimony, fiction, and even poetry will finally not matter as much as the fact that each use of language approaches in its own way the same experiential truth.

Perhaps the fullest dimensions of that truth remain ultimately inaccessible to us. Hara says in "Two Deaths" (Futatsu no shi, 1949) that his world in different from that of Hiroshima-bred Japanese not present in the city on August 6th (441). How much more so, a skeptic might wonder, for readers of entirely different generations and nationalities. But it is the appeal to our imaginations as well as our intellects that Hara's work makes that finally convinces us the horrors are real, and that impresses upon us the need for style, rhetoric, and poetry in a time largely emptied of anything but the most terse and prosaic commands, such as the order to drop an atomic bomb on a civilian target. Documents of the destruction are already many. What remains scarce are its inspired orators and poets. "I told myself that I must record these things," wrote

Hara in "Summer Flowers," again echoing the similar imperative noted by his fellow witness to atrocity, Chaim Kaplan.[53] But Hara's witness is characterized with an urgent creativity rare among the many survivors made mute by what they saw, and lived. When Hara killed himself, critic Odagiri Hideo expressed not only shock but regret that he and others had failed to understand Hara's work and its import.[54] It is a regret that points to how difficult it is for even the most astute among us to comprehend the significance of literature that would narrate, however awkwardly, the imminent collapse of the very world accustomed to granting our stories their meaning.

Yamashita Soboku, *The Blast* (Sakuretsu, 1985)

if I speak normal
words in the normal
order

who will hear me

Marc Kaminsky,
The Road From Hiroshima, 1984

Will I die
Wordless?
The fog
Is silver

Tōge Sankichi, 1938

5

Poetry Against Itself

If testimonial accounts of the bombing of Hiroshima and Nagasaki were historically the first genre of atomic-bomb literature, it was quickly joined by poetry and, quite likely, soon exceeded by it in sheer volume. Atomic-bomb lyrics and prose, however, were not so much competitive as collaborative: office clerk Doi Sadako inserted a poem between the paragraphs of her eyewitness testimony, as did more than a few hibakusha:

> A day wrapped in the vivid morning sun
> Everyone making ready to face the new battle
> One instant, in the demon light from the sky that blanketed the city
> Hiroshima became a city of death.
> Paintings of hell flash in the darkness that surrounds heaven and earth
> The voices of people screaming
> The voices of people groaning echo in heaven and earth

The night of agony ends, the summer heat desolately burns
Hiroshima, city of death, gasps for breath.[1]

The impulses to express oneself literally and figuratively often coincided, and
for causes linked not only to Japanese aesthetic traditions (traditions that mini-
mized the distinction of verse from prose) but to the exigencies of the postnuclear age. "In Hiroshima it was the poets who most quickly responded to the
atomic bombing," noted Fukagawa Munetoshi, a poet himself. "Perhaps this
was because the Japanese lyric is a conveniently simple genre, and because it
is readily adapted to circumstance."[2] "Circumstance," of course, refers modestly
to nuclear war: but it is one that apparently has inspired rather than precluded
the writing of poetry. Beginning in the spring of 1946 with the establishment
of *Chūgoku bunka* by Kurihara Sadako and her husband Tadaichi, the works of
many hibakusha poets both professional and amateur have been published regularly and widely—if not to universal critical acclaim. Dozens of editions of
single poets' works and massive anthologies comprised of poems solicited re-
gionally and nationally have appeared, albeit more often than not in small runs
and through the agency of local publishers.

Among the most widely read of the collections of individual poets is
Yoneda Eisaku's 1951 *River, Always Be Beautiful* (Kawa yo, towa ni utsukushiku);
and of the anthologies, *From Beneath the Atomic Cloud* (Genshigumo no shita yori,
1952), *Ashes of Death* (Shi no hai shishū, 1954), and *Japanese Atomic-bomb Poetry*
(Nihon gembaku shishū, 1970). One other noteworthy anthology, the award-
winning *Poetry Hiroshima* (Kashū Hiroshima, 1954), contained a record 1,753
poems by 220 poets selected by a committee from among 6,500 submissions
nationwide, thus earning the sobriquet "gembaku *Man'yō*," or the "atomic-
bomb *Man'yōshū*," a reference to the earliest extant anthology of poetry in Japan, compiled in the eighth century. The allusion is not gratuitous: one of the
striking features of popular atomic-bomb poetry is in fact its aesthetic conservatism, its reliance on traditional diction and lyrical images. Atomic-bomb poetry even produced one work in a extended form rare for a thousand years:
Nagasaki poet Shimauchi Hachirō's 1946 *chōka* (literally "long poem") "A Vow
of Peace From the Ruins" (Heiwa no chikai—haikyo ni tachite) came complete
with its equally ancient *hanka*, or complementary "envoy poem": "Mount Iwaya
still towers high above/ As if to tell us to build a nation without wars."

Despite the relative critical neglect of atomic-bomb poetry in favor of
prose literature—reflecting, perhaps, the reduced prestige of poetry generally
among the genres of modern Japanese literature—probably no other single
specific theme in Japanese poetry accounts for so many examples in such a
short span of time. The vigor of atomic-bomb poetry may suggest a particular
affinity between Japanese lyricism and the nuclear theme, or at least as it was
reflected in the immediate experience of Hiroshima and Nagasaki. Poet and

critic Ōoka Makoto, speaking broadly of the entire history of Japanese poetry, has concluded that in place of romance, "The grief of how transient life remains is the most enduring and fundamental theme in Japanese poetry."[3] Though "grief" is by no means the only emotion given expression in atomic-bomb poetry, it is certainly there in great measure, and thus seems congruent with the traditions of its genre in a way that atomic-bomb prose literature is not.

The history of Japanese poetry provided a range of precedents, of vocabulary and thematic sanctions, that perhaps made it seem an appropriate vehicle for hibakusha writing. The *Man'yōshū*'s plaintive poems of soldiers dispatched to posts far from their families or, more to the point, its most famous poet's evocation of the sorrow of a fisherman's widow who will never know her husband's final resting place, finds its counterpart in the thousands of Hiroshima and Nagasaki poems that memorialize lost relatives. Taga Kōko's 1950 poem "Ah, Mutsuko!" (Ā, Mutsuko!) describes the mournful grief of a mother over the death of her youngest daughter. Its final stanza reads:

> When you died
> With the word "Mother" on your lips
> She forgot to cry
> And simply stared
> At your body slowly losing its warmth.
> Chilled by the night winds
> And silent, forever, forever,
> She simply stared. (77)

It was a easy matter to describe a single death, as in this poem, in language and emotions continuous with those of traditional verse. In 1943 Miyoshi Tatsuji similarly memorialized the death of Admiral Yamamoto Isoroku in the skies over New Guinea with the remote, archaic language of classical Japanese poetry in a work that Yoshimoto Takaaki argues demonstrated not only "the deep roots of traditional Japanese sensibilities [*kansei chitsujo*]" but the "essence of the dominant hegemony of Japan under fascism's total control."[4] But once the war was over, and that control gone, the impetus to describe death, even mass death, in the idiomatic terms of long-standing poetic practices was irrepressible. In another example of how the theme of Hiroshima and Nagasaki was quickly, if not always successfully, assimilated in the most unexpected ways into poetic conventions, references to the anniversary of the atomic bombing (*gembaku-imi*) were domesticated as a seasonal theme (*kidai*)—linked, of course, to mid-summer—in haiku:

> Remembering the day of the atomic bomb's dead:
> In the midday skies
> Fragments of the moon.[5]

But other forces are at work in this poetry, and they are forces not particular to the cultural tradition of a millennium, nor even benignly indifferent to them. Rather, they are quite twentieth century. Or instead: our time presents an oblique lyricism with certain special opportunities and dangers. It was with this ambivalence in mind, perhaps, that Ōoka called the year 1945 "a crucial dividing line" for poetry.[6] On one hand, the jingoistic idiom imposed upon waka during the Second World War made the entire form indecorous for some after 1945; and haiku, with its fossilized cliches, was embarrassed into reform by Kuwabara Takeo's famous 1946 essay, "A Second Class Art" (Daini geijutsu).

But at the same time, perhaps it was poetry, by virtue of its consciously ironic relationship with language, that offered the hibakusha writer his best opportunity for alluding to a truth which apparently resists explicit denotative expression. Perhaps the hibakusha's historical encounter with the reality of Hiroshima or Nagasaki parallels, or can be made to parallel, the poet's literary encounter with the idea of the poem. Shortly after the war C. Day Lewis wrote that "we find poetic truth struck out by the collision rather than collusion of images."[7] His choice of violent metaphors ("collision") suggests that figural language is itself violent, and thus in itself mimetic of, for example, Hiroshima and Auschwitz.

The poet, unlike the typical writer of prose but very much like the alienated target of a nuclear attack, thinks of himself as standing outside of language. He encounters it as an obstacle before he can use it as a tool. Jean-Paul Sartre, writing shortly after the war and so presumably aware of its impact on European culture, theorized that "as the poet is already on the outside, he considers words as a trap to catch a fleeting reality rather than as indicators which throw him out of himself into the midst of things."[8] For Sartre as well as for the atomic-bomb poets to be studied here, the crisis of literature amid the violence of the twentieth century is foremost a crisis of poetics.

It is at this juncture that atomic-bomb poetry raises in its succinct form the implications that Hiroshima and Nagasaki ultimately portend for literature as the institutionalized rehearsal of our culture's values. Poetry lies at the heart of "literature" because of its specificity as "literary," its most extended "difference from ordinary discourse by an empirical individual about the world."[9] The power of language associated with poetry—the impulse of poets, in Ōoka's characterization, to seek release from form and their return to an original "state of inspiration," "spiritual authority"—is in atomic-bomb poetry re-marshalled in the case of some poets to mirror the incapacitation of form already evident in their Hiroshima or Nagasaki worlds; and in others to restore form to, not release form from, that same world.

This choice the atomic-bomb poet faces—to attempt a poetry as implacably form-less as that of their experience (a poetry oddly realistic and mimetic in its ambition), or to urge onto poetry constructive powers not usually associated with it—is a choice that leads us to the difficulties as well as the potential of a Hiroshima and Nagasaki lyricism. This is not the comfortably "paradoxical" view of modern poetry that Modernism argues. When Cleanth Brooks states, for example, that "the language of poetry is the language of paradox,"[10] that paradox does not seem to be one that drives poets to despair, or even suicide. At its most benign, the "paradox" of atomic-bomb literature can result in no literature at all. One Hiroshima writer, Tokunō Kōichi, eventually abandoned trying to write at all, saying "poetry was terrifying."[11] What deterred him from continuing were perhaps the particular processes to which poetry subjects experience: processes that challenge memory, which is to say "reality," and threaten to change it into something which stalks the hibakusha poet.

Japanese poetry, which at least since the latter half of the nineteenth century has struggled to encompass a plethora of new social and historical themes, met in Hiroshima and Nagasaki the most dramatic challenge to its traditional—both old and newly wrought—aesthetics. In one sense this challenge was opposite to that which European writers such as Paul Celan faced in composing poetry about the Nazi extermination camps: a generation earlier French Symbolists had already rejected the view of classical theories that poetry had its "natural subjects," and thereby eased the thematic restraints with the claim that language could expand endlessly to accommodate new topics. European poetry of atrocity, however, was to test that assumption, and in the opinion of some it failed. Theodor Adorno, in the most famous instance, argued that the German language had been so abused by the Nazis that it was a language no longer fit for literary expression, that words once used to order people into gas chambers could never be used for poetry again.[12] On the other hand, Japanese poetics, though far more hospitable to horrific themes in the twentieth century than previously, still clung tenaciously to the idea of natural subjects, of "good taste" in verse which rejected the "inelegant." The traditions of both European and Japanese poetry resisted atrocity as a proper theme, and Adorno's famous imperative "No poetry after Auschwitz!" finds a parallel in these lines from Tanaka Kishirō's poem "Rage" (Fundo):

> However one tries to speak
> However one tries to write
> Of human atrocity
> All tongues and pens are to no avail.[13]

The irony here of course is that Tanaka *is* trying. In many ways early atomic-bomb poetry is a species of writing which very self-consciously attempts to efface itself. Or at least explicitly exploit the inherent rhetorical ambiguity of poetic language—in this, perhaps Japanese poets were more successful than their European counterparts, since the tradition of Japanese poetry shares with the relatively new literature of atrocity an exaggerated tension between meaningful words and meaningful silences. The increasingly strict control of diction even while the thirty-one syllable waka made room for the seventeen-syllable haiku meant that any single poem (or indeed any single word) implied quite nearly as much by what it did not say as by what it did. A kind of default "intertextuality" determined an implicit field of reference in the briefer forms of Japanese poetry, suggesting to some hibakusha writers that here was a vehicle capable of speaking about the bombings without entailing the real risk of telling, and thus reducing into some number of words their complex experience.

Novelist Ōta Yōko, often quoted on the inadequacy of literature to represent the bombing of Hiroshima, noted that the waka was the first literary form nonetheless to make the attempt.[14] In fact many of the first generation of atomic-bomb poets composed in the most traditional of meters with the most conservative choice of words, for in making such aesthetic choices they took refuge in the continuity of an inherited set of rules within the larger context of a culturally discontinuous Hiroshima or Nagasaki experience. Such poets turn to the authority of a familiar repertory of symbols (including, in the less accomplished examples, clichés) in seeking a concrete idiom for the atrocity and its aftermath. Whether it were in a waka or the even more compressed haiku, the Hiroshima or Nagasaki poet might hope to write of the bomb in a kind of cultivated shorthand which would not obscure his theme with verbiage. For reasons as ancient as Homer's refusal to narrate the fiery destruction of Troy, and as Heidegger said of all poetry, "The poet's statement remains unspoken."[15] To attempt to speak can risk the loss of that faculty altogether, as Sawamura Mitsuhiro writes in poem that recalls the fate of Lot's wife:

> You   Don't look back
> You messengers of God, too   Don't look back
>
> If we look back   Then once again
> Our human words will not be able to speak of anything.[16]

Such explicit warnings reveal a theory, or perhaps a hope, implicit in early atomic-bomb poetry: that one could open imaginative doors to the interior reality of the bombing without baring its entire, and unfathomable, architecture. If, in Pierre Macherey's words, "Silences shape all speech," and if then "measuring silences" is the most appropriate way to read a text after the theoretical insights of the West's late-twentieth century, then it is also, coincidentally or not, the most ethical way of doing so after the historical events of that same century's midpoint.[17] "I find the world," wrote Hara Tamiki in one of his post-Hiroshima poems, "is lowering its voice."[18] But both the theories and the ethics soon lead to the conclusion that real silence is impossible. As even Adorno, silence's most famous partisan, understood, "Not even silence gets us out of the circle. In silence we simply use the state of objective truth to rationalize our subjective incapacity, once more degrading truth into a lie."[19] The poet's very effort to "communicate," to account for the violence that had been committed against the notion of personal or collective survival, speaks of his trust in certain of the linkages between the past and the future. Aristotle's justification for metaphor, it should be remembered, was that we apprehend new ideas and experiences in terms of the familiar.

To illustrate how conservative those linkages may be, here are four examples of waka written by Kurihara Sadako in Hiroshima within one year of the bombing:

> The bird in its cage
> Does not stir
> Outside the window
> The misty moonlit night
> Grows ever late!

> In a corner
> Of this untended field
> The pale purple
> Of one spring orchid
> That escaped.

> In the scorched city
> Spring rains fall
> And make bloom
> The life
> Of what has not been destroyed.

> One hundred thousand lives
> All killed here
> Burnt fields far away
> Winter, and wither still.[20]

Each of these poems is written in the compromise literary-style Japanese now reserved for traditional poetry. Each either uses standard poetic images ("misty moonlit night," "pale purple") or makes standard seasonal references ("spring," "winter"). None mentions either Hiroshima or the atomic bomb by name. While not quite examples of Wordsworth's definition of poetry—"emotion recollected in tranquility"—their sentiments are nonetheless conventional. They inculcate in the reader an appreciation of sadness, loneliness, and grief. Such appreciations are valuable, just as these waka by Kurihara are "true" insofar as they are accurate representations of important cultural values if not history. Or rather, not the history of August 1945: in fact, these poems are full of history, that of a millennium and more of Japanese lyrical tradition and its peculiar rhetorical habits. When James Scully offered his own definition of the "belles-lettres poem" as "a work that masters history and logic, including its own," he was ascribing both a great power and an awesome deceit to such writing.[21] The power, of course, flows from the perfection and self-sufficiency of form; the deceit, equally clear, is the essential lie told by any human expression which pretends to be fully circumscribed by its style, rather than by its practice.

It is unfair to judge Kurihara's poetry too critically on the basis of these several minor waka. Her most famous atomic-bomb poem, also one of the earliest—it was written in August 1945 and initially published in March the following year—is a longer, modern free verse inspired by a story she heard shortly after the bombing.[22] Entitled "Let Us Be Midwives!" (Umashimen ka na), it is one of the three or four most widely quoted atomic-bomb poems in Japan:

> It was night in the basement of a building now in ruins.
> Victims of the atomic bomb
> jammed the dark room;
> there wasn't even a single candle.
> The smell of fresh blood, the stench of death,
>   the sickening smell of humanity, the moans—
> out of all that, miraculously, a voice:
> "The baby's coming!"
> In this hellish basement, at this very moment,
> a young woman had gone into labor.
> In the dark, without a single match, what to do?
> Forgetting their own pains, people worried about her.
> And then: "I'm a midwife; I'll help with the birth."
> Seriously injured herself, the speaker had been moaning
>   only moments before.
> And so, in the darkness of that hellish depth,
>   new life was born.
> And so, before dawn, still bathed in blood,
>   The midwife died.
> Let us be midwives!
> Let us be midwives!
> Even at the cost of our own lives.

One of the ironies of this poem's immediate and continuing popularity is that its optimistic courage in the face of a nuclear explosion—a courage not uncommon in literature written immediately after the bombing before the full and lingering impact of the bomb was known—would in Kurihara's latter work be supplanted by a bitter cynicism.[23] The collection in which this poem was included, Kurihara's August 1946 *Black Eggs* (Kuroi tamago)—importantly, the very first book of atomic-bomb literature published in Japan—was dedicated by its author to "a society of freedom, life and peace," and to "a society without war." Of "Let Us Be Midwives!" itself, Kurihara once named its theme "the recovery of our humanity from amid the most extreme inhumanness."[24] Built about the image of blood simultaneously the sign of impending death and an imminent birth, the poem aligns itself with the solace of faith in a cyclical survival, in the ultimate conservation of human existence: a concept that Kurihara's later formulation of a "nuclear age" would call into serious question.

"Let Us Be Midwives!" and its long-standing popularity attest to how eagerly we look to our literature for succor and not for the more fearful facts of living with the likelihood of total annihilation. Kurihara's poems here, however, decline to initiate the reader into any original understanding of the radical nature of the event they carefully circumscribe. On one hand, her waka risk domesticating the atrocity by describing it in terms associated with nonatrocious disasters, and "Let Us Be Midwives" risks the same through melodrama and even bathos.

It is this and other related dangers which led some poets to seek other means for their work. These poets were frustrated by the near total exclusion of violent sentiments—rage, for instance—from verse by traditional Japanese poetics, a poetics which could not accommodate an anger that balked at even the attempt of language to profile it. It is again ironic that literary "silence" in a tradition which valorizes it means that this same tradition is handicapped in communicating some part of the *moral* silence which allowed the bomb to be dropped in the first place. What was once a poetics of inspiration was to be replaced by a poetics of expiration. It was in fact an overwhelming consciousness of a experience before or even outside language, of a historical uniqueness, which drove some of the earliest atomic-bomb poets to turn from the waka to free verse (*gendaishi*) and its potential for innovation. All things are not the same: a poem about Hiroshima or Nagasaki needs to be responsible not only to its own language, but to its special subject. It will be important, as we read atomic-bomb poetry, to distinguish between those figures of speech which are inherited and those newly forged. In the latter, it was hoped, original forms might succeed in intimating the new reality of a world that can vanish in an instance. New words, too: Hiroshima poet Sakamoto Hisashi would for example rename the horseweed (*tetsudōgusa*) that grew about the bombed ruins as "atomic-bomb weeds" (*gembakugusa*); or more strikingly, his term for those human beings killed in the bombing is "zero-speed pedestrians" (*sokudo-zero no samposha-tachi*).[25]

Many of these innovations, and indeed much of Hiroshima and Nagasaki's free verse in general, hardly strike us as poetry at all. It can seem excessively prosaic, lacking in word-play or imagery. This derives, one might argue, from a legitimate distrust of rhetorical figures which might distract from—or even displace—the factuality of the historical events they seek to inscribe. "Wailing" (Dōkoku) by Yamada Kazuko, for example, is a poem which requires no translation at all, only transliteration:

Shooji   yoo
Yasushi   yoo
Shooji   yoo
Yasushi   yoo
Shooji   yooo
Yasushi   yooo
Shoojii   yooo
Yasushi   yooo
Shoojii
Shoojii
Shoojiii.

What is narrated in this poem is presumably a dying mother's cries for her sons Shōji and Yasushi. What makes it such a powerful statement must be, in part, the way its stark recitation of names focuses our attention on those very sounds, the very witness that such syllables, squeezed out of a half-dead parent, display. But this is also a poem devoid of any familiar play of tropes or standard imagery. It, like much atomic-bomb poetry, eschews the typical for what is atypical and thus makes a kind of "poetic" sense even as it refutes "poetry." It may be an example of what Scully had in mind when he predicted "a fully realized poetry will also be a kind of anti-poetry," or in other words a poetry impervious to any reading outside of complicated and unruly historical, social contexts.

Especially salient in "Wailing" is an absence: that of any language immediately identifiable as imagistic, symbolic, or even suggestive in any literary sense. Simile, metaphor, metonymy—such devices can be rare in much Hiroshima and Nagasaki free verse. Of course, there can be no inviolable curbs on our tendency as readers to supply tropes where none were intended, or even where they are explicitly repressed. Just as Yamada's "Shooji" and "Yasushi" are no longer just the names of two orphans, but synecdochical refrains for all of "Hiroshima," "Hiroshima" itself has over time become an "old" metaphor now available for more or less cavalier application to "newer" events and experiences. The rhetorical force mustered, for example, in speaking of "the Hiroshima of Somalia" to describe mass starvation in Africa shows how both dialectical and uncontrollable the references of language are.

It also reminds us of how threatening such force can be. The status of such figures as metaphor, of course, was controversial before the Second World War. Ortega y Gasset warned in 1925 that metaphor, which "disposes of an object by having it masquerade as something else," was "the most radical instrument of dehumanization."[26] The applicability of this observation became clear when, after the violence of the 1940s, metaphor in the poetry of that violence would seem to risk reiterating precisely the process undergone by the victims of that violence itself. Hibakusha writers were understandably sensitive to the "masquerade" of tropes. Each substitution of a stylized phrase for an experience that had become the essential fact of their lives seemed to diminish that experience. The absence of metaphor from much early atomic-bomb poetry might indicate that its poets sought to avoid inflicting any such further damage atop the actual destruction.

In Ibuse Masuji's novel *Black Rain,* the central character and Hiroshima survivor Shizuma Shigematsu thinks about poetry when, four days after the bombing of his city, he sees masses of maggots devouring a corpse:

> Suddenly, a phrase from a poem came back to me, a poem I had read in some magazine when I was a boy: "Oh worm, friend worm!" it began. There was more in the same vein: "Rend the heavens, burn the earth, and let men die! A brave and moving sight!"
>
> Fool! Did the poet fancy himself as an insect, with his prating of his "friend" the worm? How idiotic can you get? He should have been here when it had all come true: when the heavens had been rent asunder, the earth had burned, and men had died. (161)

What Shigematsu objects to in poetry is Ortega y Gasset's "masquerade," an innocent use of metaphor that offends once "it had all come true." To read atomic-bomb poetry—or, more precisely, to read any poetry after Hiroshima as well as Auschwitz—we may find it necessary to, in the words of Alvin Rosenfeld, "disown the figurative use of language" and instead "interpret literally."[27] "Fire" can be no more a metaphor in atomic-bomb literature than it can be in that of the death camps.

But there is another survivor in *Black Rain* who reacts differently to his recollection of poetry amid the grotesque suffering of Hiroshima. Iwatake Hiroshi, a medical reservist injured far more severely in the bombing than Shigematsu, sees human grief that reminds him "of a poem by the Chinese poet Li Po that I had learned thirty years ago at middle school. For the first time, I realized that it was not just a piece of skillful description, but a work of intense emotion" (252). Rather than reacting angrily to inappropriate metaphor, what appeals to Iwatake in Li Po's verse is its classical representation of a common human experience repeated even before his own eyes. That the themes of poetry can be affirmed at the same time its most typical rhetoric can be rejected demonstrates the contradictions any poet, but especially the Hiroshima or Nagasaki poet, has to write mindfully within. Even the most ordinary language itself may seem metaphorical, and thus suspect: when one reads atomic-bomb poetry, its language can seem so *apart* from what it would refer to that its nature as a *substitution* can be overwhelming, and a deterrent from reading further. And when overtly metaphorical language does occur, as in Sakamoto's "zero-speed pedestrians," then as Rosenfeld said of certain Holocaust literature, "the function of metaphorical language . . . is to compare one thing with another not so much from an urge to get at the first but to get rid of it."[28]

This ambivalence over metaphor, while a hesitation found throughout modern history and among genres, assumes a heightened urgency for atomic-bomb writers. If, as Ortega y Gasset claimed, metaphor betrays "an instinctive avoidance of certain realities," then the debate is shifted onto the question whether such "avoidance" is to be approved of as morally kind or opposed as ethically cowardly.[29] But "avoidance" itself is less a fact than an idealizing projection. Readers will always search for metaphors, and we can always find or manufacture them: words themselves, after all, are somehow only "substitutions" for what they purport to signify, and it is unclear how any non-hibakusha reader could read any description of a nuclear bombing without, at some level, interpreting it as a fantastic "figure of speech." To make such an interpretation is, in turn, its own form of avoidance. If, as has been argued, "metaphor no longer has its telos in reality. . . . Instead metaphors become weapons directed against reality . . . confer[ring] on the poet's words a magical presence that lets us forget the world," that moment of "forgetting" permitted by metaphor is a moment that lets one be ignorant at the same time.[30]

Whichever contradiction one wishes to extract from atomic-bomb poetry, what is always lost is the comfort of the poem's unity. Modern poetry has been animated, in fact, by the theoretical and often contradictory allegiance to the organic completeness of the poem, and to metaphor, which necessarily opens up that aesthetic closure by leading us elsewhere to that which is substituted. Traditionally metaphor opens the work of art to something which thereby "transcends" it: so how, one asks, can there be "unity" within the poem? Actually we seem to enjoy metaphor's penchant for the disruption of erstwhile unity: the modern view of the poem is to see the sublimity of closure—itself a pleasure—erupt into play—another variety of pleasure—in rhetoric. That we read poetry with the expectation that it will charm us with both its formal structural order and its linguistic or rhetorical disorder rehearses the contradiction in "atomic-bomb literature" itself, where a cultural practice constrained with the rules and habits of an ancient civilization is put into a disarray sometimes productive, sometimes not, by a weapon meant to diminish that same civilization.

Lyricism, then, is the "crisis" of atomic-bomb literature, in the sense that it foregrounds the critical, impossible natures ascribed to language. The choices faced by the poet cast him decidedly in either the world of experience or the world of its semaphores, of fidelity to either the referent or its signifier— the tenuous relationship between which the atomic-bomb poet must be especially, if frustratingly, aware. We cannot read these poems without ourselves being aware of the struggles they subsume to find expression for Hiroshima and Nagasaki that is both part of, and apart from, those cities; without being aware of the paramount historical and ethical implications to which the poet's choice of metaphor over simile, of figural over literal, language, gives rise. The poems may as a result appear fractured, unfinished, incomplete. But as American Richard Eberhart writes near the beginning of his poem "Aesthetics After War,"

> Our own men testify to awe
> If not to aesthetic charm
> On seeing man's total malice over Hiroshima,
> That gigantic, surrealistic, picture-mushroom (57)

How very much more so, one wonders, for "their" men, for whom in recollection "that gigantic, surrealistic, picture-mushroom" is also something which, trapped within, they never saw, but instead only felt in its terrific heat and wind. Blindness, and so with it insight, here must take on different meanings for the atomic-bomb poets of Japan than it does for their critics, as indeed we shall ourselves "see."

■

In the previous chapter's discussion of Hara Tamiki's documentary memoir of Hiroshima, "Summer Flowers," it was noted that suddenly, prose failing him, Hara had to insert a poem into his account to express more adequately what he witnessed. "Red human corpses, their odd rhythms— / All that was? Or all that could have been?" Hara's brief detour into poetry is a turn to a language which would hopefully say more than it says: language which refers not only to the sights and sounds and smells which Hara recalls, but to itself, and which detains the reader to ponder, even more closely, its particular use of words. The rush of his prose, thought to be unencumbered reference to events, is interrupted ever so briefly by lines set off by wide margins, as if to alert us to the different way we are now to read and understand.

In some sense Hara is reverting to poetry not merely as an expedient tactic in his struggle to communicate, but because poetry is his most comfortable medium. He started his career as a poet—Dadaism was an important influence on his juvenilia, an influence characterized by one critic as a protest against a reality which even then he saw as "hopeless"—and never wholly ceased.[31] In fact, the majority view of critics has been that Hara was a better skilled poet than he was a writer of prose. If "Summer Flowers" is his most frequently read work, then that is most probably a reflection of the favor prose enjoys in modern Japanese literary culture. For in fact, Hara is also considered by many of those critics one of the founders of Japanese atomic-bomb poetry.[32]

Hara's most famous poems are found in a small series entitled "Atomic-bomb Landscapes" (Gembaku shōkei, 1950). The nine poems are arranged in a metonymical order and can be read as a single extended work, or separately. The first of the poems is referred to by its first line, "This Is A Human Being" (Kore ga ningen na no desu):

> *This is a* human being.
> *Please note what* changes *have been affected by the* atomic bomb.
> The body *is grotesquely* bloated,
> Male *and* female characteristics *are indistinguishable.*
> *Oh that* black, seared, smashed *and*
> *Festering* face, *from whose swollen* lips oozes a voice
> *"Help me"*
> In faint quiet words.
> *This is a* human being.
> *The* face *of a* human being.

This poem achieves its effect in three stages organized about a pattern of ironic revelation. It succeeds as it does because of the tension between the innocently expository tone of the first few lines and the horrible return to that same tone after a description of just what a "human being" can indeed be: sexless, charred, and dying. The apparently simple and straightforward declaration "*This is a* human being" is re-read after such words as "festering" and "swollen" with an altered, disturbing, and ironic awareness of how, after Hiroshima, un-human a "being" can appear. The poem turns on the dismantling of an assumption, the dislocation of an expectation. It uses the reversal associated with irony to "re-order" the experience of the reader; it attempts to change the reader, not to comfort or reassure him. Critic Kokai Eiji writes of Hara: "As a writer and as a contemporary poet, he put words to paper in order to engage with history. The 'atomic bomb' was a criminal sentence pronounced suddenly, ripping apart the clouds about our heads. But Hara sought to reverse that sentence: he stood on the side of those who would restore history to humanity."[33]

In Hara's world human beings do not resemble human beings. Nor do his poems necessarily resemble poems. Indeed a reader supplied with "This Is A Human Being" in its original Japanese is doubly struck by its unusual appearance as well as its contents. Hara wrote it in ordinary Sino-Japanese characters and in the extraordinary katakana syllabary, which I have represented in translation with italics. The effect on the Japanese reader is at least two-fold. First, the processing of the poem is considerably slowed—words appear fused, confused, even incomplete. Second, even when the poem is successfully read, its contents remain somehow associated with the contents of things more commonly written with katakana: the skeletal language of telegrams, the authoritative prose of official communications, and foreign words or slang—that is to say, language not wholly understood or sanctioned. Consequently, reading this poem is like reading under duress a cable which announces terrible news in a language, though eventually comprehensible, finally not quite one's own. The orthography effects an alienation of the reader from the work, rendering the experience it narrates slightly, significantly, incongruous.

Fellow Hiroshima poet Kurihara Sadako has suggested that the city of her birth is now written often in katakana in order to express the idea that there is a "peace which the atomic bombing has brought us."[34] In her estimation this is an ersatz, even cruel, way of turning an actual *place*—the site of a nuclear war—into its idealized opposite. Similarly, in Ōta Yoko's 1953 novel *People and the City of Evening Calm* (Yūnagi no machi to hito to), the narrator, a hibakusha returning to Hiroshima eight years after the bombing, is sharing a drink with a journalist when the question of whether "Hiroshima" should be written in katakana or not comes up. Both express a dislike for the practice, suggesting that far from signifying "Hiroshima" as an internationalized semaphore of peace, it in fact allows more, and equally abstracted, "Hiroshimas" to occur (136).[35]

But what Kurihara and Ōta protest is what happened to a katakana "Hiroshima" under the stewardship of highly politicized, and not always sincere, "peace movements." For Hara in the first years after the bombing, the reference in his use of the katakana "Hiroshima" was not to that of banners during the routine rallies of August 6th and 9th, but in part to the memory of a language intrinsically part of the original anger and hurt. Hara was not the only poet to deploy such orthographic styles. At the end of the first section of his poem entitled simply "Hiroshima" (but "Hiroshima" in katakana), Nakamura Atsushi embeds the following citation of an announcement posted shortly after the bombing, one written in the same mix of characters and katakana as Hara's *"This Is A* Human Being":

> Notification
> Those injured *by the* recent special bomb
> *May apparently* find immersion in ocean water
> Effective.
> —Western Army Regional Headquarters (34)

The language of the authorities, riddled with a retrospectively cruel and pathetic irony, is the same language in which Hara composes his poems. All but one of the "Atomic-bomb Landscapes" poems is written in this peculiar mixed script. Interestingly, however, the one exception, "Forever Verdant" (Eien no midori), is no complete exception, for within this poem each time the place name "Hiroshima" occurs it alone is spelled out phonetically in katakana, thus charging the one word that, like its European counterpart "Auschwitz," stands as synecdoche for the catalogue of modern atrocities. This is a kind of innovation that sought, oddly, both to remember and forget the place to which it refers. It is an exaggerated example of the modernist ambiguity of writing, namely the tenuous tie between words and what any author would like them to mean. Geoffrey Hartman has speculated that "writing destabilizes words, in the sense that it makes us aware at one and the same time of their alien frame of reference . . . and of the active power of forgetfulness (a kind of silencing) which it enables and which, in turn, enables us to write."[36] This destabilization of which he speaks looms so large in the world of atomic-bomb poets such as Hara that it becomes a central theme of their work. The rudimentary dislocation reflected in language by the experience of an atomic bombing forces the hibakusha writer to highlight the "alien frame of reference" of words. Hara, for instance, attempted with his purposefully unusual orthography to insulate the uniqueness of Hiroshima within a unique code.

Hara was not the only poet to experiment in such ways (others, for instance, exclusively used the *hiragana* syllabary—the script first learnt by school children—to stimulate an "emptying" of language by returning it to its "elementary" status), but unlike the Surrealists, for example, who hoped to demonstrate a basic distrust of "reality" with their corruptions of form, Hara endeavored to make his innovations reflect a basic fidelity to reality, a reality itself twisted and distorted almost unrecognizably by violence. T. S. Eliot once spoke of the poet "dislocating language into meaning";[37] his remarks seem newly relevant for a poet such as Hara, a poet writing in a world where nothing had been left, undisturbed, in its former place. The "defamiliarization" of language, to borrow a term from the Russian Formalists, that Hara practiced in his poetry by casting it in katakana may have thus made it "literary": but he surely meant it to be so in ways radically *un*familiar to his readers.

The best known of the "Atomic-bomb Landscapes" poems is *"Give Me* Water" (Mizu o kudasai). Water and its associated images have long been important in Hiroshima writing: it is a city of once seven, now six, rivers. Perhaps more to the point, rivers have long been an important source of allusions for Hara Tamiki's poetry.[38] But this particular poem refers to water in its most horrific post-Hiroshima context. The victims of August 6th, like burn victims everywhere, experienced terrible thirst and asked repeatedly for water. Tragically, however, a rumor quickly spread that water was in fact injurious to the health of the victims, and thus was apparently withheld from even those who begged for it—as if to the mythological Tantalus' already cruel punishment of unquenchable thirst had been added the irony of the gods' belief in their own charity. Hara's poem "Give Me Water" must account for one part of its affective power over readers to this fact, for some perhaps a contrite memory:

> *Give me* water
> *Ah Give me* water
> *Let me drink*
> Death *would be better than this*
> Death *would be*

> *Aah*
> *Help Help*
> Water . . .
> Water . . .
> *Somehow please*
> *Someone*
> > *Ohohohoh*
> > *Ohohohoh*
>
> *The* heavens *are* split asunder
> *The* city *has* disappeared
> *The* river
> *Is flowing*
> > *Ohohohoh*
> > *Ohohohoh*
>
> Night *is coming*
> Night *is coming*
> *In burnt dry* eyes
> *On festering* lips
> *Blistering* hot
> *This staggering distorted*
> Face's
> *Groan is that of a human being*
> *Of a human being.*

Many of the techniques used by Hara in *"This Is A* Human Being," especially that of irony, are found here in *"Give Me* Water" as well. But there is more, too: this poem moves further toward disorder. Grammarless phrases, as "staggering" and "distorted" as the face they (may) describe, are piled atop each other to create a weight of words unrelieved by a rigorous syntactical structure. Hara attempts to parallel his experience by circumventing—metaphorically annihilating—a sample few rules of language. The practiced rhetoric of poetry is pushed to the extreme to encompass an extreme. When words themselves are replaced by moans ("*Ohohohoh*"), those moans are potentially rendered artifacts of the suffering rather than translated or narrated with virtual or abstract signs. The suggestion of anarchy in this poem reflects a lack of the unity of expression, just as there was no unity of impression in August 6th. Here too lies the fundamental struggle between the rage of the victim and the order of the writer. For a man such as Hara, who is both, the struggle cannot be resolved decisively. But, as suggested earlier, this is a crucial feature of any theory for a literature of atrocity. A contradiction always underlies such artistic enterprises: on the one hand, the hibakusha writer feels an instinctive revulsion against allowing his imagination—his memory—to release the horrors he has seen since that might risk legitimizing them, while on the other hand he feels the equally compelling instinct against repressing that imagination, against the forgetting which accompanies concealment. The ambivalence generated within this contradiction becomes its own pronouncement, its own "genre," in which the understanding of an event is always fraught with the danger of its acceptance.

It is probably true that all hibakusha poets, if not all modern poets, are forced to see the difficulty of some referents for some, maybe most, words.[39] That difficulty, when it surfaces in their poems, as it must, makes those poems for us all the more "poetic." After Hara Tamiki, however, such a poetics must be seen not as any sort of sophisticated advance in the way we view language, but instead as a diminished, nearly muted, capacity for that language to mean in any fashion that would allow us still to consider ourselves fully or even sufficiently civilized.

■

Carved into the stone memorial that prominently stands in Hiroshima's Peace Park are the lines that, perhaps as a consequence, comprise Japan's most famous atomic-bomb poem:

> Give me back my father. Give me back my mother.
> Give me back the old people.
> Give me back the children.
>
> Give me back myself. And all those people
> Joined to me, give them back.
> Give me back mankind.
>
> Give me peace.
> A peace that will not shatter
> As long as man, man is in the world.[40]

This poem is the first in a collection of twenty-five entitled simply *Poems of the Atomic Bomb* (Gembaku shishū, 1951) and written by Hiroshima native Tōge Sankichi. This collection, together with Hara's "Atomic-bomb Landscapes," is considered the founding work not just of Hiroshima's, but of Japan's, atomic-bomb poetry. They are, in the words of one literary historian, "today already the classics of atomic-bomb poetry."[41] *Poems of the Atomic Bomb* has proven so popular over the years that it was adapted for dramatic performance on the stage and used as the inspiration for a cantata. It was so critically successful that it rescued Tōge, writes another critic, from ending his career as a "mediocre and sentimental lyric poet."[42] But in fact it was his encounter with the destruction of Hiroshima which made him the most public and politicized of the early

Hiroshima poets, and which in retrospect may be said to have guaranteed his poetic achievement and subsequent acclaim.

Tōge Sankichi, né Mitsuyoshi, was born in the city of Hiroshima in 1917 to an established family which until Tōge's grandfather's day, when they went into commerce, had served as leaders of a nearby village. But despite the family's relatively privileged class background, the Tōges had long been associated with progressive and even left-wing causes. Tōge's father, Kiichi, who would become a hibakusha himself, was involved with the socialist movements of the 1920s. His mother, Sute, in addition to being an amateur poet, was an admirer of the feminist Hiratsuka Raichō and publicly advocated women's causes herself. Elder sister Yoshiko embraced a liberal (and, in the context, socially critical) Protestantism, and is believed responsible for Tōge's own Christian baptism in 1942. But it was Tōge's older brother Kazuo who was the most radical. Much admired by Sankichi, Kazuo was constantly in and out of prisons for his communist activities. In fact Kiichi, alarmed at the tendencies of Tōge's older siblings, hid Kazuo's Marxist books from his younger son's view at home, and urged him to go into business, where presumably he would be less apt or able to pursue the dangerous politics of his brother.[43]

None of this was to any avail. Tōge did graduate, in accordance with his father's wishes, from the Hiroshima Prefectural School of Commerce in 1935, and dutifully went to work for the city's gas utility. But from the very next year, 1936, the poetry—largely haiku and waka—at which he had been attempting his hand since the age of fourteen took a pronounced political turn. Examples of Tōge's work survive beginning with that year, and they reveal the influence of the proletarian fiction Tōge and many of his generation had then enjoyed reading. Another factor, however, in shaping his early work was his suddenly endangered health. Although much of that work is classically lyrical and thematically romantic, like Hara's first poems it is charged with themes of powerlessness and of uncertain survival. Diagnosed with pulmonary tuberculosis, and according to his diary resigned to a life expectancy of only another two or three years, Tōge resolved to leave his mark as a poet and wrote furiously, in the words of one critic, "as if to prove he were alive."[44] There is, for example, this haiku from the late 1930s:

> Somewhere, out there
> There summons me
> The demon of death,
> A star.[45]

Tōge's morbid premonitions, however, were premature. By the year Tōge wrote this poem, he was well enough to sit up in bed; and by 1941, to get out of it. Soon thereafter one detects new influences on Tōge's poetry. One of these is the same Symbolism that had so excited Hara; another, however, was the growing awareness within Japan proper of the war abroad. The combined impact of these influences was to create a poetry simultaneously lyrical and, reflecting his family's political biases, suggestively polemical. The coexistence of these two and always potentially incompatible rhetorical modes would remain a hallmark of Tōge's verse after the Second World War and indeed for the whole of his career. It likely also accounts for Tōge's move, after 1943, away from the traditional forms of the waka and the haiku, and towards modern free verse with its greater capacity for narration and range of expression.

When Hiroshima was bombed, the evolution of Tōge's poetry was both deflected and accelerated. At the time his home was in Midori-chō, three kilometers from ground zero in the eastern part of the city. On the second floor that morning, Tōge was fortunate that the house did not collapse, though he was nonetheless injured by flying glass. Had the bombing come ten minutes later, he would have been on his way to work and in all probability killed. As if proof that he was lucky in an unlucky city, many of Tōge's relatives—his uncle Teru, a cousin and his wife, most of his brother-in-law's family—were indeed all killed outright. Tōge recalled that morning in a diary entry that would later form the basis for several of his most memorable poems:

> At 8:07 [*sic*] on August 6th, three or four enemy planes dropped a new-type bomb on our Hiroshima. It (the atomic bomb) produced waves of heat and light, as well as violent winds, over a wide area. Sparing only the suburban neighborhoods, all the city's homes were destroyed, and all people within crushed. Others were burnt to death in the fires that broke out, and many of those who were outdoors also died from the burns they received.[46]

For several days thereafter Tōge wandered the city searching for friends and relatives, but soon he began to experience such symptoms of radiation poisoning as loss of hair and diarrhea. Two weeks after the bombing he entered the Red Cross Hospital in Itozaki, a small city east of Hiroshima proper, and although he was released after a short time, never did Tōge enjoy full health again.

Nonetheless the next few years of Tōge's life, his last, were ones of tremendous energy and productivity. All the poetry of Tōge's we are apt to read today was written in the space of these few years, and it is for these poems that he earned the sobriquet "the atomic-bomb poet" (*gembaku shijin*). There is a poem, entitled "Picture Book" (Ehon) and which appears in an entry in Tōge's diary written only a few days after the bombing, that may be regarded as the first poem written about the nuclear age:

> Injured by the hands of war
> A mother soon to die   her child shows her his picture book

From a tall lattice window   one ray of late afternoon sun
Falls on the cold floor   of a receiving facility for the wounded

Held open   for the burnt and blistered face to see
He slowly turns the pages   childish drawings in red and blue
Fairy tales   so old and familiar

Eyes turned   to the burnt badger of Mount Kachi-kachi
The groans of the man nearby   Suddenly cease
The eyes of mother   staring so blankly
So far away   the drooping eyelids

The pain, the grief   even the hopes for her son
Never told   and in the stink of shit and piss
She dies
She dies.[47]

It is of course possible, and perhaps even probable, that one could read this poem and not think it refers to the atomic bombing at all. The human destruction and the pathos it narrates does not require a nuclear bomb, but simply war itself. Apparently the poem was inspired by Tōge's discovery, as he was searching for injured friends immediately after the bombing, of a young mother (identified as "K"—standing possibly for "Kawauchi"—in the later *Poems of the Atomic Bomb*) in a receiving facility. Just where her son was in fact showing her his picture book is an unanswerable question, but what can be said about this poem, specifically the absence of any mention of an "atomic bomb," is that such references were impossible, at least in a poem written in the same month as that in which the attack occurred: the very term "atomic-bomb" was unknown and thus unavailable to Tōge, or to anyone else in Hiroshima. He, like many others in the city, believed the rumors that the city had been hit by multiple rockets carrying conventional explosives.

The first specific mention of the bomb in Tōge's poetry is found in his 1946 "The Road Home from Christmas" (Kurisumasu no kaerimichi):

In this city of burnt ruins an evening rain gently dispels the fog
Christmas songs burn in the heart like myths
The young girl and I walk silently along the ruined railroad tracks

The first Christmas after the war, quiet amid the stench of smoldering
    ruins
God, behind the sorrow of war, is beautiful like candy
The young girl and I step across the mud like acrobats

The numberless atomic-bomb ruins we pass whisper in the darkness
They whisper discordant sounds about God and war
The young girl and I silently step on the tracks and straddle the rail ties

The atmosphere of this Christmas past is more gentle than the drizzle
The youth that survives is heavier than the trees shaking in the wind
Bearing that weight, the young girl and I walk
The young girl and I continue to walk
Whether God exists or not.

Tōge's Christian background might reasonably lead one to take his references to Christmas more sincerely than ironically. But a God who is "beautiful like candy," and who may exist "or not," suggests a faith shaken, if perhaps not destroyed, by the "burnt ruins" in which Tōge passes both the anniversary of Christ's birth and the first year of an era only incongruously counted anno Domini.

It is the presence, perhaps, of the young girl and not the shadowy question of God that finally means "The Road Home from Christmas" is other than a fully discouraged poem. Not alone, but rather accompanied by a companion of presumed innocence and thus of hope, Tōge preserves for himself a "road home." It was in the following year, 1947, that Tōge fully committed himself to poetry both as a professional and as a dedicated partisan. In February he joined the Hiroshima Poets Society (Hiroshima Shijin Kyōkai) that had been formed around prominent local poet Yoneda Eisaku. This membership was not simply for literary purposes but carried with an implicit commitment to left-wing political activism. The Society's journal, *Chikaku* (Nucleus), begun in June 1948, had the stated objective of using poetry to promote what they per-ceived—no doubt in the contagious euphoria of the immediate postwar years—to be progressive social change. In the founding issue of *Chikaku* Tōge published an essay entitled "The Liberation of Aesthetics" (Bi no kaihō) which may summarize what his theory of poetry may have been at the time. His remarks linked the "liberation of aesthetics" with the parallel "liberation of mankind"; he asserted that postwar poetry must join in the "democratic revolu-tion" then under way. In fact, Tōge argued, poets should lead this revolution, for by their giving up the "old aesthetics" for "the truth of the new age," poets would "provide the crystallized form for all manner of correct consciousness and thought."[48] Such an alignment of poetry with politics, of course, invited a reaction from Hiroshima's more conservative poets secure within their assump-tion that poetry had necessarily to eschew politics—an assumption, argues critic and poet Ōoka Makoto, that goes back a thousand years to the Japanese preference for the pastoral themes of classical Chinese poetry over the more explicitly controversial[49]—but it also proposed a challenge to Tōge's own po-etry. His was a poetry whose often highly subjective lyricism did not so appar-ently or necessarily lead to the revolutionary conclusions he was, in theory, now advocating. Tōge's refashioning of his own poetic practice along the lines of left-wing orthodoxy would take time; nearly all the time that his shortened life was allotted.

In the meanwhile, however, Tōge became ever more involved in a number of radical cultural and political organizations, and he eventually rose to prominent leadership positions within them. In February 1949, he joined the New Japan Literature Association (Shin Nihon Bungaku Kai), an organization expressly for "democratic revolutionary writers." Later that year, and perhaps prompted by the again rapid deterioration of his health, Tōge told his common-law wife Kazuko that before anything happened to him, he wanted to become a formal member of the Japan Communist Party. When his application was accepted that same year, news of his membership was announced that May nationwide in the JCP's party newspaper, *Akahata* (Red Flag).[50] Tōge also was involved in the local chapter of the largely communist-sponsored Culture Circle (Bunka Sākuru) movement that was established across Japan in the wake of increasingly repressive Occupation policies and the general decline of left-wing activism. After this chapter broke up in late 1949 and early 1950—in part due to the ripple effects of the national purge of communists and their sympathizers under way at that time—poets in Hiroshima still committed to activist partisan politics formed a new group, and this time around the leadership of Tōge Sankichi himself.

The Our Poetry Association (Warera no Shi no Kai), which began publishing its vehicle *Warera no shi* (Our Poetry) in November 1949, was under Tōge's tutelage committed to bringing about the creation of what was termed a "free society." The mass firings of striking workers in 1949—known as the Japan Steel Hiroshima Incident—radicalized Tōge's leftist politics even further and prompted him to integrate those politics more explicitly into his poetry. What he saw as the exposure of "class contradictions" in that particular struggle led him to strive for a "fresh literary style" combined with a "materialistic method."[51] He continued, as always, to write the occasional lyrical waka, but sought with added fervor the potential of a "new poetry" for his "new ideas." In 1950, while the Occupation's second Red Purge was under way, Tōge wrote in a manifesto attached to an anthology of antiwar poetry that "art" was a "weapon" to be deployed against the "enemies of mankind."[52] Tōge's own work in this anthology marks the first time he would attack, directly, America for its use of the atomic bomb. "The Appeal" (Yobikake) is an earlier version of the poem with the same title included later in *Poems of the Atomic Bomb*:

> What if you had tears endlessly dripping
> From a wounded heart penetrated by a brilliant light
> That that day burnt your retinas
> What if you stunk like Hiroshima, and even now

> Had bloody pus gushing from those wounds
> And were cursing war.

Tōge's "you" was gradually assuming a distinctly antagonist identity for him. Occupation policies were, by 1950, making life more difficult than previously for Tōge and his political comrades and colleagues. The 1950 purge resulted in many members of the Our Poetry Association losing their jobs. Discouraged, some of those members dropped out of the group; others became informers. At the same time the Japan Communist Party itself was breaking up into factions, forcing Tōge to take stands on a number of both minor and major controversial issues.[53]

A series of crucial events then unfolded in quick succession. In June 1950, the Occupation ordered the Central Committee of the JCP fired from public-sector jobs, and *Akahata* was ordered to cease publication—in part, apparently, because the Hiroshima bureau of the paper had published in *Heiwa sensen* (Peace Front), another Party publication, photographs of Hiroshima taken immediately after the bombing. Unfortunately for Tōge, one of his poems was printed on the cover of this offending publication. The poem, entitled "August 6" (Hachigatsu muika), would comprise the final lines of the poem by the same name included in *Poems of the Atomic Bomb*:

> In the feces and urine on the floor of the arsenal
> a group of schoolgirls who had fled lay fallen;
> bellies swollen like drums, blinded in one eye,
>   skin half-gone, hairless, impossible to tell
>   one from the other—
> by the time the rays of the morning sun picked them out,
> they had all stopped moving;
> amid the stagnant stench, the only sound:
> flies buzzing about metal washbasins.
>
> The stillness that reigned over the city of 300,000
> who can forget it?
> In that hush
> the white eyes of dead women and children
> sent us
> a soul-rendering appeal:
> who can forget it?

In August 1950, tensions ran quite high among activists in Hiroshima due to the U.S. intervention in the Korean peninsula the previous month. A mass demonstration planned for August 6th, combining both protest over the Korean conflict and commemoration of the 1945 bombing, was forbidden by the Occupation. The Hiroshima branch of the JCP decided to proceed nonetheless, and hold an illegal demonstration; unfortunately, the crowd that assembled that day in downtown Hiroshima turned into a violent melee once the police intervened. The events of that day are described in Tōge's poem "August 6, 1950" (1950-nen no hachigatsu muika):

> They come running;
> they come running.
> From that side, from this,
> hands on holstered pistols,
> the police come on the run.
>
> August 6, 1950:
> the Peace Ceremony has been banned;
> on street corners at night, on bridge approaches at dawn,
> the police standing guard are restive.
> Today, at the very center of Hiroshima—
> the Hatchōbori intersection,
> in the shadow of the F. Department Store—
>
> the stream of city folk who have come to place flowers
> at memorials, at ruins,
> suddenly becomes a whirlpool;
> chin-straps taut with sweat
> plunge into the crowd;
> split by the black battle-line,
> reeling,
> the crowd as one looks up at the department store—
> from fifth-floor windows, sixth-floor windows,
> fluttering,
> fluttering,
> against the backdrop of summer clouds,
> now in shadow, now in sunlight,
> countless handbills dance
> and scatter slowly
> over upturned faces
> into outstretched hands,
> into the depths of empty hearts.
>
> People pick them up off the ground;
> arms swing and knock them out of the air;
> hands grab them in midair;
> eyes read them:
> workers, merchants, students, girls,
> old people and children from outlying villages—
> a throng of residents representing all Hiroshima

for whom August 6 is the anniversary of a death—and the police:
pushing, shoving. Angry cries.
The urgent appeal
of the peace handbills they reach for,
the antiwar handbills they will not be denied.

Streetcars stop;
traffic lights topple;
jeeps roll up;
fire sirens scream;
riot trucks drive up—two trucks, three;
an expensive foreign car forces its way
through the ranks of police in plain clothes;
the entrance to the department store becomes a grim checkpoint.

Still handbills fall,
gently, gently.
Handbills catch on the canopy; hands appear, holding a broom,
sweep every last one off;
they dance their way down
one by one, like living things, like voiceless shouts,
lightly, lightly.

The Peace Ceremony—the releasing of doves, the ringing of
        bells,
the mayor's peace message carried off on the breeze—
is stamped out like a child's sparkler;
all gatherings are banned:
speeches,
concerts,the UNESCO meeting;
Hiroshima is under occupation by armed police and police in
        mufti.

The smoke of rocket launchers
rises from newsreel screens;
from back streets resound the shouts
of those, children too, who signed petitions against the bomb.
In the sky over Hiroshima on August 6, 1950,
spreading light above anxious residents,
casting shadows on silent graveyards,
toward you who love peace,
toward me who wants peace,
drawing the police on the double,
handbills fall,
handbills fall.

This poem, published in the September 1951 issue of *Warera no shi*, was, like "The Appeal" and "August 6," later included in the one collection of poetry, *Poems of the Atomic Bomb*, that would establish Tōge's fame. This is a renown, as should be clear from "August 6, 1950," that came not from any special poetic achievement but instead an attention to special public issues and events. The earliest of its twenty-five poems was written in May 1949, the last by April 1951. All of the poems are based on experiences that Tōge had recorded earlier in the prose accounts of his diary. But its immediate impetus was apparently President Truman's announcement on November 30, 1950 that he was thinking of using the atomic bomb in Korea—the same announcement that prompted fellow Hiroshima poet Hara Tamiki's suicide.[34] The first edition of the *Poems of the Atomic Bomb* appeared in September 1951 as a crude mimeograph done by the Our Poetry Association. Only five hundred copies were produced. In February 1952, however, Aoki Shoten, an established publisher, reissued the collection.

Any comparison of these poems with his earlier, prewar, lyrical works demonstrates clearly that Tōge's commitment to a nuanced symbolism was receding and, conversely, his pursuit of a "materialist method" being taken seriously. Poems such as "Dying" (Shi), "Blindness" (Mōmoku) and "Season of Flames" (Honoo) are extreme examples of the prosaic literalness that increasingly governs his expression, no longer strictly "poetic" but now unabashedly propagandistic. Some of the poems are best thought of as effectively documentary in nature, no doubt purposefully so given the dictates of both Tōge's experiences and the JCP's endorsement of socialist realism. For example, there is in the very title of his work "Eyes" (Me) the suggestion of a direct and testimonial mode of prosody:

Shapes I do not recognize are looking toward me.
In a lost world, a lost time,
inside a dark storehouse,
a light neither night nor day falls through the twisted bars of a window;
piled one atop the other—shapes that once were faces.
  Shapes that once were the front sides of heads.
Faces once the upper parts of human beings,
    that like flickering water
reflected life's joys and sorrows.
Now—ah!—lumps of putrid, blubbery flesh, only the eyes ablaze;
seals of the human, skin torn away,
on the ground, sinking into the cement floor;
swollen, soft, heavy round objects
not moving as if pinned down by some force;
the only movement: white gleaming from torn flesh,

watching my every step.
Eyes fastened to my back, fixed on my shoulder, my arm.
Why do they look at me like this?
After me, after me, from all sides, thin white beams coming at me:
eyes, *eyes*, EYES—
from way up ahead, from that dark corner, from right here at my feet.
Ah! Ah! Ah!
Erect, clothed, brow intact and nose undamaged,
I walk on—a human being:
eyes transfix me, hold steady on me.
From the hot floor,
from the oppressive walls, from beside stout pillars supporting the
    cavernous ceiling,
eyes materialize, *materialize*, do not fade.
Ah, pasted to me, fixed forever on me—
back, then chest; armpit, then shoulder—
I who step into this dark
in search of the one who only this morning was my younger sister—
eyes!
A straw mat on the cement floor, urine from somewhere oozing through
    its meshes; pressing into the mat,
sunken-cheeked,sippery with ointment, secretions, blood, burnt
ash—a death mask.
Oh! Oh!—
an eyeball that moves spills drops of transparent liquid;
from torn lips
red-flecked teeth
groan out my name.

In actual fact Tōge had no younger sister: the person referred to in his
poem is held to be the same as the character in the earlier poem "Picture Book,"
namely the widowed acquaintance whom Tōge sought in the bombing's aftermath and who figures in several of the pieces collected in *Poems of the Atomic
Bomb*. That so many of his verses are overtly anecdotal or, more broadly, documentary, indicates perhaps not only the influence of Marxist literary theories
upon Hara—theories which, at their simplest, mandated an allegiance to popular experience over a private, aestheticized, and subjective muse—but additionally the demands of atomic-bomb literature in general for language which
cleaves as closely as possible to the *nuclear* experience: experience unadulter-
ated by the intervening agencies of either an individual poet or, perhaps especially, his deployment of an acculturated stylistics.

But it is "Give Me Back My Father," the poem that introduces the rest in

Poems of the Atomic Bomb, which is unquestionably his best known despite the complete absence of any references to specific individuals, incidents, or facts. Carved into stone, it abruptly commands "Give me back my father. Give me back my mother." This is a poem that impels the reader with blunt imperatives rather than coax him with images. As a poem, it may strike us as simple, too thin. Its proximity to the genre of the slogan may explain why, as Robert Jay Lifton pointed out, it served as "a rallying cry for peace movements throughout Japan."[55] Its sheer power presents too few twists or turns for us to revel in as the poet manipulates language. But the imperative "give me" does supply a grave weight that insinuates, in the place of subtly crafted ambiguities, a strident, nearly antipoetic, resentment at the loss of his family and a rage at whomever is to blame. Of course, the dead cannot be returned: the command "give me" is ultimately rhetorical and even unintentionally, one can imagine, pathetic. But Tōge goes on to convert such pathos into a philosophical politics: "Give me back mankind." With this line Tōge throws open the poem to one of the more radical consequences of Hiroshima and Nagasaki, namely the abrogation of man's place at the center of the world. This is done without resort to metaphor, yet with the last stanza, "Give me peace / A peace which will not shatter / As long as man, man is in the world," Tōge suddenly transforms his previous anger into an appeal for "peace," itself potentially a tropic abstraction that allows the reader to transcend the destructiveness of rage by substituting it for a more or less conventional ideal whose premises the bomb had undermined. In a sense Tōge is asking that he be returned to the world which will again allow him to write poetry, even while it is the annihilation of that same world that is so often his theme.

It is clear from the nature of Tōge's last poems that he was attempting to do in poetry something significantly different than was, for example, Hara Tamiki. Hara moved inward, away from the world and into the play of language. Tōge, on the other hand, increasingly saw his poems as a literary adjunct to his social activism, as a kind of high-cultural agitprop which could serve both his art and his politics. It is interesting to note that, in counterpoint to Hara's use of katakana to estrange the reader, to make us read his poetry multivocally, Tōge wrote "Give Me Back My Father" entirely in hiragana, another phonetic syllabary but one, when emptied of Sino-Japanese characters, which is reminiscent of a schoolchild's elementary reading primer. The language is not rendered difficult but instead vastly simple, as if Tōge wanted no obstacles between our reading of his poem and the poem itself. Something is at stake for Tōge that precludes too much concern for aesthetics. As he wrote in one of his manifestos, "The time has come when our artistic creation is impossible without the struggle for peace."[56]

Such issues, while certainly of no slight consequence to Hara, were not placed at the center of his writing as they were for Tōge. On the title page of

the 1952 edition of *Poems of the Atomic Bomb*, Tōge dedicated the collection to—
in addition to the two atomic bombings' victims—"all people throughout the
world who abhor nuclear weapons." The commitment to both lyricism and
politics in *Poems of the Atomic Bomb* produces, upon reading it, the impression of
a revolutionary, cosmopolitan romanticism, though it is sometimes combined
with a narrower, indignant nationalism when, as in "When Will That Day
Come?" (Sono hi wa itsuka), the death of one young girl becomes a symbol
of crimes committed against all Japanese. One of Tōge's admirers, Hayashida
Yasumasa, cites Tōge's *Poems of the Atomic Bomb* to prove the possibility for an
"ethnic epic poetry" *(minzoku jōjishi).*[57] In both cases—the cosmopolitan romanticism and the racial nationalism—poetry is used to inform, propagandize, and
convert. Despite a similar melancholy and even depression in his work—a
characteristic of many hibakusha poets—Tōge finally resolves to make poetry
something less poetic and thus perhaps more efficacious in the "real" world.

After *Poems of the Atomic Bomb*, however, Tōge wrote very little. He had
planned to write an epic poem, his intended lifework, entitled simply "Hiroshima"; but he never advanced beyond a few preliminary notes for it. His last
completed poem is thought to be "The Scar" (Kizuato), a work written after
Tōge saw the following scene at an event commemorating the publication of
an atomic-bomb poetry anthology he had co-edited, the 1952 *From Beneath the
Atomic Cloud:*

> Little boy Okamoto finishes reading
> Raises his short poem high with both hands
> Finishes reading and suddenly bows his head
> A head with a bald spot far too big
>
> The destroyed house and his mother's death
> Scars directly etched onto his five-year-old head
> Now a sixth-grader
> He has an "A-bomb bald spot" that others tease him for
>
> "Things got bad after the bomb was dropped"
> Says Okamoto's poem
> As it grips all of the upstairs of the Teachers' Union Hall;
> The darkness of surviving, after losing the leaning pillars of
>   A house robbed of its workers
> And the future
> Becomes that shiny bald scar
> And gnaws into everyone's heart.
>
> The charwoman tightens her grimy fists
> The young woman who will never ride public transportation
> Behind what she covers with her mask,
> Through each of the windows

There is Hijiyama, its landslides, and
The ABCC forms a dome
There, the Americans, the A-bombers,
    Continue to certify the lethal effects

And so
Yesterday in Room No. 6 at the Red Cross Hospital
    On the dewy paths of Onaga-chō
We say goodbye to the corpse
of a pale and swollen little boy whose white corpuscles made
What was wrong even worse
The eyes of Hiroshima
Listen to this poem in silence
And even the master of ceremonies endures the silence.

Tōge's last poem is one that reflexively takes poetry itself as the theme: a small boy, himself a "text" of the bombing ("Scars directly etched onto his five year-old head"), writes a simple and descriptive poem that "grips" its audience "and gnaws into everyone's heart." This is an endorsement for a poetry that not only can come from children, but perhaps only can: whatever this poem says, it does so without sophistication but with the moving moral authority of the most innocent of victims. When the boy's words are read aloud a second time—at his funeral—"The eyes of Hiroshima / Listen to this poem in silence," the power of his language precludes any other, as if to have, indeed, the "final word."

By the time Tōge wrote this poem, his own "final word," his health, never good, had deteriorated to the point where further work was impossible. Plagued not only with genuinely life-threatening medical problems since the bombing but with a series of misdiagnoses and ill-advised treatments, Tōge died on the early morning of March 10, 1953 of respiratory disease doubtlessly complicated by his generally compromised physical condition as a hibakusha. His biographer Masuoka Toshikazu flatly claims that "what killed Sankichi was the atomic bomb."[58]

Since his death Tōge's reputation has continued to be inextricably linked to politics, and perhaps it has even been exploited for purposes Tōge may or may not have approved of. Robert Jay Lifton correctly describes Tōge as "the only Hiroshima writer to become a popular hero."[59] But apart from whatever sincere or opportunistic canonizations of Tōge have followed from such a brief, frustrated career lasting no longer than eight years, Tōge's fellow poets have often reflected upon him in less polemical terms than have the publicists for Tōge's announced or imputed politics. Kurihara Sadako, for example, has written that Tōge's "postwar verse begins with the combination of Symbolist poetry with a lyricism that cannot be thought of apart from the catastrophe of the atomic bombing."[60] It is this combination that gives Tōge's poetry its distinctiveness and distinction; it reveals the struggle of a poet both to report the world and to change it. His own work " The Shadow" (Kage), included in *Poems of the Atomic Bomb*, is perhaps the best critical comment on all his atomic-bomb poetry:

> Cheap movie theaters, saloons, fly-by-night markets,
> burned, rebuilt, standing, crumbling, spreading like the itch—
> the new Hiroshima,
> head shiny with hair oil,
> barefaced in its resurgence;
> already visible all over the place,
> in growing numbers, billboards in English;
> one of these: "Historic A-Bomb Site."
>
> Enclosed by a painted fence
> on a corner of the bank steps,
> stained onto the grain of the dark red stone:
> a quiet pattern.
>
> That morning
> a flash tens of thousands of degrees hot
> burned it all of a sudden onto the thick slab of granite:
> someone's trunk.
>
> Burned onto the step, cracked and watery red,
> the mark of the blood that flowed as intestines melted to mush:
> a shadow.
>
> Ah! If you are from Hiroshima
> and on that morning,
> amid indescribable flash and heat and smoke,
> were buffeted in the whirlpool of the glare of the
> flames, the shadow of the cloud,
> crawled about dragging skin that was peeling off,
> so transformed that even your wife and children
> would not have known you,
> this shadow
> is etched in tragic memory
> and will never fade.
>
> Right beside the street where people of the city come and go,
> well-meaning but utterly different,
> assaulted by the sun, attacked by the rain, covered over by dust,
> growing fainter by the year: this shadow.

The bank with the "Historic Site" sign at the foot of its steps
dumped out into the street pieces of stone and glass, burned gritty,
completed a major reconstruction,
and set the whole enormous building sparkling in the evening sun.
In the vacant lot diagonally across,
drawing a crowd: a quack in the garb of a mountain ascetic.

Indifferent, the authorities say: "If we don't protect it with glass or
  something,
it will fade away," but do nothing.
Today, too,
foreign sailors amble up in their white leggings,
come to a stop with a click of their heels,
and, each having taken a snapshot, go off;
the shoeshine boy who followed them here
peers over the fence, wonders why all the fuss,
and goes on his way.

The description here of the "shadow" created on the stones of the Sumitomo Bank building is itself a figure for the imprint of the bombing on Hiroshima and its subsequent literature, too: something real, but something only marginally present, a sign with a referent lost except in the memories of those who were there on the sixth of August and which "will fade away," like the shadow itself, in time. The plaintive lyricism of this poem—one especially devoid of explicit politics—seems to warn us of the fragile nature of poetry itself.

In one sense, it may have been to protect poetry from its own fragility, its ambivalent worth in post-Hiroshima times, that Tōge strove so overtly in his other verse to underscore the political and historical stakes of those same times. That Tōge now looms so uncontroversially as Lifton's "popular hero" may itself attest to the difficulty we have in judging Tōge "purely" as an individual, moderately gifted, poet. But I would choose here, certainly in Tōge's instance, not to set up any necessary tension or even contradiction between the practice of poetry and the practice of politics, and instead argue a more subtle, if unfamiliar, line. When Lifton suggests that Tōge's opus "could be viewed as a Hiroshima version of the lyrical-revolutionary tradition of Mayakovsky and Yevtushenko," that is not a tradition in either Japan's, or Lifton's own, national culture.[61] This is not to say, however, that a specific rationale for Tōge Sankichi's solution to the problem of reconciling modern aesthetics with modern crises needs to be based on unique or even rare circumstances. Some would argue, as has James Scully, that in fact "political poetry is not a contradiction in terms but an instructive redundancy."[62] With special relevance for Japanese criticism, Scully insists: "Assertions that poetry and politics don't mix are not disinterested statements but political interventions in their own right. They presume not only that 'poetry' and 'politics' are autonomous categories, but also that there is such a thing as disinterested observation."[63]

Scully's position is an absolute one. Just as all poetry is a social practice, so is it all and always political because one never speaks from anywhere but a position within history and within social structures. One may counter that the utility of the term "political" is diminished once its application is rendered so broad: certainly some of what Scully describes in poetry could alternatively be called the "ethical" or even "moral" stance of the poet. But it certainly seems valid to ask poets to remain aware of the political implications that may, intentionally or otherwise, follow from their work. Those implications can be so subtle as to seem quite nearly invisible, but the poets of Hiroshima and Nagasaki, Tōge foremost among them, have long agonized over their very implacability. If Scully's provocative claim that "writing is a struggle against stylistics" would be taken as a commonplace among atomic-bomb writers, then his charge that "writers have also to question whether their techniques have become extensions of the problems they would resolve" is precisely the bind that both stymies and stimulates those writers when they are hibakusha.[64] And it is a bind that reiterates that of the poet who would also be a social activist; who would both describe what he sees and change it, too.

One of Tōge's best poems, "Dawn" (Asa), derives its power from the uncomfortable contrast of his description of the bombing's horrors with his programmatic atomic utopianism. The survivors of Hiroshima, writes Tōge,

> dream
> of a dawn
> when the pigs in human skin
> who use the power of the earth's veins erupting,
>   of earth's crust quaking, only for butchery,
> will not be found except in fairy tales;
> when the energy ten times more powerful than gunpowder,
>   1 gram the equal of 10,000,000,
> will be released from inside the atom and strengthen
>   the arms of the people (344)

The promise of a better life for the toiling masses, versus the historical reality of "butchery," suggests a parallel with the premises of Tōge's Marxist beliefs versus the demands of Japanese poetry. Tōge died with neither set of conflicts resolved or even fully recognized. Nor could they have been, certainly not without the cost of what distinguishes Tōge as both a poet and a combative survivor. The Byronesque reputation that still attends him can strike us today as sentimental, anachronistic or even regressive in that such a reputation has to celebrate Tōge's fate in order to lionize him. But his words that that reputation is responsible for having etched into stone are nonetheless words that have doubtlessly named that humbling sense of irretrievable loss felt by the millions who have visited, and will continue to visit, Hiroshima and see the monument to both the loss and the achievement told by his few poems.

■

Shōda Shinoe is not, like Hara or Tōge, a well-known poet. Her reputation, as well as the number of her published works, is small. When her name is mentioned, it is with no little irony that she is often mistaken for a relative of reigning Empress Michiko, who shares the same family name with Shōda and nothing else. But her lack of fame points to her very representiveness as a hibakusha: the relative anonymity of both her career and her poems makes her a far more "typical" survivor-writer than any of her more renowned fellow poets. Kurihara Sadako, one of Shōda's more enthusiastic admirers, implicitly praises Shōda poetry when she describes her as having "led the classic life of a Hiroshima bomb victim."[65] That is a life, unfortunately, whose details are even more gruesome and depressing than those of either Hara Tamiki or Tōge Sankichi.

Shōda's life began in circumstances far different from those in which it ended. Born in 1910 in the town of Etajima in Hiroshima Prefecture, she was the eldest daughter of a well-to-do family that had once manufactured flour mills but which, after the Second World War and specifically because of the bombing, would be not only decimated financially but largely killed off. When she was ten the family moved to Ujina, on the outskirts of Hiroshima city, and in 1925 she entered a girls' high school run by the predominant Buddhist church in the region (indeed, in Japan at that time), Jōdo Shinshū, or the "True Pure Land" sect. One of the older forms of Japanese Buddhism—it dates back to the pessimistic era of the twelfth and thirteenth centuries, when years of both political and natural disasters seemed to portend the imminent end of the world. Jōdo Shinshū might be compared with Protestantism in its emphasis of fervent individual faith over scholasticism, as well as in its long-standing appeal among the traditionally dispossessed communities of peasants, fishermen, and especially outcast (*hinin*) groups, of whose numbers are many in the Hiroshima area.

Whether it was the influence of her schooling or her home life, Buddhism would be a major influence on Shōda's life and especially her poetry, which she began writing in earnest after graduating from high school in 1929. She would always be, in contrast with professional poets such as Hara and Tōge, a waka poet. From her first efforts published in the late 1920s in *Kōran* (Fragrant Orchid), a monthly journal founded by Sugiura Suiko—a noted disciple of the major modern poet Kitahara Hakushū—to her mature work published in Suiko's subsequent journal *Tanka shijōshugi* (Waka Aestheticism), her poems evidence a clearly spiritual, specifically Buddhist, cast that would distinguish her atomic-bomb writings as markedly different from those of her more famous colleagues who wrote under the influence of, for instance, Western stylistics and ideologies.

The early security of Shōda's life began to dissipate when her husband, engineer and family friend Takamoto Suematsu, died in 1940 and left her as a single parent charged with responsibility for raising their son Shin'ichirō. Eventually Shin'ichirō, along with Shōda's father and Shōda herself, would die of bomb-related causes, but for the duration of the war years Shōda struggled with the rest of her family to survive. In January 1945 the Shōda home in Ujina was demolished, forcing them to move to Hirano-chō, a neighborhood along the Kyōbashi river in the city of Hiroshima proper. Hirano-chō was only two kilometers from ground zero.

After the August 6th bombing and the death of her father the following February from intestinal cancer, but before Shin'ichirō fell ill with radiation sickness, Shōda was briefly married for a second time. This husband, however, was soon unfaithful to her. The loss of anyone she could have relied upon for financial help forced her to go into business for herself. First she ran a very modest inn, and then, after the city ordered her inn torn down as part of the rebuilding plans, an even more humble boarding house for students.

These tragedies and events, described in detail in her 1962 memoir *A Ringing in the Ears: The Notes of an Atomic-bomb Poet* (Miminari—gembaku kajin no shuki), were a wrenching emotional and physical strain on Shōda, and especially so once she had to provide continual care for her ailing son. Still, she found time to pursue her amateur interest in waka. As early as January 1946, Shōda took some of her poems to a former mentor, Yamazumi Mamoru, who was also editor of the Hiroshima poetry journal *Banshō* (Evening Bell). When she asked him if he would write a introduction to her poems, which she hoped to publish, Yamazumi indignantly declined on two grounds. One, he was surprised that someone as new to poetry as Shōda would presume to publish; and two, he held that the theme of her work—the atomic bombing—was quite inappropriate.[66] This would not be the last time that Shōda would encounter such a blanket dismissal of what history, despite the dictates of traditional aesthetics, had rendered her single subject.[67]

Shōda persisted in searching for a venue in which to publish, however, and in August 1946 she did place thirty-nine of her poems under the group title "Oh! The Atomic Bomb" (Ā! Genshi bakudan) in a special issue of the briefly lived journal *Fushichō* (Phoenix). These are five of Shōda's first atomic-bomb waka:

> Flash-boom!
> In the space of an instant

That silence
When it becomes the bloody carnage of Asura
That silence.

Carried on someone's back
To the emergency first-aid facility
I look before me
Beside a corpse, crying "water, water"
The last hours of a child.

Like the temple's Guardian Deva Kings
Swollen big and scorched black
Naked corpses
Piled atop each other.

Sticking out of the smoldering earth
The bag of the school teacher
Spills the grade sheets
of the pupils.

Bones interred
In a fire-damaged lunch box
Only this
Has any reality.[68]

Like many poems by hibakusha, amateur and professional alike, these
waka make what is almost standard reference to the sensory impact of the
bomb, the silence that followed, the cries of burn victims for water, the separa-
tion of children from their teachers, and the makeshift disposal of corpses. The
poems are direct, descriptive, and often narrative: aside from the mention of
the Deva Kings, they lack any metaphors or similes. Consequently, they additionally lack the typical markers of a Japanese aesthetic sensibility. Highly
praised upon their publication by Suiko, he claimed them poems "heretofore
unprecedented in the history of Japanese poetry"[69] and thus celebrated what
Yamazumi had earlier denigrated, namely their inadmissible and nonliterary
(by the strictures of conventional criticism) theme. Suiko recognized that the
departure from traditional poetic practice that Shōda's atomic-bomb waka represents was, as in the work of other Hiroshima and Nagasaki poets, an attempt
still to accommodate violence within the aesthetics of Japanese lyricism. Like
much atomic-bomb verse, they deploy instead the metonymical authority of
the pathetic anecdote—the dying child, the scattered grade sheets—to generate an appreciation of the fundamental loss that permeates the memory of Hiroshima and Nagasaki.

This overwhelming experience of loss is specifically framed in Shōda's poetry, however, by her unusual and sustained range of motifs and language

adopted from her popular Buddhist beliefs. "The bloody carnage of Asura [*shura*]" of the first waka, for example, is at once a not-uncommon expression for particularly violent bloodshed and an explicit reference to the Brahmanist, Hinduist, and eventually Buddhist figure of a fierce devil who delights in battling the gods.[70] "Guardian Deva Kings" (*niō*) refers to the giant wooden statues that stand by the entrance gate to many Buddhist temples in Japan, but whose contorted facial expressions are cited here to convey the horror of death rather that the ferociousness of their spirits. Finally, the interment of bones in the final waka is not so importantly a religious reference as is its declaration on what has "reality" (*genjitsu*), the nature of which is one of the most important questions posed in Buddhist metaphysics. Such language not only synchronizes this poetry in a long-standing religious and cultural tradition—much like European camp survivors' common allusion to the Book of Job—but it adds measurable weight and depth to the theme of the bomb's horror, collating it with general Buddhist cosmological and eschatological beliefs.

These poems were, however, only a prelude to the collection of her poetry that constitutes, in an apparently unanimous opinion among critics, her best work. In the fall of 1948, now suffering from increased symptoms of radiation disease herself, Shōda added another sixty-one waka to her previous thirty-nine for a perfect one hundred. She took these now not to Yamazumi, but to the more sympathetic Suiko and asked him not only to write a preface but to assist in locating a publisher. Suiko enthusiastically agreed.

What resulted was *Repentance* (Sange), a collection issued privately—secretly, in fact—from the print shop of a prison whose warden had been interested in literature in his youth. The costs of printing *Repentance* were borne by Shōda's seriously ill father, but only one hundred, perhaps one hundred and fifty, copies were made. Although the date on the edition states it was printed in December 1948, it was in fact done in October. Dates were falsified in order to deceive Occupation officials who might have decided to arrest Shōda—and according to the rumors of the day, put her to death—for violating Press Code provisions. In her memoir *A Ringing in the Ears* Shōda says that she was aware of the risk she was taking, but decided to go ahead with the project anyway.[71] The drama of *Repentance*'s publication is now part of the work's daring celebrity. Ōe Kenzaburō claims that its Hiroshima audience read the collection in secret, away from the eyes of an occupying army that would have presumably confiscated it.[72] As Shōda's biographer Mizuta Kuwajirō has said, "*Repentance* has long been known as the 'phantom' poetry collection, and Shōda herself has consequently become a 'legendary' figure."[73]

The Japanese title of the collection is often, understandably if inaccurately, taken as a Buddhist phrase meaning "flower petals scattered before the Buddha," and thus metaphorically, "a heroic death." But though Shōda may

very well have intended her title to carry such connotations, *sange* is in fact
another Buddhist term that occurs in the last of *Repentance*'s poems:

> We people
> Who never bear arms
> Shall live in deep faith
> With great repentance. (214)

"Repentance," like yet another Buddhist word in this poem, "deep faith" (*jin
shin*), attests to Shōda's conspicuously religious approach to her atomic-bomb
experience. She once explained her choice of title, and consequently why repentance is such an important emotion and process within her poetry:

> I believed that no catastrophe of war since the beginning of the universe
> was crueler than that of the atomic bomb. I also believed that in consid-
> ering why I had had to undergo such a horrible experience, what had to
> be blamed was not just others but in fact myself, as well. I have had no
> choice but to examine myself, my odd survival and my subsequent ill-
> nesses, and repent [*sange*]. That is why I came to entitle my collection as
> I did.[74]

This notion of guilt is expressed throughout *Repentance*, not in political
terms as a complicit citizen of a militarist state that might have brought on the
use of American nuclear weapons, or psychological terms as a traumatized victim seeking some accommodation with the source of that trauma, but in religious ones—namely the concept of the individual soul as invariably implicated
in the sin, punishment, and hope of the profane world:

> Thinking, mistakenly, his end near
> The old mother
> Whispers into the ear of the man
> "Take care in your next life."
>
> "We'll be busy
> When we're reborn into the Pure Land"
> Looking up
> Towards the heavens.
>
> Going into death with the words
> "The redemption of rebirth"
> The smile fades
> From the lips.
>
> The man who told us
> "We'll be busy in the next world"

> Has been born, I wonder,
> Into what new life.
>
> Encourage people
> To serve their fellow man
> And venerate, and pay alms:
> This is to what I dedicate my remaining life.
>
> I will live
> With deep faith, and repent
> As a citizen of a nation
> That will never bear arms. (213–14)

Such Buddhist concepts as "rebirth" (*gensō*), "redemption" (*saido*), "alms" (*fuse*), "veneration" (*aikyō*), the "Pure Land" (*ojōdo*), "care in the next life" (*goshō no daiji*), "deep faith" (*jinshin*), and "repent" (*sange*) are all precise and even technical terms. They invoke the Buddhist faith informing much of Shōda's poetry to provide a both a meaning for the suffering—life as essentially suffering—and a promised way out of it: the next life, and finally one day entry into the paradisiacal "Pure Land" to which the name of her religion refers.

It has been noted repeatedly by scholars and critics of Holocaust literature that the two-thousand year history of Jewish civilization's struggle to survive has produced both anti-apocalyptic and lamentative traditions upon which modern writers could rely as a cultural inheritance.[75] While the history of the Japanese may not similarly yield a record of genocide, both attempted and realized, that circumstance could make Japan's own literature of catastrophe "meaningful" in just the same way. Popular Buddhism's approach to human existence as essentially an ordeal to be endured until, one day, a final release is an approach that translates in Shōda's poetry into an affirmation both of the atomic bomb's earthly evil and of the promise of deliverance once the soul is freed from its material, bodily fetters. At work in Shōda's poetry is a ritual process that is at once both anti-humanistic, on the one hand, and therapeutic and spiritual, on the other. *Repentance* addresses itself not so much to us living readers but to the dead or to those on death's threshold. This oratory is perhaps not entirely rhetorical. Ōe Kenzaburō has observed that many Hiroshima hibakusha seized upon the Dantesque descriptions of hell found in the first chapters of a tenth-century primer in popular Buddhist doctrine still read today, the *Ōjōyōshū* (A Guide to Rebirth), where presumably they discerned cogent analogies for their twentieth-century experiences.[76]

Shōda's poetry is popular in the same sense not only because of her semi-professional status as a poet but also because of how thoroughly inculcated it is in the amalgam of nativist as well as Buddhist beliefs of her religious milieu. Like Tōge's poem carved in the monument in Hiroshima's Peace Park, there is a poem taken from *Repentance* that stands inscribed on a public monument—

albeit a difficult one to find—in the same city. This is a monument dedicated to the memory of the bombed faculty and young students of a school in central Hiroshima; and the poem is considered, perhaps as a consequence, Shōda's best-known work:

> The large bones
> Might be the teacher's
> Nearby are gathered
> The smaller skulls. (208)

No poem could better demonstrate the difference between Hara's experimental lyricism, Tōge's political rage, and Shōda's elegiac but purposeful pain. What is at work in this poem is a direct address to the souls once bound to these bones, those of the teacher and his or her young students. Robert Jay Lifton, in his discussion of atomic-bomb poetry, linked the frequent memorialization of the dead with the concept and practice of *chinkon*, or the "consolation of souls." This is a native Japanese ritual, also known by the Japanese expression *tama-shizume*. According to Lifton,

> [Chinkon] predates Buddhist influence, and originally referred to the ceremony for enabling the soul of a person hovering between life and death to achieve repose—either through urging it not to leave the body, or to return to the body if it had already left. As with the custom of offering water to the dying (which was sometimes part of *chinkon*), the significance was that of maintaining life, either in actuality or in symbolic continuity. . . . *Chinkon* suggests a gentle atmosphere of respect and love, and above all *a combination of continued connection with the dead and peaceful separation from them.*[77]

Unfortunately, an interpretation of Shōda's work as a kind of magic that seeks through what, after Freud, we call the "work of mourning" to restore a placable order to both the living and the dead was to be confirmed by subsequent events in Shōda's own life. After *Repentance* her work as a poet underwent a long hiatus until the early 1960s, when she published her memoir *A Ringing in the Ears.* But the story of her struggle to write, support her family, and stay healthy was cruelly undermined when in 1963, a year after publishing *A Ringing in the Ears,* she was diagnosed with a plethora of illnesses indeed reminiscent of Job. She developed breast cancer, both her red and while blood counts plummeted, her spleen became chronically swollen, and rashes broke out all over her skin; moreover, she developed ringing in her ears, headaches, lethargy, loss of appetite, night sweats, bad temper, bleeding gums, anemia, numbness in her limbs, and deteriorating vision. Finally, on June 15, 1965, Shōda Shinoe died.[78]

The final indignity heaped upon the body of Shōda Shinoe, like that of so many hibakusha, was the dissection of her cancer-riddled body at the Atomic

Bomb Casualty Commission (ABCC) research facility, the same facility scorned in her poetry. But while she had been the sickest she had taken on one new writing project. On a visit to Tokyo in October 1963 for medical treatment, Shōda visited the nearby burial site of Tokugawa Ieyasu, the shōgun who ruled Japan from 1603 to 1616. There she learnt that Ieyasu, at the end of his own life, had reportedly copied a devotional Buddhist phrase that invoked the name of the redeeming Amithaba Buddha—like Shōda, Ieyasu had been an adherent of the Pure Land sect—thirty thousand times. Inspired by Ieyasu's legendary demonstration of faith, Shōda resolved to undertake the same project and donate the resulting document to the Hiroshima Peace Museum in memory of the bombings' dead.

She began her labors on October 25 of that year and worked steadily each day. By November 18, she had reached the ten-thousandth phrase, filling some seventeen meters of paper. By December 5, she was two-thirds of the way to her goal. Finally, on January 6 in the year she would die, she completed all thirty thousand of her devotions.

The significance of this work is not, like that of her poetry, its originality or talent. It is the collusion of writing and of faith, the proof it provides that by inscribing these holy words—"I invoke the name of Lord Amithaba Buddha"—she was again consoling and perhaps even saving souls. "I invoke the name of Lord Amithaba Buddha" indicates a jointly poetic and spiritual practice, if you will, far more primitive than either Hara's Modernism or Tōge's Marxism: but as a result potentially more powerful, too. This is chinkon on a scale that Ieyasu need not have imagined—the scale of twentieth-century warfare being so much larger than in the sixteenth century—but it is a ritual that draws on similar sources of spiritual strength. It does indeed seem that such strength was finally of much greater consolation to Shōda than was art to Hara, politics to Tōge, and perhaps even poetry to Shōda. Shōda Shinoe, if discussed in histories of atomic-bomb literature at all, is described as a "housewife." But she was also a poet through whom a good deal of the confidence, compassion, and even comprehension of the more "average," nonprofessional Hiroshima writer made itself so powerfully evident.

Only ninety-nine of the one hundred poems of *Repentance* are found on its pages: the one-hundredth is printed on the inside of the cover:

> Death presses close
> A tribute to the souls
> of my brothers and sisters:
> A diary of grief. (205)

Death is objective: it was a fact of Shōda's own life, and the lives of her family and indeed the lives of everyone in the city in which she dwelled. The diary is personal: her own private record of what "death" and "life" meant. But the souls are neither objective nor personal: the "souls" is the word that escapes the miserable cycle of the living and dying that, for Shōda, was finally the spiritual ground upon which her literature was consecrated.

What is important to note here in comparison to both Hara's and Tōge's poetry is the radical anti-humanist thrust of Shōda's poetry, and anti-humanist precisely because of its attention to the spiritual, specifically Buddhist, invocation of another category and order of being. Kurihara Sadako, who perceived the quite opposite implications of Shōda's verse from her own politically engaged poetry, wondered whether only an "indirect" hibakusha such as herself could continue to celebrate the "human" (*ningensei*) over the "inhuman" (*hiningensei*).[79] Yet Hara and Tōge, like Shōda "direct" hibakusha, never amid their ethical or political indignation wrote lines as angry as these in Shōda's poem bleakly entitled "Let Everyone Die" (Minna shineba ii n da): "Human beings all throughout the world / Let them be burnt black and die" (257).

It is an irony of Shōda's religion that the fate she bitterly dictated for all of us is just the fate which, as a Buddhist funeral, would also release from our worldly ties and bear the faithful among us to the Pure Land. The simple faith Shōda so deeply professed proved no more capable of resolving the impossible contradictions of literature after Hiroshima and Nagasaki than did Hara's lyricism or Tōge's ideology.

Tsukasa Osamu, *Remains* (Nokosareta katachi, 1989)

The right vantage point from which to view a
holocaust is that of a corpse, but from that vantage
point, of course, there is nothing to report.

Jonathan Schell, *The Fate of the Earth*

We, the survivors, are not the true witnesses.

Primo Levi, *The Drowned and the Saved*

6

Ōta Yōko and the Place
of the Narrator

In Ōta Yōko's novel *Half-Human* (Han-ningen, 1954), the heroine, named
Oda Atsuko, is like author Ōta herself a famous atomic-bomb writer suffering
from severe depression. She enters the hospital in an attempt to cure an addic-
tion to tranquilizers whose intemperate use derives from very real, but to the
medical profession opaque, neuroses ultimately due to the trauma of Hiroshima. No treatment proves totally effective. Medicine can only hope to
counter illness, not history, and Oda's deepest torments remain chronic. She
continues to be plagued by a frustration linked in the novel's fifth chapter with
the three choices she has faced in the seven years since the end of the Second
World War: suicide, flight, or the writing of a "good work of literature."
Throughout the novel Atsuko dismisses suicide as not in her nature; Ōta, in
her essay "The Psychology of Survival" (Ikinokori no shinri, 1952), concludes
that no Japanese writer can abandon Japan, and her heroine here concurs. Of
Oda's three alternatives all that would seem left is the writing of a good work,

but that too seems elusive. What would constitute "good" is unclear. Just how she might recognize one ("ii sakuhin to wa nanimono ka") is a literary problem inextricably bound with Atsuko's physical and psychological problems, and all have arisen from her presence at Hiroshima's destruction.

Oda's dilemma paralleled Ōta's own. Ōta was the only Hiroshima hiba-kusha already a prominent novelist, with nine volumes of published work by the time of the attack. Her writings, so dramatically bifurcated, offer the possi-bility of assessing the impact of atomic war on a writer's genres, themes, and even confidence in language. What first strikes us is how charged her postwar fiction is with a testimonial urgency less evident in that of her nonvictim peers. Similarly, it seems complicated with an assortment of personal and public tasks seldom associated with the duties of novelists. Sata Ineko, a friend and fellow author of atomic-bomb fiction, has noted how Hiroshima presented Ōta with an irreconcilable contradiction. On the one hand she wanted to address the atomic bomb by pursuing its worst consequences, while on the other she equally sought to overcome it, exhaust it, by turning it into a "good work."[1] In Sata's view Ōta was to remain obsessed with Hiroshima even as she attempted to reduce it to literary representation, a "theme" given expression—and thus disposed of—within a figural closure. Such cross-purposes frustrate as well as animate Ōta's Hiroshima works. She herself noted that while she found it hate-ful to write the word *gembaku* 'atomic bomb,' neither could she refrain from its writing.[2] Her projected "good work" was required both to resist the residual force of the bombing with its own aesthetic power and, at the same time, tran-scend the bombing as if such force no longer mattered. This battle between engaging Hiroshima and suppressing it led Ōta to write, within a relatively short span of years, a wide variety of atomic-bomb works. That variety sug-gests Ōta was searching for that one "good" work by variously manipulating in her atomic-bomb books the relations between experience and imagination, and fact and fiction. Most of all, however, Ōta reworks the relations between herself as an author, herself as a character, and the rest of us as her readers. The inconclusiveness of those experiments would keep the act of writing, as Ōta frequently complained, "a bitter struggle" that never quite yielded the desired, perhaps impossible, results.

■

Before the nuclear destruction of Hiroshima, Ōta's work was less encumbered, though it, like her life, was apparently never free of complications.[3] Born Ōta Hatsuko in central Hiroshima in 1903, her career began in the 1920s when, during a tumultuous relationship with a journalist, she published short, and unnoticed, stories in local newspapers and coterie journals. By the end of the decade, and through her association with the short-lived but important Tokyo feminist magazine *Nyonin geijutsu* (Women and Art), she had achieved a national, if minor, reputation. Real recognition came to Ōta when she decided to turn the difficult years of her life with the journalist into a full-length novel. *Drifting Shores* (1939) was, in a major departure for Ōta at that time, explicitly autobiographical and confessional. No longer much read, it is an awkward mix of diary-like narration dressed with bits of fictionalized melodramatic conversation. As would be true of her atomic-bomb writing, *Drifting Shores* is a tragic personal account thinly disguised as a novel. "Almost two-thirds," Ōta remarks in her epilogue, "is about love" (254), but the work is anything but a romance. As the story of abuse suffered within the private confines of a sexual relationship, *Drifting Shores* is, according to Ōta's biographer Esashi Akiko, a model narrative of victimization that in Esashi's view anticipates her subsequent work on the victimization of hibakusha.[4]

Hindsight makes such inferences, whether meaningful or not, inevitable. Today no one thinks of Ōta Yōko as any sort of a writer other than one of the catastrophic bombing of her native city. The acclaim and resulting patronage that *Drifting Shores* and subsequent works brought her did nothing to insulate Ōta from the degradation she was to suffer in the last year of the war. As publishing houses burned along with everything else, and paper shortages brought a halt to periodicals, Ōta's livelihood disappeared. In mid-1944 her mother Tomi, who had been living with her in Tokyo, was evacuated to Hiroshima, and Yōko herself moved to an apartment in the suburbs to escape the worst of the U.S. air attacks. By the following January, however, she had grown so frightened of remaining anywhere near Tokyo that she joined her mother at her step-sister Kazue's home in central Hiroshima. Living alone in Tokyo had set her nerves on edge, and Ōta sought respite in the city of her birth, a place, she writes in one of her postwar novels, it was thought would be spared aerial bombing because the Americans meant to save it for a resort once they occupied the country. Unfortunately Kazue's home was in a neighborhood less than two kilometers from ground zero. On the morning of August 6th, Ōta and her family had their bags packed to relocate further into the countryside, but the attack came too early in the day for them to have been spared.

Ōta survived the initial explosion with only slight injuries. With her mother and sister, she luckily escaped the subsequent fire storms, and within a few days had found refuge in Kujima, a town west of Hiroshima. By the end of the month she published, in the *Asahi shimbun*, the first essay by a professional writer on the topic of the bombings. This brief piece, "A Light As If From the Depths—The Atomic-bomb Air Attack" (Kaitei no yō na hikari—genshi bakudan no kūshū ni atte), argues, as if to convince herself as well as her readers, that the calamity of Hiroshima had inspired its citizenry to heroism and greater patriotism. "From the moment Hiroshima was burnt into nothingness, I was a supporter of the war" (14). Perhaps this represented the last of her lingering enthusiasm for a war now, in fact, over; perhaps it was the delusion of a person still traumatized by unprecedented events. Ōta would eventually argue the contrary, that the bombing of Hiroshima was incapable of inspiring anything but shock. Descriptive phrases found in this essay such as "the beauty of the victims " would be supplanted in later work with such characterizations as "they were not so much human beings that had lost their lives as they were simply wretched inanimate objects."[5] This early essay already demonstrates how difficult Ōta found it to represent Hiroshima without recourse to familiar concepts that would later have to be discarded as inadequate. Dignity was one such concept; humanity, another. In 1945 she believed it feasible to declare "a weapon cannot raze the human spirit," but six years later a character in one of her novels would alternatively conclude that nuclear weapons might "finally and utterly destroy the human spirit."[6]

Ōta's ambivalence over which of our values, beliefs, and ideas might survive into the post-Hiroshima age extended even to language. Words are predicated, it is typically thought, on a consensus over their referents, and a doubtful Ōta repeatedly grappled with the problem of the uniqueness of the experiences she hoped to communicate to her nonvictim readers. She insisted the bombing of Hiroshima marked a break with the past so total that tools formerly available the writer now failed to function. Looking back on her various attempts to make her postwar novels conform to a world that, from her perspective, was utterly changed, Ōta noted with exasperation: "I feel ashamed whenever I plan a work making use of traditional Japanese literary techniques. I feel so ashamed that I shudder. I live in a nation that has experienced the unprecedented; I am unable to cling to the ordinary sorts of literature that we had before."[7]

It was not because her literary techniques were "traditional" or "Japanese," and thus somehow inferior to newer or imported ones, that Ōta despairs. What she is pleading for are "techniques" that will do more than play with words; she wants the means to address and even repair the diverse damage wrought by a weapon of heretofore unimagined power. In the preface added to her first atomic-bomb novel, Ōta states that the "unearthly spectacle" of the bomb is "impossible to describe, difficult to convey" for any writer holding "a conventional view of words."[8] How wrong those people are, regrets Ōta, who assume "that turning the atomic bomb into literature is no great deal, that it's like a natural disaster which happened to befall Hiroshima and Nagasaki, far from our own lives."[9] Ōta's is not so much a position taken on linguistic or literary theory as it is a militant declaration on her ethical right as a victim to retain, as a minimum consolation, her experience of degradation against that act of degradation itself. Other early atomic-bomb writers embraced similar skeptical views on language inspired by similar assertions of historical privilege. A mayor of Hiroshima spoke collectively for all the hibakusha of his city, and on behalf of their right to resist our efforts to understand (and thus supersede) them, when he called the bombing "an inhuman act that surpasses human imagination and powers of expression."[10]

In Ōta's work the articulation of that same right is phrased in terms of the diminished powers of the writer, or rather, the expanded notion of the real. She despairs, for example, of the language to describe a young girl whose breasts have been ripped off.[11] But in fact we do not need the "new language" Ōta calls for to do so. The old one suffices. That is not to say, however, that we will ever have, as Ōta did, the experience of seeing such a scene and thus knowing it can happen. The real problem is not the relationship of the writer divorced from the means of delineating a new reality to that elusive means, but rather that of a writer fully initiated in that reality to a readership which cannot or, in consideration of the consequences which might ensue, should not be. What Ōta asks is how does she, as victim, preserve that moral difference in entitlement to the experience even as she seeks in her writings to share it with us? Her essay "The Stance of the Writer" (Sakka no taido, 1952) comes close to restating this issue of "language" as such when she wonders how a literature of atrocity can be both realistic and humanly readable (323). "Realistic" means true to her experience of atrocity, and "humanly readable" means still comprehendible to us. What has changed, then, is not so much the frame of reference in which our language and our literature can function, but our assurance as to whom has rights to a language and literature suddenly responsible for isolating some forms of knowledge as well as propagating them.

The problem of whether words for describing atrocity exist is thus inextricably joined with the issue of *whom* should narrate it. When George Steiner said that "the world of Auschwitz lies outside speech as it lies outside reason" (a remark suggestive of critic Kurihara Sadako's frequent characterization of Hiroshima as "absurd" [*fujōri*]), he used "reason" not in any sense of "logic" or "science," but rather in its sense of "moral acceptability."[12] The crisis of the postwar writer made skeptical of the "good work" begins with the problem of how to represent a moral order in which individual human lives must somehow matter—such a moral order implicit in much modern fiction—against a backdrop of mass indiscriminate violence that seems to mock such assumptions. That same crisis soon includes, however, our locating ourselves, both authors and audience, somewhere within that moral order. Who, in other words, judges whom?

Ōta claimed that her search for a new language was for one predicated on new assumptions, one that would impress Hiroshima's import onto us with its force of words. Yet at the same time it paradoxically seems a search for a language that would bar us, the nonvictims, from fully understanding that language. Or rather, from *speaking* it: Ōta requires a language whose novelty establishes in our minds as well as hers a form of "one-way communication." She

requires our appreciation of what happened to her but would bar our reiteration, or worse, opinion of it. When Ōta called for "new methods of description
and expression" that would communicate "a reality that cannot be told without
first creating an original language suited to it," she revealed a kind of thinking
perhaps purposefully circular.[13] A unique story, if told in a corresponding
unique language, would remain unavailable to those of us outside it: but that
might very well be the only solace left a survivor otherwise bereft of meaningful possessions. Her call for a new language is, in fact, effectively the same as
Elie Wiesel's famous plea for an "accumulation of silence" about the Holocaust.
A new language, then, or perhaps none at all: either way the victim remains
the sole proprietor of a historical moment which, even in its terror, represents
in itself a new kind of historical knowledge that commands a compensatorily
powerful view of modernity.

Ironically, Ōta became the most prolific of atomic-bomb writers, just as
Wiesel has been of the Holocaust. Moreover, despite these early insistences
on new and enlarged languages, there is nothing radically innovative about
any of Ōta's Hiroshima writing. It consists of readily recognizable first-person
accounts, documentary novels, and autobiographical fiction. All its words are
found in the dictionary. What distinguishes her postwar work formally is its
struggle to situate Ōta, her narrator-characters, and her audience in a configuration that satisfactorily represents a valorized hierarchy of the historical experience of Hiroshima, a configuration that would somehow keep the experience
her own while sharing some degree of awareness and even responsibility for it
with others. Her first three atomic-bomb novels, *City of Corpses, Human Rags*
(Ningen ranru, 1951), and *Half-Human*, constitute not only her principal efforts
in juggling both her and her readers' identification with the material presented—and thus her efforts in establishing moral prerogatives to that material—but, along the way, the most sustained effort by any one writer to document a nuclear holocaust and its aftermath.

In each of these novels is found Ōta's conviction that Hiroshima divides
human history into a past now lost us and a restricted, reduced present. In
Human Rags she terms the world after Hiroshima one in which none of us can
ever again live "completely" (kanzen ni wa) due to the needless "half-human,
inhuman" suffering there (207). Whatever "completely" means, its preclusion
marks a loss of some part of our humanity in proportion to the inhumanity
demonstrated by the use of nuclear weapons: it means that none of us lives
enjoying our full potential. This is a conviction that must change the way its
holder can view fiction. A diminished faith in the human potential for life is
also a diminished belief in the potential of literature. Ōta's belief in the moral
efficacy of literature comes into conflict with her insistence on the moral bank-
ruptcy of her age. Is she to proceed as if "good" writing can exist apart from
the "bad" it chronicles, or is she to abandon such ideas as hopelessly naive?

Her heroine Oda Atsuko has no idea what a good work would be; but Ōta herself, when asked rhetorically in *City of Corpses* if she could ever write of the human carnage still smoldering before her eyes, instantly replies that she must. It is "the responsibility of the writer" who has witnessed such things (73). This passage is often cited as an example of Ōta's early resolve as an atomic-bomb novelist. It also marks, however, the source of her quandary. It is a responsibility that is successfully carried out only with the continued belief in the moral force of such testimony, and what she testifies to has made her suspicious of such beliefs. One of her characters in *Human Rags* pointedly observes that "the atomic bomb illustrated the moral collapse [*seikaku hasan*] of the entire world" (258). If Ōta believes this as well, to whom is her work as a writer addressed? To us readers, who must have been spared that collapse if Ōta's work is to make effective appeal?

Ōta was aware of the contradictions lurking within her writings, just as she was aware of the conflicting demands made by the theme of mass violence on modern literature in general. In the essay "The Terror of Literature" (Bungaku no osoroshisa, 1956), Ōta complained that while she remains pledged in her work to the "factuality" (*jijitsusei*) of the bomb, she is convinced of, and thus pursues in that same work, "literature's unique essence," which is to say its absolute value in an otherwise worthless landscape. "This is precisely my contradiction. And it is this terror of literature that strikes at my very core" (323). Ōta wrote in the preface to *City of Corpses* that whenever she thinks of how it would be inconceivable for the tragedy of Hiroshima to be without lasting significance, she finds herself unable to grant any credence to a concept of fiction dependent upon possibly capricious invention. Yet in the novel itself, she declares that she cannot begin to tell of Hiroshima unless her account is going to be something more than a compendium of damage reports gathered from the newspapers. The prerogative of exercising her writer's imagination comes into conflict with what Wallace Stevens called "the pressure of reality": the force of modern history that risks turning our poems, and presumably our stories, into pointless nostalgia.

The dilemma lies in how to articulate post-Hiroshima nihilism within terms and forms that do not, because of their very existence, contradict it. Ōta's problem is that the "originality" and "essence of literature" already imply the presence of a constructive force—that of a productive, validating creativity—in which she resists believing. Factuality is damning, fictionality is potentially saving; but to abandon what she is also at pains to preserve as the *truth* of her experience would be tantamount to saying it, like fiction, never really happened. Modern writers often struggle with literary forms that might seem a probable reflection of the shapes into which their experiences fall. But Ōta, resolute in her view of Hiroshima as not properly translatable into terms non-victims should be able to appropriate, struggled particularly hard. The word "history," in her parlance virtually synonymous with "fact," occurs frequently as shorthand for that experience of atrocity resistant to literary representation. After Hiroshima Ōta could not imagine literature without "history," but she also seemed to fear, and hope, that for the rest of us "history" would remain (dangerously, or mercifully) unimaginable. Should such history in fact stay unavailable to us, then by default it reverts to Ōta and her fellow victims. Her immediate project in authoring the most complete body of atomic-bomb literature we have today was devising the right calculus of mediated reception in her representation of Hiroshima. How is she to preserve her status as a single author yet one of many victims, as well as the audience's status as nonvictims made aware of the facts of Hiroshima but not of its ultimate significance for the survivors, a significance that from their point of view must remain restricted if it is ever to console.

The answer, at least for Ōta, lay in variously dictating her readers' understanding of where "Hiroshima" was located in any given work by shifting who tells the story to whom, how reliably and with how much access to what Ōta, both victim and author, controls as the final arbiter of the experience. It was Ōta's battle to remain in control of our responses to her writing no matter what particular arrangement of story, narrator, and audience she devises. It is important to remember that every representation *of* something is also a representation *to* someone; and indeed "the ultimate problem in the rhetoric of fiction," as Wayne Booth identified it, is "that of deciding for whom the author should write."[14] Ōta always seemed aware of her readers both as a jury that needed to be convinced and as a jury with finally no right to pass sentence, and that awareness shapes her atomic-bomb works in ways distinct from books concerned with other, more genteel, themes.

Those distinct shapes are the cumulative result of a series of decisions one can imagine Ōta made each time she approached her material. Initially her choice is whether Hiroshima should be narrated or dramatized. If the former, then she is committed to treating the experience of the bomb as objective fact, as "news" to be, as succinctly and unambiguously as possible, stated and understood. If the former, however, Ōta must believe in the efficacy of analogy. Moreover, she must trust in the reader to respond to such "news" with the shock she expects and not the indifference she fears. If the latter, then Ōta must re-create Hiroshima through its representation, and consequently give her writing a creative "life," as it were, of its own not only at odds with the mortal totality of Hiroshima but subjected to the risk of readers interpreting for themselves, of readers detaching the bombing from "history." Perhaps we will empathize with the victims too much, and think ourselves victims, too; or perhaps we will decide it was not "all that bad" for them after all. Again, the issue is just how much to empower the non-victim reader to make any story Hiroshima his own; what would have seemed a great literary accomplishment for any other kind of novelist—the seduction of the reader—might strike an atomic-bomb novelist as a potential betrayal of other victims, or indeed an act of cruelty in itself.

The next rhetorical choice that Ōta conceivably confronted was the construction of her implied reader. To whom is Ōta trying to communicate Hiroshima? Every representation *of* is a representation *to;* her rhetoric is directed towards assisting the reader in grasping the work in a predetermined way. Such coercion, however gentle, is bound up with contending premises, both on the author's part and our own, over rights to certain knowledge and consequently power. Ōta wondered, for example, if her readers would ever truly accept what her characters say is true as true—a doubt not of the limits of her "art" as a writer but of our moral imagination. In her short story of 1953, "Fireflies," Ōta wrote, "The eyes and souls of the visitors from Tokyo, who had never experienced the intense light of radiation, were different from ours" (94). Eyes that perceive, souls that comprehend: the "ours" that are the victims of Hiroshima are opposed to the implicit "theirs" or "yours." Here is a fundamental differentiation, a basic alienation that already seems to threaten the implicit contract that ordinarily links author and audience in a mutual exchange of interested assurances. Ōta no longer so firmly believes in what we still may, namely the joint participation of author and reader not just in a common language but in a common history leading to consensus over moral entitlement. What, post-Hiroshima, Ōta did come to believe was that only the most cynical relation was possible between an author and his readers. In her extended essay "Astray in the World" (Yo ni mayou), published posthumously in 1964, Ōta states that writers, regardless of intentions, "deceive the reader. And I have come to think that stealing that reader's time, his energy, and the money he spent to buy your book, is no different from how a geisha in her line of work treats the customer."[15]

Although it would take Ōta more than a decade after August 6, 1945, to arrive at this discouraged view of literature, the issue of how an author should configure himself, his material, and his audience is one that consistently surfaces in Ōta's postwar writings. What are the values she is at the most pain to preserve when forced to choose between Hiroshima and her commitment to literature? The issue is not solely thematic, but unfolds even at the level of which narrative voice, point of view, and assumption of readership she elects in, and for, any given work. "Moral questions," declares Wayne Booth, are not "irrelevant to technique."[16] The moral question at stake here, though hardly accounted for in Booth's survey of choices, is just how detachable the experience of a mass atrocity should be from those who underwent it in distributing its knowledge among the various constituencies of author, narrator, character, and reader. This is a question of the appropriateness (another way of saying "righteousness") of maintaining the power to critique, whether as a victim or in the place of a victim. For a philosopher such as Berel Lang, whose theory of writing as well as of morality never fails to account for twentieth-century atrocity, "the *fact* of writing reflects a moral judgment, through its implied claim that writing will usefully add something to what the subject otherwise, *un*written, would fail to disclose of itself."[17] The humiliation and powerlessness of a person who has experienced atrocious violence runs up squarely against the transfer of authority involved in engendering a communicative work of "art" about that experience. Hence, the recurrent twentieth-century resistance to an excess of aesthetic concern, an excess that inevitably threatens, as Lang argues, to render "moral judgment . . . at best irrelevant, or a defect."[18]

In his essay "The Position of the Narrator in the Contemporary Novel," Theodor Adorno noted that Franz Kafka—the prewar writer most prescient of postwar writers' necessary battles with both history and language—completely abolishes the distance between narrator and reader:

> Through shocks, he destroys the reader's contemplative security in the face of what he reads. His novels, if indeed they even fall under that category, are an anticipatory response to a state of the world in which the contemplative attitude has become a mockery because the permanent threat of catastrophe no longer permits any human being to be an uninvolved spectator; nor does it permit the aesthetic imitation of that stance.[19]

Few other, if any, writers could however forego, as did Kafka, the demands of a "good work" if even their grasp of modern times was as perspicuous as his. Ōta Yōko, a Japanese who did not voluntarily choose to reinvent the schema of the contemporary novel but instead had that task imposed upon her by the burden of history, constantly resisted the transfer of authority Kafka so easily ceded. *City of Corpses, Human Rags,* and *Half-Human* will in each its own way construct the basis and extent of that wary transfer by variously defining the reader's relationship to the Hiroshima story they collectively tell.

■

Ōta began writing *City of Corpses* only one month after the bombing. At the time she was living above a saké shop in Kujima, twenty kilometers outside of Hiroshima; large numbers of refugees from the city, many dying, were still arriving there to seek the same escape Ōta had found. *City of Corpses* was a work written under extraordinary circumstances. The original manuscript is little more than scraps of paper, including bits of *shōji* screen and toilet tissue. Every inch is covered with packed, minuscule handwriting and suggests that memory as well as paper was a valuable commodity. Ōta writes in her preface written in 1950 that "from August to November of 1945 I hung on the edge between living and dying. I wrote *City of Corpses* living from one moment to the next, never knowing when I would be dragged into death" (301). This sense of only a provisional, temporary survival is doubtlessly why Ōta also states in the preface that she "had to complete [the work] before I died" and thus "had no time to structure it as a work of fiction" (300).

But if *City of Corpses* is not fiction, then what is it? Ōta herself defended it as literature (bungaku) because "within it I have described human actions."[20] This sweeping definition of literature as whatever tells of people is perhaps the understandable response of someone who has survived the use of a weapon meant to eliminate them. Critics, however, have found more selective vocabulary to classify this first book-length instance of atomic-bomb literature. It has been variously labeled a "document" (*kiroku*), "documentary literature" (*kiroku bungaku*), and "literature with documentary qualities" (*kirokusei no aru bungaku*). Each of these phrases identify the factual content of the work and privileges it over the imaginative or dramatic. One critic, echoing many, called *City of Corpses* "an important source of information for posterity in understanding how one person reacted to the first atomic bomb attack in world history."[21]

"Information" and "history" are terms commonly associated with *City of Corpses* and indeed with nearly all the atomic bomb prose literature written by actual survivors. Ōta's work does, in fact, chronicle in detail a wide range of personally experienced or reported (largely via the newspapers) events in and around Hiroshima from August 6th to late autumn, most of which occurred from the time of Ōta's flight from the city on the 9th to her subsequent relocation in the exurbs. The work is divided into seven lengthy sections made of the thirty chapters of its original serialization in the journal *Chūō kōron* (Central Forum). The first two sections, the middle three, and the final two form convenient thirds for dividing the work up into an essay on the current state of the city, the central section which actually details its destruction, and a concluding explanation of how and why Ōta came to initiate the writing of the very book we are reading. The circular and reflexive course of the work, in addition to the frequent highly stylized passages, distinguishes it from the more amateurish testimonial writing produced by those survivors not professional writers. But in fact *City of Corpses* is testimonial, and in a way which needs to be distinguished from documentary.

Both documentary and testimonial writing share a concern for facts. Historical veracity in either instance is posited as the most valuable, indeed definitive, feature of the work. But in the testimonial as opposed to the documentary, there is in addition to a nearly palpable urgency with which the facts are presented by a very specific narrating subject who relates and mediates those facts to us. A documentary will more often than not attempt to arrange its information "objectively," i.e., as if that information is all the more trustworthy because it is detached from an explicitly involved narrator and thus from interpretation.

In testimony, however, the involvement of a narrator is paramount: we do not read of events, we are *told* of them. Ōta so addresses us in *City of Corpses,* and nowhere more so than in the center chapters of the work, "Hiroshima, City of Doom" (Ummei no machi—Hiroshima), "The City is a Tattered Mat of Corpses" (Machi wa shitai no boromushiro), and "Vehicles in which to Rest" (Ikoi no kuruma). She begins her testimony with a brief idyll. She recalls her seaside Hiroshima as a romantic and picturesque place with a long history shattered only when "an ominous blue light flashed soundlessly in the sky":

> I had no understanding of what could have caused everything around us to change so in just one instant . . . something truly different, something nothing to do with war. . . . The newspaper reported that a single moment turned everything into the fiery hell foretold by Buddhism, but whoever wrote that was thinking in conventional terms. . . . In fact, we were invaded by a calm so complete that one would have thought that every living thing had died at once. (47)

Ōta goes on to tell us of how she and her family fled the fire storms and spent their first night among the dying in the dry Kandagawa river bed, eventually fleeing the city by train and then bus for Kujima. There, Ōta experiences the shock of Japan's surrender on the 15th and the hunger that was even worse. She relays stories told her by other victims and which inspired her, once out of immediate danger, "to get my life back as a writer" (120). Indeed, by the conclusion of *City of Corpses* Ōta is ready to write the work the reader has in hand. "I am fortunate that the fire in my writer's soul now burns again" (152), and it was this energy that produced the present account. In tracing its origins *City of Corpses* becomes not only reflexive but, like much testimony, beholden to the quirks of history for its existence. "Here is how I have come to speak"— as if to explain, perhaps apologize, for this exception to the otherwise silent, leveled landscape.

Like most testimony, the events of Hiroshima are consistently narrated in *City of Corpses* by a first-person voice ("watakushi") unmistakably Ōta's own. In part because of the supposedly unmediated presentation of experiences in this first-person account, Ōta's first atomic-bomb book has generally been regarded as an impressively effective, which is to say comprehensive and unambiguous, record of the events it set out to describe. One prominent postwar writer, Noma Hiroshi, has remarked that "Reading *City of Corpses* allows [us non-victims] to experience today the atomic bombings."[22] What Noma says here gives pause, however. Does he *really* mean "experience" the bombings? Even Ōta herself hesitated to claim the knowledge—the right—implied in Noma's phraseology. In her preface she maintained that her own "narrow and shallow" experiences could hardly represent the scale of what "really happened" (301). All that is left to Ōta to do, true to the nature of this genre she initially adopted, is to mediate that scale through herself and in a sense to herself; the point of view which Ōta selected in *City of Corpses* insured that the map of Hiroshima she was to draw would be precisely the frantic route she herself took out of the city.

This choice has its consequences. Whenever a narrator is positioned within the structure of a literary work, the rest of that work's topography is concurrently mapped and certain epistemic perimeters marked. In the testimonial novel, for example, representation is principally mediated through the agency of a testifying subject. In *City of Corpses* that subject is single, unitary, and ubiquitous within the narrative. Any information that reaches the reader comes to her via an act of transmission by the narrator. If our access to information is through this first person, our ability to extrapolate, deduct, or infer is equally dependent on that person. We find ourselves in a world of highly restricted ways of knowing and imagining. We are in a world where, as readers, there is scant choice but to register, and accept without argument, what we are told.

In *City of Corpses* the first-person narrator is closely identified with the persona of the author. "Watakushi" debuts on the novel's first page ("I did not know when death would come to me" [6]). Soon that same "I" is established as belonging to Ōta herself. The lack of distance between narrator and author suggests that we are to trust that narrator to be reliable, but in fact we have no other choice. The narrator talks directly to us; we do not eavesdrop on the narrative, we are its goal. More importantly, however, the author/narrator has herself only a limited command of information. Since the point of view never shifts, neither does it expand. "Watakushi" is not allowed to be anyone but Ōta. No experiences are constituted as real other than her own; other people's stories become hers in the retelling. Even we readers exist only as the addressed audience of her monologue. She tries hard to make us as knowledgeable as possible—she brings in newspapers, other people's reported testimony, and in one odd scene even interviews her own mother in the midst of the destruction in the attempt to communicate to us all she can. But finally, all that knowledge is never more than what she herself has been able to gather, synthesize, and convey.

The corollary of this is that other characters in *City of Corpses* are ancillary, supplemental and corroborative in function. They matter only as accessories to the narrator's experience. We are offered no interior views. Everyone else, including members of Ōta's own family, is hardly distinguishable from the bombed terrain of the city. Indeed, they seem continuous with the charred Hiroshima landscape, barely animate figures in an otherwise inanimate expanse. As such, Ōta usually encounters these other human beings as inscrutable enigmas—at one point she goes on at length about their "indifferent appearance" (*muyoku gambō*)—in a way that does indeed seem to render them inor-

ganic. In fact, the crucial demarcation in *City of Corpses* is between the author/
narrator on one hand and the landscape of hardly differentiated physical ruins/
human victims on the other. Burnt buildings, burnt people—an unrelieved
range of inert carnage against which only one center of consciousness rails:
that of Ōta/"watakushi."

The reader, to whom this consciousness narrates Hiroshima, may also represent a consciousness—otherwise, why address us?—but we are hardly a contending one. Despite the fact we participate in the narrative when we read it,
we are not necessary or even relevant to its effect. *City of Corpses* excludes us
from the factual landscape built through the narrator's reportage. Noma Hiroshi notwithstanding, we are meant to remain outside of this experience. We
might be termed postatomic voyeurs: it is not impossible to imagine a reader
guiltily embarrassed as he proceeds through Ōta's Hiroshima, much as if he
were prying into someone else's private affairs. Unlike a work in which we are
invited to sympathize with a character, in *City of Corpses* the only one with
whom that might be conceivable, Ōta herself, refuses to let us share any of her
experiences, resorting as she does to her strident rhetoric of the "impossibility"
of our ever "understanding" what has happened. Indeed, that would appear to
be one of the purposes of the novel: to remind us, lest we forget, that we were
not there in the first place. The reader, then, is left superfluous and disenfran-
chised. One aim of *City of Corpses* might very well to render us, instead of the
victims, redundant and surplus.

With negligible distinction either between narrator and author or among
the human characters surveyed by that narrator/author, everything within *City
of Corpses* collapses into a monologue delivered by the one cognizant victim to
many ignorant nonvictims. No lever is given us to break Ōta's grip on perspective, knowledge, and insight. In the Hiroshima of such a work the narrator fills
and accounts for everything, and nothing can challenge her authority. It should
be noted, however, that such authority is itself contingent. The narrator's own
knowledge of herself is obtained no differently than her knowledge of all else
found in the rubble of postatomic Hiroshima. Her own image is mediated by
those whom she sees. "No one was capable of knowing what had happened to
his own face. We could only guess by looking at others" (58), she observes in
a remark indicative not only of an environment now devoid of mirrors or calm
reflective waters, but of the mutual identity of victimhood, the sign by which
the narrator knows herself and, conversely, by which we cannot. The narrator,
who cannot see herself, imagines herself in the others she has created for us.
In this sense the narrator herself slips back into the atomic landscape herself;
it mediates *her* as she mediates *it*. She is a victim, too; the looks of others tell her
so. Nowhere in this bizarre arrangement is there room for us: we are excluded
categorically. We feel ourselves outsiders, and we are not entitled to a place
anywhere in the stark world that *City of Corpses* posits.

There is a moral valorization implicit in Ōta's selection of narrative voice and point of view. First, the author Ōta appropriates the testifying voice for herself within the work: that is already an assertion of privilege. Second, that voice is not shared, or even interrupted. It issues from and returns to the one victim alone. Third, complementary characters are left essentially mute, at least insofar as no one speaks without Ōta speaking for them. Fourth, the reader, which is to say the world outside of Hiroshima, is not only denied real participation in the novel, but consideration as well. We are tangential, an audience for the news of atrocity but in no way empowered to interpret it, or offer opinion. What emerges is a hierarchy of privilege to experience, information, and thus the prerogative to judge. The world in *City of Corpses* is one in which the hibakusha, otherwise indistinguishable from each other or even the leveled city they inhabit, seize a kind of power unavailable to the rest of us; but only there. This is a kind of rhetorical gesture that we might dismiss as gratuitous, as only a self-dramatizing posture. But to argue that is to place again the victim beyond the center, to put her somewhere on the margin of where we ourselves safely stand. That would dangerously resemble the conditions of August 6th, when the entire citizenry of Hiroshima was reckoned dispensable. The force of *City of Corpses* is precisely that such positions are reversed. In place of our usual intercession with the victim, the victim discards us altogether as she constructs a Hiroshima narrative in which we simply do not either exist as characters or operate, in our role as interpretive readers, as significant figures.

Ōta pays a price for making her first Hiroshima novel so thoroughly testimonial. An "I" that narrates is necessarily limited. She has access to only some information. That "I" standing between us and the events she narrates is tempted to dramatize herself. That she does: throughout *City of Corpses* Ōta is as much aware of herself as a writer privileged to be present at a historic moment as a person victimized by that same moment. At one point in the novel Ōta says "I have got to see everything" (149); she wants to know everything in order that it serve her account. One recent critical reader, Sawada Akiko, has said that "while reading this work I could not forget that I was in a world of invention [kyōkō]. . . . This was because the atrocity of the bomb seems itself unreal, but more so because the work is 'literary' insofar as Ōta was aware of herself as a 'writer.'"[23] In other words the book seems obviously the product of a professional author (and less that of a victim) because Ōta cannot write without contemplating the implications of writing. The awkward coexistence of Ōta's status as a writer with her status as a victim led, in fact, to her stated dissatisfaction with *City of Corpses*.[24] Because the novel was so testimonial that it excluded the imaginative participation of the reader, Ōta concluded that she needed a more flexible and less confining structure for her second atomic-bomb book. In a few years' time Ōta would turn from the testimonial memoir to the documentary novel. Unfortunately, in a pattern that characterizes most of Ōta's post-Hiroshima work, solving some problems seemed only to create others.

■

By 1951 Ōta was no longer quite so apprehensive whether she would, like many of her fellow victims did in the fall of 1945, die at any moment. Now living in Tokyo and again making a living as a writer, Ōta completed a book begun in the previous year: the work of "literature" about Hiroshima forecast in the final lines of her preface to *City of Corpses*. Ōta had boldly declared she intended to write a book that would somehow, in spite of its theme, express a "love of mankind." She wished, it seemed, to redeem what had been forsaken in her first atomic-bomb novel.[25] Six years after the bombing Ōta was concerned less with the plain documentation of an unprecedented event than with the more elaborate, and perhaps more prestigious, artistic achievement that a Hiroshima epic would represent. Atomic-bomb literary historian Nagaoka Hiroyoshi states that of all Ōta's works either before or after the war, it was this one, *Human Rags*, into which she poured her greatest measure of literary skill and passion. Nagaoka considers *Human Rags* Ōta's attempt to fashion a "single literary work"—single in the sense of comprehensive, literary in the sense of possessing lasting value—out of what she only crudely chronicled in *City of Corpses*.[26] Some opinion holds that Ōta succeeded: insofar as *Human Rags* probes the problem, argues her biographer Esashi, of "inner man," this novel might be interpreted as a work that reasserts the idea of human integrity. That is not, however, to say that any notion of integrity, post-Hiroshima, also restored Ōta's faith in human potential: we shall have to examine just what "inner man," post-Hiroshima, meant to Ōta Yōko.

Human Rags is the fictional tale of half a dozen diverse characters brought together by circumstance in the aftermath of the atomic bombing. This novel, a lengthy one, takes its characters through a full year and a half of life and death in post-bomb Hiroshima. The survivors persevere, they rebuild, they fall in love. They become sick and die, they betray each other, they flourish and fall. In brief, they do the sorts of things people usually do in novels as well as real life. The one difference is that they they do those things under an unusual burden of memory. At first glance *Human Rags*, like the prewar *Drifting Shores*, takes as its central problem the troubled relationships between men and women. The backdrop for those relationships, however, perverts them in ways that regularly draw the reader's attention to August 1945. It is hard to imagine a typical romance transferred, intact, to a wasted Hiroshima, and in fact it is this incongruity that gives *Human Rags* its peculiar effect.

The novel is divided into three titled sections. The first, "Summer 1945" (Senkyūhyaku yonjūgo-nen natsu), opens on the morning of the 6th on Kanawajima, an island one kilometer off the coast from Ujina and four kilometers from the city of Hiroshima itself. At the time it was used as a site of repairs for the Imperial Navy. Sugita and his girlfriend Kikue, students conscripted to work on the island, make their way back into the burning city after witnessing the tremendous explosion across the water. The details of their unanticipated journey into and through the burning city are supplemented with the similar accounts Ōta supplies the reader through the eyes of other characters, including Sugita's mother Sumiyo, his father Eizō, and Eizō's mistress Yae. These accounts are also retrospective in that they supply the reader with details of the characters' pasts. Indeed, from the very start of *Human Rags* the bombing of Hiroshima as a theme must compete for the reader's attention with a soap-operatic web of complicated sexual relations. In addition to the distrustful triangular relationship of Sumiyo, Eizō, and Yae, there are for example Sugita's troubled, and correct, suspicions: is someone other than Sumiyo his real mother? Could the father of Kikue's child be a man other than himself? Such doubts over whom is related to whom often seem to produce at least as much anxiety as the atomic bombing. Ōta wants these people to be real to her readers—hence the little dramas—but the effect can just as easily seem absurdly unreal because it is so contrived.

The second part of the novel, "Maggots" (Uji), brings more characters and more complications into the cast. Principal among them are Umehara, the doctor who—in a scene far more graphic than any other in the novel—helps Kikue through her miscarriage amid the smoldering ruins; and Toshiko, Sugita's aunt (in fact, his true mother), recently returned from China with her husband, who is killed in the bombing. Eventually all the principal characters, save Sumiyo and Eizō who set up makeshift shelter on the outskirts of the city, move into Umehara's crowded clinic. Soon they begin to suffer, to varying degrees, the radiation sickness that afflicts the other anonymous patients providing the grim backdrop of the novel. By the time of *Human Rags'* final section, "Falling Apart" (Kuzurete yuku), the members of the circle have largely recovered from their physical malaises but are further plagued by greater passion and intrigue. Umehara has fallen in love with an unresponsive Toshiko; Toshiko, aware that her coldness is due to something that snapped within her the day of the bombing, is driven to drugs; Yae, jealous of the love that Toshiko spurns, eventually sinks into a depraved and degraded life as a addict-prostitute who even suggests to Sugita that he "lend" her Kikue for purposes of "commerce"; Sumiyo, who at one point suddenly disappears, is rumored to have to become a stripper also available for a price. As one year and then half of another go by, even Sugita, once the eternal optimist, finds himself numbed to life—too demoralized and too cynical to resist even when a thief makes off with his coat, an example of the deteriorating moral climate in postwar Hiroshima. *Human Rags* ends in a discouraged and unmitigated silence. It is peopled with characters both major and minor who are left with nothing to say to each other. As Umehara notes, "All that the people [living in the clinic] have in common is that they are victims of war. All were subjected equally, at the same time on the same day, to the fierce and fiery ravages . . . and that sense of equality was what consoled them in the face of that unchangeable fact" (186). Such consolation, however, is ironic and useless; no one is cheered, only discouraged, by the odd sort of democracy the atomic bomb brought to Hiroshima.

Throughout the novel there are moments of individual courage and, especially on the part of Sugita, selfless concern; but still, "in the face of that unchangeable fact" the reader searches in vain for any sign of a "love of mankind." More typical than love is, in fact, utter estrangement from feeling. Toshiko, for instance, is fond of coldly killing insects in acts of small but nonetheless gratuitous violence she can only attribute to the violence done to her. At the time of the writing of *Human Rags* Ōta was herself suffering from emotional disorders and drug abuse, problems further acerbated by the escalating Korean War and the suicide of Hara Tamiki. In place of any uplifting message, what functions as a synthesizing element in *Human Rags* is the imperious dominance of the bombing over the lives of its characters. No amount of passing time mitigates its presence. Indeed, here as in much atomic-bomb fiction, the narrative is not bounded or even coordinated by a governing point of view, but rather by that one weighty historical experience. Unlike *City of Corpses*, which created a unified and exclusive narrative vantage point under the aegis of an autobiographical "I," *Human Rags* proceeds in an opposite direction. A multitude of points of view come variously to the fore only to fade soon back into the background; a crowd of victims briefly invited to speak rushes past the reader much as other crowds rushed throughout Hiroshima on the 6th.

This disconcerting parade of narrators has lead to the novel's near-universal critical reputation as a failure. Nagaoka Hiroyoshi notes that from its first publication the work was attacked as a novel without a hero.[27] Sugita, initially expected by the reader to be the central character, disappears as a meaningful presence from the novel's second half. Ōta's fellow atomic-bomb writer Agawa Hiroyuki added that the characterization of Toshiko, herself a leading contender for the role of "main character" at one point, is so tenuous that whatever sections of the novel she dominates are unacceptably weak.[28] Another critic, Tanabe Kōichirō, while judging *Human Rags* a failure, buffers his criticisms by suggesting that Ōta's subject—Hiroshima hibakusha culture—contributes its loss of faith in humanity to a similar tenor in the work itself, namely a loss of faith in any of the characters to sustain the reader through the entire tedious length of the novel.[29] *Human Rags* tells of survival without surviving; it is structured, minimally, by a simple chronology informed by the fictive legacies of a pre-bomb past (Sugita's confused parentage, Eizō's infidelity, Toshiko's hiatus in China, etc.) but dominated by the diminished prospects for a post-bomb future. Somehow none of the characters ever move beyond the ruins, the "rags," of their former existences.

For these reasons it seems hasty to dismiss *Human Rags* as "poor" writing without undertaking an assessment of how the nature of Ōta's theme makes "good" novel-writing problematic. What disturbs us most, the novel's plurality and tentativeness of character, might be Ōta's attempt to replicate something new to us which we instead only find odd. At least one critic, in noting the artistic ambitions of the novel, has seen within them an experiment to convey the breadth of the violence through its multiple third-person perspectives.[30] But what finally remains most noteworthy about *Human Rags* is Ōta's troubled efforts to suppress the personal, testimonial voice—to efface the first-person singular "I"—and leave in its place a work more conventionally "literary," to "show" rather than "tell" by eliminating certain overt signs of the author's presence. This impersonal narration may have contributed to the failure of *Human Rags*, but from the stance of a victim it may signal its ironic success as well. To understand Hiroshima as one "event" in a continuous process of dehumanization that resists being restricted to a single moment ("August 6th") or single subject ("I") is to suggest that such an understanding is a profound one, indeed.

Human Rags is a documentary work, not a testimonial one. At first the distinction may seem trivial, since both documentary and testimony are dedicated the preservation of historical fact. Yet not only the means of recording such fact, but the status of "fact" itself, differs between the two. Gone from documentary is the first-person narrator, and with her the reliance on surfaces and the limitation of depths. They are replaced by an abstract and omniscient author with access to interiors provided by inside views. Irony is thus inevitable. *City of Corpses* is built with observed measurements; *Human Rags* with psychological insights. If *City of Corpses* is a "true" work of Hiroshima, then *Human Rags* strives to be a "truthful" one, perhaps less literally factual but nonetheless commensurate with Ōta's lived experience. As a result, the information is presented neither as urgently nor as directly as in testimony, but with the force of imagination. The reader takes a more circuitous route to Hiroshima in *Human Rags*, and the pay-off, presumably, is that this more novelistic work will read that much more powerfully; that the reader will find himself in Dr. Umehara's clinic along with the others.

In lieu of the single narrator in *City of Corpses* we have the many of *Human Rags*. Ōta herself seems disassembled and distributed among them. Toshiko often seems similar emotionally to the image Ōta presents of herself in other works. Sugita often articulates in his private thoughts views on the war that are traceable to Ōta's own; Umehara possesses her intellectual acumen. Yet Ōta remains content not to have any one of these characters wholly identified with her. Here, unlike in *City of Corpses*, Ōta has surrendered center stage. She is willing to let others speak for her. But on the other hand, if Ōta is less present for having separated her authorial self from her narrating self, she has reserved for herself somewhat greater cognitive powers than in the first novel. She unavoidably reveals herself as storyteller each time she redirects the point of view, but she reveals herself even more forcefully each time she shows a character's inner thoughts, something she must do to construct the psychological dimension associated with novels. Whereas in *City of Corpses* Ōta's knowledge was scant, here it is total. She retreats personally from the action but intervenes in her characters' assessment of it. By giving her characters proxy to speak on her behalf, *Human Rags* becomes fractured, multi-voiced, and even contentious. But the important thing is that the totality of her presence in *City of Corpses* has been supplanted by the totality of her knowledge in *Human Rags*. This makes our experience in reading the two works quite different. In *Human Rags* Ōta sets up characters we are free to like or dislike, trust or suspect. We ourselves are now empowered in the new schema. Ōta, the implied author, grants us the power to know things about the characters they do not know about themselves. Along with irony, judgment suddenly becomes possible. The author, powerful in her new way, retreats just far enough for us to form guided opinions about the characters—one surely prefers the honorable Sugita, Toshiko, and Umehara over the devious Eizō, Yae, and Kikue—and thus we are allowed, perhaps dangerously from Ōta's perspective, to valorize the world she has given us. In *City of Corpses* we had no choice but to accept it unquestioningly. Here, however, we interpret and thus critique. If we do so as Ōta wishes, she has won our sympathies and thus potentially our deeper understanding. But there is no guarantee that we will do so.

By sharing some measure of her control in *Human Rags*, Ōta differentiates the moral implications of this novel's representation of Hiroshima from those in *City of Corpses*. The more complex legislation of knowledge in this second work results in a more crowded ethical condominium of victim and nonvictim. Ōta may provide us with more information than ever, yet now we, in reacting variously to the moral character of those who are described by that increased information, inevitably form opinions as to their relative worth. In *Human Rags* we can, and indeed do, embrace or reject the victims, an action which elevates some them above us and degrades others. The characters' status as hibakusha seems secondary to their "fundamental" nature as people both good and bad. *Human Rags*, in moving us closer to the readers' expectations associated with conventional novels, sets in motion an audience process of evaluation that Ōta cannot wholly prescribe. She is only one hibakusha now among many, hardly conspicuous in her own book; and we, in addition to thinking we know what being a hibakusha is like, choose which one we would *rather be*. The world is no longer just Hiroshima victims. It is now the nonvictim, too, once those people exist among "us." Here is the start of moving those victims simultaneously away from the moral center and towards the periphery, thereby clearing a space that we are free to fill. As Hiroshima recedes in importance among the sundry themes of the work—after all, the lives its hibakusha lead seem somehow part of their own doing as well as the bomb's—what takes its place is the very ordinary world that once appeared to Ōta to have been the weapon's co-conspirator. The frustration that Ōta experienced at the conclusion of *City of Corpses* and which inspired *Human Rags* was followed with similar feelings of failure even before that second work had reached completion.

■

With the publication of *Half-Human* in 1954 it was recognized that Ōta was attempting yet another kind of Hiroshima novel.[31] Here was an Ōta novel none of whose incidents took place on August 6th, or in 1945, or even in Hiroshima at all. Rather, its material was drawn from Ōta's private and much later emotional and physical problems, which had been aggravated during the writing of *Human Rags*. In "The Psychology of Survival" Ōta stated that she shared a common "emotional paralysis" with Hara Tamiki, the writer who had killed himself—reputedly because of his despondency over the possible use of nuclear weapons in the Korean war—as she was working on *Human Rags*. In both this essay and in "The Terror of Literature" Ōta confesses that, unable to forget the bombing, she had sought the help of drugs, which only contributed to further irritability, distress, and exhaustion. Perplexed doctors diagnosed her as suffering from "nervous paralysis." Ōta disagreed, convinced that ultimately the trauma of the bombing was the source of her troubles. After finishing *Human Rags* she entered a University of Tokyo hospital for sixteen days of sleep treatment in the hope that complete rest would calm her. This was a treatment that Ōta admits succeeded in part, but only in part, since the real root of her problem was one she felt even Japan's best doctors could not begin to understand much less cure.

This hospitalization becomes the story told in *Half-Human*. Ōta wrote it soon after being discharged. Unfortunately it was poorly received, and Ōta recalls in "The Terror of Literature" that the novel's critical failure ironically worsened the psychological problems it described, since she began to worry if she had during the course of the treatment forgotten not the bombing, but how to write.

In fact *Half-Human* is very much about a writer trying to write. Its nine chapters are told from the third-person point of view of Oda Atsuko, a famous atomic-bomb writer undergoing the same medical treatment Ōta did herself. Like Ōta, Oda has been told her illness is "anxious nervous disorder," vague medical jargon never explained in much detail. The symptoms, however, are quite real. For some time Oda has found normal social interaction impossible.

Her biggest problem is insomnia, a condition she has treated with ever larger dosages of antihistamines, doses which are increased each time she hears of preparations for war somewhere in the world. Eventually she finds herself in a university hospital room with several other patients, all suffering from similarly "anxious," even insane, mental states ultimately traceable to their pitiable experiences in postwar Japan. One of the women, impregnated by an African-American U.S. serviceman, bore a child who soon starved to death. Now, Oda overhears with horror, she wants to kill all foreigners, but hating herself for such thoughts she had attempted to kill herself instead. Another woman, the wife of an unemployed bureaucrat, had turned to a new postwar religious cult for consolation but, having only been swindled out of what savings remained, now has only her own "neurosis." Indeed, none of Oda's roommates puts her at any greater ease than she had been outside the hospital. The world outside the ward and the world within it are likewise wrenched, impaired, corrupted: despite Oda's hope that passing through its doors would "isolate her from society" (265), what she experiences instead is the institutionalized refuse of that same unsympathetic society.

Her stay in the hospital takes on the quality of a sublime torture. Patronizing male physicians and indifferent female nurses ask her meaningless questions, and dismiss her own concerns with their professional contempt. Oda soon senses the absurdity of her situation as a "patient": though she recognizes her state of mind as "pathological" (*byōteki*) she does not have much confidence in a cure. Rather, what she seeks is oblivion in drugged unconsciousness. Oda manages her first two nights in Room 7, before the sleep therapy is begun, by secretly giving herself antihistamine shots. Still, their effect is incomplete: Oda does not achieve "liberation from her anguish." Once the sleep treatments commence a day later, they too seem hardly effective. Constantly waking and sleeping, never sure of which state she is in—the toll of temple bells dissolves into the sterile silence of her room—Oda falls repeatedly out of bed, sleepwalks at all hours, and confuses reality with dream and dream with memory. Tied down to the bed to prevent injury to herself, weeks of terrifying hallucinations involving disfigured hibakusha (the "Atomic Bomb Maidens") and Class A war criminals become intertwined with the recollection of the drone of a plane overhead. In a sense the medical treatment makes Oda more fearful and nervous, acting only to intensify her nervous apprehensions. She fights consciousness and continues to seek the respite of a numbed, unthinking sleep, but the more she struggles to stay asleep the more she involuntarily recalls the past.

In fact, medical treatment fails to improve the condition of any of the women in her room. Treatment itself is a source of fear. No cure, Oda reflects, can be gentle these days. "Even holding one's life dear nowadays seems a joke" (326). Oda is incapable of any enthusiasm. When one well-meaning doctor offers her a private room in which she might resume writing, she declines, thinking to herself that she lacks the presence of mind to scribble even a post-card. When this same doctor suggests to Oda that her hallucinations might serve as literary inspiration, she snaps back in reply that all she wants is a "peaceful life." To her doctors there is no scientific reason why she cannot have one, but to Oda such things have little to do with choice.

The only member of the hospital staff who seems to understand Oda and her predicament is a kindly nurse who rescues her from sleepwalking one night, encourages to get well so that she can "write for peace," and who, in the final scene of *Half-Human*, takes Oda for a comforting stroll one moonlit evening. The message at the novel's conclusion seems to be, as Oda put it at its start, that "no matter what sort of condition people find themselves in, they try to go on living" (265). It is left to us to decide whether such perseverance is brave or perhaps only pathetic.

Perhaps here is the "love of mankind" Ōta professed to express. Then again, perhaps it is only a further moment of drugged delusion; the reader doubts that Oda has undergone a catharsis. This "condition" refers to the range of victimized states in which the women of *Half-Human* represent. Noting this, Sata Ineko has acclaimed *Half-Human* as a miniature map of postwar Japanese society.[32] The novel does repeatedly invoke the suffering that many, bomb victims or not, experienced in postwar Japan, and like many novels, its detail leads to certain insights into the larger social world that informs it. But finally *Half-Human* is not a social novel, or even a historical one. It is rather a very individual one, planned apparently with an intent not to "map" a milieu or demarcate an era, but to make a confession. Consequently, *Half-Human* has of-ten, and with derision, been typed as an example of shishōsetsu, or "personal fiction" in which the implied author seems withdrawn from every world other than one of his own making.

Thinking of the prewar *Drifting Shores*, some critics have emphatically ar-gued that Ōta should not be thought an atomic-bomb writer at all, but instead, as if the two cannot coincide, a shishōsetsu novelist. "No matter what the work," says Kuroko Kazuo, "Ōta never seems to exceed her shishōsetsu frame-work."[33] There is, adds Adachi Yukizō, no "action" (*kōdōsei*) in her work.[34] If one thinks of shishōsetsu as idly reflective or indulgent confessional writing in which the narrator is identified with that of the author, then *Half-Human* might minimally qualify. But it is also possible that this perceived lack of "action" is not an aesthetic choice but a consequence of recording faithfully the phenom-enon of a hibakusha's willed inaction in the face of robust, non-hibakusha, vitality. The origin of Oda's affliction lies in the paralyzing impact of a nuclear attack; the portrayal of Oda as a sensitive writer acutely aware of her own "condition" without interacting with it may be typical of much shishōsetsu, but it is also typical of how some survivors come to (dis)regard their environment;

inert, abstract, and without consequence, the world of the hibakusha becomes so alienated from the self of the hibakusha that the resultant narrative becomes groundless in ways indeed reminiscent of the highly introspective tradition of shishōsetsu.

Noting such parallels between *Half-Human* and a particularly self-absorbed sort of autobiography, however, neither exhausts what can be said about the novel nor leads to any useful alignment of it with Ōta's earlier atomic-bomb literature. In *Half-Human* the relationships among author, narrator, characters, and readers are reworked in ways that elaborate and contrast with those in the earlier works. As in *City of Corpses,* there is but a single narrator who commands all narrative authority; but Oda, unlike *City of Corpses*'s Ōta, is a third person and thus only an adjunct to the implied author. Not wholly identifiable with that author herself, Oda Atsuko is herself an objectified re-construction towards whom the real Ōta Yōko's stance is uncertain. All information in the novel comes via this source termed "she," but as a reconstruction she is not entirely reliable—which is to say, what Ōta may think and what her character Oda may think are possibly cleaved by the narrative distance placed between them. The frequent quotation of the third-person narrator's thoughts gives us enough interior views to encourage our sympathy for her. But our sympathy is stubbornly qualified. Whatever its cause, Oda clearly suffers from some sort of mental disorder: her hallucinations, paranoia, and general state of high tension make her less than a wholly trustworthy narrator. Perhaps the doctors are right, and not she; perhaps nothing, in fact, is quite as Oda Atsuko tell us it is. At times we would like to bracket our doubts, give in to our sympathies, and join with Oda in her indignation at an insensitive world. But we do so aware of how tentative such solidarity is; one false, or insane, move on her part and we will shift our allegiance to her doctors. The final scene of the novel—the one in which a nurse's kind friendship to Oda suggests to some an affirmation of human feeling, human communication—might also suggest how fragile such an affirmation can be. As a weakened Oda sits on a bench with the nurse and watches other pairs of nurses and patients stroll in the evening air, she asks her if her maid Takeyo—herself a deeply troubled woman—has survived the suicide Oda recently learned she attempted. The nurse replies, maybe a bit too quickly, that Takeyo is fine. One wonders if Oda is not being shielded from less pleasant news. Maybe she is even being humored; maybe she truly is mad. We cannot be sure, and that unsureness extends back through the novel to undermine many of our conclusions about Oda and the post-Hiroshima world she inhabits.

The novel's other characters—the maid, the nurses and doctors, the other patients—are, again as in *City of Corpses,* available to the reader only through the narrator's agency. In other words they exist only through the active mediation of the narrator's own, admittedly skewered and drugged, perception. Consequently, the reader must treat Oda's perceptions suspiciously, and since he has no other access to the scene, the entire story told becomes tentative. Aesthetic distance is heightened; Oda Atsuko, the dramatized narrator, extends Room 7 to include us as well. Like her doctors, we might prefer to humor rather than question her. The result in *Half-Human*, far more than in the earlier two works, is skeptical relations between readers and everyone else, including author, narrator, and characters. Moreover, the ill-ease which derives from the bracketed contingency of those relations carries with it its own moral implications for the non-hibakusha reader encountering the hibakusha literary character. More than ever in Ōta's atomic-bomb literature, the reader is thrust into a position of authority. He must make judgments concerning the reliability of what he is told and thus its status as fact. Ōta guaranteed that such a situation would arise when she decided to create such an ambiguous portrait of herself as Oda Atsuko. The reader, left to conclude that only he is in sure possession of lucidity, is tempted to feel superior to the variously impaired figures of the novel, and to Oda most of all. We emerge with a sense of healthy wholeness from the experience of reading *Half-Human*, and that sense can translate into a dismissive smugness; or worse, the thrill of being free of what oppresses and terrorizes Oda/Ōta. Though we may be sympathetic to her plight, we are nonetheless less threatened by it than we were in *City of Corpses* and *Human Rags* because now the problem—Hiroshima, and by extension the nuclear extinction of the human race—seems so much more personal, even idiosyncratic, than it does historical. In *Half-Human* Ōta has created a work we are at liberty to enter or leave as we will; to stand on either side of the ward door which so terrifies her. We possess a freedom as total as the hospitalized women's constriction; we can accept or reject the political implications of *Half-Human* on the basis of their being either sane or insane. The literature of the atomic bomb represented by this third Hiroshima book of Ōta's is a work suggesting madness. As such, it nearly reverses the militantly testimonial authority of *City of Corpses* and the epic ambition of *Human Rags*. The end result of *Half-Human*—or at least the end result of its critical reception—has been to justify Ōta Yōko's reputation as a bitter, disturbed, and perhaps even deranged woman whose writings on Hiroshima deserve to be discounted as equally bitter, disturbed, and deranged themselves.[35]

■

Ōta's reputation, while largely the legacy of Japanese critics' attacks on her for pursuing a theme—the atomic bombing—not properly literary,[36] is not contradicted by her prominent position as a hibakusha informant within the work of Robert Jay Lifton. *Death in Life: Survivors of Hiroshima*, Lifton's landmark 1967 study of hibakusha psychology, relies more heavily for its data on Ōta

Yōko and her works (especially *City of Corpses*) than on any other single source. Ōta becomes the most important proof of his hypothesis, in short that the survivor of violence as complete as Hiroshima copes through a "psychic closing-off process . . . a means of creating emotional distance between himself and the intolerable world immediately around him" (34). Lifton refers to Ōta's doubts that language can communicate her experiences as a sign of her "psychic numbing," her inability to transform Hiroshima into the symbols that language would represent. He generally invokes Ōta as a example of atomic-bomb impairment; caught "in a characteristic A-bomb writer's bind . . . her increasing dissatisfaction with the memoir approach to A-bomb literature, and her inability to evolve an alternative one, undoubtedly contributed to her 'anger' at the A-bomb" (404–5).

There are, however, several problems in using Ōta Yōko to these psychoanalytic ends. Aside from the methodological criticism that might arise from Lifton's selective reading of a creative author's literary texts as generally indicative of hibakusha attitudes (a hibakusha who is a writer might be, after all, *expressively* a very different kind of hibakusha than the very many to whom Lifton's thesis no doubt applies), there is conceivably an ethical criticism: to speak of Ōta's literature—indeed, her life—as frustrated because of an "impairment" caused by the bomb is to make her even more a victim. Rather than think of Ōta's admittedly complicated stance towards the possibility of an atomic-bomb literature as part of her "problem" as a hibakusha, perhaps it can be thought of as her "solution." To do so would grant her a kind of power, not to mention dignity, that Lifton's analysis does not. Secondly, it leads to a more satisfactory account of the considerable body of literature that Ōta did author.

When Ōta Yōko originally scribbled her story of Hiroshima on the bits of scrap paper that became *City of Corpses*, she wrote narrowly, as a single victim. It was inevitable, however, that as a survivor of nuclear war the initial "I" struggling to speak in that first work would eventually seek, in later efforts, to extend itself and thus address both the actual scale and historical import of the violence. In a sense each of Ōta's atomic-bomb novels represents a negotiation with her readers—how much of Hiroshima should, could, be exchanged to secure our understanding of, and moral participation in, the events of August 1945. If Ōta was, in fact, the bitter and failed artist that the literary establishment long considered her, or if she was the emotionally handicapped victim that Lifton sees, then perhaps it was because the writer in Hiroshima is indeed faced with extraordinary tasks. Ōta seemed to doubt that the contractual relationship between author and reader would actually allow her audience to accept what her hibakusha characters say is true; and the rhetoric required to convince that audience raises the question asked by Wayne Booth, for instance, whether such rhetoric is ultimately compatible with art.

In "Fireflies" Ōta tells of visiting the ruins of Hiroshima Castle several years after the bombing. "Turning my back on the stone walls, I began walking. It seemed as though those stone cliffs, turning into flames, were collapsing behind me. The feeling was not a false one. To me that was the ultimate truth" (88). "Ultimate truth" may finally not fall within the purview of a genre, that of the novel, ofttimes defined as fundamentally ambiguous over issues of fiction versus factual reality; but as a survivor of nuclear war aware of just that fact, Ōta tried to offer to us her own "ultimate truth" in the very restricted way such truth can ever be made portable. In my own reading of her work I have noted how point of view, and its relation to character and to reader, variously determine not just what might be known, but our ethical stance towards that knowledge. These three novels trace, in other words, moral positions as well as perceptual: positions on how the world should "look" after Hiroshima for all of us as well as for the victims themselves. That the positions change from work to work reflects, I believe, the inadequacy of any single one. Ōta's empowering desire to remain the victim of (and identical with) the experience of atrocity, and the plain need to warn the rest of us by sharing it, may be irreconcilable and in hindsight the exacting price Ōta paid for being, as she frequently boasted, "Japan's atomic-bomb writer."

From the mid-1950s until her death from a heart attack in 1963 Ōta repeatedly complained she wished nothing more than to "throw away her memory of Hiroshima" and "flee from its use as a subject."[37] Her work in the last years of her life turned increasingly to themes of loneliness and isolation. In the *People and the City of Evening Calm*, the narrator—again Oda Atsuko—returns to Hiroshima seven years after the war and witnesses the distressed squalor in which her fellow survivors still wallow. If that work still permits the possibility of hope, however, the advent of even more powerful nuclear weapons heralded by the 1954 Bikini Atoll tests drove Ōta to an unprecedented despair in such works as the 1956 "Half-Vagrant" (Han-hōrō), in which Ōta declares her wish to "flee everything."[38] Then, in her final collection of short stories, *Eighty-four Years Old* (Hachijūyonsai, 1961), Ōta confesses painful resentment at where and how she had ended up as a writer. One might conclude, with Lifton, that such frustration was due to the inefficacy of writing for her after Hiroshima. Then again, it might be a frustration that only grows with an author's awareness of her difficult relations with "author-ity."

There is a scene in "Fireflies," for instance, in which Ōta pays a call on the young woman who is the most horribly deformed of the all the Hiroshima hibakusha. Throughout their moving conversation, Ōta cannot escape thinking of how she is speaking with her not as a fellow victim, but rather as a *writer.* "The calculations of an author consciously rose in my mind" (107). This, in fact, is Ōta's bind; she is interior to the atomic-bomb experience as a hibakusha herself, yet she is exterior to it as a writer. "I look," she wrote in *City of Corpses,* "with the one eye of a human being and the one eye of an author" (73). In other words, she is both subject and object, an proprietor of Hiroshima and one seeking to exchange her propriety for our understanding. Her status vis-à-vis Hiroshima is complicated by the discursive hierarchies implicit in the telling of it. The same remains true of our own experience as readers encountering Ōta's works. Never sure how well we "know" what we are told, never really confident enough to judge even as we are invited to, and never comfortable with the ease with which we come and go from the novels, "the calculations of the reader" continually arise among ourselves and force us to contemplate humbly just how very different are the circumstances in which we, compared to Ōta, regard the tasks of atomic-bomb literature.

Hongō Shin, *Mother and Children in the Storm*
(Arashi no naka no boshi, 1960). Peace Park, Hiroshima

If, they say, a single one of the atoms which constitute the
universe were annihilated, there would result a catastrophe
which would extend to the entire universe, and this would
be, in particular, the end of the Earth and of the solar system. This metaphor can be of use to us here. The For-
itself is like a tiny nihilation which has its origin at the
heart of Being; and this nihilation is sufficient to cause
a total upheaval to *happen* to the In-itself.
This upheaval is the world

Jean-Paul Sartre, *Being and Nothingness*

7

Ōe Kenzaburō: Humanism
and Hiroshima

In the 1980s Ōe Kenzaburō emerged as the unrivaled spokesman among
Japanese intellectuals for atomic-bomb literature in Japan.[1] This is a role for
which he had been preparing himself since the start of his career in the late
1950s. But what most famously established his credentials was his publication
of a series of essays in the literary journal *Sekai* (The World) based on a number
of short visits to Hiroshima conducted between the summer of 1963 and the
end of 1964.[2] Ōe later collected these essays in a single volume entitled *Hiroshima Notes* (Hiroshima Nōto, 1965), which was published shortly after he finished his acclaimed novel *A Personal Matter* (Kojinteki na taiken, 1964). Although Ōe is now often thought of as an editor and publicist of atomic-bomb
writers whom he feels have been unfairly excluded from the canon of postwar
Japanese literature, he in fact has written of Hiroshima himself yet has hardly
suffered from critical neglect: *Notes* has been a widely read and appreciated
work.[3]

Unlike most of the atomic-bomb writers whom he champions, Ōe belongs to the distinct second generation of authors to make Hiroshima their theme. At the time of the bombing Ōe was only a young boy and far from Hiroshima in a Shikoku village. He is not, then, a victim-writer who has sought to convey a lived experience to a non-victim audience, but is rather himself a reader of history inversely attempting to comprehend a situation directly accessible only to its immediate victims. This difference in the relationship of the writer to his material necessitated for Ōe an equally different narrative approach. *Notes*, although (or perhaps because) it is a collection of essays arguably the most famous since the Second World War, nonetheless raises the question of the status and utility of the essay within a thematic genre, that of atomic-bomb literature, composed principally of documentary fiction and lyric poetry. In other words, adding to the problems which Ōe inevitably faced as a non-victim daring to define the victims' condition for an audience which surely included some of his subjects, Ōe also needed to claim for the discursive prose of *Notes* the capacity to initiate his readers into a state of understanding which some theorists of a literature of atrocity insist is possible in "imaginative" writing alone.[4] Such arguments typically hold that in fiction the reader is rhetorically manipulated and thus seduced into identifying with the characters whose experiences then become his own. Ibuse Masuji, the author of the most widely read novel ever to deal with the Hiroshima bombing, *Black Rain*, obliquely faulted *Notes* as "too rational."[5] Such remarks imply that writing on the theme of Hiroshima must take the form of "contradictory" works of imaginative "art" if they are to produce more essential "truth." Ōe's position appears to be that at least some part of what is significant about Hiroshima can be reported in the clear and orderly language of the essay, and it was ostensibly as a journalist—and not as a novelist—that he traveled to that city.[6]

Nonetheless Ōe has been at pains to protect *Notes* as a work of "literature." He has somewhat defensively declared it such, on the grounds that it is finally concerned with the question of what it means to be human ("ningen to wa nani ka").[7] This humanist definition of literature, leaving aside the problem of just what species of writing would *not* qualify, risks seeming oddly anachronistic in a post-Hiroshima age when the relatively recent invention of "Man" has been displaced, literally vaporized, by the alignment of modern physics and modern warfare. Yet no matter what the eventual implications of Ōe's privileging the notion of an anthropocentric world, the theme of *Notes* is certainly about what it means, in a familiar moral sense, to *be* human. Or rather, a particular kind of human: as Ōe states several times, *Notes* is his retrospective study of the development of hibakusha culture as the nuclear age reached maturity twenty years after the first use of fission weapons. *Notes* thus qualifies, though not without ironic difficulties, as a humanist manifesto to be read as a work which, like most atomic-bomb literature, seeks to (re-)define our character and place in a century dominated not only by our past, but also potentially by our future crimes of atrocity against our "human" selves.

Ōe's choice of nonfiction, specifically interpretative nonfiction, for this inquiry into what is as well a general theme in his fiction implies the presence of a special process in nonfiction that aims for the realization of a special knowledge: the explicit intellectualization of the human condition and the objective understanding of Ōe's place within it.[8] In the conclusion to *Notes* Ōe cites the various titles he had once considered for the work: *Hiroshima and Thoughts on Mankind, Hiroshima Within Us,* and *How Shall We Survive Hiroshima,* all titles which attempt to identify the broad humanist and intellectual project of the book. The final choice of *Hiroshima Notes* suggests a compilation of journalistic or scientific observations, an encounter with discernible facts in the tradition of dry scientific treatises. Ōe reflects in *Notes*:

> When I published *A Personal Matter* last year I wrote in an advertisement for it that I had "attempted the novel as a radical 'file' to 'polish' the many themes already present in the world of my writings." I have come to write this series of essays on Hiroshima with again the same intent in mind. Perhaps it is Hiroshima that is my most radical and sharpest file. In the attempt to see in Hiroshima the expression of my fundamental thought I am hoping to affirm the fact that I am a Japanese and a writer. (158–59)

While using Hiroshima as a "file" for the systematization of his philosophy ("my fundamental thought *[shisō]*"), he is at the same time exploiting the aftermath of an atrocity in which tens of thousands died in order to reassert his identity as a kind of privileged and individualized being ("writer," "Japanese"). Ōe is inviting us, telling us, to read his *Notes* both biographically and intellectually against the background of his own life and those beliefs essential to his work; the context as well as the theme of the essays is extended beyond what any reader might have at first assumed.[9]

The ideas contained in *Notes*, while uniquely Ōe's own, are phrased in a lexicon rather starkly and conspicuously existentialist in character. Much of Ōe's work over the years has shown a debt to modern French literature, his field of study at the University of Tokyo in the early postwar period when the prestige of the existentialist writers was at its zenith. Existentialism has had more of an influence on literature than has any other twentieth-century philosophy, and the author most famously associated with it, Jean-Paul Sartre, was the one in whom Ōe is the most deeply read.[10] Ōe has claimed that the work of Sartre, together with that of Norman Mailer and the Japanese writers who emerged immediately after the war, comprise the triad upon which his own writing is built.[11] In fact, the references both direct and oblique in *Notes* to existentialism are many. He invokes Camus when he terms the atomic bomb "the most modern of *pestes*" and quotes him outright on the problem of God;

but more importantly for any reading of *Notes*, Ōe incorporates the discourse of existentialism *par* Sartre with his free and frequent borrowing of such seminal concepts as "authentic" *(seitōteki)*, "dignity" *(igen)*, and "shame" *(kutsujoku)*.

None of these words is used without an awareness of their history and power. Although Ōe actually met Sartre in Paris only a few years before beginning work on *Notes*,[12] he explains in it that he had long found in French literature the articulation of certain key problems which have troubled him since childhood and which still command his attentions.

The relationship between Sartre's works and Ōe's cannot be viewed as either insignificant or derivative. Existentialism, even if we speak of it in the singular, is pluralistic, stretching from at least Nietzsche to Sartre and beyond. It represents, as Sartre notes in *Existentialism and Humanism* (1946), "a spontaneous movement in contemporary European thought." Perhaps not only European: if Walter Kaufmann is correct, and existentialism is the thought of those who have contemplated philosophy from an "extreme situation," the Japanese counterpart of Europe's such situation was its defeat in the Second World War. That defeat, marked by the unprecedented use of nuclear weapons, itself an extreme situation, produced in Japan, as in France, a generation of writers who sought a philosophy that could restore some chance for dignity and liberty to their people.

The particular features and applications of Sartre's thought in *Notes* include the notion of absolute freedom, the insistence that "existence precedes essence," and the final absurdity of a world in which we all, no matter what, will die. But what is most central in *Notes*, and equally fundamental to Sartre's philosophy, is the concept of the Other. Existentialism has long been concerned with first proving the existence of the Other and then detailing the range of its possible relations with the Self. The use of these terms in existentialism is not initially social or political: it is purely ontological. In *Notes*, too, the idea of the Other is neither a strategy for creating "character" nor for attacking academic politics. Ōe himself may very well not be aware that his attempt to define in *Notes* an Other after the fashion of the existentialists informs the entire work in such an ontological way, since it is ostensibly a product of political journalism and not philosophy. But his interest in maintaining the distinctions between, for example, himself and the hibakusha, the Japanese and the Americans, the past and the present, and good and evil nonetheless sets up certain others as Other, i.e., beings who matter only insofar as they are not Ōe or do not participate in the culture with which he identifies. Because Ōe proceeds in a manner so suggestive of the French existentialists, it might be useful to outline the concept of the Other in Sartre's principal statement, *Being and Nothingness* (1943), to see how Ōe in writing of Hiroshima conforms to, or deviates from, the particular logic of the philosophy which has so influenced him.

■

Of the many terms for the different phases of being used by Sartre, the two most important are Being-for-itself (human consciousness) and Being-in-itself (all which is not human consciousness; already a term which, from the point of view of the For-itself, is potentially Other). The For-itself becomes aware of its existence when it realizes it is not the In-itself. In one sense the For-itself is, thanks to this negation, already "outside" one kind of being, isolated from the fullness some seem to enjoy. For Sartre, this is our liberation. The For-itself is rendered radically free, able to choose its own definition and to invent itself continually. Choice, consciousness, and freedom are ultimately traced to the same origin in this original differentiation of being.

Into the world of any For-itself, however, inevitably comes the day when it encounters a kind of being whose existence cannot be defined by an absence of consciousness. One day, in other words, all of us meet another human being who is as capable of treating us as an object as we are of him. At this point we are both "subjects" and "objects," and joining the company of the For-itself and the In-itself is now the For-other, i.e., a human consciousness aware of itself as the perceived object of another consciousness. This discovery of an Other who can do to us what we do to him is, naturally enough, unsettling and potentially lethal. Sartre writes in *Being and Nothingness*: "The Other is the one who excludes me from being himself, the one whom I exclude by being myself. Consciousnesses are directly supported by one another in a reciprocal imbrication of their being" (319). We are locked in a confrontation with our Other because it is just powerful enough to reify and render us an In-itself robbed of our freedom. If we define freedom as the potential for perpetual decision-making, and if the Other can decide for itself what we are, then one part of our freedom is threatened or even blocked.

Sartre has built into his social ontology the inevitability of conflict. He writes in *Existentialism and Humanism*:

> I cannot obtain any truth whatsoever about myself, except through the mediation of another. The other is indispensable to my existence, and equally so to any knowledge I can have of myself. Under these conditions, the intimate discovery of myself is at the same time the revelation of the other as a freedom which confronts mine, and which cannot think or will without doing so either for or against me. . . . It is in this world that man has to decide what he is and what others are. (45)

As we fear this power which the Other exercises over us even as we require its presence, the Other becomes our obsession. Our strategies are many: we can attempt to seduce it or conquer it, flee from it or embrace it. Any of these choices, however, traces its impetus back to a conflict between ourselves and our Other which Sartre characterizes as "absurd" because we can never eliminate the Other's threat to us. Moreover, it is also absurd to exercise freely our choice of relations (the initial encounter) or end them (our death). This is the concept of "absurdity" which led to attacks on existentialism as nihilistic, and which led Sartre to tell a skeptical Simone de Beauvoir that it was no more absurd to die at eighteen than at eighty.[13] To live one day in order to live another, to "exist" (a transitive verb in Sartre's French) a life knowing that one day life will no longer be existed, is patently absurd. For an existentialist the incontrovertible fact of death, however commonplace, presents a vast obstacle which we must clear before we can live as freely as we potentially can; if that fact reinforces the notion that existence is absurd, it may infect all other choices. Death, even more than the discovery of our own freedom, shapes life according to our desires and becomes the guiding condition of every life. Yet since the principle is so unsettling, it is also life's greatest absurdity, because death is the condition beyond which there is no "other." It must become one of the most important elements in our exercise of choice. As Heidegger, Sartre's philosophical forebear put it in *Being and Time* (1927), "Being-in-the-world is being towards death." His younger contemporary Maurice Blanchot expressed it in a more Gallic fashion: "The death of the Other: a double death, for the Other is death already, and weighs upon me like an obsession with death."[14]

Our battle with the Other, then, takes place against an absolute constraint which we cannot alter but must accommodate. This dark sketch of the human condition which Sartre draws prefigures the state of Hiroshima described by Ōe in *Notes;* but also like Sartre, Ōe holds out the promise of living fully under that constraint. Ōe's hibakusha, too, discover that it is up to them to realize their freedom by seizing it. That a Sartrean hero such as the communist Hoederer in *Dirty Hands* (1948), a character totally dedicated to social justice, should so resemble the brave hibakusha activists whom Ōe describes in *Notes* points to a shared belief in the possibility of good works in an evil world. This shared belief follows from a shared definition of the human condition. For both Ōe and Sartre man is confronted with two terminal points (birth and death) over which we have no control, yet between which we remain, in theory, free. Similarly for both of them, the practice of that freedom begins with an exercise of will: it is up to each of us to decide how, and what, we will be. Ōe invents in *Notes* a term for those who have survived Hiroshima and yet have refused to accede to their circumscribed status as victims: "Hiroshima-teki na ningen," or "Hiroshima Man." Sartre, while he does not have an equivalent phrase to describe his rare compatriots who act freely because they have resolved to be free, has nonetheless dedicated his literature to them. Again, there is a significant coincidence in this. One might characterize most of Sartre's postwar fiction as one steady and courageous effort to fight against despair amid circumstances which would seem to allow for no other reaction: fiction simultaneously free and absurd, free because its characters choose to revolt and absurd because most of the time despair is finally too pervasive to dispel. The despair of the twentieth century seems particularly permanent since it has been so "extreme." If, as Frederick Hoffman has stated, existentialist literature is the most modern of literatures since its primary direction is to present, "in terms of a succession of instantaneous experiences encounters of the self with objects, the full nature of the self and of its situational dilemma," then the literature which will be the most modern will be the one in which that "situational dilemma" is the most "extreme."[15] In Sartre's multi-volume work *The Age of Reason* (1945–49) that extreme situation was the wartime occupation of France, a time in his life when he was confronted with a clear existentialist dilemma: how to act authentically, i.e., as a free Frenchman, in the face of an overwhelming Other—a Nazi regime—continually imposing its own will.[16] Sartre discovers that there are many ways to act authentically in such circumstances, just as Ōe discovers that there are many ways to live as a hibakusha with dignity.

Indeed, if the presence of the Wehrmacht in Paris was an extreme situation, then so certainly was the nuclear incineration of a city. Twenty years after the bombing, Ōe would observe in *Notes* that Hiroshima was "the most weighty, the most dominant, existence" in his life. Interestingly, Ōe terms Hiroshima an "existence" (*sonzai*), as if it too partakes of being; and in the sense that the whole of that city's suffering does represent for him a fearful yet compelling Other, Hiroshima can be said to "exist" in much the same way a human consciousness does. In fact, much as Ōe is faced with the usual Sartrean range of responses to Hiroshima and its survivors (love, hate, fear, anger, etc.), his encounter with the atrocity also serves as a "praxis"—the existentialist call to action prompted by an individual's doubt-evoking experience—that governs his future encounters. Hiroshima is clearly treated as such a praxis: in Ōe's own words it is the ultimate "extreme situation" (*kyokugen-jōkyō*), and his tense confrontation with it is precisely the confrontation of self with the menacing world that existentialism posits for all of us.

In *Notes*, for example, as in other of Ōe's works, there is a special attention paid to ethnic minorities in Japan. Among those whom Ōe meets in Hiroshima are Korean and Okinawan hibakusha, survivors who are identified with a double marginality that strengthens Ōe's stark contrast of himself against the Other. In the third chapter of *Notes*, entitled "Hiroshima, City of Moralists" (Morarisuto no Hiroshima), he sets out to visit a hibakusha who is at once female, old, Korean, and Christian: all characteristics which neither Ōe nor his dominant society favor. Although she once hated America for dropping the bomb, and Japan for the war which was the justification for its use, her only available emotion now is the wish that it not happen ever again. Ōe marvels at her attitude. In a phrase Ōe uses repeatedly in his descriptions of the hibakusha, he praises this victim as one who has "freed herself" by realizing that she is at liberty to live a life not wholly determined by her past: in renouncing her anger, she has thrown off some part of the bomb's hold on her. She is, in other words, an existentialist. The knowledge that she will one day die—more likely than not for bomb-related causes—in no way mitigates her struggle. The hibakusha, who live each day as a reprieve from a mortality seen more clearly by them than by the rest of us, can choose to endow their lives (whether long or short, it makes no difference) with a purpose, and that ability to choose is just as crucial to Ōe's message in *Notes* as it is to the whole of Sartre's philosophy.

Ōe notes several times that his objective in visiting and writing about Hiroshima is to comprehend Hiroshima Man, people who, like Sartre's resistance fighters, represent unambiguous examples of existentialist action in the world. It is important to point out, however, that these examples do not find the exercise of that action either easy or innocent. Sartre argues it is bad faith (*mauvaise foi*, perhaps better translated as "self-deception") which prevents us from realizing our freedom. One of his examples in *Being and Nothingness* is that of a woman who, though she has no intention of rewarding a prospective suitor with her affections, endlessly defers acting in such a way as to make that clear to him (96–97). Bad faith also prevents us from realizing what anguish there is in being free: by remaining outwardly noncommittal, she does not have to face the problem of letting him know how she truly feels. But eventually, if we are lucky, a crisis comes along which forces us to consider our values, and then we do face our freedom, and the terrible power it gives us, in anguish. When we are bereft of all our usual ways of thinking, we realize that we may value anything we please, that we are not bound by any "essence." Consequently we experience anguish at our fundamental emptiness which is identical with our freedom. This is why Ōe has found in the hibakusha of Hiroshima his perfect existentialist model: the annihilation of their city has rendered them acutely aware of their emptiness, their anguish, and thus potentially of their freedom as well.

Ōe comes to Hiroshima and its survivors not only with this vision of their heroic exercise of freedom but also with a very personal past which has led him to seek out such an exemplary, and galvanizing, exercise. Ōe explains that past in a central chapter of *Notes*:

> I was a child in a Shikoku mountain village when the war ended, and I was troubled by a single terrifying dilemma. It arose from an episode in a film which I had seen in our local theater. A young soldier, taken prisoner by the enemy and afraid that he would confess military secrets under torture, promptly commits suicide. This story shook me. The deep impression it made caused me to shudder with fear. I was sure that I, too,

would be faced by a similar predicament at some point in the war. An important problem of choice loomed before me. I was moved by the young soldier's death but, like the child that I was and so very attached to my own life, I doubted there was anything in this world which I would protect at such a cost. Still a newcomer in this world, with nothing yet accomplished, I thought the idea of my death so fearful that I had no way to speak of it. If I were ever forced to make a choice between a secret and my death, I would reveal everything. When would I ever become the sort of human being who could resist until death? I asked my father, with whom I had seen the film and who would soon die afterwards, why the young soldier had committed suicide. I hid my dilemma behind a boy's innocent expression. Until that moment I had never heard words from an adult as shocking as my father's short reply. It was his irritated way of punishing his son's feigned innocence.

"That soldier? Even if he hadn't committed suicide, they'd have killed him after they made him talk." (85–86)

This "fearful dilemma," as Ōe terms it elsewhere, is how to convert himself from one type of person—the sort who has nothing to die for—to another, a man who will live, and die, in accordance with his chosen beliefs. Yet what complicates the dilemma, and what makes it classically Sartrean, is the cruel absurdity that Ōe's father used to destroy his innocence: no matter what we choose, death remains inescapable. Choice, then, does not alter our condition but only our dignity possible within it. In this brief anecdote we learn why Ōe found existentialism so compelling a philosophy. He would be able to link his anxious encounter with the young soldier of the wartime film with Sartre's abstract, but equally anxious, encounter of the For-itself with another For-itself, that is, the Self with the Other: both Ōe's childhood incident and Sartre's reasoned ontology force upon the subject an awareness of itself as an object, and both look upon that awareness with a mixture of curiosity and fear.

Sartre, in his study of Jean Genet, *Saint Genet* (1952), imagines his criminal-homosexual-artist subject's first "conversion," that is, that "fatal instant' which labels one's being forever, to have taken place in his life "sometime between the ages of ten and fifteen." (Ōe was ten when he attended the theater with his father.) Genet's conversion took place, theorizes Sartre, when he was innocently reaching into a kitchen drawer and an adult, of whose presence he had not been aware, shouted out the damning charge "Thief!" From that moment Genet *is* a thief, and his life will be spent reconciling his freedom with that identity. If Ōe's conversion was that "fatal instant" in the theater when he confronted his emptiness (at the time confused with cowardice), then we can expect him to be as obsessed with that particular indictment as Genet was with his. Both Genet and Ōe were introduced to their Others at equally tender ages, and both have pursued in their careers as writers the possibility of exceeding the limits which such Others would seek to impose.

This is not to say that either Genet or Ōe would wish to banish or destroy their Other; the former is glad to be a thief, and the latter somewhat relieved to be a coward. (In a chapter of *Saint Genet* entitled "I Went to Theft as to a Liberation, as to the Light," Sartre writes that Genet's association with a professional thief "woke him up, freed him from his fate, made a man of him" [435]; and in the fourth chapter of *Notes* Ōe is quite aware that his fear of dying like the young soldier in the film is what, ironically, keeps him alive.) Sartre incessantly reminds us that the discovery of the Other is the primal and reciprocal discovery of ourselves: "To be other to oneself—the ideal always aimed at concretely in the form of being *this Other* to oneself—is the primary value of my relations with the Other" (*Being and Nothingness*, 476). The Other is a necessary if threatening force in the completion of our human existence, and our original confrontation with it is one that simultaneously emboldens and threatens us. This was true when Ōe saw the young soldier on film, and it was true when he actually met the hibakusha of Hiroshima. The survivors of the world's first use of nuclear weapons painfully reminded Ōe of what he is and what he is not. He aspires to be both what they are (heroes) and what they are not (healthy "normal" people); he both seeks and fears what they might have to teach him. The hibakusha, like the celluloid soldier, are acutely aware of their approaching deaths, yet in the face of this inalterable fact both the soldier's decision not to confess and the hibakusha's resolve to persevere strike Ōe as doubly brave, and moreover authentic, gestures of their total existentialist freedom to make whatever they wish from that which circumstances have dealt them.

Against this background of a search to find, and preserve, the human will and the dignity it generates in a world increasingly intolerant of individual autonomy, *Notes* reads as an extended and meandering definition of the hibakusha—women and men who struggle against their reification by atrocity—as Ōe's feared and respected Other. Finally that definition will have to overlap with that of himself. Sartre writes that "to-be-in-the-world is to haunt the world, not to be ensnared in it; and it is in my 'being-in-the-world' that the Other determines me. Our relation is not a *frontal* opposition but rather an *oblique* interdependence" (*Being and Nothingness*, 331). Ōe discovers the truth and relevance of this interdependence once he attempts to fix his own relation to the hibakusha. In the prologue to *Notes* Ōe initially sees himself, correctly, as "other" in the eyes of the survivors when he bifurcates all people as those who are "of" Hiroshima ("Hiroshima no hito") and those who are, in a phrase reminiscent of Sartre, "outside" Hiroshima ("Hiroshima no soto no hito"). Later in *Notes*, however, this radical division is complicated when Ōe finds himself identifying with, and even envying, those who would exclude him from their

terrible experience. Conversely, the hibakusha themselves can seek to appropriate Ōe's Otherness in resolving *not* to live as victims. This is what Sartre was
describing when he termed relations between the Self and Other as a "reciprocal imbrication of their being."

What emerges in *Notes* is Ōe's ambivalence towards the hibakusha, which
is in truth an ambivalence towards himself and his own being. The Sartrean
schema of struggling relations between the Self and the Other is in part predicated upon a like ambivalence: "There is no dialectic for my relations toward
the Other," Ōe states in *Notes*, "but rather a circle" in which Self and the Other
continually pursue and flee from each other.[17] Ōe points out, for instance, that
we admire the activist hibakusha who risk their frail health in the service of
world peace, but at the same time we deny the implications of such risk-taking
for ourselves: "Do not we who are left alive in the world deny the gamble of
their deaths and refuse to pay off their wagers?" (96). In other words our lack
of the hibakusha's courage is one proof of their existence as "Other" even while
our admiration of it would challenge that opposed status. We use that ambivalence to affirm ourselves. At one point in *Notes* Ōe tells the story of an old man
who, unable to provide his hibakusha grandson with proper medical care, went
insane with grief once the boy died. When Ōe then asks, "Is there any despair
from which it is impossible to recover more miserable than that which the old
man felt, the despair that comes from having to reproach oneself for another's
suffering?" (72), he is using the notion of "despair" ambivalently. First, it points
to the pathetic and victimized lives that Ōe's hibakusha lead. Second, it leads
the way to a kind of authentic and aware existence Ōe covets. "Miserable
despair" is a phrase with a considerable lineage within Sartre's existentialism: it
is a key concept for his map of anyone's journey towards the realization of
freedom. He writes in *Existentialism and Humanism:*

> As for "despair," the meaning of this expression is extremely simple. It
> merely means that we limit ourselves to a reliance upon that which is
> within our wills, or within the sum of probabilities which render our
> action feasible. . . . When Descartes said, "Conquer yourself rather than
> the world," what he meant was, at bottom, the same—that we should
> act without hope. (39)

The despair of Ōe's bereaved old man forces him to realize how radically
alone in the world any of us is, and from that understanding begins the exercise
of our freedom: Sartre would surely say that Ōe's old man *chose* insanity as a
way of "being" which expresses his relations with others. Ōe may feel sorry
for him, but he also describes him with admiration, perhaps because he too
recognizes insanity as a "brave" choice in a world which has, after the "rational"
decision to drop an atomic bomb, so devalued sanity.

Nothing the old man could have done would have saved his grandson, and that renders his insanity the act of a free man. Freedom is only true freedom if it is exercised without the assumption that it will lead to a change in the world. The despair and the hopelessness of the hibakusha consequently can lead them to pursue objectives which, absurdly, they know will not be achieved. For Ōe the most absurd of such objectives is the peaceful world envisioned by Hiroshima's committed activists. The nihilism persistently associated with existentialism (and with good reason, despite Sartre's protests) extends to the lives of those Hiroshima survivors who, with only a few years to live, struggle to abolish nuclear weapons though nations increasingly covet them. Yet, one recalls, it is only through the "nihilism" of negating the In-itself that Sartre says the For-itself can come into being: as he writes in the epigraph to this chapter, it has "its origin at the heart of Being." The annihilation of Hiroshima similarly serves in Ōe's essays as that "total upheaval" which results in our consciousness of the world. *Notes* can be read as an attempt to interpret Hiroshima and its aftermath as an existentialist situation so extreme that it in fact outlines in bold relief and on an immense scale the entire economy of Being, a new world which both grants us an existence ("bomb victim," much as Genet was a "thief") and also menaces that existence (bomb victims will die, just as thieves must be imprisoned). Ōe's world, even more so than Sartre's, is one in which For-themselves flee from each other even as they strive to exchange existences with each other; and it is one in which all such Sisyphean struggles nonetheless take us to the same, unalterable, and finally very un-free conclusion.

■

Ōe's prologue to *Notes* itself begins with a prologue: an explanation of his profound despair before he even left Tokyo for Hiroshima. As he prepared to attend the Ninth World Conference against Atomic and Hydrogen Bombs in the summer of 1963,[18] his infant son was in the hospital "on the verge of death" with "utterly no hope of recovery"; his editor and traveling companion Yasue Ryōsuke had just lost his oldest daughter; and both of them were upset over the death of a mutual friend in Paris who, in anguish over the possibility of a world nuclear war, had killed himself. Ōe's state of mind had already concluded that the world which allowed Hiroshima was a world entirely consistent with its tragedy; attending this extraordinary Conference would only be a reminder of what ordinary life had dictated. "I had never previously set out on a trip so deeply exhausted, depressed, and melancholy" (9).[19]

Ōe began his journey to Hiroshima in anguish, but an anguish which carried with it a responsibility. Ōe felt responsible not just for having brought a severely ill child into the world but also for having undertaken a trip to Hiroshima to unearth something which will make his friend's choice to commit suicide a decision that he himself would not have made. However, it was his friend's freedom to have selected that course which, just as Sartre would have predicted, incited the greatest anxiety in Ōe. From the very start *Notes* reads as an investigation of any individual's ethical courses within the context of anguish either affirmed in the exercise of freedom or wholly surrendered to in the face of seemingly overwhelming constraints .

The actual Conference sessions only deepened Ōe's depression. Riddled with scandal and plagued by politics and egotistical grandstanding, the discussions struck Ōe as inauthentic, insincere, and even embarrassing. But then something happened: "Yet a week later, as we were leaving Hiroshima, we both realized that we had found a way to climb out of the deep pit of melancholy into which we had fallen and move towards an authentic recovery. The only reason for this frankly had been our encounter with people who embodied the characteristics of Hiroshima Man" (10).

Each of Ōe's subsequent trips to Hiroshima was an attempt to continue such encounters with the very special kind of men and women that the atrocity had ironically produced. Moreover, each trip was an attempt to understand more of himself, both what he is and what he is not, by comparing his own life with theirs. The discovery of Hiroshima Man is Ōe's discovery of the Other. Ōe himself understands this when he notes, "I hoped to re-examine, using Hiroshima as a tool, as some sort of lens, all the thoughts, morals, and sensibilities which I had assumed were mine" (10). Since he earlier defined Hiroshima as something he is not ("Hiroshima no soto no hito"), he can only find himself in it if it functions, as in Sartre, as a consciousness which illuminates his own by challenging it. That illumination, again as in Sartre, is not a gift freely offered but one won in a confrontation. Ōe writes in the prologue about a letter he received from a Hiroshima doctor and victim of the bomb who symbolizes for him what he, as an outsider, will never be able to know about the lives of the hibakusha. When, for example, the doctor and Ōe seem in agreement over the hibakusha's right to silence about the atrocity, the doctor still insists that a non-hibakusha such as Ōe cannot know why the hibakusha would choose to exercise that right. This criticism does not bother Ōe in the least. He gratefully accepts it, for it actually supports his vital opposition of Self and Other. The doctor, in fact, is an excellent example of what Ōe seeks: as the first of the hibakusha Others whom we encounter in *Notes*, it is telling to observe that Ōe portrays him to be exercising one of the freedoms for which Ōe yearns. The doctor, complaining in an essay he once wrote that atomic-bomb literature has focused exclusively and to its detriment on only those victims who have died in tragedy, argues that he and many other hibakusha have *chosen* to lead quite different sorts of lives: "I have especially warned myself not to indulge in that hibakusha tendency to think of themselves as 'victims.' Although I was there in Hiroshima, I have nonetheless worked to heal myself and all of mankind, and I have come to hope for a death not due to the bomb but rather entirely my own" (13).

Ōe's hibakusha doctor has freely chosen to revolt not against his condition (just as Genet never tries to stop being a criminal) but within it. He asserts his power to assume whatever attitude he wishes towards the circumstances in which history has placed him, and he scorns those who have surrendered that power. His will to live as he pleases is an expression of existentialist freedom: a freedom not to alter reality ("I was there in Hiroshima") but to regard it in whatever fashion still preserves one's dignity. Frederick Hoffman observes in *The Mortal No: Death and the Modern Imagination:*

> The most profoundly charged act of the modern self is an act of will: it is the "adventure" of choice. The self must choose what he is, what he will be, what he will do by way of assuming a position with respect to his death. The expectation of dying becomes a major issue. As an ultimate boundary situation, one which no one can avoid, it offers additional kinds and degrees of challenge and stimulates new exercises of the will. (317)

The existentialist person uses this act of will consciously in confronting a terrifying world to locate a mode of existence deliberately patterned after, although not enslaved by, that world. Ōe seeks to perceive and be the Other ("When would I ever become the sort of human being who could resist until death?") while the Other similarly seeks to perceive and be Ōe ("I have come to hope for a death not due to the bomb but rather entirely my own"). The question for each of us, hibakusha doctor and famous author alike, is how much responsibility we will accept for a world that is created by forces outside our direction or control. When that world is Hiroshima, as it is for the doctor, or when it is a place whose fearful encounters are epitomized by a visit to Hiroshima, as it is for Ōe, its inhabitants can feel especially powerless in the face of an atrocity that killed tens of thousands. Yet, as in the case of the doctor who has resolved to live his irradiated life as if it were not, Ōe too hopes there is still a chance that he can choose to be as brave as that young soldier he once saw in a film.

The first chapter of *Notes,* "The First Journey to Hiroshima," describes Ōe's discovery of atomic-bomb survivors who have chosen to be brave by struggling for an improved life even as they emphasize their status as victims, and it promises him personally a similar opportunity for authenticity. Ōe contrasts his hibakusha heroes with the demoralized non-hibakusha participants at the Conference:

> At the political meetings I sometimes felt like an unknown and lost traveler. There I was, just running in circles from one session to the next. Yet

once I left the conference hall, I encountered what was for me the new, and true, Hiroshima. I attempted to enter into it and become intimate with it. . . . I felt that I would try to understand the real Hiroshima Man on each of the trips I would make here. . . . What opened my eyes and inspired me was a meeting of hibakusha which went on until late at night. . . . (42–43)

Most prominent, however, among these hibakusha who led Ōe into "the new, and true, Hiroshima" were those in their final stages of life. Highlighting the Conference was the annual Peace March, which made its way across the city in a public display of concern for the past, and potentially future, victims of nuclear weapons. Ōe followed the march and observed as it passed in front of the Atomic Bomb Hospital, a facility reserved for the treatment of the hibakusha. Several of the patients there for treatment emerged from the entrance to greet and encourage the marchers, oblivious perhaps to the political squabbling which had marked the earlier proceedings. One of the patients, a diminutive middle-aged man named Miyamoto Sadao, attracted Ōe's attention with his brief speech (nearly drowned out by the loudspeakers wielded by the marchers themselves) expressing his sincere hopes for the Conference's success.

Ōe encountered many more terminally ill hibakusha at the Atomic Bomb Casualty Commission (ABCC)—a grim institution which Ōe describes as "a land of the dead"—and at Hiroshima's Red Cross Hospital as well. At these facilities, however, the one who interested Ōe most was a hibakusha who was not a patient but the chief of staff. Dr. Shigetō Fumio served as the head of both the Atomic Bomb Hospital and the Red Cross Hospital. Although injured in the blast, Shigetō had been ambulatory enough, and altruistic enough, to attend to those more seriously hurt. For the next two decades Shigetō continued his care of, and research into, the hibakusha as well as involve himself in a number of social and political causes linked to their plight. However, his work, like so many of our actions in the existentialist world, has been often in vain. Ōe was as intrigued with the ongoing struggle against these overwhelming odds as he had been frightened by his father's remarks on the inevitability of death. He notes on the evening that commemorates the destruction of Hiroshima eighteen years earlier: "No doubt there were many people this night everywhere in Hiroshima who slept. At the Atomic Bomb Hospital doctors struggled without a moment's rest. Their fight was for naught. They worked hard to save a young girl, but she died" (32).

Shigetō and the other "activist" hibakusha whom Ōe met comprise the intentional object of Ōe's search for a mode of existence that will provide him with a reflection of his own potential for freedom: his heroes, Hiroshima Man, the Other. One year later, in events related in the second chapter of *Notes*,

"Hiroshima Revisited" (Hiroshima saihō), Ōe is again drawn to their courageous example. We learn that almost fifty patients in the Atomic Bomb Hospital have died since Ōe last visited, despite the careful and continuous attentions
of Dr. Shigetō and his staff. Against the background of a conference even more
racked by politics in 1964 than it had been in 1963, the death of one of these
victims especially affects Ōe: Miyamoto, last year's Peace March spokesman
for the hospitalized hibakusha, has been dead since the beginning of winter.
Ōe eulogizes Miyamoto as "the last man" not only because this year no other
hospital patient has come forward to take his place as a representative but also
because Miyamoto represents for Ōe a completed, final ideal. In his own words
left behind in a testament, Miyamoto describes how his life, and death, could
embody an ideal: "I appeal from Hiroshima, from the city in which the human
race first experienced the atomic bomb and where there are still many who,
suffering day and night from radiation sickness, anemia, and liver damage, continue their struggle towards a miserable death" (50).

Fully aware, as the existentialists teach, that our terminus is always death,
Miyamoto and his comrades choose to struggle towards, never against, the fact
of that death. Only because of that choice can they also realize their freedom
to "live" as they wish prior to their deaths. Others, Miyamoto tells us in the
same testament, commit suicide when diagnosed with radiation sickness, but
he himself selected instead to dedicate his remaining days to a cause—that
of world peace—which, Ōe learns, contributed to the exhaustion that soon
killed him:

> His words full of sadness and suspicions, Dr. Shigetō questioned why
> Miyamoto, too, had died so easily from general weakness—a question
> he had asked himself of so many other patients. The doctor, who had
> seen countless deaths of bomb patients due to general prostration, con-
> cluded that in this instance as well the bomb had more likely than not
> destroyed something essential in that part of us which resists.
>
> When, in order to announce his belief in the success of the Ninth
> World Conference, this small middle-aged man appeared in the front
> garden of the hospital at the hottest hour of the day, he surely shortened
> the path towards the end of his life by straining himself. For that price,
> he purchased the opportunity to express his will (even though nearly
> none of the marchers heard him above the din of their loudspeakers) and
> thus withdraw with the satisfaction, and dignity, of a man who had let
> his hopes be known. (47–48)

"For that price" Miyamoto is also numbered among the freest of Ōe's existentialist men and women. Ōe is moved by a victim who would freely choose
to hasten his own death in order to live in accordance with his principles. It
makes no difference that no one heard him "above the din" or even that the

Conference was doomed to fail: what does matter is that Miyamoto himself was the one who chose to commit his remaining strength as he willed. By exercising that prerogative, Miyamoto realized it was his to make and achieved not only an awareness of his freedom but, to use a word with powerful reverberations in both *Notes* and Sartre's literature, dignity.

In keeping with the existentialist theory of the Other, however, it must be recognized that this exercise of freedom on Miyamoto's part wins not only Ōe's admiration but inspires a fearful envy. Ōe, momentarily once again the small boy troubled both by a young soldier's bravery and by his father's contempt of that bravery as absurd, is confronted by the fact that Miyamoto's courage is his own cowardice. Upon reflection, the implications of that bravery for Ōe are not wholly comfortable, or without contradiction. If, after all, we are free under all circumstances to select our responses to those circumstances, the fact yet remains that any one of the responses available to us may result in a worsened situation, not because we wish it so but because we cannot predict all the consequences of the response we choose. The world of action, to phrase it in explicitly existentialist terms, is vaster than any of our paltry attempts to influence it. Miyamoto may have acted "authentically," but he is nonetheless dead; he may have been courageous, but it was a courage inspired by a terrible wrong.

Ōe might agree with Sartre when he says it is no more absurd to die at eighteen than eighty; Miyamoto was going to die one day anyway, not because he was a hibakusha but simply because he was mortal. We cannot choose our deaths, only our lives, and that is what Miyamoto and the rest of Ōe's Hiroshima Men (and Women) do. The existentialist tradition holds that we all come into the world as surplus being ("geworfen," "de trop"); we feel ourselves to be marginal, extra, and supplemental since the world has gotten on very well without us. The hibakusha in a sense are far more acutely aware of their marginality than we are of ours, for they experience tremendous shame and guilt at having survived what many of their neighbors did not. Moreover, they think of themselves as useless in a world of "normal" non-hibakusha. Only through their perception of that marginality as one imposed upon them by the Other, only through refusing to live in bad faith and choosing their own lives, do hibakusha—or any of us—in fact live authentically. When Sartre writes that "existentialism, in our sense of the word, is a doctrine that does render human life possible" and when Ōe writes that his Hiroshima Man "survives in Hiroshima through the most horrifying experience and then, as one who survives, lives the most authentic life,"[20] they are both independently concluding that men and women such as Miyamoto have achieved a mode of existence that defines "life," and have exercised a freedom that potentially grants us our freedom, too.

This idea of a symbiosis linking the extraordinary lives of the hibakusha with the ordinary choices facing the rest of us is amplified in the third chapter of *Notes*, "Hiroshima, City of Moralists." The survivors who have so impressed Ōe on his trips to Hiroshima seem to him gifted with special insights into the human condition. The "concrete yet personal" meanings they attach to words such as "courage," "hope," and "authenticity" mark the survivors as those whom Ōe says were once called *jinsei hihyōka* (literally, "critics of human nature"), although he now glosses this Sino-Japanese compound with the English word "moralists." Aligning the notion of "critic"—Ōe's own profession—with the notion of ethical action—defined by Sartre in *Existentialism and Humanism* as behavior in accordance with one's authentic self—renders Ōe's life work parallel to that of the hibakusha heroes he celebrates.

The "crisis" of Hiroshima which has precipitated Ōe's perfect examples of existentialist freedom shares with the "criticism" he practices in order to enjoy that freedom for himself a common root: Greek *krinein*, "to divide" and thus by extension "to decide." Both are terms in which difference, either between an earlier era and the present one or between what is valued and what is not, matters greatly; and just as Ōe the critic seeks the difference of his hibakusha Other, the moralists of Hiroshima seek in the crisis of atrocity the difference between how one might have acted in good faith before the bomb and after it. Ōe proclaims Miyamoto to have been the "representative Hiroshima moralist," but his most compelling example of the "moral" nature of his hibakusha Other is found in the story of a young woman deformed by the bomb who, years later, gave birth to a stillborn and similarly deformed baby. In keeping with standard medical practice, this woman was never shown her dead child before it was disposed of. Later, when she laments, "If only I had seen the child, what courage I could have summoned!" (68), Ōe is tremendously struck by her conspicuous use of the charged word "courage" among her otherwise sorrowful expressions of grief and lifelessness. Ōe comments that her courage "belongs to the depth of meaning newly given the word by the existentialists" (68–69); a depth that derives from the importance that the choice to act as one wills has for the entirety of existentialist being. Courage, for instance, is very much the theme of Sartre's *Troubled Sleep* (1949), in which ordinary Frenchmen living under the German Occupation of Paris evidence a courage: not a momentary emotional reaction, but rather a considered decision to *be* free men and thus reveal the possibility of freedom even in a world which seems to scoff at the very idea.

The young woman of whom Ōe writes would have found courage in seeing her stillborn child because she would have confronted herself and "realized" her own being. The reasons why this would be so, Ōe points out, may not be easily apparent to the rest of us. We might think that it was kindest (Ōe uses the word *hyūmanisutikku*, 'humanistic') of the hospital not to expose a young mother to the sight of her deformed baby, since we ordinarily need to observe the limits of what we may "gaze upon with human eyes" and still remain human. But a hibakusha, who has already lived through the most inhuman of experiences, may be inured to things we are not. A survivor of that which Ōe again refers to existentially as an "extreme situation," this young woman now contemplates herself as inalterably different, a post-Hiroshima human being: the Other. She would have looked upon her child and seen herself in the confrontation with an object empowered to render her the same. In realizing her own self, she would have gained the courage to be whatever she willed within that self, just as the Nazis made Sartre's Frenchmen understand their own freedom under tyranny. In Ōe's words, such a confrontation would produce a new humanism which surpasses ordinary humanism, a humanism "born out of the 'Hiroshima catastrophe'" (69).

Sartre argues in *Existentialism and Humanism* that "existentialism is a humanism" because he believed that to realize one's own freedom was to realize freedom for everyone. In *Notes* Ōe reverses the argument. The issue for Ōe in *Notes*, as elsewhere in his writing, is always humanism—existentialism seems simply a way to preserve it intact.[21] "Humanism is an existentialism" because recognizing the true character of the bomb's victims necessarily entails recognizing one's own character, i.e., one's freedom. The relationship between the hibakusha and their comprehension of freedom even within their highly restricted lives is one which increasingly absorbs Ōe's critical attentions in *Notes*. For instance, he tells the story of a young girl who hanged herself after being diagnosed with cancer. Initially Ōe sympathizes: he "cannot criticize" what was in one sense an exercise of courage, and he is grateful that Japan is not a Christian country which would have censured her choice. But Ōe cannot see her death as an exercise of freedom. Sartre, for his part, usually considers suicide a senseless act since the commentary one hopes to make with an act whose effects one is not even around to witness only plunges us more deeply into absurdity. Ōe, too, saves his greatest respect for those victims who "do not commit suicide, in spite of everything," because *that* is a choice in line with the sincere acceptance of their condition. It is not inconsistent to admire the courage of the young soldier who kills himself along with the courage of the hibakusha who do not. These are kinds of courage categorically different from each other, just as the hospital's "humanism" is not the "humanism" of a mother who has survived a nuclear attack. The first courage is pre-atrocious, a gesture of drama in a world that was guaranteed to acknowledge it, while the second, the courage of those who watch the world disintegrate, is the barest, most meager sign they can make to retain any sense of themselves. Ōe senses clearly here his own "otherness," his inability to live as decisively and as freely as the hibakusha whom he documents. He indicts himself as one "rotten by the mold of powerlessness" because he cannot stop others from suicide. After all, he too might kill himself were he stricken with cancer; the hibakusha, then, are all the more "other" to him if they choose not to. Their special courage, the kind Ōe lacks, is finally the product of their "fundamentally and thoroughly human moral sense."

Whereas it was once a suicide that challenged Ōe to examine his own nature when he was a boy, as an adult in the postwar, post-Hiroshima world it is now those who do not kill themselves "in spite of everything" who challenge his sense of self. In one chapter of *Notes* Ōe mentions three elderly hibakusha in particular—a butcher, a music teacher, and a pensioner—as examples of how some survivors can choose to accept their condition and realize their freedom within its confines. This they do by joining a group of other atomic-bomb victims. It is a move which affirms their identity on one hand while it liberates them from it on the other. These people too use the word "courage" to express that which confronting their Other, and thus themselves, has provided them. Ōe's hibakusha, like Sartre's Genet, are individuals who have been reified by society to the point where their freedom of action is severely restricted by the function (that of a passive victim) assigned them. The hibakusha can then either accept this reduced portion and lose their right to accede to the fullness of their humanity, or, like Miyamoto, they can take risks and assert their will. It *is* risky: to leave the small space in life which we are given means we might lose even that. Only some hibakusha are courageous because for most an authentic act would result merely in further alienation from the world that surrounds them.

In the seventh chapter of *Notes*, "Other Journeys to Hiroshima" (Hiroshima e no samazama na tabi), Ōe tells the moving story of a young male hibakusha who has recently died of radiation sickness. He had been diagnosed with the disease for two years, but rather than quit his job and stay in bed—the recommended treatment—he, in Ōe's words, "attempted to live." And love as well: but the woman he had intended to marry committed suicide shortly after his own death. Ōe calls her suicide a "hopeless choice": as Sartre interprets Descartes, only in acting without hope does our despair lead us to freedom. What she chose to do was the "maximum." There was no inauthentic self-sacrifice in it, only the "violence of a decisive love." Ōe theorizes that "she had completely involved herself in the life of her young man in participating in his fate: this was her own single most radical choice of fate" (136). This was the risk we take when we act freely. The girl's decision to do the "maximum" led, tragically, to her death. Loving a victim of the atomic bomb resulted in the loss of two lives, two small spaces now eliminated. This is a dilemma for the men and women of *Notes*, and for all of us in the existentialist view of life, of which Ōe seems aware but seldom pursues to its fullest logical conclusions. For no matter how much of an existentialist Ōe may seem to be, he resists the cruelty of the gamble we make when we embark on a truly free course of action, and he does not want every action to conclude always in absurdity. It is important, perhaps too important, to Ōe that he find something whole in Hiroshima amid the rubble.

The growing fissure in Ōe's attempt to fashion heroes out of victims is apparent in the fourth chapter of *Notes*, "Of Human Dignity" (Ningen no igen ni tsuite), in which he explores the dichotomy between dignity and shame. Both are words, he admits, whose full moral and philosophical force he learned to appreciate through his reading of French literature. At the same time, however, they echo the difficult choice he has faced since childhood: it is here that Ōe relates his anecdote of going to a movie theater with his father at age ten. Could Ōe, too, choose to die with dignity rather than be killed in shame? "When could ever I, the sort who would be meaninglessly killed after being shamed, convert myself into one who would die by my own hand, and with dignity?" (88). In this chapter we are told that the dignity found in the hibakusha is Ōe's most vital discovery in Hiroshima, something "beyond that which words can trace." Ōe goes so far as to claim that the only way he knows of finding dignity himself is never to lose sight of that of the Hiroshima people; his self-worth becomes entirely tied up with the Other he perceives to exist at the site of an atrocity of whose ultimate meaning he remains "outside."

Again it is the Other that embodies a quality to which Ōe is attracted yet either fears or remains distant. Miyamoto and others like him are held up as increasingly idealized examples of people who have led their lives with dignity. Dignity, moreover, is a particularly crucial quality. Ōe calls it the most "human" of characteristics, and that which he has personally coveted since his childhood. Ironically, however, it is also true that Ōe finds dignity in others because they are *not* him. The hibakusha have been through a conversion which, were Ōe to duplicate it, would threaten his own life just as the young woman who loved the dying man had to kill herself in order to "participate in his fate." For Ōe to partake of the hibakusha's dignity would be to partake of their Otherness, which, even if it were possible, would result in his becoming a victim as well.

An equally difficult term for Ōe to reconcile with atrocity is the opposite of dignity: humiliation. He gives us the example of a young woman disfigured with keloid scars. Typically for such victims, she perceives all people in the world as divided into only two categories: other women disfigured with keloid scars and everybody else. Like tattooed numbers, keloids are the twentieth century's special stigmata. Her body becomes the basis of her relations with all others. Sartre explains at length in *Being and Nothingness* that our physical selves constitute "the necessary condition of the existence of a world," and that the body itself leads to the realization of our finitude and potentially our freedom:

Even this disability from which I suffer I have assumed by the very fact that I live; I surpass it toward my own projects, I make of it the necessary obstacle for my being, and I cannot be crippled without choosing myself as crippled. This means that I choose the way in which I constitute my disability (as "unbearable," "humiliating," "to be hidden," "to be revealed to all," etc.). But this inapprehensible body is precisely the necessity that *there be a choice*, that I do not exist *all at once*. (432)

Similarly, the keloid victim can use her condition as a liberating means toward full, and human, being. First, her physical difference becomes the basis for a radical Other-ing of the rest of the world. Second, she and the other victims suffer the consequences of this Other-ing, for they are the ones who feel the shame and humiliation of being different. They are the ones who fell *de trop*, and their status as "surplus" people unleashes a Sartrean chain reaction whose three major links are shame, confrontation with the Other, and alienation from the world. This is precisely what happens to Ōe's keloid victim. What sort of life, he asks, does she choose for herself? Like most such victims, she hides and refuses to participate in the world: they allow the Other and their shame before it to rob them of their freedom. Ōe will not acknowledge this flight as an exercise of freedom because it is not truly as they wish to live; but he will once again canonize those keloid victims who take a third step and confront the world with their difference. These victims make weapons out of their scars and wield them so that others will not have to. Consequently, they free themselves from shame and fear and realize their complete humanity. Ōe gives us an example of such a liberated keloid victim in "Other Journeys to Hiroshima" when he writes of once moderating a round-table television discussion featuring not only well-known local hibakusha activists but a woman named Murato Yoshiko. Murato, who suffers from terrible disfigurement, is lauded by Ōe as a "classic example of a hibakusha who has not surrendered."[22]

At first Murato had wanted her beauty—her "lost" beauty—back. Ōe notes that the shift in her life toward the realization of her freedom and toward authentic being began when she abandoned that vain hope: again, we are free only when we act "without hope." How did she, unlike so many others, save herself from suicide or madness?, Ōe asks. At the inaugural World Conference against Atomic and Hydrogen Bombs in 1955 Murato first learned that there were others like herself, and that in joint action there could be a struggle which would grant significance to all their lives. With the decision to, among other things, appear before television cameras with the famous Ōe Kenzaburō, Murato realized her freedom. She accepted her scars and thus removed them as an obstacle to action. She underwent a Sartrean conversion (*kaishin*), a transformation which enabled her to account openly for her victim status as one part of being and not its total master. In Murato's confrontation with the Other—

the "everybody else" in the world—she is challenged to come into complete freedom and authentic being by fighting the Other, all of "outside of Hiroshima" who do not know how the world has been changed by the use of nuclear weapons. Ōe applauds Murato and her activism: she ranks high among his examples of Hiroshima Man. Her form of activism, however, is simply appearing in public, all over the world, without "shame." The problem arises that although Murato achieves full humanity by resolving to act in life without being controlled by the humiliation of her scars, she is effective as an activist only insofar as those who view her judge her as somehow "less than human," that is, as a victim of a terrible tragedy. In other words, were the cause of her "shame" not visible, she would not have been invited to appear on Ōe's talk show; he must continue to perceive her as "impaired" to perceive her as a heroine. Ōe, typically, wants to have it both ways: he requires that the destruction of Hiroshima be seen as an event which forever altered humanity while he also requires that it preserve it. This contradiction parallels Ōe's personal relations with the Other, relations which necessitate both fear and envy.

Ōe repeatedly argues himself into a corner. In this same chapter he tells of a friend he had at the University of Tokyo who, though a survivor of Hiroshima, never spoke of it. "Naturally he had a right to silence," allows Ōe (94), and he has previously acknowledged that one also has the right to flee either "inwardly or outwardly" from Hiroshima. But Ōe does not really approve of the exercise of those rights. After a hibakusha confronts the reality that he will possibly, probably, die of a bomb-related disease, he is forced to accommodate that reality by denying it through silence, fleeing it through suicide or madness, or struggling with it through activism. It is clearly the third of these options that Ōe wishes to celebrate in *Notes*. Indeed, those hibakusha who elect to struggle, who embrace a dignity defined as the desire to ameliorate the world, are proclaimed by Ōe to be "saints" (*seija*). Sartre calls Genet a saint because he is also a criminal: he writes in *Saint Genet*: "He hopes for Saintliness, he wants to acquire it. What is it that he wants? To be. To be a saint, to be an evildoer, it doesn't matter: to be his being" (263). What does matter is that saints are the Other, that they are what we are not. Saints challenge what we may mean by the "human condition." But Ōe borrows this nomenclature innocently, and uses it without irony. Saints do *not* challenge Ōe's concept of the human condition because their existence is held out as a promise of real good in the world, an essential feature of his liberal world view. We can be saints only if we embrace the choices which Ōe's hibakusha heroes have made.

Ōe elaborates in the fifth chapter of *Notes*, "People Who Do Not Surrender" (Kuppuku shinai hitobito), that sainthood is conferred upon those hibakusha who embody the "absolute good" generated in reaction to the "absolute evil" of the atomic bomb. This is a popular view of human history; Erich Auerbach, in tracing the entire course of Western literature, wrote that in "epochs of atrocious occurrences the great vital forces of the human soul reveal themselves: love and sacrifice, heroism in the service of conviction, and the ceaseless search for possibilities of a purer existence."[23] It is a view that Ōe is at great and uncomfortable pains not to abandon.[24] He discerns in the lives of the Hiroshima doctors like Shigetō the presence of a good which perseveres even if it accomplishes nothing, and the presence of that good renders the entire world "purer" than it was before. The world after Hiroshima, in Ōe's estimation, is a world in which none of our choices have been eliminated but rather one in which those choices are starker than ever. The hibakusha featured in "People Who Do Not Surrender" are those who, as in Miyamoto's words, "struggle towards a miserable death," and out of that struggle comes the reaffirmation of an optimistic world view that Ōe will not allow the annihilation of a city to contradict: "Genuine humanists were made keenly necessary in Hiroshima by that summer of 1945. There were many such people there. It was in that city that for the first time a hope existed which survived the most evil hopelessness ever known to the human race" (110).

In other words Ōe's Hiroshima Man does not experience full freedom because he continues to act with hope; Ōe finally cannot accept the world which Sartre's existentialism gives us because he cannot leave us entirely in despair. He retreats from the necessary conclusion that the exercise of freedom is truly free only if it is made without the sanction of an ideology that approbates it.

This hesitation to view the world as Sartre does, radically devoid of an intrinsic "essence," leads to a similar ambiguity in Ōe's characterization of his relation with his hibakusha Other. Ōe's heroes know that their efforts can do nothing to alter the effects of the nuclear catastrophe that continue to kill people, but they nonetheless elect to conduct their affairs in a way which implies hope. This is true of Ōe's "humanists," his "people who do not commit suicide in spite of everything," those "who do not surrender" and, since he both aspires to their stature but is terrified of how they achieved it, his "Other" as well. This admission of hope is a theme reiterated in the sixth chapter of *Notes*, "An Authentic Human Being" (Hitori no seitōteki na ningen). The title refers to Dr. Shigetō, who is once more held up as a "hero" who "does not surrender." Additionally he is now described as an "authentic Human Being," a modern Sisyphus who chooses to struggle though the struggle's end is nowhere in sight. Long after others have concluded that the frightful effects of the atomic bomb have run their course, and that all who will die have already died, Shigetō still harbors doubts. These doubts keep him dedicatedly at work. He and his associates eventually uncover an unusually high rate of occurrence of leukemia in the local hospitals. Once they make the connection between the bomb and this delayed reaction, Ōe's "authentic human being" is placed in direct confrontation with his worst fears: remember that Shigetō, too, is a hibakusha who now knows there may be a time bomb ticking away inside him. With a heightened awareness of his mortality, and more generally of a human condition endlessly threatened, Shigetō's struggle against the lethal aftereffects of the bomb takes on the character of a free existentialist choice exercised in the face of an absurd situation. But then Ōe comments that his efforts to cope with the disease "were something to invite a very human inspiration. . . . His method of trial-and-error implied the very human and natural expectation of ever-brighter hopes" (121). The situation, then, cannot in all honesty be called absurd. One day Shigetō's experiments might pay off in a cure for leukemia, and once again Hiroshima will have given rise to an "absolute good."

In *Notes'* conclusion, "Epilogue: Out of Hiroshima" (Epirōgu: Hiroshima kara), Ōe contemplates the significance of a hibakusha's choice to struggle. He defines the bombing of Hiroshima as our realization that history and technology may conspire to render us literally no longer human—that radiation can, in fact, so alter the make-up of our blood and cells that its first malevolent use in Hiroshima is the beginning of the end of our species. In other words it is the most extreme situation imaginable.[25] Yet still out of this horrible encounter with our destiny arise men and women, Ōe's Hiroshima Man, who comprehend the full dimensions of the atrocity and choose to live not in despair but with a dignified courage made possible with hope however remote. It is no paradox that within such people Ōe recognizes for the first time authenticity. The Other in existentialism always holds out the possibility of our own full being. The Hiroshima hibakusha is shunned as tainted and even, as if a criminal, somewhat guilty for having been there on the 6th in the first place.[26] But as Sartre indicates when he quotes Hegel in *Being and Nothingness* to the effect that "the Slave is the Truth of the Master" (321), the Other holds the key to our being even as it is prohibited from participation in full being itself. In Ōe's world the hibakusha Other, though impoverished and discriminated against, contaminated and dreaded, necessarily embodies that which it is dangerous to see in ourselves. We reject the Other because we fear the power it holds over us; we covet it because of that power. But Ōe finds it difficult to regard his hibakusha Other as a menace to his own freedom because he is so eager to portray that Other as an unquestionable hero. In his concluding remarks he states that "there is no way for us to live as conscious human beings other than as comrades of the hibakusha" (161). Later he adds that "I would like to be in solidarity with those people whom I view as the most authentic, post-bomb Japanese" (162). Ōe would also have liked to have been in solidarity with the young soldier who killed himself in that wartime film, but his courage frightened him for years afterwards; perhaps Ōe wishes to be a "comrade" in order to defuse the power that surviving an atrocity has given the hibakusha. Ōe's confused notion of the Other both enables his own existence and threatens it. His attempt to define the Other as a "victim" who must acknowledge an unchangeable fate necessarily conflicts with his existentialist urge to grant this same Other the freedom to exist in whatever manner chosen. For Sartre, such a contradiction is happily part of the endless warfare of his social ontology. For Ōe, however, it is a disquietingly stubborn obstacle to his attempt to make grand saviors out of the hibakusha. Quite contrary to its author's stated intent, *Notes* thus reads not as a simple ode to heroic, if tragic, martyrs, but rather as a commentary on the impossibility of such sentimental ideals after a nuclear atrocity.

■

Camus wrote that "man's first faculty is forgetfulness."[27] Ōe, as if to offer proof, notes that those of us "outside of Hiroshima" have connived to forget what happened on August 6th. For Ōe, this is a forgetfulness tied to our private attempts to erase the memory of personal tragedies. In his own life those tragedies might include his son's mental retardation and in a larger sense his long frustration as an activist writer in a society that remains stubbornly indifferent to political change. Ōe, like Sartre, seeks to change his reader. Both consider themselves "committed" writers. Ōe states in *Notes* that the role of committed intellectuals like himself should be to work with the hibakusha in order to realize their aims (148–49). But here Ōe, and other existentialists, face a predicament. In the epilogue to *Notes* he states that his essays on Hiroshima have served him as a tool which he has used to understand himself as a "Japanese writer": while his experiences in that city have made him appreciate the "human dignity" of his people, those experiences have also made it possible for him to imagine, concretely, human authenticity. In other words Ōe has aims of his own, aims which may not be the same as those of his heroes.

One may doubt whether many of the hibakusha care if Ōe understands himself as a "Japanese writer" or not, especially if that understanding will necessitate the distortion of their own lives. It has been argued that in his later writings Sartre ceased being an existentialist once he became *too* interested in making people different, in changing the choices for which they may opt. To succeed in that would mean denying people their freedom to behave as they would will. The same line of argument concludes that existentialism can never be a humanism, for when Sartre claims, as he does in *Existentialism and Humanism*, that choosing freedom for oneself is choosing freedom for everyone, he is contradicting his earlier position that there are *no* universal values.[28]

Existential humanism would be impossible, then, because one's relations with the Other are always in conflict. Neither could there be an existentialist moral theory: it is a philosophy that merely attempts to describe our place in the world, not one that dictates how people should actually regard each other. Ōe, in trying to prove that the hibakusha are both free *and* his ideal of correct moral behavior, finds himself in a similar bind. He is not a hibakusha: he is their Other, and they his. The hibakusha struggle with Ōe to achieve the same "full being" that he possesses, and he struggles with them to ascend to their high moral ground. In some respects Ōe's problems in *Notes* are the problems of any non-hibakusha striving to make heroes out of the hibakusha in a society which would prefer to forget them. Moreover, Ōe easily forgets an important lesson of existentialism, that to be "free" is to be "condemned to be free." The anguish that should accompany the hibakusha's realization that they are free because they are finally and terribly alone in the world is replaced in *Notes* with a confident solidarity shared among activists convinced they will accomplish a good for everyone.

Ōe is at work in *Notes* not so much as a journalist or a philosopher than as a highly literate propagandist. One notes, for instance, how he shifts his position vis-à-vis the hibakusha. Although he generally portrays himself in the essays as the hibakusha's Other, a person "outside of Hiroshima," at one point in *Notes* he identifies with the hibakusha as a fellow Japanese (and fellow victim) in opposition to the American "Other" who dropped the atomic bomb, in an extended sense, upon his entire nation. Although most of Sartre's *Being and Nothingness* is a description of how our relations with the Other constantly vacillate and equivocate, Ōe's reason for re-defining exactly who are the victims, and of what, is not traceable back to a complex ontology but rather to his own private agenda. In *The Savage God* A. Alvarez notes that the victim-survivor in modern literature has been raised to the status of a moral hero, and in *The Mortal No* Hoffman even more perceptively sees that modern writers themselves often assume the status of victim-survivors in their own works in order to assure the sympathies of the reader.[29] If this is indeed some part of Ōe's own motive in writing of the hibakusha, then it is necessarily a motive that risks distorting the truth of an atrocity that he admits to being "outside" of.

Ōe's own friend, the journalist and Hiroshima activist Kanai Toshihiro, has faulted him for precisely such a misrepresentation. He charges Ōe with seeking a Hiroshima that is not necessarily the real Hiroshima but rather one that inspires him and many others to locate within its tragedy the genesis of a "human renaissance" (*ningen kaifuku*) not actually there.[30] The propagandist in Ōe is that part of him which must believe in the continuing possibility of such a renaissance, just as it is in the nature of Ōe's work to preserve at nearly any cost the artistic endeavor of his writing as humanist in a world which is often inhuman (or, as some might argue after Hiroshima, "ahuman"). Like Sartre, Ōe reserves for literature that which the rest of the world so insistently and ruthlessly has set out to destroy: a place for men and women to remain whole and enjoy freedom. "Art could call itself humanist because society remained inhuman," wrote Sartre in 1950, five years after the carnage of the Second World War was still re-directing the possibilities of literature.[31] Ōe's view of Hiroshima is similarly predicated on the assumption that art could survive the implications of mass violence intact. On one hand Ōe readily admits that Hiroshima spelled the death knell for one kind of (older) humanism: how could an atrocity on such a scale result in anything other than the abrogation of the individual as the center of a universe that reflects him? Yet on the other hand Ōe is not prepared to abandon entirely the possibility of meaningful individual action in that universe, and this is why he repeatedly argues in *Notes* that the nuclear incineration of a city can be the birth of another (newer) humanism through the intervention of an existentialist praxis whenever a survivor is inspired by his condition to take decisive and positive action. Consequently Ōe himself continually risks falling back into the totality of the inhuman world not only because he sees himself as one of the victimizers of the Hiroshima victims (he is always their Other) but because the rarity and futility of such decisive and positive action suggests that there may in fact be no other world.

If this is in fact the case, and Hiroshima is only a place where we have demonstrated our ability and resolve to annihilate whole populations, then Ōe's claims in *Notes* for the heroism of his hibakusha sound hollow and even cruelly hypocritical. In Sartre's short story "The Wall" (1939) the narrator, Pablo Ibbieta, is a Republican taken captive by Franco's forces. His death, like that of Ōe's hibakusha, is certain. He knows exactly when and where he will face a firing squad. His one remaining hope is to die with dignity. Unfortunately his body revolts by profusely sweating, and his desire to appear unshakably calm in his last hours is frustrated by the close presence of a doctor who is doing research into the mental state of men condemned to die. At times Ōe reminds us of this doctor. His literary forays into the lives of the hibakusha reduce them to passive objects, the objects of a famous writer's notes, as ultimately reifying as the atomic device which originally exploded over their heads. Ōe is uncomfortably stranded in the position of salvaging "courage," "authenticity," and "freedom" out of a world in which, were such values to survive, they would so alter the sum effect of a nuclear holocaust as to risk minimalizing its radical significance for civilization.

It is at this point in Ōe's dilemma that one can see the contradiction of a "humanist atomic-bomb literature" mirroring the contradictions of other postwar literatures also caught between present history and nostalgia for earlier ideas. Elie Wiesel, for instance, has written in his own collection of essays entitled *One Generation After* that modern times have made messengers of writers, messengers who bring us the "news of history." Sometimes, however, we resist that news and wish the messenger gone. But we must remember that the messenger is not synonymous with what he tells us, and that for the messenger-writer himself the evil events of our age—or rather, the men who order them—constitute their own Other. For that reason Wiesel also cautions the messenger-writer:

Therein lies the dilemma of the storyteller who sees himself essentially as a witness, the drama of the messenger unable to deliver his message: how is one to speak of it, how is one not to speak of it? Certainly there can be no other theme for him: all situations, all conflicts, all obsessions will, by comparison, seem pallid and futile. And yet, how is one to approach this universe of darkness without turning into a peddler of night and agony? Without becoming other? (16)

To become the other in Wiesel's nightmare is to exacerbate the victims' suffering by telling of it. Ōe, himself a witness quite aware of this dilemma, confesses in *Notes* that he is troubled by how the brave hibakusha are canonized. He implies moreover that the canonization is performed by people just like himself out of a repressed guilt which often assumes the form of envy. But Ōe does not seem aware that such patronizing treatment of the hibakusha is a last-ditch attempt to defend his basic assumptions about human life and our potential for freedom: assumptions that authors who were there in Hiroshima on August 6th do not necessarily share. Kurihara Sadako, for instance, has complained that Ōe's "idealization" (*bika*) of exceptionally brave hibakusha in *Notes* makes it impossible for all the hibakusha to understand what it is that determines their common condition as victims, and therefore undermines the chances for the full life that Ōe hopes for them.[32]

In a 1968 essay entitled "Erasmus in the Nuclear Age" (Kaku-jidai no Erasumusu), Ōe comes close to admitting how impossible, if admirable, is the set of complementary fears and hopes he shares as both a humanist and a post-Hiroshima intellectual:

My courage to believe that finally humankind will survive the nuclear age . . . comes from knowing that, even as history prepares us for war with nuclear arms, there can never be an end to the humanist enterprise. . . . Yet how can there ever be a humanist defense against an "accidental launch," or a "miscalculation"? That is indeed what the nuclear age is precisely all about. (275)

Ōe, however, cannot act in consistent good faith with this rare and devastating realization, even as the existentialist lurking within prohibits him from any other response to the atrocity of Hiroshima. When Camus states in *The Rebel* (1951) that "despairing literature is a contradiction in terms" only a few pages after quoting Nietzsche's famous dictum, "No artist tolerates reality," he seems to be concluding that despair arises out of the reality which writers must refute in their works. Sartre, for his part, argues in *Anti-Semite and Jew* (1947) that an anti-Semitic novel is "impossible" because the very idea of the novel does not tolerate evil falsehood. In other words the existentialist tradition firmly maintains the incompatibility of a world aimed at oppressing us and a literature designed for liberating us. Ōe's essays on Hiroshima cannot tolerate "reality" or "despair": his *Notes* must unfold as if the atomic bomb has not permanently and disastrously altered our way of being in the world, as if a threshold has not been crossed which would render absurd the notion of humanist values at work in a civilization where human lives in the aggregate no longer mattered. Ōe's conclusion, that humanism was changed by Hiroshima yet nonetheless survives, may be true but is certainly misleading. Yes, there are brave hibakusha, but in truth only a handful; like Sartre's resistance fighters so prominent in his novels, somehow their small historical presence pales beside that of the majority of their countrymen. That men such as Miyamoto and Shigetō in *Notes* should loom so large—larger than "life"—is a telling indication that Ōe's existentialist reading of Hiroshima requires such distinct Others; and the fact that they are required for Ōe to understand himself hardly leaves those Others very free.

Finally, there is a great deal of Ōe in the pages of *Notes* and little else. Just how much does the reader really know about Ōe's hero Miyamoto when he is done with the book? Not much more than Ōe's own complicated emotional reaction to him. Ōe's journey in these collected essays is not towards Hiroshima but rather through his imagination: out of fragments he has created his own universe and his own self within it. The result is a work at odds with the experience he had hoped to memorialize, and indeed threateningly subversive of it altogether: the attempt to discern "freedom" and "dignity" in the "absurdity" of Hiroshima is to dissolve the doctrine of existentialism into another pre-Hiroshima mode of thinking that militates against the lessons modern atrocity has taught. The survivors who "struggle towards a miserable death" finally seem neither free nor noble, but rather frightening reminders of what the decision to incinerate cities has done to our former, now obsolete, myth of human dignity.

Shigematsu's Family. Still photograph from the 1989 film version of *Black Rain*

> In ideology men do indeed express, not the relation between
> them and their conditions of existence, but *the way* they live the
> relation between them and their conditions of existence: this pre-
> supposes both a real relation and an *"imaginary" "lived"* relation.
> Ideology, then, is the expression of the relation between men and
> their *"world,"* that is, the (overdetermined) unity of the real rela-
> tion and the imaginary relation between them and their real con-
> ditions of existence. In ideology the real relation is inevitably
> invested in the imaginary relation, a relation that *expresses a will*
> (conservative, conformist, reformist, or revolutionary), a hope
> or a nostalgia, rather than describing a reality.
>
> Louis Althusser, "Marxism and Humanism"

8

Ibuse Masuji:
Nature, Nostalgia, Memory

I begin by juxtaposing this epigraph, Althusser's famous definition of ideology as the representation of our imaginary relationship to the real conditions
of existence, with an example from where that definition has found its most
fertile application: a novel. This is another oft-quoted excerpt—the first paragraph of Ibuse Masuji's *Black Rain*, Japan's best-known work of atomic-bomb literature:

> For several years past, Shigematsu Shizuma, of the village of Kobatake,
> had been aware of his niece Yasuko as a weight on his mind. What was
> worse, he had a presentiment that the weight was going to remain with
> him, unspeakably oppressive, for still more years to come. In Yasuko, he
> seemed to have taken on a double, or even a triple, liability. That no
> suitable marriage was in sight for her was a circumstance simple enough
> in itself. The real trouble was the rumor. Towards the end of the war, it

ran, Yasuko had been working in the kitchens of the Second Middle School Service Corps in Hiroshima City. Because of that rumor, the villagers of Kobatake, over one hundred miles to the east of Hiroshima, were saying that she was a victim of radiation sickness. Shigematsu and his wife, they claimed, were deliberately covering up the fact. It was this that made her marriage seem so remote. People who came to make inquires of the neighbors with an eye to a possible match would hear the rumor, would promptly become evasive, and would end up by breaking off the talks altogether. (9–10)

The typical in medias res opening of a novelistic narrative; its *Pride and Prejudice* bourgeois concern with the marital disposition of a young woman dependent upon the family patriarch; and a succinct statement of the "problem" which the remainder of the novel must endeavor to resolve—all mark *Black Rain* as precisely the kind of work for which Althusser's formulation of ideology as sets of variously "real" and "imaginary" representations has proved so analytically useful. The European novel of manners, attractive to Marxist critics since Marx himself for the sake of its rich display of implicit ideological constructions of an "everyday life" afforded by the fruits of capital, seemingly finds a ready parallel in the first lines of this Japanese novel from the mid-1960s. If the classic realist narrative "turns on the creation of an enigma through the precipitation of disorder which throws into disarray the conventional cultural and signifying systems,"[1] then *Black Rain*'s basic problem of how to marry off Yasuko—how to "exchange" her, were we to think of matrimony as implicated in our "cultural and signifying systems"—would seem to qualify the novel as precisely the kind of literature that a Marxist critic could claim reproduces, as an "Ideological State Apparatus," the relations of production.[2]

But at the same time, something very un-European and un-nineteenth-century intrudes before the paragraph can conclude: the reference to "radiation sickness" and its fatal social as well as physical repercussions suddenly thrusts the novel into a specific and ghastly history that makes it a novel about a very new theme, certainly for Western readers, as well as one at least as old and familiar as Jane Austen. This conjuncture, as we have seen in other works purporting to be "literature" about the "atomic-bomb," is always an unstable one: but nowhere more, perhaps, than here. "A genre committed to life or even to death in the bosom of the nineteenth-century middle class," writes Berel Lang, "would simply fail as the vehicle for a subject that challenged the very possibility of social existence."[3]

From another perspective *Black Rain* is again a striking anomaly. For a reader accustomed to the documentary approach of a Hara Tamiki, or the direct and angry address of atomic-bomb literature by such authors as Ōta Yōko, Ibuse's work seems so much more an ordinary "novel." This impression, even while it charges the novel with its own particular energy, namely that between the telling of a story many families might find cognizant and the telling of one nearly all would find extraordinary, is responsible for *Black Rain's* unprecedented degree of success. Until now this genre has been described in this study as marginalized and even suppressed: but now, as we encounter atomic-bomb literature two decades after its inception, there is this one notable exception. There is no doubt that Ibuse Masuji's 1966 novel is far more widely read, translated, and taught than any other single example of Japanese atomic-bomb literature: its status as a "curriculum" for the lessons of Hiroshima makes an analysis of precisely what it teaches, and with what implications, especially significant. Like all good novels, the story that seizes our attention is in part congruent with our own lives and experiences, which is precisely why *Black Rain* proposes itself as a proof-text for how, as Althusser and others suggest, our "lives" and "experiences" may seem intuitively known to us but are in fact social representations with their own histories, uses, effects, and consequences.

It is *Black Rain's* power as a work of literature that the domestic is so believably and convincingly combined with the historical. When Yasuko is finally approached by a suitor who almost seems "too good for her," Shigematsu thinks the best way to ward off the usual round of destructive rumors is to send the go-between Yasuko's certificate of good health. But that unfortunately only raises suspicions, and the go-between comes back to Shigematsu wanting to know what Yasuko did, and where, from the day of the bombing to her return to Kobatake.

It is this situation which inspires Shigematsu to copy out the relevant entries from his niece's 1945 diary. Shigematsu, himself diagnosed with mild radiation disease, has heretofore spent his time fishing, and most recently started a small carp nursery with two other hibakusha in the village. It comes as a shock to Shigematsu as he recopies Yasuko's diary that she, too, was pelted by the radioactive "black rain" which fell across the city a few hours after it was bombed:

> And yet, he told himself, at something past eight on August 6, when the bomb fell, Yasuko must have been more than ten kilometers from the center of the blast. He himself had been at Yokogawa, only two kilometers from the center, and his cheek had been burned, but even so he was alive, wasn't he? He had heard that some people who had been in the same area but had escaped without burns were now leading perfectly normal married lives. (35)

So Shigematsu decides additionally to copy out his own diary, entitled simply "The Journal of the Bombing" (Hibaku nikki), to send along to the go-between for purposes of comparison. Indeed, the whole family collaborates. Shigeko, Yasuko's aunt and Shigematsu's wife, appends her own document, "Diet in Wartime Hiroshima." Perhaps predictably, however, before he is finished with his labors the rumors about Yasuko become prophetic, and with the onset of her symptoms the marriage talks break off. Powerless to help his niece in any other way, Shigematsu continues to assemble and recopy for the benefit not only of her doctors but himself such additional documents as Shigeko's "Diary of the Illness of Yasuko Takamaru"; the story of one hibakusha's miraculous recovery entitled "Notes on the Bombing of Hiroshima, by Hiroshi Iwatake, Medical Reserve"; and "A Record of Mrs. Iwatake's Recollections of Events at That Time." It is, however, Shigematsu's own "Journal of the Bombing" that itself takes up over half the length of *Black Rain,* and it is as Yasuko's illness terminally worsens that both Shigematsu's recopying of his diary and the novel itself rather abruptly conclude.

This brief outline of *Black Rain* identifies the two characteristics that best qualify it: its documentary, historical detail and its seductive, almost melodramatic fictional narrative. The combination has proved a successful one for both the novel and Ibuse personally. In addition to the aforementioned international popularity of the work, it has been used for psychoanalytical purposes in Robert Jay Lifton's study of hibakusha psychology, *Death in Life: Survivors of Hiroshima;*[4] its prose appears as verse in poet Marc Kaminsky's *The Road From Hiroshima;* and it is the only work of atomic-bomb literature that has been adapted for both television and film, the latter—a 1989 production directed by Imamura Shōhei—indeed winning five Japanese Academy Awards. If John Hersey's documentary account *Hiroshima* stands as the dominant American reading of the first atomic bombing, then Ibuse's novel *Black Rain* is the Japanese: a source of anecdote, myth, history, reference, and, most importantly, a source for the intimation of the human scale of the atrocity. The importance of this work, which is to say its emblematic representation of "what happened," means that in some real sense the perceived importance of Hiroshima itself now hinges upon what it says, and does not say.

This is most true in Japan itself, where the novel has no commercial equal among other works of atomic-bomb literature. According to 1981 figures, the Japanese edition had sold 263,000 hardback copies and 1,160,000 paperback ones.[5] Perhaps more significantly, a survey of leading Japanese intellectuals published in 1987 declared *Black Rain* the most important Japanese book written on *any* topic since 1945. The critical and popular contrast with other works of atomic-bomb literature—works resisted by publishers, dismissed by critics, suppressed by censors—is both striking and grounds for the first point of departure for any reading of *Black Rain.* Even before the work had appeared in its entirety during its 1965–66 serialization in the literary journal *Shinchō* (New Tide), it was enthusiastically hailed by some of Japan's most respected critics as a masterpiece. Saeki Shōichi, for instance, wrote in the *Asahi shimbun:*

Ibuse has placed himself amid overwhelming and extraordinary events as a very reserved, ordinary [*nichijōteki*] spectator. He is a unperturbed observer who records the smallest details of what was eaten at meals; of how fish are raised; of the seasonal ceremonies and festivals of farming families. And into the framework of a Jane Austen-like domestic novel, he embeds what was "Hiroshima." This is a nearly unbelievable triumph. . . . Perhaps it is nothing other than the very essence of Japan [*Nihonteki na gokui*] [6]

This review iterates two of the most common critical observations made of *Black Rain* at the time of its publication. First, there is the "reserved, ordinary" discourse of Shizuma Shigematsu's description of the bombing and life afterwards. This is a discourse which is implicitly in contrast to those of other, presumably less reserved and less ordinary atomic-bomb writers. In fact, Saeki and others have attributed one part of *Black Rain*'s power to the universal identification with the character of Shigematsu that his very "ordinariness" allows— an identification that earlier writers such as Hara Tamiki and Ōta Yōko, by virtue of their irrepressible sense of themselves as "different," resist.[7] Second, there is the suggestion, indeed the outright assertion, that there is something ineffably "Japanese" and thus authentic about Ibuse's use of rural and familial detail which makes this work a "triumph" where others are not.

Such views advertise a kind of cultural, national, or racial collectivity allegedly expressed in Ibuse's novel, an expression that wins it not only the appellation of "literature," but that of "Japanese literature." Yamamoto Kenkichi, an important conservative critic somewhat older than Saeki's generation, frankly explained why this work of atomic-bomb literature found favor with him and why those by Hara and Ōta did not:

[Other works of atomic-bomb literature] are too strenuously serious. They are too sullied by politics. Or too full of simplistic catch-phrases. Had Ibuse not written this novel, I would never have been able to feel better about myself as a Japanese.

That such a novel as *Black Rain* was written is a triumph for Ibuse and his approach to literature. Sartre came to Japan and stirred up our intellectuals; but it was Ibuse who, with the calm and unperturbable attitude of a common, ordinary Japanese [*Nihon no heijōshin*], wrote this book. We might think about whose attitude—Sartre's or Ibuse's—is the stronger, the more authentic.[8]

Yamamoto's term for "authentic" is *chi ni tsuita*, literally to have one's feet on the ground. (In fact, the title of the essay from which the above is quoted is "Chi ni tsuita heijōjin," or "An Ordinary Person with his Feet on the Ground.") The metaphor suggests some nostalgic reference to the peasant, the simple backbone of the nation—precisely the opposite of the critical, politicized urban intellectual who, in the person of Ōe Kenzaburō (surely implicated as one whom Sartre "stirred up"), had recently monopolized public discourse on Hiroshima. *Black Rain* becomes a "triumph"—here the same language as Saeki's—which is at once a nationalistic emblem and a reactionary attack on liberal or left critiques. In fact, most of the praise for *Black Rain* from major literary critics shared an admiration for the novel's lack of political content; its choice of a rural landowner and former white-collar worker such as Shigematsu for a hero rather than an urban intellectual; and most importantly its supposed endorsement of traditional Japanese culture and values.

Uniting conservative critical commentary on *Black Rain* is its approbation of what is held to be the "common man" and "non-intellectual" nature of its story and its complementary rejection of "ideology" as a consideration in the narration of the Hiroshima bombing. As one observer has noted in recent years, "The critical reception of *Black Rain* made exceedingly clear the Japanese literary establishment's definitive emphasis on political transparency and its insistence on de-ideologization."[9] Such a reception takes place, in Japan of the 1960s, amid a great deal of literature—by no means not only that of the atomic bomb—charged with highly explicit political intentions and even consequences. Ōe's *Hiroshima Notes* had been a prime example of precisely what some senior critics meant to rail against: literature that was held to exploit the moral indignation of Hiroshima and Nagasaki to score anti-Western, pro-communist points. In this atmosphere of larger geopolitical controversies, little note was taken of Ibuse's own modest stated intentions in writing *Black Rain*—simply to tell the story of a friend, named Shigematsu Shizuma in real life, who was "exposed to the Hiroshima atomic bomb."[10] Instead, grand and boldly provocative claims were made on behalf of *Black Rain* by critics who, according to the most cynical interpretation, sought more to attack other writers and other works more than they meant to praise Ibuse.

No such claims were finally more controversial than those made by Japan's most prominent conservative literary critic today, Etō Jun. As a young man whose precocious work in the 1950s on Natsume Sōseki still stands in many ways unsurpassed more than thirty years later, Etō was originally sympathetic to the progressive approaches and critiques of Japanese literature and culture made by his peers such as Ōe Kenzaburō. But by the time of *Black Rain* Etō had begun to argue against rather than for the left, a shift which his review of *Black Rain*—the most famous of all of its reviews—made quite clear.

Etō's essay, entitled "Extraordinary Events Told Ordinarily: Atomic-bomb Fiction Without Rancor" (Heijōshin de kataru ijōji: kioi no nai gembaku shōsetsu), begins as did Yamamoto's with a general and blanket statement dismissing all atomic-bomb literature written heretofore:

I have never liked what is called "atomic-bomb literature." In fact, I have myself refrained from writing or speaking of the bombings. I felt that I wished that others had done likewise when I read Hara Tamiki's "Summer Flowers" and Ōta Yōko's series of novels. I also felt that Ōe Kenzaburō's *Hiroshima Notes* was fundamentally in error somewhere. John Hersey's *Hiroshima* is the product of a good conscience, but finally I've never rid myself of the impression that it is sensationalist.

Etō pinpoints more precisely what it is that dissatisfies him about these examples of atomic-bomb literature when he points to their irreconcilability of "experience" (*taiken*) and "expression" (*hyōgen*). Etō is not the first, of course, to identify this as an issue in atomic-bomb literature, and quite likely he is influenced by some of the theoretical contradictions identified by the same atomic-bomb writers—Hara, Ōta, and Ōe—whom he here dismisses as failures. But Etō's statement of irreconcilability is not, as it is for others, the incommensurability of atrocious violence with cultural meaning. Rather, for Etō "expression" refers to intellectual, and specifically oppositional intellectual, discourses. It is *their* expression that fails to convey experience, not expression itself as language. This is why Etō was subsequently able to represent Ibuse and his novel as a counter-example, a successful work of atomic-bomb literature where expression and experience fortuitously intersect. Ibuse's achievement lies precisely in the fact that he is not an intellectual, or that at least in *Black Rain* none of his characters adopt the practiced critical stance of one. Shigematsu, Etō declares with approval, is *not* an intellectual; he is a small landowner (*shōjinushi*) who is deeply involved in all the family and village life such a figure typically is. There is a web of what Etō refers to as *ningen kankei*, or "human relations," which constitutes the local society and culture upon which the impact of the atomic bombing of nearby Hiroshima is measured.

In Etō's estimation and that of his like-minded colleagues, such an environment represents the "real Japan," the everyday reality of life that exists in contrast to the Westernized, politicized, urbanized life of the intelligentsia—ironically the life presumably led by Etō Jun himself. It is just this unfashionable rejection of the metropolis and its literary-left milieu that thus enables *Black Rain* to be an honest and reliable work where others are not: a work without, Etō claims, ideology: "No other work of fiction has so looked at the atomic bombing with an eye so unclouded with any ideology." By "ideology" Etō would mean, first of all, the various expressions of anti-Americanism linked in postwar Japan with left-wing politics. In fact *Black Rain* does seems a novel with little to say on America at all, either one way or another. It is a novel expressly novelistic in its focus: the tragic story of a family whose lives are affected and potentially destroyed by the bombing, a story that unfolds against a background nonetheless recognizably familiar, at least to readers well versed in the other families of modern literature if not actual life. In *Black Rain* rural daily life seems dominated with such matters as marrying off one's daughter, arguing with one's wife, or gossiping with the neighbors. *Black Rain*, unlike much other atomic-bomb literature, is never didactic, polemical, or argumentative. It is a work that, in some respects not unlike *The Diary of Anne Frank*, resorts to sentimental (in fact, quite sparingly so) but nonetheless always dignified examples of individual lives subjected to collective violence in order to represent a totality of "Hiroshima" within its carefully circumscribed descriptions of the lives of one small "typical" family. It is, as a result, a very moving work.

But what precisely within us is "moved" must be examined in light of the claims made for the novel by its conservative champions. When Etō Jun chose to associate the term *heijōshin* (a word coined by a novelist in the late nineteenth century and explained as "a unexceptional and typical calm state of mind"— unperturbedness, in a word) with Ibuse's method in *Black Rain*, he was converting the atomic bombing into an event that *was* "ordinary," or at the very least capable of an ordinary retelling. The first effect, not necessarily unintentional, is to remove the bombing from the political history in which it is typically inserted. The second effect is to separate the left intelligentsia from their perceived monopoly of the atomic bomb and its discourse in contemporary Japanese culture. Etō's "heijōshin"—literally "normal heart"—was a term that found widespread favor, perhaps due to its appeal as metaphor, among other conservative and reactionary critics in writing of *Black Rain*. For example, Yamamoto Kenkichi, writing in the Hiroshima newspaper *Chūgoku shimbun*, claimed that Hiroshima natives Hara Tamiki and Ōta Yōko notwithstanding, no writer before Ibuse Masuji had produced a work of atomic-bomb literature with a style "so everyday [*nichijōteki*], so unsacrificing in its ordinariness [*heijōshin*]."[11]

Such comments as these conflate the presence of an ordinary style with ordinary, i.e., apolitical, views of world events. Indeed, it is precisely the fact that in *Black Rain* an atomic bombing is no longer a "world event" but an entirely local, even familial one, that seems to produce the aesthetic charm of the work for so many critics. There is a clear connection between the presence of this withdrawal from political history and the subsequent celebration of the novel's status as the representative account of Hiroshima. The great restraint of the novel, both politically and artistically, is interpreted as proof of its intrinsic literary merit, a merit not earned by the works of atomic-bomb literature that preceded it. Its minute scale—even while it intimates something immense— together with its comfortable domesticity, resonates with the important tradition of introspective writing, the writing of manners, which constitutes the dominant and critically sanctioned mainstream of modern Japanese literature.

This became the view of the novel everywhere. C. P. Snow, in his widely quoted review of the work, referred explicitly to the welcome "aestheticization" of the atomic bombing in *Black Rain*:

> Some subjects are too big for art . . . too far removed from the human scale. Most writers have the self-protective cunning to keep off them, or to touch on them only glancingly. . . . Yet here is a novel by an elderly Japanese writer which turns Hiroshima into a major work of art, utterly unsentimental, unsparing but not at all sensational, telling us what we are like as human beings and what horrors we assist at, and perhaps leaving us with a vestige of stoical hope.[12]

To maintain that *Black Rain* "turns Hiroshima into a work of art" is to say a great deal not only about "Hiroshima" and "art"—Snow implies that here, at least, the two can be coterminous—but about the power of a writer to effect such a conversion. If *Black Rain* tells "us" (non-victims) what "we" are like as human beings, then it is because here is a novel that tells of the similarities between ourselves and the victims rather than the differences. This is the crucial point, and this is perhaps why the book has been received so enthusiastically. It proposes, in place of the historical fissure argued by a Hara Tamiki or Ōta Yōko, a common nature: something essentially "human" and thereby linked to what is most properly the subject of "art."

It is also an appeal to something essentially "Japanese," which is to say something that is "cultural" as opposed to historical or political. Thomas Rimer, an American scholar of Japanese literature, states:

> Ibuse . . . might be said to be representative of those authors who maintain an older, humanistic view of human character in general and of the Japanese situation in particular. Untouched by any of the fashionable postwar literary movements imported from Europe and the United States, Ibuse was long considered an exemplar of a gentler and perhaps more circumscribed tradition in Japanese literature. . . . Ibuse's novel, which has already gained the status of a classic in Japan, looks at the horrors of war without political bias and seemingly without lasting bitterness, no small achievement in itself.[13]

This evaluation derives from, and contributes to, the critical consensus that Ibuse and his novel are more purely Japanese, more authentic and "real" than those writers and their works who might be "touched" by non-Japanese literary influences, "political bias," or "bitterness." When this is acclaimed as "no small achievement," the implication is that atomic-bomb literature is usually, *Black Rain* aside, some or all of these things. Rimer, in synchrony with the Japanese critics cited earlier, goes to the heart of what makes *Black Rain* so attractive to readers seeking the kind of catharsis that allowed Yamamoto to "feel better about [him]self as a Japanese," namely its nature as a work that has "changed," "transformed," or "reworked" Hiroshima as a real event in human history. *Black Rain* does something to the popular representation of Hiroshima not achieved earlier: it is a near-organismic cultural operation (hence such terms as "older" and "circumscribed") performed *on* Hiroshima, an operation that recasts the place and occurrence marked as "Hiroshima" as a literary "classic" fully part of the organism. It is more than coincidence that the aesthetic satisfaction that *Black Rain* provides as a "true work of literature" derives from a novel whose principal theme is the neat congruency of human and natural life, despite the vagaries of history. Such "organicism," defined by Terry Eagleton as the signification of "social and aesthetic formations with the supposedly spontaneous unity of natural life-forms" in his examination of English literature from Arnold to Joyce,[14] is precisely what is celebrated by Ibuse's conservative admirers when they boast of his Japanese authenticity, sensitivity, and stoicism.

■

Ibuse himself did not encourage critics in their exuberant claims for his novel. In fact, he was somewhat embarrassed by all the attention it initially caused, and even expressed some measure of regret over ever having written it, disowning it as a "failure" because it did not communicate just how horrible hibakusha told him Hiroshima really was.[15] When asked in later years to speak about *Black Rain,* Ibuse abruptly responded that he had nothing to say on the subject.[16] He did not, in other words, take deliberate professional advantage of the critical view of him as, in place of Hara, Tōge, Ōta, or Ōe, the representative writer of Hiroshima.

This is quite in keeping with his modest character. Born in 1898 in a village in eastern Hiroshima Prefecture, and dead only recently at the age of 95, Ibuse has been not only one of twentieth-century Japan's most long-lived writers but one of its most approved.[17] His reputation was secure long before *Black Rain,* and is built upon works more often noted for their sympathetic, but never sentimental, descriptions of ordinary people than for their intellectual insight. It is true generally of Ibuse what Rimer says specifically of him in the postwar period. While never entirely free of fashion, Ibuse was in comparison to his peers relatively free of the political and artistic trends that swept through Tokyo literary circles, especially between the two world wars. Ibuse did not subscribe to any noteworthy commitment to either the left-wing enthusiasms of the 1920s or the reactions to them in following decades. Neither was he in the postwar period much given to the imposed ideologies of American-style democracy or the post-Occupation retreats from that democracy. Indeed, the most common critical impression of Ibuse, a writer who began his career in 1923 with the simple story of a salamander who makes friends with a seahorse, and who devoted himself in his last years to personal memoirs, is the epitome of the politically indifferent, perhaps even naive, author. Sequestered in his study, immersed in his world of the picturesque (and often picaresque) village "folk" and city "eccentrics," Ibuse Masuji was indeed one of those Japanese writers from whom one would least expect a polemical novel. Critics looking for an author who could write of Hiroshima without reference to postwar history—either that of the nation, or of the literary establishment—found in Ibuse their perfect champion.[18]

Naturally, it is difficult to imagine that a writer whose career bridges such a turbulent century would create a body of work wholly free of references to history and politics. Where such references do exist in Ibuse's work, they have been ignored or repressed by most critics: but they are there. Early on, under the influence of the proletarian literature movement that held sway in the late 1920s and early 1930s, Ibuse wrote a short story ("Tankōjitai byōin," or "The Mining Town Clinic," 1929) which, in its depiction of the lives of coal miners, was certainly influenced by its concerns. In the 1930s Ibuse's historical fiction, and its frequent theme of past civil conflicts and uprisings, clearly had implications for Ibuse's views on the war in which his country was then currently entangled. And of course after 1945, with the dramatic changes wrought by the Allied Occupation, Ibuse's stories were not immune to such changed contexts. If one were to characterize the net effect of such tumultuous national history on Ibuse, it would be as a conceit: he is famous for his wryly affectionate depictions of a rather commonsensical "folk wisdom" that suffices among the everyday, often rural, Japanese people in lieu of an overtly ideological extremism of any ilk.

This conceit, too, can easily and properly be critiqued as political. It is the construct of some ahistorical, inoffensive national "character" that perseveres to survive intact the ravages of cruel history, whether man-made or natural. It is a representation of Japanese national character that is attractive—American culture has its own versions of it—even as it is resistant to change. It is precisely this disposition towards change, its impossibility just as much as its possibility, that makes Ibuse's work amply capable of sustaining a political reading, even if it itself is not political in the plainest sense.

Such readings do exist. The early, enthusiastic endorsement of *Black Rain* by mainstream conservative intellectuals inspired a few rejoinders from critics and readers who, while just as impressed with the literary talent of Ibuse's work, were nonetheless disturbed and even made suspicious by its rapid elevation to the ranks of the "modern classics" of Japanese prose literature. Many of these doubts came from hibakusha themselves, who perhaps understandably resented the fact that such success was to be earned not by one of their own, such as Hara or Ōta, but by a non-hibakusha such as Ibuse. In fact, though *Black Rain*, like Ōe's earlier *Hiroshima Notes*, was and is highly regarded outside of Hiroshima, within the city itself voices in some quarters felt the need to qualify it as a good work by a "non-victim." Moreover, by novelizing the event of the bombing, Ibuse made the experience comparable to other novelistic situations. Such comparisons may inevitably render Hiroshima a less epochal, even less real event: and that demotion is contested by hibakusha who insist that their experience cannot be freely borrowed, interpreted, or domesticated.[19] Toyoda Seishi wrote five years after *Black Rain* was published that it "most certainly does not enjoy a high reputation among Hiroshima writers. 'It's written just too cleverly.' 'It's nothing more that a skillful adaptation of actual diaries.' 'Ibuse has always turned his back on literature with political themes in favor of his little vignettes. He is incapable of grappling with this kind of story.' These were the sorts of critical reviews *[Black Rain]* received."[20]

As noted earlier, Ibuse himself termed his work a failure and reportedly vowed never to write about Hiroshima again—a promise he kept—on account of the criticism his novel generated in the city he sought to memorialize. One might try to discount such negative reactions among Hiroshima readers as the predictable, if sincere complaint of victims who fear their lives compromised even further through their objectification by outsiders. But in fact the criticism leveled against *Black Rain* was more than that, and not completely restricted to Hiroshima and its understandably sensitive hibakusha.

Rather, this broader criticism was not so much an attack on Ibuse or his novel as it was a criticism of the eagerness of the literary establishment to embrace it, to declare it a triumph in language that denigrated earlier atomic-bomb literature (as "political" and thus "artless") even as it promoted *Black Rain* (as "artistic" and thus "apolitical"). Kaneko Hiroshi, for instance, has noted that it was this loose establishment, and not Ibuse himself, that endeavored to cast *Black Rain* as an example of such apolitical subgenres as "domestic" or "personal" fiction.[21] Similarly, Sakurai Mikiyoshi, while acknowledging *Black Rain'*s critical status as "a work representative of the 1960s," suggests there is nonetheless something amiss about its reputation among mainstream critics.[22] From the point of view of a critic sympathetic to the two decades of atomic-bomb writing that preceded Ibuse's novel, such belated praise raises more suspicions than perhaps it does appreciation.

The most astute questioning of the motives of the literary establishment in welcoming *Black Rain* into the ranks of genuine literature at the expense of all previous atomic-bomb writing was conducted by Ōe Kenzaburō. Responding specifically to Etō Jun's essay that proclaimed *Black Rain* to be the first worthwhile atomic-bomb literature by virtue of Ibuse's application of heijōshin—his "everyday tack of mind"—to the famous events told in the novel, Ōe argues that this notion of heijōshin is simply another way of identifying the narrator of the text as an outside observer, unperturbed by history in the manner of classic realist writing. Shigematsu's journals thus serve as a means for relativizing the events of the bombing in a way that appealed to the aesthetic and political conservatism of the literary establishment. Ōe's point is persuasive. Ibuse's serene language is no less a rhetorical mode of oratory than would be strident polemic, and by placing the historical event of August 6th in the frame that such a mode provides, the potential of that event to disrupt the form of the narrative—and perhaps more—is literally contained.

Ōe suggests this conflation of Ibuse's dispassionate authorial stance with the "proper" attitude towards Hiroshima is a misleading interpretation of a novel by which Ōe is himself impressed. There is, according to Ōe, no actual *heijōshin* in *Black Rain*. Rather, the calmness, the ordinariness for which it is mistaken is in fact the surface effect of the submerged *shock* than runs through the novel.[23] Etō's reading remains no better than cursory, according to Ōe. In fact, *Black Rain* intimates in its very quietude a deep, albeit numbed, response to the violence; the novel invites us to read it as ironically as we would the outwardly placid account of any victim of trauma.

Ōe's reading is encouraged by his conviction that any act of writing about Hiroshima naturally and indeed even necessarily entails political issues. In his nonfictional writings over the past thirty years, Ōe has insisted, perhaps jingoistically, that the use of two nuclear weapons was perhaps the single one most important advance for twentieth-century American power, and it allowed in large measure the unequal relations the United States has imposed upon non-nuclear nations, including Japan. Consequently, "Hiroshima" and "Nagasaki" are terms which have taken on, in addition to their literal references, the nature of metaphors that indicate Japan's humiliating submission to the superior military prowess of a superpower. In other words, any discussion of nuclear war must involve the fact of a massive exercise of power, literally and in the extended sense of the organizations of human societies in ways that enabled and authorized the production and execution of that power. Moreover, and more apropos the themes of atomic-bomb literature, responses among the Japanese to that use of power mirror similar power relations within the configuration of Japanese society itself. The marginalization, for instance, of the hibakusha community (a marginalization insured in government legislation as well as in cultural life) is itself an exercise of power, one that identifies the aftermath of the Second World War—an aftermath which is always potentially a reminder of Japan's expansionist ambitions—as something best repressed. Atomic-bomb literature for Ōe can never meander far from history, and from a particularly brutal history which records the clash of modern states intent in establishing their own international and national hegemonies.

But it is precisely the exploration and narration of this kind of broadly geopolitical history which has been so difficult for Japanese atomic-bomb writers, indeed for Japanese writers of all sorts. The relative paucity of modern

Japanese literary works that take up political themes is well noted and is even held up for admiration on occasion by native and foreign critics alike. The critically received modern canon is marked by its resistance to certain explicitly political or social discourses. Since the late nineteenth century, when the intellectual writer of fiction found himself no longer licensed to write about issues of power, and when simultaneously an aesthetics denuded of social critique was made a criterion of evaluation, the great narratives of history have been eliminated as proper themes for art. Thomas Rimer, in the same essay quoted earlier, states that "traditionally, Japanese literature has not lent itself to political debate in any particularly direct form."[24] Konishi Jin'ichi, dean of Japanese literary historians, has gone even further to state categorically that "the scarcity of political topics is, in fact, a characteristic of Japanese literature."[25] This may or may not be true, of course, depending on how broadly or subtly one wishes to define "particularly political" and how one interprets "tradition," but it seems valid to claim that, for the twentieth century at least, "pure literature" (jun-bungaku) is a critical appellation thoroughly invested with the sanctioning value granted works eschewing political debate in favor of the subtlety and intricacies of individualized, psychological identity.

It is important to add, however, that even these works of "pure literature," despite their alleged apolitical character, are sometimes conceded to be embedded within broad historical contexts which include the "influence" of politics. This is true of *Black Rain*. Ibuse himself has declared that his novel was written in a political context, and what is more, out of a political intent. The context and intent were not those of the Second World War but instead of a war more immediate to the years in which Ibuse was writing. "I wrote *Black Rain* just as the Vietnam War was raging," Ibuse explained. "I tried to make it reportage that, while faithful to the facts, also included an antiwar sentiment. Unfortunately it was wholly ineffective against the proponents of war."[26]

This "antiwar sentiment" is expressed in the work via its occasional references to the failure of politics in Japan at the end of its own war. To some extent the documentary ambitions of the work for historical veracity necessitated the insertion of references to militarist sloganeering and paraphernalia, particularly at its beginning. Yasuko's diary, for instance, is described as having the icon of a Rising Sun printed on its cover. Other emblems of empire, some as pathetic as the crude bamboo spears that young draftees took with them from their villages, abound in *Black Rain* and always appear against the irony of the ignominious defeat that had long been certain by the summer of 1945. But Ibuse's position is not easily identified with that of any rote left-wing orthodoxy. In fact, it is crucial to the novel's effect that any "position" taken vis-à-vis "politics" be ridiculed—and that, in fact, is what comprises the subtlety of the politics in and of *Black Rain*.

This is an excerpt from Yasuko's diary:

Both Mr. and Mrs. Nojima are always doing things for the other people who live in the same district. People say that Mr. Nojima has been friendly for years with a left-wing scholar called Mr. Matsumoto, and that since the war got more serious he's been making himself especially nice to everybody in the district so that the authorities won't get suspicious. Mr. Matsumoto, who went to an American university and used to correspond with Americans before the war, has been called before the military police any number of times. So he, too, is always on his best behavior with the people at the city hall, the officials of the prefectural office, and the members of the civilian guard, and whenever there's an air raid warning he's always the first to dash outside and rush around calling out "air raid! air raid!" He's never been known to take off his puttees, even at home. They say he even offered to take part in bamboo spear practice with the women. It's really pathetic to see a reputable scholar like him trying so hard to please. (20)

Such cynicism is used to dismiss political activity after the war as well, when it takes place on the left rather than the right. One of Shigematsu's friends and fellow hibakusha declaims, for example, that "everyone's forgotten. Forgotten the hellfires we went through that day—forgotten them and everything else, with their damned anti-bomb rallies. It makes me sick, all the prancing and shouting they do about it" (30). In effect any political action, in support of the war or against it, for the bomb or against it, is indicated in *Black Rain* to be spurious, inconsequential, vain, and even silly. What looms as real are only the lived experiences of those who suffered during a war without meaningful categories of "good" and "bad." What seeks to convert such experience into a program for action is human organization, which is represented on a small scale by, for instance, the aforementioned "anti-bomb rallies" but on a larger scale by the larger unit of this organization, namely the apparatuses of national government.

   In the eleventh of *Black Rain's* twenty chapters Shigematsu describes two soldiers who were engaged in cremating corpses shortly after the bombing. Exhausted, one of the soldiers remarks to the other, "If only we'd been born in a *country*, not a damn-fool *state*" (162). Country (*kuni*) is preferred over state (*kokka*) because it connotes an idyllic place rather than a coercive organization; a people peaceably inhabiting it rather than a powerful government imposing its regimen upon that people. Such nostalgia for "country" dismisses one kind of politics; it dispenses with the decisions to be made between "left" and "right" even while it seems earnestly "antiwar," for without the authority of a state there is no center of power, and even no voice with which to declare one. When Shigematsu goes into the ruins of Hiroshima and notes that city hall has been destroyed (a "desolate sight"), what has been symbolically destroyed along with it is the apparatus of power that turned the Japanese islands into a Japanese state and led to the destruction Shigematsu now surveys.

This is not an endorsement of anarchism. That, too, is another of the political idealisms which *Black Rain* repudiates as useless and, more to the point, a distortion of the "natural" state of human life. Perhaps this makes *Black Rain* an apolitical or even antipolitical novel; then again, maybe it makes it merely a discouraged political novel. The late Irving Howe once proposed a careful, highly circumscribed working definition of "political novel" that might initially help in understanding the critical controversy that attends *Black Rain*. Howe wrote:

> By a political novel I mean a novel in which political ideas play a dominant role or in which the political milieu is the dominant setting—though again a qualification is necessary, since the word "dominant" is more than a little questionable. Perhaps it would be better to say: a novel in which *we take to be dominant* political ideas or the political milieu, a novel which permits this assumption without thereby suffering any radical distortion and, it follows, with the possibility of some analytical profit.[27]

For Howe only some novels are strictly, meaningfully, political. For political ideas to be "dominant" in mimetic fiction would seem to limit the political novel to instances in which the setting and characters are recognizably part of a society's formal institutions for the exercise of its power. Howe's examples of the political novel include Stendhal's *The Red and the Black*, Conrad's *Under Western Eyes*, Orwell's *1984*; Henry James's *The Princess Casamassima* is cited only as a book that fails to explore politics as the "collective mode of action" Howe wishes to make a minimal requirement.[28] As a critic he is at pains to avoid any "radical distortion" of a political criticism that seeks to extend the definition of "political ideas" beyond such formal boundaries and so risks diluting the efficacy of such ideas where they might really exist.

It seems advisable to allow Howe his careful definition, and to calculate rather that a much larger range of—indeed, perhaps all—novels which may be thought as *ideological* if not political. That is the concept with which critics after Howe have often permitted themselves to look at literature as implicated in the way social organization is imposed even if the "politics" of that imposition are not thematically present. An ideological novel, whether radical or conservative, will treat the issue of existence, of *being*, as problematic: as a construction of property, people, and institutions that has undergone change and will undergo it again. It is the provisional character of those arrangements, the necessity of an attitude within the novel towards change and therefore toward "time" or "history," that makes what is ideological in literature also the potentially political. Fredric Jameson, writing in the late 1960s, defined "political ideology" as "first of all a certain attitude towards Being itself . . . towards the

Being of objects and the world, of social institutions, of people and of their positions in the world."[29] For Marxist critics such as Jameson, the Hegelian vocabulary of "Being" would soon be replaced with Lacanian and Althusserian language of "representation," which holds that ideology is no longer a set of illusions but a system of signification: not just the *real* relations of how people live, but the *imaginary* ones. Ideology is a concept—a process—that thus partakes of both the real and the fictive.[30] As such, it is abundantly present in those literary representations defined as simultaneously real and fictive, i.e., the mimetic or historical novel. Whereas for Howe "political novels" are ones which thematically take up "politics" and thus are limited in number, presumably for Jameson the "ideological novel" is a tautology, and exists everywhere. Terry Eagleton has put this point more literarily himself: "Ideological language, then, is the language of wishing, cursing, fearing, denigrating, celebrating, and so on. And if this is so, then perhaps the closest analogue we have to ideology is nothing less than literary fiction."[31]

■

To look at how the range of social, political, and economic relations are organized, maintained, and altered within culture in terms akin to how a given situation in fiction appears "real" to us is to look at the brief exchange between Etō Jun and Ōe Kenzaburō as one which elides a crucial point. If we agree that *Black Rain*, as a representation of Hiroshima, must make of Hiroshima not only an "event" in history but a statement, a position, on "Being"—on what can and can *not* be—then Etō's and Ōe's common premise that *Black Rain* is not a political novel has aided the circumvention of critical readings of its ideological character. Moreover, this premise has served to make the debate over the work one which has displaced the real issue today, namely how this novel has come to be accepted so readily and so widely as an ideal example of the Japanese cultural response to Hiroshima and Nagasaki; and as an internationally available primer in one of the lessons of twentieth-century mass violence everywhere.

The ideological work of *Black Rain* is displayed in ways familiar to us from other works of modern mimetic fiction. Whether we are talking about Jane Austen's *Pride and Prejudice* or Erich Segal's *A Love Story*, novels both high and low construe as "real" those practices and structures that reiterate the conditions of socialized (including the "individual") life in modern societies. But those encoded practices and structures nonetheless yield a discernible ideology insofar as they reproduce the "deformed representation" which any literary realism has to be, since the very concept is at root oxymoronic. There, in the inevitable lapses and gaps, looms the possibility of critical reading. The deformed representation is not stable: it is the product of internal tensions between ideology and representation in a process that makes spurious noises which, when we labor to make sense of them, account for the fact that some novels seem explicitly to undermine dominant ideologies while others reinforce them. Jameson writes: "Ideology is not some thing which informs or invests symbolic production; rather the aesthetic act is itself ideological, and the production of aesthetic or narrative form is to be seen as an ideological act in its own right, with the function of inventing imaginary or formal 'solutions' to unresolvable social contradictions."[32] As a process of symbolic systems both verbal and otherwise that determines specific representations of events, and as the process by which particular versions of reality are represented as naturally true and unconstructed, ideology in fiction tends to act in conformity with a perceived "status quo," which is to say some hegemonic formulation of historical, economic, and social relations. The radical—whether from the left or the right—wishes, again according to the early Jameson, "to alter Being; the conservative wishes to associate himself with the permanence of Being, its massive quality. The conservative always has the advantage in literature: his attitude is *already* an esthetic one. The conservative has no need to single out political activity from the rest of Being. . . . His program is already achieved when he has interested you in Being itself."[33]

The built-in advantage that the novelist has in choosing to reproduce the existing social and ideological relations that obtain in his society is maximized, in fact, whenever critics such as Etō and Ōe cite works like *Black Rain* as "apolitical" or "non-political." When they, like Howe, mark some texts as "political" and others not, they are labeling those that are "not" *as* ideological by repressing the structures of power which the novelist, if he is to be taken as "realist," must mimic within his writings.

A major project of literary critics in Japan, not all of them Marxist, has been to identify precisely what ideological work conducted in novels has been masked as "aesthetic." *Black Rain* has been subjected to this critique. In Japan, apart from the Etō-Ōe controversy, the most vociferous criticism of the novel came from hibakusha who felt that a non-victim writer such as Ibuse had exceeded the boundary of ethical privilege in writing about the atomic bombing of Hiroshima. But this a criticism that is made of many works, and is in a sense unfair. The sort of literature written by a non-victim should not be required to "compete" with one written by a hibakusha, if for no other reason than because the premises of how knowledge of Hiroshima and Nagasaki is to be grasped is so utterly contrary between any two such works.

It is unfortunate that Etō and other critics have not distinguished between different orders of atomic-bomb literature predicated upon the different backgrounds and ambitions of their authors. Hiroshima is not a theme that Ibuse, painfully aware of the chasm that looms between his own life and those of the hibakusha, approached cavalierly. Raised not far from the city, he had wanted to write for a long time about what happened on August 6th. But by the 1960s Ibuse, who first published in 1923, was already a senior writer already thought to be in semi-retirement. Ibuse did not need to write *Black Rain*—though it would become his most overwhelmingly popular work—in order to enjoy a reputation as one of Japan's most important twentieth-century writers. A few years before he began work on *Black Rain*, it seemed likely that Ibuse would soon cease writing altogether. In a 1959 essay he complained that the years now race by, that he wished he could "apply the brakes . . . or put up a stop-light" to halt what he feared was the decline of his talents.[34] Moreover, he complained elsewhere of a writer's block; unable to write, "no matter what the theme," he resolved to dedicate his remaining energies to projects already begun but not yet finished. These projects are three, he writes, the last of them being the story of a hibakusha friend named Shigematsu.

The difficulty of finishing such a story, of course, was how to do it responsibly and within the bounds of historical authenticity. Ibuse was familiar with the atomic-bomb literature both of hibakusha novelist Ōta Yōko (from whom, after the success of *Black Rain*, he would inherit the mantle of "Japan's A-bomb writer") and of the non-hibakusha Ōe Kenzaburō;[35] and he had already written in the early 1950s a short story that dealt obliquely with the destruction of Hiroshima. Ibuse had, in other words, already given what must have been considerable thought to the problems of representing, accurately and ethically, an atrocity which one is guiltily spared. In that early short story, "The Iris" (Kakitsubata, 1951), the elected method was to locate the scene of the narrative not in Hiroshima proper but in the nearly town of Fukuyama and then to note the repercussions of the bombing on those citizens rather than on the Hiroshima population itself.[36] In *Black Rain*, the displacement would be of another sort, one with a long and useful lineage in Ibuse's work.

From the late 1920s to the present day, Ibuse's longer works of prose literature have often assumed the form of the diary—more precisely, the journal—kept by invented characters. Such novels and stories as the 1938 *Waves* (Sazanami gunki), the 1943 "A Young Girl's Wartime Diary" (Aru shōjo no senji nikki), and the much later *A Record of Tea Parties at Tomonotsu* (Tomonotsu chakaiki, 1983), have used the conceit of a personal archival record to organize individual experience in the midst of important events in history: respectively the twelfth-century Gempei wars, the Battle of Singapore, and the late sixteenth century. Ibuse narrates the public history of these events through the mechanism of private memory; through the detailed recollections of the direct participants in, or close observers of, those events. He once characterized journals *(nikki)* as a particularly "powerful" *(tsuyoi)* genre of literature:[37] this is a choice of words that suggests diaries (and to some extent all the extratextual materials comprising, or quoted in, his works) confer upon his narratives and their themes an authenticity, a specific and personal historicity. This grounding

of the text in an anterior, external chain of denoted events results in a calculated effect crucial to *Black Rain's* success as a novel of violence. Its use of diaries
allows the everyday trivia of conventional life to overlap and thus contrast with
the trauma of a nuclear explosion. It also acts to constrain the typical centrifugal tendency of the novel to move away from strict historical representation
and towards the imaginative exploration of private psychologies. Much as Shigematsu attempts to arrange a match between his niece and a suitor, so do the
diaries mediate the pre-bomb and post-bomb realities of their authors. In this
regard Yasuko, the first of *Black Rain's* diarists, is akin to earlier Ibuse heroes—
and to Ibuse himself when, as a diarist stationed in Southeast Asia during the
Second World War, he retreated from his "public" role as an occupying soldier
into a writer's privacy.[38] All share a common purpose: the subjectivization and
consequent appropriation of experience through making it a story. The manipulation of testimony—and what masquerades as testimony—is both the literary charm and ideological feat of *Black Rain*. Like any documentary narrative,
it is a work assembled from historical accounts, real or invented, that seeks to
authenticate and thereby naturalize a particular interpretation of that history.

   Black Rain is Ibuse's most extended and complex use of journals to create a
work of fiction. Its many journals—some inserted intact, others more or less
imagined—were acquired from or through Ibuse's real-life hibakusha acquaintances. Shigematsu Shizuma (whose family and given names were reversed
when Ibuse made him a novelistic character) first made Ibuse's acquaintance
just after the war. Shigematsu, a farmer in the actual village of Kobatake in
Hiroshima Prefecture, told Ibuse the story of his hibakusha niece Yasuko who,
after marrying and bearing two children, came down with symptoms of radiation disease and soon died. Shigematsu offered to send Ibuse her diaries, but
when Ibuse did ask for them later, it was discovered that other relatives had
destroyed them.

   Ibuse broadened his search for documentary sources. In the days immediately following August 6th, villages throughout the prefecture dispatched relief
teams into Hiroshima to assist the authorities. Ibuse notes, however, that of
each village's team "only one survived."[39] Ibuse assembled five or six of these
informants, intending to transcribe their accounts for use in his novel, but he
had trouble with his tape recorder and abandoned the idea.

   At this point Shigematsu again came to Ibuse's aid. Shigematsu himself
had gathered much material on Hiroshima, a collection of records that he,
like his counterpart in *Black Rain*, planned to bequeath as archives to future
generations. His accumulated documents amounted to over three hundred
pages. Once lent to Ibuse, these personal accounts of the bombing and its
aftermath constituted the single greatest source of testimonial data for use in
Black Rain. As Ibuse stated, the novel "could not have been written from simple
speculation."[40] Additionally, Ibuse personally conducted a detailed investiga-

tion of the events of August 1945. He said in an interview with the *Asahi shimbun:*

> Since I had no first-hand knowledge of what happened, I was left with no choice but to gather as much material as I could. I collected all there was to be collected, as if I were raking it in. Both before and after I began to write, I went to Hiroshima to hear the stories of more than fifty survivors. I listened to people who, as members of the fire brigades, had gone into the hills. When the talk turned to those who had searched through the "ashes of death," everyone turned silent. The ashes were a forbidden subject. I was told that everyone who passed through them had died.[41]

Ibuse thus commenced his work on *Black Rain* as he would with historical fiction, by researching facts before imaginatively manipulating them. Ibuse has repeatedly stressed the documentary character of his novel, noting how he has embedded within it the stories of many hibakusha. But of course the work is hardly an interpretation-less and value-free assemblage of survivors' accounts—author Ibuse intervenes everywhere to make their stories his own. "The writer, as the producer of a text, does not manufacture the materials with which he works," writes Pierre Macherey, in a reference to Marx's own comment on the material conditions in which men make their own history. "Neither does he stumble across them as spontaneously available wandering fragments."[42] Ibuse would find that the diaries he acquired, as well as those he invented, proposed their own ethical and ultimately ideological response. He stated in the same interview with the press:

> Once the writing was under way, I grew quite serious. It was a seriousness that came not from the act of writing, but from the transient world itself. I asked myself: Why did this happen? Everything seemed senseless. I kept thinking to myself that I must continue writing. There was no justice, no humanity, no anything in what happened. Everyone died. The more research I did, the more terrible it became. It was too terrible.[43]

By relying upon the diaries Ibuse was perhaps able to maintain a kind of epistemic distance from the material which was also experiential: it always remained *their* story and never became empathetically *his.* There are many diaries in *Black Rain* besides that of Shigematsu, but it is through his that Ibuse actually describes how one comes to write about—and *not* write about—Hiroshima as an event in history. The use of diaries means that Ibuse creates for his reader a textual hall of mirrors in which "Hiroshima" is made textual in ways that make its relationship to history a mediated one. Traditionally, diaries often seem to occupy a unique position exactly where the lines of historical and literary representation cross. But diaries within a novel, deployed as a rhetorical trope of the eyewitness, seem fully "novelistic" because they are there in lieu of an author's right to imagine others', here atrocious, experience. Ibuse demurs to represent "Hiroshima" himself: he writes instead about people who represent it. He avoids direct description of the bombing itself and leaves that to the writers he has invented, or whose words he has borrowed, to characters or sources who possess that "first-hand knowledge" of which he pointedly admits a lack. The function of the town of Fukuyama in the earlier story "The Iris" as an extended figure for the impact of the war on people and their ability to make sense of it becomes the function of the Shizuma household in *Black Rain*. Through this family, the novel works dialectically as life inspires writing and then writing inspires life. The reader is led from diary to diary, each corroborating the others and demonstrating the central work of the novel, namely, the articulation of a new vocabulary of violence through the creative project of writing. Against the destructive power of the bomb stands the constructive power of words, language, writing. The reader notes, for instance, how, on the one hand, some hibakusha struggle to identify and name the bomb, while, on the other hand, other characters easily compare names for fish in their various native dialects. The diaries of *Black Rain* cease to be vehicles for stories and become the story itself.

Ibuse makes this the most evident when he works with Shigematsu's diary. Unlike Yasuko's diary, which was merely recopied, Shigematsu's "Journal of the Bombing" is, by virtue of the work of memory, essentially rewritten. Shigematsu adds new interpolations and explanations as he seems to relive the experience of the bombing even while safe in his study. Yet far from recoiling, he now rejoices. The diary becomes a project of which Shigematsu is genuinely proud:

> "I should have had to copy it out decently soon at any rate, if I'm going to present it to the Primary School Library for its reference room. I'll show it to the go-between before I give it to them."
>
> "Surely Yasuko's diary will be enough for the go-between, won't it?"
>
> "Yes, but this will be a kind of appendix to it. Either way, if it's going to go in the school reference room, it'll have to be written out properly sometime."
>
> "Won't you just be making yourself more work?"
>
> "I don't care. It's my nature to keep myself occupied. The diary is my piece of history, to be preserved in the school library."
>
> Shigeko said no more, so with a smug air he went and got out a fresh notebook, then set about rewriting his own account of the bombing. (36)

At this early stage in the novel we can already see how on the one hand "fact" is made into "fiction," and on the other "fiction" into "fact." Ibuse relies upon eyewitness testimony, he has told us, because he himself was not present in Hiroshima. The surrender of his own subjectivity in exchange for that of the victim is an expression of his humility: it is his politically and ethically sensitive act of contrition. But at the same time he makes that testimony, as he renders it his own by reproducing it, a kind of novelistic fiction—a particular type of narration embedded within a general narration identified less with the historical or documentary record than with the discourse of the novel. The original testifying voice of Shizuma Shigematsu is detached from its historical position and inserted into a literary one, a movement that must then effectively "fictionalize" it. One Hiroshima critic, perhaps embittered by Ibuse's popular success, has complained that Ibuse relied so much on Shigematsu's diary that Shigematsu himself should have been cited as the *Black Rain*'s co-author. Hospitalized at the time the novel appeared, Shigematsu, it is hinted, was victimized in new ways that are partially Ibuse's own responsibility, too. "Ibuse was very lucky to have had the Shigematsu diary," is the derisive way this critic characterizes the allegedly disingenuous relationship between the two works.[44] But in an important sense *Black Rain* is absolutely no part of Shigematsu's memoir. Ibuse fundamentally alters its status as testimony once he introduces it into an aesthetic practice, namely, that of the literary work, in ways not just epistemological (for example, the way we readers comprehend that testimony via its function as a device advancing plot) but including the ideological. With the introduction of the authorial narrator and the dismissal of the hibakusha narrator from the narrative center, the hibakusha becomes *represented*, part of a broader interpretation of the novel's events as something suddenly less individual and now more generally "Hiroshima."

This new implicit narrator, an "implied author" with whom the reader may more readily identify than he would with Shigematsu, represents an exteriorized cognitive register (whether we call it "Ibuse Masuji" or "ourselves") within which we—and certainly critics—are at considerably greater ease. The "position," if you will, is an ideologically comfortable one. The "timeless," "traditional," and "authentic" virtues associated with Ibuse Masuji's storytelling skills are manipulative as well as artful. The conditioning of bourgeois humanism encourages us to imagine that we are suprahistorical readers rather than the products of particular social and cultural conjunctures: the proof of the presence of such humanism in *Black Rain* may be the fact that, unlike any of Ōta Yōko's novels, the reader emerges from it intact. While Shigematsu is clearly central as a character in *Black Rain*, the multiplicity of explicit narrative viewpoints in the novel produces both an "Ibuse" who assembled those viewpoints and similarly communicates the impression that the author does not identify uniquely with any own of his characters. The result is that no one character, and especially not the doomed Yasuko, is singled out for any special fate or fortune; and the corollary is that the reader does not feel uniquely bound to that fate or fortune either. Instead, where one is bound is precisely that place the author, a person much like ourselves, speaks to us. In one sense

Ibuse is thus able to avoid turning *Black Rain* into a melodrama, the shortcoming of many critically less "successful" atomic-bomb novels.

But, as was seen in the earlier discussion of Ōta's novel *Human Rags*, there are potentially less welcome consequences as well. In her case, fracturing unified narration and point of view imbued *Human Rags* with a kind of pluralizing structure which the more circumscribed genre of personal testimony cannot. But at the same time, it opens up the work to the reader as well, and in ways that give the reader a figural space within which to interpret and even judge. For Ōta this was a problem, since such autonomy for the reader means a proportional reduction in her own propriety as a hibakusha. Ibuse's problem in *Black Rain* is different, of course. He is not a victim, and has no "truth" of his own to protect in its dissemination. Rather, his use of a number of viewpoints is in the service of representing Hiroshima as a historical event to which he can lay no privileged claim. This, I would argue, places Ibuse inevitably if inadvertently in the position of having to endorse an ideological structure rather than, as in Ōta's instance, a moral one. What is at stake in Ibuse's novel is not the *right* of a hibakusha to any particular knowledge not shared generally in society, but instead how society will make "knowledge" out of that hibakusha.

In other words, the organization of *Black Rain*, lacking a single hibakusha narrator whose story dominates the novel as in much atomic-bomb literature, aims for a general *cultural* representation of Hiroshima where those other works were concerned first and foremost with a survivor's personal, even private, representation. It is the public duty served by such a social representation—a duty noted when, for example, Saeki Shōichi calls *Black Rain* "the very essence of Japan"—that can so easily and even necessarily lead to ideological effects and then political implications.

Every representation of the past has ideological implications insofar as that representation is a choice among modes of representation. In the case of modern literature in general and atomic-bomb literature in particular, each of those choices strives to naturalize itself as "realistic," "authentic," or "true-to-life." But if that is the similarity between these choices, the differences lie in the rhetorical contingencies that initiate models of *relationships* within plot, characterization, and interpretation beginning, however, in language. Hayden White has argued that "the crucial consideration for him who would represent [past facts] faithfully are the notions he brings to his representation of the ways parts relate to the whole which they comprise."[45] Among the atomic-bomb writers already discussed we have noted a variety of ways in which "parts" of Hiroshima are related to its "whole," but perhaps the most commonly utilized is the metonymical strategy nearly always embedded within the testimonial mode.

One example of this is Hara Tamiki's "Summer Flowers." As an actual survivor, Hara's account of August 6th and its aftermath is highly personal and subjective, governed by a first-person narrator whose epistemic limits are fixed by the particular and individual encounters this single "I" has. "I felt as if I were standing stage center in a tragic play," Hara writes, suggesting that initially his experience was one radically singular, isolated, alone. The part of Hiroshima his narrator surveys as he makes his way from one refuge to another effectively reduces all of "Hiroshima" to that path—what else can the highly circumscribed field of vision of the testimonial survivor do? Yet at the same time, in reducing the whole of the bombing's impact to that on the single individual, there is presupposed a *difference* between that part and the whole. Hara writes in "Summer Flowers" that he "scarcely knew the truth about the air raid then" (54–55), just as fellow hibakusha Oda Katsuzō writes in his memoir "Human Ashes" (Ningen no hai, 1966) that neither he "nor anyone else had the slightest idea what had brought about this sudden freakish event" (70).

What is important here, and what leads to an awareness of the ideological structure of how Hara represents the Hiroshima experience and thus its historical significance, is that the part is more "real" than the whole, if only because the whole is so epistemically remote as to be unknowable and thus only conjectural. Hara's insistence on the radicalness of his experience ("Oh, the world stripped of all in an instant," as Hara wrote in the poem he embeds in "Summer Flowers") is related to the radicalness of this metonymical mode of narration, in which unity is undone by this dissolution into parts. Hara begins many of his sentences with a first-person pronoun, despite the Japanese language's reluctance to do so, and so he forces on to us the militancy of his testimonial mode. Concomitant is his rejection of a totalizing, metaphorical mode, to argue instead the ideological implication that the phenomenal field defined in "Summer Flowers" is one that does not readily submit to tropic organization resulting in a synthesis of individual experience into a communal, social economy.

There is in *Black Rain* a similar move that might be associated with the testimonial. Shigematsu's diary, while far less immediate in its witness than Hara's memoir, is much like "Summer Flowers" in that it is a first-person narrative that operates metonymically to reduce the whole of the bombing to the part of an average white-collar worker within an "Everyman" whose records are meant to intimate the expanse of history.

Indeed the whole project of testifying is explicitly narrated and contextualized as a theme in the novel. Worried that the description in Yasuko's diary of the literal black rain that fell shortly after the blast may compromise her chances for marriage, Shigematsu resolves to append his own diary to hers. If he, only two kilometers from ground zero, has survived, then surely Yasuko, many times that distance away, has been spared any ill effects. But unlike Yasuko's diary, which was merely recopied, Shigematsu adds new interpolations and explanations—it becomes a project more ambitious than originally intended, and a project with an intended audience much wider than Yasuko's prospective suitors—hence his characterization of his "Journal of the Bombing" as "history."

The "Journal of the Bombing" is both a record of Shigematsu's own suffering and a general history of a major event. Consequently, it is written to be part of an institution, the school library: as "history" it is now a public document, a representation that in time will be synonymous with the event it depicts. That is, it is precisely what *Black Rain* the novel is today in Japanese and perhaps even American culture.⁴⁶ What seems to foreshadow such a special place for Shigematsu's journal is the solemnity with which he undertakes its recopying and revision. Writing the diary is a special responsibility for Shigematsu, at first perhaps only to assist in his niece's marriage negotiations but later as a survivor of Hiroshima whose experience needs to be preserved and propagated. This urge recalls Hara's remark that he had to write in the urgent detail that he did in "Summer Flowers" before events "became distorted in time,"⁴⁷ or Ōta's insistence that she "had to complete [*City of Corpses*] before she died."⁴⁸ It also parallels, as Terrence Des Pres once pointed out, Chaim Kaplan's characterization of his role as a writer in his *Warsaw Diary* as a "duty," a "mission," and a "sacred task."⁴⁹

But there is a difference between Shigematsu and other chroniclers of the most intimate details of atrocity. The grotesque landscape noted in Shigematsu's "Journal of the Bombing" accuses modern civilization as did Hara's poem did in its line "world stripped of all in an instant"; but that same journal, in its important practical value as an accessory to marriage negotiations, or as a contribution to a library, buttresses traditional institutions, the conservative constructs of acculturated life as it was lived before the bomb. In part this is in keeping with the fact that while Ōta and Hara are modern writers—and thus positioned to be disaffected critics of modern society—Shigematsu is not an intellectual, rather a former white-collar worker who is now a semi-retired country gentleman. He is, in other words, a person—not a writer—already integrated into society as any "part" is into a whole. Shigematsu's efforts at writing can never be aesthetic, but rather are purely functional and thus reiterative of his, and Japan's, social imperatives.

Such demands extend to and govern, for example, how Shigematsu approaches his work as an amateur historian. In the fourth chapter Shigematsu, in response to a remark by Shigeko that perhaps he is too concerned with his writing style ("some sort of 'isms'"), defends his brand of amateur historiography as nothing but "crude realism" (*akushajitsu to iu bunshō*). In other words his diary is meant to present "Hiroshima" without the mediation of aesthetics, form, rhetoric, or even language. Shigematsu rejects anything that might bracket his representation of Hiroshima as subjective and not objective.

This is because on another, and possibly conflicting, level, the metonymical testifying mode in *Black Rain* opposes the superseding theme of the Shizuma family after the bombing, a theme which as synecdoche shifts our attention from the witnessing "I" to the socialized and socializing "we." For example, the testifying "I" searches for relatives: the novelistic "we" has them all assembled in the household. In contrast to the primacy given the part in a metonymical scheme, in synecdoche the difference between the whole and its constituent parts is made only in order to identify the whole as a totality that is identified with those parts. Thus, while metonymy is *reductive* (in the sense that the part matters *more* than the whole), synecdoche is *representative* in that the part is cited only on behalf of the whole. While Shigematsu as survivor-witness in his journal is a metonymical figure, Shigematsu as the family patriarch, the country gentleman, the amateur historian, is a synecdochial one. He now *represents* Hiroshima and its aftermath as a kind of middle-class hibakusha John Doe. In effect the switch is from the Shigematsu of the diary as someone extraordinary to Shigematsu as someone much more ordinary, even "natural" in the way he responds to his crisis.

Black Rain abounds with details that make Shigematsu and his family highly recognizable and familiar to us, which is to say to readers accustomed to those representations of bourgeois life most commonly found in novels. Domestic details crowd the pages of *Black Rain*, creating a rich portrait of intimate family life. Shigematsu was, until the bomb reduced him to a semi-retiree, a precursor of the postwar *sararīman*, or white-collar worker. Shigeko, both before and after the bombing a housewife much busy with the usual litany of chores involved in caring for a family, writes in her diary "Diet in Wartime Hiroshima" that "I imagine you could call our family's diet 'lower middle grade' as far as ordinary white-collar workers' families went" (71).

After the war, set up in a quasi retirement in Kobatake village, the Shizuma family resumes a more "normal" life, which is to say one that resonates comfortably with our notion of modern life. The main concern of the family now, it should be remembered, is marriage: a theme that unites this work with so many other examples of bourgeois realism in Japan, such as Tanizaki Jun'ichirō's *The Makioka Sisters* (*Sasameyuki*, 1948).[50] "Shigematsu," who as a witness to atrocity in his journal stood alone as a disconnected voice seeking intelligible terms for a nuclear explosion and its immediate aftermath, becomes the "Shizuma family" in Ibuse's *Black Rain*, no longer so much a narrator as now the narratee, a Japanese Everyfamily whose troubles, while hopelessly complicated by its status as hibakusha, now seem more to resemble our own than to differ.

The effect of this is to exaggerate the internal tensions in the novel, already a conservative vessel struggling to restrain radical contents. By making the Shizuma family a synecdoche emphasizing the wholeness or unity of the survivors, and by replacing Shigematsu as a metonymy representing the shattered parts of what once was a whole but is now ironic, Ibuse has written in *Black Rain* a novel where the traditional unities of form and the social organism seem to supersede—"heal" in more anthropological terms—the damage so powerfully described in the journal. *Black Rain* can consequently be read simultaneously in varying, even contradictory ways—as Etō's *and* Ōe's comments make plain—that yield either stabilizing or destabilizing histories of Hiroshima; either politically conservative or revolutionary imports. But the fact that, Ōe notwithstanding, most commentators have seen in the book the work of a tranquil but totalizing "heijōshin" is proof of the potency and appeal of synecdoche over metonymy, of our predisposition to value wholes over parts—that itself a demonstration of our modern tendency to prefer the genre of the novel over other literary forms. *Black Rain* continually lobbies for such privileging, not only through the utter volume of detail dedicated to the description of the Shizuma family, but through its particular rhetorical strategy of replicating on several levels, thematic as well as formal, the integration of parts into a whole.

■

The device for this movement towards the production of unity and closure most methodically deployed throughout *Black Rain* is that of the ceremony or ritual. "Device" implies that something is imposed by the literary text upon raw experience, but in fact the novelistic Shigematsu's interest, for example, in reciting the Buddhist funeral liturgy has its analogues in testimonial accounts. Robert Jay Lifton, for example, quotes one of his hibakusha informants:

> In the midst of the disaster I tried to read Buddhist scriptures continuously for about one week, hoping that my effort could contribute something to the happiness of the dead. . . . It was not exactly a sense of responsibility or anything as clear as that. It was a vague feeling—I felt sorry for the dead because they died and I survived. I wanted to pacify the spirits of the dead. . . . In Buddhism we say that the souls wander about in anxiety, and if we read the scriptures to them, they lose their anxiety and start to become easy and settle down. So I felt that if I read the scriptures, I could give some comfort to the souls of those who had departed.[51]

Ceremony, or more precisely its irretrievable loss, is a frequent topic in atomic-bomb literature. "Those killed without ceremony," writes Sasaki Yutaka in a waka, "we gather and place in the bonfire without ceremony."[52] The nature of mass death means the suspension of many civilities, including those of burial: in Hiroshima and Nagasaki, the exigencies of a death toll in the tens of thousands meant that bodies had to be disposed of quickly and easily, without the luxury of religious or civil ritual. Early in Agawa Hiroyuki's novel *The Devil's Heritage* (Ma no isan, 1954), a character explains to a visitor to Hiroshima that the stench outside his home is due to the dead horses and human beings indiscriminately buried together on his neighbor's property (105). The loss of a proper grave represents much more than that, in fact an entire assumption one may have once held apropos the value of life itself as well as of death. In Takenishi Hiroko's aptly titled short story "The Rite," protagonist Aki sees a portrait of an ancient Egyptian nobleman and imagines his death with a nostalgia made meaningful only by its contrast with the aftermath of Hiroshima and Nagasaki:

> There without a doubt was a fitting way to start out on death's journey, with the dead well tended and watched over by the living. Thinking of that man who had left behind a part of his own flesh, and his people who had taken it into their keeping, in what was surely a most dignified and solemn ceremony, it seemed to Aki that there was a secure and reassuring way to die. (173)

With Ibuse's *Black Rain*, however, the theme of ceremony's loss meets with that of its recovery. Every chapter is enriched by Ibuse's emphasis on ritual, custom, and tradition. This broad motif permeates the lives of his characters at each stage of the novel. Even as Shigematsu and his family were fleeing the burning city on August 6th, he paused long enough to reflect that the parched rice they were eating was a foodstuff travelers in older times were certainly wise to carry. Returning to events earlier that same day, Shigematsu notes in his diary that when he had stumbled out of Yokogawa Station he had found himself in front of a shrine, or rather what remained of it. Within the shrine grounds lay bleeding, disfigured victims of the explosion. The scene suggests the disintegration of religious structures (in both the literal and abstract senses) under the force of the bomb and their subsequent replacement by images of violence that potentially refuse the succor of faith.

Shigematsu's fear and confusion have the effect of driving him back into the reassuring rites of his pre-bomb existence. For instance, he is suddenly inspired to do his usual morning calisthenics as if they were a "Shinto purification ceremony." Even—especially—when the narrative moment of the novel returns to the present, Shigematsu remains dedicated to regulating his life through ritualized activities. At the end of the third chapter Shigematsu, done with his copying for the day, is having dinner with Shigeko when he recalls how poorly they ate during the war. Perhaps, he suggests, she could write her own account of their deprivations as an appendix to his "Journal of the Bombing." Shigeko has her own idea: why not commemorate Hiroshima by having, each August 6th, the same breakfast they had on that day in 1945? This would preserve, in effect ritualize, their suffering in a kind of reverse feast of thanksgiving. Shigeko remembers exactly what she prepared that day, and indeed, she remembers much else.

Soon the entire Shizuma household is busy writing. Shigeko's contribution to the family project, though brief, is entitled "Dietary Life in Wartime Hiroshima." It is a fascinating summary of the largely nutritional hardships endured by the civilian population in the last years of the war. This journal, like others in *Black Rain*, supplies interesting details on how ingeniously people respond when faced with serious shortages. By obtaining foodstuffs in the country or on the black market, or by substituting homemade concoctions for hard-to-get necessities, the women of Shigeko's neighborhood exhibit the resourcefulness which figures as the principal talent of *Black Rain*'s characters.

Shigematsu approves of his wife's literary labors. After reading her account, which notes how hungry children were given insects to eat, it is with no little irony that he leaves to attend a ritual dedicated to the souls of vermin:

> The Mass for Dead Insects was a rite performed on the day after the [harvest] festival, when farmers would make rice dumplings as an offering to the souls of the deceased insects they had inadvertently trodden on as they worked in the fields. (71)

Such historically agrarian customs are some of the traditions of the pre-bomb world that Shigematsu brings with him into the post-bomb world. They are modes of symbolic behavior, validated by centuries of common observances intimately connected with a social sense of full integration. They ensure, to whatever extent, the continuity of key cultural structures. Shigematsu, stripped of those structures by the Hiroshima bomb, now realizes what subtle purposes such old folklore can serve. The belief is one in the sanctity of life, the most important of all faiths for Ibuse's hibakusha characters. Throughout *Black Rain* the hero will find himself recalling a host of obscure rites from the past, all of which serve as powerful talismans against further attacks on a social matrix already weakened by atrocity. Ibuse writes at the beginning of chapter seven:

> Still Shigematsu continued the transcription of his "Journal of the Bombing." This month, he reflected, was a succession of festivals. The Mass for Dead Insects had gone by already; the Rice-Planting Festival came on the eleventh, and the Iris Festival, by the old lunar calendar, on the fourteenth. On the fifteenth there was the River Imp Festival, and on the twentieth the Bamboo-Cutting Festival. In all these countless little festivals he seemed to sense the affection that the peasants of the past, poor though they were, had lavished on each detail of their daily lives. And as he wrote on, and the horrors of that day came back to him ever more vividly, it seemed to him that in their very insignificance these farmers' festivals were something to be loved and cherished. (101)

Shigematsu treasures the "simple ceremonies" of modern life as well—Shigeko's celebration of her August 6th breakfast, and his own attention to the raising of carp. One of the festivals observed in Kobatake, however, can predict the future, with consequences not necessarily favorable for either the village or Yasuko. Just before her prospective fiance breaks off negotiations because of disturbing talk that will not subside, Ibuse writes:

> June 30th was the day of the Sumiyoshi Festival in Onomichi harbor. In Kobatake village, the occasion was marked by a festival at which lanterns were set afloat on the river to call the attention of the god of Sumiyoshi and invoke his protection against flood. Four small floats, named after the four seasons, were made of plain, unvarnished wood, lighted candles were placed inside them, and they were set afloat on one of the pools of calm water that occurred along the mountain stream. The longer they drifted about the dark surface of the water, the more favorable the omens were said to be. If the autumn float, for example, was promptly carried away out of the pool, it was believed that there would be a danger of floods in the autumn. (126)

Ritual in *Black Rain* is tied not only to the private regeneration of one hibakusha family but to the general movement of the human and natural world. "Ideology," observed Althusser, "has no history," and in fact nature comes close to replacing history entirely by the conclusion of Ibuse's famous novel.[53] Indeed, Shigematsu's recopying of the diary is itself an activity that, conspicuously marked with words found like those on the Sumiyoshi Festival floats, functions much as a modern, literary amulet: a demonstration of how one of ideology's functions is to circulate "culture" and "nature" and render both synonymous.

The various sorts of ceremonies and rituals alluded to in *Black Rain* include the religious, the doctrinal, the aesthetic, the literary, and even the personal. They often function together, however, as elaborate patterns of mitigation, which is to say as ideological mediation, assimilation, and naturalization. What is negotiated and converted into a set of political relations is the gap suddenly presented by the atomic bomb between the individual subjectivity of the hibakusha and his place in the objective environment—"reality." To gargle water, recite a sutra, float a lantern, or write a journal are conceivably diverse attempts to effect a similar reconciliation: that of Shizuma Shigematsu with his world by providing him with a role empowered to induce, ritualistically, the "natural" course of that world. In the end all these rituals collectively imply that their enactment comes to signify more than any given fact—however intensely a part of his experience that fact may be. The project of this revival and the institutionalization of such ceremonies is to identify and define a transient human life as part of a greater cycle of living and death which provides a kind of consolation or even compensation for the victim.

It is important to note that the role performed by ritual and ceremony as a pattern of mediation is akin to the role of ideology. As Althusser has defined it in the epigraph that stands at the head of this chapter, ideology "is the expression of the relation between men and their 'world' . . . a relation that expresses a will (conservative, conformist, reformist or revolutionary), a hope or a nostalgia."[54] Applied to the rituals described in *Black Rain*, it is through the empathetic magic exercised by Shigematsu the Priest, the Farmer, the Guardian that he hopes his will, his hopes, and his nostalgia might bring about a normal, "natural" world in which he and his family will survive. Ideology here as elsewhere is a *process*, a way of life that naturalizes itself, subsuming the subject's real relations within his imaginary relations. In *Black Rain* we typically welcome these processes as powerful antidotes to the destruction continuously distorting the lives of its characters. But just because we are grateful for a representation of Hiroshima that redeems something whole out of what has disintegrated, we should not pretend that just because such constructs are necessary they are not "imaginary," and thus part of an ideological apparatus. Fredric Jameson states "the ideological representation must . . . be seen as that indispensable mapping fantasy or narrative by which the individual subject invents a 'lived' relationship with collective systems which otherwise by definition exclude him."[55] *Black Rain*'s principal "individual subject"—Shigematsu—dramatically, as in the role he serves as priest, "invents" repeatedly such a "lived" relationship with a "collective system." It is just this repetition that makes Shigematsu the major architect of the ideological ground of the novel—that of a "natural" world coterminous with a folk tradition that simultaneously accommodates and repairs the inordinate violence represented by the atomic bomb.

"Nature," as a continuum of order that suffices in lieu of those offered by civilization, permeates every chapter of *Black Rain*. There are all kinds of "nature": the nature of animal life, plant life, the skies, the rivers; and of course "human nature." The first chapter, which introduces the problem of Yasuko's inability to find a husband, inaugurates what is essentially a problem of "nature"— of sexual maturity threatened by the great thwarting of nature in the novel, the atomic-bomb and its lingering contamination both physical and social. The second chapter reiterates this initial theme with the story of Shigematsu's raising of baby carp, a parallel to the relationship he has with his niece. Additionally, as we learn in chapter four, Shigematsu is "the head of a farming household," i.e., the patriarch of another unit linked to cyclical, generative, and natural activity.

In fact it is crucial to *Black Rain*'s message that after the war Shigematsu, who had previously been a white-collar worker in a light industry, leaves the city and returns to the country, which is to say "nature": a place before industry, before modernity, where urban rules are suspended and folk practices and beliefs come to the fore to govern life in its rhythms. The disorder of the world in which the bombing of Hiroshima took place is contrasted within the *order* of a world where human society follows a course determined by its fauna, flora, and human myths. It is an order to be "loved and cherished." Culture is naturalized; nature is cultivated. At the same time Shigematsu begins his duties as a substitute priest. His is a *cultural response* to an atrocity interpreted in one sense as something *natural*. As political authority in Hiroshima breaks down all around him—leaderless soldiers loot, for example—the work that Shigematsu performs once again as the mediator of a natural cycle seeks to restore moral authority. "In olden times, people used to say that in an area badly ravaged by war it took a century to repair the moral damage done to the inhabitants; and it began to seem as though they might have been right," Ibuse writes in the conclusion to the tenth chapter (149).

This restoration of moral authority in the person of Shigematsu anticipates the rejuvenation of nature soon after the bombing, again a substitute for political authority. A week after the bombing, Shigematsu, ostensibly on a mission for his company, travels back into a still-smoldering Hiroshima only to be surprised at what he finds in addition to the ruins:

Insects and plants, indeed, were thriving as never before. Yesterday, I had seen a new shoot a foot and a half long on a plantain tree in what had been the back garden of a noodle shop. The original stem had been snapped off by the blast and had disappeared without a trace, but a new shoot, encased in a sheath like bamboo, was already growing in its place. Today, the shoot was a good two feet long. Familiar with trees as I was, after a childhood spent on a farm, I was astonished. (191)

The power of the natural world rushes in to fill the void vacated by the collapse of political power. "Abstract phrases" mouthed by the remaining civil and military officials in chapter fourteen "were of no comfort at all" to Shigematsu; such authority is now counterfeit and ersatz. But the survivors of Hiroshima are not left in anarchy as a result. Rather, the "natural" world of the flora, fauna, and, most importantly, the village, takes over. In a sense the city *becomes* a village: Shigematsu is constantly running into acquaintances from Kobatake in Hiroshima. In chapter fifteen, Shigematsu notes how it is only a relief squad made up entirely of Kobatake volunteers that does any effective good in Hiroshima.

There is a direct line connecting this "natural" resurgence in Hiroshima with the "natural" life Shigematsu and his family lead in Kobatake five years later. At the beginning of the sixteenth chapter Shigematsu thinks he would like to finish recopying his diary entry for August 15th, but Yasuko, who now evidences sure and undeniable signs of atomic-bomb disease, suddenly preoccupies his thoughts instead. To distract himself Shigematsu heads off for his fish pond, where the carp are about to spawn. Later, a long description of this spawning follows immediately upon news of Yasuko's deteriorating condition:

> Approximately eighty percent of the fry hatched from the two lots of spawn they had gathered had perished. That left—assuming that one spawning produced about twenty-five thousand fry—some ten thousand in the hatching pond. They were about the same size as killifish. At this stage, they were called *kego*. About two months after hatching, their backs would begin to turn bluish and they would reach a length of from one to two-and-a-half inches. At this stage they were called *aoko*, and were released into the main pond. Those that were a year or more old were called *shinko*, and those that were big enough to eat were called *kirigoi*. . . .
>
> When he arrived home, Shigematsu got out an almanac—Daigaku Katō's "Treasure Almanac," it called itself—and studied it carefully. It was the seventeenth of the sixth month by the old lunar calendar—the "seventeen-day old moon," when it was appropriate, according to the almanac, to sow certain varieties of giant radish, kidney beans, and a particular kind of Chinese cabbage on the soil where one's carrots, marrows, and the like had been. A good piece of advice that, thought Shigematsu—it was obviously based on the farmers' experience in taking advantage of the Indian summer that regularly occurred in September. On the same principle, carp fry should do nicely, too. It also occurred to him that there were only three days to go to the anniversary of the Hiroshima bomb, which occurred on the sixth and was followed on the ninth by the anniversary of the Nagasaki bomb. (271–72)

The synchronization of the destruction of Hiroshima and Nagasaki (including Yasuko's delayed illness) with the life cycle of fish—and the human ritualization of that cycle—acts to subordinate that destruction under and within a general concept of the "routine natural," a belief in an essential organismic character of human, botanical, and zoological culture. This same strategy of de-historicizing "bad" events by rationalizing them within a "good" natural world is perhaps most powerfully demonstrated in *Black Rain*'s final chapter, when Shigematsu recopies his journal entry for August 15th, the day of the Shōwa Emperor's radio broadcast announcing the national surrender. Five minutes before the broadcast Shigematsu, on an impulse, left the building where all his fellow workers were assembled before the radio. What he saw was as "exterior" as what he flees was "interior":

> The courtyard was silent and deserted. Three sides were enclosed by company buildings, while the other faced the slope of a hill where oak

trees grew. An irrigation canal some six feet wide flowed from among the oaks into the courtyard and out again via the gap between the office building and the building housing the engineering section, bringing a cool breeze with it. The damp soil on this side of the canal had thick-growing clumps of tall plants with small, pink flowers. Here and there, there were tall white flowers with large yellow pistils. (296)

Once the imperial broadcast began, Shigematsu remained outside in his verdant, virtually human-less landscape. His attention was focused not on the collapse of the state but on the almost magical resurgence of the natural world:

How had I never realized there was such an attractive stream so near at hand? In the water, I could see a procession of baby eels swimming blithely upstream against the current. It was remarkable to watch them: a myriad of tiny eels, still at the larval stage, none of them more than three or four inches in length.

"On you go, on up the stream!" I said to them encouragingly. "You can smell fresh water, I'll be bound!" Still they came on unendingly, battling their way upstream in countless numbers. They must have swum all the way up from the lower reaches of the river at Hiroshima. Newborn eels usually swim into the rivers from the sea in mid-May. Within the first mile from the estuary they are still flat and transparent, like willow leaves, and the fishermen of the bays around Hiroshima call them "sardine eels," because of their likeness to sardine fry. By the time they reached here, though, they looked like real eels, about as big as a large loach but far slenderer and more graceful in their movements. I wondered where they had been swimming on August 6, when Hiroshima had been bombed. I squatted down by the edge of the canal and compared their backs, but all I saw was different shades of gray. None of them showed any signs of harm. (296–97)

When Shigematsu finally, and reluctantly, returned inside the building to learn that, in fact, Japan had surrendered, his tears at the news reminded him of another natural scene:

My own tears had dried up. . . . If the truth be told, I suspect they had not been tears genuinely shed for that moment—that moment, shortly after noon, on a particular day of a particular month—but for something quite different. They reminded me of the time when I was very small, and used to go out to play around our house. At those times I was often tormented by a village lout, almost a half-wit, called Yōichi, but I would never let myself weep in front of him. No—I would run home instead, and badger my mother into baring her breast for me; and it was only then, at the sight of that familiar haven, that I burst into tears at last.

Even now, I can still remember the salty taste of her milk. The tears I shed were tears of relief, and I believe that my tears this day were of the same kind. (298)

Two pages later the novel is over. Shigematsu hopes for a natural sign—a "familiar haven"—in the form of a multicolored rainbow that might portend Yasuko's recovery. The correspondences between the ambiguously construed human world and the very unambiguous world of carp, plantain trees, and even atmospheric phenomena are articulated in ways not so much Romantic— where such natural images would be recognized *as* images—but literal. The symbolic order of nature is proposed, in fact, as its actual order; otherwise, the damage done by the atomic bomb could not both be expressed by its distortion of the natural world and repudiated by its occasional repair of that distortion. Here is why, perhaps, John Bester could reasonably and sincerely claim that "*Black Rain* is not a 'book about the bomb' at all."[56] So successful is the dissolution of one of the greatest atrocities of the century into stories of baby carp and other nostalgic signs of a long-gone pastoral, that the novel's translator can say that its theme is precisely opposite what the public assumes. "A hope or a nostalgia, rather than describing a reality," wrote Althusser of the "imaginary relation" defining ideology: and, one might add, both the appeal and terror of *Black Rain*.

■

The function of these themes in *Black Rain* is to create a context that explains, orders, and governs the lives, the deaths, of the Shizuma family: a family who stands as the first synecdoche of all hibakusha and, indeed, conceivably all Japanese. This is the primary charge of this novel's particular ideology, but it is well in the way of things ideological anyway that in *Black Rain* "nature" is fused and conflated with "history." If "false consciousness" is where we would look for the product of ideological reasoning, then Shigematsu Shizuma's imaginary relationship with the social world around him lies in his conviction that it is not social at all, but natural. Hiroshima as a event in *time* is repressed in favor of Hiroshima that is a *place* where the forces of violence demonstrate anew their power. Hiroshima of course remains a horrible tragedy, but it is one that, equipped with the collected tranquility ("heijōshin") of a propertied family patriarch, is reconciled within the sanctions of the traditional understanding of how, perhaps after all, things are meant to work. Ideology, conceived here as the sum of the ways in which people both live and represent to themselves their relationship to the conditions of their existence, operates in *Black Rain* through the hegemony of its well-considered picture of nature. In Raymond Williams's formulation, Ibuse's natural world, as well as ideology itself, is "the central, effective dominant system of meanings and values, which are not merely abstract but are organized and lived."[57]

Such definitions allow us to see in *Black Rain,* and in particular in Shigematsu's view of the world around him, how meanings and values are "naturally" implied. "As he wrote on, and the horrors of that day came back to him ever more vividly, it seemed to him that in their very insignificance these farmers' festivals were something to be lived and cherished." The "insignificance" of these ritual reenactments of man's place in the world could not be otherwise, if they are to be ideological. To the extent that ideology equals the commonsensical, it obscures the real conditions of life by prescribing partial truths. Shigematsu "sees" in nature a model that offers some hope of regeneration, of redemption, but such sight requires an equal degree of blindness, in this instance to the very contingent circumstances, not "natural" at all, that allowed nuclear war. When Shigematsu intuits a correspondence between the events of August 6th and the way an earlier peasant society is organized about commemorative observances in order to guarantee the reproduction of the relations of agrarian production—the reproduction entrusted to ideology—he rationalizes *those* events as well as *that* society. The effect is to extend the ethos and practice of those observances forward, into the aftermath of the Second World War, and rewrite that aftermath as another marker in the periodically catastrophic lives of ordinary people. There is a kind of universalization of Hiroshima at work here that, insofar as that is also its moment of naturalization, is ideological.

But "universalization" is also doubtlessly what has made the novel so popular, because finally it seems so "real," so close to "experience," and thus surely congruent with dominant forms of ideology. By universalizing this particular brand of nostalgic rural life, *Black Rain* concurrently represses other post-Hiroshima cultures, and indeed propagates the illusion that there is only one genuine culture, post-Hiroshima or otherwise, and moreover a culture that reiterates features—perhaps most importantly that of the patriarchal family—that may hold a special appeal for conservative critics. This legitimization of a particular familial organization akin to a *natural* organization in *Black Rain* is coterminous with its ideological work. This work emplots human history along a "continuum" that in turn reconstitutes both pre- and post-Hiroshima life as a seamless unity, a unity no less monolithic for being comforting to readers eager for such reassurance.

Ideological naturalization, this accommodation of a forced unity of history with nature, is replicated in the unity of *Black Rain* as a literary work. By combining the testimonial, discursive content of the diaries with its narrative argument as a "novel," *Black Rain*—even beyond its explicitly ideological functions—imposes a reiterative and reproductive form. Critics such as Etō Jun and Yamamoto Kenkichi find the design of *Black Rain* as a "true literary work of art" so admirable because it, like all such successful forms, satisfies just those desires and expectations that it arouses. *Black Rain's* hybrid status as a novel with testimonial passages finds establishment approval because it meets the criterion that an "objective" world would be re-presented, aesthetically, as a subjective experience, and moreover as a subjective experience linked to "our" own subjectivity. The effect, politically, is one of domination rather than of resistance. This is where *Black Rain* is at its most conservative, though this is not by any means necessarily a bad thing. It continually restores "forms"—the vital conjunction—among past, present, and future endangered in modern culture by mass death. Shigematsu never knows when, or if, he will succumb to a worse case of life-threatening atomic-bomb disease, but he does know that his little carp, as the hardiest of them grow from *kego* to *kirigoi*, will continue to affirm that precious continuity of life so much at stake in this novel.

The powerful processes at work in *Black Rain*, and afterwards in the works of its impressed critics who have aimed to make the novel so singly representative of Japan's nuclear destruction, are processes we should identify not with the individual struggle of, say, a Hara Tamiki or Ōta Yōko to create an atomic-bomb literature, but rather with a general reaction on the part of established and powerful cultural circles to do so. In an obituary that appeared in the *Asahi shimbun* the day after his death in 1993—an obituary far more extensive than that usually accorded writers, but one in keeping with Ibuse's immense reputation—it was said he "wrote of the important contemporary theme of the atomic bombing by looking at it in the context of everyday life, and it was characteristic of him to do so with a calm and unperturbed state of mind."[58] The author of the obituary expressed "calm and unperturbed state of mind" in Japanese with the single word "heijōshin"—the word first used to describe Ibuse and *Black Rain* by his more conservative reviewers, but which now inevitably appears whenever his most read and critically praised novel is cited. There is in *Black Rain* and its critical reception traces of the forging of a Hiroshima equivalent of a nostalgic, and politically expedient, medieval "Matter of Britain" or "Matter of France." As troubadours once wove together myths with history to create a field upon which the collective imagination might draw in being "British" or "French," so now does *Black Rain* serve as a similarly romantic expression of how "the Japanese" experienced and answered their history.[59] Such expression, or at least its uses, may be criticized; but in its being if not particulars, it is probably inevitable. "Only a horizon ringed about with myths," says Nietzsche, "can unify a culture," and it attests to the success of Ibuse's benevolent myth-making that another of his eulogizers declared him "the epitome of a Japanese."[60]

It is a powerful imagination that Ibuse leaves us, one with ethical and pragmatic dimensions we might well recognize as salutary. But we realize, along with Irving Howe, that it is in the nature of the political novelist that he "urges his claim for a moral order beyond ideology," and that "the receptive reader, even as he perseveres in his own commitment, assents to the novelist's ultimate order."[61] But this ease of assent testifies to the ideological promise of *Black Rain*—that we, while (or perhaps because we are) horrified by the terrors told in Ibuse's novel, are nonetheless strangely reassured by the strengths its victims summon even in the face of the atomic bomb's inexorable toll. I say "promise" because the ideological work performed by *Black Rain* is only provisional, full of countervailing doubt and its own undoing—and that, too, is part of the book's power. If it is true, as has been argued, that "the effectively ideological is also at the same time necessarily utopian,"[62] then *Black Rain's* ideological content can hardly be said to be wholly effective—the world of Kobatake, while one that we may indeed inhabit, is not the one we would unambiguously wish for ourselves. Around its edges *Black Rain* lets us know that perhaps the hopes and certainties upon which Shigematsu relies to get through his and his family's troubles are private ones born of a particular desperateness: an inference that has a great deal more in common with the messages of Hara and Ōta than Etō and Yamamoto might care to acknowledge. Like the lives of the victims it portrays, *Black Rain* too is a struggle, albeit one between not life and death but rather between the wholeness of life and our recent, irrefutable evidence to the contrary.

Kozaki Kan, *The Holy Statues* (Seizō, 1974)

August 9, 1945, is the present. . . . August 9th is nothing but
the present. . . . We have not moved even one step forward.
Even when we think we have, when sense returns
we are still standing on August 9th.

Hayashi Kyōko, "Document"

9

Nagasaki and the
Human Future

"Ikari no Hiroshima, inori no Nagasaki": Hiroshima rages, Nagasaki
prays. This common characterization of the marked difference between the
social and cultural responses of the number one and two cities to be subjected
to a nuclear attack speaks a widespread prejudice: Nagasaki is the second city,
the silent city, the city that, because of its early familiarity with the Western
science that would one day facilitate its destruction, perhaps even invited that
fate. The slogan frequently heard at protests throughout the world, "No more
Hiroshimas!" makes no mention of Nagasaki. Whereas the place name "Hiroshima" is now the metonymy of all "Hiroshimas" past and future, Nagasaki
remains just "Nagasaki," conceivably better known around the world because
of an Italian opera than because of an American air raid. There exists in the
historiography of the nuclear age a hierarchy—Hiroshima and then, only
sometimes, Nagasaki. The plutonium bomb exploded over Nagasaki was more
powerful than the uranium one dropped on Hiroshima, yet its use is not ac- 301

counted for even in the feeble apology offered for Hiroshima ("A demonstration had to be made"). Nagasaki seems less consequential and certainly less
historic. As one historian put it, "There was a vast difference between the two
missions and the two bombs. Photographers and high brass had been on hand
for the lift-off of the historic *first* 'A-bomb' mission. . . . The second atomic
drop was being left to the professionals."[1] One Japanese story makes much the
same point, but from the perspective of Hiroshima hibakusha who listened to
the radio three days after the attack on their own city: "Everyone was silent at
the news of Nagasaki. It had, after all, been expected."[2]

This is precisely why, however, the destruction of Nagasaki is so crucial
in history. A redundant act within the logic of the Second World War, it represents the exercise of a technological and scientific capacity for curiosity's sake,
and the exercise of a postwar military capacity for power's sake. If Hiroshima
initiated the nuclear age, Nagasaki confirms it. This makes the event of Nagasaki perhaps more terrible, despite its lesser carnage: its annihilation converted
what might have been an unique aberration in the history of warfare, had the
atomic bomb been retired once its effects were known, into a pattern. It turned
a strategy into a tactic, one more easily applied to our own cities today wher-
ever they are.

Abetting the usual relegation of Nagasaki to the margins of history—a
move justified by the contempt in which the city is held for its relative mute-
ness—is the undeniable fact, however, that the canon (if we may speak of one)
of atomic-bomb literature is overwhelmingly dominated by Hiroshima writers
and Hiroshima works. Nagasaki atomic-bomb literature, for whatever reasons—they are many—is quantitatively smaller and critically less favored. Yamada Kan, a prominent poet and native of Nagasaki, has admitted that nothing
strikes him as more anomalous than the paucity of atomic-bomb poetry that
has come out of his city. It is a place, he notes, with a tradition of poets—he
rightly cites, for example, Saitō Mokichi—but after August 9th, very little
to recommend it.[3] Elsewhere Yamada has also observed that other genres of
atomic-bomb literature are similarly stunted: few testimonial accounts, for example, have been published by Nagasaki survivors.[4] This disturbs Yamada, as
if the lack of literary activity might indeed indicate a lesser historical importance for his city's tragedy, which would translate into Nagasaki's lesser significance generally as an atrocity. But quite significantly, what troubles Yamada is
something which, from time to time, has attracted the speculation of other
writers and critics throughout Japan.

Exactly ten years after the bombings, the Nagasaki Literature Society (Nagasaki Bungaku Kondankai) published in a special issue of the local literary
journal *Chijin* (The Native) the results of a survey conducted among two dozen
well-known writers, including Inoue Mitsuharu, Odagiri Hideo, and Noma
Hiroshi. The survey consisted of just two questions. First, why has Nagasaki,

unlike Hiroshima, not produced a real *(honkakuteki)* atomic-bomb literature? Second, what should writers do in response to the anti-bomb movement then prominent in the mid-1950s? Responses to the second query were fairly uniform. As Noma said, it is the duty of writers to write, and Nagasaki writers must write documents of their experiences. To the first question, however, numerous, diverse, and occasionally even contradictory explanations were suggested. Hayashida Yasumasa, in his summary of the survey's results, includes the following quotes. "Hiroshima was first," "There were few professional writers in Nagasaki," "The mountainous geography of the city limited the damage to only one area." These factors, however, Hayashida considers simply coincidental to Nagasaki's lowered postwar literary production. He goes on to enumerate reasons he judges more essential: "Nagasaki's negativity *[shōkyokusei]*," "Nagasaki's lyricism," "The inappropriateness of the social environment," "Nagasaki's historical and regional nature," "The popularity of traditional shorter poetic forms," "The lack of democratic influences," "The clannishness of its citizens," "Journalism's inhospitality," and finally—one might have cited it first—"The difficulty of the atomic bomb as a subject."[5]

Ironically it is Hayashida's "coincidental" reasons that in hindsight make some degree of sense. Hiroshima, as the first target of a nuclear weapon and the site of the most killed, does attract the attention of victim and non-victim writers everywhere. Hiroshima and its environs were in fact the temporary home of a number of professional writers who had been evacuated from Tokyo;[6] and quite unlike the flat delta upon which Hiroshima was built, the topography of Nagasaki, resembling a hand with its fingers outstretched, did serve to minimize the impact of the explosion outside its immediate vicinity.[7] But Hayashida's list of "intrinsic" reasons, in the few instances where they are intelligible, reveal nothing so much as the deeply held prejudices both against Nagasaki as that major city most distant from Tokyo and thus one of the country's most literally provincial, and against any broad interpretation of what manifestations an "appropriate" atomic-bomb literature might assume. Cryptic references to Nagasaki's "social environment," "negativity," and "clannishness" are apparently meant to contrast with the cosmopolitan character of other Japanese cities, and the suggestion that the popularity of "traditional shorter" poetry stymied atomic-bomb literature implies that "lyricism" fails to communicate the—prosaic?—truth of nuclear war. But most of all, Nagasaki is clearly perceived, and for reasons not plainly stated by those surveyed, as markedly different from other Japanese cities, which is to say different from other regional cultures collectively and affirmatively held to be somehow more consistently "Japanese."

Indeed, Nagasaki atomic-bomb literature is guaranteed to proceed differently than that of Hiroshima precisely for this reason: Nagasaki itself occupies a unique position in Japan's history and thus Japan's modern imagination. A visitor to Nagasaki today, for instance, is shown a city that boasts of its uniqueness not as a target—for in that sense, of course, it is *not* unique—but as an international entrepôt during Japan's centuries of national isolation, when contact with foreign nations was strictly forbidden outside of Nagasaki. Nagasaki city boosters still prefer to think of its local culture in terms of Dutch estates and Chinese temples, and decidedly not as the A-bomb city which, nonetheless, it is. Especially within Japan itself, Nagasaki has sought to exploit its exoticism, which is to say its carefully cultivated "foreignness." It has made a tourist industry out of being benignly alien. Reconciling the irony of being a city which, due to the early influence of European traders, introduced much of modern Western technology to the rest of Japan with the fact of its destruction by the twentieth-century results of that same technology is certainly not part of the city's promotional rhetoric. But it is nonetheless an irony that can unnerve the unprepared visitor, and an irony that can thus make a trip there more pathos-inspiring than any to Hiroshima.

A history of important contacts with the West in the sixteenth century has led to other particular, popular distinctions concerning Nagasaki that continuously inform the ways its literature are written and read. "Perhaps Japan's most significant historical community," wrote Norman Cousins, Nagasaki "pioneered in everything the West has had to offer, all the way from fine art to explosive plutonium."[8] But the image of Nagasaki in the Japanese popular imagination seems most closely tied to Japanese perceptions of Christianity. Nagasaki has long been the Japanese city with the highest percentage—though it is still a small minority—of Christian adherents, and this historical circumstance has led to the making of a number of tenuous connections with the city's equally conspicuous status as the target of an atomic attack. In *An American Hero*, for example, novelist Iida Momo exploits the obvious irony of a Christian bombing crew targeting Japan's most Christian city (193). Others have gone further, however, and make the curious and unsubstantiated suggestion that Nagasaki was selected as such a target precisely because it *was* "Christian." This argument hinges on either a special martyrdom divinely mandated for the city's faithful, or towards a perverse, even sadistic logic followed by the bomb's Western, i.e., Judeo-Christian, innovators. Looming behind much of the discussion of Nagasaki's atomic-bomb literature—and present in some of that literature itself—is a strange mythology: namely that in Nagasaki Christians themselves reconcile their fate as bomb victims with Christianity's, and perhaps in particular Japanese Christianity's, special regard for martyrs. In 1597, twenty-six foreign and Japanese Christians were crucified in Nagasaki; later, other Christians would be tortured to death in the hot springs of nearby Unzen. These and subsequent acts of suppression, known collectively as the "Urakami *kuzure*," or the Urakami Persecutions, drove tens of thousands of Christians underground for centuries, thus keeping Christianity alive, if not wholly intact, in Japan despite successive and increasingly bloody pogroms lasting well into the late nineteenth century. A certain historical memory was created, then, that resonates with the horrors that would be visited upon Ura-kami in the summer of 1945, as well as a certain historical tradition of surviving such horrors by internalizing and "hiding" one's identity, be it that of a Christian or, mutatis mutandis, a hibakusha. As one long-time Jesuit resident of Japan and translator of Nagasaki atomic-bomb literature has remarked, "Martyrdom was a glorious act of which the Nagasaki Christians are justly proud. And those who died in the atomic holocaust are no less martyrs than their illustrious ancestors who were crucified on mountains or who died hanging over the sulfur pits of Unzen."[9]

In 1960 Inoue Mitsuharu published a short story, "The House of Hands" (Te no ie), which explicitly links the history of Nagasaki's centuries-old secret Christian sects, the hidden believers, and its atomic-bomb survivors. Underground Christians most successfully kept their faith alive on those small islands off the coast of Nagasaki most remote from the authorities. It is on one of those islands that Inoue locates his story of another, more modern, secret that its young women keep. "The House of Hands" is a title that refers to a orphanage established to care for hibakusha girls, the fact of whose existence is concealed from everyone not native to the island, much as their Christian faith was and to some extent still is. The plot of the story revolves around the visit of an off-islander who had been hoping to conclude arrangements for the marriage of one of these girls; unfortunately, she dies suddenly and ironically of a vaginal hemorrhage. The story's point, however, is about a historically marginalized village that, despite the suffering it must therefore bear in silence, does not wish to be ostracized any further. Inoue overlays a Christian legacy atop an atomic one to produce a doubly powerful account of how one community works to survive by means tested and proved as nowhere else in Japan, and it is that strength lent by three centuries of patient endurance that does, in fact, underlie much Nagasaki atomic-bomb literature.

Inoue's sympathy and admiration for Nagasaki's Christians, however, are not universally shared. Other non-Christian Japanese, indulging prejudices long held, saw some sort of perversely just retribution in the fact that it was, after all, the foreign-tainted Japanese Christians who were bombed. "The bomb was not dropped on Nagasaki; it was dropped on Urakami," older residents of the city once reportedly and ungenerously quipped in a reference to the particular neighborhood suffering the worst damage and, coincidentally (since the bomb was dropped off-target), housing the highest concentration of Christian populations. Urakami is, for example, the site of Nagasaki's Catholic cathedral, and was the most notable locale destroyed in an attack described by *Life* magazine in August 1945—presumably without any knowledge of Nagasaki's Christian martyrs and the sadistic means of their deaths—as one that, in contrast to the one which had "blown [Hiroshima] off the face of the earth," merely "disemboweled" Nagasaki—a metaphor that grotesquely resonated with that city's own sense of a special victimization.[10]

A long history of persecution had resulted in the ghettoization of Nagasaki Christians most conspicuously in Urakami proper, where they were and still are subject to defamation and more serious discrimination in matters of employment, housing, and marriage.[11] When some 9,000 of the 17,000 Christians in Nagasaki were killed in the bombing, and the irradiated rest subsequently made susceptible to the additional prejudice easily exercised against hibakusha, certain sympathetic voices compensatorily interpreted events as a trial of faith: a Christian God testing his newly Chosen People. Less sympathetic, indeed outrightly hostile, voices obversely saw the work of Japanese gods taking vengeance on heretics. In either rationale the rage directed outwardly in so much Hiroshima atomic-bomb literature was conversely directed inwardly in Nagasaki, where the phenomenon of "blaming the victim" served to curb what impulses to record, document, and write might have otherwise flourished. Indeed, the Christian heritage of Nagasaki is the factor most frequently cited as the root cause for the paucity of the city's contributions to atomic-bomb literature. Hayashida, for instance, called Christian "influences" the "real" hindrance to Nagasaki's literary activities.[12] Just why Christianity, at least in its Japanese manifestations, should obstruct an atomic-bomb literature apparently lies in the widespread impression that Christianity is a religion which exploits guilt and which countenances extreme violence as legitimate within the ken of divine action. Japanese contempt for Christianity as a "foreign," "alien" system of unhealthy, certainly unpeaceable, beliefs is popularly conflated with another intractable contempt for atomic-bomb literature itself as an unnecessarily, uncomfortably morose genre of writing.

Traditional xenophobia, coupled with an internalized self-hatred within pockets of the Japanese Christian community itself, has to some extent doubtlessly impeded the production—certainly the critical validation—of what atomic-bomb literature Nagasaki might have offered. "Christianity" or "Catholicism," repeatedly invoked with little elaboration as the cause of Nagasaki's taciturnity, soon fails, however, to account for the complete range of difference in local literary cultures. Quite frankly, religion of any sort is of less consequence in modern Japan than in most Western nations, and seems of especially little concern to writers. More explanatory, perhaps, would be the view that references to Christianity and its exotic overtones simply serve as a rhetorical shorthand for reiterating prejudices already inclined to sequester Nagasaki writing further within the already compromised genre of atomic-bomb literature throughout Japan.

This double burden under which Nagasaki atomic-bomb literature labors has resulted in a body of writing even more preoccupied than that of Hiroshima with its reasons to exist, its right to speak, and the nature of "survival." Many of its works reflect with particular passion on the predicament of modern historical and imaginative writing concerned with atrocity, or more precisely the textual representation of mortal violence perpetrated without restraint by one community against another. The continual danger that Nagasaki literature runs of being subsumed within Hiroshima literature, and thus effectively disappearing, parallels the struggle of the literature of atrocity in general wages against a long-standing tradition of literature as an aestheticized and aestheticizing practice. But at the same time this multiple suppression offers Nagasaki atomic-bomb literature multiple opportunities to conceive and develop its themes in conjunction with other current themes in modern writing. Figuring prominently in Nagasaki literature are the problems, for example, of women and ethnic minorities: problems displayed against and within the context of an alterity already established by the literally vital difference between those who are hibakusha and those who are not. By focusing attention not so much on the physical damage wrought by the bomb but rather on its repercussions for a group or groups in society already denied full participation, Nagasaki atomic-bomb literature can foreground one of the more important contradictions of the nuclear age: that now, just as subordinated minorities in modern societies are made to understand, all of our survivals are continually and mortally challenged by majority interests.

The most engaging works produced about Nagasaki by Nagasaki writers are largely distinguished by their paramount concern with the long-range consequences of the use of atomic weapons on human beings. This theme, though pursued in various ways, is one narrating and postulating a continuing legacy of victimization, and the examples cited to illustrate that victimization will frequently be expressed in terms of religious, gender, and racial or ethnic difference. Nagasaki atomic-bomb literature exploits both written and unwritten narratives of the already unenfranchised to represent what is perhaps the ultimate alienating and humbling inference of the post-Hiroshima world: that we are perhaps, even at the level of our physiological being, the last intact human generations to know the world.

■

Nagasaki atomic-bomb literature, though less voluminous than that of Hiroshima at every point in its history, developed in its first decades along lines roughly parallel. Anthologies of poetry were compiled early in both cities, for example, and Hara Tamiki's celebrated 1947 documentary treatment of August 6th, "Summer Flowers," compares in many ways with Ishida Masako's *Masako Will Not Succumb: An Account of the Nagasaki Atomic Bomb* (Masako taorezu: Nagasaki genshi bakudan ki), published two years later and in which a fifteen year-old girl narrates in a testimonial mode the August 9th bombing and its aftermath. Well received by critics (though characteristically for a work of Nagasaki writing, it is seldom mentioned in atomic-bomb literary histories or listed in chronologies), it is still cited as the preeminent example of early Nagasaki documentary accounts. A later, and also acclaimed, documentary account is Fukuda Sumako's 1968 *I Am Still Alive* (Ware nao ikite ari). The fact that both of these works were written by women already points, however, to a significant difference between Hiroshima and Nagasaki, namely the conspicuously wider participation of female authors in the literature of the latter. Possibly accident, this distinction should not be overworked—for example, female Hiroshima writer Ōta Yōko's novel *People and the City of Evening Calm*, which details the degraded lives led by Hiroshima hibakusha, is matched in Nagasaki by male writer Inoue Mitsuharu's 1963 *People of the Land* (Chi no mure), a novel set in a hibakusha ghetto just as alienated and discouraged as any in Ōta's Hiroshima. But Inoue's work, with its steady impulse to describe the lives of the people of Nagasaki in comparison with those of the untouchable *burakumin* caste, stigmatized Koreans, and other ethnic minorities in Japan, as well as communists and coal miners, again points to another of the common divides between Nagasaki and Hiroshima literature, namely the underlying context of traditional forms of marginalization and victimization—be it organized on the basis of gender, race, or ethnicity—that seems to influence so much of Nagasaki literature and, by comparison, so little of Hiroshima's.

Events in *People of the Land* take place in a small fictional community over a twenty-four hour period on the eve of the seventeenth anniversary of the bombing of nearby Nagasaki. It explores how three generations of victims—not just of the bomb, but of prejudices widespread before the war as well as after—are forced to live continually and painfully aware of their pasts. The central character, a thirty-seven year-old alcoholic doctor named Unan Chikao, seems in other respects much like author Inoue himself, who once implied in an interview that he invented the novel's village of "Kaitō Shinden"—a name of such recent vintage that, like "Soweto," it already suggests some system of apartheid—to show how social discrimination insinuates and perpetuates itself, and to consider how one lives, when living itself is a dilemma.[13] Those dilemmas include the unfathomable but inexorable progress of radiation illness, the rape of a burakumin girl, and the murder of that same girl's mother, possibly for having raised awkward questions about others' long-hidden ethnic identities. No character in the novel is redeemed, or even has his or her suffering ameliorated. But unlike the nihilism that overwhelms the work of Hiroshima writers, here the desperateness derives not solely from the bombing but from stubborn forms of insidious bias practiced in Japan long before the Second World War.[14] Hiroshima literature has not produced a novel ambitious in quite this way. It has fallen to Nagasaki, with its historical sensitivity to social discrimination, to place the atomic bombings in literary contexts that directly address issues of class, racial, religious, and gender difference.

Another example of the roughly parallel course of the development of atomic-bomb genres and the roughly dichotomous course of atomic-bomb themes in the two target cities is theater. Hotta Kiyomi's 1957 Hiroshima conventional drama *The Island*, the story of a young man whose chances for a normal married life are ruined by his earlier exposure to "contaminating" radiation, was followed in 1959 by Nagasaki native Tanaka Chikao's more powerful work *The Head of Mary* (Maria no kubi). Tanaka, one of Japan's most noted modern playwrights, used a large cast led by women characters to recreate the conspiracy of a group of Catholics to collect the fragments of the statue of the Virgin Mary that once stood in front of the city's cathedral in order to reassemble her in their own secret place of worship. Similarly scarred by the bomb, these new "secret Christians" chose the Virgin as their special saint for veneration. At the end of the play, the partially repaired statue miraculously responds to the prayers of her hibakusha supplicants. The last lines of the play are those of a song sung from off-stage:

> Hear, sweet Mother, hear the weary,
> Borne upon life's troubled sea;
> Gentle guiding Star of Ocean,
> Lead thy children home to thee.
> Still watch o'er us, dearest Mother,
> From thy beauteous throne above;
> Guard us from all harm and danger,
> 'Neath thy shelt'ring wings of love. (181)

The Head of Mary clearly pivots upon a Christian religious motif not typically encountered in Hiroshima atomic-bomb literature. Tanaka, who himself holds Roman Catholic beliefs, wished to explore in his play the relationship between a providential god and the fate of his city, or least that of the Christian community within it. Such literature, while inconspicuous in Hiroshima, is plentiful in Nagasaki. It is not impossible to find some in Nagasaki who have written approvingly of God's will in the dropping of the bomb. Such reasoning represents a powerful undercurrent in Nagasaki atomic-bomb literature, an undercurrent not wholly without parallels in Jewish concentration and death camp literature, where some writers have been equally concerned with the special trials seemingly reserved for a "chosen" people. It is tempting to interpret such attitudes as yet another proof of our compensatory psychological mechanism capable of discerning in any tragedy some value. It might be simpler in the instance of Nagasaki, however, to regard this embrace of martyrdom as a response to the continuing legacy of the degradation and humiliation of Christians, and by extension hibakusha, in Japan.

This view of the Nagasaki bombing is exemplified in the works of Nagai Takashi, and especially his *The Bells of Nagasaki* (Nagasaki no kane, 1949). It is without a doubt the single best-known work of Nagasaki atomic-bomb literature, selling 70,000 copies soon after it was first published. At the time of the attack Nagai was the thirty-seven year-old dean of radiology in the medical school at the University of Nagasaki, a facility located in Nagai's own words "between three and seven hundred meters from the center of the explosion . . . within the radius directly affected by the bomb" (11). Nagai's retrospective account of the fires which enveloped his school, and of the often Herculean efforts expended by him and the few other surviving medical personnel to provide assistance to the injured in and around the city, as well as of his own battle with radiation sickness, leukemia, and his "miraculous" recovery therefrom, was inspired by a friend who, visiting Nagai while bedridden with radiation illness, suggested that he leave a "record" behind. It was completed in the summer of 1946, but publication was delayed until 1949, no doubt in anticipation of Occupation reaction to the disturbing effect the memoir would have on readers. In fact, that power is still felt today. *The Bells of Nagasaki* remains one of the most alarming and poignant first-person accounts of either of the atomic bombings, and its English translation has meant that its impact has traveled far beyond its Japanese readers.

The carnage both material and biological so close to the epicenter in Nagasaki was immense, a result of the more powerful isotopes carried in America's last atomic bomb of the war. It produced, in Nagai's words as well as those of other survivors, "a world of the dead." After struggling to save both buildings and people obviously beyond saving—that effort more an existential choice than a real rescue—Nagai had finally to conclude late on the day of August 9th that "our Nagasaki School of Medicine . . . was reduced to ashes" (34). Later, as new and unfathomable diseases struck down initial survivors weeks and even months later, Nagai would witness human lives as well leveled by what he recognized from the moment he was hit as "no ordinary event." As in other accounts, *The Bells of Nagasaki* records a steadily deepening realization of the power of a weapon total in its lethal, and long-term, effects. Distant neighborhoods as devastated as near ones; men and women dying who were not even present in the city on the 9th: the bomb presented Nagai with mysteries both as a scientist and as a Christian. For Nagai, such mysteries were on one hand to be pondered and solved, and on the other simply accepted as the work of a greater, purposefully obscure, power. This paradox distinguishes Nagai's memoir from others as famous. When Norman Cousins, writing after Nagai's death, observed that Nagai's "one-room bungalow," located not far from the Urakami cathedral, "is fast becoming a shrine," he noted the unique role this man now posthumously performs: that of canonized saint, like Christopher a patron of Japan's most miserable Christians, and one whose powers to heal are now wholly a matter of faith and not of science.[15]

Apart from the polished literary style of many passages—including surprising moments of a deftly handled black humor—*The Bells of Nagasaki* probably remains the most scientifically accurate first-hand document of the ground-level effects of nuclear weaponry. One part of the post-atomic world is eminently comprehensible for Nagai: the world in which reality is now very much atomic particles invisible to the eye, but whose aggregate effect is the obliteration and contamination of human tissue. Nagai brings to this reality—as a radiologist, not an entirely new one for him—his trained curiosity. The education he possesses made him more knowledgeable, and even dispassionately interested, in both the abstract science of the bomb and the pathology of its effects than any other well-known survivor-writer. Descriptions of the damage and suffering are punctuated with well-written and informative detours into the history of international nuclear research, the rudiments of fission, and the close physiological relationship between atomic radiation and human health. Other survivors, of course, also incorporated various scientific addenda into their testimonies and documentary accounts. Ōta Yōko's *City of Corpses* is one such example. But what sets Nagai so decisively apart is the distinct moral position he takes on the advent of nuclear energy. Or rather, which he does not take: for in fact throughout *The Bells of Nagasaki* Nagai is uncomfortably ambivalent towards the technology that would finally, in 1951 at the age of forty-three, end his own life. (He died the victim of a heart attack prompted by leukemia linked either to his career as a radiologist, or to his status as a hibakusha, or to both.) One part of Nagai understood this experience—this victimhood—as the consequence of a epochal, monumental, scientific and technological achievement which he could hardly welcome. "There will be no beautiful stories, no songs, no poems," writes Nagai of the post-Hiroshima world, and with no less bitterness than an Ōta Yōko or Hara Tamiki, "no paintings, no music, no literature, no research. Only death" (104).

Yet another part of him, perhaps that part attempting to salvage something of value in the midst of Nagasaki's destruction, rejoiced in the atomic bomb—if not its use—as proof of the inevitability of human progress, as a sign of the birth of a new age. The original title of *The Bells of Nagasaki* was *The Curtain Rises on the Age of the Atom*: proof of an early impulse to describe the science of atomic energy as one that might, not merely potentially but probably, bring the human race unimagined benefits. The bomb for Nagai is also "the triumph of physics" (51). Evident throughout his account is a stubborn faith in the fundamental righteousness in the quest of science, even when it improves upon the technology of killing. Of course, at the same time, that faith was shaken as Nagai came to understand how the very civilization proposed by the ideology of modern science, an ideology usually recognized as a kind of liberal humanist morality, was also potentially unraveled or at least compromised by it. Nagai sensed in his confusion of two moralities—that of science's promise of progress and that of his commitment as a doctor to preserve human life against the onslaught of that same "progress"—an initially irreconcilable contradiction that his *The Bells of Nagasaki* would have to address.

As his narrative continues, Nagai discerns a way—unique among atomic-bomb testimonial literature—to supersede that contradiction through an appeal to a Christian concept echoing the scientific: the idea of spiritual progress, of the inevitable march towards a redemptive apocalypse, that parallels science's pledge of a similar material liberation. The contradiction is first rendered mundane by juxtaposing it with another mystery—a proper, in the sense of appropriate, sacred mystery embraced by Nagai as a Christian. *The Bells of Nagasaki* serves as Nagai's Christian apology, the vehicle for confessing his suddenly deepened convictions as a believer in essential, imponderable mysteries. His faith in God, far from being shaken, is strengthened by his witness of an atrocity: it eventually supplants what he had earlier expected from science.[16] Nagai writes: "The human race, with this discovery of atomic power, has now grasped the key to its future destiny—a key to survival or destruction. This is the truly awful thought. I myself believe that the only way to the proper use of this key is authentic religion" (116).

The conflict of Nagai's scientific "subjectivity" and his targeted "objectivity" is solved through a convenient Christian fusion of the two through the implied invocation of human will to elect sin or salvation on the one hand, and the inevitability of an apocalyptic climax to that election. Nagai insists, in fact, on the relevance of the workings of "authentic religion." ("Authentic" here is opposed to the "false" religion of the Japanese deities appropriated in Japanese wartime propaganda.) In the words of Nagai's translator, William Johnston, Nagai was a "deeply religious" person, a Catholic married to a Nagasaki Christian who traced her ancestry back to her city's famous martyrs.[17] In the August 15th entry of Nagai's account, the day Japan announced its surrender, he subtitles the date as the "Feast of the Assumption of the Virgin Mary." It is a day of particular note: Nagasaki Christians have traditionally had a special devotion to Mary, and the Urakami Cathedral, as noted in Tanaka Chikao's play, is consecrated to her. Moreover, before turning to the obviously momentous events of that day, Nagai notes his attendance at mass that morning (77). The very title *The Bells of Nagasaki* refers to the bells of the cathedral which, Nagai writes stirringly, were restored just before Christmas 1945 in time to ring out across the city and signal the resurrection that Nagai believed both the city and the spiritual soul were experiencing. As Nagai states, "Faith alone is the motivating force behind the reconstruction of Urakami" (114).

Christian symbols and analogies are distributed liberally throughout the work. Not only do references to the "big, red cathedral"—either destroyed or rebuilt—occur regularly, but so do references to the "eternal soul" and to the omniscient powers of the Christian God. Nagai, as he wanders the hills north of the city seeking out those who might need medical attention, seems to imagine himself a modern-day Samaritan: he reenacts a biblically inspired story that, happily, culminates in divine approbation. But the most important, and governing, Christian narrative among those incorporated into *The Bells of Nagasaki* is that of sacrifice winning salvation. Nagai tells of his desire—spoken as if with the authority of the entire Nagasaki Christian community—to *be* a sacrifice, one consecrated not only for his fellow human beings but for his abiding faith in the greater, unknowable designs of God. This theme, apparently quite nearly irrepressible in Nagasaki literature whatever its theme, is united historically, sentimentally, and theologically with that city's own special narrative, that of martyrdom.

Although there are plenty of like indications both direct and indirect throughout the work, the eleventh chapter entitled "Visitors to My Hut" expresses most succinctly the perceived link between the atrocities committed in Nagasaki in the past and those of the present. Nagai engages his friend Ichirō, a recently demobilized soldier, in a debate on the moral and theological implications of the atomic bombing of Nagasaki. To Ichirō's doubts over whether God would in fact deign to destroy innocent people, Nagai confidently retorts, "In fact, I have the opposite view. The atomic bomb falling on Nagasaki was a great act of Divine Providence. It was a grace from God. Nagasaki must give thanks to God" (106). Nagai later elaborates his opinions at length in an address delivered at the Urakami Cathedral. He argues that far too many curious circumstances—such as the selection of Nagasaki, "this sacred territory of the East," as a target; the fact that the bomb was dropped off-target only to destroy the small Christian community and its church; the fact that the war ended on an important Catholic feast day, and so on—are present to think that the city's special relationship with the Church, and thus with God, is wholly coincidental to its nuclear destruction. Nagai argues: "Is there not a profound relationship between the destruction of Nagasaki and the end of the war? Nagasaki, the only holy place in all Japan—was it not chosen as a victim, a pure lamb, to be slaughtered and burned on the altar of sacrifice to expiate the sins committed by humanity in the Second World War?" (107)

Without doubt this was a daring hypothesis—Urakami as Calvary, the site of a divine, compensatory violence not inspired by men but rather by their sins. This is a reading of events certainly controversial even among Nagai's like-minded Christians. There are, after all, other biblical allegories that might have been borrowed to "explain" Nagasaki. But none quite as flattering: Nagasaki becomes, in Nagai's narrative, an Old Testament story of a wrathful God combined with a New Testament promise of deliverance by that same God.

Nagai makes no mention, it will be noted, of Hiroshima: if that city "commenced" the nuclear age, then Nagasaki "ended" the war, and thus is of greater moment.

Equally controversial, we can imagine, was Nagai's assertion that it was the blameless innocent who were killed outright by the bomb and called to heaven, whereas those who had transgressed in life—he includes himself among their number—were merely injured in order to remain in the post-atomic purgatory of an irradiated Nagasaki. In effect, Nagai is rhetorically drawing a connection between the "blood of martyrs" spilled in Nagasaki long ago and that same blood of his own time. Like the joy of Saint Joan at the stake, Nagai sees—perhaps out of genuine faith, perhaps out of psychological or egotistical need to retrieve something of worth—something he calls "noble," "splendid," and "beautiful" from the flames that devoured Nagasaki's Christians. He does this with ample precedent. "It is characteristic of Christian anthropology from its beginnings," observed Erich Auerbach, "that it emphasizes man's subjection to suffering and transitoriness. This was a necessary concomitant of the idea of Christ's Passion as part of the story of salvation."[18] But one effect of such an argument in Nagasaki is to remove the event of the bombing from the world of people and what people are both willing and capable of doing to each other and to place it in the traditional and impenetrable universe of divine will, and in the particular Christian mechanism of violent sacrifice as prerequisite to salvation. Nagai's *The Bells of Nagasaki* is a fervent and sincere reading of spiritual intervention into the profane world found nowhere else in atomic-bomb literature.[19] It is consequently a powerfully compelling accounting of an atrocity which, in the estimation of other writers, seems to defy interpretation much less explanation. It is also a view, however, that links August 9th with the long tradition of inspired suffering—one might say "privileged" suffering—that the Christian history of Japan has associated with the name of the place, "Nagasaki." The connection in Nagai's work is between past tests of faith and present-day ones—tests in which believers should rejoice—from the first martyrs through to his own generation. The atomic attack on Nagasaki is provided the context of a precedence, a history that validates as well as prefaces the event. The bombing is integrated into a pattern with greater—greater in both historical and moral senses—significance, enabling its victims (a word Nagai himself hesitates to use) to accept, understand, and endure with dignity. This is a line of reasoning not often encountered in Hiroshima atomic-bomb literature. Ōta Yōko, for instance, looks back nostalgically in *City of Corpses* to Hiroshima's history as a compromised pastoral Golden Age and interprets its bombing as a tragic rupture of that history. But Nagai, proceeding in an opposite direction, discerns in the dark passion of Nagasaki a confirmation of Job's trials; a darkness that, in God's wisdom, leads us to light.

Other writers, one is not surprised to learn, have cited the atomic bombing of Hiroshima and Nagasaki as proof of precisely the opposite, namely the death of the Judeo-Christian God, or at least of the full abrogation of his promises. At the end of his notes on the events of August 6th, Hara Tamiki wrote: "Think, if you will, on the phrase 'Suddenly one day': can anything be 'sudden' for God?"[20] But the deepest skepticism about God's existence or intentions— as well as the deepest faith—is found in Nagasaki literature, where, for example, one character in *People of the Land* considers the decapitated statue of Mary the very symbol of God's failure to honor his covenant (26). And with the succinct brevity that is the hallmark of Japanese poetry, "In the Cathedral in the ruins of boundless expanse," reads one Nagasaki waka, "I stayed one night cursing God."[21]

If these sentiments approach a kind of blasphemy, then Nagai's *The Bells of Nagasaki* represents another extreme Christian reading of modern atrocity, one echoed in that Holocaust literature that takes the biblical persecution of the Jews as a model for German campaigns of genocide. Later Nagai's sanguine views would be ridiculed and would embarrass and even anger other Nagasaki citizens. Kurihara Sadako quotes one such reader, himself a physician, who considers Nagai's views on the bomb both "ingratiating and servile" vis-à-vis the United States.[22] But Nagai's oft-noted obsequiousness was not without its purposeful ironies: when Occupation officials, concerned over how *The Bells of Nagasaki* might be received by the public, required its publishers to append a description of Japanese atrocities in Manila, Nagai wrote in his own preface that he could "hardly contain [his] thanks over the extremely good result of the Occupation Army's having this published together with a description of Manila," rather clearly making his point that both events should be judged war atrocities.[23] In general, Nagai's writings continue to insist upon a notion not unusual—if less overt—in many of the Nagasaki writings that would follow: that the city's history of persecution makes its atomic-bomb literature ring with special irony. This is an irony, moreover, that might explain the infamous recalcitrance of Nagasaki's survivors to write, and rage, at their fate. Was the August 9th bombing, in other words, another instruction from a God intent on testing the faith of his chosen? And is not silence one way to prove one's willingness, even joy, to bear such challenges? For one sort of Christian, perhaps yes; for others, no. This long line of suffering identified by Nagai in *The Bells of Nagasaki* as the mark of his city would, in the hands of his fellow Nagasaki writers to follow, be a line extending far into the future: and a line with far less capacity to console.

■

The writer now most closely identified with the bombing of Nagasaki is not Nagai Takashi but Hayashi Kyōko. Although born in Nagasaki in 1930, she was not even one year old when the family moved to Shanghai, where her father worked for Mitsui Industries. Well known for her stories of wartime China as well as for those of the bombing of Nagasaki, Hayashi wrote in one of them that she "was a child who, while Japanese, was also one steeped in the customs and manners of the Chinese."[24] Consequently, when she, her mother, and her three sisters left their father behind to return to Nagasaki in early 1945, she was an exotic in a city itself exotic. As a repatriated Japanese who was not quite a full Japanese culturally (but someone more than a Japanese, at the same time), her sense of alienation is one that has long remained with her, if her stories and novels are any indication.[25]

When she returned to Japan in 1945, it was doubtlessly because the home islands were thought the safer places to be as the war grew closer. Her mother and two sisters took up residence in the old castle town of Isahaya in the Naga-saki exurbs, but Kyōko, in order to attend higher school, boarded in the city proper. Even more unfortunately for Hayashi, she was conscripted with her classmates to work at the Mitsubishi munitions works, less than a kilometer and a half from the bomb's epicenter: she became a hibakusha only days before her fifteenth birthday. Seriously ill for several months thereafter, Hayashi claims she has never enjoyed full health as an adult. "I was bombed in Nagasaki when a junior at the girls' high school, while mobilized as a worker. I was 1.4 kilometers from ground zero, within the 'special zone' where all forms of life both above and below ground were said to have been exterminated."[26]

Nonetheless, she has survived to become a strikingly prolific writer. After an impoverished adolescence made difficult when her father became unem-ployed as a result of the Occupation's dissolution of Japan's prewar conglomer-ates, and after the failure of a singularly unsuccessful marriage, Hayashi began writing in the early 1960s and won major critical attention a decade later. Her short story "Two Grave Markers" (Futari no bohyō, 1975), published on the thirtieth anniversary of the Nagasaki bombing, is generally representative of her work. Fourteen year-old Wakako is, as was Hayashi, a mobilized student-worker who survives the blast and extricates herself from the collapsed ruins of her factory building, but who must then witness helplessly the wretched deaths of her classmates, including that of her best friend Yōko:

> The maggots swarming in Yōko's open wounds would soon become flies, and it would be their turn to create new lives. They were devouring Yōko's flesh at great speed as they prepared to bring forth the next gener-ation. They would turn into flies, and then assault Wakako. . . . Wakako tried to move away from Yōko without attracting her attention. . . . "Don't leave me alone," Yōko shouted. Wakako covered her ears with both hands and raced down the slope.

Wakako did not start to walk slowly until she had reached level ground. (33–34)

Eventually Wakako makes her way back to her and Yōko's home village, but she hides Yōko's demise from everyone: both the details of that death, and in particular Wakako's own abandonment of her, are too terrible for the young girl to recount. Soon Wakako, too, falls ill. Festering wounds in her back caused by embedded shards of glass again attract maggots, and exacerbating her own present agony is the belated realization of how unbearable her friend's must have been. Wakako, soon hovering near death, falls into delirium and screams about the vermin now eating her flesh. She nears her own end with the added pain of an unconfessed guilt over how she forsook her closest friend only to be meted out the same degrading fate.

This story iterates a theme, namely the guilt that one victim can feel towards others even more victimized, that occurs regularly in Hayashi's atomic-bomb stories:

> I was made a hibakusha in the summer of my fourteenth year. I survived with no visible injuries, and made my way to my mother and sisters evacuated to Isahaya. Isahaya is an old castle town some seventeen miles from Nagasaki. The victims of the bombing had fled to cool, intact Isahaya; the town's schools and government buildings were overflowing with hibakusha. They died never having seen a doctor. They died, even those with no injuries.[27]

Part of Hayashi's project as an atomic-bomb writer has been to demonstrate and contemplate the range of both the injury and the survival of injury, the complex net of often contradictory feelings that a hibakusha feels toward himself and other hibakusha either living or dead.

Steadily productive since her entry into the corps of major contemporary writers in the 1970s, Hayashi published a full-length novel in 1981 entitled *As If Not.* As the story of four hibakusha women who were classmates in 1945 Nagasaki, two of whom are now, thirty years later, dead from bomb-related causes, *As If Not* discusses a wide range of historical incidents, political issues, and ongoing hibakusha concerns. Of special import to the two surviving women—an unnamed narrator and her old friend Haruko, married to an American who deserted the military during the Korean War—are the fears and hopes associated with their decisions to have borne children. But what emerges as a unique problem for the narrator alone—a narrator evenly split between an "I" who recounts the events of the past, and another noted simply as "the woman" (*onna*) who inhabits the narrative present—is additionally the act of narration itself:

Since suffering the atomic attack on August 9, 1945, my life has not moved one step forward from that point in time. However, I bear the responsibility to pass on my experience to the next generation. I write fiction in the attempt to be the tribal chronicler *[kataribe]* of August 9th.[28]

Hayashi's narrator's ambition to be a "tribal chronicler," a kataribe, is an ambition to serve as a communal memory. It is a term that reaches back before the advent of literacy in Japan, when clans *(be)* were charged with certain functions, among them the role of performing the recitation *(katari)* of key genealogies and cosmologies. The most famous of the historical kataribe was Hieda no Are, a woman who was commanded by Emperor Temmu to "recite . . . the 'royal genealogy' and 'the legends of antiquity'" for the compiler of the eighth-century *Record of Ancient Matters* (Kojiki) because—presumably due to a growing number of contending versions—"they had reached a perilous state."[29] In this context to be the kataribe of Nagasaki means to speak for it with a special authority and special responsibility, and to speak of it for the future. Indeed, Hayashi Kyōko herself has worked hard to earn that authority and carry out that responsibility. Her experiences have been recorded in her stories and novels in a perhaps piecemeal and fragmented way over the past two decades. Together, however, they constitute a collective and consistent stand on the broader implications of nuclear war as well as of Nagasaki.

But it is a stand nonetheless riddled with questions, doubts, and even self-recriminations. In one sense, the ambition to become Nagasaki's kataribe is a plea for the rest of us to listen, and that plea is heard so frequently in Hayashi's writings that it has precipitated a backlash against her work among impatient critics. At the same time, however, Hayashi like many hibakusha does not easily believe in our ability to understand what we are asked to listen to. The question is whether a kataribe would speak of Nagasaki in order to change the world, or to change Nagasaki itself. "The woman resolved to become the kataribe," Hayashi writes in *As If Not*, "because she wanted to prevent, if only by a little, Nagasaki from becoming routine. But ironically, her very speaking of August 9th was beginning that process of routinization" (77).

At the conclusion of the novel, the narrator suddenly sees her dilemma clearly. She understands the principal contradiction of her life over the thirty years that have passed since the bombing. To the world, she looks like nothing other than what she is, a hibakusha. But she herself has always wanted to a "normal person." When her husband of twenty years finally leaves her, he tells her that their entire marriage had been a marriage with a hibakusha. If you truly want to be a kataribe, he admonishes, then all you need do is describe your own, everyday life. This advice startles her: all these years of fearing the label "hibakusha," of repressing her identity, is ironically exactly what a hibakusha's life is all about. "It was precisely because I am a hibakusha, that I wanted to be a normal person. . . . Could anything have been more precious a waste?" (216).

Despite the sincere pathos of *As If Not*'s conclusion, its long and tedious discourses on contemporary Japanese and world politics have led it to be ranked critically as one of Hayashi's least successful works. Another of her pieces seems likely to retain its reputation as her most famous work, and indeed as one of the most celebrated works of Nagasaki atomic-bomb literature. "The Site of Rituals" (Matsuri no ba) stands both chronologically and thematically at the head of her long list of works concerned with the theme of demoralization in hibakusha culture; according to one assessment, it forms a single trilogy in combination with *Cut Glass, Blown Glass* and *As If Not*.[30] First published in 1975, "The Site of Rituals" won *Gunzō*'s New Writer's Prize and then the most prestigious literary honor for new Japanese writers of promise, the Akutagawa Prize. Adopting the narrative format she would use in most of her later stories, Hayashi employs a first-person narrator to relate the accounts of herself and her fellow Nagasaki hibakusha. Here the narrator—again a fourteen year-old schoolgirl ordered to work in a Mitsubishi munitions factory—describes in exact detail, with much objective scientific and journalistic data marshalled along the way, the fate of her classmates, teachers, family, and relatives. The "site" of the story's title refers to a concrete courtyard at the factory; the "rituals" to the send-off dance that the high school boys, also mobilized as munitions workers, would perform whenever one of their number was sent to the front. "By that time, students were sent to battle everyday," Hayashi writes. "That concrete, brutal factory courtyard had become their site of rituals" (38). More than forty of them would be enacting their "sad, pantomime-like dance" when the bomb explodes overhead:

> The students who were dancing their farewell dance in the courtyard died instantly, or were so seriously burnt that they survived only a hour or two. One was thrown to the concrete by the pressure of the blast and had his intestines squeezed out of him; so young, his screams were horrible. A friend who had heard those screams while fleeing himself, must even now cover his ears when speaking of it. (40–41)

Most of "The Site of Rituals," however, is concerned with Hayashi's own female classmates and family. Like Hayashi herself, the narrator of "The Site of Rituals" was the only member of her immediate family in the city proper that morning. Her father was still abroad, and her mother and sisters safely evacuated to Isahaya. "Not one of them imagined that Nagasaki, twenty-five kilometers away, had been bombed and was now aflame" (33). Later on the 9th, as bits and scraps of clothing—pieces, literally, of Nagasaki—fall from the sky, as then does an odd black rain, rumors gradually reach Isahaya that, indeed, Nagasaki had been the target of an air strike. But surely, reasons the narrator's mother, the whole city could not have been bombed; surely her daughter is safe.

The next day, with the added information that in fact much of Nagasaki did sustain damage, the narrator's mother just as easily believes her daughter must be dead. Yet she has survived, miraculously and so far; thirty years later, the narrator still notes of her friends that "fragments of glass remain in their bodies" (37). Her survival is extraordinary. For the majority of her classmates working on that factory floor, death was quick and presumably without comprehension. For them, the narrator reflects, "there was neither light nor sound" (38). She recalls the horrible fires that swept through the factory and notes that "in an atomic attack, the best thing is to die immediately" (42). The narrator continues to be amazed at her exemption from the otherwise universal rule of death: "Living and dying were separated by less than a thin sheet of paper" (43).

After the initial explosion, she crawls out of the factory and makes her way, with difficulty, to a neighborhood closer still to ground zero. She sees disfigured victims whom she describes in detail so complete as to repel some readers. Moreover, she does so in the local Nagasaki dialect, rendering the written description oral, testimonial, and thus all that more powerfully real. She is grateful whenever she spots someone who has managed to retain any semblance of humanness, be it an eye, a nose, or any recognizable feature. Many have not. Hayashi—like Ōta in *City of Corpses*—skillfully intersperses dry statistics and scientific reports on the mass impact of the bomb with wrenching, anecdotal details, such as those of her own vomiting that set in approximately two hours after the blast. In her ill condition she is acutely sensitive not only to the degradation of her surroundings but to their absurdity as well. After noting how her nausea was soon compounded with diarrhea, she goes on to observe also how both destruction and a strangely detached calmness in the face of it can coexist. It is this coexistence that makes "The Site of Rituals" a successful combination of the two scales of destruction that the bombings wrought: at once both a historical crisis and a very individual terror. For instance, next to a report on the statistical death rate for those victims suffering from diarrhea, Hayashi juxtaposes her private memories of the unnerving silence that settled over her leveled high school. A descriptive and narrative rhythm is established in the story through the alternation of public information with first-person accounts. A representation of "Nagasaki, August 9th" is assembled with diverse data, the exercise of memory, and a carefully deployed literary pathos. Within the "site" in "The Site of Rituals," the narrator steadily descends into the typical "death-in-life" compromised existence of the hibakusha. "Amid the countless dead of Urakami, I had become as indifferent as a robot" (58).

Eventually the narrator is found in Nagasaki and brought out to Isahaya on foot, where many other refugees have come only to have fallen ill. Many have already died. Some—as in the case of one of the narrator's former teachers—go insane just before death. It is fear, she thinks to herself, that does that; and it is fear that wracks her own body once she notices her hair has begun to fall out. So distraught is she by the onset of the symptoms of radiation disease that her mother takes her comb away. This first sign is soon followed by others, and her family can do nothing but stand by helplessly. Lethargy renders the narrator immobile. As her blood count reaches critical levels, uncomfortable tensions rack the house. She begins to think of herself as a burden to others, and even concludes that it is her duty to die quickly rather than prolong the inevitable. But fortunately her condition stabilizes a month later, and she even becomes capable of humor, albeit cynically black. When she receives a check for eighteen yen for her last two months' work at the munitions factory, for instance, she wryly jokes that the money might best be spent on flowers for her funeral.

Her mother tries various folk remedies to help her, but it is only after special attention from an American doctor that the inflammation recedes and her wounds begin to heal. Still, other survivors, some of whom are the narrator's friends, continue to die. When school reopens in October, and she attends the opening ceremony against her doctor's advice, the eulogies delivered in memory of the deceased classmates make her guilt in surviving all that more sharp. Indeed, some of the schoolgirls who were alive in October die soon afterwards, and still die. The seemingly endless menace of radiation disease and its complications ironically undermines the last sentence of "The Site of Rituals," itself an ironic remark made after noting how the narration of an American film on the bombing concluded so eloquently: "Thus the destruction came to an end" (68).

In fact the thematic thrust of Hayashi Kyōko's atomic-bomb literature has been to show how the damage associated with the bombings has not and cannot so easily, if ever, come to an end. This is the theme throughout "The Site of Rituals," a first-person memoir that steadfastly refuses to deal with the events of August 1945 as some isolated if nightmarish incident in a past history now over. Rather than reiterate what other survivors, such as Nagai Takashi, have already amply demonstrated to have been an unprecedented terror, Hayashi endeavors to make the bombing a present-day problem for a world that only looks as if it is at peace. "Fragments of glass," the narrator reminds us, "remain in their bodies." Or, as another character in *As If Not* puts it, "a nation at peace does not mean an individual person is at peace" (141). Perhaps more than any other atomic-bomb writer, Hayashi Kyōko has considered the problem of the hidden but still festering wounds that continue to torment in spite of whatever outward healing might have taken place. It is for this reason that Nakano Kōji, for one, considers Hayashi the writer who "best carries on the tradition of atomic-bomb literature."[31]

This responsibility, however, has placed a special burden on Hayashi. The jurors of the 1975 Akutagawa Prize praised "The Site of Rituals" effusively, noting in particular "the weight of its facts" (Inoue Mitsuharu), "the vividness of the experience" (Haniya Yutaka), and "the power of its material" (Ōoka Shō-hei),[32] but they also expressed doubts over the work's literary style. They posed familiar questions: Is this fiction? Reportage? Or criticism? Like the work of Ōta Yōko, of whom other critics asked the same questions more than twenty years earlier, "The Site of Rituals" is not a narratively unified work. Within it, all manner of perspectives compete with each other. It is a work in which it is impossible for a reader to sympathize with a hero or to submerge himself in a fictional premise. In her attempt to represent Nagasaki as both a point in time and a continuing condition, Hayashi's work can become difficult to read. The chronology is shuffled, and more than any one person's story is dealt with at any given instant. This is, of course, part of the power of "The Site of Rituals." It reaches for a inclusiveness when it describes August 9th not just from Haya-shi's own point of view but with information she learned later. "Nagasaki" re-fuses to be experienced as an individual matter in any of Hayashi's work. It argues instead an entire history. But perhaps as it is for every atomic-bomb writer, that history, however total, always seems to fall short of the mark. "When I began writing 'The Site of Rituals,'" Hayashi herself has admitted, "I rejected every vestige of fictional themes. I vowed to put down in words, as much as possible, just what happened. I also planned to end my career with its completion. But in fact the results were just the opposite."[33]

In other words, the story that was meant to tell "just what happened," did not. Hayashi's rejection of the fictional failed, as we have seen in the case of other writers, to be sufficiently full and exhaustive. Perhaps that is why only a year after "The Site of Rituals," rather than give up her writing career, Hayashi began serializing the stories later collected in *Cut Glass, Blown Glass*. This collec-tion tracks the direction her atomic-bomb literature has steadily grown to pur-sue: about how the world has been forever changed by atomic bombs, changed in ways attested to by wounds that do not heal and memories that are never erased.

One of the *Cut Glass, Blown Glass* stories, "Yellow Sand" (Kōsa, 1977), deals with Hayashi's bittersweet childhood memories of her Chinese upbringing, and in particular her innocent friendship with a Japanese prostitute. Another, "Echo" (Hibiki, 1977) combines her account of fleeing Shanghai with her mother and the parallel account of fleeing Nagasaki four days after the bomb-ing. A third story, one of the best, "Young Men" (Seinen-tachi, 1977), is about the deep and unconfessed fears both Hayashi and her son have, despite his apparent good health, over his one day developing a fatal ailment inherited from his hibakusha mother. All the other nine stories, however, revolve around Hayashi's return to Nagasaki from Tokyo after three decades to attend the annual memorial service for the atomic-bomb dead, and to see old school class-mates, hibakusha like herself who are holding their reunion concurrent with the August 9th public observances.

"The Empty Can" (Akikan, 1977) introduces the reader to the former girls' high school as well as to Hayashi's private guilty feelings over having survived what few did; "Mount Kompira" (Kompirayama, 1977) leads us further into the company of Hayashi's small group of women friends with whom she grew up, attended school, and worked in the same wartime munitions plant. They are all hibakusha. But, and this is a major theme of the collection, most of them suffered more than Hayashi, who in fact lost no close relatives or retained any visible physical scars. These women will turn forty-six years of age in the year in which this story is set, and they express a sad relief at being—finally—beyond their childbearing years. Their complex and conflicting apprehensions as hibakusha are focused especially upon the special risks associated with child-birth for hibakusha, namely the inordinate loss of blood, stillbirths, genetic defects and most of all a lifetime of concern over whether their children will be inherently susceptible to bomb-related cancers. The women blame the bomb for the high incidence of uterine myoma in Nagasaki, as well as for other problems that seem to afflict hibakusha in unexpected numbers. These women, the reader soon learns, have spent the decades that have passed since the bombing uneasily waiting for something terrible to happen, "something" whose exact details remain an intimidating mystery.

This is the dominant theme of *Cut Glass, Blown Glass*. In the title story Haya-shi accompanies a friend while visiting Nagasaki on her fruitless search for a some antique glass, a famous craft of the city. Each piece they examine con-ceals somewhere an imperfection, a hairline crack perhaps, that suggests it too was damaged internally, nearly invisibly, by the force of the atomic blast over thirty years ago. As Hayashi looks at one sample of glass fused by the heat—a piece that was further away from the epicenter than she herself had been—she knows the "truth" of Nagasaki all over again. As she writes in "Document," another of the collection's stories, August 9th looms over Hayashi's, and by implication all hibakusha's, lives however much time may pass. "Even when we think we have moved one step forward, when sense returns we are standing on August 9th" (166).

This ever-present realization—described by Hayashi's son in "Young Men" as "like being condemned to an innocent death" (84)—has a permanent effect on these women. Some have refused to marry, others to bear children. Haya-shi, who has done both, feels she has somehow inadvertently betrayed the others, and thus inflicts upon herself another reason to suffer guiltily. The im-pact of these stories is that of an impression of dire, exitless oppression. The characters of *Cut Glass, Blown Glass* comprise a community of women for whom the terror of Nagasaki has never fully receded or even measurably lessened. Hayashi portrays this dread with an acute sensitivity since she believes herself spared the absolute worst of it, but for her too it is a fear possibly infinite in its ability to persist through time into succeeding generations. The survivors of Nagasaki Girls' High School are understandably concerned with what effects of their exposure, be they physiological or psychological, might be passed on to their offspring. The issue is a consequential one, and is taken seriously by science. "Whole body irradiation injured the nuclei of the cells and . . . may lead . . . to alteration of genes," states one study. "One should never forget that such momentary injurious action of an atomic bomb can have aftereffects for years and generations to come."[34] This is an issue explored repeatedly in literature, too—"I'm frightened of children," confesses a woman considering an abortion in Natsubori Masamoto's "The Woman from the Hallowed Ground" (Seichi no onna, 1975). "I've seen in Hiroshima just how much the child of a hibakusha can look less like a human being, and more like something else" (318). But no one author has so relentlessly and depressingly thought this problem through in its most complete psychic and historical repercussions as Hayashi Kyōko.

For Hayashi the crux is the relationship between nuclear weapons and the biological survival of the species. More immediately, the concern is whether, even after direct hibakusha like herself have died, the indirect hibakusha—the *hibaku nisei* or "second-generation victims"—might not themselves face some number of the unsettling health apprehensions their parents felt; and more generally the concern is whether the species will ever wholly repair itself of the insidious damage inflicted in August 1945. "I raised my son worrying of nothing but whether he would be attacked by radiation disease," Hayashi has written. "Now I have the same apprehension for his own child."[35]

"In the Fields" (No ni, 1978), the concluding story of *Cut Glass, Blown Glass*, has Hayashi returning to Tokyo and reviewing the events of her busy week in Nagasaki. Recalling how some of her classmates had died instantly, she guiltily marvels anew at her own continuing fair health. Her provisional survival, however, in no way lessens her obsession with bombing and its perversion of life afterwards. A character in *As If Not* asserts that "all people alive today, throughout the world, may quite properly be hibakusha" (205); and in "In the Fields" it is Hayashi's conclusion that all, hibakusha and non-hibakusha alike, are caught in the events of Hiroshima and Nagasaki. "Everyone alive today feels terror towards the nuclear age, and not just on the days of August 6th and 9th. Just to think of it is to induce anxiety" (243). For Hayashi that anxiety is a broad and omnipresent one, rendering every moment of her life a critical one. Every revived worry suggests catastrophe: that the sword will finally descend and all life will be terminated, just as the nightmare she lived through as a young girl seemed to portend. Moreover, that critical moment is not hers alone, but her generation's and indeed the human race's. "These are wounds inflicted by human beings," Hayashi writes at the end of "In the Fields." "These are deliberate wounds precisely calculated and inflicted by human beings. On account of these calculations, the very life that we would pass on to our children and grandchildren has sustained injury" (243).

These comments succinctly express both Hayashi's anger and her fear: her sense of a crime having been perpetrated against her and the rest of her immediate world, and her frightened sense that the crime may also have been perpetrated against future generations not even yet conceived. For those who would like Hiroshima and Nagasaki to be, if a tragedy, then a tragedy now safely ensconced in history—"a lesson learned," "a mistake never to be repeated"— Hayashi's writings are disturbing, upsetting, and potentially even subversive of our typical mechanisms for the repression and sublimation of the nuclear scenarios prepared for us. For Hayashi herself, however, one could conclude that the dismal future predicted by her fears constitutes nothing worse than what has already transpired. The history of Nagasaki—like Hayashi's own, a history inextricably tied to Japan's turbulent relations with China and then the Western powers—has already demonstrated a violence that continues today and into future days. In "Young Men" Hayashi finds herself trying to deny the possibility that what has happened to other children of hibakusha—death from cancer—could ever happen to her own son. Maybe one day he will indeed fall ill, she finally forces herself to admit. Her fear has long prevented her from contemplating such possibilities: but they are there, and they are possibilities conspicuously highlighted in the literature by Nagasaki writers—perhaps because, in recent years, they have been largely women—who have paid special attention to the long-term disruption of fertility, marriage, and childbearing. "Woman gives birth," writes Hayashi. "And what of men? His wife's baby is surely his own, but he has no history of having carried the child in his womb."[36] Such biological determinism may be in disfavor among many critics; but from Hayashi's point of view, what is at stake is less the definition of the feminine and more the source of her gender's arguably unique insight into the crisis of the species.

Unlike Nagai's treatise on a wise patriarchal God whose will included the use of the atomic bomb, Hayashi's stories of women alone and impaired from being fully female ("Women, to one degree or another, all have the maternal instinct")[37] are markedly forlorn and bleak, lacking any of the hope that Nagai confidently proclaims. In *As If Not* Hayashi's present-day narrator ("the woman") notes that it had always been her hope to "give birth to a healthy child and raise him to be strong, even though she was fearful of childbirth" (210–11), while her narrator of the past ("I") admitted that she "was anxious whether he had passed on to her son the vitality necessity to grow into adulthood" (156). But very much like Nagai, and very much like mainstream Nagasaki writing, Hayashi's works pursue a chronology of suffering far more extensive than that demarcated by Hiroshima writers. Nagai, in invoking the Shimabara martyrs, extends August 1945 backwards to the seventeenth century; Hayashi, fearing genetic damage, extends the legacy of the bombing into the future. This represents a complementary, common ground with Nagai, ground important in defining what constitutes "Nagasaki atomic-bomb literature" as distinct from that of Hiroshima. But it also sets her apart morally and emotionally from Nagai, for in condemning the future rather than mourning the past she legislates a world not only without end but without any chance of salvation: precisely the salvation in which Nagai so earnestly believes. For Nagai, the bombing provided more opportunities for the demonstration of, and commitment to, faith. For Hayashi, and indeed for many hibakusha who have written for us, there is absolutely nothing in which to believe.

This deep nihilism in Hayashi has culminated in what is the most cynical pose and writing style of any major atomic-bomb writer.[38] When Hayashi speaks of "human dignity," for instance, it is always within brackets. She frankly does not believe that such terms, post-Nagasaki, retain any identifiably meaningful referent. For her, such anachronistic notions can now apply only ironically. Equally useless to her are such concepts as "humanity" or "modernity," ideas implying an ameliorable, civilized condition: an implication that she regards as void in the wake of the barbarity of nuclear weapons.[39]

One example of Hayashi's bitter cynicism is this passage from "The Site of Rituals":

> At present, were I to die, I would receive money for my funeral from the state. The amount would be 16,000 yen. This is the amount designated for "special hibakusha." However, it is not enough simply to die. Certification of a bomb-related cause of death is required.
>
> A "special hibakusha" is one who carries a special hibakusha health record. One who qualifies in Categories I through V of the Atomic Bomb Medical Treatment Law Enforcement Ordinance Clause Six.
>
> I am a Category I Special Hibakusha. This is limited to those hibakusha and their interuterine children who were directly hit within three kilometers of the blast. It also includes other special areas, such as those where the black rain fell. Isahaya apparently does not qualify.
>
> In order to receive the 16,000 yen, one must submit the following: a Funeral Expense Allowance Application Form, a death certificate, one's Residence Card cancelled for reason of death, one's Special Hibakusha health record, and one's legal seal.
>
> I intend to leave instructions that my 16,000 yen be used to purchase flowers. That should buy eighty tulips even at winter prices. That should make for a gorgeous funeral. If that is not acceptable, giant radishes will

do fine. You could buy eighty of those. Their price is going up even as I write: fifty-three giant radishes. (90–91)

It is easy to sympathize with Hayashi's sarcasm at how non-hibakusha culture would seem to discharge its guilt and moral responsibility with pathetic, patronizing, and even insulting gestures. In this, Hayashi is among the most scathing of the survivor-writers. Unable to countenance the ersatz nurturance that distant authorities legislate for her, she rejects it with skepticism and even contempt. At the same time, however, Hayashi rejects something else as well. She jettisons, along with the outside world's meager sympathy, the readers presumably inhabiting that outside world and who must feel themselves equally the target of Hayashi's accusations. She once described her writings as intended "medical charts, hopefully of use when they dissect me after I'm dead."[40] At the root of Hayashi's cynicism is the thought behind what her character Wakako rhetorically asks in "Two Grave Markers": "How could anyone who had not been there understand?" (26). Supposing that this is indeed Hayashi's own sentiment, then apparently she shares the views of earlier atomic-bomb writers such as Ōta Yōko that their common experience in Hiroshima and Nagasaki is in fact not common, but radically singular. Moreover, she would appear to use her proprietorship of that experience as a weapon: her insistence on incommunicability leads to her denunciation of the nonvictim world as inevitably cruel in its ignorance.

One might argue that Hayashi's many stories and novels contradict those sentiments and on the contrary proclaim her steadfast belief in the communicability of her experience. Yet the overwhelming impression a reader takes away from Hayashi's work, especially "The Site of Rituals," is that what Hayashi is at pains to tell us is not the experience of Nagasaki per se but rather the empty void which that experience occupies, paradoxically, in culture. In other words the insistence that "understanding" is limited works as a foil in her fiction, a manipulation meant to direct our attentions toward other issues, issues of the continuing states of victimization decades—perhaps even generations—later. For some critics Hayashi's often arrogant cynicism defeats her as a writer insofar as she discourages readers from sympathizing with her. Perhaps this is what novelist Nakagami Kenji meant when he histrionically accused Hayashi of "atomic fascism."[41] For Nakagami, Hayashi's cynicism was so total as to curb any sympathetic encounter with her work; the readers end up confronting a door-less wall denying them the right to proceed, or even perceive, past it.

But the stories of *Cut Glass, Blown Glass* show that this is not absolutely or necessarily true, and that Nakagami's charges reveal his own blindness to the worth of work by an author admittedly melancholy and obsessed. Although there is surely a place in this century for writers who, at their most despondent, sound a message unrelieved by either self-deprecating levity or the inclination to forgive others—it was Bertolt Brecht who said "He who can still smile has not yet heard the news"—in fact Hayashi does not hold the reader so much in contempt as she irritably insists that we admit, under the pressure of her bitterness, that her world *is* different from ours. This is a fact she would force us to accept, and it is not surprising some of us do resist. What strikes some critics as indulgent arrogance is perhaps, more compassionately understood, a pathetic chasm between experiences that fiction finally does not bridge.

It is hard to imagine a greater contrast to *The Bells of Nagasaki,* a work that earnestly strives to discern in the bombing a good thing, a thing belonging to all us and which comes from the same God who, in delivering upon his promises for our salvation, sacrificed his own Son. Hayashi's work refuses even her own son a moment of respite from the anxiety, doubt, and anger Nagai was able to dispel through the reaffirmation of his Christian faith. Nagai, I suspect, will in time have more readers: Hayashi's works may be simply too devoted to their own relentlessly self-absorbed agony to be popular with either readers or critics who perhaps are themselves more interested in rewriting history than contemplating it. But finally one must conclude that it is not Hayashi's contrary or perverse will at work in her stories, nor a will culpable for apparent excesses. One should conclude instead that the discomfiture those stories provoke must incite us to indict the same history that so single-mindedly commands her attention.

To that extent—to the extent they are both hibakusha—Nagai and Hayashi are similar. Atomic-bomb writers, even those who proceed as differently in their writings as these two, are often labeled as less than first rate because of the narrowness of their themes. Yet Nagai's sincere attempt to work out a Christian theological response to modern atrocity by linking it with past examples of God's often humanly incomprehensible will, and Hayashi's insistence on projecting her presence as a young girl in Nagasaki on the 9th onto a world fundamentally changed, can hardly be thought themes modestly conceived or without significance. In fact Nagasaki atomic-bomb literature in general seems distinguished by the widened scope of its ambition. Perhaps free of the burden of having to describe the first atomic attack, Nagasaki writers have been able to turn their attentions to the issue of the insidious and stubborn effects of the second, and the fear of a third or fourth. As Hayashi writes in the final pages of "In the Fields," her scars "are scars that human beings have inflicted on us . . . [and] on the lives we would pass on to our children and grandchildren" (243).

In 1975 Hayashi Kyōko traveled to the museum that displays the famous Hiroshima murals of painters Maruki Toshi and Maruki Iri. Her essay describing this trip dwells on one mural in particular. Entitled *Water* (Mizu) in reference to the thirst of the burn victims, the painting portrays a various crowd of hibakusha: but Hayashi, who elsewhere has declared the bond between mother and child "the origin of love,"[42] is drawn to that one pathetic depiction which

Twentieth-century image of madonna and child: detail from the fifth panel of *Water* by Maruki Iri and Maruki Toshi[43]

bears the caption: "The twentieth-century image of madonna and child: an injured mother cradling her dead infant." Hayashi interprets: "What the dead infant signifies must surely be the lack of any future awaiting us."[44] She might just as well as have been addressing the meaning of her own art.

■

Gotō Minako does not rank among the better known atomic-bomb writers discussed in this study. Even more so than the poet Shōda Shinoe, her reputation is largely a local one. But unlike Shōda, whose single small collection of poetry was included in this study in order to suggest the diversity of atomic-bomb verse, Gotō and her one novel are of critical value in indicating the degree of similarity among works of Nagasaki atomic-bomb literature, at least that by women. The coincidences are many, and they are not limited to the writings themselves: born in Nagasaki in 1936, Gotō is the daughter of a doctor who taught at the Nagasaki Medical College and who quite probably knew Nagai Takashi. Unlike Nagai but like Hayashi Kyōko's, however, Gotō's father was not in Nagasaki, in fact not even in Japan, when the atomic bombing took place: like Hayashi Kyōko, Gotō, her mother, and her brother were subjected to the attack without him present.

These circumstances have provided Gotō with the basic concerns of her work as an adult writer. After graduating from a junior college with a degree in English, and after working for many years at a publishing company, Gotō published in the November 1971 issue of the prestigious literary monthly *Bungei* a short novel that not only won her that journal's annual literary prize but which consequently lifted her from obscurity and for a time placed her in the company of Japan's promising newer writers. *Tug of Time* (Toki o hiku) remains, however, Gotō's principal statement. Her other pieces are essentially retellings of the same autobiographical story. But it is a story of such power and consequence that it has become one of most frequently noted works of Nagasaki atomic-bomb literature.

The novel opens in 1970 as Yōko (narrating from a first-person point of view), a young woman recently married, is taken by her new husband Michio to visit his mother in Tokyo. Yōko, identified at first as a native of "Kyushu" rather than of the more tell-tale "Nagasaki," is nervous not only on account of this imminent encounter with her mother-in-law, but just by being in the immense and unfamiliar capital city. But she is intimidated beyond all expectation when her mother-in-law sadistically probes into why Yōko's own mother did not attend the recent wedding, though of course she knows very well why. An embarrassed Yōko can only reply, in her provincial accent, that her "ailing" mother is still "weak."

In truth Yōko's mother is mentally incapacitated and confined to an institution. Telling the reasons why occupies the first part of the novel. Yōko and her
mother are both Nagasaki hibakusha. In August 1945 they and Yōko's older
brother were living in Urakami while Yōko's father, a doctor, was serving with
the military in the South Pacific. On the morning of the 9th her brother had
already left the house and was working in a factory when the bomb was
dropped, killing him outright. Yōko and her mother were able to flee the city
and take refuge in a small village, but the shock of her son's death soon drives
the mother insane, so mad in fact that at one point she even tries to murder
Yōko. The effect of all this on Yōko, only a young child, is to render her (as
Gotō writes in no small understatement) "terribly alone and isolated," a survivor not only of Nagasaki but a survivor of the destruction of her own family.
Nagata, a friend of Yōko's father and himself a physician, moves in with them
to see to it they are at least provided for. Provided for, in fact, more than
materially: there is the suggestion that Nagata and Yōko's mother briefly enjoyed the kind of rare intimacy between acquaintances, surely more importantly emotional than physical, that the trauma of disaster permits and perhaps
even encourages. But Nagata cannot alter the fact that Yōko's brother is dead;
that her mother has become a menacing stranger to her; and that her father
remains thousands of miles away. When her father is finally demobilized after
the surrender and returns to Japan that winter, he hardly seems like anyone she
ever knew. Not present when the bomb exploded over Nagasaki, he has not
experienced what she has, and that makes for a crucial difference. The gap
between them is more alienating that the tie of parent and child is uniting. He
himself has, of course, experienced hardships overseas at the front, but these
varieties of suffering do not readily compare, and he remains ignorant of the
depth of his daughter Yōko's psychological handicaps. Insensitive to her feelings as a survivor, he takes her and her mother back to Urakami in the spring.

Yōko is incredulous to find people trying to lead "normal" lives there, but
that is precisely what Yōko's father intends for the three of them to do. He
resumes his teaching at the local medical college, and his career advances
quickly, but any notion of normalcy is his alone. "Mother lives in a world only
of herself" (42), and Yōko is painfully torn between her love for her mother
and her desire to leave that part of her life which her mother's madness represents behind her in the past. Both sets of feelings erupt openly on the day that
father commits mother to a mental hospital. Yōko detests him for what she
sees as his unforgivable betrayal, yet she is also guiltily conscious of her relief
at the fact that mother is indeed now gone. Nonetheless, Yōko angrily confronts her father. Has he considered the possibility that he might be making a
mistake in committing her? After all, he was not there on August 9th; he cannot
realize how impossible it is that mother will, whatever the treatment, ever be

"cured." Just what sort of life does he expect her to live? These arguments, less rhetorical than Yōko's own sincere and unanswered questions, fall on uncomprehending deaf, non-hibakusha, ears.

One day Yōko pays a call on her mother at the hospital. Unfortunately, she soon regrets having made the trip. "I have no idea what it would mean for my mother to 'get better'" (54). Nor, for that matter, do the doctors. One of them asks Yōko about the onset of her mother's illness. Yōko replies that there is nothing to say. The doctor—who, we are told, comes originally from Tokyo—is annoyed by Yōko's lack of a ready response. Irritated, he wonders aloud why no one in Nagasaki is forthcoming in their answers to even his simplest questions. He protests that he had friends who were in Hiroshima; none of *them* are so taciturn. Nagasaki, he continues to lecture Yōko, is "way behind Hiroshima":

> Here there's absolutely no self-expression. They're not even angry. No matter what I ask them, they just sit there in silence and smile at me. When I go ahead and press for answers, they look at me with eyes begging for forgiveness, as if they had done something wrong. . . . Adults, children, women, men: they're all the same. I feel as if I'm being made a total fool of. Having been bombed is nothing to be ashamed of. (57)

The doctor's remarks point to how impossible it is for him, a physician but nonetheless a non-hibakusha physician, to begin to comprehend the difference between his world—a world of questions and their answers—and the discontinuous world of his atomic-bomb patients. None of his remarks, however, strikes Yōko as more typical of non-hibakusha than "They're not even angry." The doctor's reaction, however plausible it may be, indicates a perspective inaccessibly remote to those whose frames of reference are so dislocated that they cannot locate an object at which to express even rage. Yōko's personal situation—the deterioration of her home life—makes her especially unable to relate as others might. Her father shuts her entirely out of his life in the attempt, she is sure, to pretend that the past never happened. That, she reasons, is perhaps the only way people can go on and live acceptable lives; that is also why the exasperated Tokyo doctor cannot get his Nagasaki patients to talk about that past.

Yōko herself is no exception. She, too, would like to forget. After she graduates from a junior college, she meets her future husband Michio. She revels in his love because for the first time she feels "liberated" from her incessant thoughts of August 9th and its aftermath, if only because she is momentarily distracted. Michio pays attention solely to her. He never mentions the bombing; apparently he is not aware that she is a hibakusha. Michio comes to represent to Yōko everything that Nagasaki is not: kind, healthy, fully formed. She soon decides that she wants to marry him and move—move away—to

Tokyo. When, after a few of her manipulations, Michio finally does propose marriage, she realizes, "Rather than be pleased, I thought to myself that this was all I could do" (64). She does not dream the typical dream of a perfect life with her fiancé—such feelings, like anger, are beyond her—but hopes only for a "mute, average happiness."

A week before going to Tokyo for the wedding, Yōko pays a call—another visit she would soon regret—on Nagata. Yōko is curious how he is doing. She finds him back in Urakami running a prosperous clinic and remarried with two children. What does he recall of that "summer day," and of the life he and her family shared in the village afterwards? What of her and her mother, now? Yōko is full of questions, but Nagata is disconcerted, and even shamed, by them. Although he apparently harbors deep and painful memories, his restored affluence—symbolized by a pool of expensive carp in his garden—belies his desperate efforts to put, just as Yōko is about to do, his past behind him. One of the carp, Yōko notices, is different from the rest: spotted, marred like a victim of the bomb. And indeed so are all of us, she reflects. She feels sorry that she has tried to make Nagata remember, against his will, those days.

Tug of Time has now come around to the point of time at which its narrative began, with Yōko's awkward visit to her mother-in-law's. Things between her and her husband's mother never seem quite right afterwards. Her life with Michio, too, is not so much peaceful as it is merely "blank" (*kūbaku*). She gradually feels herself slipping away once more into her intensely private, melancholy, and isolated world as a survivor of an atomic attack, into a sense of alienation that finally overwhelms her one night as she and Michio chat in bed. In a conversation that comprises the central scene of the novel, Michio casually observes out loud that Yōko has no keloid scars on her body. Shivers run up her spine as Yōko hears him speak these words. Is he talking to her, she wonders. She feels accused of a crime, or as if she were naked in front of a crowd. "From the outside," adds Michio to make matters worse, "you don't look any different from a normal person" (75). After trying to comfort her obvious hurt by denying that her victimhood has in any way figured in his feelings, he reveals that his feelings are in fact wholly changed when he mentions, as if it were an obvious truth, that of course "we can't have children" (77). Yōko realizes that Michio has known for some time that she is a hibakusha. Her attempts to pass as otherwise (that is, as a "normal" person) are over. She learns that her father told Michio everything just before they were married, thereby both dooming the marriage and betraying his daughter just as he had earlier his wife. For Yōko that next morning, everything is changed:

When I picked up Michio's pajamas in my arms and began to walk towards the washer, the smell of his body rose up into my nostrils and filled me with a violent sensation of nausea.

"We can't have children."

As I crouched down the words Michio spoke last night came back vividly.

"We can't have children," I whispered to myself alone in the room. At that moment I knew I was clearly meant to know fertility—before it had been only a feeling. Is it really impossible for me to have children? Should I really not have any? I wanted to ask someone, anyone, these questions.

Whom? Whom should I ask? How about God, if God exists. Someone will answer my question, surely. I, who had not once imagined far into the future; I, who was now stripped of my freedom to imagine it, now more than ever felt ludicrous over wondering whether I would be able to have children. (79)

In this passage Yōko confronts what for the reminder of the novel is her ultimate alienation. Earlier she was cut off from the worlds of her father, her husband, and all non-hibakusha: now she is cut off, abruptly, from her own biological possibilities. The sudden realization that she might not have children—for physiological or social reasons, it is not made clear, nor need it be—"strips her of her freedom to imagine" the future and leaves her stranded in the events of August 1945. That next day, the day after her husband's unfeeling pillow talk, Yōko can do nothing but reflect repeatedly upon the existential lacuna that seemingly separates her forever from anyone who was not present in Urakami that day. How can they ever imagine what it was like, she asks rhetorically, and with deepening despair:

I believe that those of us who happened to be on Urakami that day have a right to forget that summer of fear. Even if that right is the pitiable right of the weak, a right unable to hinder the fall of the human race. If I suppose that I have survived this far only in order to forget, and if I suppose that I have a right to that forgetfulness, then I must also conclude now that I also have the right to cut myself off from the future. (81)

"To cut [one]self off from the future" means to inhabit the future only as a victim, a biologically or socially infertile hibakusha marking a human existence whose past and future properties have been collapsed into a single moment in the late morning of August 9th. Like many victims, but perhaps in additional ways particular to women hibakusha, Yōko is permanently grounded in the brief time and small space of that victimization's origin. She can calculate her past and probable future only in the stark terms of that instant. Yōko is a "survivor" for whom surviving makes little difference; she is trapped in the time in which her reproductive potential died along with her brother.

The deaths continue, albeit in ways that always retrieve memories of the first. Three months after her now shattered marriage, and on the occasion of a reunion with her father—one in which neither has much to say to the other—Yōko learns that Nagata, too, is now dead. For an instant Yōko does not believe this news that her father so casually mentions to her. How healthy he was, she says in way of a protest, but then instantly realizes how silly such words sound. Nagata realized as well as she, as well as anyone on Urakami that August 9th but left alive, just how provisional life "afterwards" is. But Nagata had seemed so confident of his new life; Yōko cannot bear the thought of him wasting away, dying slowly and in the throes of radiation disease. Yet that is exactly what happened.

Typically, Yōko's father attempts to change the uncomfortable subject of their conversation. He is going to be promoted to the chair of his department, he tells his daughter, and just as triumphantly informs her that he is divorcing and will remarry. His "good news" dazes an already stunned Yōko even further. Not one word, Yōko notes to herself, has been said about her mother; and it is just at that instant that father announces she has gone to live with her own mother back in the rural village where she was raised. Surely she will happier there, he says and, unprompted, goes on to diagnose her mental illness as the result of having lost a child, Yōko's brother—and only then "maybe" to her exposure to the atomic bomb itself. Yōko is dumfounded. Could her father *not* have realized this from the start? No longer able to restrain herself, she launches into an attack. Your cold attitude, she accuses, is no different from that of the foreign doctors who came to Nagasaki to observe us. You treat mother like a stranger. You have abandoned the both of us. But the only defense her father can summon is a feeble and rote "There's nothing that can be done about it."

To hurt him further, Yōko brings up the details of Nagata's past intimacy with her mother. She wishes to wound her father by pointing out his inconsequentiality in their lives. When he counters that in the jungles of New Guinea, where even "walking was war," it was bad for him, too, Yōko insists that no matter how terrible his suffering was, it is over for him now. Yet for hibakusha, suffering is without end: finally Gotō reiterates plainly the same point made in so many ways by her fellow Nagasaki atomic-bomb writers.

How ironic it is, Yōko reflects, that father—who did, after all, go off to war—survived while Nagata, at home, was the one who died. She is frightened by the menacing implications of his fate. For her part, she does not want to wait simply to die. She wants to struggle, fight back. But fight what? Whom? With what? Yōko now cries for the first time, feeling her body as if on fire. As she cries out her regrets as well as her gratitude to Nagata, she is reminded by the red of her fingernails of the flames of August 9th. *Tug of Time* ends with its narrator caught more inescapably in the closed dimensions of the Nagasaki atrocity than at any other point in the novel. She is a character left with no choices but to remain a victim and, just as she has feared, await a miserable and lonely death.

Tug of Time, Gotō's award-winning work, elaborates at the greatest length themes treated in such short stories as "The Weight of Three Spikes" (Sambon no kugi no omosa, 1972) and "The Town Where It Rains Coal Dust" (Tanjin no furu machi, 1972). These are works which, like the novel, feature a young female first-person narrator who has a mother made insane by the bombing of Nagasaki. In "The Town" this crazed mother even tries to assault the Emperor, shouting wartime cries of "banzai!" as if to refute the deceptively peaceful atmosphere of postwar Japan. In each of Gotō's works she stubbornly pursues what are in her view the irreparable wounds inflicted upon the spirit by the bomb above and beyond its literal wrecking of flesh, concrete, and steel. Gotō's principal strategy for doing so is through her recurrent theme of "blood": a metonymy, of course, of the bombing itself, but something literal, too. Her characters' complex relationships with their common, insane mother, as well as their anxious apprehensions about their own children, are conditions "related" with blood. Gotō writes, for example, through her narrator in "The Weight of Three Spikes": "I wonder what sort of life has been decided for me, me with the blood of my insane mother, and blood assaulted by the atomic bomb? Am I to go on living the way this blood dictates? With my own wishes irrelevant?" (144).

This notion of a powerful and determinate genealogy, blood as vehicle for irradiated genes, seems a notion especially connected with Gotō's assumption of women as the biological architects of the species. Unlike Hayashi Kyōko, Gotō does not attempt to be a chronicler of Nagasaki. Her ambitions are at once more humble, if equally far reaching: she writes about one small family, but with implications that rehearse Hayashi's fear of a now irreparably corrupted genetic pool. Moreover, Hayashi and Gotō each depict a world of Nagasaki hibakusha that is predominantly a world of women, one in which gynecological injury, or fear thereof, engenders a common understanding of their hibakusha victimization. This world constantly draws attention to their biological (and hence psychological and cultural) difference from men. This affects their identity even more fundamentally than it might a male hibakusha's. In fact, what is most diabolic about the use of nuclear weapons for Gotō is how they have forced upon their surviving targets a distorted life that abandons the naturalness of the human family. As demonstrated in *Tug of Time*, concepts of "family," "love," and "children" are assaulted and even dismissed entirely. Her mother insane, her father indifferent, her husband a stranger, Yōko cannot imagine what being a "family" might mean. Her own doubts and fears over her suddenly precluded motherhood reflect the impossibility of ever repairing this insidious effect of the atomic bomb, which is to wreak havoc with the very notion of human love and biological survival.

Gotō Minako was only nine years of age when Nagasaki was bombed. When asked why she writes of an event that occurred so early in her life, she answered, "For me, writing means unearthing the 'grave' I had once tried to bury for good."[45] As the climatic encounter in *Tug of Time* between Yōko and her father shows, the suffering of the victims continues beyond the grave. It is a suffering without such a proximate terminus, a suffering that extends into future generations or even the lack thereof. This is not, as Hayashi was criticized for supposedly doing, to indulge a somehow unattractive Japanese penchant for taking delight in an egocentric "victimization" but is rather a legitimate recognition of issues raised, and raised uniquely, by nuclear war. Here those issues are the particular and cruelly attenuated effect of irradiation, both physical and psychological. The victims never know if they are "safe" or "spared." They must live in dread of the little symptoms that will one day evidence themselves. This theme—an uncomfortable one to read of today, given its resonance with our apprehensions over ecological catastrophes and retroviruses—insinuates itself throughout the greater part of Nagasaki atomic-bomb literature. It does so nowhere more than in the most noted novel to come out of Nagasaki, one by neither Hayashi Kyōko or Gotō Minako. For just those reasons, this last example of the second city's literary response may be the most frightening and disturbing work of atomic-bomb fiction to come out of either the 6th or the 9th of August 1945.

■

Sata Ineko, like Ōe Kenzaburō and Ibuse Masuji, is a distinguished writer with a long-standing reputation earned largely apart from her works dealing with the atomic bombings. Her life and her career—the two have always been closely intertwined—have been among the more dramatic of Japanese women writers in this century. Born in Nagasaki in 1904, the illegitimate daughter of two adolescents, Sata grew up in Tokyo amid squalid poverty once her unemployed father took her there after the death of her mother. A dropout from the fifth grade, Sata worked as a young girl in sweatshop conditions later detailed in her debut short story, "From the Caramel Factory" (Kyarameru kōba kara, 1928), and subsequently as a store clerk and waitress. Her first marriage, to a man who soon proved emotionally unreliable, ended in failure in 1924. Soon thereafter, however, she became acquainted with a group of writers associated with the coterie journal *Roba* (The Donkey) and who encouraged her to write. Her talent soon made her one of a small but very prominent number of women associated with the best of that era's considerable body of left-wing writing.

Her colleagues also encouraged her nascent interest in radical politics: Sata joined the Japan Proletarian Writers Federation in 1929, and then, in 1932—a most inauspicious year in which to commit to a revolutionary movement—the Communist Party. Despite what some consider to have been her tacit collaboration with the government during the Second World War, after the defeat she resumed her participation in radical politics and energetically returned to the writing of fiction and autobiography. Since the early 1960s Sata has again been one of the more celebrated writers in Japan: her novels, memoirs, and biographies have won numerous distinguished literary prizes.

Few of her works, however, can be considered atomic-bomb literature, nor was it ever inevitable that Sata would indeed turn to that genre. Sata was not present in Nagasaki on August 9th. The theme of her native city's destruction—as opposed to the theme of the entire war itself—was not one Sata felt compelled to write about, as did a direct hibakusha like Ōta Yōko. Quite to the contrary, Sata long felt that it would have been improper, even "arrogant," of her to write about such experiences solely from information and impressions gained second hand, or worse, imagined. What changed her inclination was a chance encounter with a hospitalized victim of the Nagasaki bombing who convinced Sata that she had a duty, as a writer and as a city native, to write about Nagasaki.[46] Initially, in a series of short stories with titles such as "A Series of Visits" (Rekihō, 1951) and "The Colorless Paintings" (Iro no nai e, 1961), Sata began exploring the theme of Nagasaki and its hibakusha culture. At the same time she rehearsed a set of dramatic incidents and characters that would later be incorporated into her most renowned and prize-winning Nagasaki novel—and her only atomic-bomb novel—*The Shade of Trees* (Juei, 1972).

The best-known of these stories, "The Colorless Paintings," is the first-person narrative account of a woman's visit to an exhibition of paintings at a national museum in Tokyo. She has come to find in particular those paintings done by "K," a Nagasaki friend of hers now dead of radiation-related causes. Viewing the paintings with her is "Y," also from Nagasaki but a businesswoman of Chinese descent who was quite friendly with K. K's paintings are distinguished from all the others in the exhibition by their emphatic lack of color, a feature which stands in marked contrast with the bold hues favored by other contemporary artists. Studying the works in a shared silence, the narrator reflects on why K, alone amid all these painters, might have elected to reject color. Perhaps, she speculates, it was to reflect the pure and singular nature of the violence he underwent. Certainly, she observes, his paintings are all the more powerful for their blank monochromy.

Y, too, suffers from the aftereffects of the bomb. The narrator is surprised that people once as robust as K and Y would one day fall victim to something that happened so long ago, something all the more treacherous for its invisibility. It is this imperceivable part of their lives, and the lives of other Nagasaki survivors, that is present by its absence in the metaphor of the paintings' color-lessness. It represents what Sata calls in this first atomic-bomb story an "un-nameable grief." The story ends with the narrator wondering rhetorically just what measure of the "unnameable" will ever be evident in these paintings to the casual museum patron.

In "The Colorless Paintings" Sata has essentially laid out the groundwork for *The Shade of Trees* a decade later. This lengthy novel would, however, expand the stories of the characters first identified here only by cryptic initials. More-over, it would tell those stories from their own points of view, which is to say from the points of view of two hibakusha themselves. *The Shade of Trees* is the epic and romantic tale of Ryū Keiko—the daughter of an immigrant Chinese father and a second-generation Chinese-Japanese mother—and Asada Su-sumu, a struggling painter who is already married and the father of a family. The setting is postwar Nagasaki: but over the decades of subsequent history chronicled in the novel, many motifs and themes are developed with an intri-cate and engrossing complexity. First, there are the dynamics of Keiko's and Asada's semi-illicit affair; then, too, there are the wider political issues associ-ated with the "interracial" nature of their relationship, issues which in Japan's postwar history involve not only societal prejudice but the specter of the Chi-nese Revolution itself. Keiko's identity as an ethnic minority—only gradually important to either Keiko or the reader—gives Sata Ineko the opportunity to discuss racism, the internal turmoil that arose within Japan's Chinese commu-nity over events on the mainland, and the implications of a successful Asian communism for Japan.

The main focus of the novel, nonetheless, is the nature of the hibakusha subculture in Nagasaki, itself a newly wrought if almost invisible minority com-munity comprised of people of many different racial and national backgrounds. Crucial to this portrait is its historical and geographical setting in a city that slowly and then only vaguely, perhaps even grudgingly, understood the extent of the damage it had sustained as well as the consequences that would, perhaps indefinitely, persist. This central theme is introduced with foreshadowing in *The Shade of Trees*' opening paragraph:

> Did those people speak of nothing? Could they really have spoken of
> nothing? No, certainly not much. That is part of their nature. There is
> no doubt something difficult about them, but there is also a gentleness
> that makes them shy: this is first of all why they do not speak. Perhaps
> they do not share what they really feel even when among themselves.
> Perhaps what renders them mute is both their wish to protect each other,
> and a repressed anger. Can we not say that they have even substituted
> self-reproach for their feelings of concern for each other, and for that
> repressed anger? The fact that the way these people love is not normal

for this world doubtlessly comes from the fact that the minute reality of that day, that day, has upset their very emotions, and it is in that fact that they now entrust themselves. Somewhere in their minds those emotions serve as a wishful cover. Can we say it is because of that cover, that those people have repressed the anger and terror that lurks in their deepest recesses? That is inevitable for ordinary human beings. That is why these people do not speak. Almost nothing is put into words. Their anger and terror cannot be spoken of even between just two people. Perhaps even this realization is cheated them, as they are aware of such feelings only as some faint shadow. Such overlapping frustrations have been with these people's lives all the past ten years, and while their misery is about to become public before too long, there was nothing but to notice how, finally, that shadow was ripping them apart. (47)

Sata begins her most ambitious novel with a statement of the essential estrangement of bomb victims from the non-hibakusha culture about them. "These people" refers, of course, to the Nagasaki atomic-bomb survivors. But soon, the reader discovers, it will also refer specifically to "just two people." The mention of the necessarily distorted way in which they love predicts the particular devotion that will develop between Keiko and Asada: a love with a "faint shadow" that precludes talk of "that day, that day." *The Shade of Trees* is an impressive fictional representation of hibakusha (and not just "Japanese" hibakusha), perhaps the most impressive to date, in part because the novel seeks to establish why in fact hibakusha's lives are so difficult to represent in the first place. The novel's achievement lies in portraying just how and why such hibakusha indeed say so little even as "their misery is about to become public," if only via their obituaries.

The Shade of Trees is organized in twenty-one chapters that span the more than two decades between the bombing and 1967. Commencing three years after the war, the novel makes clear that Nagasaki still bears signs of its destruction. Parts of the city may benefit from the boom of postwar reconstruction, but other neighborhoods continue to remind the city of the special fate it, with Hiroshima, was meted. Keiko and Asada come to know each other in this transitional milieu. The sole support of her family, Keiko is an ethnic Chinese who knows nothing of China yet is not accepted as a Japanese. She asks Asada for his professional help, himself estranged and alienated albeit from—at first—a wholly distinct set of circumstances. An impoverished, unfashionable, and provincial artist unsure of his talent, he still suffers from the aftereffects of his detention during the war on account of his left-wing views. What Keiko first seeks from Asada is his expertise in the design and refurbishing of a small coffee shop, the income from which she hopes will support her father and sisters. Both businesswoman Keiko and artist Asada wish to forget the past and proceed with their lives and their ambitions. Neither thinks of himself or herself as a hibakusha—after all, they came into central Nagasaki only *after* the blast—and thus their futures, though financially uncertain, can still be hopeful. Both are attracted to each other at once, though neither speaks openly of that attraction. After the shop opens and does moderately well, and as Asada's work earns some degree of recognition in Tokyo, they continue a casual association not quite yet openly erotic, but certainly affectionate and potentially much more.

This situation alone might have been sufficient for an intriguing novel: an exotic setting, two even more exotic characters, and the seeds of an extramarital affair. But on top of this Sata builds a work that elaborates on something vastly historical as well as specific. Her subtle insinuation of deeper troubles to come renders the novel a document of a world increasingly typical of our own today at the end of the century. At first, that trouble is negligible. Keiko starts to suffer from a cough and other cold-like symptoms. She visits a hospital occasionally, always stopping along the way to visit Asada at work in his studio. Asada himself does not feel all that well, and when he, like Keiko, is diagnosed with a "chest ailment," he—possessing a darker, more easily depressed personality than Keiko—imagines this the first sign of something terminal. Perhaps, he fears, he has contracted tuberculosis.

But Sata does not dwell long or deeply on illness in the early chapters of the novel. Rather, Asada's and Keiko's common visits to the hospital serve as the convenient pretext for bringing them closer together. Sharing a lethargy that stands in stark contrast to the bustle of an energetic postwar Japan, they do indeed fall in love with each other. To varying degrees their love inspires both of them to persevere and dream even of prosperity. Although Asada has a wife, and Keiko's own family cautions her about getting too involved with a Japanese, they draw on each other's differentness, their akin senses of alienation, and out of those things fashion reservoirs of personal strength. At moments they dare to indulge their most romantic thoughts, sharing even the common lovers' fantasy of, one day, Paris. The world they create between themselves is an exceptionally private one, even for two young lovers. But it is a privacy in part forced upon them: "The two of them boarded up their relationship in a locked shack. Yet whenever they tried to imagine their's somehow a world apart, they were struck in many ways by the reality without" (80).

As time passes Asada seems to enjoy rather better health than Keiko, but he nonetheless persists in blaming his maladies for his not yet achieving greater fame as a painter. Discouraged, he even uses one of his paintings to cover a leak in his roof. Keiko, alternatively, endures her illness—an illness compounded by the stress of running a business—in stoic silence. Their relationship, one wholly satisfactory to neither because it is so constrained, is intertwined with their compromised physical, psychological, and financial states.

They seem never able to enjoy ever any truly carefree happiness. The backdrop of the novel, a residually radioactive Nagasaki, slowly moves to the fore in the novel as its citizens, even the busy Keiko and Asada, are inexorably condemned to realize that the damage sustained by their city is at base different from that of a conventionally bombed Tokyo or Osaka. Sata skillfully charts a rising consciousness in Nagasaki of its legacy as an atomic-bomb target. Some of Keiko's family's acquaintances, for example, fall ill and die from radiation sickness, even as post-Occupation antinuclear mass movements organize and militate. But by this point, it is a decade since 1945, and Keiko and Asada, though they individually think of it frequently, have yet to breach in conversation the topic of the bombing between themselves. "It was certainly not the sort of thing," Sata writes, "one could reminiscence about" (115).

This recalcitrance is no doubt attributable in part to a painful if unarticulated awareness of how their relationship is constantly threatened not only by social or racial prejudice, poverty, and frustrated ambitions, but by illness. Sata's success in *The Shade of Trees* lies in its portrayal of a romantic relationship defined within the boundaries of a hibakusha subculture, even if the two central characters do not identify with that subculture. Both Keiko and Asada sense that their feelings for each other are qualified by their seemingly incurable, if only vaguely defined, ill-health. Thus there is a ceaselessly present but suppressed tension between them. Their love for each other becomes a way of declaring their resolve to live, as if to stop loving would mean acknowledging the fragility of their lives. This tension is reenforced by other ones in the novel. Keiko envies Asada his art; what, she sometimes thinks resentfully to herself, does she have? Asada, on the other hand, is most proud of one painting in particular, one produced by his new self-proclaimed "simplified" method, entitled "Wall." It is a work that mystifies, exasperates, and even irritates Keiko, at least until she finally comes to understand its sheer blankness once Asada tells her that if she were to ask why he doesn't leave his family for her, the answer would be that he is too weak to leave anyone.

As the novel progresses it is in fact increasingly dominated by weakness: *The Shade of Trees* becomes the very portrait of a world of weakness. Keiko is alarmed at every new ache and pain. For days at a time she feels terrible. Unable to climb stairs or properly attend to the demands of her business, and reduced by attacks of diarrhea to near total immobility on some days, Keiko finds herself slipping further and further away from even the fantasies of the romantic happiness she had earlier imagined for herself and Asada. Yet she, like her lover, never speaks of her own illness. Indeed, this tacit agreement to keep silent results in Keiko believing Asada has wholly recovered. In 1956, when the second World Conference Against Atomic and Hydrogen Bombs is convened in Nagasaki, Keiko and Asada hardly take notice. He is busy with his painting, she with the café, and both with their secret, worrisome symptoms. Neither has yet allowed himself or herself to link, explicitly, their reduced states of health to the nuclear blast.

It is at this point, in the ninth chapter of the novel, that Sata allows Keiko to dwell on the events of August 1945; events that she is sure saved her from becoming a hibakusha. Like Asada, she was not in the city proper that day. Rather, she was in the outskirts of Nagasaki, safe where her father had taken her and her sisters after his premonition of an imminent air raid over the city. Six days passed before Keiko had the chance to see the center of the explosion, a scene she recalls as "defying reality." But that constitutes the extent of her memories. She does not think of herself as a victim because, like so many in Hiroshima and Nagasaki in the 1950s, she remains unaware of the secondary effects of the bombing, which is to say the delayed but lethal atomic-bomb disease lurking in tens of thousands of people who, even weeks later, returned to city centers thinking themselves well past any danger.[47]

Their ability to rationalize and deny, however, eventually reaches its limits. Asada begins to experience new symptoms. Troubled by a rising panic over his mortality and his seemingly impossible predicament in loving two women, he starts to drink heavily. He refuses, intellectually, to entertain his premonitions of death seriously. He tells himself that he must continue painting. Yet finally he breaks down and confesses his fears to Keiko. This brings *The Shade of Trees* to its emotional climax: Sata cannot long let things continue this way in this aggravated state of dread, apprehension, and ironic foreshadowing.

Just at this halfway point in the novel, Asada notes he has suddenly developed purple spots on his left wrist. He goes to Keiko at once, and though she calmly advises him to visit the hospital—it is thirteen years after the war now, and Nagasaki has its own A-Bomb Hospital—each of them is stunned. Asada never thought of himself as a hibakusha. But after all, he says to himself as well as to Keiko, he *was* exposed to radiation. Like so many others, adds Keiko, as if those "others" had been guaranteed some exemption to just the fate that Asada now faces. Asada went into Nagasaki shortly after the bombing to search for his nephew and found himself caught in the infamous "black rain" that pelted the city with radioactive ash. He recalls the numberless dead he saw, and that he had always thus thought himself spared the worst. Looking back, he knows now he was stupid to have walked about the ruins so much. But who could have known? He has never spoken of these things because they are still so painful to him. Keiko, moved by Asada's stories, confesses to him for the first time that she, too, had traversed ground zero.

This scene and its confessions dramatically change the relationship between Keiko and Asada. "Keiko had, until now, never really thought much about her own anxieties; and she could hardly bear the idea that they might be related to Asada's purple spots, both of them the result of an event thirteen years in the past" (144). Her anxiety—as well as Asada's own, and by implication that of all hibakusha—is scrutinized in close detail in *The Shade of Trees*. It is a secreted and cloaked anxiety not glibly expressed in political or social terms, but instead one that seeks to disguise itself as something else. It is an anxiety documented nowhere in atomic-bomb literature as well as in Sata Ineko's novel:[48]

> Every day now, thirteen years after the end of the war, was spent by both Asada and Keiko catering to their states of poor health. The development of what was pronounced a "chest ailment" doubtlessly meant that the life they had once eagerly anticipated would now never come. Yet the suffering that ensued was an inducement to keep on living. One could say that the suppression of their fears, as well as the strain of their infirmities, was now part and parcel of their lives. Both of them had health worries, and those worries were the reason behind their psychological deterioration. Nagasaki's ordeal of thirteen years ago was something from which the city was recovering, but that was the consequence of how normal people get on with their lives. It had nothing to do with how those who were sick might think. Neither of them, until now, had imagined what illness might actually mean. Even now, as it was sinking into their consciousness, they denied its import. But such evasion itself was the work of their weakened state. The anxiety brought about by the spots that appeared on Asada's wrist made a mockery of their charade. Asada was aware of this now, but he also sensed that his anger over how stupid he had been to go into Nagasaki back then was wrapped up with an undefinable fear. This fear produced in Asada certain anxieties. Weren't his physical listlessness, and the lethargic state of mind that went along with it, much like the symptoms that develop after exposure to radiation? Such heretofore unimagined ideas now assailed Asada. (144)

A frightened Asada finally does go to consult a doctor, who assures him—as Japanese doctors routinely do—that all is fine. Asada is eager to believe him, and indeed the purple spots do eventually fade and vanish. Both he and Keiko throw themselves back into their work. Asada, however, is still stalked by morbid nightmares. In his mind he goes over and over his movements that August now long ago, seeking ways to blame himself for what he suspects is to be his inevitable fate. His mental state interferes with the execution of his art. He still has enthusiasm for painting, but no longer any confidence. At one point Asada thinks about atomic-bomb writers, and how *motivated* their work is—why isn't his? He concludes not only that the visual arts are different from the literary, but that he, unlike those writers, is not a hibakusha. Asada's desperate struggle to deny his victimhood resumes and thus acerbates his psychological struggles.

That same year he hears—incorrectly, as it turns out—that none of his submissions have been selected for inclusion in the annual Tokyo exhibition of contemporary art. He becomes despondent, muses about killing himself, and ends up passed out from drunkenness in a bar. Keiko feels powerless to help him. Neither of them mentions his evermore frequent lapses into a drugged despondency, for to do so would necessitate broaching the forbidden subject. Keiko tells herself that his loneliness is the sort that only he, and no one else, can do anything about. Their relationship continues to mutate: it is much colder, more measured and rehearsed than before. They grow ever sicker, both physically and emotionally. Asada will not tell Keiko of his new symptoms of diarrhea; meanwhile, Keiko suffers in her own self-imposed silence even more aggravated symptoms. Her level of resentment occasionally rises to near anger. Asada after all, she thinks to herself, has his art, his family, his leftist causes— what has she got? What right does he have to be depressed? She tells herself that Asada enjoys much better health than she, a misconception given further credence when, in the spring of the following year, she discovers purple spots on her own body. When she describes them to Asada, his only response is to worry about himself. Nothing is left of the old days, when they traveled, in love, to the hospital together.

Now on the rare occasions they visit doctors, it is alone. On one such visit Asada is diagnosed with "liver trouble." The doctor tells him that he will have to be hospitalized for treatment. Asada confesses to Keiko his mounting terror that this might be the consequence of radiation disease. In fact, it is: once in the hospital—the same hospital that brought him and Keiko together—he will never leave. Half a month passes; his condition does not improve, and the diagnosis is still ambiguous. Asada is shocked, then terrified, to learn that his hospital bills are being paid by the government since his illness has been, provisionally, classified as "atomic-bomb disease." The hospital insists that this is only an expedient, a way to spare Asada private expense. But his fears remain unassuaged. Still, he does not protest too much: he is too weak to do so. All that is left him are his mental capacities, and even they are increasingly compromised by fear. His doctor may continue to assure him he does not have atomic-bomb disease, but Asada reasons that since no one knows what *is* wrong with him, his illness might very well be the consequence of his exposure to the aftereffects of the bomb.

Keiko watches as Asada loses much of his weight. She tries, for his sake, not to look concerned. Her nursing of him (she provides more care than does Asada's own wife) adds to her own exhaustion. Eventually she learns Asada has liver cancer (a diagnosis never shared with the patient himself) but by that point she is not surprised. Nonetheless, it makes being with Asada, who has convinced himself he is recovering, even harder on her emotionally.

The time of year is August, and the weather is hot. One day Asada coughs up blood. An alarmed Keiko asks if she should call a doctor: and those words are the last she would ever utter to a coherent Asada. He dies soon thereafter, his entire body hemorrhaging. Keiko, after watched him suffer in ignorance of his true condition, is relieved for him.

The funeral is a family affair, and Keiko is not included in the plans. But gone with him is ten years of her own life. Later, she travels to Tokyo to see his last paintings displayed posthumously in a scene much like that described in the earlier "The Colorless Paintings." The year is 1961 now, and Asada's plain representational paintings are out of place among the loud and abstract themes shown as the exhibit. His works possess a calm whiteness, a colorless-ness that has a powerful effect on Keiko. The effect is one, however, of loneli-ness and isolation, for there is no sign of their love in any of the paintings. Rather, "they seemed to say that he was withering to death" (208).

Outwardly, Keiko's life after Asada's death continues much as it had when he was alive. Inwardly, however, she is emptied. She wishes herself dead in order to be with him, and to apologize to him for her part in allowing the distance that seemed to separate them in their last years together. She is tor-tured by how little she understood him, and by how little her love had seemed to change anything for the better.

For several years thereafter, Keiko's life is filled with new and compensa-tory concerns. Her interest in China, originally awakened by Asada's left-wing views, motivates her to become involved in political activities in the local Chi-nese community and eventually to open a Chinese-language bookstore. Per-haps she throws herself into such things in order to forget; perhaps it is because she wishes to honor Asada's memory. But in the end, the tremendous exhaus-tion of these activities, coupled with the running of now two businesses, takes its toll. One autumn morning Keiko simply collapses. She will not allow a doctored to be summoned—no, she just hasn't had enough sleep, she insists. But that night, she falls again, and by the time help arrives she is dead at the age of forty-six. Like Asada, in fact more so, Keiko had worked hard to survive; but it was those very efforts that may have helped to kill her.

She is buried in the Chinese fashion, with a large box filled with fresh foods placed before her grave. *The Shade of Trees* concludes with a description of another grave near her own:

> A huge gravestone shaped like a scroll was today just as it had been left by the violent force of *that time.* It was proof of the reality of that single instant that had lasted for twenty-two years. It laid face up on the with-ered grass, and a single crack ran through the Chinese characters carved into it. (253)

The Shade of Trees ends as it began, with an oblique reference to the bombing of August 9th. Between the beginning and the end, and between those two references, lies a romance that runs its course never far from the consequences of that bombing. At nearly every turn, the lives of Ryu Keiko and Asada Susumu are governed, restricted, and destroyed by history: leftist politics, the Chinese Revolution, the Security Treaty riots, but nothing more than the atomic bombing of Nagasaki itself. Like much atomic-bomb literature, the organizing scheme of the novel is not a narrative point of view, or a plot: it is a historical event of such proportions that it makes every moment of the work an adjunct demonstration of the very scale of those proportions. The scale is both immense and microscopic. There is the stealth of the invisible rays that kill Asada, perhaps Keiko, too; there is also the insidious nature of a single weapon that even the force of love, exerted over the course of decades, is unable to ameliorate, and so assumes a scale as "immense" as the actual power of the blast itself. Here is where Sata Ineko's work intersects with that of Hayashi Kyōko and Gotō Minako. Nagasaki, unlike Hiroshima, signifies the insidious, permanent, and seemingly endless suffering of the bombing on the most private and intimate levels: mother and son, father and daughter, man and woman. In each of these three women's works is described a Nagasaki that disrupts the most essential structures of romantic love, families, the birth of children: it is a "Nagasaki" described from the point of view of women and mindful of their differences from men. This is not to say it is "domestic" and thus ancillary, of lesser importance. Rather, it is a literature which takes up the very issue of biology and culture, and thus our literal and symbolic survival, that makes atomic-bomb literature the terrifying literature it is.

■

The Nagasaki writers examined in this chapter have been commonly concerned in different ways and to varying degrees with the historical conditions—past and future—of victimization. For a committed Christian such as Nagai Takashi, victimization is, and has been since the early days of Japanese Christianity, part of the transformation of believers into the body of Christ. Nagai's own transformation of a modern and very secular atrocity into an articulation of historical, theological metaphors and allegories reads the events of August 1945 as the replay of a divine judgment. It is also an early rehearsal of the Apocalypse, in which only the good are as yet saved (by their instantaneous deaths) and thus spared the manifold dread that the sinners (read hibakusha) must now endure in the Purgatory of a postwar Nagasaki.

The representations of Nagasaki victimization fashioned by Hayashi Kyōko, Gotō Minako, and Sata Ineko could not be more different, though theirs, too, are just as historical. Far from being redemptive, the radiation that not only withered flesh but rearranged genes and spoilt fertility is totally without rationale, design, or sense. There is no comfort anywhere. There is only damage, horrible enough in its initial manifestations but subsequently the source of anger, madness, and death that threatens to persist, perhaps infinitely, beyond the targeted generation itself and into its heirs. In Kurihara Sadako's most famous poem, "Let Us Be Midwives!" a bomb victim gives birth to her baby at the cost of her own life. It is a poem that, despite its tragedy, suggests that that tragedy is transient and finite. "New life was born," Kurihara wrote, "Even at the cost of our own lives." For Kurihara, of course, writing in the immediate aftermath of the bombing, there was no knowledge of the tenacious aftereffects of radiation, nor any expectation that in all likelihood this "new life" too would soon die. There is an irony in "Let Us Be Midwives!" that was unavailable to Kurihara when she composed these lines, but which was paramount by the time Nagasaki women writers such as Hayashi and Gotō emerged in the 1970s. These later writers know better: as if to reverse the terms of Kurihara's poem, in *As If Not* and *Tug of Time* it is relatively healthy women who fear for their real or prospective children's well-being. And in Sata's *The Shade of Trees*, Keiko dies childless, presumably not only because she never married but because of her sickly health.

Perhaps it would have to be women writers, culturally if not biologically more sensitive to issues of survival, who would create that branch of atomic-bomb literature dedicated to pursuing the widest implications of nuclear weapons and their institutions on the human species and our history. The blood that according to Christian symbolism must be the sign of God's sacrifice for us of his own Son, is from the perspective of at least one woman hibakusha writer "the blood so easily susceptible to radiation, the blood that will always be of special concern to the female sex, the blood we fear."[49] Perhaps, too, it would have to be Nagasaki writers, writers from a place whose fullest historical significance is seldom recognized, who would produce writings that predict an import in fact not yet fully apprehended. Theirs is a literature of things that have only begun to happen.

Secretary of War Henry Stimson notified Prime Minister Winston Churchill of the successful detonation of the world's first nuclear device with the single sentence: "Babies satisfactorily born": a reassurance that neither Hayashi nor her fellow women hibakusha would ever dare permit themselves to believe. "These are wounds inflicted by human beings," wrote Hayashi Kyōko. "These are deliberate wounds precisely calculated and inflicted by human beings. On account of these calculations, the very life that we would pass on to our children and grandchildren has sustained injury." In Hayashi's analysis the advent of nuclear weapons is first expressed as a human, not divine, act, and second, as one heralding a possibly permanent, certainly inter-generational, distortion of life as it was known before, in ways simultaneously physiological and psychological. This is why Nagasaki atomic-bomb literature may convey the genre's most disturbing import. To imply that the fundamental assumption we grasp in the world—that we are part of a human continuum—is changed, and changed in ways graphically etched into human flesh and sentiment that no volume of concrete, no groves of newly planted trees, no institutionalized memorial observances, can quite efface, is to deny readers the consolation such gestures offer. The agony of Hayashi's portrait of a mother worrying for the health of her son, of Gotō's portrait of a daughter pondering the depth and extent of her mother's madness, and of Sata's figure of a lonely woman frightened herself of the fate meted out to her dead lover, is a fear writ large throughout life now. It is a fear that does not pass briefly, but is rather one marking an era in which warfare and its technology leave no part of human existence whole, or intact. The contribution of Nagasaki atomic-bomb writers and their works is to guarantee that the unbelievable stories initiated in Hiroshima do not end in Nagasaki but continue as long as does the threat of annihilation, either in the past or future, by weapons whose insidious effects still remain imaginatively estranged from us, yet still too near to view in their terrible entirety.

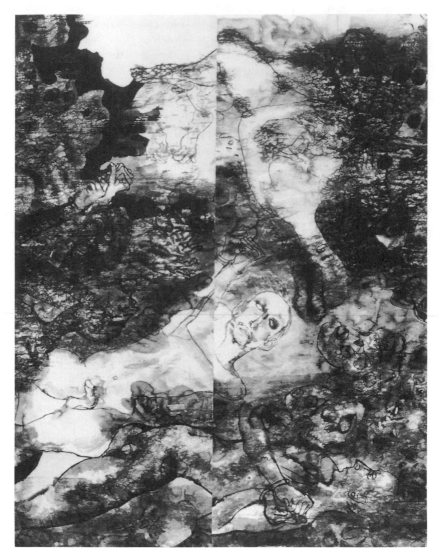

Maruki Iri and Maruki Toshi, *Death of the American Prisoners of War*, left half
(Beihei furyo no shi, 1971)

War can only be understood in its totality if the writer has a perspective
which enables him to understand the forces that lead to war.

Georg Lukács, *The Meaning of Contemporary Realism*

There is no totality.

Friedrich Nietzsche, *Will to Power*

10

The Atomic, the Nuclear, and the Total: Oda Makoto

T he 1980s were conspicuously and even urgently the most "nuclear" decade of the post-Hiroshima era. Commencing with the traumatic event and
nervous aftermath of the Three Mile Island near-catastrophe—a crisis tragically repeated in the real catastrophe of Chernobyl—wholly predictable "accidents" revived popular concern over and resistance to nuclear power and nuclear weaponry. In the popular media the 1980s are to large measure
retrospectively defined by two alternative visions of the human future. The
first is offered by Jonathan Schell's immensely influential *The Fate of the Earth* and
environmental activist Helen Caldicott's even more disturbing predictions.[1]
The second is Edward Teller's and Ronald Reagan's common dream of a post-
nuclear Strategic Defense Initiative ("Star Wars") with, in its closing years, the
tentative hope of a partial disarmament of the global nuclear terror as the then-
Soviet Union and the United States sought to reconfigure superpower prerogative. For reasons both contingent and necessary, nuclear issues were paid an

attention unrivaled since the years immediately following the Second World War.

It was therefore appropriate and perhaps even imperative that popular discussion of the "nuclear," heretofore generically remote from literary studies in the West, would now be submitted to the sorts of discursive analyses associated with contemporary textual and cultural theories that had often obliterated the intellectual restrictions on what constitutes the "proper" object of study in a university's departments of literature. In America the immediately popular term "nuclear criticism" first widely circulated in the summer of 1984, when a special issue of the academic journal *Diacritics* was dedicated to this new field.[2] The editors' preface to this issue explained that in April of that year the journal, in conjunction with Cornell University's Department of Romance Studies, had held a colloquium on nuclear criticism, selected proceedings of which comprised the contents of this issue.

Diacritics declared, in the manner of a manifesto, that by "nuclear criticism" it meant the application of literary and critical theory to the logic and rhetoric of nuclear war. One of its more famous contributors even predicted that universities would soon be establishing "programs and departments" of a then presumably capitalized (in both senses of the word) Nuclear Criticism.[3] It was thus something "positive" and "new," a project self-consciously critical and even interventionist (if only in the classroom), but at the same time (and in a not entirely compatible complementary gesture) open to all points of view.[4] *Diacritics* boasted of the seven collected essays that "the principle of their selection is mainly the wish to demonstrate . . . diversity, in order to open this field to the greatest plurality of voices and to calculate on the most unexpected sources for whatever may prove to be politically enabling."[5]

Yet despite the stated commitment to "diversity" and to "unexpected sources," the inclusion of an essay by a Japanese critic or of an essay that at least introduced a Japanese (or, in an equally interesting omission, Soviet) perspective was not to be. Just what is signified by "diverse" or "unexpected" when the presence of even one intellectual from, to date, the only nation subjected to nuclear attack was not deemed absolutely necessary is both clear and not clear. If a theoretical diversity (poststructuralism, feminism, etc.) suffices in lieu of possibly crucial racial, national, cultural, and historical differences, then *Diacritics* may have succeeded. If, however, that kind of curious displacement also guarantees a kind of theoretical homogeneity—as indeed it seems to have, given its Western parochialism—then the proclaimed "diversity" proposes the same kind of ironic reading of *Diacritics'* nuclear criticism that that very conference meant to undertake of nuclear war itself. All the contributors to the special issue were apparently Western—certainly their intellectual references were—and while that was of course no insurmountable curb on the content of their essays, in fact none wrote as if the Japanese could have meaningfully commented on the issues at hand. Nuclear criticism has been, from the start, a conversation among critics gathered in the only nation that has used nuclear weapons. That fact, despite the great weight given in the academy today to the problem of identity and context, was not cited to qualify, inter se, the confidence with which any ideas were asserted in *Diacritics*.

There are, one can imagine, a number of possible reasons for this Western monopoly of nuclear criticism, some more innocent than others. Japanese critics and academics are not usually participants in our conferences outside of the sciences. To be fair, this is not solely attributable to ethnocentrism, or at least to its most virulent form, for the critical idioms of Japanese literary and cultural theorists are not always readily intelligible to Western critics, some of whose belief in the global applicability of much current theory may, in fact, not be quite so demonstrable. That said, it is also clear that the work involved in making these theoretical differences intelligible would certainly be worth the effort. In an emerging "nuclear criticism," if nowhere else, one might reasonably assume that abstract vocabularies, if not national experiences, could overlap or at least profitably clash; one might moreover assume that a dialogue between intellectuals in that culture which invented nuclear war and intellectuals in that culture which has had to live with those weapons' intellectual as well as material implications might be, at long last, imaginable as well as imperative.[6]

This expectation, however, arises from a set of assumptions not necessarily shared by the initial seven architects of Western nuclear criticism. The organizers of the *Diacritics* colloquium did not have to intervene to prevent Japanese participation, since the critical framework had already made such participation irrelevant or even, given the assault launched by these presumably representative essays on the usefulness of diachronic history, counterproductive. The most engaging and influential essay of the seven published in *Diacritics* was Jacques Derrida's "NO APOCALYPSE, NOT NOW (full speed ahead, seven missiles, seven missives)." Its arguments, no less for their perspicuity, explain why Japanese attendance at an international colloquium on nuclear criticism is not required. While Derrida repeatedly tells us that he takes the threat of nuclear weapons to "humanity" as "real" (though the brackets with which his essay usually sequesters those terms also gives him a way out of that blanket reference), he also argues that any implied nod to a historically specific "origin" for the issues at stake—a nod that the presence of a Japanese critic would have inevitably brought—is to be avoided if the programmatic work of nuclear criticism is to proceed. It is a fundamental corollary to Derrida's claim that what we now call "the nuclear age" has always been with us (there is, he states "no radical new predicate in the situation known as the 'nuclear age'" [21]) that, through his own recourse to history, nuclear war has never taken place. The destruction of Hiroshima and Nagasaki—places Derrida never mentioned directly by name (as if those words have a force that might make them "real" without the mediation of quotation marks)—is marked only by a telling circumlocution: he states "American bombs in 1945 ended a 'classical,' conventional war; it did not set off a nuclear war" (23). In other words, for Derrida;

> Nuclear war has not taken place, it is a speculation, an invention in the sense of a fable or an invention to be invented in order to make a place for it or to prevent it from taking place (as much invention is needed for the one as the other), and for the moment this is only literature. (28)

It is key to Derrida's argument here, and consistent with his theoretical project in general,[7] that "nuclear war" (as opposed to nuclear *weapons*) be a term without a referent grounded in the phenomenal world; that it be instead left a tenuous signifier with meaning only in tandem with other, equally fragile, signifiers. Here specifically, those signifiers are all those implicated in the "balance of terror" that threatens world-scale, nuclear apocalypse (a word, Derrida tells us, that "means Revelation, of Truth") but always deters/defers it. It is, in fact, on this ground of both metaphysical "meaning" and atomic wars regularly threatened but never waged that Derrida's one-time excursion into nuclear criticism overlaps with his long-time concern with the deconstruction of Western philosophy's canonical texts' struggle to suppress their rhetoricity in favor of transcendental signifiers.

This relationship is anything but casual. Derrida speaks of a special relationship between deconstruction and the nuclear age, and it is a relationship which explains his interest in nuclear criticism and, additionally, what he is at pains to preserve in it besides human survival. "Total destruction watches our deconstruction, it guides its footsteps," writes Derrida, taking advantage—as he will repeatedly—of a pun-like congruency of the terms most key in his essay. "That is why deconstruction, at least what is being advanced today in its name, belongs to the nuclear age. And to the age of literature" (27). Deconstruction and the nuclear age, that is to say, each make literature "precarious": they threaten its assurances of sure meaning and a future. This is an insight which helps explain not only the resistance to deconstruction in the West, but to atomic-bomb literature in Japan—here, Derrida is absolutely correct. But Derrida's "nuclear epoch" is again pointedly characterized as something fully independent of the Manhattan Project and 1945 (indeed, Derrida's examples of the writers who most seriously deal with this epoch—an epoch that has been with us ever since there has been a modern "literature"—are Mallarmé, Kafka, and Joyce). Nuclear criticism for Derrida, despite whatever benefits it might bring us as a means of defusing the superpower rhetoric under which we lived in 1984, is finally and perhaps even equally importantly a means for again demonstrating how provisional and reversible our signifying structures—Ronald Reagan's as well as Rousseau's—really are.

Derrida, quite fairly, insists on not being misunderstood in making this link between the discursive production of the nuclear and the philosophical production of truth. He does not intend "to paint with verbose vanity the horror of the nuclear catastrophe," but rather "to think today, retrospectively, the power and the essence of rhetoric" (24). But one does have to pause at the idea of an "essential rhetoric" and wonder what new foundational ground may have just been substituted for an older one. If Western philosophy had, long before Derrida, been detached from the absolute requirement of a fixed referent and linked only nostalgically—*rhetorically*—to the signified, then the more recent advent of an equally discursive "nuclear age"—described by Derrida as "a certain type of colloquium, with its particular technology of information, diffusion and storage, its rhythm of speech, its demonstration procedures, and thus its arguments and its armaments, its modes of persuasion or intimidation" (21)—corroborates how right we were to part paths with ontological reference in the first place.[8] Nuclear war, like any other transcendental ideal, remains a "belief" that can never be submitted to test. It must be a phrase, in "other words," as emptily self-referential, as paradoxically *sous rature*, as such terms as "Being" earlier submitted to Derridean deconstruction. And presumably a "nuclear war" now permanently encased in brackets cannot, as Gayatri Spivak explains of Derrida's theory of all signs, "be taken as a homogeneous unit bridging an origin (referent) and an end (meaning). . . . It must be studied 'under erasure,' always already inhabited by the trace of another sign which never appears as such."[9]

I am well aware that it is a common error of those who have not read deconstructionist critics attentively to complain that they reject any relation of language to reality. "In a genuine semiology," wrote Paul de Man (who in fact may be more easily charged with just this implication), "the referential function of language is not being denied—far from it; what is in question is its authority as a model for natural or phenomenal cognition."[10] But in the specific application of poststructuralist theory to postwar nuclear strategizing, once the "authority" of superpower rhetoric is disposed of as "as a model" for understanding the nuclear era, the two facts of Hiroshima and Nagasaki are also discarded. When Derrida speaks of the nuclear epoch, for example, as having its own "arguments and armaments," he takes advantage of his own alliterative rhetoric to conflate two things of very different orders—geopolitical *language* and material *weapons*. A similar clever tropic pun is found in the very title of Derrida's essay, in which "seven missiles" are "seven missives": despite Derrida's insistence that he knows the "real" danger of actual weaponry, that insistence is itself undermined, if not implicitly deconstructed, by such wordplay.[11] If Derrida himself has always been on the lookout in philosophical treatises for those words that combine different registers of signification—the remedy/poison of Socrates' *pharmakon* being perhaps the most famous example—in order to isolate what is highlighted and what is repressed in rhetoric-rich "logic," one might respectfully suggest that here, in Derrida's own writing, such play is also in evidence.

It is precisely in this easy elision of the discursive and nondiscursive aspects of the nuclear age that Hiroshima and Nagasaki—with no brackets—risk dissolving and disappearing entirely in Derrida's contribution to Western nuclear criticism. In Derrida's own assertion that "the terrifying reality of the nuclear conflict can be only the signified referent, never the real referent (present or past) of a discourse or a text," the parenthetical insertion of "past" seems intended to pointedly dismiss the nuclear destruction of two large Japanese cities as a conceivably "real," i.e, fixable, referent for a "nuclear war" that must never be realized in order to remain the perfect example of a metaphysical idea parading as reality. Such a war's "essential feature is that of being *fabulously textual,* through and through . . . fabulously textual . . . to the extent that, for the moment, a nuclear war has not taken place: one can only talk and write about it" (23). Again, it is revealing to look at the rhetoric that Derrida himself deploys in making just this point. "A non-localizable nuclear war has not occurred," he writes in an awkward sentence straining to retain a curious double negative. A sentence with an argumentative force quite different than if he had said "A localizable nuclear war has occurred," it scrambles to avoid a *positive* assertion that might have led readers to wonder, after all, why more has not been said of that war which *has* "occurred." In contrast with such tortured circumlocutions, Japanese critic Nakajima Kenzō has argued, in an essay which attempts to define atomic-bomb literature, that "our inability to ignore any longer the conditions that obtain before literature—or, put another way, the conditions that produce the literary work—may indeed characterize contemporary writing."[12]

It is not hard to imagine, however, why within his own critical framework Derrida must make nuclear war a product of *doxa* and not of history. Derrida's fourth missile/missive—"*As for the aporias of the nuclear referent, we don't believe in them*"—is countered in the fifth missile/missive with "*But we do not believe . . . in anything except the nuclear referent.*" The point, however, is precisely that we either *believe* or *don't believe;* that the referent is either there or "not there" as an effect of *doxa.* Derrida's point here is neither banal nor inconsequential. My own engagement with his essay is not for the purpose of proving it right or wrong, although I mean to demonstrate how different Japanese positions on just this issue of *doxa* versus history are. I find Derrida's reading of the theory of the Cold War impressively useful in a very real-world way. If there is to be nothing "beyond the text," then that language that terrifies us the most with its supposed presence, the talk of nuclear brinkmanship, must and can accordingly be exposed as the rhetoric it is. Neither is it hard to imagine how eagerly, and with relief, we accept such arguments in the West. The saber-rattling arguments of the American and former Soviet governments are indeed deconstructable as the oratorical acts they surely are. But that is not an original insight (who really believed that Khrushchev literally meant to "bury" us?), and even apprised of it, the weapons and a history of their use still remain. What is worrisome is that whatever Derrida's intentions, it is entirely in keeping with the history of Western, specifically American, intellectuals since 1945 to repress the consequences of Hiroshima and Nagasaki and to speak of "nuclear war" only as something that has not happened. Most nuclear literature in the United States, for example, is science fiction, which is to say a perpetual deferment of an historical fact into an immaterial future. Indeed, the absence of a discussion of nuclear (i.e., post-Hiroshima) culture in the works of American intellectuals[13] is precisely the trace of its conspicuous presence—just the kind of rhetorical trope so often identified by contemporary theorists, and so characteristic, in fact, of the *Diacritics* special issue and its intentional or unintentional (it makes no difference) exclusion of any sign (pun intended) of Japanese nuclear criticism.

■

There is, as of course one might have reasonably predicted, a Japanese nuclear criticism, regardless of whether it has an audience in the West or not. First of all, there is the long tradition of what one might call an "atomic criticism," i.e., a body of historical, scientific, literary, and philosophical discourse on Hiroshima and Nagasaki. Much of this criticism, especially its cultural arm, has been frequently cited throughout this study. Even more of it was anthologized just around the time that Western nuclear criticism was commencing its own work: in August 1983 the small Tokyo publishing house Horupu issued the fifteen-volume—five more than planned—*Atomic-bomb Literature in Japan* (Nihon no gembaku bungaku), the first and heretofore only ostensibly complete record of the testimonial, prose, poetic, dramatic, and critical record of the bombings of Hiroshima and Nagasaki. Ōe Kenzaburō, the most prominent member of the committee that edited this anthology, has stated that the original impetus behind the project was to carry out what was thought to be writers' responsibility to guarantee that fiction chronicling the "nuclear holocaust" not be forgotten.[14] Fellow editor Itō Narihiko notes, however, that finding a publisher for such a "guarantee" proved difficult. Before Horupu agreed, other houses turned it down as commercially unfeasible.[15] In other words this important reference work—the de facto canon of Japanese atomic criticism—encountered much the same critical resistance as had the authors, such Ōta Yōko, who it sought to keep in print. In fact, such resistance may finally be as constitutive, even definitive, of the genre of atomic-bomb literature as is its concern with the events and aftermath of August 6th and 9th; it is also this resistance that makes *Diacritics'* conspicuous neglect of those events unfortunately typical of four decades of willful blindness, and little insight.

Yet at the same time, the events recalled at the head of this chapter had their own impact in Japan. These events, in their broad implications, served to encourage a debate in Japan better described as "nuclear" than "atomic" because of its acute awareness of a postwar balance of terror initiated by Hiroshima and Nagasaki but no longer wholly attributable to them. The 1982 Writers' Appeal Against the Dangers of Nuclear War sparked a public controversy (see chapter 3), and the general alignment of intellectuals along opposing political lines that the Writer's Appeal engendered led to other projects and further bitter debate. In ways both revealingly similar to and dissimilar from the *Diacritics* special issue, a number of Japanese literary and cultural critics came together in the Fall 1982 issue of the literary journal *Bungakuteki tachiba* (Literary Perspective) to argue, and in effect officially inaugurate, a "nuclear criticism." The parallels with *Diacritics* come, most certainly, from a shared historical sense of urgency and a reinvigorated will among critics, East and West, to engage political issues. The differences, however, can be sensed even in the title given the *Bungakuteki tachiba* issue—"What Can Be Done in Literature?" (Bungaku ni nani ga dekiru ka?). The differences in fact derive from the persistence, in contemporary Japanese nuclear criticism, of certain key assumptions of an earlier atomic criticism inseparable from the events of Hiroshima and Nagasaki. [16] Against that prominent shift in Western literary thinking that is often, if reductively, interpreted as meaning that subjectivity and agency are produced or enabled within the social practice of language, the contributors to this Japanese project steadfastly endorse the view that literature could and even *must* serve as a practical tool for engaging and battling the politics of a nuclear age that Derrida and others would subsequently argue was "real" only within the rhetoric of brackets.

At the same time, the Japanese have acknowledged a particular crisis of agency in and for literature, albeit of a more explicitly political than philosophical character. In the published round table discussion that formed the centerpiece of the *Bungakuteki tachiba* issue, Hoshino Mitsunori succinctly sketched the concern, assumptions, and central contradiction of this emergent Japanese nuclear criticism:

> We are faced today with the "nuclear" as the ultimate phenomenon of humanity's alienation from itself; we are faced, too, by the phenomenon of the forfeiture of our humanness on account of that alienation. I thus believe it is absolutely incumbent upon us to ask again what precisely it

is that each of us can do that cannot be done in literature. This is not an question that must necessarily result in the writing of some actual literary work. It is, however, natural for writers, given that this is not solely a literary problem, to wonder just what should be done.[17]

If the rise of nuclear criticism in the West is an analogue to the turn among many leading critics—Edward Said, Frank Lentricchia, Fredric Jameson, and Gayatri Spivak, for example—to the analysis of suddenly paramount political and social forces with strategies honed within literary theory proper, then Japanese nuclear criticism has likewise recognized a rupture between the literary on one hand and the political and social (read nuclear) on the other, and has also acknowledged the special potential that literary theory and criticism may possess for comprehending how that rupture occurs and with what repercussions. It was just this set of awkwardly linked assumptions that led, again through the intervention of Ōe Kenzaburō, the International P.E.N. Congress held in Tokyo in May 1984 to adopt as its theme "Literature in the Nuclear Age—Why Do We Write?"[18] The question was ambivalently rhetorical. The underlying assumption is that "the nuclear age" is indeed a proper theme for writers, but just why, or to what end, seemed stubbornly unclear not just to the Congress's invited literary luminaries but even to its organizers. Yet such doubts never apparently undermined the determination of writers to persist in addressing the nuclear age as a largely cultural, and indeed literary, problem. Despite the claims made by both *Diacritics* and *Bungakuteki tachiba* for the general, even universal, crisis of the nuclear, none of either's contributors is anything but a textual specialist; indeed, all the *Diacritics* authors are additionally academic ones.

There are, of course, many grounds for challenging both the perception of a contemporary "nuclear" crisis and the appropriation of the theory of that crisis, if it does exist, by writers and their critics. It is not inconceivable, although certainly not my own view, that the resurgence in atomic-bomb literature and nuclear criticism around the world in the past decade lies in the public view that, in fact, nuclear issues have been effectively severed from the "East-West" history of military and political brinkmanship—i.e., that it is now "safe" for professors of literature to talk about nuclear weapons because, quite frankly, those weapons now (like professors of literature themselves) matter so little. The *Diacritics* essays were attacked (both cogently and less so) for what was considered their insouciant use of theory,[19] and—in an extension of the torrent that engulfed the Writers' Appeal two years earlier—Japan's conservative critic Etō Jun publicly attacked the political biases, and sloppy reasoning, of the P.E.N. Congress's Japanese patrons.[20] Alain Robbe-Grillet, one of the Congress's leading invitees, declared unarguably, but doubtlessly still to the dismay of the organizing committee, that "the nuclear issue alone does not account for all our problems today."[21] In fact, most speakers at the Tokyo conference simply ignored its announced theme, and talked about whatever they wished.

Despite the many problems both intellectual and institutional faced by nuclear criticism, Western or Japanese, there are important and even vital common points of concurrence between the two practices that neither set of founding critics commented upon. The basis of nuclear criticism in both the West and Japan is a radical and ironic cleavage inserted, either by philosophy or modern warfare, between the signifier and its proposed referent. If the irony made preeminent in late twentieth-century sophism is, in the words of Paul de Man, the "systematic undoing . . . of understanding,"[22] then the historical experience of Hiroshima and Nagasaki introduced into Japanese theories of literature, and moreover into some practices this study has surveyed, an outwardly similar ironic cleavage between signifier and referent that also challenges the confidence with which we might have once approached the work of language. Signs, one might observe, are in trouble the world over.

The nature and specific histories of these perhaps coincidental ironic cleavages are, however, radically different from each other. While one would find ready agreement among Japanese critics that indeed "nuclear war" and even "Hiroshima" and "Nagasaki" do constitute discursive formations, and thus to one degree or another are governed by the words with which they are spoken, they would add that they are also effectively real, i.e, traceable to and identifiable with referents not only prior to language but clearly at the root of language's noted failure to signify what the events of Hiroshima and Nagasaki are believed to mean. What is undermined in Japanese literary theory argued amid a critical awareness of post-Hiroshima culture, what constitutes a native Japanese "nuclear criticism," is a disbelief in the integrity of the sign because it is the signifier, not the referent, that now seems unworkably remote. Reality remains unscathed, remains "real" and is even reaffirmed. Instead, it is language, so often taken in the modern West as the only proper *ground* for knowledge, which becomes elusive, shadowy, untrustworthy: un-real. Kuroko Kazuo, the Japanese critic who perhaps could best respond to the positions taken by nuclear critics in the West, has written:

> To think about "atomic-bomb literature" is to be made acutely aware that "literature" proceeds with the world not as its telos but as its fundamental condition. That is to say, insofar as "language" locates it basis in actuality, however much it may be "fictionalized" a literary work performs its own role in the actual world. The very existence of an atomic-bomb fiction leaves us with no alternative but to recognize this.[23]

The disengagement of literary languages from the assumptions underlying the projects of Western metaphysics would, if applied to the assumptions of their own work, strike more than a few Japanese critics of atomic-bomb literature as a dangerous move towards the dismissal of history, a move towards the often politically suspect rhetorization of two tangible atrocities. The irradiated material condition of life in Hiroshima and Nagasaki is not noted in Western nuclear criticism; it is, however, the historical and *moral* starting point of any investigation for Japanese nuclear criticism. In "No Apocalypse" Derrida declares prescriptively, "*As for the aporias of the nuclear referent, we don't believe in them,*" but for critics such as Kuroko, it is not a question of believing or not believing. It is a matter of absolutely massive, self-evident history. In remarks which take on special significance in light of Western nuclear criticism and deconstruction's privileging of this trope of aporia, Kuroko asks:

> Is our "future" in fact open to us? Or is it closed? For us, forced to live under a "nuclear civilization" unimaginably enlarged in the world's structural "cold war" since August 6th and 9th in Hiroshima and Nagasaki, that question is the original aporia we are made to confront.[24]

It can seem as if Derrida and Kuroko, while both modern skeptics, speak entirely different languages: not that of "French" versus "Japanese," but rather the language of one who stands convinced of the reality of nuclear war, and doubts culture's ability to articulate that, and one whose equal conviction is only of the figural force of those blasts, whose equal doubt is only that of sure meaning behind the words that would make that force more than figural. Both know their aporias: but for Kuroko, his has an un-deconstructable origin; it even has a date and time of day. The term "nuclear criticism" subsumes at least two very different criticisms. There is "nuclear war criticism," and there is "nuclear politics criticism," and, I would argue, on the basis of what critics like Kuroko do with the former and critics like Derrida do with the latter, that they are very different things: one is a criticism of human, lethal, events, the other of human talk of more such lethal events.[25]

But we must also see the common historical context that underlies both criticisms. Maurice Blanchot, for instance, orders us in *The Writing of the Disaster* to "write in order not simply to destroy, in order not simply to conserve, in order not to transmit; write in the thrall of the impossible real, that share of the disaster wherein every reality, safe and sound, sinks" (38). Blanchot is insisting upon something in *language*: the "impossible real" is "impossible" for those who have not seen everything, once "safe and sound" in fact sink. On the other hand, Karl Popper stated in 1982—though he acknowledged his arguments were "partly rational, partly ad hominem, and partly even ethical," that "any argument against realism which is based on modern atomic theory— on quantum mechanics—ought to be silenced by the memory of the reality of the events of Hiroshima and Nagasaki."[26] Popper warns against what is so risky in positions such as Blanchot's and Derrida's. To make nuclear war the "impossible real" is to separate from significant history the very conditions that must govern a largely rhetorical discourse of "nuclear (politics) criticism." Not to do so, borrowing Derrida's own terminology, means subscribing to more "white mythology," to a metaphysics that imperfectly hides its own rhetoricity in order not just to establish its claims to truth but, in addition, to dis-establish the very unambiguous, clearly understood, and precisely executed chains of signs—a military command—that resulted in two chain reactions: chain reactions that resulted, for Japan, in a "death of the author" far more literal than that intended by Western literary theory.

Thus a Japanese nuclear criticism will be a criticism that takes Hiroshima as both its start and finish; it is a criticism that takes the *practice* of Hiroshima as also the first draft of the *theory* of nuclear war. It is a criticism that will seek a *totality* in the nothingness of that bombing; it is a criticism that is historical, political, and *lived*. In all these ways it distinguishes itself from the deconstruction of the rhetorical acts of superpowers, and takes as its object instead the literal threat indeed behind those acts—acts that are not merely potential, but actual. This criticism, its theory as well as practice, is significantly located within an ongoing tradition of creative fiction, and for reasons that include the pursuit of a totality perhaps only realizable through the novel's modernist exercise of imagination. "In the nuclear age," writes Ōe Kenzaburō, "writers have a duty to continue to create individual models of the future, thereby challenging readers who may in fact share in a yet unimagined nuclear catastrophe, to widen their *horizons of expectation*. For this purpose, the novel is an effective tool. . . . A novel is a device of language through which the elements of humanity as a *whole* can be brought to life."[27]

This notion of a "whole," of a "totality"—not to mention that of "humanity"—may strike us as philosophically and politically quaint, perhaps even perilously romantic. But, as I will presently argue, they are notions which arise out of a very specific and well understood set of historical circumstances anything but illusionary or anachronistic. Japanese nuclear criticism will, in fact, in its concern with totality—that of "total war" as well as of "total understanding"—argue its own implicit deconstructionist critical practice, if one with a radically different impetus and markedly different implications.

■

In her 1981 novel *As If Not*, Hayashi Kyōko describes how new public controversies over nuclear weapons only exacerbated the anxieties long felt by her Nagasaki hibakusha characters; she thereby also describes what questions a Japanese "nuclear literature," as opposed to a "atomic-bomb literature," might address:

They had now survived more than thirty years. In that time none of the women's relatives had had to go off to war. A state of peace continued. But now, at the start of the decade of the 1980s, issues of Japan's military and national defense were being publicly discussed: issues such as rearmament, the most controversial. Just what did the "re-" of rearmament— needed to defend against some hypothetical enemy—mean for the past and future of these women's country? Why did a return to military conscription have to be entertained as a possibility? What sort of peace is "the peaceful use of nuclear energy"? (136–37)

The policy debates in Japan alluded to here by Hayashi were contentious in the early 1980s precisely because Japan's role in the world, in particular its relation with the United States, was then in the initial stages of a major revision. The nuclear literature that *As If Not* begins to define, as well as the nuclear "criticism" it was also part of, could not and cannot proceed without reference to the very "real" places of Japan and America: Japanese nuclear criticism at every stage particularizes as it historicizes a relation of "difference" as geopolitical as it may be semiotic. Those particulars and that history are consequently irreducible to a matter of rhetoric. In recent years Japan, now more of an economic rival than a military and diplomatic dependent, has had to rethink its long-standing imagination of itself as America's "victim," the "target" of first the atomic bombs and then the postwar hegemony of an imperial United States. Such rethinking was bound to effect atomic-bomb literature, in which the relationship of the victim to the victimizer had never been a simple one at any stage in its history.

There are many reasons for this complexity. It is not attributable to any instinctive hesitation on the part of postwar Japanese writers to criticize an ally or, more accurately, patron state. Of all its causes, the one inseparable from the fact of twentieth-century atrocity is the problem of circumscribing the perpetrator, and with it the nature of his power. The lines between the victimizer and the victimized can be obscured by the presence of collaborators, both active and passive; or by those who conceive of lethal decisions and those who execute them; or indeed, they can be obscured by alternative sets of ethics in competition with each other in pursuit of the purported "least evil." The attempt, however imperative, to define evil against all else requires a willful, moral (as well as technological and legal) refusal to entertain ambiguity, a bold resolve to approbate some actions while holding others culpable, even if all are equally bound up in a single, seamless continuum toward the same unbelievable but irrefutable end. This quandary arises from the fact that no parts of the bureaucratic, technological operation collectively dubbed contemporary civilization—Weber's "iron cage"—are easily detached, identified, and purged.

The victimizer exists only diffusely, distributed in the relationships between the human parts, and systemic processes, that operated death camps in the middle of Europe and or built nuclear piles beneath a college football field.

We do not accept this diffuseness without resistance. When it results in works of literature that do not accuse, we can be disappointed or frustrated. The story we are told seems to lack an appropriate ending. Contrary to the usual expectations of non-hibakusha readers—who perhaps would have wished their feelings of ill-ease and even guilt assuaged through their literary and thus suitably distal indictment—little atomic-bomb literature notes, much less denounces, the human hand that ultimately inflicted the suffering. This hand, despite the difficulty noted in defining it (Is "hand" literal? A metaphor? Or a synecdoche?), is sometimes assumed to be the militarist clique that led Japan into war, or Truman, or Einstein, or alternatively simply human nature in general. But most of the time it is thought of as "America," that corporate entity that conceived, financed, and largely staffed the research, development, production, and delivery of Fat Man and Little Boy. In some literal and important sense, of course, the "cause" of the violence can be mechanically traced through a chain of deliberate and identifiably "American" decisions. As one hibakusha put it, "An atomic bomb is quite different from a landslide. One never falls unless someone drops it."[28] It is with an insistence that has grown only more shrill over the decades, as if this simple information were in danger of being forgotten, that one Hiroshima writer recently said: "There is only this unalterable fact: that two cities were deliberately bombed—by American airmen, by the order of an American president, and with weapons made in America and loaded onto American planes."[29] Yet though we all know who (or, at least, that someone) dropped the bomb, "America" remains relatively absent from the pages of atomic-bomb literature—almost as if it were too remote, or perhaps too large, an idea to encompass meaningfully in works otherwise occupied with detailing the minutiae of the immediate deaths of Japanese individuals.

Throughout the history of Japanese atomic-bomb literature this absence has inspired controversy with very large stakes. Ōe Kenzaburō was vociferously criticized for his near total neglect of human responsibility for the bomb in his *Hiroshima Notes*. Why, some of his subjects queried, does Ōe seem to equate the bombing of Hiroshima with a "plague" or a "flood"? Where, others suspiciously wondered, is the assailant in Ōe's account of the victims? Even more accusatory is the character in Takahashi Kazumi's novel *The Melancholy Faction* who makes this criticism of his friend's manuscript on the lives of Hiroshima survivors:

> You are trying to turn the atomic bomb into an eschatological theory, as if it were related to apocalyptical thought, the cooling of the universe,

natural selection, or a near-miss with Halley's Comet. Well, I can't go along with you. The atomic bomb is a military weapon. And just as there are its victims, there are also without a doubt those people who dropped it on them. (122–23)

But such an accusation, and all it legitimately implies, might just as well have been pointed at the testimonial and documentary work of such pioneering hibakusha writers as Hara Tamiki and Ōta Yōko, neither of whom felt compelled to advertise or even determine culpability. Seeing America as the cause of Hiroshima, noted Ōta, is finally an emotional response, however satisfying: what of Japan, which doggedly pursued a war already over?[30] Indeed, despite the widespread reputation of atomic-bomb literature as anti-American, in fact "America" recedes from view in most examples of the genre, stubbornly irrelevant to the significance of Hiroshima if not its history. The scale of atomic-bomb writers' grief suggests it is only minimally consolable through the catharsis of rage. It also suggests that here is a grief whose roots are hardly comprehensible as the work of a "nation," a concept intellectually valid but emotionally worthless. In Ochi Michio's 1969 short story "The Life Left Us" (Izō sareta seikatsu), two Hiroshima hibakusha find that the imminent birth of their child inspires a decidedly mixed set of feelings. "Assuming that nothing happens to terminate the life of this fetus, his birth will be the very best revenge we are capable of," they reason. "But revenge against what? The *Enola Gay*? Truman?" (221). It is as if the victims were so overpowered by the bomb's effects that its culpable origins are rendered hopelessly abstruse and even ultimately pointless. "Against whom," wonders Marguerite Duras in *Hiroshima Mon Amour*, "the anger of entire cities?" Nowhere in Tōge Sankichi's *Poems of the Atomic Bomb*, for example, do the words "America" or "United States"— possible retorts to Duras's question—occur (nor does "atomic bomb," despite the collection's title), and perhaps for the reasons powerfully stated in Takenishi Hiroko's story, "The Rite":

The great anger, the deep hate, come after the event. The thing . . . that made me cower all night in a hollow in the ground—if I could catch the real nature of that thing and fling the fullness of my anger and hate at it, I would not be in torment this day, well over ten years after, tied to this fierce anger that still finds no proper outlet. I would not be tortured by this nameless hate that yet finds no clear object. (194–95)

Holocaust literature, to cite what may be the closest thematic parallel, seems largely spared of the problems faced by Japanese atomic-bomb writers attempting to fix responsibility for their anger and suffering. It is easier, one imagines, for camp survivors to hate a notion of a proximate "Germany," and to make such an abstraction the target of their anger. Although many victims of the Nazis presumably felt betrayed when the culture that had nurtured them suddenly turned on them, it was still with relatively few complications that Jews could render Adolf Hitler's Germany a consummate evil, a country linked to the fate on one man upon whom rage could be focused. This could not so easily be done by the Japanese regarding America. In the minds of many, America did bring an unpopular war to an end. It is still not hard nowadays, despite how well the facts are known, to find Japanese who will eagerly tell an American how America did "us" a favor by dropping the bomb.

In point of fact, America (in a formulation that coincides with the bomb-dropping "America") did introduce many reforms during the postwar Occupation which progressive Japanese, including a number of hibakusha, surely welcomed. Feelings toward America in Japan have long been ambiguous, tinged with both envy and resentment. The United States has been in relatively quick historical succession a model, an enemy, an occupier, an ally. Since the war and until rather recently, America has been linked in the minds of many Japanese as materially and ideologically the source of much that is desirable. The especially contradictory feelings of identification and estrangement that some Japanese—in particular intellectuals—have harbored quietly and not so quietly for America have complicated the genre of atomic-bomb literature and its reputation from their very beginnings. In her story "In the Hills" (Sanjō, 1953), Ōta Yōko describes an encounter with an American officer who has come to caution her about the implied anti-American content of her work. She curses herself for having been courteous to him, but she could not have done otherwise. Robert Jay Lifton has noted "the special psychological use Japanese have made of their relationship to America and Americans in their struggles for self-definition and autonomy; their need to absorb what they perceive to be 'American' as a means of creating themselves. More than simply a mentor, America becomes a kind of psycho-historical 'double' or alter ego."[31]

It is all too easy, though misleading, to read the views of Japanese intellectuals towards the United States in such psychological terms. There is a history to take note of here that has little to do with Oedipus. As I have suggested, there might just as well be more compelling, and generic, factors related to the particular nature of modern atrocity that makes the application of the traditional antagonist-protagonist axis unsatisfactory. These are factors perhaps symbolized by Hiroshima and Nagasaki, but they have been surely evolving over time as "antagonist" and "protagonist" is an evermore dubious choice of nomenclature. The First World War, certainly, came as a technological surprise to its participants: poison gas and the machine gun enabled killing on a massive, and impersonal, scale achieved in no prior European conflict. As a result literature between the wars increasingly dwelled on the newly problematic relationship between the victim and assailant. Works like *All Quiet on the Western Front* take place in a world of trenches, the enemy unseen. Yet, he is still imaginable; the soldier's counterpart is there, just over the ridge, in his own trench.

Technology by Remarque's time may have already rendered the force destroying us perceptually untenable, but it would not be until the Second World
War that that force became morally overwhelming as well. And *under*whelming:
putting men in planes saves them from Hannah Arendt's famously stated problem of "the animal pity by which all normal men are affected in the presence
of physical suffering."[32] Matsumoto Hiroshi, attuned to this shift, has noted the
complexity—indeed, the impossibility—of ever defining the terms "victim"
(*higaisha*) and "victimizer" (*kagaisha*) within modern technological civilization
and the totalizing state.[33] Iida Momo in his *An American Hero* has an American
character note that "the dead aren't only Japanese. Chinese, Koreans, Indone-
sians, Burmese, Thais, White Russians and our own guys, white and black"
(390). In other words, the spectrum of victims can conceivably mean that any
of us are potentially fellow victims; there is also the implicit suggestion that
the victimizer is also ourselves, i.e., indistinguishable from "victim." Indeed,
the bomb did not discriminate; it did not check passports. When the prized
product of modern civilization is pitted against itself, the victimizer might in
fact be victimizing himself, especially when that person's means—in the case
of Hiroshima and Nagasaki, aggressive adaptations of nuclear fission—are seen
as suicidal. A kind of closed circle is created: an origin-less chase of death
triggered by irresolvable issues, dominated by technology beyond our, much
less any one individual's, control.

The survivors of Hiroshima and Nagasaki often seemed to intuit the rami-
fications of these weapons for our traditional models of a "crime": hence the
unexpected scarcity, perhaps, of strident anti-American sentiment in their
works. Their concern is with something even more disturbing, but perhaps less
conventionally available: as Kurihara Sadako has written, "One might say that
human beings are human when they respond to an inhuman act with hate. Not
being able to respond with hate is to be in a state less than human."[34] That is
precisely the state of Kurihara's mind: it is unreasonable to assume hibakusha
will act normally when they have been treated so *ab*normally. Our desire to
experience the brunt of their absent hate is our insistence on seeing them as
less damaged than they are. We seek their recuperation so as to excuse ourselves.

But in fact the victimizer is diffuse, unnameable in whole; and the victims
are stunned into a silence on the question of blame that only further incapaci-
tates in a way that prefigures our own recent powerlessness under the nuclear
hegemony, the hegemony that Western nuclear criticism sought to disclose as
rhetoric masquerading as *realpolitik*. For the Japanese, however, and for their
atomic-bomb literature, the result has been the conspicuous lack of the dramatic confrontation of "good" versus "evil," murderer versus innocent that our
narratives until the twentieth century have usually readied us for. Who, after
all, is really putting Kafka's K on trial? The modern world has ceased to worry

greatly about the absolute origins of its actions (indeed, their lack of such is one important premise of our present Western nuclear criticism); yet, and so graphically for the Japanese, the ends of those actions remain unquestionably here with us. We might find this unsettling, not only because it leaves us historically uncertain and ethically empty-handed, but because so much atomic-bomb literature categorically declines to cooperate with any form of emotional compensation, which is to say any further sanction of the violence. An atomic-bomb literature that proclaims a hate for things American would make things "equal" between us; that has not happened. What does occur is that each reader of atomic-bomb literature is drawn into a moral quagmire: if the sum total of the story is not simply an elaboration of exchange between victim and victim-izer, there is suddenly and uncomfortably new room provided for the reader, too. Where, after all, is the bystander (those of us not American or Japanese; those of us born after 1945) in the ethical implications of Hiroshima and Naga-saki? Perhaps squarely with evil: for anyone reading today must ask if survival is complicit with the political and technological regimes that leave us provisionally alive.

■

Oda Makoto, born in 1932, is an exceptional essayist, novelist, and activist who nonetheless typifies in many ways the post-Second World War Japanese intellectual both attracted to American cultural and political idealism and disillusioned by the blatant abuses of American power and wealth. Raised in Osaka—a city so devastated by conventional bombing that it was not seriously entertained as a target for either of the atomic bombs—Oda was in his first year of middle school when the war ended. Although he had, along with so many Japanese, suffered hunger, displacement, and air raids in the last years of the war, Oda recalls that he reacted to Japan's defeat with "neither joy nor sadness," a remark that already points to the adult Oda's estranged relationship with state authority and national identity. Nonetheless, the surrender and all it implied about his country's touted superiority certainly made an impression on the adolescent Oda. It was an impression he put into words when, soon after, he precociously embarked on a writing career. While still in high school he wrote and had published a novel entitled *Notes on the Day After Tomorrow* (Asatte no shuki, 1951), in retrospect not much more than juvenilia but which at the time attracted attention and marked Oda as someone to watch as a writer of promise. In 1952 he entered the University of Tokyo and selected the unfashionable major of classical Greek, though in fact he spent most of his time writing fiction. Upon graduation he supported himself as an English teacher until, in the spring of 1958, he won a Fulbright Scholarship to study at Harvard.

While abroad he traveled (on the proverbial "one dollar a day" budget) widely through Canada, Mexico, and India. He returned to Japan in 1960 just in time to participate in the most radicalizing event of his generation, namely the mass demonstrations and eventually riots in Tokyo against the renewal of the Japanese security treaty (*Ampo*) with the United States. Oda, who enjoyed his time in the United States, had no problem opposing what was widely seen as the imposition of American imperialism over Japanese sovereignty; even then in Oda's mind, there was apparently America the "country" and America the "state," and the distinction would remain a crucial one for him and indeed for his generation of like-minded left-wing Japanese intellectuals.

After resuming his duties as an English teacher, he wrote an entertaining travelogue account of his extensive and, for the time, exceedingly rare international travels, *I'll Give Anything A Look* (Nan de mo mite yarō, 1961). This best-seller established Oda's fame as a writer and his credentials as a social critic, as well as his claim to be a spokesman for a postwar generation ready to experience the world outside of Japan. Ōe Kenzaburō lauded it for its frankness, and consequently Oda was welcomed to the ranks Ōe already inhabited, namely those of liberal or leftist critics of the West—which is to say, of America—who were nonetheless steeped in and dedicated to the celebrated American, at the time specifically Kennedyesque, ideals of individual freedom and social egalitarianism.

Oda soon completed another and perhaps his most famous novel, *America* (Amerika, 1962). *America* is the story of a Japanese trading company employee sent to business school in the American south. His mission is to help pave the way for his company's expansion into the American market, but what happens instead is that this employee forsakes his identity as a company man and consequently "finds himself" through his interaction with American friends, his participation in the civil rights movement, and an affair with a white woman. He comes to view life as he knew it in Japan as unacceptably straitened—he not only turns down the hand of his company president's daughter in marriage, but he seems to have irrevocably decided to stay in America forever, as an "American." In a remark typical of the novel, the hero says "I want to be myself . . . I want to live my own life my own way." Such freedom is equated with the American identity: *America* is a novel which struck a responsive chord in its readers, despite the continuing resentment of America after the security treaty riots. The dream of an unencumbered life in America was one shared by many of Oda's generation, as was the realization that such freedom was not always enjoyed by the citizens of America's client states elsewhere in the world, or even by all Americans.

In one brief essay Oda is quite candid about his obsession with America, an obsession that led him to write this novel:

No doubt I wanted to possess my own "America." Ever since I can remember I have always had "America" in front of me. . . . In the deepest
recesses of my mind—no, my body—"America" has always existed. The
"America" of skyscrapers, the "America" of the Texas desert, the
"America" of small Midwestern towns . . . the "America" of Vietnam,
the "America" of Son My, white "America," black "America," yellow
"America" . . . all the "Americas" deep inside me intertwined and mixed
together. Nonetheless, there has always been one wall over there, one
that I would, should I give it a name, would have to be my "America."
Yet that, probably, is in fact my very own self.[35]

Oda's projection of his "self" onto his imagination of a bracketed "America"
serves as a dialogue he conducts between the private real and the social ideal.
None of this would be unusual for other postwar Japanese intellectuals both
enthralled by American cosmopolitanism and disenchanted with the same's betrayal of its own professed principles, but in Oda Makoto the split, and exceedingly personal, nature of his contradictory feelings of affection for American
culture and of resentment against American power is conspicuously stark.
America is an example of that half of his work which describes the affection: but
only a few years later, Oda career would take an explicitly political direction
that seemed to punctuate the depth of the resentment.

In the spring of 1965, Oda was one of the founding intellectuals of the
League of Citizens' Movements for Peace in Vietnam (Betonamu ni heiwa o!
Shimin Rengō), more familiarly known in English by its Japanese acronym,
Beheiren. The umbrella organization for the anti-Vietnam war movement in
Japan, Beheiren repudiated the notion of a "leadership" but was, in fact, coordinated largely by Oda. He led the organization in often dramatically subversive
activities. Soon recognizing the need to go beyond simply educating the Japanese public on the issues at stake in Vietnam, Beheiren went so far as to set up
antiwar underground cells on American military installations in Japan, and
even to assist U.S. soldiers who wished to desert. Beheiren was from the start
an organization that engaged "America" far more than it did "Vietnam," a fact
not inconsistent with Oda's announced interests and even obsessions. Addressing his role in encouraging U.S. Army desertions, Oda has said "I could
sympathize easily with the young American draftees because I had been in the
United States. I saw the draftees as victims of their own government as well as
aggressors against the Vietnamese."[36] In other words, Oda's actions in Beheiren
both undermined and bolstered his "America." He worked against government
policy while helping individual Americans victimized by that same policy. He
was able both to assert his values of self-determination for the Vietnamese, and
to put himself in a position to help Americans be, in his view, more genuinely
American.

At the same time, within Beheiren Oda was able to put into practice his theory of the individual's relationship to power. The "young American draftees" were perfect examples of that relationship: both the victimizers of the Vietnamese and the victims of their own government, they—like all of us, Oda would argue—are implicated as the subjects and objects of power. It is only the propaganda of the state which convinces us we are one or the other. In fact, we are both. This idea of the individual and his multivalent relationship to state authority applied full well, in Oda's argument, to the Japanese themselves. Early in 1967 Oda wrote: "Realistically speaking, we [Japanese] are all guilty of complicity in the Vietnam War. We must recognize that each of us is among the perpetrators."[37] But elsewhere Oda has noted that Japan was a victim of that same war as well, and that in fact those two conditions are necessarily intertwined:

> Our country was a kind of "forced aggressor" in the [Vietnam] war. Because of the security treaty, Japan had to cooperate with the American policy of aggression. In this sense Japan was a victim of its alliance with that policy, but it was also an aggressor toward the small countries in Indochina.[38]

In one sense this complicity of the victimized with the victimizer made Oda's anti-American rhetoric, while vitriolic, forgiving as well. Even as he wrote about American aggression with distaste, he continued to write about an essentially "good" American culture with affection, and with an affection in direct conflict with the disdain he has for the values of his own society. For example, from the very start Beheiren had close relations with the New Left in the United States. Oda often traveled to America to meet with its leaders and express solidarity with the "struggle" of the American "people," a struggle described in strikingly similar terms to that of the Vietnamese. Oddly, Beheiren allowed Oda to be evermore distinctly *pro*-American and *anti*-American: the "Americas" "intertwined" "deep inside" him were played out on the very public stage of the international antiwar movement. When the political scientist Rōyama Michio stated that activist "Beheiren people believed in the ideals of American liberalism," he surely could have cited Oda Makoto as a prime example.[39]

Once Beheiren officially disbanded, Oda continued to perfect his theory of the complicated and ambivalent nature of modern citizenship by exploring the specific relations between Americans, Japanese, and other Asians. Under the title *Son My* (Son Mi) he translated Seymour Hersh's *My Lai 4: A Report on the Massacre and Its Aftermath*, an American work by an American author about an atrocity perpetrated against Asians. It is a book that in both English and Japanese translation powerfully contrasts the naivete of U.S. soldiers with the depravity of their actions. But in the Japanese edition alone do we read of a translator, Oda Makoto, who identifies with both Hersh and the Vietnamese villagers. As he writes in his translator's introduction, what is so fascinating as well as horrible about Son My is Lieutenant Calley's very ordinariness: ordinary like us, and thus so little different. Victimizer, victim, and even reader are construed as essentially overlapping identities, albeit placed in provisionally different circumstances. Unlike many Japanese intellectuals, for whom their Japanese identity is crucial to the way they choose to interpret the world, Oda Makoto looks upon such national labels as ideologically imposed and regulatory.

The point here is not to hold Oda up as someone unusual among Japanese intellectuals. Peers who are both attracted and repulsed by American rhetoric and American power are rife, and are found of course among American intellectuals as well. Rather, the point is to establish the very important concerns and passions that would have to inform a work of atomic-bomb literature written by such an intellectual. For Oda, the theme of such a work cannot possibly remain narrowly "Hiroshima" or "Nagasaki" for long. Indeed, from the first page there will have to be an "America" too, and "America" as a source of not only what destroys but what sustains as well. Such a work will have to draw not into a contradiction—but rather a dialectic—Hiroshima, Nagasaki, and the American challenge, ideological and otherwise, to a world that despite quiet misgivings and loud protests continues to admire much of the famed American way of life.

■

Before Oda Makoto himself turned to these themes, there were a small but significant number of works of Japanese atomic-bomb literature that had already explored the relationship between America, Japan, and the ethical issues of nuclear war. All these works interestingly chose to work loosely with the historical figure of Major Claude Robert Eatherly, famed pilot of the weather plane (*Straight Flush*: a reference not to cards, but to a toilet) that flew with the *Enola Gay* over Hiroshima and whose later mental illness was widely (though erroneously) attributed to that assignment. In 1960, for instance, Hotta Yoshie published *The Judgment* (Shimpan), a novel whose principal character "Paul," a crew member of the Hiroshima bombing mission, ends up in a mental ward; a Japanese character, Takagi, similarly pays a heavy price for his complicity in Japanese atrocities committed in China. Miyamoto Ken's stage drama *The Pilot*, produced in 1965, also contemplates the fate of an Eatherly-based American character. Both works are notable for their attempt to view the bombings from the perspective of one who facilitated its initial deployment, rather than solely from that of those who suffered its effects and consequences. Matsumoto Hiroshi, for example, said of *The Judgment* that it was a work in which Hotta, not himself a hibakusha, dealt with issues—namely the extent and nature of ethical responsibility—Hiroshima writers themselves would have to face; and *The Pilot* was hailed by another critic as "the model for a literature of the victimizer."[40]

But it was Iida Momo's 1965 *An American Hero* that most spectacularly and controversially reassigned the typical point of view in Japanese atomic-bomb literature, and so forced it to reinterpret the historical and moral contexts of Hiroshima and Nagasaki. "Unprecedented in the history of Japanese litera-ture," writes Tsurumi Shunsuke of Iida's work; "No Japanese character appears in the whole of the long novel."[41] Its first person narrator, never named, is like Claude Eatherly a participant in the mission over Hiroshima, but it is never made clear precisely what his role was. Similarly, despite the novel's combina-tion of "mockery, fluidity, and Marxist dogma in its forays through madness and sanity, guilt and retribution,"[42] it is never clear whether this American char-acter is normal, insane, or criminal. As if a mystery novel, *An American Hero* begins with its character in a Texas mental hospital—just why we do not know. As his past becomes somewhat clearer (but never clear), the reader travels with him through an America reminiscent of the images propagated in Hollywood movies and television.[43] Eventually this character, who has called himself "the first criminal of the new age" (140) and who was "destroyed in that single strike against Hiroshima" (326), makes a visit to postwar Nagasaki and confronts the impossibility of ever reconciling himself to what a history for which bears par-tial responsibility has wrought, an impossibility that prompted one critic to call *An American Hero* "a modern *Don Quixote*."[44]

It is just such surfeit of irony, however, that makes *An American Hero* an intriguing example not merely of atomic-bomb literature but of the Japanese intelligentsia's highly conflicted fascination with the power and appeal of the United States in the early 1960s. In his "Afterword" to the novel, Iida speaks plainly of this. He says that *An American Hero* is his "essay on the United States of America," and he likens himself to a small boy in a Japanese village ponder-ing "Number One" North American civilization—a civilization that, in its de-cline, reminds him of the now-lost Mayans, Aztecs, and Incas. Yet while he sees America as a culture perhaps fatally flawed, Iida admits to his obsession with it, and moreover to his faith in the "American proletariat" (428).

Oda Makoto's own attempt to combine in fiction the events of August 1945 with a discourse on the nature of American culture and life, his novel *Hiroshima* (Hiroshima, 1981), also exhibits on nearly each page a similar split between a desire to identify with Americans and a need to criticize their collec-tive complicity in a terrible history. *Hiroshima* is the only work of Japanese atomic-bomb literature mentioned in this study which has a Roman letter, i.e., English, title. From the very start it is a work American in its settings and char-acterizations. Moreover, it is not a novel properly "about" Hiroshima at all. Only a very few pages speak of August 6th, and even those are from a non-Japanese perspective. *Hiroshima* is a long, nearly epic, work that not only chronologically spans the dense history from the eve of Pearl Harbor to an indeterminate present day, but geographically ranges across America and the South Pacific as well as Japan. Its more than eighty characters include Americans of European, Japanese, African, and Native American ancestry; even the characters in Japan are not all Japanese, but include in their number Koreans, Southeast Asians, Japanese-Americans and, as P.O.W.'s, white Americans, too. There is a sweep of history and locale here not encountered in any other work of Japanese atomic-bomb literature. The "totality"—*zentaisei*, an word often used in the book's reviews—of the work's scope usurps the place of any single main character. Its ambition is to describe the thrust of an apparently unstoppable movement of institutional, even cosmological, forces: *Hiroshima* strives to be a sum of diverse parts constituting what life in an international "nuclear age" might really mean. Oda attempts to dislodge talk of the atomic bombings from the Japanese victims' perspective and shift it, imaginatively, elsewhere. Of course such efforts excite some readers as a bold work pioneering a genuinely new direction, while they disturb others as a trivialization of an event that in its destruction was effectively Japanese and not otherwise (one reviewer called its characters "cartoonish" and "stereotypical";[45] this the price, perhaps, of reaching for an imaginative breadth rather than depth). But these same efforts seem to parallel in interesting ways the movement of nuclear criticism in the West to universalize, as "discourse" or "textuality" instead of literal occurrence, much the same history as does Oda.

Yet as is nearly always the case, Japanese writings on Hiroshima trace their origins to a lived experience and not a theoretical precept, and this is true of Oda Makoto as well. Oda's consistent interest in the relations between victimizer and victimized—actually, the relations between each self's role as both victim and victimizer, relations subsumed in Oda's term "complementarity"[46]—is one inspired by his own wartime experiences in Japan in conjunction with his experiences as an ambivalent purveyor and critic of American values after 1945. In the same essay where he writes "it is impossible to speak of the experience as victim without including the experience as victimizer,"[47] Oda reminisces about his childhood:

> Having endured the Osaka air raids on three occasions in my youth, I later became obsessed with curiosity about how the scene must have looked from the air, from the perspective of victimizer. I embraced that strange curiosity for twenty-one years after the war, but I only understood its true meaning in the library of a small, rural college in the United States. There, when I saw a *New York Times* news photo, my heart leapt. The caption read, "Osaka Air Raid." I realized that I had been under all that smoke, and in that instant I relived my own experience as victim,

and that of each of my countrymen. On second thought, I saw that photo itself was unimpressive, nothing but tall, black columns rising into the air. It was just an abstract, impersonal picture of smoke—the sort I had glanced indifferently at in the past. If we were to carry this indifference a step further, is it clearly distinguishable from the indifference displayed by the pilot as he calmly drops bombs, calling forth a hell of suffering and smoke? (159)

Oda's ease in regarding himself as both the subject and object of the exercise of alienated violence replicates his duality as both a Japanese and an Americanized intellectual. This stimulates his desire to make plain the interrelations between this version of history mutually implicating both sides of his own experience and that of historical Japanese-American ties. The essay from which the above is quoted, "The Ethics of Peace," was written in 1968 at the height of Oda's involvement with another war. But the questions he then asked, and the propositions he then put forth, seem to be the ones he sought to explore the most fully in his atomic-bomb novel written over a decade later. *Hiroshima* is the work in which he most earnestly tries not so much to "relativize" notions of victim and victimizer as to *fix* them solidly within the individual lives of his novel's American, Japanese, and other characters. *Hiroshima*, then, is the response to the need noted by Oda with frustration some dozen years earlier:

Why have we no records of wartime experience as victimizer? Not objective, third-person accounts, but personal records similar to all those relating experience as victim. If that's too much to ask, just a collection of candid war stories, blurted out to close friends after a couple of beers, would do. When placed side by side with all those experiences as victim (they might be written by the same people) their intertwining complicity would become clear.[48]

This "intertwining complicity" is in fact the theme of *Hiroshima*. Unlike any other work of atomic-bomb literature, Oda's novel seeks to retell the events of August 6th as an example of how many peoples, not just the Japanese, are governed by the dictates of the modern state telling us which side we are on, when in fact the issue of "sides" is too hopelessly contradicted by the complexities of our actual lives to allow an unambiguous resolution. It is in this sense that Oda's *Hiroshima* anticipates the West's high-academic practice of "nuclear criticism." It is also in this sense, however, that *Hiroshima*, as a work written by an author who saw the Osaka air raids from the ground, implicitly criticizes that same nuclear criticism for its insufficient account of the history that underlies not only the postwar atomic age but also such intellectual discourse itself.

■

Hiroshima is divided into three parts, but the first alone accounts for over three-fourths of the novel's length. It opens in rural New Mexico, near White Sands, in the year 1941. Joe Clancey, Oda's initial central character, is a nineteen year-old ranch hand whose simple life ends when he is drafted into the military after the attack on Pearl Harbor. Others find their lives changed just as suddenly. For a moment, the venue of the novel shifts to Southern California, where the Japanese-American Nakata family—minus youngest son Tommy, who is studying in Japan near Hiroshima—finds itself abruptly ordered to an internment camp. One of the older Nakata boys, Henry, eventually enlists in the American military. The other, Norm, becomes a "no-no boy" who is sent to prison for his refusal to declare his loyalties either way.

Tommy, however, is the Nakata who figures most prominently in *Hiroshima*, especially once Oda shifts the setting of his story to Japan. Tommy—now renamed Tomio—becomes fanatically pro-Japanese once his learns of his family's treatment in racist America. Oda goes on to describe, however, similarly degrading conditions in Japan, primarily through the depiction of the life of Ulsun, a Korean woman brought to Japan as a child and now living in a Hiroshima slum. She is the victim both of individual prejudice and economic oppression because of her ethnicity; but similarly ostracized is Sakaguchi Keiji, a classmate of Tomio's. Like Tomio, Keiji found himself taunted in school, not for being American but for being from the big city of Osaka. Keiji wishes to be treated like everyone else, which is to say as a patriotic Japanese and not as an effeminate weakling unaccustomed to country life. While on his morning run one day—"running" is the one common link all of Oda's sympathetic male characters share—Keiji wonders if there is not someone like himself in America, someone for whom each other is the enemy:

> While running a thought came to him. It came suddenly, and it filled his mind completely. At first it was the question of what, at just this moment, this very instant, a young man his own age far away on the other side of the Pacific, in the enemy country of the United States, might be doing. . . . This question, which had never before occurred to Keiji, at some point turned into the idea that a young man his own age, with the same thin physique and skinny limbs, was at this exact time himself running intently somewhere in the enemy nation across the ocean. Keiji could clearly picture that youth running and panting, just like himself. He was the "enemy." Then it dawned on Keiji that *he* was that boy's own enemy. (148–49)

Such moments in *Hiroshima*, when characters suddenly perceive not only their own situations but see them as mutually imbricated with those of others, are many. It seems key to Oda's purposes in his novel that the experiences of his characters overlap, duplicate, predict, and, most powerfully, render ironic those of each other. For just this reason, the most sustained treatment of any nationality in this Japanese novel is that of the Americans, or more precisely that of Americans neither European nor Japanese in ancestry but rather Native American. Like some other Japanese intellectuals of his generation, Oda Makoto evidences a special fascination for Native Americans, apparently in part because of a perception of their intermediary position as "Americans" genetically if distantly as "Asiatic" as the Japanese themselves. Native Americans, in other words, represent an imaginatively vicarious point of view for the Japanese—certainly for Oda—and it is for just this unique perspective that guarantees the Native Americans in *Hiroshima* the pivotal role.

Near the town where Joe worked before enlisting is a Hopi settlement. The tribe, however, once occupied what is now White Sands, a place it still considers an important ceremonial ground. Most prominent among Oda's Hopi characters in the first part of the novel is a former Olympic runner named Chuck. As caretaker of his tribe's ancient myths, Chuck decides to pass them on to the next generation through his nephew Ron. The essence of these myths, as revealed to Ron, consists of a cosmology of four worlds, each of a color corresponding to the principal human races but of which the first three have, save for the few good people, been destroyed by a Hopi god angry each time humankind forgot its essential unity and began to differentiate languages and skin color. Chuck warns Ron that time may be running out for the present and fourth world—1942 is a violent year—and preparations must be maintained for the preservation of the good people once more.

Chuck shows Ron a covered pit in the middle of the White Sands desert. This is the most sacred site of the tribe, the hole into which the good people will flee when the god of the Hopis sees fit to destroy the fourth world for its sins. Chuck has foreseen this coming in his dreams. Indeed, it is not long afterwards—but following Chuck's death—that Ron is led one day by a mysterious voice resembling that of his uncle back to White Sands. Driven to obey, Ron scales the barriers erected by the military to hide its secret weapons project and hides in the Hopi sanctuary pit. He waits and watches as soldiers scurry about a single tall tower, and just at the moment he stands atop a ladder to get a better view, a powerful explosion knocks him down and burns into his eyes the brilliant scene of the end of the world foretold in the tribal myths. What Ron has witnessed, of course, is the July 16, 1945 test of Trinity—the world's first nuclear bomb. Ron has been made the world's first hibakusha. Soon he falls quite ill, and loses all his hair. Neither a citizen of Hiroshima nor even a

Japanese (but, importantly, a person whose roots are both Asian and North American), Ron represents in Oda Makoto's nuclear age the perfect trope of the modern victim: an uncomprehending and innocent casualty whose identity is not readily equated with that of any one nation or culture.

With this dramatic start of the nuclear era—here dated several weeks earlier than in any other work of Japanese atomic-bomb literature—Oda moves the reader much closer to the climax of his novel. The story shifts to the South Pacific, where Joe Clancey finds himself in the summer of 1945 on a small island—unnamed, but surely Tinian—for a brief refueling stop. He is headed for Okinawa, where he will participate in aerial bombing raids against the Japanese home islands. Joe nervously jokes with his friends that God in his wisdom made Tinian in the shape of an aircraft carrier. He hears that a ship has recently brought a secret weapon—something like a rocket—to the island. It is a weapon, he hears, that will kill a lot of Japanese.

Joe is still ignorant as to the true nature of the secret weapon when, on a conventional bombing sortie, his plane is shot down over the Hiroshima suburbs and he becomes a prisoner of war. We are now at the penultimate moment of the long-deferred culmination of the novel—no other major work of atomic-bomb literature so keeps the reader waiting for the events of August 6th— but still Oda refuses to present the actual blast over Hiroshima as it typically has been told. Although he returns the action to Hiroshima—actually, to a hospital just outside of it—the precise moment is narrated through the eyes of minor character Iwata Kyōko, who is paying a sick call on Abdullah Hassan, an Indonesian student. Just as Iwata walks into Hassan's room, she hears screams and then sees a flash. Here, with no further elaboration save a possible allusion to the *Iliad,* with its opening scene of an angry Apollo raining down arrows upon the men of Akhaia ("Nine days the arrows of the god came down"),[49] the novel's first part comes to its conclusion. In other words, Japan's nuclear conflagration is predicted with imagery borrowed from the Hopi and described with imagery taken from the Greeks whom Oda studied at university. He forcefully makes his point that Hiroshima was in many ways an international event.

This ambitious project, namely the redefinition of August 6th as a broadly human and not just Japanese historical event, proceeds not only with these cosmopolitan references at the end of the novel's part one, but culminates in its part two—a part as brief (eight pages) as the first was long. As it begins, we readers have arrived at the point we have anticipated, but we are still kept at arm's length from a direct view, or indeed at first from any view at all. In part one we were left in a suburb in the company of minor characters; we expect part two to describe the actual destruction of the city, perhaps through the eyes of Tomio or Keiji. But such a picture of Hiroshima, and such a release from the dramatic tension developed thus far in the novel, is not to be. Our considerable suspense as the second part of *Hiroshima* opens—namely, from which of the many perspectives Oda has created will the incineration of the city be described?—is frustrated, turned back onto itself and reversed, almost as if Oda is suggesting that this is the wrong question for us to ask. It is only very gradually that Oda makes his narrative perspective plain. The second section starts: "How, or to where, he was walking, there was no way to guess" (321). All that the antecedent-less "he" knows is that "he" is being pursued by fires. How many days since he was brought to this place, he does not know. Rather, understanding stops at the fact that he darkness he experiences now is different from the darkness of his cell.

At this point the reader has sufficient clues to guess the identity of Oda's Hiroshima narrator. The interior monologue that comprises the entirety of the brief second section of *Hiroshima* transpires within the thoughts of P.O.W. Joe Clancey. Our guess is confirmed when his mind flashes back to his hometown; next, in a dizzying race of free associations, he recalls being dragged out of his cell into the open several days earlier by the Japanese military police as an air raid siren wails. "That is your country coming to bomb us," he is told by a guard. "That is your country coming to kill you" (233). And indeed, it was in that prison courtyard that Joe was standing when America—his "own country," whatever that notion means by this point in Oda's novel—does subject him to a nuclear attack.

Blinded and disoriented, Joe stumbles through the hot rubble. His body feels as if burdened with a heavy weight. The darkness seems infinite, and he is unable to gauge the passage of time. The world, he intuits, is destroyed; he knows he is in a sea of fire, corpses, fragments of tile. Only gradually does his sight, and his ability to infer from what he increasingly senses, return; and it is accompanied by a growing incredulity. If only he knew what time it is, he says to himself, he could go on living. Miraculously, he finds a watch; its hands, however, have stopped at eight-fifteen.

As consciousness returns, so does his awareness of exhaustion and thirst. "Give me water," he moans repeatedly as he nears the center of the city—the center that so many of *Hiroshima*'s characters earlier strolled—and encounters more fire, more dead. Some of the corpses—no, surely their ghosts, Joe reasons—move towards him. They are so horribly disfigured they must come from another world; and then Joe realizes he looks no different himself.

One of the "ghosts"—one who reminds Joe of the Indians back home—sees that Joe, despite his disfigurement, is not Japanese. "You American!" he gasps, and soon word spreads that the enemy is there among them. Many "ghosts" start to move towards Joe; a voice from Joe's life back in the desert warns him to run, run as fast as he did on the desert plain of White Sands. But such advice is too late, or perhaps Joe is simply unable to summon such energy.

It was too late to do anything. The ghosts were coming to attack a ghost. They were summoning what little strength remained in their bodies to pounce upon him, another ghost. The dying ran over the dead—the dead over the dying—in getting to him. Using all his might he tried to push through them to run away, but the ghosts kept piling atop themselves in wave after wave, and he was unable to move at all underneath the weight of the heap. . . . Only the dead were within the flames. They were the only ones left behind. Both the ones trying to finish one off, and the one trying not to let that happen, were piled up like so much garbage in the dark depths of a hell burning high with crimson flames; both died excruciating deaths even as they lived by struggling with each other with what little strength remained in their moribund state. He had now closed both of his eyes, but he thought he could see clearly how it all looked. His progressively weak consciousness of himself ("I . . .") and his words that would follow (". . . am here for what . . . ?") changed to take a plural subject. ("We . . .") Those were the final words that passed through his mind.

A rain began to fall upon the heap of garbage. It was a rain like black mud. (238)

Despite this section's brevity, in it Oda has accomplished something without precedent in Japanese atomic-bomb literature. The selection of an American as point of view into the actual site of the atomic explosion may seem unusual, even insensitive in its promotion of an atypical victim, but it is a choice entirely respectful of the promise he once made to the effect that there are some things only a hibakusha has the right to describe.[50] For Oda the line of demarcation is between the supple states of victimhood and nonvictimhood, not between "American," "Japanese," or any other variety of reified national identity. For him to have chosen a character to represent Hiroshima who is not Japanese is in effect to make that less a "Japanese" event and more a "historical" event that should resist any one nation's, as opposed to any one individual's, claim to a unique victimization. Joe Clancey's shift from his personal "I" to a collective "we" is a reference to a collective hibakusha community, which was international already on August 6th, 1945, and indeed potentially global by the early 1980s.

This universalizing of what happened on a New Mexico testing ground and then in Hiroshima is the task of *Hiroshima*'s third and most boldly imaginative section. In part three the venue shifts from Hiroshima in 1945 to the United States in the present. It is only a vague present, however, because the whole of the novel's third section (a section which might easily be read as a short story in its own right) continues the dream-like mood of the second. Its sometimes real but often surreal narrative involves, once again, characters of diverse racial and national backgrounds brought together under a contemporary nuclear terror. This third part of *Hiroshima* aims for a representation of the modern condition initiated by Hiroshima and Nagasaki unparalleled in earlier atomic-bomb literature. It is ambitiously conceived and executed, and it leads the reader into an area of the fantastic that exploits the skittish post-Hiroshima imagination to encompass a theme of unusual scale.

"Everyone thinks I'm going to die soon," begins part three (241). Again, an unidentified "I" only gradually allows the reader to become aware of place and time. "I" is revealed to be a Native American dying of lung cancer in a charity hospital somewhere in the American Southwest. One of his doctors, a Paris-educated Congolese implausibly named "Winslow," tells him his cancer is likely the consequence of working, like so many of his tribe, in the local uranium mines. He never wanted to go into those mines: located on soil sacred to his people, it was always known that their desecration would lead to something terrible. Winslow is sympathetic. His own father was a miner. Winslow points out to his patient that these uranium mines produced what destroyed Hiroshima and Nagasaki so many years ago, and that the victims in those two cities were from many nations, including red and black men like themselves.

Oda establishes at the outset of this third and final part to his novel that not only is its time that of the present day, but that the international nature of the Hiroshima tragedy described in the first and second parts has now led to the cosmopolitan crisis of a nuclear age, one initiated in a single city—or single test site—but which now extends around the world and is especially acute among those marginal populations most easily discarded. Nuclear technology, in the forms of weapons production and electric power generation, is allowed by the state to ruin the lives of ordinary people. Much of part three goes to great lengths to establish the mutual fate of, and even the possible karmic ties between, men of diverse generations and races universally subordinated by authorities armed with lethal technologies and amoral political wills. One character dreams of another; one race imagines the purgatory of another; one young man relives in terror the suffering of an older one. Most importantly, however, no one victim is spared from having to realize his own acts of victimization. In one dream, for instance, the Native American is told by Winslow that the dead have no names, no genders, no ages; you are Everyman, he is told, and everyone has been burnt black, rendered wretchedly the same by what has been hurled down upon the earth. The Native American protests. He was not responsible. He neither made or dropped "what" was that thing. The dead corpses that surround him in this dream, however, remind him that he did dig "it" up, and is thus an accomplice. What choice did I have? the Indian cries, my children have to eat. "But you dug it up" is all that the dead keep repeating.

As this section progresses we learn that the growing number of patients in the hospital room are—or think they are—reincarnations of characters initially introduced in part one. The first Native American, named Dan, is soon joined by a younger one of a different tribe named Ralph. Though the reader to led to think that Ralph—who is dying of uranium waste-related cancer—is Ron's nephew, Ralph insists on calling himself Ron and on calling Dan "Chuck," i.e., by the name of his own uncle's uncle. As Oda continues to have the lives of his present-day dying patients overlap with the lives (and deaths) of earlier characters, the novel grows almost unmanageably complex. Not only in their dreams but in their insane waking moments, the horrors of what they—or their previous incarnations—once lived through are relived. The third new patient in the room, Glen Taylor, is a bigoted white Marine sergeant who earned a distinguished service record in Vietnam. But it turns out that even he is connected to the fate of the others. His cancer, too, is related to the work he did in the Vietnam War era with a special unit conducting tests with tactical nuclear weapons. His nightmare memories of Vietnam merge with the others' memories of another Asian atrocity, Hiroshima. In yet another twist of the story linked to Oda's notion of our dual roles as both victims and victimizers, the dead return in the patients' fantasies to kill their killers. Everyone is mutually imbricated in an infinite regression of responsibility and suffering. As the dying men in the hospital room grow progressively weaker, the circle of death expands to encompass everyone. In the final scene, Glen, drugged with morphine, believes he has been invited to the White House for a special award ceremony. Dr. Winslow, trying to convince him that cannot be true, notes that in fact tomorrow the Japanese Prime Minister—someone "famous," someone whose name begins with "H"—will be having dinner with the President.

That night, the Ralph/Ron character rouses the Dan/Chuck character. We're all going to Washington now, he explains. Glen is already waiting for them in the helicopter. Piloting the craft, Glen makes an unscheduled stop— presumably at White Sands—to pick up a present to give the heads of government then attending a state dinner at the White House. But at the exact center of history's first ground zero, what they actually pick up is just enough irradiated dirt to fill the lead, coffin-shaped box they had brought with them.

Later, as they approach the White House and catch sight of two flags— the Stars and Stripes and the Rising Sun—the helicopter passengers and pilot are wearing protective radiation suits, the "proper, appropriate" wardrobe for such an occasion. They spot the two national leaders coming out of the White House wearing tuxedos and mounting a special dais. "Time to dump the dirt," says Dr. Winslow, yet another of the passengers; it contains enough radiation to kill them, and so those who killed will now be killed themselves.

But Glen Taylor loses control of the aircraft when he tries to stand upright within the helicopter at the sound of his national anthem being played outside the White House. They crash atop the dais, killing themselves as well as the prime minister and the president. In the final lines of the novel, the reader is taken back to the original charity hospital room, where Dr. Winslow has just pronounced all his cancer patients dead. The fanciful attack on the White House—though hardly more fantastic than much in *Hiroshima*—concludes rather humbly with something quite expected and even routine: the death of cancer victims. But when Winslow says to himself, albeit aloud, "They're all dead," he refers not only to his few patients but in fact to all the characters of *Hiroshima* save himself. "They" may refer specifically to the three deceased patients, but more generally it also includes each important name in *Hiroshima*. This is a novel in which nearly everyone is indicted for his complicit, if varied, role in producing the modern terrors of the atomic bomb, nuclear energy, and state totalitarianism.

At the same time, the entire world is made its own victim, too. Instances of individual victims include Joe Clancey, an American in Japan, or like the Nakatas, Japanese in America; collective instances include the Native Americans, resident in North America but ultimately of Asiatic origins. As symbols of human culture before the imposition of the nation-state and its ideology, the Native Americans may have a special, prescient knowledge of the workings of the world, but they are not spared its fate. No matter whom, all these characters are caught up in a hopelessly intertwined and confused cycle of victimization and victimhood: in other words, in the ways we are forced to live under the obligatory conditions of the nuclear age. *Hiroshima* takes its title from the name of a Japanese city, but its theme hopes to address something more than the local. It purports to be about modern history, ethics, and politics. It is a work that has strayed a long way away from that of the first atomic-bomb writers who found it difficult, at times even impossible, to say anything. Oda is trying, in his way, to say everything.

Hiroshima is not an elegant or even well-written novel. Its message is told somewhat less than subtly, and its characters are embarrassingly one-dimensional. Oda is much more an essayist than he is a novelist. But in his sincere attempt to "say everything," he has brought us not so much to the fringes of an atomic-bomb literature commenced in 1945 as to the start of something quite new, a literature decisively "nuclear" in the way the 1980s have seen that word become one of global concern. Although the literal history of Hiroshima informs the entire work, this novel shares little with that earlier atomic-bomb literature which nearly always described the bombings in terms of those emotions in individual and subjective responses. *Hiroshima* certainly deals "with" the destruction of Hiroshima, but it is "about" something more, and it is that something which insists upon a new critical framework in order to account for all its ambition. After Oda Makoto, Japanese atomic-bomb literature is now nuclear literature in two senses: it chronicles two fission weapons used to destroy two cities, but it also thematizes a cluster of causes and implications of those historical weapons for the general political order under which we live. And importantly, unlike earlier atomic-bomb writers who bemoaned the loss of moral principles demonstrated in the annihilation of Hiroshima and Nagasaki, for Oda that loss is ironically the predictable and deserved destiny of a specific political order.

Atomic-bomb literature, as we have seen, has commonly used first-person narration, a testifying "I," to deal with a situation originally unique to a relatively limited number of actual surviving hibakusha. Perhaps this feature may function retrospectively, in fact, as one practical definition of early "atomic-bomb literature." But *nuclear* literature seems predicted upon a state of powerlessness not limited to an ever fewer number of survivors, but rather expanded to include to all citizens of the nation-state. Oda Makoto's novel is not the only example of Japanese nuclear literature, nor is it rare for a hibakusha to turn to these "post-" atomic-bomb literature issues. "Everyone in the present age is gripped with a terror not only of August 6th or 9th," writes Hayashi Kyōko writes in her short story "In the Fields," "but of the nuclear" (243). In *As If Not*, another Hayashi character speculates that "Perhaps everyone alive in the world today is, in fact, a hibakusha" (205). *Hiroshima*, with its immense number of characters and its theme of inextricably joined experiences of victimhood and victimizing, seeks a global perspective in appropriate scale to the complexity of those seemingly paradoxical experiences. In other words the novel posits a *totality* that comprehends the diverse political conditions of modern life under the nation-state; it would also have to posit that this totality can be described within a single work of fiction.

That such conditions are both real and realizable is an opinion that Oda has repeatedly endorsed in his nonfiction writings. They are conditions determined through the constant, heavy intervention of what Oda broadly terms the "state" (*kokka*). For example in his 1968 essay "The Ethics of Peace," he asserts that "in time of war, the state compels the individual to fight. As he fires the shot which knocks over the enemy, he stands as victim in relation to the state and victimizer in relation to the enemy" (160). In other words, the overlapping identity of the atomic-bomb perpetrator and the atomic-bomb target described in *Hiroshima* through the key character of Joe Clancey is an identity which Oda had postulated at the height of his own country's complex involvement—both as victim and victimizer—with America at the height of the war in Vietnam. Oda is unambiguous on this point: parting company with some on the left, for whom postwar Japan is an unambiguous casualty of the imposition of American power around the world, Oda is always careful to indict such reductive identities as "victim" or "victimizer" as rhetorical and ideological strategies on the part of the state to create a national consensual order. Oda writes in this same essay:

> Our own victimization, now skillfully portrayed as the ordeal of the Japanese people collectively, has become, willy-nilly, a state experience. The state has adopted our victim experience as its own [as a basis for nationalism]; it is now viewed as only one element, or aspect, of the victimization of the state itself. In the course of that transformation, we have again identified ourselves with the state, depended upon it, and fallen into its grasp. (168)

In other words, it is the nature of modern government to appropriate one part of its citizens' experience and identify itself wholly with that part. Such a move is not only a reduction of history, a masking of complicity and power, but a dangerous justification for further coercive acts. The complex matrix of victim/victimizer, filtered through and reduced by ideology, turns history into a melodrama in which important questions of real authority are never allowed to be posed. It is against this rhetoric of the "victim" and the "victimizer," heretofore nearly always coincidental in atomic-bomb literature with national or racial categories of identities, that Oda presents his novel. Its aim is to repudiate the propaganda of national power which has turned Hiroshima into a rationale for a disturbing new Japanese identity that downplays its own "victimizing" history and the renewed potential for more. In his translator's afterword to *Son My*, Oda states:

> One thing made clear by this incident [at Son My] is how the state coerces the individual in all sorts of matters. To that extent, the individual is made a victim by the state. Yet by the very fact that the individual is a victim, he in turn becomes a victimizer of unparalleled cruelty. There is no incident in history which makes this mechanism of "victim-equals-victimizer" more clear as this.[51]

Already by 1968 we can see the outline of the connection Oda would draw between the way Hiroshima is now represented to the Japanese people and the basis of authority which the postwar Japanese state enjoys:

> Whenever I see pictures of the atomic mushroom clouds over Hiroshima and Nagasaki, I wonder why we have never sought to assign personal responsibility to the airmen who dropped the bombs. . . . It is our duty . . . to carry out this accusation. . . . By adding a realization of the complementarity between our roles as victim and victimizer, it is possible for us to adopt universal principles directly without the mediation of the State. (164–65)

By renouncing the commonplace labels we are assigned by the state as victims or victimizers, and by realizing that participation in modern life inevitably means being both, Oda postulates that we need to detach ourselves from these national identities used to mobilize us for the agenda of the state. What we would then enjoy, without this ideological "mediation," would be the exercise of "universal principles," spelled out more fully in this same essay as the "universal brotherhood of mankind." At first such ideas seem unabashedly liberal and fully at home in the American tradition, including its tradition of the "melting pot" rhetoric with which national identity is typically phrased. Oda might retort that these ideas are not so much Jeffersonian as they are Hegelian, with "brotherhood" the issue of a dialectic in which our imbricated roles as victim and victimizer produce a complex ontology in fact not easily manipulated by state propaganda. Such thinking can lead one to Marxist or Sartrean elaborations of being, existence, and power; and indeed, it is precisely from these traditions, as they were received into postwar Japan, that Oda formulated the specifically literary and political ideas explored in *Hiroshima*.

The notion of the "universal" is linked closely here to that of the "total," an idea which Oda takes quite seriously in his epic novel. In fact, in a very particular usage, the term "total" (*zentai; zentaisei*) was frequently cited in discussions of *Hiroshima* both by its author and its critics. When the book was first published, some reviewers described it by reviving a phrase often heard in the 1950s and especially the late 1960s, just those years when Oda was personally involved in the radical student movement: *zentai shōsetsu*, or "total literature." The term has a complex history, with ultimate roots at least back to Hegel. In his 1859 foreword to *A Contribution to the Critique of Political Economy*, Marx refers to man as a synthesis of historical forces that are the sum "total" (*Gesamtheit*) in how they determine our being.[52] But the history of this term "total literature" in Japan comes via its application in the writings of Sartre, who in his 1939 essay "François Mauriac and Freedom" adapted that synthesis of historical and material forces to the field of literature. He asked the question of how an author was to fix both the exteriority and interiority of his characters and still permit them "freedom"—a literary problem that soon reflected itself in real life, as French intellectuals would soon wonder where their freedom could lie under a German occupation. The answer, articulated by Sartre during his days as a graduate student, lay in his identification of the imagination as a way for people to exceed their situation and grasp their freedom. Imagination then becomes the necessary tool for people to exercise the freedom they can, existentially, will for themselves.

Such an important role for the imagination, and such an attractive prize it might win, found great appeal among some of Japan's own writers demoralized in the wake of the war. One of them, Noma Hiroshi, whose work is usually taken as the start of postwar Japanese literature, summarized Sartre's project this way:

> Sartre termed humanity "homme total." In other words, mankind is a total existence. If mankind cannot be grasped solely from the exterior, neither can he be understood solely from the interior. Mankind, as something defined in total simultaneously from both the inside and outside, must be grasped just as that, in one fell swoop. Sartre's view of humanity was emerged after the war, but it had crystallized in him as a result of having lived through it.[53]

Noma's own epic novel *The Cycle of Youth* (Seinen no wa, 1947–66) is the most famous example of a literary work by a Japanese writer attempting to achieve this same representation of humanity as a totality. Noma defined what he meant by total literature in the context of his own work in 1969:

> I personally think that art must be understood to include all those pieces that mask the whole *[zentai]*—shall I call it the unity of the natural and social worlds in which mankind now finds itself placed, the worlds in which we all now live? By grasping that we each exist within such a total situation, and that it is there that we all transcend our individuality, we can come to see just what freedom for each of us might mean, and then begin to realize that goal. Art can perform that function for us. I believe that the power of those writers who pursue this aim is the power that creates fiction.[54]

Such language might strike us today as impossibly utopian and naive. But so was that of the Western philosophers who initially suggested that such a powerfully redemptive "art" was indeed possible. The best-known passage in Sartre on his concept of a total literature occurs in his essay "Situation of the Writer in 1947" where, in the context of discussing the demoralized world in which the postwar writer writes, he defines "total literature" in equally unattainable, idealistic terms: a literature that has "finally understand its essence" as literature, that has "made the synthesis of *praxis* and *exis*" (234). Total literature is dialectical: it is a process, and as a process, it can "totalize" literature as a dynamic system rather than as a static arrangement of objects described. Sartre subsequently gives a concrete example of what he means, and it is one useful to us in seeing what Oda Makoto himself has attempted:

> If our desires could be realized, the twentieth-century writer [of a total literature] would occupy between the oppressed and those who oppress them an analogous position to that of eighteenth-century authors between the bourgeois and the aristocracy, to that of Richard Wright between the blacks and the whites, read by both the oppressed and the

oppressor, furnishing the oppressor with his image, both inner and outer, being conscious with and for the oppressed of the oppression, contribut- ing to the formation of a constructive and revolutionary ideology. (234–35)

Sartre's example of literature which functions dialectically—i.e., literature which mediates and synthesizes otherwise diametrically opposed categories of being ("oppressors" and "oppressed")—is the direct forebear of Oda Makoto's attempt in *Hiroshima* to similarly place such concepts of "victim" and "victim- izer" in a similar dialectic leading to a similarly "constructive and revolutionary ideology." Some Japanese critics have even seen Oda accomplishing just what Sartre abandoned. French literature scholar Hirai Hiroyuki, for example, while he calls both Oda and Sartre "writers of engagement," sees the former suc- ceeding with *Hiroshima* where the latter failed with his *The Age of Reason*.[55] In other words, Oda's novel, unlike Sartre's unfinished series, achieves a kind of Hegelian totality within, and perhaps on account of, its diverse geographical terrain and temporal span. Kamata Sadao, writing of *Hiroshima*, has explained this widely heralded triumph of the novel in more detail:

> [Oda] has put forth a [Sartrean] "novel of *situation*," a work which unites metaphysical absolutes with the relativity of historical facts. What he wants to describe is not the memory of the past but the tension of the past and the future lurking in the present; the confrontation of hope and hopelessness; and the perspective of the human struggle therein.[56]

It might be embarrassing to have one's work described in such ambitious and ebullient terms; but Oda, like Sartre, has depicted the task of the modern writer with just such monumental phrasing. In his 1964 essay "The Path to a New 'Total Literature'" (Atarashii "zentai shōsetsu" e no michi), Oda argues that after Sartre the Balzacian model of "total literature," i.e., literature in which an omnipotent author takes the place of God, is clearly impossible. Rather, what writers today must do when they strive to create a total literature is create "fiction constructed with the complex fields of vision of a great many human beings" (133). This program is consistent with Oda's oft-stated enthusiasm for an engagement with "reality," which in Oda's parlance typically means the dis- courses of nuclear and Third World politics.[57] It is also certainly the intellectual motive behind Oda's writing of *Hiroshima*, a work that he says he started out writing as fiction but which along the way became, somehow, something else.[58] That something else is a work that aimed to mirror philosophically the oppres- sion, the "situation," under and by which we now "live" in the nuclear age.

This would be, however, a kind of totality not fully anticipated by Sartre or Japan's Noma Hiroshi. Different historical moments are held to determine different types of a total literature—hence the great variety of writers, from Dostoyevsky and Balzac to Proust and Sartre, each said to have attempted it—

but every such instance must be dominated by some philosophy or worldview that synthesizes just that moment. For nineteenth-century French fiction, it was the microcosmic world of the individual; for Sartre, the problem of the Other. For Oda, what produces the total is more often a historical event than it is a concept. "When the Vietnam War was under way," he stated in a recent interview, "the Vietnam War was everything."[59] Similarly, Hiroshima the occurrence is the now distinctly contemporary frame of the "nuclear" that functions to coordinate both the material and ideal conditions of our existences in Oda's total literature. The clarity of the frame does not make Oda's ambition any easier to achieve: Sartre and Noma eventually despaired of attaining such a unity of exis and praxis even when such a unity did not yet involve plans for orbiting satellites armed with neutron bombs.

In fact, the much proclaimed achievement of Oda in *Hiroshima* fails, in my view, even more quickly on account of the vast scale which now such "totalities" must encompass. In a certain sense Oda's concession to his characters of an imaginative power—and thus self-willed act—can be seen consistent with the path to personal freedom made part of the definition of total literature by Sartre and Noma: a freedom achieved only by attaining the synthesis of the "total." But in Oda's world such terms as "total" and "freedom" take on particular contexts, and thus meanings. The question of just what the meaning of "freedom" could be for Oda, if his notion of the "total" is the "'nuclear age" ushered in by Hiroshima, is a question not just for literary critics but a paramount issue for all of us who, like Oda's imaginary characters, live beneath it.

In the brief second part of *Hiroshima*, when the individual "I" of Joe Clancey's consciousness becomes a common—totalized—"we," the ethical distinction (in Sartrean terms, the "situation") between victim and victimizer is exceeded and a totality, admittedly grotesque, is presented us. In this interpretation, no doubt one shared by such enthusiastic critics as Hirai Hiroyuki and Kamata Sadao, *Hiroshima* does indeed become an example of "total literature." For Oda, the genealogy of such totality must be the "totality" engendered through the exercise of America's nuclear hegemony in the postwar period—the same totality against which Oda's antiwar Beheiren movement struggled. It is a totality made up of the side which destroyed Hiroshima and Hiroshima itself. It is the totality we now refer to through the short-hand of the phrase "the nuclear age." In 1984 Oda wrote that "the act of dropping the atomic bomb entailed the three issues I call ideology, everyday life, and system."[60] Nuclear war—and the nuclear age it ushered in—already and always comprises the absolute totality under which we all live today, regardless of nationality or race.

This is already a more specific, considerably more phenomenal and less philosophically obtuse totality than is Sartre's or even Noma's. But where the real divergence between these two ideas of "totality" looms the most conspicuously is the way "freedom" is treated in *Hiroshima* and the way it is in, for example, Sartre's *The Age of Reason*. It has been noted that introducing such ideas as existentialist "freedom" into a Marxist or Hegelian totality inevitably raises problems. Sartre's existentialism may be one of the "private religions" that Fredric Jameson scorns in the course of ridiculing the precise assumption that would seem to underlie the theory of a *littérature total*:

> To imagine that, sheltered from the omnipresence of history and the implacable influence of the social, there already exists a realm of freedom—whether it be that of the microscopic experience of words in a text or the ecstasies and intensities of the various private religions—is only to strengthen the grip of Necessity over all such blind zones in which the individual subject seeks refuge, in pursuit of a purely individual, a merely psychological, project of salvation.[61]

Oda, though his alternate faith in "materiality" may be that solely of nuclear warheads, makes a somewhat similar point in how the characters of his novel realize the emptiness of "freedom." In the third part of Oda's novel, the Americans brought to the verge of their deaths by weapons experiments and the atomic power industry can realize "freedom" vis-à-vis the authorities represented by the American president and the Japanese prime minister only in the form of an impotently imaginative revenge. Finally what Oda's story seeks is not the un-ironic realization of freedom imagined by the existentialists, but rather a bleak description of a bleaker "totality"—that of the nuclear age—which can *not* be exceeded, and which cannot, therefore, lead to any promise of liberty. It is in this sense that even if *Hiroshima* fails (as surely any work of literature does) to be "total," it still succeeds, just as a scientific experiment that disproves a hypothesis is nonetheless a valuable advance. Through the imagination exercised by Oda via his characters, literature does come closer to approaching the total reality of an inescapably menacing world order. The irony, however, of Oda's notion of totality is as oppressive as Sartre's and Noma's was intended to be liberating—those same characters are, after all, dead by the end of the novel. Oda writes:

> It was the "Manhattan Project" that produced the atomic bomb, but its officer in charge, General [Leslie R.] Groves, makes some interesting remarks in his memoirs. Although the Manhattan Project was begun by Roosevelt and inherited by Truman, "Once such an immense project commences, no one can stop it. Even a president is no more than a child on a sled that has begun to move." The president, the highest authority, should be expected to be able to halt such a project if he saw fit to do so, but Groves writes quite candidly that once an entire organization begins to operate, not even a president can stop it. . . . When a single system, a single society, starts to move in its entirety, even the most pow-

erful cannot stop it. I believe that this is something that we must contemplate.[62]

The atomic bomb, one prominent example of such a modern "system," possessed an unstoppable momentum that assured one sort of an autonomous "totality." And since it was "total," individual victimhood as well as individual responsibility stumbles as a workable concept. Here is where Oda's theory of the total inverts that of his Marxist and existentialist predecessors and discloses their key term of "freedom" as one more inaccessibly lofty signifier. As the distance between *Hiroshima*'s victims and victimizers shrinks, it is not any "situation" which is "dominated" by a totality, but rather the "situation" which dominates and thus comprises all of the "totality." While not quite the elegant or clever performance of a deconstructive critic, Oda has nonetheless unbalanced and frustrated an erstwhile symmetry—albeit by referring us to something that is indeed *de hors-texte*—with the same skeptical force.

This results in a work of literature not so much philosophical as explicitly political. The same can fairly be said, in fact, of all Japanese "nuclear criticism" and "nuclear literature." *Hiroshima* may be a work that seems to describe, with an imaginative power inspired by history, the absolute and terrifying "totality" of a nuclear age under which all races and nationalities survive only provisionally. But it is more accurately a work of "total literature" that, instead of liberating us through the achievement of an elusive "freedom," is in fact an anti-total literature that, in its own impossible aporia, expresses a totality which constantly menaces us and does not allow "freedom." A word as confident as "freedom" takes on only an ironic meaning in a world as depressingly circular as *Hiroshima*'s. In the present day described by Oda in this novel, any "totality" which makes freedom possible is already anachronistic.

There is a distinct incompatibility between the postwar Marxist or existentialist "total literature" and the sort of nuclear literature proposed by Oda Makoto—as well as an odd congruence of the latter with the Derridean deferment of signification, meaning, and presence. The failure of Oda's *Hiroshima* to establish a realm of freedom thematizes the similar failure of *The Age of Reason* and *The Cycle of Youth*: Oda makes the total as ungraspable as does deconstruction's rhetorical reading of Western metaphysics. At the same time, it should be clear that there is also a degree of incompatibility between such nuclear literature as Oda's and the atomic-bomb literature discussed earlier in this study, particularly the testimonial accounts left by hibakusha. The problem begins with a literature that assumes its subject is the *particularity* of Hiroshima and Nagasaki, and a literature that alternatively takes as its theme a generality that follows from that particularity, i.e., the "modern condition" of the "nuclear era." In his essay on total literature Oda argues that there are two trends in modern literature: one, to describe the world of the individual, and two, to describe the world of politics.⁶³ Oda would like to see fiction unite the two, and for his most enthusiastic critics that is just what happens in *Hiroshima*. Nakano Kōji, for example, praised the novel for having "done away with national borders."⁶⁴ Not even Oda himself would likely agree with this, but what the novel does do, in this latest phase of Japanese writing given its original impetus by the 1945 atomic bombings, is move to undo the frequent insistence of earlier atomic-bomb literature that Japan is "unique" because "it" uniquely suffered the only nuclear attack in history: when Oda reverses the logic of this assertion, he exposes the duplicity of rhetoric in nuclear politics at least as effectively as the contributors to *Diacritics*.

Such an amendment of course contradicts at the same time a great deal of atomic-bomb literature, and indeed dismisses some major part of it. The choice of an American to narrate the devastation was surely a purposefully provocative one. In a sense it was ahistorical because the American hibakusha is so anomalous.⁶⁵ There were non-Japanese residents and captured enemy personnel in Hiroshima on the 6th, but in such small numbers that its bombing still remains, intentionally and effectively, a "Japanese" tragedy. But Oda is not a historian. He is a social critic and a political activist. He would likely retort that we, in order to survive, must view nuclear weaponry as a global threat. There is a tension as well as a continuation, then, between earlier atomic-bomb literature and the nuclear literature that may be succeeding it. As the events of Hiroshima and Nagasaki in literature have receded to allow the national and international politics that manipulate more powerful weaponry to come to the fore, those initial events nearly achieve the status of tropes, fainter impressions of something which now we, mostly born after the Second World War, look upon as a significant, if distant, sign of the modern world: a world in which we have never *not* known nuclear terror. As Kuroko Kazuo, Japan's preeminent critic of atomic-bomb literature and himself born in 1945, has put it: "The biggest issue is not whether one has or does not have the experience [of the bombings], but rather the fact that we are alive today."⁶⁶

Danger lurks: the risks of perversion, of trivialization, of mythologizing. To veer from the literal facts, as Oda has done and as such hibakusha writers as Hara and Ōta well understood, is possibly to supplant them with lies. Indeed, *Hiroshima* borders on the fantastic, a world wholly apart from that of so-called realistic fiction. Here, unlike in "Summer Flowers" or *City of Corpses*, there is not a single "fact" in the entire novel. In its place there is only Oda's imagination. It is however an imagination haunted by facts, and all the fanciful writing leads us back to the incontrovertible presence of August 6th in the world that fuels Oda's imagination. Whether atomic-bomb literature or nuclear literature, it has two tasks today: to remind readers of the past and to warn them of the present. This is the whole which Oda's novel describes. *Hiroshima* is an awkward, sincere attempt to tell within a single book a great many small and large stories. It succeeds in part only because all the stories are linked by a common thread: nuclear technology which, now coupled with economic, political, and ethical systems ready to exploit it, has changed not only the way some of us died but indeed how all of us now live.

This returns us back to the juxtaposition with which I began this chapter, namely the different directions which "nuclear criticism" in the West and in Japan has taken. In the works of European and North American theorists, the place of the imaginary is not in our response to the "nuclear threat," but in fact that threat itself, part of the irrepressible work of language to always pretend it indicates the real when in fact it points only to itself. "The terrifying reality of the nuclear conflict can be only the signified referent, never the real referent (present or past) of a discourse or a text," Derrida instructs us, and the lesson is an important one. The postwar superpower (and no longer just superpower) strategy of "mutually assured destruction" (MAD: an acronym custom-ordered for rhetorical unpacking) did and does indeed depend upon a deterrence/deferment, a perpetual threat of omnicide in order to perpetually survive. That threat must, impossibly, be both "real" and infinitely unrealizable, and it is just that aporia which, once identified, might allow us to fear it less. But that "it" will still be *words*, and not the warheads aimed at us. None of what a Western nuclear criticism discloses should undermine our appreciation of the convinced passion with which Japanese theorists of the nuclear believe in the literal and real reference of an atomic war that was *not* deferred. This crucial difference between being an intellectual in the West, where nuclear war has been little more than game theory, and being one in Japan is not a structural one: it is demonstrably historical and tragic.

That difference may explain why, for Oda and others like him in Japan, the paradox of efficacious action in the world has never resulted in a withdrawal from it. In his life as well as his writings, Oda has always, if sometimes artlessly, struggled to elucidate those conditions he firmly believes do make for real differences not only in the way we interpret the world, but in the way we live it. In the late 1980s, when a number of deconstructionist critics were forced to detour back to a time before the "nuclear" and consider just how sincere, or "fabulously textual," the wartime anti-Semitic writings of one of their number might have been, Oda Makoto was considering running on the Socialist ticket for mayor of Tokyo. Similarly, *Hiroshima* is a novel which grapples sincerely with a problem many other writers in various ways have sought to minimize, even explain away: namely, how do we think of ourselves as citizens, as people, on a planet over which hover all manner of weapons whose control, much less inner workings, partake of a complexity that makes anachronistic older notions of accountability? I would propose that if we are in need a radical deconstruction of the forces that tell us we labor beneath a nuclear terror, then it could be Oda Makoto to whom we might turn, as well as to the West's contemporary theories. In Oda's replay of history, we also find a dismantling of the ideas we thought forever fixed: the idea of victim and victimizer, of peaceful uses of nuclear energy and the belligerent ones, of the citizen of one nation-state and another, of intellectual and worker. But most vitally, the lessons Oda Makoto brings might additionally prevent us from going to our fiery deaths condescendingly believing, all the while, that the ample warnings were only delusionary exercises in rhetoric.

A page from the English translation of Nakazawa Keiji's *Barefoot Gen* (Hadashi no Gen, 1973).

The world, I realize, is drugged on metaphor, the opiate of the age. Nobody's scared. Nobody's digging. . . . Nuclear war. It's no symbol. Nuclear war—is it embarrassing? Too prosaic? Too blunt? *Listen*—nuclear war—those stiff, brash, trite, everyday syllables.

Tim O'Brien, *The Nuclear Age*

Where else in the world would you be able to buy shoes with the brand name *A-BOMB*? Nowhere, except Japan of course.

The Japan Times, January 29, 1987

11

Concluding Remarks: *And Then*

The second part of this book began with Japan's earliest acknowledged atomic-bomb writer, Hara Tamiki, and has concluded with one of its most recent, Oda Makoto. The distance between them is not only that of more than thirty years but that of several intervening generations of writers who, ever more remote from the actual events of Hiroshima and Nagasaki, have devised ever more imaginative—which is not to say less accurate, or truthful—means of representing the contemporary significance of those cities' names. This is not because those of us born after 1945 have "forgotten" anything about the events those names keep before us, and thus somehow need to invent new stories to replace those no longer available to us—though one may well agree with Michael Geyer that "the preeminent post-modern, post-contemporary question is what to do when no one who lived the events of World War II is still alive."[1] One of the points I have hoped to make in this book is that even the first hibakusha writers themselves did not pretend to "know" Hiroshima or Nagasaki in ways exhaustive of those events' import either for us or themselves. Rather, the experiments of an Ōe Kenzaburō, an Ibuse Masuji, a Sata Ineko, an Oda Makoto, and other non-hibakusha writers, following upon those of whom, like Hara Tamiki, Tōge Sankichi, and Ōta Yōko, were there on the 6th and 9th, are experiments that diversely seek to enlarge upon something already so boundless that some had thought it beyond the expressiveness of words and thus the effective limits of writing.[2] They are experiments—and more, one can safely predict, will follow—that serve to remind us not of the failure of the first atomic-bomb writers to say it all, but rather their subtle success in not doing so.

The past dozen years in Japan have—unlike any decade heretofore—not seen the emergence of a new wave, or even any additional individual examples, of atomic-bomb writers, though several of those studied here have continued to publish steadily.[3] At the same time, the theme of Hiroshima, Nagasaki, and their consequences has provoked cultural responses around the world that have even been imported back to Japan in a kind of "multinational economy," if you will, of nuclear terror. Tim O'Brien's recent novel *The Nuclear Age*—whose story of a man obsessed with the likelihood of a third world war and his family's survival of it recalls Kurosawa Akira's 1955 film of a Japanese family patriarch who wants his entire extended household to emigrate to South America for just those same reasons, *Record of a Living Being* (Ikimono no kiroku)—created a sensation when published in Japan. Its translator, Murakami Haruki, himself an immensely popular novelist, shares membership in O'Brien's postwar generation and recognizes the particular set of morbid concerns history has imposed on them both: in his translator's afterword, he goes so far as to call *The Nuclear Age* "the complete novel of our age" *(gendai no sōgō-shōsetsu)*—not "total literature" in Oda's or Sartre's openly ideological sense, perhaps, but certainly akin in its capture of what makes "our age" essentially ours.[4]

It is tempting, then, to devise a chronology of "periods" for atomic-bomb literature, and to describe the present, globalized phase as one which effectively marks both the end of an exclusively Japanese enterprise and the start of a cultural collaboration as international as the technology and politics it protests. But periodization is inconceivable without the premise that we stand somewhere beyond the same history we would hope to transcend by punctuating: and this is where the lessons of an atomic-bomb literature still meaningfully "Japanese" intrude. Oda Makoto, my last writer, has written an essay on Hara Tamiki, my first, and so makes my ostensible line of authors a circle. In "To Say 'And Then'" (Sore kara, no koto, 1980), Oda pays homage to the initial writer of prose in post-nuclear Hiroshima and to the original challenge of Hara's work that inspired his own decades later. Oda says that Hara's stories were written on the very edge of fiction, perilously close to a precipice where they might have tumbled into an abyss of meaninglessness. What places Hara's literature in such a precarious position, and what consequently is instructive for how "literature" in the twentieth century can survive, is the fact that here there are not, as in other fiction, the actions of individuals. In their stead loom only the actions of humankind: Hara does not distinguish between the single person and the collectivity of victims, who are perhaps the entire species.

Unfortunately this achievement—for Oda it is no small one—was accomplished at the cost of being in Hiroshima when the bomb was dropped, for it was from there that Hara perceived what Oda and other postwar writers have so earnestly sought. There in the carnage of his native city, Oda believes Hara "saw the dead as a totality" (195). Hara, in other words, lived what others have tried to imagine: that place in which all the forces that govern modern life are synthesized, albeit in the terminal act of policide. Ironically, that synthesis was forged in the fires through which Hara had to traverse in order to survive, a carnage that we survey in the legacy of memoirs, poems, and stories in order to understand. The implication of a literature, "total" or otherwise, that narrates such experiences and such lessons is not that it can, as the humanists might hope, free us. Indeed, it may restrict our liberty further, even to the point of an enforced reticence. "I suspect that the 'individual' is now subsumed in 'humankind,' and not the other way around. That in itself might be fine," writes Oda, "but then the problem becomes: is fiction possible?" (199).

Oda's doubt is the doubt of the nuclear age, of culture after the reduction of individual human worth to a unit that, in the discourse of defense strategists, is cited only in the millions. Perhaps, post-Gorbachev, the binary opposition of an East versus a West is to be replaced by a far greater multiplicity of possible enemies and disposable cities. According to an American government report leaked in 1992, "the U.S. arsenal is to be disengaged from a singular enemy to operate in many interlocking scenarios, with weapons targeted at 'every reasonable adversary.'"[5] But one thing remains the same, no matter where the missiles are trained: what kind of fiction should we now be writing, if modernity's "individual" is now an inconsequential part of a aggregate target? One thing is sure: the theme of high-technological atrocity, like that of love, will never disappear from the literature of the future. The question is, what can such a misanthropic literature look like? Perhaps, Oda wonders, one could write epic poetry or Greek tragedy—but not fiction as we once knew it, fiction that pursued our sense of a collective human life through the unique particulars of the single hero. Oda speculates that, given the atomic bomb and its guarantee of an undifferentiated landscape of the indiscriminately slaughtered, such writing can no longer lay claim to realism. In his own Hiroshima novel, however, what Oda gave us was neither epic poetry or Greek tragedy. What we read instead is the unmetered prose of everyday life, but it is indeed prose which speaks, like that of the Mediterranean ancients, of a world not provincially but universally menaced.

The course of atomic-bomb literature in Japan, then, poses much the same question in its latest works as in its earliest. The implications of that question— namely, what form is modern culture to take once its ethical foundations and an attendant trust in the viability of the individual and his dignity are debased— threaten to unravel much upon which we once could instinctively depend. Ironically the "value" of reading and studying atomic-bomb literature lies precisely in understanding that those foundations and that trust *are* debased, and that we cannot proceed as we have, whether as "victims" or "victimizers"—for Oda the distinction ultimately disguises the mechanisms that can make us both—and not risk complete destruction this time around.

As Oda Makoto says in his homage to Hara Tamiki, it is difficult to write "and then." Our once reflexive faith in the certitude of a next moment has been undone by writers, worldwide, whose lives were spared by the whim of the camp officer or the (in-) accuracy of the bombardier. Half a century after the events of the Second World War, our literature of atrocity is no longer a documentary record of separate outbreaks of barbarity, but instead a cumulative contemplation of how we are to live in the present culture such barbarity bequeaths. Understandably, we would prefer our former faiths restored. But the courage of Japanese atomic-bomb writers in committing their stories to paper, despite the dread that such exercises of memory and imagination must have revived, should be matched on our part by an equal bravery in taking their still very contemporary experiences as painfully distinct and profound warnings of what we have abundantly proved ourselves capable.

It would be in keeping with the intellectual vanity of literary studies today to wonder: What can we critics say about Hiroshima and Nagasaki? But the real discovery might be the answer to: What do Hiroshima and Nagasaki have to say about us critics? And our little world of words? How accountable to history are we? What are our responsibilities to the terrible story, the dead storyteller? I take the events of August 6 and 9, 1945 as sufficiently dramatic in their narrative effect to question and even shatter our explanatory paradigms otherwise thought so elastic. These two days contest our aesthetics of the poem and the novel; our philosophies of the subject; our politics of the modern and postmodern world. Other events, too, undermine our conviction in the worth of structures, be it the grandeur of an ideology or the comfort of a habit. But Hiroshima and Nagasaki do so in a way, and from a far place, that by their unprecedented nature would seem to supply the final, irrefutable proof of this rip in history, morality, common sense. And they will continue to do so, in ways that we cannot now foresee, for even if those two days in August are thus far unique, our future interpretations of them will not be. Still, the one unchanging lesson of Hiroshima and Nagasaki is that there might yet be an end to our talking. "And then," Oda Makoto writes. There he stopped, invoking a silence that echoes over the banal cacophony of what, some fear, may be our last chance to speak.

Notes

Preface

1. Nakayama Shirō, "Shi no kage," 42.

2. Takahashi Kazumi, *Yūutsu naru tōha*, 298.

3. The Committee for the Compilation of Materials on Damage Caused by the Atomic Bombs in Hiroshima and Nagasaki, *Hiroshima and Nagasaki: The Physical, Medical, and Social Effects of the Atomic Bombings*, 105–6. I refer readers generally to this impressive compendium of information on Hiroshima and Nagasaki not only for its wealth of scientific data but for its occasional and welcome lapses from the objective language of the statistician, the physicist, and the doctor to speak instead of the import such data has for the moral, as well as material, aspects of human culture post-Hiroshima.

4. Norman Cousins, "Foreword," in Nagai Takashi, *We of Nagasaki*, vi.

5. Brigadier General Thomas F. Farrell, quoted by Major General Leslie R. Groves in his secret memorandum to Secretary of War Henry Stimson, July 18, 1945; quoted in Martin J. Sherwin, *A World Destroyed: The Atomic Bomb and the Grand Alliance*, 310.

6. Ōe Kenzaburō, for example, not only notes this fact, he argues for its importance in how the Japanese people should think of themselves as a people: not in the regressive form of a "nation," but rather as inhabitants of the nuclear age charged with finding the means to survive it. "The personal experience [*taiken*] of the atomic bombings," Ōe wrote in 1968, "is now the public experience [*keiken*] of not only hibakusha but of an extremely broad stratum of Japanese" ("Gembakugo no Nihonjin no jiko-kakunin," 211).

7. I recognize, of course, that some of us are more immediately faced with extinction by older means because of ethnic, racial, or religious hatred, or poverty and disease—and that such threats will remain even if atomic weapons were to disappear. But they will not, and what finally separates the terror under which historically besieged peoples live from the Faustian strategy of nuclear deterrence in place worldwide is not just the latter's global universality. On some level most now believe racism and anti-Semitism vestiges of a history whose irrationality we can clearly see; but I wonder

whether we are still convinced by a more recent rhetoric that claims the logic of science, even as applied to bombs, as a badge of our progress as a species.

8. More typical of the genuinely complicated feelings of Japanese towards the atomic bombings and the end of the war—events now permanently and hopelessly fused in the popular historical memory—are expressed by the narrator of Kokubo Hitoshi's story "The Mark of Summer" (Natsu no kokuin, 1976). Assuming that the silence of the United States to explain its use of nuclear weapons beyond their value in shortening the war and "minimizing damage" is tantamount to saying "We did you the favor of saving you [surviving Japanese] your own lives," he regards the deaths of those in Hiroshima and Nagasaki as "needless deaths, meaningless deaths, in other words wasted deaths *[inujini]*." The impact of this realization on the narrator is less anger and more "a pathos compounded by powerlessness"—until he also realizes that the war *would* have gone on longer without the atomic bombings. Finally, he concludes that it is not the United States that did any Japanese a favor: it was the dead victims of Hiroshima and Nagasaki (335–36).

9. Edward Said, *The World, the Text, and the Critic*, 4–5.

10. Berel Lang, "Genocide and Omnicide: Technology at the Limits"; Michael Geyer, "Man-made Transcendences: Consumerism, Violence, and the Problem of Memory."

11. Kuroko Kazuo, *Gembaku to kotoba: Hara Tamiki kara Hayashi Kyōko made*, 134. No literary critic of atomic-bomb literature in Japan has been more thoughtfully sophisticated than Kuroko, and I recommend this book, as well as his subsequent *Gembaku bungaku ron: Kaku-jidai to sōzōryoku* (Atomic-Bomb Literature: The Nuclear Age and the Power of Imagination, 1993).

12. Jonathan Culler, *The Pursuit of Signs: Semiotics, Literature, Deconstruction*, 218.

13. Hasegawa Ken, quoted in Kin'ya Tsuruta, "Akutagawa Ryūnosuke and I-Novelists," 18.

14. Kurihara Sadako, *Dokyumento Hiroshima nijūyonen: Gendai no kyūsai*, 26–27. Kurihara is another name that will appear repeatedly in this study; all of her books on the atomic bombings make for valuable reading, but none more so than this 1970 collection of essays and poetry. While only its third section deals explicitly with atomic-bomb literature, the first and second parts usefully sketch both the past history and then-current state of hibakusha culture and the Japanese peace movement.

15. See Peter Schwenger, *Letter Bomb: Nuclear Holocaust and the Exploding Word*. I recommend this work to anyone interested in the themes and problems I raise here in my own study of Japanese literature; Schwenger pursues many of the same in contemporary Western literature and thought. See also his essay, "Writing the Unthinkable."

16. *The Anchor Bible: Job*, 65, 69.

Introduction

1. Iida Momo, *Amerika no eiyū*, 403. This novel is discussed in the final chapter of this book, "The Atomic, the Nuclear, the Total: Oda Makoto."

2. Karl Jaspers, *The Fate of Mankind*, 3.

3. Czeslaw Milosz, *The Captive Mind*, 29.

4. Albert Einstein, quoted in the Committee for the Compilation of Materials on the Damage Caused by the Atomic Bombs in Hiroshima and Nagasaki, *Hiroshima and Nagasaki: The Physical, Medical, and Social Effects of the Atomic Bombings*, xxxix.

5. Margaret Thatcher, quoted in Martin Amis, *Einstein's Monsters*, 11.

6. Lord Zuckerman, once chief science advisor to the British government, wrote just before his death in the spring of 1993:

"That there are now no secrets about how to make a nuclear warhead . . . has in fact created a future more uncertain and possibly more menacing than it was in the days of the cold war, when we had become habituated to the knowledge that nuclear weapons exist, without much thought of what the consequences would have been had they been used" ("The New Nuclear Menace," 14).

7. Martin Amis, *Einstein's Monsters*, 28.

8. Sugimoto Naojirō, "Gembaku ni atta hi," 72.

9. Len Giovannitti and Fred Freed, *The Decision to Drop the Bomb*, 110.

10. For a popular account of this incident, see Ralph E. Lapp, *The Voyage of the Lucky Dragon*.

11. Tanuma Hajime, *Gembaku hibakusha shomondai*, 20.

12. Ōe Kenzaburō, "Hiroshima, Amerika, Yōroppa," 205.

13. See, for example, Günter Anders, *Endzeit und Zeitenende: Gedanken über die atomare Situation;* Jacques Derrida, "NO APOCALYPSE, NOT NOW (full speed ahead, seven missiles, seven missives)."

14. Anonymous article, quoted in Masuoka Toshikazu, *Hachigatsu no shijin: Gembaku shijin Tōge Sankichi no shi to shōgai*, 311.

15. Committee for the Compilation of Materials on the Damage Caused by the Atomic Bombs in Hiroshima and Nagasaki, *Hiroshima and Nagasaki*, 114, 366.

16. Itasaka Gen et al., eds., *Kodansha Encyclopedia of Japan*, 1:109.

17. From *Hiroshima wa uttaeru*, quoted in Masuoka Toshikazu, *Hachigatsu no shijin: Gembaku shijin Tōge Sankichi no shi to shōgai*, 300.

18. Saotome Katsumoto, "Heiwa wa aruite kite kurenai," 305.

19. Anthony Tucker and John Gleisner, *Crucible of Despair: The Effects of Nuclear War*, 51.

20. Hashioka Takeshi, "Hachigatsu nijūsannichi no koto," 368.

21. Brigadier General Thomas F. Farrell, quoted in Paul Boyer, *By the Bomb's Early Light: American Thought and Culture at the Dawn of the Atomic Age*, 66.

22. Toyoshima Yoshio, "'Hiroshima' e no kanshin," 57.

23. It is interesting to note that when the first atomic bombing was announced to the American people, President Truman chose to identify, incorrectly, Hiroshima not as a city but as "an important Japanese Army base." Such language suggests that Truman was himself aware that an atrocity had in fact been committed, and was sufficiently ashamed or frightened to lie to the public. See Barton J. Bernstein and Allen J. Matusow, eds., *The Truman Administration: A Documentary History*, 39.

24. The United States Strategic Bombing Survey, quoted in Edwin Fogelman, ed., *Hiroshima: The Decision to Use the A-bomb*, 87.

25. Admiral William D. Leahy, quoted in Leon Giovannitti and Fred Freed, *The Decision to Drop the Bomb*, 323.

26. Gar Alperovitz, *Atomic Diplomacy: Hiroshima and Potsdam*, 114. I am sure that many will disagree with my characterization of the atomic bombings as gratuitous violence—as far as the Second World War was concerned—and regret my cursory references to the voluminous scholarly material on just this point, perhaps one of the most controversial in modern military history. I am well aware of the academic challenges to the conclusions of historians such as Alperovitz—as well as the inevitable counter-challenges, and so on. I am also sure that a generation of Americans who were convinced their own lives hung upon the allegedly imminent decision to invade or not invade the main Japanese islands will find it difficult to sympathize with the position that my more detached reading has led me to assume—a position that I recognize is prompted in part by strongly held hopes as well as demonstrated evidence. However, finally this particular debate is of less significance than the issue which has always mattered most to the bombings' survivor-writers themselves: not the violence's strategic rationales or its political repercussions, but its proof of an unacceptably enlarged tolerance for cruelty—a word neither whose essence nor limits are beyond contention, but whose applicability to what occurred Hiroshima and Nagasaki seems as close to an intuitive truth as we are apt to find.

27. Major General Leslie R. Groves, quoted in Len Giovannitti and Fred Freed, *The Decision to Drop the Bomb*, 253.

28. Nakano Kōji, "Tamashii no kiroku," 164.

29. The Committee for the Compilation of Materials on Damage Caused by the Atomic Bombs in Hiroshima and Nagasaki, *Hiroshima and Nagasaki*, 337–78.

30. Frank Kermode, *The Sense of an Ending: Studies in the Theory of Fiction*, 95.

31. Suga Hidemi, quoted in Kuroko Kazuo, "Han-hankaku no shisō-teki kōsō," 99; Cynthia Ozick, "Innovation and Redemption: What Literature Means," 244. In trying to account for why "a gifted and respected American writer" might say such a thing, Ozick speculates that in his view surely "to be responsible as a writer is to be responsible solely to the seizures of language and dream" (245) and not to any particular moral subject. Ozick's explanation is as generous a one as I can imagine for Suga's remarks.

32. Zygmunt Bauman, *Modernity and the Holocaust*, 87.

33. George Steiner, "The Long Life of Metaphor," 160.

34. Robert Jay Lifton, *History and Human Survival*, 195. I am aware of no one who, more than Lifton, has both discerned the common terror of the Holocaust and Hiroshima and predicted more dire consequences. In his book *The Life of the Self: Toward a New Psychology*, Lifton writes: "I have emphasized the importance of holocaust in our symbolic vocabulary—of the recent past (Nazi death camps, Hiroshima and Nagasaki, Vietnam), the present (beginnings of massive starvation in Africa and on the Indian subcontinent), and the future (the imagery of ultimate destruction by nuclear weapons, environment pollution, or other means). Now we see the imagery of the holocaust coming together with the experience of postmodern cultural breakdown: our loss of faith not so much in this symbol or that but in the entire intricate web of images, rituals, institutions, and material objects that make up any culture" (136).

35. Berel Lang, "Genocide and Omnicide: Technology at the Limits," 115, 120.

36. Kurihara Sadako, "Hiroshima no bungaku o megutte–Aushubittsu to Hiroshima," 260. Just what Kurihara means by her metaphor of the "machine" is best explained in the following observation by Zygmunt Bauman: "Lucy S. Dawidowicz objects against equating the Holocaust with other cases of mass murder, like the wiping out of Hiroshima and Nagasaki: 'The purpose of the bombing was to demonstrate America's superior military power'; the bombing 'was not motivated by a wish to wipe out the Japanese people.' . . . Having made this evidently true observation, Dawidowicz nevertheless misses an important point: the killing of the two hundred thousand Japanese was conceived (and executed) as a searched-for effective means to implement the set goal; it was, indeed, a product of rational problem-solving mentality" (*Modernity and the Holocaust*, 210).

37. Hibakusha writer Kamezawa Miyuki makes the connection explicit between Germany's deception of its victims in the interests of efficiency and the similar effect of America's deceptively innocent means of delivery in Hiroshima. She compares the deaths of Japanese school children who had no idea that the sole parachute they saw in the sky carried the bomb that would kill them, with those of Jews sent to a gas chamber they thought was a shower ("Hiroshima junrei," 456). In neither case could there have been the chance to revolt and escape, or to dive for cover: in both cases ignorance insured the technology's maximum effectiveness.

38. Fukunaga Teruhiko, *Shi no shima*, 2:279.

39. Ishihara Kichirō, quoted in Nagaoka Hiroyoshi, *Gembaku bunken o yomu*, 16.

40. Ian Clark writes in *Nuclear Past, Nuclear Present: Hiroshima, Nagasaki, and Contemporary Strategy*: "It is a widely held belief that the bombings were not only politically efficacious but also morally justified: by putting an early end to the war, they saved lives, Japanese as well as American. In the great utilitarian calculus, the lives lost at Hiroshima and Nagasaki were deemed to be justified by the other lives that were spared: the bomb brought to an end the fire bombings of Japan and avoided an invasion of the Japanese home islands. . . . The bombings taught the lesson that atomic weapons could be used, not only to good military-political effect, but with full moral approbation" (5).

41. Elie Wiesel, *One Generation After*, 220.

42. Ōta Yōko, "Hotaru," 187–88.

43. Kamata Sadao, "Jūgonen-sensō to gembaku bungaku," 169–218.

44. Winston Churchill, quoted in Michael Mandelbaum, *The Nuclear Revolution: International Politics before and after Hiroshima*, 3.

45. Toyoshima Yoshio, "Bungaku ni okeru kōsōryoku," 31.

46. Shiina Rinzō, "Sensō ron," 26.

47. Kuroko Kazuo, *Gembaku to kotoba: Hara Tamiki kara Hayashi Kyōko made*, 189.

48. Kunioka Akikazu, "Gembaku ni ikite," 128–32.

49. Elias Canetti, *The Human Province*, 9.

50. Lawrence Langer, *The Age of Atrocity*, 63.

51. Lewis Mumford, *Technics and Civilization*, 268.

52. Lewis Mumford, quoted in F. J. Hoffmann, *The Mortal No: Death and the Modern Imagination*, 156–57.

53. Erich Kahler, *The Tower and the Abyss: An Inquiry into the Transformation of the Individual*, xiv.

54. Inokuchi Motosaburō, "Kyōten," 25.

55. Philip Morrison, quoted in Paul Boyer, *By the Bomb's Early Light*, 215.

56. Brown Miller, *Hiroshima Flows Through Us*, 9.

57. Ian Clark, *Nuclear Past, Nuclear Present*, 107.

58. Oda Makoto, "Han-kaku hansen," 31–32.

59. Kuroko Kazuo, *Gembaku to kotoba*, 33–34.

60. Nellie Sachs, quoted in Sidra Dekoven Ezrahi, *By Words Alone: The Holocaust in Literature*, 139–40.

61. "In fact the means of killing in Auschwitz was not revolutionary," wrote critic Nakayama Shigeru, "but the atomic bomb was a revolutionary development for both the history of science and technology and the history of industry" ("Sekai no gembaku bungaku," 25).

62. Marius Jansen, quoted in John W. Dower, "E. H. Norman, Japan, and the Uses of History," in E. H. Norman, *Origins of the Modern Japanese State: Selected Writings of E. H. Norman*, 56.

63. Hayashi Kyōko, "Buji—Seireki senkyūhyaku hachijūichi-nen: gembaku san-jūshichi-nen," 45.

64. Lawrence Freedman, *The Evolution of Nuclear Strategy*, 22.

65. Ōe Kenzaburō, "Kaku-jidai e no sōzōryoku," 102.

66. Uchimura Yoshiko, quoted in Publishing Committee for "Children of Hiroshima," ed., *Children of Hiroshima*, 265.

67. Robert Jay Lifton, *Broken Connection: On Death and the Continuity of Life*, 337.

68. William Faulkner, quoted in Michael Mandelbaum, *The Nuclear Revolution: International Politics Before and After Hiroshima*, 210.

69. Anonymous, quoted in Robert Jay Lifton, *Death in Life: The Survivors of Hiroshima*, 369.

70. Col. William S. Parsons, quoted in Paul Boyer, *By the Bomb's Early Light*, 232.

71. Nihon rekishi daijiten henshū iinkai, ed., *Nihon rekishi daijiten*, 2:347.

72. Nadezhda Mandelstam, *Hope Against Hope*, 45.

73. Günter Anders, quoted in Oguro Kaoru, "Hiroshima no sei to shi," 195–96.

74. David Rousset, *The Other Kingdom*, 168.

75. George Steiner, quoted in Lawrence Langer, *The Holocaust and the Literary Imagination*, 15.

76. Walter Benjamin, "The Storyteller: Reflections on the Works of Nikolai Leskov," *Illuminations*, 83–84.

77. Kuroko Kazuo, "'Shūmatsu' e no chōsen," 450.

78. Ozaki Kazuo, "Kaku-heiki: shiröto no shimpai," 422.

79. Ōe Kenzaburō, "Hiroshima, Amerika, Yōroppa," 197–98.

80. Noma Hiroshi, quoted in Abe Tomoji, "Gembaku to bungaku," 80.

81. Kurihara Sadako, *Dokyumento Hiroshima nijūyonen: Gendai no kyūsai*, 280.

82. Abe Tomoji, "Gembaku to bungaku," 80.

83. Ōe Kenzaburō, "Introduction: Toward the Unknowable Future," 15.

84. Toyoshima Yoshio, "Bungaku ni okeru kōsōryoku," 28.

85. Nagaoka Hiroyoshi, quoted in Kurihara Sadako, *Kaku-jidai ni ikiru: Hiroshima—shi no naka no sei*, 212.

86. Kokubo Hitoshi, "Futatabi 'gembaku bungaku' ni tsuite," 254.

87. John Whittier Treat, *Pools of Water, Pillars of Fire: The Literature of Ibuse Masuji*, 199–200.

88. Milan Kundera, *The Book of Laughter and Forgetting*, 3.

89. Ōe Kenzaburō, "Nani o kioku shi, kioku shitsuzukeru beki ka," 248.

90. Walter Benjamin, "The Storyteller," *Illuminations*, 94.

91. Hannah Arendt, *Eichmann in Jerusalem: A Report on the Banality of Evil*, 212.

1   Atrocity into Words

1. Hashimoto Kunie, "Wasureenu shinsetsu," 97.

2. Tōge Sankichi, *Gembaku shishū*, 145.

3. Hara Tamiki, "Sensō ni tsuite," 589.

4. Hachiya Michihiko, *Hiroshima Diary*, 55.

5. Mary McCarthy, quoted in Paul Boyer, *By the Bomb's Early Light: American Thought and Culture at the Dawn of the Atomic Age*, 183.

6. Tokunō Kōichi, quoted in Masuoka Toshikazu, *Hiroshima no shijin-tachi*, 63.

7. Fumizawa Takaichi, "Gembaku kō," 302.

8. Primo Levi, *Survival in Auschwitz*, 22.

9. Kijima Katsumi, "Kiesaranu kuyami", 91.

10. Albert Camus, quoted in Robert Jay Lifton, *Death in Life: Survivors of Hiroshima*, 534.

11. Takenishi Hiroko, "Hiroshima ga iwaseru kotoba," 322–23.

12. Ozaki Shirō, "Romanteki seishin no ikitsuku tokoro," 141.

13. Lawrence Langer, *The Holocaust and the Literary Imagination*, 37.

14. Richard Poirier, "Writing Off the Self," 216.

15. Berel Lang, *Act and Idea in the Nazi Genocide*, 151.

16. Ōta Yōko, "Bungaku no osoroshisa," 322.

17. Hara Tamiki, quoted in Kuroko Kazuo, *Gembaku to kotoba: Hara Tamiki kara Hayashi Kyōko made*, 134.

18. Gotō Minako, *Toki o hiku*, 222–23.

19. Ōe Kenzaburō, "Nani o kioku shi, kioku shitsuzukeru beki ka," 251.

20. Paul Fussell, *The Great War and Modern Memory*, 137–44.

21. Perhaps the most striking use of Buddhist motifs in the representation of Hiroshima and Nagasaki can be found in the paintings of Maruki Iri and Maruki Toshi. See John W. Dower and John Junkerman, eds., *The Hiroshima Murals: The Art of Iri Maruki and Toshi Maruki*.

There are, of course, accounts of large-scale natural and man-made disasters in classical Japanese literature. But whether they tell of fires and earthquakes or civil wars and acts of wanton cruelty, no recluse's memoir or military epic has provided any hibakusha writer with a narrative model for Hiroshima or Nagasaki. Perhaps classical Japanese literature is too highly aestheticized, or too religiously devout, to serve twentieth-century history. Or perhaps such literature is still too closely associated with the propaganda of the regime that led Japan into war. In any case, the allusion to classical culture among representations of the atomic bombings remains the sole purview of the visual arts, where no language and its particularly suspect rhetoric intrude.

22. Roland Barthes, "Writing Degree Zero," 14.

23. E. D. Hirsch, *Validity in Interpretation*, 31.

24. Ibid., 11.

25. Takenishi Hiroko, "Hiroshima ga iwaseru kotoba," 321.

26. José Ortega y Gasset, "The Dehumanization of Art," 18.

27. Harold Bloom, *A Map of Misreading*, 32.

28. Wayne Booth, *The Rhetoric of Fiction*, 116.

29. Roland Barthes, "Writing the Event," 149.

30. Maeda Masahiro, "Ani mo michigaeta kao," p. 67; Satō Makoto, *Nezumi Kozō: The Rat*, 278–92 passim.

31. Maurice Blanchot, *The Writing of the Disaster*, 28.

32. Bruno Bettelheim, quoted by Christopher Browning, "German Memory, Judicial Interrogation and Historical Reconstruction: Writing Perpetrator History from Post-War Oral Testimony."

33. Anonymous, quoted in Leslie Todd Pitre, "Of Patience, Faith, and Beloved Enemies," 5.

34. Toyoshima Yoshio, "Bungaku ni okeru kōsōryoku," 25.

35. Ōta Yōko, "Shikabane no machi jo," 305.

36. Frank Kermode, *The Sense of an Ending: Studies in the Theory of Fiction*, 133.

37. See Edward Said, *The World, the Text, and the Critic*, esp. 31–53.

38. Kuroko Kazuo, *Genbaku to kotoba: Hara Tamiki kara Hayashi Kyōko made*, 201.

39. Terrence Des Pres, *The Survivor: An Anatomy of Life in the Death Camps*, 147.

40. Kurihara Sadako, quoted in Nagaoka Hiroyoshi, *Genbaku bungaku shi*, 147.

41. Konaka Yōtarō, "Kyō no kaku-jōkyō to bungakusha no hankaku seimei," 45–46.

42. Frank Kermode, *The Sense of an Ending*, 130.

43. Wallace Stevens, *Opus Posthumous*, 165.

44. Elie Wiesel, quoted in Raul Hilberg, "I Was Not There," 23.

45. Ōe Kenzaburō, "Kaku-jidai e no sōzōryoku," 107. Imagination and its political

utility have been by Ōe's own admission one of his writings' two or three most frequent themes. Imagination is such a central concern because of its relationship with event, history, the real; and because of its relationship to how we are able to remake ourselves in light of—or despite—those things. In his 1967 essay "Kaku-kichi ni ikiru Nihon-jin—Okinawa no kaku-kichi to hibakusha-tachi," Ōe argues that imagination is just what we need to understand and confront what nuclear strategists otherwise have in store for us (214): imagination, in other words, is not only the means of recreating the past, but determining the future.

46. Frank Kermode, *The Sense of an Ending*, 164.

47. Hayashi Kyōko, quoted in Nakayama Kazuko, "Sakka annai," 238.

48. Yaguchi Hisayo, untitled testimony, 210.

49. Yamamoto Yasuo, "Maboroshi," 20.

50. Robert Jay Lifton, *Death in Life: Survivors of Hiroshima*, 201.

51. Elie Wiesel, *The Gates of the Forest*, 172.

52. Hayashi Kyōko, "Mumyō," 216.

53. Takahashi Shinji, *Hiroshima no rinri*, 130.

54. Saul Bellow, quoted in Wayne Booth, *The Rhetoric of Fiction*, 118.

55. Sata Ineko, "Kaisetsu," 338–39.

56. Kokubo Hitoshi, "Futatabi 'gembaku bungaku' ni tsuite," 253.

57. Walter Benjamin, "Edward Fuchs, Collector and Historian," *Illuminations*, 359.

58. Tadeusz Borowski, "Auschwitz, Our Home (A Letter)," 130–34.

59. Sidra DeKoven Ezrahi, *By Words Alone: The Holocaust in Literature*, 2.

60. Miyoshi Tatsuji, "Kennin-jikyū," 121.

61. Takekoshi Yoshio, "Shi to gembaku," 143.

62. Susan Sontag, "Against Interpretation," 7.

63. Nakajima Kenzō, "'Gembaku bungaku' no imi," 375.

64. Unno Jūza, "Genshi bakudan to jikyū bōei," 20.

65. Ōta Yōko, *Shikabane no machi*, 28.

66. Roland Barthes, "Writing Degree Zero," 17.

67. Kurihara Sadako, "Gembaku bungaku ronsō shi (shō)—Ōta Yōko o jiku ni," 277.

68. Kenneth Burke, *The Philosophy of Literary Form*, 1.

2   Genre and Post-Hiroshima Representation

1. José Ortega y Gasset, "The Dehumanization of Art," 47.

2. The Committee for the Compilation of Materials on Damage Caused by the Atomic Bombs in Hiroshima and Nagasaki, *Hiroshima and Nagasaki: The Physical, Medical, and Social Effects of the Atomic Bombings*, 34.

3. The United States Strategic Bombing Survey, *The Effects of Atomic Bombs on Hiroshima and Nagasaki*, 15.

4. Erich Auerbach, *Mimesis: The Representation of Reality in Western Literature*, 20.

5. Terrence Des Pres, *The Survivor*, 199.

6. Hayashi Kyōko, "Kiroku," 165.

7. Doi Sadako, "Tomo ni tasukeraretsutsu," 23.

8. Kanaya Masako, "Keroido o nokoshite," 43.

9. Sera Megumi, untitled memoir, 256.

10. Hara Tamiki, quoted in Nakahodo Masanori, *Hara Tamiki nōto*, 247.

11. Iwamoto Hakuzō, "Ko no shikabane o yaku," 210.

12. Kitayama Futaba, "A, rakkasan da," 20.

13. Yamashiro Tomoe, "Jo," 114–15. There is a brief account of Yamashiro's own life, as well as a translation of one of her stories, in Mikiso Hane's *Reflections on the Way to the Gallows: Voices of Japanese Rebel Women*. See the last chapter, "The World of the Stars: Yamashiro Tomoe," 213–52.

14. Kamata Sadao, "Kaisetsu (2)—Nagasaki no hibaku taiken kiroku," 516.

15. Kitayama Futaba, "A, rakkasan da," 16.

16. Toyoshima Yoshio, "Bungaku ni okeru kōsōryoku," 27.

17. John Hersey, *Hiroshima*, 23.

18. In December 1946, General Headquarters (GHQ) originally forbade the publication of Hersey's *Hiroshima* in its Japanese translation, but relented in the spring of 1949. An initial run of fifty thousand copies published by Hōsei University sold out almost immediately.

19. Nagaoka Hiroyoshi, *Gembaku minshūshi*, 139.

20. Ronald Weber, *The Literature of Fact: Literary Nonfiction in American Writing*, 69.

21. Anonymous, quoted in Paul Boyer, *By the Bomb's Early Light: American Thought and Culture at the Dawn of the Atomic Age*, 206.

22. Ibid.

23. These remarks were originally made in MacDonald's October, 1946, review of Hersey's *Hiroshima*. This review is anthologized in Dwight MacDonald, *Memoirs of A Revolutionist: Essays in Political Criticism*, 179–80; this particular quote is from 180.

24. Kuno Osamu, quoted in Nagaoka Hiroyoshi, *Gembaku bunken o yomu*, 135.

25. Berel Lang, *Act and Idea in the Nazi Genocide*, 138.

26. Anonymous, quoted in Robert Jay Lifton, *Death in Life*, 19. I have rearranged Lifton's quote into four lines in order to more closely resemble the poetic genre, the *tanka* (waka), to which Lifton ascribes it. Unfortunately, Lifton does not identify the professor by name.

27. Yamada Kan, "Kaisetsu (4)—Nagasaki no gembaku shika," 524.

28. Theodor W. Adorno, "Engagement," 125–27.

29. Ōhara Miyao, "Hiroshima—Nagasaki to gembaku shi no shihan seiki," 264.

30. Akiya Yutaka, "Fuyu no shudai," 219.

31. Ōhashi Kiichi, "Gembaku to watakushi ni totte no gekisaku," 269.

32. Berel Lang, *Act and Idea in the Nazi Genocide*, 132.

33. *Nezumi Kozō: The Rat,* as well as the other plays discussed in this chapter, have been translated and briefly analyzed in David G. Goodman's valuable translation and study, *After Apocalypse: Four Japanese Plays of Hiroshima and Nagasaki.* While my view of these plays, and particularly of Satō's, is more critical than Goodman's own, I am indebted to his work for raising a number of issues crucial to any theory of the dramatic representation of atrocity.

Other important Japanese plays treating the atomic bombings, but not discussed by Goodman, would include Miyamoto Ken's famous work about Claude Eatherly, *The Pilot* (Za pairotto, 1965); Koyama Yūshi's *Beneath the Magnolias* (Taisanboku no ki no shita de, 1963) and *A Flower in Winter* (Fuyu no hana, 1970); Hara Gen'ichi's *The Harbor* (Gyokō, 1959); Fujita Asaya's *About the Tears About Hiroshima* (Hiroshima ni tsuite no namida ni tsuite, 1968); and Ōhashi Kiichi's prize-winning *A Record of Zero* (Zero no kiroku, 1968).

34. David G. Goodman, trans. and ed., *After the Apocalypse,* 262.

35. George Steiner, "Dying as an Art," 301.

36. Albert Camus, *Notebooks,* 119.

37. David G. Goodman, trans. and ed., *After Apocalypse,* 12–13, 187.

38. F. J. Hoffman, *The Mortal No: Death and the Modern Imagination,* 140.

39. Theodor W. Adorno, *Negative Dialectics,* 367.

40. F. J. Hoffman, *The Mortal No,* 159.

41. Terrence Des Pres, *The Survivor,* 5.

42. In early 1958 Tanizaki began serializing a novel entitled *An Account of Brutality* (Zangyakuki), the protagonist of which had been rendered impotent by the atomic bomb. He abandoned the project in November of that same year.

James Agee attempted a novel about the A-bomb from an American point of view soon after Hiroshima, but he despaired even more quickly than did Tanizaki. See Paul Boyer, *By the Bomb's Early Light,* 243–44.

43. Takeda Taijun, quoted in Yamamoto Kenkichi, "Shijin no shi no imi suru mono—Hara Tamiki no shi ni tsuite," 589.

44. José Ortega y Gasset, "Notes on the Novel," 58.

45. Frank Kermode, *The Sense of an Ending,* 167.

46. Kaga Otohiko, "Kaisetsu," 69.

47. Fukunaga Teruhiko, *Shi no shima,* 1:70.

48. Albert Camus, *Notebooks,* 21.

49. In the specific instance of Japan, Jay Rubin has shown that "realism" was feared as subversive ever since novelist Oguri Fūyō's *Making up for Bed* (Ne-oshiroi) was banned in 1896. See Rubin, *Injurious to Public Morals: Writers and the Meiji State,* 42.

50. Odagiri Hideo, "Genshiryoku mondai to bungaku," 195.

51. Kurihara Sadako, *Dokyumento Hiroshima nijūyonen: Gendai no kyūsai,* 172.

52. Theodor W. Adorno, *Negative Dialectics,* 367–68.

53. Rolf Hochhuth, "The Deputy," 248.

54. Satō Hachirō, "Yomu made to yomioete to," 126–27.

55. Paul Fussell, *The Great War and Modern Memory,* 7.

56. Kitayama Futaba, "A, rakkasan da," 11.

57. See Northrop Frye, *Anatomy of Criticism: Four Essays*, especially the chapter "Theory of Modes," 33–67.

58. Kuroko Kazuo, *Gembaku to kotoba: Hara Tamiki kara Hayashi Kyōko made*, 167.

59. Frank Kermode, *The Sense of an Ending*, 67.

60. Inokuchi Motosaburō, "Kyōten," 26.

61. Karl Popper, *Quantum Theory and the Schism in Physics*, 2.

62. Takenishi Hiroko, "Hiroshima ga iwaseru kotoba," 321.

63. Theodor W. Adorno, *Negative Dialectics*, 362.

64. Hanada Kiyoteru, "Genshi jidai no geijutsu," 204.

65. In a conversation with Giairo Daghini in 1984, later translated into German and published in *Immaterialität und Postmoderne*, Lyotard states "Die Moderne ist jedoch nicht 'unvollendet,' sondern sie wurde 'liquidert.' Nach Auschwitz und dem Stalinismus lässt sich gewiss nicht behaupten, dass die Hoffnungen, die sich mit der Moderne verbanden, erfüllt worden sind. Allerdings sind sie nicht vergessen, sondern zerstört" (37–38).

66. Alvin Rosenfeld, *A Double Dying: Reflections on Holocaust Literature*, 33.

67. Mieko Hara, untitled memoir, 244.

68. Theodor W. Adorno, *Negative Dialectics*, 362.

69. Michael Geyer, "Man-made Transcendences: Consumerism, Violence, and the Problem of Memory."

70. Hayden White, "Historical Employments and the Problem of 'Truth.'"

71. Fredric Jameson, quoted in Anders Stephanson, "Regarding Postmodernism— A Conversation with Fredric Jameson," 21.

72. Berel Lang, *Act and Idea in the Nazi Genocide*, 155.

73. Theodor W. Adorno, *Negative Dialectics*, 631.

74. In some ways, the task of the atomic-bomb survivor-writer remains unequalled in its impossible demands, despite the newer instances of mass death since the end of the Second World War. For example, novelist Andrew Holleran, despairing of any literary genre's ability to describe the AIDS epidemic, has suggested in an essay entitled "Reading and Writing," that "the only other possible enduring thing would be a list of names" (18). The logic that informs such stark minimalism—much like the design of Maya Lin's controversial Vietnam War Memorial—shares with Japanese atomic-bomb literature a retreat from the dangers of rhetorical elaboration. But how would one assemble such a list for Hiroshima and Nagasaki? Where the enormous number of casualties, as well as the means of death, precluded something so basic as even record-keeping? So much greater, then, the onus of the atomic-bomb writer to undertake what, for Holleran, is writing's pathetic last resort.

3   The Three Debates

1. Elie Wiesel, *The Accident*, 7.

2. Anonymous, quoted in Itō Narihiko, "Kaisetsu—'kaku' o mitsumete kita me 1945–1983," 518.

3. Arisue Seizō, quoted in Len Giovannitti and Fred Freed, *The Decision to Drop the Bomb*, 268.

4. Nagaoka Hiroyoshi, "Gembaku bungaku no keifu," 225–26.

5. Kurihara Sadako, *Kaku-jidai ni ikiru: Hiroshima—shi no naka no sei*, 261.

6. George M. Kren and Leon Rappoport, *The Holocaust and the Crisis of Human Behavior*, 1.

7. Okuno Takeo, *Nihon bungaku shi*, 184. Okuno is both right and wrong. There are many, and a few outstanding, postwar novels that describe and indict barbarous acts of the Japanese during the war. Takeda Taijun, Agawa Hiroyuki, Hotta Yoshie, and Ōoka Shōhei wrote of the depths to which the military sank in China and the Philippines; Endo Shūsaku has exposed the complicity of civilians at home in war crimes. But apparently all these novels are limited to the point of view of the Japanese themselves, and never includes that of their victims. There is, as far as I know, no novel for the Rape of Nanking, for example, that tells that horrible story from the stance of the Chinese, though there is a very large nonfictional and journalistic literature in Japan on just that topic, as well as a famous mural painting by Maruki Iri and Maruki Toshi, the artists most closely associated with the visual representation of Hiroshima and Nagasaki. One recalls the remarks of the film executive who, when explaining why all references to the Rape of Nanking were expunged from Japanese showing of *The Last Emperor* (over the strenuous objections of its director, Bernardo Bertolucci), said that no one wished "to confuse the Japanese public about what happened."

But before one criticizes the Japanese for their failure to produce a literature of their own atrocities that parallels that of Hiroshima and Nagasaki, we should note that American culture is similarly silent on indigeneous genocide and the violence of Vietnam as well as, of course, its atomic bombings. Like Japan, the United States has produced voluminous materials of a scholarly and reportative nature on just these sad chapters of its history; but again like Japan, the novel seems conspicuously absent from those materials. Can we speculate that, worldwide, the power of imaginative writing— powerful because it makes us *live* the stories it tells—will inevitably make it the last genre to remind us of the histories we inherit, the legacies that make us what we are?

8. See Nakano Kōji and Nagaoka Hiroyoshi, "Gembaku bungaku o megutte," 21.

9. Throughout this book I will use the word "canon" to describe those works of Japanese literature that meet one—typically more—of the following conditions: (1) it is regularly reprinted or anthologized, (2) it is commonly taught in the schools, and (3) it is subject to a sustained and high level of critical study. The fact that Japanese has no word exactly corresponding to "canon" does not mean that neither the concept nor the practice exists: terms such as *taikei* "system" and *meisaku* "masterpiece" often semantically approximate it, and *bungaku* "literature" itself seems practically to serve a similar principle of conservative stewardship.

Just as the Buddhist canon traditionally tends to emphasize inclusiveness as against a biblical canon based on exclusiveness, the modern Japanese literary canon is probably more diverse and tolerant than the current debates here would seem to indicate our own, American versions are: a liberality that makes the struggle for atomic-bomb writers and their sympathetic critics to gain admission for their works all the more resentful.

10. Kuroko Kazuo, *Gembaku to kotoba: Hara Tamiki kara Hayashi Kyōko made*, 58–59.

11. Ochiai Naobumi, Ikebe Yoshikata and Hagino Yoshiyuki, quoted in Michael Brownstein, "From *Kokugaku* to *Kokubungaku*: Canon Formation in the Meiji Period," 444.

12. Tony Siebers, *The Ethics of Criticism,* 8.

13. Katō Shūichi, *A History of Japanese Literature,* vol. 3: *The Modern Years,* 273; Donald Keene, *Dawn to the West: Japanese Literature in the Modern Era (Fiction),* 963.

14. Jay Rubin, "From Wholesomeness to Decadence: The Censorship of Literature under the Allied Occupation," 71.

15. Kurihara Sadako, *Dokyumento Hiroshima nijūyonen: Gendai no kyūsai,* 165.

16. In light of the overwhelming problems that faced Japan in the immediate aftermath of the defeat, the cruel triage that the Allied Occupation carried out left no doubt that the cities of Hiroshima and Nagasaki were to be abandoned entirely: "On 6 September 1945, the General Headquarters of the Occupation forces issued a statement that made it clear that people likely to die from A-bomb afflictions should be left to die. The official attitude in early September was that people suffering from radiation injuries were not worth saving." Committee for the Compilation of Materials on Damage Caused by the Atomic Bombs in Hiroshima and Nagasaki, *Hiroshima and Nagasaki: The Physical, Medical, and Social Effects of the Atomic Bombings,* 14.

17. Nagaoka Hiroyoshi, *Gembaku bunken o yomu,* 16.

18. Yamamoto Kenkichi, "Shijin no shi no imi suru mono—Hara Tamiki no shi ni tsuite," 581.

19. Etō Jun, quoted in Jay Rubin, "From Wholesomeness to Decadence," 71.

20. Kurihara Sadako, *Dokyumento Hiroshima nijūyonen,* 192.

21. Jay Rubin, "From Wholesomeness to Decadence," 88. See also Matsuura Sōzo, "Senryōgun no genron dan'atsu: gembaku hōdō wa hitoku sareta."

22. Mizuta Kuwajirō, *Gembaku o yomu,* 40.

23. Satō Tadao, *Nihon eiga shisō shi,* 329.

24. Nakano Shigeharu, "*Gembaku shishū* ni tsuite," 131.

25. "Chūgoku" refers to the city of Hiroshima and its geographical region of western Honshū, the largest of the Japanese islands. Sponsored by the Chūgoku Culture Federation (Chūgoku Bunka Remmei) founded in October 1945 by Kurihara Sadako and Kurihara Tadaichi, *Chūgoku bunka* was published nineteen times between March 1946 and the end of 1948. It was the first issue, however, a special one organized exclusively around the theme of the bombing, that was an important milestone in postwar literature both nationally and in Hiroshima itself. Acclaimed by Masuoka Toshikazu as "the first general-interest magazine founded in postwar Hiroshima, and the first to publish a special issue on the atomic bombing," it managed to avoid Occupation censorship by strategically and occasionally making such assertions as "it was the bomb that gave us peace." See Masuoka Toshikazu, *Hiroshima no shijin-tachi,* 98.

Kyōyū, founded at approximately the same time as *Chūgoku bunka* by Maekawa Noritaka and the two dozen other writers (including Shijō Miyoko, discussed later) associated with the mainstream Hiroshima literary society Fiction Study Group (Shōsetsu Benkyō Kai), published twenty-one issues by its demise in July 1949. For details of how these two journals functioned in a complementary opposition with each other, see

Iwasaki Seiichirō, *Hiroshima no bungei—chiteki fudo to kiseki,* especially chapter 4, "Hon-ryū—bungei fukkō ki," 66–118.

26. At the time of its publication, a number of mainstream Japanese critics, most prominently Etō Jun, hailed *Black Rain* as a "masterpiece," the first "literary" treatment of the atomic bombings. This praise, of course, meant that no prior atomic-bomb writing should be considered literary. Ōe Kenzaburō speculated at the time that the Ibuse's novel won such unprecedented favor because of its lack of overt anti-Americanism, or indeed lack of any political references at all, and thus naturally attracted the patronage of conservative intellectuals. See the later chapter "Ibuse Masuji: Nature, Nostalgia, Memory," as well as "Ibuse, *Black Rain,* and the Present Day," in John Whittier Treat, *Pools of Water, Pillars of Fire: The Literature of Ibuse Masuji,* 199–201.

27. The ratification of the U.S.-Japan Security Treaty in 1959–60 was one of the most controversial and violent events of postwar Japanese history. This treaty—commonly referred to as "Ampo" in Japanese—allows for the presence of, and freedom of action for, U.S. bases and military personnel in Japan and was a condition of the San Francisco Peace Treaty signed by both nations in 1951. Overwhelming popular opposition to the renewal of the treaty culminated in mass demonstrations that largely immobilized the Japanese government in the spring of 1960. It was nonetheless automatically renewed (as it routinely is now every ten years) four days after Kamba Michiko, a protesting college student, was crushed to death in a riot at the Diet building in Tokyo.

28. Odagiri Hideo, "Genshiryoku mondai to bungaku," 192–93; Nagaoka Hiroyoshi, "Gembaku bungaku sakuhin mokuroku."

29. Esashi Akiko, *Kusazue: Ōta Yōko hyōden,* 150–51.

30. For discussions of the Japanese bundan in English, see Irene Powell, *Writers and Society in Modern Japan,* and Edward Fowler, *The Rhetoric of Confession: Shishōsetsu in Early Twentieth-Century Japanese Fiction,* especially 128–45.

31. Masao Miyoshi, *Accomplices of Silence: The Modern Japanese Novel,* xii.

32. Donald Keene, *Dawn to the West: Japanese Literature in the Modern Era (Poetry, Drama, Criticism),* 550.

33. Nagaoka Hiroyoshi, *Gembaku minshūshi,* 162–63.

34. Maekawa Noritaka, quoted in Iwasaki Seiichirō, *Hiroshima no bungei—chiteki fudo to kiseki,* 70.

35. Yamamoto Kenkichi, quoted in ibid., 106. In fact, Yamamoto's severe criticisms, which appeared in the widely read national monthly *Bungakkai,* prompted something of a revolt among the younger contributors to *Hiroshima bungaku.* Beginning with its third issue, editorial policy seemed to have changed: works of atomic-bomb literature started to appear, and by the fourth issue authors associated with Maekawa's earlier *Kyōyū* ceased to publish in *Hiroshima bungaku* at all.

36. Iwasaki Seiichirō, *Higure no machi,* 228–29.

37. Leslie Epstein, "Writing about the Holocaust," 263.

38. Nagaoka Hiroyoshi, "Gembaku bungaku to sengo nashonarizumu," 376.

39. Kokubo Hitoshi, "Futatabi 'gembaku bungaku' ni tsuite," 254–55.

40. Ōta Yōko, "Sakka no taido," 242–45.

41. Shijō Miyoko, "'Gembaku bungaku' ni tsuite," 250.

42. Kurihara Sadako, "Gembaku bungaku ronsō shi (shō)—Ōta Yōko o jiku ni," 273.

43. Iwasaki Seiichirō, *Higure no machi*, 234.

44. Hirakushi Kenjirō, quoted in Kurihara Sadako, "Gembaku bungaku ronsō shi (shō)—Ōta Yōko o jiku ni," 277.

45. Aono Suekichi, "Hiroshima to heiwa," 64.

46. Kokubo Hitoshi, "Futatabi 'gembaku bungaku' ni tsuite."

47. Anonymous, quoted in Robert Jay Lifton, *Death in Life: The Survivors of Hiroshima,* 79.

48. Iwasaki Seiichirō, "'Hachigatsu muika' o kaku dainishū kaisetsu," 339–40.

49. Odagiri Hideo, "Genshiryoku mondai to bungaku," 180–97.

50. Abe Tomoji, "Gembaku to bungaku," 88.

51. Matsuhara Takahisa, quoted in Kurihara Sadako, "Gembaku bungaku ronsō shi (shō)—Ōta Yōko o jiku ni," 169.

52. Fukagawa Munetoshi, "'Kanashimi o taete'—'gembaku bungaku' ron o chūshin ni," 257.

53. Perhaps no other atomic-bomb critic has had the audience, and impact, as Kurihara. The most important collections of her work are *Dokyumento Hiroshima nijūyonen: Gendai no kyūsai, Hiroshima no genfūkei o idaite,* and *Kaku-jidai ni ikiru: Hiroshima—shi no naka no sei.* For additional information on Kurihara, and particularly her poetry, see the later chapter, "Poetry Against Itself."

54. Kurihara Sadako, "Gembaku bungaku ronsō shi (shō)—Ōta Yōko o jiku ni," 289.

55. Matsumoto Hiroshi, "Fumō de nai bungaku no tame ni: Kurihara Sadako-shi e no hanron," 264.

56. See the subsequent chapter "Nagasaki and the Human Future" for a more detailed discussion of Hayashi's major atomic-bomb writings.

57. Karatani Kōjin, Kawamura Jirō, and Nakagami Kenji, "Sōsaku gōhyō," 288.

58. Claude Lévi-Strauss, quoted by Sande Cohen, "Historians' Histories and the 'Final Solution' as Dispossession."

59. See Nakano Kōji, "'Hankaku' ni goryū shita bungakusha no nikusei."

60. Ōe Kenzaburō, "Japanese Intellectuals at Bay," 6.

61. See Nakano Kōji, "'Bungakusha no seimei' ni tsuite."

62. "Kaku-sensō no kiken o uttaeru bungakusha no seimei." The "Three Non-Nuclear Principles" (*Hikaku sangensoku*), or the promise that "Japan will not produce, possess, or let others bring in" nuclear weapons, was announced as a national policy by Prime Minister Satō Eisaku (who subsequently won the Nobel Peace Prize in 1974) in January 1968 and adopted as a resolution by the Diet in 1972. A number of years later, however, persistent rumors that in fact Japan had allowed the U.S. military to bring nuclear weapons onto its territory were publicly confirmed by a former ambassador to Japan, Edwin O. Reischauer.

63. Kinoshita Junji, quoted in Masuoka Toshikazu, *Gembaku shijin monogatari*, 184.

64. See Nishida Masaru et al., "Futatabi kaku-sensō no kiki ni bungakusha wa dono yō ni tai suru ka."

65. Ayukawa Nobuo, quoted in Itō Narihiko, "Gembaku bungaku to kyō no mondai," 98.

66. Suga Hidemi, "'Kaku-sensō no kiken o uttaeru bungakusha no seimei' o yomu."

67. Nakagami Kenji, "Karasu," 83–84. The Imperial Rule Assistance Association (Taisei Yokusan Kai) was established in 1940 as the single political party meant to replace the several that had existed until that time. It soon, however, was used as the mechanism for the extension of state control of many, if not all, aspects of national life. Although several postwar historians have likened the IRAA to Germany's Nazi Party, in theory *every* Japanese subject (which would have included colonial peoples) was a member; it is this totalizing feature of the IRAA that proposed it as an apt analogy for Nakagami in his critique of the Japanese antinuclear movement.

68. See Konaka Yōtarō, "Kyō no kaku-jōkyō to bungakusha no hankaku seimei," 52–53. Hayashi Kyōko might accept the validity of a charge of "andropocentism" or "unabashed humanism" against the Writers' Appeal and, by extension, her own work. But her humanism is one she has chosen to define for herself, and thus perhaps it is in a way distinct from that of those who find the word, and the thought behind it, unacceptable. In her essay "'Water,' 'Crows,' and 'Boys and Girls'" (Mizu—karasu—shōnen shōjo, 1976) Hayashi thinks about the children her fellow Nagasaki hibakusha have borne—children whom worried authorities, Hayashi reports, have suggested should have been barred from being born in order to spare the state the probable cost of their eventual medical care: "They enjoy excellent health and lead wonderful lives. Because, by virtue of their parentage, they bear the burden of being second-generation hibakusha, they know each day of those lives the preciousness of life and the humility involved in prizing every moment of time. All right, let's suppose that they've been struck down by atomic-bomb disease: they are still *human beings*. Who has the right to govern even these children's own progeny?" (35)

69. Suga Hidemi, "'Kaku-sensō no kiken o uttaeru bungakusha no seimei' o yomu."

70. See Yoshimoto Takaaki, *"Hankaku" iron.*

71. While Karatani himself makes no such explicit connection, the Writers' Appeal's deployment of such language as "overcoming" "ideology" perilously resembles that of the infamous "Overcoming the Modern" (*Kindai no chōkoku*) discussions of July 1942, when leading Japanese intellectuals convened in Kyoto under the auspices of a leading literary journal to theorize a postmodern, i.e, post-Western, Japan in the context of the state's anti-Western propaganda. See H. D. Harootunian, "Visible Discourses/Invisible Ideologies," especially 67–71.

72. Karatani Kōjin, "Hankaku apīru ni tsuite," 237.

73. Ibid.

74. See Nishida Masaru et al., "Futatabi kaku-sensō no kiki ni bungakusha wa dono yō ni tai suru ka," 27.

75. Kuroko Kazuo, "Han-hankaku no shisōteki kōsō," 99.

76. Tanaka Yasuo, quoted in Nishida Masaru et al., "Futatabi kaku-sensō no kiki ni bungakusha wa dono yō ni tai suru ka," 27.

77. Ibid., 44.

78. Ibid., 16.

79. Matsumoto Ken'ichi, ed., *Ronsō no dōjidai shi*, 333.

80. Nishida Masaru et al., "Futatabi kaku-sensō no kiki ni bungakusha wa dono yō ni tai suru ka," 28.

81. Masuoka Toshikazu, *Gembaku shijin monogatari*, 7.

82. Ibid.

83. Yoshimoto Takaaki, "Sekai ron," 22.

84. Nishida Masaru et al., "Futatabi kaku-sensō no kiki ni bungakusha wa dono yō ni tai suru ka," 17.

85. Kurihara Sadako, *Dokyumento Hiroshima nijūyonen: Gendai no kyūsai*, 283.

86. Abe Tomoji, "Jobun."

4 Hara Tamiki and the Documentary Fallacy

1. See Ōta Yōko, "Hara Tamiki no shi ni tsuite," 600–601.

2. Ōe Kenzaburō, for instance, calls Hara "a master of poetic prose suffused with gentleness" in his introduction to a collection of atomic-bomb literature including both an abridged version of Hara's "Summer Flowers" and "The Land of Heart's Desire" (Shin-gan no kuni). In an editor's preface to a 1973 Japanese anthology of Hara's postwar writings, Ōe goes so far as to say "Hara Tamiki is the greatest author in contemporary Japanese literature to have described the experience of the atomic bomb." See Ōe, "In-troduction: Toward the Unknowable Future," 10–11; "Hara Tamiki to wakai hitobito to no hashi no tame ni," 182.

3. Honda Shūgo, "Kaen no ko," 579.

4. For a detailed account in English of Hara's life, see Richard H. Minear, *Hiroshima: Three Witnesses*, 29–40.

5. Kokai Eiji, *Hara Tamiki—shijin no shi*, 23.

6. Ibid., 83.

7. Hara discusses the death of his father in "A Break in the Clouds" (Kumo no sa-keme, 1947). Tsuru's death is referred to often in Hara's work, but it is treated in the greatest detail in "Honoo."

8. See Yamamoto Kenkichi, "Shijin no shi no imi suru mono: Hara Tamiki no shi ni tsuite," 584–85.

9. See Kokai Eiji, *Hara Tamiki—shijin no shi*, 24.

10. Ibid., 34.

11. See Nagaoka Hiroyoshi, *Gembaku bungaku shi*, 93.

12. Terada Tōru, "Hara Tamiki," 608.

13. Katsumoto Seiichirō, quoted in Kuroko Kazuo, *Gembaku to kotoba: Hara Tamiki kara Hayashi Kyōko made*, 131.

14. Nakahodo Masanori, *Hara Tamiki nōto*, 54.

15. Donald Keene writes, "If any movement in Japanese literature of the twentieth century can be described as central, it is doubtlessly Naturalism *(shizenshugi)*. . . . Its influence is not yet spent." *Dawn to the West: Japanese Literature in the Modern Era (Fiction)*, 220. Mailer's comments on the continuing force of Naturalism are paraphrased in Shinohara Shigeru, *Ōe Kenzaburō ron*, 133.

16. Shimazaki Tōson made an important contribution to the assimilation of Naturalist thought in Japan with *The Broken Commandment* because, though it is a work featuring many themes and images reminiscent of Romanticism, it also describes, in the tradition of Zola, the life of its hero as the aggregate of a complex array of forces acting upon him as their focus. It is with Tayama Katai, however, that readers learn how those forces that determine men and women can turn dark and even potentially lethal. That this historically critical turn should have taken place in Katai's writing is doubly significant, for Katai fulfilled much the same role in Japan as did Zola in France in formulating and propagating the explicit terms of Naturalism. The Japanese equivalent of *Le Roman experimental* was Katai's essay "Straightforward Description" (Rokotsu naru byōsha, 1904), in which his attack on *gikō*, or "stylistic artifice," in fiction represented an attempt to render writing transparent (which is to say, documentary), to replace rhetorical figures with what Katai considered a prior reality, a reality continuous with that of perceivable objects and forces. Katai's own fiction demonstrates both this displacement of an interior set of laws (rhetoric, style) with an exterior set ("natural" phenomena) and the subsequent evolution of a literature predicated on the centrality of forces that must increasingly dominate character. *The Quilt*, for instance, evokes the power of the libido and its control of a teacher attracted to his student. The sexual force establishes itself as potentially lethal, and certainly autonomous, on the novel's very first page when Katai refers to a "hidden force" that could destroy everything in his character's life. By the middle of *The Quilt*, the origin of this force at work on the teacher has clearly shifted to the exterior and grown actively hostile; most significantly, the force of lust now alters people rather than simply accounts for them. "He always regretted being controlled by this strength, but sooner or later he was always beaten and forced into submission by it" (50). By this point in *The Quilt*, a work that stands at or near the beginning of naturalistic writing in Japan, the destructive potential of the forces used to construct the narrative is already noted. By 1912 and his short story "The Railroad Tracks" (Senro), violence in Katai's writing has become so prominent that the work opens with a nameless five-year-old child being run over by a train. Both the first and last thing the reader knows about the victim is his/her death beneath a massive, insurmountable force; any possibility of the story that follows granting the child a "character" has been precluded by the fact of that train. The central experience of Katai's life was his experience as a journalist at the front during the Russo-Japanese War; Hara's was his presence in Hiroshima on August 6, 1945; a direct line can be drawn between the former's naturalist writing at the beginning of the century and the latter's documentary at its halfway point.

17. Kurita Tōhei, "Seidōshoku no yami," 298.

18. See for example "Motion" (Idō, 1935), "A Parable" (Hiyu, 1935). "Sparrows" (Suzume, 1935), and "A Stroll in the Summer Heat" (Manatsubi no sampo, 1935).

19. Sigmund Freud, "Thoughts for the Times on War and Death," 289.

20. Nagata Hiroshi, "Kaisetsu," 545–46.

21. Hara's dependence on his wife was extreme, and her importance to him is amply reflected in his writings both early and late. She is always portrayed as a loving and supportive wife, one whom Kokai Eiji claims "harbored [Hara] from the world and its storms" (86). Among the many essays that mention the touching role Sadae played in her husband's life, one of the best is Satō Haruo, "*Hara Tamiki shishū* jobun."

22. The principal works are "A Painfully Beautiful Summer" (Kurushiku utsukushiki natsu, 1949), "Autumn Diary" (Aki nikki, 1947), "Winter Diary" (Fuyu nikki, 1946), "On the Brink of a Beautiful Death" (Utsukushiki shi no kishi ni, 1950) and "A View Into Death" (Shi no naka no fūkei, 1951).

23. Itō Sei, quoted in Kokai Eiji, *Hara Tamiki—shijin no shi*, 132.

24. Hara Tamiki, quoted in Masuoka Toshikazu, *Hiroshima no shijin-tachi*, 8–9.

25. Kurihara Sadako, *Dokyumento Hiroshima nijūyonen: Gendai no kyūsai*, 258.

26. Nagaoka Hiroyoshi, *Gembaku bungaku shi*, 210.

27. The Committee for the Compilation of Materials on Damage Caused by the Atomic Bombs in Hiroshima and Nagasaki, *Hiroshima and Nagasaki: The Physical, Medical, and Social Effects of the Atomic Bombings*, 61.

28. Tōge Sankichi, *Gembaku shishū*, 145.

29. Ōta Yōko, "*Shikabane no machi* jo," 300.

30. See the next chapter, "Poetry Against Itself," for a fuller discussion of Hara's, and other atomic-bomb writers', use of nonstandard orthographies.

31. Nagaoka Hiroyoshi, *Gembaku minshūshi*, 164.

32. See Terada Tōru, "Hara Tamiki," 607.

33. See Hara Tamiki, "Chiisa na mura," 97.

34. "Prelude to Annihilation" is a powerfully ironic description of Hiroshima in the days just before the bombing. It is filled with highly ironic foreshadowing of the destruction to come; it concludes: "There were still a little over forty hours until the atomic bomb would call on the city." "From the Ruins" is a somewhat less interesting story of Hara's life in the nearby village of Yawata from August 1945, through the end of the year.

35. Hara Tamiki, quoted in Mizuta Kuwajirō, *Gembaku o yomu*, 39.

36. Masuoka Toshikazu, *Hiroshima no shijin-tachi*, 9.

37. Richard H. Minear, *Hiroshima: Three Witnesses*, 40. For a detailed discussion of "Summer Flowers'" status as documentary, see Udō Toshio, "Hara Tamiki ron."

38. For a discussion of how writers have used documentary in a variety of ways to describe the Nazi death camps, see Sidra DeKoven Ezrahi, "Documentation as Art," in *By Words Alone: The Holocaust in Literature*, 24–48. For a discussion of how that same documentary constitutes a rhetorical mode, see James E. Young, *Writing and Rewriting the Holocaust: Narrative and the Consequences of Interpretation*, 52–80.

39. Mutsu Katsutoshi, "Kaeranu tamashii," 104.

40. Kuroko Kazuo, *Gembaku to kotoba: Hara Tamiki kara Hayashi Kyōko made*, 132–33.

41. Sasaki Kiichi, quoted in Egusa Mitsuko, "'Natsu no hana,'" 53.

42. In a postscript to the 1949 edition of the collection of short stories published under the omnibus title of *Summer Flowers*, Hara briefly spoke of the context in which he had written his recent work: "This book is a commemoration of unprecedented personal experiences. I wrote 'Summer Flowers' first, immediately after the disaster and in the midst of terrible exhaustion and hunger. 'From the Ruins' was the following year, when I forced my starved body to work at the oil drum I was using as a desk. The other four stories in this collection were done after I returned to Tokyo but was still hounded by poverty and malnutrition. The fact that I could write under such preposterous conditions is itself one of the unprecedented personal experiences I mean to record here" (quoted in Kuroko Kazuo, *Gembaku to kotoba: Hara Tamiki kara Hayashi Kyōko made*, 134).

43. Kaikō Takeshi, "Hara Tamiki 'Natsu no hana' no baai," 138–39.

44. See Robert Jay Lifton, *Death in Life: Survivors of Hiroshima*, 19–30.

45. "Many at once concluded, 'It was a direct [bomb] hit!' They feared for their lives and started to protect themselves, to get away from the bombed area." See Committee for the Compilation of Materials on Damage Caused by the Atomic Bombs in Hiroshima and Nagasaki, *Hiroshima and Nagasaki*, 485ff.

46. Robert Jay Lifton describes similar scenes reported to him by his Hiroshima interviewees: "Part of this [dream-like] aura was the 'deathly silence' consistently reported by survivors. Rather than wild panic, most described a ghastly stillness and a sense (whether or not literally true) of slow-motion: low moans from those incapacitated, the rest fleeing from the destruction, but usually not rapidly. . . . As Dr. Hachiya described the scene in his classic, *Hiroshima Diary*, 'the outsiders could not grasp the fact that they were witnessing the exodus of a people who walked in the realm of dreams'" (*Death in Life*, 25).

47. One passage in Poe's story may echo particularly how Hara apparently felt in Hiroshima on August 6th: "What was it—I paused to think—what was it that so unnerved me in the contemplation of the House of Usher? It was a mystery all insoluble; nor could I grapple with the shadowy fancies that crowded upon me as I pondered. I was forced to fall back upon the unsatisfactory conclusion, that while, beyond doubt, there *are* combinations of very simple natural objects which have the power of thus affecting us, still the analysis of this power lies among considerations beyond our depth" (231).

48. Hayden White, *Tropics of Discourse: Essays in Cultural Criticism* 121.

49. Ibid., 69–70.

50. Chaim A. Kaplan, *Scroll of Agony: The Warsaw Diary of Chaim A. Kaplan*, 34.

51. Hara Tamiki, "Haikyo kara," 68–69.

52. Hotta Yoshie, "Hara Tamiki no bungaku to gendai," 613.

53. Kaplan wrote: "I sense within me the magnitude of this hour, and my responsibility toward it, and I have an inner awareness that I am fulfilling a national obligation, a historic obligation that I am not free to relinquish. My words are not rewritten; momentary reflexes shape them. . . . My record will serve as source material for the future historian" (*Scroll of Agony*, 104.)

54. Odagiri Hideo, quoted in Nagaoka Hiroyoshi, *Gembaku minshūshi*, 167.

5   Poetry Against Itself

1. Doi Sadako, "Tomo ni tasukeraretsutsu," 34–35.

2. Fukagawa Munetoshi, quoted in Masuoka Toshikazu, *Hiroshima no shijin-tachi*, 112.

3. Ōoka Makoto, *Shi no Nihongo*, 20.

4. Yoshimoto Takaaki, "'Shiki' ha no honshitsu—Miyoshi Tatsuji o chūshin ni," 125.

5. Okada Yasuo, quoted in Kōno Nankei, "Haiku to gembaku," 154.

6. Ōoka Makoto, "Modern Japanese Poetry: Realities and Challenges," 19.

7. C. Day Lewis, *The Poetic Image*, 72.

8. Jean-Paul Sartre, *What is Literature?* 14.

9. Jonathan Culler, *Structural Poetics: Structuralism, Linguistics, and the Study of Literature*, 162.

10. Cleanth Brooks, *The Well-Wrought Urn: Studies in the Structure of Poetry*, 3.

11. Tokunō Kōichi, quoted in Masuoka Toshikazu, *Hiroshima no shijin-tachi*, 72.

12. Theodor W. Adorno, "Engagement," 125–26.

13. Tanaka Kishirō, quoted in Takekoshi Yukio, "Shi to gembaku," 143.

14. Yoneda Toshiaki, "Gembaku to tanka," 148.

15. Martin Heidegger, *On the Way to Language*, 160.

16. Sawamura Mitsuhiro, "Hiroshima—waga maboroshi."

17. Pierre Macherey, *A Theory of Literary Production*, 85, 87.

18. Hara Tamiki, quoted in Robert Jay Lifton, *Death in Life: Survivors of Hiroshima*, 450.

19. Theodor W. Adorno, *Negative Dialectics*, 367.

20. Kurihara Sadako, quoted in Nagaoka Hiroyoshi, *Gembaku bungaku shi*, 86.

21. James Scully, *Line Break: Poetry as Social Practice*, 42.

22. Kurihara wrote in 1981: "'Let Us Be Midwives!' was my first poem after the war. It was written at the end of August in the year of the Bombing. It is a work that describes the emotion with which Hirano Mikiko, who died last year at the age of seventy-two, gave birth to her daughter Kazuko, now 36, in the basement of the old Hiroshima Depository destroyed by the bomb" (*Kaku-jidai ni ikiru: Hiroshima—shi no naka no sei*, 7).

23. Ōta Yōko, of whose work Kurihara would become its most perspicacious critic and staunch defender, is an even more dramatic example of how an atomic-bomb writer's initial bravery and resistance to nuclear war are eventually displaced by a profound and despairing hopelessness. See the next chapter, "Ōta Yōko and the Place of the Narrator."

24. Kurihara Sadako, quoted in Masuoka Toshikazu, *Hiroshima no shijin-tachi*, 97.

25. Masuoka Toshikazu, *Hiroshima no shijin-tachi*, 171.

26. José Ortega y Gasset, "The Dehumanization of Art," 33–35.

27. Alvin Rosenfeld, *A Double Dying: Reflections on Holocaust Literature*, 26.

28. Alvin Rosenfeld, quoted in James E. Young, *Writing and Rewriting the Holocaust: Narrative and the Consequences of Interpretation*, 90.

29. José Ortega y Gasset, "The Dehumanization of Art," 32.

30. Karsten Harris, "Metaphor and Transcendence," 78.

31. Kokai Eiji, *Hara Tamiki—shijin no shi*, 70.

32. See Masuoka Toshikazu, *Hiroshima no shijin-tachi*, 213.

33. Kokai Eiji, *Hara Tamiki—shijin no shi*, 137.

34. Kurihara Sadako, "Kaisetsu (1)—Shūmatsu e no yokaku to kokuhatsu," 512.

35. It is perhaps ironic, however, that Ōta herself never writes "Hiroshima" in Sino-Japanese characters in this novel. Rather, it is denoted with the capital Roman "H," or more commonly, referred to obliquely as "this city." This is another example of how Ōta Yōko consistently finds herself constrained to deploy certain language, or subterfuges thereof, despite her stated resistance.

36. Geoffrey H. Hartman, *Saving the Text: Literature, Derrida, Philosophy*, xxi–xxii.

37. Cleanth Brooks writes: "T. S. Eliot has commented upon 'that perpetual slight alteration of language, words perpetually juxtaposed in new and sudden combinations,' which occur in poetry. It *is* perpetual; it cannot be kept out of the poem; it can only be directed and controlled. The tendency of science is necessarily to stabilize terms, to freeze them into strict denotations; the poet's tendency is by contrast disruptive" (*The Well-Wrought Urn: Studies in the Structure of Poetry*, 9).

38. See Kokai Eiji, *Hara Tamiki—shijin no shi*, 67.

39. In his review of an international anthology of poems whose themes are the atrocities of the twentieth century, John Bayley begins by arguing that the existence of such a book as proof that Adorno's dictum (that poetry after Auschwitz "is barbaric") is wrong; but soon he amends his dismissal to say that "Perhaps the feeling behind Adorno's words has generalized to a point where our contemporary poetry is engaged primarily in distrusting itself, and in defeating its own traditional powers. . . . Poets must bear witness against themselves, as they bear witness to what we do to each other" (Review of *Against Forgetting: Twentieth-Century Poetry of Witness*, 22).

40. Tōge Sankichi, "Chichi o kaese."

41. Masuoka Toshikazu, *Hiroshima no shijin-tachi*, 213.

42. Katsuhara Sumio, "Tōge Sankichi shōron: *Gembaku shishū* seiritsu no haikei," 42.

43. See Richard H. Minear, *Hiroshima: Three Witnesses*, 277–300, for a fuller treatment of Tōge's life. Minear's information, like my own and that of anyone studying Tōge today, derives in large measure from the several works of literary historian Masuoka Toshikazu, most notably *Hachigatsu no shijin: Gembaku shijin Tōge Sankichi no shi to shōgai* and *Gembaku shijin Tōge Sankichi*.

44. Katsuhara Sumio, "Tōge Sankichi shōron: *Gembaku shishū* seiritsu no haikei," 43.

45. Tōge Sankichi, quoted in Masuoka Toshikazu, *Gembaku shijin Tōge Sankichi*, 26.

46. Tōge Sankichi, quoted in Masuoka Toshikazu, *Hachigatsu no shijin: Gembaku shijin Tōge Sankichi no shi to shōgai*, 302.

47. The "badger of Mount Kachi-kachi" presumably refers to the old Japanese children's story of a rabbit who seeks revenge on the behalf of an old man whose wife had been killed by a badger; and "burnt" presumably to the destroyed pages of the picture book telling this story.

48. Tōge Sankichi, quoted in Masuoka Toshikazu, *Gembaku shijin Tōge Sankichi,* 121–22.

49. Ōoka Makoto, "Modern Japanese Poetry: Realities and Challenges," 19.

50. Masuoka Toshikazu, *Gembaku shijin Tōge Sankichi,* 132.

51. Ibid., 139.

52. Ibid., 163.

53. Ibid., 196.

54. Ibid., 186–89.

55. Robert Jay Lifton, *Death in Life,* 441.

56. Tōge Sankichi, quoted in Masuoka Toshikazu, *Gembaku shijin Tōge Sankichi,* 173.

57. Hayashida Yasumasa, "Atarashii minzoku jōjishi no hōga—gembaku bungaku e no kitai."

58. Masuoka Toshikazu, *Hachigatsu no shijin: Gembaku shijin Tōge Sankichi no shi to shōgai,* 225.

59. Robert Jay Lifton, *Death in Life,* 441.

60. Kurihara Sadako, *Dokyumento Hiroshima nijūyonen: Gendai no kyūsai,* 247.

61. Robert Jay Lifton, *Death in Life,* 443.

62. James Scully, *Line Break,* 54.

63. Ibid., 3–4.

64. Ibid., 116.

65. Kurihara Sadako, *Dokyumento Hiroshima nijūyonen: Gendai no kyūsai,* 240.

66. Mizuta Kuwajirō, *Me o akeba shura: Gembaku kajin Shōda Shinoe no shōgai,* 47–48.

67. Nor, as the earlier chapter "The Three Debates" disclosed, was Shōda the only poet to meet with such antipathy. Kurihara Sadako, in retelling this anecdote of Shōda's, adds that she herself "has been viewed as heretical by that sort of poet [as Yamazumi]" (Kurihara Sadako, *Dokyumento Hiroshima nijūyonen: Gendai no kyūsai,* 22).

68. Shōda Shinoe, quoted in Mizuta Kuwajirō, *Me o akeba shura: Gembaku kajin Shōda Shinoe no shōgai,* 52–55. These poems appeared in rewritten versions in Shōda's *Repentance,* 205–6.

69. Sugiura Suiko, quoted in Mizuta Kuwajirō, *Me o akeba shura: Gembaku kajin Shōda Shinoe no shōgai,* 57.

70. See the *Japanese-English Buddhist Dictionary,* 12.

71. Shōda Shinoe, quoted in Mizuta Kuwajirō, *Me o akeba shura: Gembaku kajin Shōda Shinoe no shōgai,* 22.

72. Ōe Kenzaburō, "Hara Tamiki o kinen suru (kōen)," 176.

73. Mizuta Kuwajirō, *Me o akeba shura: Gembaku kajin Shōda Shinoe no shōgai,* 202.

74. Shōda Shinoe, quoted in Mizuta Kuwajirō, *Gembaku bungaku o yomu,* 21–22.

75. Sidra DeKoven Ezrahi cites the work of David Roskies, Alan Mintz, and Robert Alter as examples of this thesis, even while she persuasively argues that the Holocaust and the literary efforts of some of its survivors precipitated a radical break in the mainstream, rabbinical tradition of representing Jewish history as a redemptive narrative. See Ezrahi, "Considering the Apocalypse: Is the Writing on the Wall Only Graffiti?"

76. Ōe Kenzaburō, "Kaku-jidai e no sōzōryoku," 107–8.

77. Robert Jay Lifton, *Death in Life*, 409.

78. See Masuoka Toshikazu, *Hiroshima no shijin-tachi*, 179.

79. Kurihara Sadako, *Dokyumento Hiroshima nijūyonen: Gendai no kyūsai*, 24.

6   Ōta Yōko and the Place of the Narrator

1. Sata Ineko, "Kaisetsu," 338–41.

2. Uranishi Kazuhiko, "Kaisetsu," 341.

3. For a fuller account of Ōta's life and literary career, see Richard H. Minear, *Hiroshima: Three Witnesses*, 117–42.

4. Esashi Akiko, *Kusazue: Ōta Yōko hyōden*, 44–52.

5. Ōta Yōko, *Ningen ranru*, 76.

6. Ōta Yōko, "Kaitei no yō na hikari—genshi bakudan no kūshū ni atte," 17; *Ningen ranru*, 268.

7. Ōta Yōko, "Bungaku no osoroshisha," 323.

8. Ōta Yōko, "*Shikabane no machi jo*," 302.

9. Ōta Yōko, "Sakka no taido, " 243.

10. Hamai Shinzō, "Hajime ni," 3.

11. Ōta Yōko, "*Shikabane no machi jo*," 302–3.

12. George Steiner, "K," 123.

13. Ōta Yōko, "*Shikabane no machi jo*," 301–2.

14. Wayne Booth, *The Rhetoric of Fiction*, 396.

15. Ōta Yōko, "Yo ni mayou," 399.

16. Wayne Booth, *The Rhetoric of Fiction*, 378.

17. Berel Lang, *Act and Idea in the Nazi Genocide*, 124.

18. Ibid., 120.

19. Theodor W. Adorno, "The Position of the Narrator in the Contemporary Novel," 34.

20. Sata Ineko, "Kaisetsu," 339.

21. Tanabe Kōichirō, "Gembaku no bungaku," 171.

22. Noma Hiroshi, "Gembaku ni tsuite," 148.

23. Sawada Akiko, "*Shikabane no machi*," 65.

24. Ōta Yōko, "*Shikabane no machi jo*," 301.

25. Esashi Akiko, *Kusazue: Ōta Yōko hyōden*, 166.

26. Nagaoka Hiroyoshi, "Kaisetsu," 345.

27. Ibid., 347.

28. Agawa Hiroyuki, quoted in Nagaoka Hiroyoshi, "Kaisetsu," 350–51.

29. Tanabe Kōichirō, "Gembaku no bungaku," 174.

30. Nagaoka Hiroyoshi, *Gembaku bungaku shi*, 16.

31. See, for example, Esashi Akiko, *Kusazue: Ōta Yōko hyōden*, 178–82; Kuroko Kazuo, *Gembaku to kotoba: Hara Tamiki kara Hayashi Kyōko made*, 46–51.

32. Sata Ineko, "Kaisetsu," 341.

33. Kuroko Kazuo, *Gembaku to kotoba: Hara Tamiki kara Hayashi Kyōko made*, 52.

34. Adachi Yukizō, quoted in Kurihara Sadako, "Gembaku bungaku ronsō shi (shō): Ōta Yōko o jiku ni," 284.

35. Esashi Akiko's curious and often gratuitously vituperous biography of Ōta, *Kusazue: Ōta Yōko hyōden*, may be responsible for the widespread view of Ōta as a psychologically troubled writer. Esashi writes, for example: "When I first started reading those works by Ōta that dealt with the atomic bombing, I was made uncomfortably aware of her willfulness to write again and again of the conditions it had wrought, but I took no note of the author's own unpleasantness [*iyarashisa*] that underlies that willfulness. As I researched her past, and then read her prewar works, I began to see that unpleasantness. Her arrogance, immodesty, tight-fistedness, narrow-mindedness, spoiled attitude, gloominess, cruelty, and a selfish disregard for others are all factors tied to her distorted views as a writer" (82). Esashi, like even some of the more sophisticated critics of Ōta's writings, would presumably have preferred that a hibakusha author be made "pleasant" by his experiences of a nuclear attack.

36. See Kurihara Sadako, "Gembaku bungaku ronsō shi (shō): Ōta Yōko o jiku ni," as well as the earlier chapter, "The Three Debates."

37. Esashi Akiko, *Kusazue: Ōta Yōko hyōden*, 88.

38. See Kurihara Sadako, "Gembaku bungaku ronsō shi (shō): Ōta Yōko o jiku ni," 282.

7   Ōe Kenzaburō

1. Among Ōe's activities in the past decade have been his participation as an editor of the fifteen-volume anthology of atomic-bomb literature and criticism, *Nihon no gembaku bungaku*; his editing of a single-volume anthology of atomic-bomb writers entitled *Nan to mo shirenai mirai ni* and which appeared in English translation under the title *The Crazy Iris and Other Stories of the Atomic Aftermath*; his prominent role within the Japan P.E.N. Center as an organizer of such antinuclear events as the 1982 "Writers' Declaration on the Danger of Nuclear War" and the 1983 International P.E.N. Congress, which chose as its theme "Literature in the Nuclear Age—Why Do We Write?"; and most importantly, his many essays and public lectures in which he has stressed the importance of atomic-bomb writers to postwar Japanese literature, a debt unrecognized by any other critic of Ōe's stature.

2. These were not Ōe's first trips to Hiroshima. In 1960, at the time of the second atomic-bomb literature debate in the pages of the *Chūgoku shimbun* (see the earlier chapter, "The Three Debates"), a group of local writers calling themselves The Young Hiroshima Club (Wakai Hiroshima no Kai) and led by Matsumoto Hiroshi invited Ōe and Kaikō Takeshi—as "Tokyo writers"—to come to Hiroshima and debate the question whether an atomic-bomb literature was possible. Fumizawa Takaichi recalls his surprise to hear many in the audience argue with Ōe's claim that what was needed was more documentary writing on the bombing; what was required instead, they claimed, was a

"philosophy of the bomb" (*gembaku no tetsugaku*). This is precisely what Ōe then went on to do several years later in *Hiroshima Notes.* See Mainichi Shimbun Sha, ed., *Gembaku 25-nen*, 117.

3. For remarks on the reception of *Notes*, see Nagaoka Hiroyoshi, *Gembaku bungaku shi*, 75. Nagaoka points out the enthusiastic response generated by *Notes* among the "younger generation."

4. See, for example, "Documentation as Art," in Sidra Dekoven Ezrahi, *By Words Alone: The Holocaust in Literature*, 24–48.

5. Ibuse Masuji, quoted in Matsumoto Tsuruo, *Ibuse Masuji ron*, 193.

6. That position, as we shall presently see, is one that creates one set of problems even while solving another. Edward Said, in *The World, the Text, and the Critic*, summarizes Georg Lukács' discussion of the essay form and its inherent limitations in his *Die Seele und die Formen.* The essay is held to express "a yearning for the conceptuality and intellectuality, as well as a resolution to the ultimate questions of life. . . . Thus the essay's mode is ironic, which means first that the form is patently insufficient in its intellectuality with regard to living experience and, second, that the very form of the essay, its being an essay, is an ironic destiny with regard to the great questions of life" (51–52). It is precisely such irony that works to undo both the themes and the language in which they are worded within *Notes.*

7. Ōe Kenzaburō, "Kaisetsu," 382.

8. For a general study in English of Ōe's fiction, I refer the reader to Susan J. Napier's *Escape from the Wasteland: Romanticism and Realism in the Fiction of Mishima Yukio and Ōe Kenzaburo.*

9. Ōe was of course neither the first important Tokyo writer to visit postwar Hiroshima, nor the only who realized that his visit served to make clear his own thoughts and emotions. Nobel Prize winner Kawabata Yasunari wrote of his 1950 trip to the city: "It may be no exaggeration for me to say that in Hiroshima I experienced a kind of miraculous revival. It was not just that I was pleased at this experience. I was also surprised, ashamed, and challenged. I could not help reflect on how uncanny my own life, my work, has been. I hesitated to let my shock in Hiroshima show. This catastrophe that befell the human species stirred me. The deaths of two hundred thousand people made fresh my own sense of life" (Kawabata Yasunari, quoted in Itō Narihiko, "Kaisetsu—'Kaku' o mitsumete kita me 1945–1983," 528).

10. Sartre's influence on postwar Japanese literature, and particularly atomic-bomb literature, is profound. Many other Hiroshima and Nagasaki writers, such as Kurihara Sadako and Oda Makoto, as well as such major figures generally as Noma Hiroshi and Abe Kōbō, explicitly cited the precepts of French existentialism as part of their own personal philosophical and political orientations. Nor has existentialism's usefulness been wholly depleted in Japan, as perhaps it has elsewhere: "I have been enchanted by existentialist philosophies," stated Ōe in 1988, "and naturally I am an existentialist author." See Sanroku Yoshida, "An Interview with Kenzaburō Ōe," 372.

11. See Shinohara Shigeru, *Ōe Kenzaburō ron*, 91. Shinohara notes in his study that Ōe was required to read the older French classics for school, but that he read nothing but Sartre for himself. It was Sartre's unfinished series of novels about wartime France,

Les chemins de la liberté, which inspired Ōe to select French literature as a major and which also convinced him that his future lie in fiction rather than scholarship.

12. In his essay "Kaku-jidai e no sōzōryoku," Ōe discusses this meeting, which took place in the winter of 1961 and during which Sartre reportedly discussed, in fact, politics in the nuclear era (105).

13. See Axel Madsen, *Hearts and Minds: The Common Journey of Simone de Beauvoir and Jean-Paul Sartre,* 55.

14. Maurice Blanchot, *The Writing of the Disaster,* 19.

15. Frederick J. Hoffman, *The Mortal No: Death and the Modern Imagination,* 453.

16. David Craig and Michael Egan have noted how Sartre was so readily able to reconcile his philosophy with the events of the Second World War in their study *Extreme Situations: Literature and Crisis from the Great War to the Atom Bomb:* "The point here is that both these writers [Sartre and Camus] entered the war with nearly-formed philosophies that enabled them to conceive of it as an intensification of the human condition at large. They already thought of life as a matter of creating something authentic in the face of the 'absurd" flux of unrelieved existence; they were already anguished at the provisional character of such strivings. The war did not burst in on them" (27). Perhaps Ōe, too, approached Hiroshima in much the same way, as an "intensification of the human condition" which "did not burst in on" him but rather represented an important example of what he had already come to believe about human existence.

17. See the third chapter of *Being and Nothingness,* "Concrete Relations with Others," esp. 471–74.

18. The Ninth World Conference was held August 6–8, 1963 in Hiroshima under the sponsorship of the Japan Council Against Atomic and Hydrogen Bombs (Gensuikyō), a highly politicized organization. On the day before the Conference opened, the delegates split into factions, one affiliated with the Japan Communist Party and another affiliated with the Japan Socialist Party, on account of arguments over the Conference slogan "Opposition to All Nuclear Tests by All Nations." It was the position of the JCP that the development of nuclear weaponry by communist states was a defensive reaction in the service of world peace.

19. In the introduction to his translation of several short novels by Ōe, John Nathan briefly discusses the conjuncture of *A Personal Matter* and *Notes.* "Ōe was of course asking that the books be considered together; in one he chronicled the survival of an actual atomic bomb, in the other he sought the means of surviving a personal holocaust" (xvii). While the rhetorical use of the word "holocaust" may be inappropriate, Ōe's *Notes* does encourage the reader to consider his essays as paradigmatic for lives other than those of Hiroshima hibakusha: his term "Hiroshima Man" does not refer solely to that city's survivors—it is in fact our species' most recent evolutionary stage.

In the 1980 afterword to an edition of his collected essays on Hiroshima, Ōe briefly commented on the relationship between historical atrocity and the fate of his own life as, among other things, the father of a handicapped child: "When I regarded Hiroshima from the perspective of its absurd devastation, the massive numbers of the death, the injuries, the aftereffects of radiation, the deadly symptoms of leukemia—and what is more the indication that they could be inheritable—I discovered there, on its vast and total scale, the accidents [*akushidento*] that have occurred in my own private life. It only

served to deepen the sense of decay that had imposed itself, with such negative consequences, onto my own individual circumstances" ("Mirai e mukete kaisō suru—jiko-
kaishaku (ni)," 284).

20. Jean-Paul Sartre, *Existentialism and Humanism,* 34; Ōe Kenzaburō, *Hiroshima nōto,* 64.

21. In *A Personal Matter,* the hero Bird cannot decide whether to help his infant son
survive a congenital defect or to abandon him to indifferent doctors who will "allow"
the baby to die. It is while in a bar owned by a old friend—a friend who has chosen to
embrace his homosexuality, to *be* a homosexual—that Bird experiences his existentialist
epiphany and decides to choose how he will live. It is the frequent observation of readers, however, that Bird's final resolve to be a father and save his baby happens to be the
socially approbated—and humanist—choice as well as, coincidentally, the "existentialist." Perhaps, it is argued, a more thoroughly existentialist response would have been
for Bird to become his own child's murderer. It is hard to imagine, however, how an
author who in fact has a handicapped child of his own could, even in a novel, entertain
a course of action that human decency—humanism?—would brand monstrous. Like
Sartre himself—and here is the critique of *Existentialism and Humanism*—Ōe's philosophical theory thankfully results in the affirmation of human values that may leave us less
"free" but with our humanity uncompromised.

22. Other keloid victims, of course, make less admirable but perhaps more human
existential choices. In his short story "Shi no kage" (Shadows of Death, 1967), which is
about a group of Hiroshima hibakusha who were bombed when middle school students,
Nakayama Shirō observes: "There was . . . a difference between those whose skin was
more easily affected by keloid scarring and those who were not. There was also a difference between those who had immediately received medical attention and those who
had been unable to receive sufficient care. The form of the scars on a given individual
was the result of a number of such factors. However, as the years went by, the feelings
of those who bore the keloids changed from a mutual joy at having survived the bombing, to a private satisfaction that occurred whenever one saw somebody whose scars
were more ugly than one's own" (42).

23. Erich Auerbach, *Mimesis: The Representation of Reality in Western Literature,* 59.

24. In a subsequent essay explicitly Sartrean even in its title—"What is Literature?"—Ōe puts Hiroshima's well-known mayor Hamai Shinzō through a similar process of saintly "canonization" for his efforts on behalf of his city's hibakusha. See Ōe,
"Bungaku to wa nani ka?"

25. In one passage of *Notes* Ōe argues that the destruction of Hiroshima was a
greater atrocity than even the genocide of European Jewry by the Nazis: "The scope of
Nazi Germany's murder of the Jews at Auschwitz is well known around the world. But
one cannot say that Hiroshima is sufficiently known—despite the fact that it was a
human tragedy surpassing that of Auschwitz, and despite the fact that we face today a
crisis which could result in the same catastrophe happening again (and in the eyes of
those cynical enough to believe in an international, political Machiavellianism, for the
same purposes [as Auschwitz])" (143).

26. See Robert Jay Lifton, *Death in Life: Survivors of Hiroshima,* 35.

27. Albert Camus, *Notebooks,* 85.

28. See Mary Warnock, *Existentialism,* 124.

29. A. Alvarez, *The Savage God: A Study of Suicide,* 118; F. J. Hoffman, *The Mortal No,* 162.

30. See Ōe, "Kaisetsu," 382. One of the most brutal attacks on Ōe's Hiroshima writings occur when a Hiroshima bartender in Natsubori Masamoto's 1975 short story "The Woman from the Hallowed Ground" (Seichi no onna) bitterly complains, "This 'humanism' is a lot of sugary nonsense. To begin with, chanting 'humanism' like some kind of mantra isn't going to fill anyone's belly. I hate being lectured to about humanism by someone really interested in himself" (325).

Ōe, to his credit, has always been one of his own most honest critics. In his essay "Hiroshima, Amerika, Yōroppa," Ōe records some of the local Hiroshima complaints over his *Notes:* "'We aren't that pure [*kirei*],'" pointed out one hibakusha" (200). But Ōe's, and by extension our own, admiration of atomic-bomb survivors is presumably predicated upon their collective right to a higher moral entitlement, not necessarily any one individual's exercise of that entitlement.

31. Jean-Paul Sartre, "The Artist and his Conscience," 143.

32. Kurihara Sadako, *Dokyumento Hiroshima nijūyonen: Gendai no kyūsai,* 272. Kurihara's criticism stands as one of the most thoughtful, and radical, statements on how profoundly the use of nuclear weapons in Hiroshima and Nagasaki has altered the terms in which human beings and their culture can be represented in literature. It is curious that Ōe remains far better known as "the Hiroshima critic," or perhaps merely indicative of how eager we are to continue to believe in values undermined by recent history.

8 Ibuse Masuji

1. Catherine Belsey, *Critical Practice,* 70.

2. "Ideological State Apparatus" is Althusser's term; it refers to the means by which social norms are inculcated, nominally without resort to violence, among the public. Its complement is the "Repressive State Apparatus," such as the police, who contain rather than cultivate behavior. Last on Althusser's list of ISAs is "the cultural ISA (Literature, the Arts, sports, etc.)," though it is naturally that which has received the most attention from literary critics ("Ideology and Ideological State Apparatuses," 137).

3. Berel Lang, *Act and Idea in the Nazi Genocide,* 104.

4. See Robert Jay Lifton, *Death in Life: Survivors of Hiroshima,* 543–55.

5. See "Kaku no genjōkyō wa 'Fuyukai da na.'"

6. Saeki Shōichi, "Shōsetsuka to kirokusha."

7. See Kitahara Takeo, Noma Hiroshi and Saeki Shōichi, "Sōsaku gappyō."

8. Yamamoto Kenkichi, "Chi ni tsuita heijōshin."

9. Kaneko Hiroshi, "*Kuroi ame,*" 85.

10. Ibuse Masuji, "Kataware sōshi," 310.

11. Yamamoto Kenkichi, quoted in Toyoda Seishi, *Gembaku bunkenshi,* 83. Such remarks were not limited to the 1960s, nor to Japanese critics alone. In 1985, the distinguished American translator of Japanese literature, Edward Seidensticker, opined that Hara Tamiki and Ōta Yōko were Hiroshima's "chief propagandists," but that Ibuse's *Black*

Rain is "much the best book that has been written about Hiroshima" (*"Injurious to Public Morals: Writers and the Meiji State,"* 221.).

12. C. P. Snow, quoted on the back cover of *Black Rain*.

13. Thomas Rimer, "Nationalism in the Literature of Japan," 7–8.

14. Terry Eagleton, *Criticism and Ideology: A Study in Marxist Literary Theory*, 103; 102–61.

15. See Esashi Akiko, *Kusazue: Ōta Yōko hyōden*, 199.

16. Ibuse Masuji, quoted in "Kaku no genjōkyō wa 'Fuyukai da na.'"

17. At the time of his death Ibuse was considered Japan's best hope for a Nobel Prize in literature, but the wry humor for which he was so widely appreciated among his Japanese readers was probably untranslatable. In any case, it was widely reported among his friends that he would have declined the honor, for which other authors (including Japanese) have not been shy to campaign.

18. For a general study of Ibuse and his works, see John Whittier Treat, *Pools of Water, Pillars of Fire: The Literature of Ibuse Masuji*.

19. See Matsumoto Hiroshi, "Genten to shite no Hiroshima," 401–2.

20. Toyota Seishi, *Gembaku bunkenshi*, 78.

21. Kaneko Hiroshi, *"Kuroi ame."*

22. Sakurai Mikiyoshi, "Sei to shi o mitsumete—Ibuse Masuji *'Kuroi ame'* o megutte," 110.

23. Ōe Kenzaburō, *"'Kuroi ame'* to Nihon bundan." Ōe returned to Etō Jun's effusive praise for *Black Rain* in a 1967 essay entitled "Hibakusha no jiko-kyūsai undō" (The Hibakusha Self-Help Movement). There he again charges Etō with a self-interested agenda in proclaiming the novel, in distinction to all previous atomic-bomb literature, one in which Ibuse "'looked straight into an unprecedented experience'" and "'with a calm attitude [*heijōshin*] grasped, for the first time, the context of this extraordinary event'" (167). Ōe approves of the novel, too, but for a very different reason, one grounded in its mimetic failure: any hibakusha who reads *Black Rain*, and reacts with the thought that his own experience was so much more worse than Ibuse describes, "moves one step closer to the truth of the atomic bombing" (168).

24. Thomas J. Rimer, "Nationalism in the Literature of Japan," 7.

25. Konishi Jin'ichi, *A History of Japanese Literature*, vol. 2: *The Early Middle Ages*, 324.

26. Ibuse Masuji, quoted in Fukuda Kyoto and Matsumoto Takeo, *Ibuse Masuji*, 224.

27. Irving Howe, *Politics and the Novel*, 17.

28. Ibid., 150.

29. Fredric Jameson, "On Politics and Literature," 17.

30. Throughout this chapter I discuss the "ideology" of *Black Rain* as if that were an immanent "content" of the work: but that is simply for the sake of convenience. My own view is that ideology, like "meaning" (which of course it is one part of), is the product of a process impossible to imagine without the contexts of readers who will, within certain generalizable constraints of their culture, class, socialization, etc., construe that "ideology" or "meaning" for themselves. And as such a contingent "product," it cannot be spoken of with any absolute guarantees of either identity or function. Thus,

a novel that in Japan may have worked to buttress certain conservative, even reactionary, *idées fixes* of national identity, can still when transported to the American classroom be a powerful and shattering revelation for students: a revelation whose implications might undermine some of our own stubborn truisms.

31. Terry Eagleton, "Ideology, Fiction, Narrative," 65.

32. Fredric Jameson, *The Political Unconscious: Narrative as a Socially Symbolic Act*, 79.

33. Fredric Jameson, "On Politics and Literature," 17.

34. Ibuse Masuji, "Kinō no kai," 16.

35. See Sakurai Mikiyoshi, "Sei to shi o mitsumete—Ibuse Masuji 'Kuroi ame' o megutte," 110.

36. "The Iris" is discussed in John Whittier Treat, *Pools of Water, Pillars of Fire*, 201–6.

37. Ibuse Masuji, quoted in Nakamura Akira, *Sakka no buntai*, 23.

38. See John Whittier Treat, *Pools of Water, Pillars of Fire*, 110–29.

39. Ibuse Masuji, quoted in "Kaku no genjōkyō wa 'Fuyukai da na.'"

40. Ibid.

41. Ibid.

42. Pierre Macherey, *A Theory of Literary Production*, 41.

43. Ibuse Masuji, quoted in "Kaku no genjōkyō wa 'Fuyukai da na.'"

44. Toyoda Seishi, *Gembaku bunkenshi*, 85.

45. Hayden White, *Tropics of Discourse: Essays in Cultural Criticism*, 125.

46. I know of no statistics showing how prevalent the teaching of *Black Rain* may be in American schools, but my impression, garnered from my conversations with Washington State and California undergraduates, is that it is assigned in a small but significant number of secondary schools.

47. Hara Tamiki, "Nagasaki no kane," 577.

48. Ōta Yōko, *Shikabane no machi*, 300.

49. Terrence Des Pres, *The Survivor: An Anatomy of Life in the Death Camps*, 30.

50. The Makioka and Shizuma families, of course, hardly come from the same stratum of the bourgeoisie, but there are instructive parallels. The former is in possession of a declining merchant-class fortune before the war in the Pacific, and the latter's claim to property in based on land holdings whose worth after that same war would have been, in real life, presumably devalued. What links the two families is the common blow dealt them by the events and outcome of the war: that neither should survive intact (what Japanese reader does not imagine the fate of Tsuruko's family, living in a poorly built Shibuya house, during the Tokyo air raids?) is the fact which the historical record imposes upon the work of writers as different as Tanizaki and Ibuse.

51. Robert Jay Lifton, *Death in Life*, 375.

52. Sasaki Yutaka, quoted in Kyoko and Mark Selden, eds., *The Atomic Bomb: Voices from Hiroshima and Nagasaki*, 132.

53. Louis Althusser, "Ideology and Ideological State Apparatuses," 150.

54. Louis Althusser, "Marxism and Humanism," 234.

55. Fredric Jameson, "Imaginary and Symbolic in Lacan: Marxism, Psychoanalytic Criticism, and the Problem of the Subject," 394.

56. John Bester, "Translator's Preface," 8.

57. Raymond Williams, "Base and Superstructure in Marxist Cultural Theory," 38.

58. Mayuzumi Tetsurō, "Gekisezu utawazu sambun seishin." This same issue of the *Asahi* carried its lead article on Ibuse's death—noting that *Black Rain*'s 1966 English translation met with "the highest praise" in Britain and the United States, and "introduced [Ibuse] worldwide"—on the front page: another indication of the unique position he occupies among all Japanese writers who have attempted to write about Hiroshima or Nagasaki. ("Ibuse Masuji-shi ga shikyo")

59. Imamura Shōhei's recent film version of *Black Rain* has brought this representation to new audiences: but with considerably less opportunity for hope than did the novel, and certainly without romance. Ibuse himself approved of the film (earlier in his career he had forbidden the sale of film rights, no doubt because of his fears of what even more commercialization of Hiroshima might mean), but it is far from a faithful translation of his original novel. Imamura—a director noted for his melancholy themes—not only writes in the deaths of Shigeko and Shigematsu's fishing companions but ends his film with the clear implication that Yasuko, too, will soon die: the novel's ambiguity is replaced with an oppressive, even devastating, message of despair.

60. Friedrich Nietzsche, *The Birth of Tragedy*, 136; Takahashi Hideo, "Ibuse Masuji-shi sono hito to shigoto."

61. Irving Howe, *Politics and the Novel*, 24.

62. Fredric Jameson, *The Political Unconscious*, 286.

9 Nagasaki and the Human Future

1. Frank W. Chinnock, *Nagasaki: The Forgotten Bomb*, 10.

2. Nishihara Kei, "Shōdo," 94.

3. Yamada Kan, "Kaisetsu (4)—Nagasaki no gembaku shika," 524.

4. Yamada Kan, "Nagasaki no gembaku kiroku o megutte," 223.

5. Hayashida Yasumasa, quoted in Kurihara Sadako, "Gembaku bungaku ronsō shi (shō)—Ōta Yōko o jiku ni," 287.

6. See Kurihara Sadako, *Kaku—tennō—hibakusha*, 165.

7. See Yamada Kan, "Nagasaki no gembaku kiroku o megutte," 223.

8. Norman Cousins, "Foreword" to Nagai Takashi, *We of Nagasaki*, v.

9. William Johnston, "Introduction" to Nagai Takashi, *The Bells of Nagasaki*, xix–xx.

10. *Life*, August 20, 1945, quoted in Paul Boyer, *By the Bomb's Early Light: American Thought and Culture at the Dawn of the Atomic Age*, 8.

11. See Kurihara Sadako, *Kaku-jidai ni ikiru: Hiroshima—shi no naka no sei*, 31.

12. Hayashida Yasumasa, "Atarashii minzoku jōjishi no hōga—gembaku bungaku e no kitai," 210.

13. Inoue Mitsuharu, quoted in Kumaki Tetsu, "Chi no mure," 74.

14. Mizuta Kuwajirō quotes Inoue on his purposes in *People of the Land*, saying that he meant it to be his attempt to understand the relations between hibakusha and those around them, between victims and victimizers, and to understand how all have managed

to live in Japan after 1945. "I used the 'atomic bombing,'" noted Inoue, "to understand postwar ideology" (*Gembaku o yomu*, 175).

15. Norman Cousins, "Foreword," viii.

16. Nagai's affirmation of his religious faith was hardly unique, as the discussion of hibakusha-writer Shōda Shinoe and her post-Hiroshima, richly Buddhist poetry in the earlier chapter "Poetry Against Itself" demonstrated. What is striking, however, about that affirmation when it is Christian, however, is its unusual euphoria, as in this account by Hashimoto Eiichi, a Hiroshima school teacher and A-bomb survivor: "My presence in Hiroshima when it was bombed was, at least to a certain point, one of the factors prompting my conversion to Christianity. This was entirely my own matter—my having been bombed. In that undescribable, vacant state after the blast, in the midst of that mushroom cloud—I can't say exactly what color it was, I was exhausted, maybe it was yellow, I don't know, yes yellow, in that indescribable, vacant instant that I experienced beneath the atomic cloud—I attained salvation. No one came to save me, there wasn't a sound, it was a silent, still instant. After the end of war, when amid the ruins of Hiroshima I read Jesus' prophecy of the destruction of Jerusalem, I was suddenly struck. I felt like a voice was saying to me, 'Ah, Hiroshima, Hiroshima'—and that's when I became a Christian" ("Hachi—roku no imi suru mono 4," 62).

17. William Johnston, "Introduction," viii.

18. Erich Auerbach, *Mimesis: The Representation of Reality in Western Literature*, 249.

19. Christian interpretations in the West of the atomic bombings, by contrast, either have judiciously avoided the rhetoric of sacrifice and instead emphasized human fallibility before God's grace, or have mocked the use of such rhetoric to rationalize acts of profanity. My own first introduction to Hiroshima or Nagasaki, outside of a purely historical account, took place as a boy when I somehow came across Thomas Merton's prose-poem, *The Original Child Bomb: Points for Meditation to Be Scratched on the Walls of a Cave*. In his narration of the July 16, 1945, Alamogordo test—a test dubbed "Trinity"—Merton writes:

> Many who saw the experiment expressed
> their satisfaction in religious terms. A
> semi-official report even quoted a religious book
> —The New Testament, 'Lord, I believe, help
> thou my unbelief.' There was an atmosphere
> of devotion. It was a great act of faith.
> They believed the explosion was exceptionally
> powerful.

20. Hara Tamiki, quoted in Kokai Eiji, *Hara Tamiki—shijin no shi*, 133.

21. Suga Takeshi, in Kyoko Selden and Mark Selden, *The Atomic Bomb: Voices from Hiroshima and Nagasaki*, 139.

22. Anonymous, quoted in Kurihara Sadako, *Kaku-jidai ni ikiru—Hiroshima: shi no naka no sei*, 213–14.

23. Nagai Takashi, quoted in Nakazato Yoshiaki, "Hyōgen katsudō ni miru Nagasaki no hibaku ishiki," 355.

24. Hayashi Kyōko, "Hibiki," 119.

25. Kuroko Kazuo suggests that without her Shanghai background, Hayashi never would have written of Nagasaki in quite the explicitly "critical" or "intellectual" fashion that she does (see Kuroko, *Gembaku bungaku ron*, 103–10). Perhaps Kuroko means to imply that her literal geographical distance for many years from the city of her birth has resulted in an unusually detached and even coolly analytical stance towards it postwar fate. In any case, Hayashi's long residence in a major outpost of Japanese imperialism has indeed produced—despite what her critics such as Nakagami Kenji claim (see the earlier chapter, "The Three Debates)—a certain historical depth and irony evident in many of her atomic-bomb as well as Shanghai stories.

26. Hayashi Kyōko, "Arumi no yōki," 10.

27. Hayashi Kyōko, "Kodoku to iu koto," 106.

28. Hayashi Kyōko, quoted in Kuroko Kazuo, "Gembaku bungaku o nokoshita hitobito," 262.

29. Konishi Jin'ichi, *A History of Japanese Literature*, vol. 1: *The Archaic and Ancient Ages*, 254–56. Postwar Japanese literature has designated a number of such "kataribe." The late Ōoka Shōhei, author of such acclaimed novels of the Second World War as *Nobi* (Fires on the Plain, 1949) and *Furyoki* (A Prisoner of War's Story, 1952), was dubbed by critics the "kataribe of August 15th" in a reference to the day of the Japan's surrender. More recently, Kuroko Kazuo has identified the atomic-bomb graphic novels (*manga*: also known, inappropriately in this instance, as "comic books") of Nakazawa Keiji, beginning with *Kuroi ame ni utarete* (Pelted with the Black Rain, 1968) and achieving international recognition with *Hadashi no Gen* (Barefoot Gen, 1973-), as inspired by the same desire to keep intact the memory of Hiroshima as Hayashi Kyōko's of Nagasaki. See Kuroko, *Gembaku bungaku ron: Kaku-jidai to sōzōryoku*, 118–32.

The important difference, however, remains Hayashi's explicit self-identification with the ritual work—and possibly the historical female character—of the kataribe. This stated intention is consequently woven into the themes of her memoirs, fiction, and essays, and it makes that writing reflective of the simultaneously old and new social as well as artistic function of the (woman) hibakusha who possesses her people's most important stories and the voice with which to tell them.

30. Kawanishi Masaaki, "Onna-tachi ga kataru hachigatsu kokonoka," 233.

31. Nakano Kōji and Nagaoka Hiroyoshi, "Gembaku bungaku o megutte," 14.

32. See Ōsato Kyōzaburō, "'Matsuri no ba,'" 98.

33. Kōuchi Nobuko, "Hayashi Kyōko ron," 50.

34. The Committee for the Compilation of Materials on Damage Caused by the Atomic Bombs in Hiroshima and Nagasaki, *Hiroshima and Nagasaki: The Physical, Medical, and Social Effects of the Atomic Bombings*, 115–16. The Committee also reports: "From the theoretical aspects of radiation genetics, Y. Tajima (1972) estimated the number of children born to the exposed, between 1946 and 1980, to be 63,000 in Hiroshima and 42,000 in Nagasaki. Based on individual radiation doses and relative biological effectiveness (RBE) of neutron to gamma ray, the estimated number of affected offspring of the exposed would be increased by 11 percent to 16 percent in Hiroshima and by 5 percent to 7 percent in Nagasaki, when compared with the rate of abnormal offspring born to non-exposed controls. Tajima also pointed out the possibility of spreading re-

cessive traits in the heterozygous condition in subsequent generations. Further studies are obviously needed to test his hypothesis" (327).

35. Hayashi Kyōko, "Kāki-iro kara kon-iro sedai e," 58.

36. Hayashi Kyōko, "Yobun na omoi," 73–74.

37. Ibid., 74.

38. Other writers can be just as categorical, even those not hibakusha themselves. One of Fukunaga's characters in his novel *Shi no shima* says: "I wonder if it is possible for those of us who have experienced an atomic bombing to believe in anything. I find it very odd that a hibakusha might believe in Christ, or in medical science, or in the world's peaceful coexistence. Isn't it strange, after having been put through such utter absurdity, that someone could still have faith in something?" (2:339).

39. In her 1979 essay "Jisho" (Dictionaries) Hayashi notes with characteristic sarcasm how elusive just one of these words can be: "The other day I was watching television when I heard [one authority] say that our language today is in disarray, and that it would be good if each family had a dictionary of the Japanese language available at home. He was saying that there is no need to look up each and every word, but that we should realize that the national tongue *does* have its standards. I was impressed by his comments, but surely no human being has a dictionary that can stipulate what, in fact, a 'human being' is" (158–59).

40. Hayashi Kyōko, quoted in Otsu Kunsō, "Genten kara," 42.

41. Karatani Kōjin, Kawamura Jirō, and Nakagami Kenji, "Sōsaku gōhyō," 290.

42. Hayashi Kyōko, "Ai no genten," 79.

43. John W. Dower and John Junkerman, eds., *The Hiroshima Murals: The Art of Iri Maruki and Toshi Maruki*, 40.

44. Hayashi Kyōko, "Mizu—karasu—shōnen shōjo," 33–34; the translation of the caption to the painting is taken from John Dower and John Junkerman, eds., *The Hiroshima Murals: The Art of Iri Maruki and Toshi Maruki*, 39.

45. Gotō Minako, quoted in Kuroko Kazuo, *Gembaku to kotoba: Hara Tamiki kara Hayashi Kyōko made*, 138.

46. Sata Ineko, "Kaisetsu," 340–41.

47. "[One] portion of the population was not affected by primary atomic bomb radiation but was assumed to have received only secondary radiation. At the time of the explosion, these people were at a distance beyond the effects of the primary radiation; and they either came or stayed near the hypocenter after the explosion when the remaining radioactivity had not decreased, or they were living in the suburbs of Hiroshima and Nagasaki, where the fallout was heavily distributed" (Committee for the Compilation of Materials on Damage, *Hiroshima and Nagasaki*, 149).

48. What is unique about *The Shade of Trees* is its depiction of the atomic-bomb disease sufferer's anxieties and fear; there is a great deal of Japanese literature, however, that has explored the actual pathologies and treatments of that disease (actually set of diseases). One of the best is Tsukuda Jitsuo's 1963 novella *Aka to kuro no moshō* (Armbands of Red and Black). Set principally in the ward of a Hiroshima hospital, its characters are for the most part terminal patients and their sometimes well meaning, but sometimes callous doctors and nurses (the hospital's fiscal budget, for instance, is a constant, and

oft spoken-of, worry). The tone of the work, aside from its highly technical concern with specific afflictions and their care, is summed up in its last lines, as one dying patient cynically reflects that another's hope for some medical good to come out of the autopsy of his corpse is in fact what will probably enable his doctor to earn an advanced degree.

49. Hayashi Kyōko, "Kompirayama," 37.

10 The Atomic, the Nuclear, and the Total

1. See, for example, Helen Caldicott's 1980 *Nuclear Madness: What You Can Do! With a New Chapter on Three Mile Island*. It is interesting to consider how apprehensions over the nuclear arms race and concerns over the safety of nuclear power plants converged in Caldicott's appeals for popular activism against both. This may reflect a fear that the "nuclear," whether military or civilian, was on the verge of being "naturalized," made routine and thus no longer debatable, not only in the sphere of public policy but in our own everyday thinking. It is also interesting to consider how now, in the early 1990s, the environmental arguments once marshalled against nuclear power plants are now being used to argue against their fossil-fuel or hydraulic alternatives; and how the post-Cold War rhetoric of a peaceable "New World Order" insists upon the need for a new breed of tactical nuclear weapons for use in endlessly multiplying "trouble spots" in lieu of the strategic weapons now being dismantled in the once binarily opposed, but now coincidentally named, United States and the Commonwealth of Independent States.

2. The intellectual contexts—one will not say origins—of nuclear criticism are of course traceable to earlier arguments. Its theoretical tenets go back at least to structuralism, and probably in the most extended sense to philosophy's Kantian critique of ontology and its displacement by epistemology. More specifically, however, Jean Baudrillard, in his highly influential 1981 work *Simulations*, declares that "the nuclear is the apotheosis of simulation" (58), which is to say rather categorically that it is without basis in material actuality. Like the *Diacritics* writers, Baudrillard does not believe in the probability of a real nuclear war; it is a performative feigning, a pretense. It is tempting, if admittedly flippant, to speculate whether there is a particularly French position vis-à-vis nuclear war, given De Gaulle's own "performative," surely rhetorical, national nuclear policy of maintaining a *force de frappe* arsenal in the face of massive NATO and Warsaw Pact armaments. Derrida himself pointed out that the French equivalent of the English phrase "strategy of deterrence" is literally "strategy of dissuasion," and that the "rhetoric of dissuasion is a performative apparatus" ("NO APOCALYPSE, NOT NOW," 24). If their own "feigning" and "pretense" of nuclear preparedness could have been taken seriously by French intellectuals, then perhaps the ideas expounded at a conference in Cornell's Department of Romance Studies were consistent with their institutional context.

3. Jacques Derrida, "NO APOCALYPSE, NOT NOW," 30.

4. "Proposal for a *Diacritics* Colloquium on Nuclear Criticism," 2.

5. *Diacritics*, 1.

6. The single Western critic to my knowledge who has infused contemporary and theoretical nuclear criticism with certain insights learned from Japanese atomic-bomb literature is Peter Schwenger. In his book *Letter Bomb: Nuclear Holocaust and the Exploding Word*, Schwenger cites the novels of Ōta Yōko—as well as the theories of Jacques Der-

rida, Jacques Lacan, and Fredric Jameson—in the course of his inquiry into the relations, post-Hiroshima, between history, the unconscious and the imaginary. See especially the chapter "Hiroshima in the Morning," 47–67.

7. J. Fisher Solomon suggests that the impetus behind Western nuclear criticism is not solely deconstructionist, but in fact is the result of an increasingly exclusive emphasis on discursivity in contemporary thought in general: "For the thrust not only of Derrida's work but of post-structuralist criticism in general has been precisely against such a ground, against any appeal to a referentially determinate 'reality' outside the figural paradigms of our discourse. Whether structuralist, post-structuralist, or even Marxist, criticism has maintained the irreducibly discursive nature of our understanding and knowledge, attacking the identity of the referent on behalf of a play of historical and tropological differences" (*Discourse and Reference in the Nuclear Age,* 29). Against this view, Solomon calls along lines familiar to any reader of Japanese essays on the nature of the nuclear age for "criticism to rethink its rejection of the referent on behalf of a renewed approach to a referential reality that subsists outside the forms of textuality" (33). For Solomon, such a "renewed approach" means going as far back as Aristotle to rediscover Western philosophy's once traditional linkage of potentiality and the real. For Japanese critics, however, the approach quite nearly always proceeds from the intuitive conviction that, as Sasaki Kiichi put it referring specifically to Hara Tamiki's "Summer Flowers," "All words and sentences emit a explosive light as material as rock"—the rock presumably the ore from which the uranium isotopes that destroyed Hiroshima and Nagasaki were derived (Sasaki Kiichi, quoted in Nakahodo Masanori, *Hara Tamiki nōto,* 121).

8. In his famous reading of Saussure's *General Course in Linguistics,* Derrida writes of how the move to signify always involves a deceit or a paradox that makes the referent— the "origin"—evermore inaccessible to us: "Representation mingles with what it represents, to the point where one speaks as one writes, one thinks as if the represented were nothing more than the shadow or reflection of the representer. A dangerous promiscuity and a nefarious complicity between the reflection and the reflected which lets itself be seduced narcissistically. In this play of representation, the point of origin becomes ungraspable. There are things like reflecting pools, and images, an infinite reference from one to the other, but no longer a source, a spring. There is no longer a simple origin. For what is reflected is split *in itself* and not only as an addition to itself of its image. The reflection, the image, the double, splits what it doubles. The origin of the speculation becomes a difference. What can look at itself is not one; and the law of the addition of the origin to its representation, of the thing to its image, is that one plus one makes at least three" (*Of Grammatology,* 36).

One can imagine a number of retorts to the inevitability of this impasse in representation. Christopher Norris, for one, cites Ludwig Wittgenstein's linguistic philosophy as a potential corrective (should one be motivated to seek it) to the more radically skeptical implications of the deconstructionist theory of the sign: "If our ways of talking about the world are a matter of tacit convention, then skepticism is simply beside the point, a misplaced scruple produced by a false epistemology. Wittgenstein sees the history of philosophic thought as both deviled and largely sustained by such self-created puzzles. His line of reply is understandably attractive to those who reject deconstruction and seek a philosophy of meaning to put in its place. From a Wittgensteinian viewpoint, there is a basic and persistent error of thought in the post-Saussurian textual theory which makes a startling phenomenon of the split between 'signifier' and 'signified'. To see this as a problem or paradox is to repeat the traditional mistake, that which comes of expecting language to relate directly to objects or ideas" (*Deconstruction: Theory and Practice*, 130).

When practitioners of deconstruction less able than Derrida make much, in what is to Norris an obvious point, of a given text's paradoxical "double reading"—its logic of the narrative order of events versus its own logic of narrative—they fall victim in his view to "what philosophers would call a 'category mistake', a confusion of logical realms or orders of discourse" (134). I would suggest that this is just what befell *Diacritics'* ruminations on the state of post-Hiroshima nuclear culture. In my own distinction between a "nuclear criticism" and a "nuclear politics criticism," I am attempting to differentiate those "orders of discourse" and render at least the former one that significantly lies prior to and beyond (a second-order) textuality—to render it, in other words, "worldly." This is, I would add, a distinction that at least at times Derrida himself, urgently if with qualification, presses upon us. "But who can fail to recognize the massive 'reality' of nuclear weaponry. . . . One has to distinguish between this 'reality' of the nuclear age and the fiction of [future nuclear] war" ("NO APOCALYPSE, NOT NOW," 23).

9. Gayatri Chakravorty Spivak, "Translator's Preface," xxxix.

10. Paul de Man, "The Resistance to Theory," 11.

11. I would like to point out at this juncture that, just as Derrida uses the language of contemporary literary criticism to make ironic the language of the arms race—he likes, for instance, to speak of "stockpiling" in connection with writing and with the process of archivizing as well as with weapons—the use of paramilitary metaphors in general throughout that same literary criticism (more so in others' work, perhaps, than Derrida's own) is notably salient and suggestive. Texts, we often read nowadays, have particular "strategies"; readers, however, can "resist." Critics, "armed" with theories, "deploy" their arguments, "interrogate" and "intervene" in those texts, usually in response to some "crisis." Our experience can be "deterritorialized" and "reterritorialized"; consciousness is "colonized" or, alternatively, "liberated." Our readers often need to be "mobilized." To peruse academic journals in the humanities today is often to feel as if one is going off to the front, not the classroom—but my point is not to mock such language, only to ask whether this convergence of post-Hiroshima military jargon with that of literary studies is not another indication of how really recent, historical, and omnipresent our nuclear age may really be—or perhaps the nostalgia it inspires for a past when individual, heroic agency—that of soldiers as well as professors—could win wars.

12. Nakajima Kenzō, "'Gembaku bungaku' no imi," 375.

13. Those few American intellectuals who do engage their nations's own nuclear culture routinely cite this conspicuous silence on the part of their colleagues. See, for example, Paul Boyer, *By the Bomb's Early Light*, xv.

When one does discover a thoughtful American response to the post-Hiroshima world, as in Japan it is usually within the confines of fiction. In 1985, author Tim O'Brien finished a novel, *The Nuclear Age*, that would subsequently and tellingly attract more attention in Japan than in the United States. In the novel's last line, its narrator (who has been busy digging a bomb shelter to the chagrin of his wife and daughter) makes a point that may explain some part of the perverse hope which motivated the architects of American nuclear criticism—and at the same time, make such hope impossibly ironic: "I will live my life in the conviction that when it finally happens—when we hear that midnight whine, when Kansas burns, when what is done is undone, when fail-safe fails, when deterrence no longer deters, when the gig is at last up—yes, even then I will hold to a steadfast orthodoxy, confident to the end that E will somehow not quite equal mc^2, that it's a cunning metaphor, that the terminal equation will somehow not quite balance" (312).

14. Ōe Kenzaburō, "Ikinobiru kibō to shite no bungaku," 65.

15. Itō Narihiko, "Gembaku bungaku to kyō no mondai," 81.

16. In fact, *Bungakuteki tachiba* is largely the editorial enterprise of Odagiri Hideo, whose anthology *The Problem of Atomic Power and Literature* almost thirty years earlier was, in the view of Kurihara Sadako and others, the first real work of atomic-bomb literary criticism. See Kurihara, *Kaku-jidai ni ikiru: Hiroshima—shi no naka no sei,* 155.

17. Nishida Masaru, et al., "Futatabi kaku-sensō no kiki ni bungakusha wa dono yō ni tai suru ka," 17.

18. The Congress, P.E.N.'s forty-seventh worldwide but only the second held in Tokyo, was convened from May 13–19 at the Keio Plaza Hotel. It was attended by 604 people, approximately two-thirds of them Japanese. Many of the proceedings from this conference, including those by Alain Robbe-Grillet, Ba Jin, and Kurt Vonnegut as well as Ōe Kenzaburō, were published in English by the Japan P.E.N. Club under the title *The Voice of the Writer, 1984: Collected Papers of the 47th International P.E.N. Congress in Tokyo.*

19. For one of the more astute challenges to the theoretical premises of *Diacritics'* nuclear criticism, see J. Fisher Solomon, *Discourse and Referent in the Nuclear Age;* for an example of the more conventional resistance to literary critics who even address themselves to such issues, see Tony Siebers, "The Ethics of Nuclear Criticism: Conclusion" in his book *The Ethics of Criticism,* 220–40.

20. Etō Jun, "PEN no seijigaku."

21. Alain Robbe-Grillet, quoted in Isoda Kōichi, "A Survey of Literature in 1984," 1.

22. Paul de Man, quoted in Harold Bloom, "The Breaking of Form," 4.

23. Kuroko Kazuo, *Gembaku to kotoba: Hara Tamiki kara Hayashi Kyōko made,* 134.

24. Ibid., 167.

25. Derrida does, I emphasize, repeatedly and vigorously distinguish between "the reality of the nuclear age and fiction of war." But even putting aside the objection that, from the point of view of many Japanese, that war has already taken place, Derrida links his "reality" with his "fiction" in a way that reduces both to "doxa," and thus to an ultimately referent-less discourse: "For the 'reality' of the nuclear age and the fable of nuclear war are perhaps distinct, but they are not two separate things. It is the war (in other words the fable) that triggers this fabulous war effort, this senseless capitalization of sophisticated weaponry, this speed race in search of speed, this crazy precipitation" (23).

An opposing view is expressed succinctly by, once again, the narrator of Tim O'Brien's *The Nuclear Age*, who echoes the hibakusha writer's common rejection of anything that pretends to "resemble" Hiroshima or Nagasaki: "There are no metaphors. There is only science when I say, 'Nuclear war'" (126).

26. Karl Popper, *Quantum Theory and the Schism in Physics*, 2. Popper is arguing specifically against subjectivism in physics. "The central issue here is *realism*," Popper insists. "That is to say, the reality of the physical world we live in: the fact that this world exists independently of ourselves; that it existed before life existed, according to our best hypotheses; and that it will continue to exist, for all we know, long after we have all been swept away. . . . The attack on realism, though intellectually interesting and important, is quite unacceptable, especially after two world wars and the real suffering—unavoidable suffering—that was wantonly produced by them." Perhaps only a scientist could find comfort, as did Popper, in a world that endures after all human life is extinct.

27. Ōe Kenzaburō, "Postwar Japanese Literature and the Contemporary Impasse," 2.

28. Anonymous, quoted in Ōe Kenzaburō, *Hiroshima nōto*, 152.

29. Ozu Kunsō, "Genten kara," 43.

30. Ōta Yōko, *Shikabane no machi*, 23.

31. Robert Jay Lifton, *Death in Life: Survivors of Hiroshima*, 330–31.

32. Hannah Arendt, *Eichmann in Jerusalem: A Report on the Banality of Evil*, 106.

33. Matsumoto Hiroshi, "Hachi—roku, Hiroshima no imi suru mono."

34. Kurihara Sadako, "Hachi—roku no imi suru mono," 83.

35. Oda Makoto, "Kono kan no tame no kiwamete mijikai chūshaku."

36. Oda Makoto, quoted in Thomas R. H. Havens, *Fire Across the Sea: The Vietnam War and Japan, 1965–1975*, 143–44.

37. Ibid., 120.

38. Ibid., 27.

39. Rōyama Michio, quoted in ibid., 70.

40. Nakayama Shigeru, "Sekai no gembaku bungaku," 19.

41. Shunsuke Tsurumi, *An Intellectual History of Wartime Japan, 1931–1945*, 103.

42. Robert Jay Lifton, *Death in Life*, 478.

43. Indeed, fellow novelist Maruya Saiichi has said of *An American Hero* that its difficult style, much like that of a work poorly translated from English, recalls nothing more than a Hayakawa (i.e., pulp) mystery novel ("Shinsensa ni kammei," 3). Oda Makoto himself has more kindly described its language "not elegant prose [*bibun*]," and attributes it to Iida's attempt to describe clinical insanity with an objective style, rather than the more typical subjective one ("Katarikuchi no migotosa," 5).

44. Sō Sakon, "Sugurete osoroshii shōsetsu," 1.

45. Ian Buruma, "The Devils of Hiroshima," 16.

46. Oda Makoto, "The Ethics of Peace," 160.

47. Ibid.

48. Ibid.

49. Homer, *The Iliad* (Fitzgerald trans.), 13.

50. Oda Makoto, quoted in Shigeoka Tōru, *"Hiroshima,"* 108.

51. Oda Makoto, "Yakusha atogaki," 245.

52. Karl Marx, *A Contribution to the Critique of Political Economy*, 11.

53. Noma Hiroshi, *Zentai shōsetsu e no shikō*, 203.

54. Ibid.

55. Hirai Hiroyuki, "Kaisetsu—'dō' to 'sei' no chishikijin ga torikunda 'kaku,'" 338–39.

56. Kamata Sadao, "Jūgonen sensō to gembaku bungaku," 215.

57. See Oda Makoto, "Gendai bungaku wa kore de ii no ka."

58. Oda Makoto, quoted in Shigeoka Tōru, *"Hiroshima,"* 108. It is interesting to note that Oda's novel, as it moved from being fiction to "something else," reverses the shift that hibakusha writers such as Ōta Yōko noted when their testimonial or documentary literature evolved to become more pronouncedly fictional. This is a difference that may reflect the epistemic gulf between hibakusha and non-hibakusha writers: the former seek to make an experience communicable, the latter to gain imaginative access to that same experience.

59. Oda Makoto, "'Kochira-gawa' o dō kaku—Oda Makoto-shi o kiku," 126.

60. Oda Makoto, "Hankaku—hansen o tsuranuku shutaisei," 27.

61. Fredric Jameson, *The Political Unconscious: Narrative as a Socially Symbolic Act*, 20.

62. Oda Makoto, "Hankaku—hansen o tsuranuku shutaisei," 31–32.

63. Oda Makoto, "Atarashii 'zentai shōsetsu' e no michi," 129.

64. Nakano Kōji, in Nakano Kōji and Nagaoka Hiroyoshi, "Gembaku bungaku o megutte," 17.

65. Like so much in *Hiroshima*, however, Oda's imagination of Joe Clancey's death is based on the historical record. While far many more prisoners of war were to die in Nagasaki, a few were indeed in Hiroshima on the 6th: "There was no POW camp in Hiroshima City proper, but some captured American bomber crews were turned over to the military police and kept there. Of the POWs who had parachuted from the B-24 *Lonesome Lady*—which left Okinawa on 28 July 1945 to bomb the battleship *Haruna* at Kure—6 were taken to Hiroshima where all died in the atomic bombing" (The Committee for the Compilation of Materials on Damage Caused by the Atomic Bombs in Hiroshima and Nagasaki, *Hiroshima and Nagasaki: The Physical, Medical, and Social Effects of the Atomic Bombings*, 480). Oda's Joe Clancey—who wonders to himself just what kind of place this "Kure" target of his could be—is clearly meant to be one of this unfortunate half-dozen.

66. Kuroko Kazuo, in Hayashi Kyōko, "Nagasaki soshite Amerika—Hayashi Kyōko ni kiku," 175.

11   Concluding Remarks

1. Michael Geyer, "Man-made Transcendences: Consumerism, Violence, and the Problem of Memory."

2. Proof abounds that those limits have retreated as a direct result of the assimilation

of the lingo of atomic war into everyday speech; or conversely, that such lingo has been so voided of its original reference that the limits remain intact. Andrew Holleran, in writing of what AIDS has of late wrought in his Manhattan neighborhood, can say: "The bomb seems the best metaphor as I wander the Metropolitan. 'Oh,' people say when they learn someone left New York in 1983, 'you got out before the bomb fell'" ("Ground Zero," 22). We may permit him that trope because he is, after all, using it to describe a large-scale catastrophe. Yet how we to react when one of his fellow New Yorkers, in reviewing an art exhibit, notes of a Minimalist painter that "his interest in a kind of ground-zero painting began to seem pertinent to a '90s zeitgeist" (Brooks Adams, "Stephen Rosenthal at Stark," 98)? Accuse the critic of a poorly chosen phrase? Or perhaps conclude that it is the perfect choice, and see in these real canvases as blank as Asada's in *The Shade of Trees* the apt expression of our post-Hiroshima, nuclear era?

3. Inoue Mitsuharu, for example, has written two novels on the nuclear power industry and its dangers (*Saikai genshiryoku hatsudenjō*, 1986; *Yusō*, 1989); among his many essays and fiction concerned with the complex terror of the nuclear age, Ōe Kenzaburō's *Hiroshima no "Inochi no ki"* appeared in 1991; Kurihara Sadako's collection of writings, *Towareru Hiroshima*, was published in 1992; and most prolifically, Hayashi Kyōko has produced a volume of work on Nagasaki almost annually (e.g., *Rimbu*, 1989; *Yasuraka ni ima wa nemuritamae*, 1990; *Shunkan no kioku*, 1992).

4. Murakami Haruki, quoted in Kuroko Kazuo, *Gembaku bungaku ron*, 97. There is some irony when Murakami, a writer whom Ōe Kenzaburō has chided for his novels' indifference to the serious issues of contemporary history and society, cites O'Brien's *The Nuclear Age* as the paramount statement of our time on precisely those questions to which Ōe has long devoted himself. Indeed, it is in a spirit that Ōe well understands that O'Brien writes and Murakami just as succinctly translates: "Nuclear war: just a fault line in the imagination" (311).

5. Quoted in Roger Luckhurst, "Nuclear Criticism: Anachronism and Anachorism," 95.

References

The most complete bibliography of materials pertaining to the atomic-bomb literature of Hiroshima and Nagasaki is the "Gembaku bungaku shi nempyō" compiled by Kuroko Kazuo. In English, it is Wayne P. Lammers and Osamu Masaoka's *Japanese A-Bomb Literature: An Annotated Bibliography*.

The works listed here are those quoted from or, if thematically concerned with Hiroshima or Nagasaki, cited in the course of this study. When a source is identifed both by its Japanese original and English translation, whichever comes first is the version to which my textual references apply.

It is a consequence of the mass violence perpetrated upon the populations of Hiroshima and Nagasaki that many of the writings it subsequently inspired were by ordinary citizens and not professional writers. This fact, coupled with the notoriously various and even intentionally eccentric readings of Japanese personal names, makes it impossible to guarantee absolute accuracy in the romanization of some of the names listed in this bibliography. Where no verification of a particular romanization was possible, I have opted for what I believe the most likely possibility. I am well aware, however, that often it is the least obvious reading that in the end proves right, and I apologize for the inadvertent errors I have surely made.

Abbreviations

GTK   Hiroshima-shi Gembaku taikenki kankōkai, ed. *Gembaku taikenki* [Atomic-bomb Testimonies]. Tokyo: Asahi Shimbun Sha, 1965.

HTZ   Hara Tamiki. *Hara Tamiki zenshū* [Hara Tamiki Collected Works]. 2 vols. Tokyo: Haga Shoten, 1965.

NGB   Kaku-sensō no kiken o uttaeru bungakusha, ed. *Nihon no gembaku bungaku* [Atomic-bomb Literature in Japan]. 15 vols. Tokyo: Horupu Shuppan, 1984.

OYS   Ōta Yōko. *Ōta Yōko shū* [Ōta Yōko Collected Works]. 4 vols. Tokyo: San'ichi
         Shobō, 1982.

Works Cited

Abe Tomoji. "Gembaku to bungaku" [The Atomic Bomb and Literature]. *NGB*,
15:80–88.

―――. "Jobun" [Preface]. In *Genshiryoku mondai to bungaku*, ed. Abe Tomoji and Odagiri
Hideo. Tokyo: Shakai Sha, 1955.

Adams, Brooks. "Stephen Rosenthal at Stark." *Art in America* 81, no. 6 (June 1993): 97–98.

Adorno, Theodor W. "Engagement." In *Noten zur Literatur*, 3:109–35. Frankfurt: Suhrkamp
Verlag, 1965.

―――. *Negative Dialectics*. Trans. E. B. Ashton. New York: The Seabury Press, 1973.

―――. "The Position of the Narrator in the Contemporary Novel." In *Notes to Literature*,
ed. Rolf Tiedemann, trans. Shierry Weber Nicholsen, 1:30–36. New York: Columbia University Press, 1991.

Agawa Hiroyuki. "Hachigatsu muika" [August Sixth]. In Agawa Hiroyuki, et al., *Shōwa
sensō bungaku zenshū 13: Genshi bakudan tōka saru*, 219–38. Tokyo: Shūei Sha, 1966.

―――. *The Devil's Heritage*. Trans. John M. Maki. Tokyo: Hokuseidō, 1957. *Ma no isan*.
Tokyo: Shinchō Sha, 1954.

Akiya Yutaka. "Fuyu no shudai" [Winter, The Assigned Theme]. In *Nihon gembaku shishū*,
Hotta Yoshie et al., eds., 219–20.

Alperovitz, Gar. *Atomic Diplomacy: Hiroshima and Potsdam*. New York: Vintage Books, 1965.

Althusser, Louis. "Ideology and Ideological State Apparatuses." In *Lenin and Philosophy and
Other Essays*, trans. Ben Brewster, 121–73. New York: Monthly Review Press, 1971.

―――. "Marxism and Humanism." In *For Marx*, trans. Ben Brewster, 219–47. New York:
Pantheon Books, 1969.

Alvarez, A. *The Savage God: A Study of Suicide*. London: Weidenfeld and Nicolson, 1971.

Amis, Martin. *Einstein's Monsters*. New York: Harmony Books, 1987.

The Anchor Bible: Job. Trans. with notes and introduction by Marvin H. Pope. Garden
City: Doubleday and Company, 1973.

Anders, Günter. *Endzeit und Zeitenende: Gedanken über die atomare Situation*. Munich: C. H.
Becksche, 1972.

Aono Suekichi. "Hiroshima to heiwa" [Hiroshima and Peace]. *NGB*, 15:62–65.

Arendt, Hannah. *Eichmann in Jerusalem: A Report on the Banality of Evil*. New York: Viking
Press, 1963.

Aristotle. *Poetics*. Trans. S. H. Butcher. Introduction by Francis Fergusson. New York:
Hill and Wang, 1989.

Auerbach, Erich. *Mimesis: The Representation of Reality in Western Literature*. Trans. Willard R.
Trask. Princeton: Princeton University Press, 1973.

Barthes, Roland. "Writing Degree Zero." In *Writing Degree Zero and Elements of Semiology*,
trans. Annette Lavers and Colin Smith, 3–73. London: Jonathan Cape, 1967.

————. "Writing the Event." In *The Rustle of Language*, trans. Richard Howard, 149–54. Berkeley: University of California Press, 1989.

Baudrillard, Jean. *Simulations*. Trans. Paul Foss, Paul Patton, and Phillip Beitchman. New York: Semiotext(e), 1983.

Bauman, Zygmunt. *Modernity and the Holocaust*. Ithaca: Cornell University Press, 1989.

Bayley, John. Review of *Against Forgetting: Twentieth-Century Poetry of Witness*, edited by Carolyn Forché. *The New York Review of Books* 40, no. 12 (June 24, 1993): 20–22.

Belsey, Catherine. *Critical Practice*. London: Routledge, 1980.

Benjamin, Walter. "Edward Fuchs, Collector and Historian." In *One-Way Street and Other Writings*, trans. Edmund Jephcott and Kingsley Shorter, 349–86. London: NLB, 1979.

————. *Illuminations*. Ed. Hannah Arendt. Trans. Harry Zohn. New York: Schocken Books, 1969.

Bernstein, Barton J., and Allen J. Matusow, eds. *The Truman Administration, A Documentary History*. New York: Harper & Row, 1966.

Bester, John. "Translator's Preface." In Ibuse Masuji, *Black Rain*, 5–8.

Betsuyaku Minoru. *The Elephant*. In David G. Goodman, trans. and ed., *After Apocalypse: Four Japanese Plays of Hiroshima and Nagasaki*, 193–48. Zō. NGB, 12:213–75.

Blanchot, Maurice. *The Writing of the Disaster*. Trans. Ann Smock. Lincoln: University of Nebraska Press, 1986.

Bloom, Harold. "The Breaking of Form." In *Deconstruction and Criticism*, 1–37. New York: The Seabury Press, 1979.

————. *A Map of Misreading*. New York: Oxford University Press, 1975.

Booth, Wayne C. *The Rhetoric of Fiction*. Chicago: University of Chicago Press, 1983.

Borowski, Tadeusz. "Auschwitz, Our Home (A Letter)." In *This Way For the Gas, Ladies and Gentlemen*, trans. and selected by Barbara Vedder, 98–142. New York: Penguin Books, 1985.

Boyer, Paul. *By the Bomb's Early Light: American Thought and Culture at the Dawn of the Atomic Age*. New York: Pantheon Books, 1985.

Brooks, Cleanth. *The Well-Wrought Urn: Studies in the Structure of Poetry*. New York: Harcourt, Brace and Company, 1947.

Browning, Christopher R. "German Memory, Judicial Interrogation and Historical Reconstruction: Writing Perpetrator History from Post-War Oral Testimony." Lecture. April 27, 1990. University of California, Los Angeles.

Brownstein, Michael. "From *Kokugaku* to *Kokubungaku*: Canon Formation in the Meiji Period." *Harvard Journal of Asiatic Studies* 47, no. 2 (December 1987): 435–60.

Bungaku Jihyō Sha, ed. *Igi ari! Gendai bungaku* [I Dissent! Contemporary Literature]. Tokyo: Kawai Shuppan, 1991.

Burke, Kenneth. *The Philosophy of Literary Form*. Berkeley: University of California Press, 1973.

Buruma, Ian. "The Devils of Hiroshima." *New York Review of Books* 37, no. 16 (October 25, 1990): 15–19.

Caldicott, Helen. *Nuclear Madness: What You Can Do! With a New Chapter on Three Mile Island.* With the assistance of Nancy Herrington and Nahum Stiskin. New York: Bantam Books, 1980.

Camus, Albert. *Notebooks.* Trans. J. O. O'Brien. New York: Alfred A. Knopf, 1963.

———. *The Myth of Sisyphus and Other Essays.* Trans. Justin O'Brien. New York: Alfred A. Knopf, 1955.

———. *The Rebel.* Trans. Anthony Bower. New York: Alfred A. Knopf, 1954.

Canetti, Elias. *The Human Province.* Trans. Joachim Neugroschel. New York: Seabury Press, 1978.

Chinnock, Frank W. *Nagasaki: The Forgotten Bomb.* New York and Cleveland: New American Library, 1969.

Clark, Ian. *Nuclear Past, Nuclear Present: Hiroshima, Nagasaki, and Contemporary Strategy.* Boulder: Westview Press, 1985.

Cohen, Sande. "Historians' Histories and the 'Final Solution' as Dispossession." Lecture. April 29, 1990. University of California, Los Angeles.

The Committee for the Compilation of Materials on Damage Caused by the Atomic Bombs in Hiroshima and Nagasaki. *Hiroshima and Nagasaki: The Physical, Medical, and Social Effects of the Atomic Bombings.* Trans. Eisei Ishikawa and David L. Swain. New York: Basic Books, Inc., 1987. *Hiroshima-shi Nagasaki-shi no gembaku saigai.* Tokyo: Iwanami Shoten, 1979.

Cousins, Norman. "Foreword." In Nagai Takashi, *We of Nagasaki,* trans. Ichiro Shirato and Herbert B. L. Silverman, vi–viii. New York: Duell, Sloan and Pearce, 1958.

Craig, David and Michael Egan. *Extreme Situations: Literature and Crisis from the Great War to the Atom Bomb.* London: Macmillan, 1979.

Culler, Jonathan. *The Pursuit of Signs: Semiotics, Literature, Deconstruction.* Ithaca: Cornell University Press, 1981.

———. *Structuralist Poetics: Structuralism, Linguistics, and the Study of Literature.* Ithaca: Cornell University Press, 1976.

de Man, Paul. "The Resistance to Theory." *Yale French Studies* no. 63 (1982): 3–20.

Derrida, Jacques. "NO APOCALYPSE, NOT NOW (full speed ahead, seven missiles, seven missives)." Trans. Catherine Porter and Philip Lewis. *Diacritics* 14, no. 2 (Summer 1984): 20–31.

———. *Of Grammatology.* Trans. Gayatri Chakravorty Spivak. Baltimore: The Johns Hopkins University Press, 1976.

Des Pres, Terrence. *The Survivor: An Anatomy of Life in the Death Camps.* New York: Oxford University Press, 1976.

Diacritics 14, no. 2 (Summer 1984).

Doi Sadako. "Tomo ni tasukeraretsutsu" [Helped by a Friend]. *GTK,* 28–36.

Dower, John W., and John Junkerman, eds. *The Hiroshima Murals: The Art of Iri Maruki and Toshi Maruki.* Tokyo and New York: Kodansha International, 1985.

Duras, Marguerite. *Hiroshima Mon Amour.* Trans. Richard Seaver. New York: Grove Press, Inc., 1961.

Eagleton, Terry. _Criticism and Ideology: A Study in Marxist Literary Theory._ London: Verso Editions, 1904.

———. "Ideology, Fiction, Narrative." _Social Text_ 1, no. 2 (Summer 1979): 62–80.

Eberhart, Richard. "Aesthetics After War." In _Undercliff,_ 56–62. New York: Oxford University Press, 1953.

Egusa Mitsuko. "'Natsu no hana'" [On "Summer Flowers"]. _Kokubungaku kaishaku to kanshō_ 50, no. 9 (August 1985): 53–59.

Epstein, Leslie. "Writing about the Holocaust." In Berel Lang, ed., _Writing and the Holocaust,_ 261–70.

Esashi Akiko. _Kusazue: Ōta Yōko hyōden_ [Spoiled Grass: A Critical Biography of Ōta Yōko]. Tokyo: Nami Shobō, 1971.

Etō Jun. "Heijōshin de kataru ijōshin: kioi no nai gembaku shōsetsu" [Extraordinary Events Told Ordinarily: Atomic-bomb Fiction Without Rancor]. _Asahi shimbun,_ Evening Edition, August 25, 1966.

———. "PEN no seijigaku" [The Politics of P.E.N.]. _Shinchō_ 81, no. 7 (July 1984): 206–17.

Ezrahi, Sidra Dekoven. _By Words Alone: The Holocaust in Literature._ Chicago: University of Chicago Press, 1980.

———. "Considering the Apocalypse: Is the Writing on the Wall Only Graffiti?" In Berel Lang, ed., _Writing and the Holocaust,_ 137–53.

Fogelman, Edwin, ed. _Hiroshima: The Decision to Use the A-bomb._ New York: Charles Scribner's Sons, 1964.

Fowler, Edward. _The Rhetoric of Confession: Shishōsetsu in Early Twentieth-Century Fiction._ Berkeley: University of California Press, 1988.

Freedman, Lawrence. _The Evolution of Nuclear Strategy._ New York: St. Martin's Press, 1983.

Freud, Sigmund. "Thoughts for the Times on War and Death." Trans. James Strachey. In _Standard Edition of the Complete Psychological Works of Sigmund Freud,_ 14:273–300. London: Hogarth Press and the Institute of Psycho-analysis, 1953–74.

Friedlander, Saul, et al., eds. _Visions of Apocalypse: End or Rebirth?_ New York and London: Holmes and Meier, 1985.

Frye, Northrop. _Anatomy of Criticism: Four Essays._ Princeton: Princeton University Press, 1957.

Fujita Asaya. _Hiroshima ni tsuite no namida ni tsuite_ [About the Tears About Hiroshima]. _NGB,_ 12:359–407.

Fukagawa Munetoshi. "'Kanashimi o taete'—'gembaku bungaku' ron o chūshin ni" ["Enduring the Sadness": The Theory of "Atomic-bomb Literature"]. _NGB,_ 15:256–57.

Fukuda Kyoto and Matsumoto Takeo. _Ibuse Masuji._ Tokyo: Shimizu Shoin, 1981.

Fukuda Sumako. _Ware nao ikite ari_ [I Am Still Alive]. Tokyo: Chikuma Shobō, 1968.

Fukunaga Teruhiko. _Shi no shima_ [Island of Death]. 2 vols. Tokyo: Shinchō Sha, 1977.

Fumizawa Takaichi. "Gembaku kō" [Reflections on the Atomic Bomb]. _NGB,_ 15:302–8.

Fussell, Paul. *The Great War and Modern Memory.* London and Oxford: Oxford University Press, 1975.

Gembaku higaisha no shuki hensan'inkai, ed. *Gembaku ni ikite—gembaku higaisha no shuki* [Surviving the Bomb: Atomic-bomb Victim Memoirs]. Tokyo: San'ichi Shobō, 1953.

Gendai shijin kai, ed. *Shi no hai shishū* [Ashes of Death Poetry Anthology]. Tokyo: Hō-bunkan, 1954.

Geyer, Michael. "Man-made Transcendences: Consumerism, Violence, and the Problem of Memory." Lecture. April 27, 1990. University of California, Los Angeles.

Giovannitti, Len, and Fred Freed. *The Decision to Drop the Bomb.* New York: Coward-McCann, Inc., 1965.

Goodman, David G., ed. and trans. *After Apocalypse: Four Japanese Plays of Hiroshima and Nagasaki.* New York: Columbia University Press, 1986.

Gotō Minako. "Atogaki" [Afterword]. In *Toki o hiku,* 222–23.

———. "Sambon no kugi no omosa" [The Weight of Three Spikes]. In *Toki o hiku,* 107–78.

———. "Tanjin no furu machi" [The Town Where It Rains Coal Dust]. In *Toki o hiku,* 179–220.

———. *Toki o hiku* [Tug of Time]. Tokyo: Kawade Shobō Shinsha, 1972. 5–105.

Hachiya Michihiko. *Hiroshima nikki.* Tokyo: Asahi Shimbun Sha, 1955. *Hiroshima Diary.* Ed. and trans. Warner Wells. Chapel Hill: University of North Carolina Press, 1955.

Hamai Shinzō. "Hajime ni" [Foreword]. *GTK,* 3–4.

Hane, Mikiso, trans. and ed.. *Reflections on the Way to the Gallows: Voices of Japanese Rebel Women.* New York: Pantheon Books, 1988.

Hanada Kiyoteru. "Genshi jidai no geijutsu" [Art in the Atomic Age]. *NGB,* 15:199–208.

Hara Gen'ichi. *Gyokō* [The Harbor]. *Shingeki* 6, no. 2 (February 1959): 2–45.

Hara, Mieko. Untitled memoir. Publishing Committee for "Children of Hiroshima," ed. *Children of Hiroshima,* 244–46.

Hara Tamiki. "Aki nikki" [Autumn Diary]. *HTZ,* 2:263–75.

———. "Akumu" [Nightmare]. *HTZ,* 2:572–73.

———. "Chiisa na mura" [A Small Village]. *HTZ,* 2:87–104.

———. "Eien no midori" [Forever Verdant]. *HTZ,* 2:233–49.

———. "Futatsu no shi" [Two Deaths]. *HTZ,* 2:440–50.

———. "Fuyu nikki" [Winter Diary]. *HTZ,* 2:276–86.

———. "Gembaku saiji no nōto" [Notes on the Atomic Destruction]. *HTZ,* 1:529–32.

———. "Gembaku shōkei" [Atomic-bomb Landscapes]. *HTZ,* 1:474–79.

———. "Gyōretsu" [The Procession]. *HTZ,* 1:238–250.

———. "Haikyo kara." *HTZ,* 2:67–84. "From the Ruins." In Richard H. Minear, trans. and ed., *Hiroshima: Three Witnesses,* 61–78.

———. "Hametsu no jokyoku." *HTZ,* 2:13–49. "Prelude to Annihilation." In Richard H. Minear, trans. and ed., *Hiroshima: Three Witnesses,* 79–113.

———. "Hiyu" [A Parable]. *HTZ*, 1:39.

———. "Honoo" [Flames]. *HTZ*, 1:106–14.

———. "Idō" [Motion]. *HTZ*, 1:14.

———. "Kiri" [Fog]. *HTZ*, 1:18.

———. "Kore ga ningen na no desu" [*This Is A* Human Being]. *HTZ*, 1:474.

———. "Kumo no sakeme" [A Break in the Clouds]. *HTZ*, 2:351–60.

———. "Kurushiku utsukushiki natsu" [A Painfully Beautiful Summer] *HTZ*, 2:253–62.

———. "Manatsubi no sampo" [A Stroll in the Summer Heat]. *HTZ*, 1:46.

———. "Mizu o kudasai" [*Give Me* Water]. *HTZ*, 1:478.

———. "Mune no uzuki" [A Troubled Heart]. *HTZ*, 2:541–43.

———. "Nagasaki no kane" [The Bells of Nagasaki]. *HTZ*, 2:576–72.

———. "Natsu no hana." *HTZ*, 2:50–66. "Summer Flowers." In Richard H. Minear, trans. and ed., *Hiroshima: Three Witnesses*, 45–60.

———. *Natsu no hana* [Summer Flowers]. Tokyo: Nōgaku Shorin, 1949. *Summer Flowers.* In Richard H. Minear, trans. and ed., *Hiroshima: Three Witnesses*, 45–113.

———. "Sensō ni tsuite" [On War]. *HTZ*, 2:589–590.

———. "Shi no naka no fūkei" [A View Into Death]. *HTZ*, 2:301–13.

———. "Shi to ai to kodoku" [Death, Love and Loneliness]. *HTZ*, 2:540–41.

———. "Shingan no kuni." *HTZ*, 2:397–405. "The Land of My Heart's Desire." Trans. John Bester. In Ōe Kenzaburō, ed., *The Crazy Iris and Other Stories of the Atomic Aftermath*, 55–62.

———. "Suzume" [Sparrows]. *HTZ*, 1:57.

———. "Utsukushiki shi no kishi ni" [On the Brink of Beautiful Death]. *HTZ*, 2:287–300.

———. "Yume to jinsei" [Dreams and Life]. *HTZ*, 2:361–71.

Harootunian, H. D. "Visible Discourses/Invisible Ideologies." In *Japan and Postmodernism*, ed. H. D. Harootunian and Masao Miyoshi, 63–92. Durham: Duke University Press, 1989.

Harries, Karsten. "Metaphor and Transcendence." In Sheldon Sachs, ed., *On Metaphor*, 71–88. Chicago: University of Chicago Press, 1978.

Hartman, Geoffrey H. *Saving the Text: Literature, Derrida, Philosophy.* Baltimore: The Johns Hopkins University Press, 1981.

Hashioka Takeshi. "Hachigatsu nijūsannichi no koto" [August Twenty-third]. *NGB*, 11:368–81.

Hashimoto Eiichi. "Hachi–roku no imi suru mono 4" [What August 6 Means, 4]. In Oguro Kaoru, ed., *Hiroshima no imi*, 55–65.

Hashimoto Kunie. "Wasureenu shinsetsu" [Unforgettable Kindnesses]. *GTK*, 96–103.

Havens, Thomas R. H. *Fire Across the Sea: The Vietnam War and Japan, 1965–1975.* Princeton: Princeton University Press, 1987.

Hayashi Kyōko. "Ai no genten" [The Origin of Love]. In *Shizen o kou*, 76–84.

————. "Akikan." In *Giyaman bīdoro*, 7–26. "The Empty Can." Trans. Margaret Mitsutani. In Ōe Kenzaburō, ed., *The Crazy Iris and Other Stories of the Atomic Aftermath*, 127–43.

————. "Arumi no yōki" [The Aluminum Containers]. In *Shizen o kou*, 9–22.

————. "Buji—seireki senkyūhyaku hachijūichi-nen, gembaku sanjūshichi-nen" [Safe—1981 A. D., 37 Atomic Age]. *Gunzō* 27, no. 1 (January 1982): 32–57.

————. *Giyaman bīdoro* [Cut Glass, Blown Glass]. Tokyo: Kōdansha, 1978.

————. "Giyaman bīdoro" [Cut Glass, Blown Glass]. In *Giyaman bīdoro*, 47–65.

————. "Hibiki" [Echo]. In *Giyaman bīdoro*, 109–27.

————. "Jisho" [Dictionaries]. In *Shizen o kou*, 158–61.

————. "Kāki-iro kara kon-iro no sedai e" [From the Khaki Generation to the Denim Generation]. In *Shizen o kou*, 52–62.

————. "Kiroku" [Document]. In *Giyaman bīdoro*, 151–67.

————. "Kodoku to iu koto" [This They Call Loneliness]. In *Shizen o kou*, 102–10.

————. "Kompirayama" [Mount Kompira]. In *Giyaman bīdoro*, 27–45.

————. "Kōsa." In *Giyaman bīdoro*, 87–105. "Yellow Sand." Trans. Kyoko Selden. In Noriko Mizuta Lippit and Kyoko Selden, eds. and trans., *Japanese Women Writers: Twentieth Century Short Fiction*, 207–16. Armonk: M. E. Sharpe, 1991.

————. "Matsuri no ba" [The Site of Rituals]. *NGB*, 3:26–68. "Ritual of Death." Trans. Kyoko Selden. In Morty Sklar, ed., *Nuke Rebuke: Writers and Artists Against Nuclear Energy and Weapons*, 21–57.

————. "Mizu—karasu—shōnen shōjo" ["Water," "Crows," and "Boys and Girls"]. In *Shizen o kou*, 33–43.

————. "Mumyō" [In the Darkness]. In *Giyaman bīdoro*, 211–28.

————. "Nagasaki soshite Amerika—Hayashi Kyōko-shi ni kiku" [Nagasaki and America: An Interview with Hayashi Kyōko]. With Kuroko Kazuo. In Bungaku Jihyō Sha, ed., *Igi ari! Gendai bungaku*, 167–84.

————. *Naki ga gotoki* [As If Not]. Tokyo: Kōdansha, 1981.

————. "No ni" [In the Fields]. In *Giyaman bīdoro*, 229–47.

————. *Rimbu* [Round Dance]. Tokyo: Shinchō Sha, 1989.

————. "Seinen-tachi" [Young Men]. In *Giyaman bīdoro*, 67–86.

————. "Shizen o kou" [Wishing Life As It Should Be]. In *Shizen o kou*, 23–32.

————. *Shizen o kou*. [Wishing Life As It Should Be]. Tokyo: Chūō Kōron Sha, 1981.

————. *Shunkan no kioku* [The Memory of an Instant]. Tokyo: Shin Nihon Shuppansha, 1992.

————. "Tomo yo" [Friend]. In *Giyaman bīdoro*, 169–88.

————. "Two Grave Markers." Trans. Kyoko Selden. *The Bulletin of Concerned Asian Scholars* 18, no. 1 (January-March 1986): 23–35. "Futari no bohyō." *NGB*, 3:69–93.

————. *Yasuraka ni ima wa nemuritamae* [Rest Now in Peace]. Tokyo: Kōdansha, 1990.

————. "Yobun na omoi" [Feelings to Spare]. In *Shizen o kou*, 69–75.

Hayashida Yasumasa. "Atarashii minzoku jōjishi no hōga—gembaku bungaku e no kitai" [The Birth of a New Ethnic Epic Poetry: The Hope for Atomic-bomb Literature]." *NGB*, 15:209–21.

Heidegger, Martin. *Being and Time*. Trans. John Macquarrie and Edward Robinson. New York: Harper and Row, 1962.

————. *On the Way to Language*. Trans. Peter D. Hertz. New York: Harper and Row, 1971.

Hersey, John. *Hiroshima*. New York: Alfred A. Knopf, 1956.

Hersh, Seymour. *Son Mi* [Son My]. Trans. Oda Makoto. Tokyo: Sōshi Sha, 1970.

Hilberg, Raul. "I Was Not There." In Berel Lang, ed., *Writing and the Holocaust*, 17–25.

Hirai Hiroyuki. "Kaisetsu—'dō' to 'sei' no chishikijin ga torikunda 'kaku'" [Critical Afterword: "Nuclear" as Understood by Active and Passive Intellectuals]. *NGB*, 8:338–52.

Hiroshima no shi henshū iinkai, eds. *Hiroshima no shi*. Hiroshima: Chūō Kōminkan, 1955. *The Songs of Hiroshima*. Hiroshima: YMCA Service Center, 1955.

Hirsch, Jr., E. D. *Validity in Interpretation*. New Haven: Yale University Press, 1967.

Hochhuth, Rolf. *The Deputy*. Trans. Richard and Clara Winston. New York: Grove Press, Inc., 1964.

Hoffman, Frederick J. *The Mortal No: Death and the Modern Imagination*. Princeton: Princeton University Press, 1964.

Holleran, Andrew. "Ground Zero." In *Ground Zero*, 19–28.

————. *Ground Zero*. New York: New American Library, 1988.

————. "Reading and Writing." In *Ground Zero*, 11–18.

Homer. *The Iliad*. Trans. Robert Fitzgerald. New York: Anchor Press/Doubleday, 1974.

Honda Shūgo. "Kaen no ko" [Child of Fire]. *HTZ*, 1:579–81.

Horupu Shuppan henshūbu, ed. *Hankaku: Bungakusha wa uttaeru* [Anti-Nuclear: Writers Appeal]. Tokyo: Horupu Shuppan, 1984.

Hotta Kiyomi. *The Island*. In David G. Goodman, trans. and ed., *After Apocalypse: Four Japanese Plays of Hiroshima and Nagasaki*, 19–104. *Shima*, *NGB*, 12:9–83.

Hotta Yoshie. "Hara Tamiki no bungaku to gendai" [The Literature of Hara Tamiki and the Present Day]. *HTZ*, 1:612–15.

————. *Shimpan* [The Judgment]. Tokyo: Iwanami Shoten, 1963.

Hotta Yoshie, Kinoshita Junji, and Ōhara Miyao, eds. *Nihon gembaku shishū* [Japanese Atomic-bomb Poetry]. Tokyo: Taihei Shuppan Sha, 1972.

Howe, Irving. *Politics and the Novel*. New York: Horizon Press, 1957.

Ibuse Masuji. "Aru shōjo no senji nikki" [A Young Girl's Wartime Diary]. In *Ibuse Masuji zenshū*, 10:98–116.

————. *Black Rain*. Trans. John Bester. Tokyo: Kodansha International, 1978. *Kuroi ame*. In *Ibuse Masuji zenshū*, 13:3–298.

————. *Ibuse Masuji zenshū* [Complete works of Ibuse Masuji]. 14 vols. Tokyo: Chikuma Shobō, 1964–1975.

————. "Kakitsubata." In *Ibuse Masuji zenshū,* 5:3–22. "The Crazy Iris." Trans. Ivan Morris. In Ōe Kenzaburō, ed., *The Crazy Iris and Other Stories of the Atomic Aftermath,* 17–35.

————. "Kaku no genjōkyō 'Fuyukai da na'" [The Present Nuclear Situation: 'Not Very Pleasant']. *Asahi shimbun,* evening ed., August 3, 1981.

————. "Kataware sōshi" [A Story in Pieces]. In *Ibuse Masuji zenshū,* 8:301–12.

————. "Kinō no kai" [The Banquet Last Night]. In *Ibuse Masuji zenshū,* 12:16–24.

————. "The Salamander." Trans. John Bester. In *Lieutenant Lookeast and Other Stories,* 59–65. Tokyo: Kodansha International, 1971. "Sanshōuo." In *Ibuse Masuji zenshū,* 1:3–11.

————. *Sazanami gunki.* In *Ibuse Masuji zenshū,* 1:370–480. *Waves: A War Diary.* Trans. David Aylward and Anthony Liman. In *Waves: Two Short Novels,* 26–103. Tokyo: Kodansha International, 1986.

————. "Tankōjitai byōin" [The Mining-Town Clinic]. In *Ibuse Masuji zenshū,* 1:61–71.

————. *Tomonotsu chakaiki* [A Record of Tea Parties at Tomonotsu]. In *Ibuse Masuji jisen zenshū,* 13 (supplemental): 7–130. Tokyo: Shinchō Sha, 1986.

"Ibuse Masuji-shi ga shikyo" [Ibuse Masuji Dead]. *Asahi shimbun,* July 11, 1993.

Ienaga Saburō, Odagiri Hideo, and Kuroko Kazuo, eds. *Hiroshima Nagasaki gembaku shashin kaiga shūsei* [Hiroshima and Nagasaki: The Atomic Bombings As Seen Through Photographs and Artwork]. 6 vols. Tokyo: Nihon Tosho Sentā, 1993.

Iida Momo. *Amerika no eiyū* [An American Hero]. Tokyo: Kawade Shobō Shinsha, 1977.

Inokuchi Motosaburō. "Kyōten" [Catastrophe]. *NGB,* 14:25–27.

Inoue Mitsuharu. *Chi no mure* [People of the Land]. Tokyo: Kawade Shobō Shinsha, 1963.

————. "The House of Hands." Trans. Frederick Uleman and Kōichi Nakagawa. In Ōe Kenzaburō, ed., *The Crazy Iris and Other Stories of the Atomic Aftermath,* 145–68. "Te no ie." *NGB,* 5:10–30.

————. *Saikai genshiryoku hatsudenjō* [The Saikai Atomic Power Plant]. Tokyo: Bungei Shunjū, 1986.

————. *Yusō* [Transport]. Tokyo: Bungei Shunjū, 1989.

Ishida Kōji. "Kumo no kioku" [Memory of a Cloud]. *NGB,* 10:257–82.

Ishida Masako. *Masako taorezu: Nagasaki genshi bakudan ki* [Masako Will Not Succumb: An Account of the Nagasaki Atomic Bomb]. Tokyo: Hyōgen Sha, 1949.

Isoda Kōichi. "A Survey of Literature in 1984." *Japanese Literature Today,* no. 10 (March 1985): 1–5.

Itasaka Gen et al., ed. *Kodansha Encyclopedia of Japan.* 9 vols. Tokyo: Kodansha, 1983.

Itō Narihiko. "Gembaku bungaku to kyō no mondai" [Atomic-bomb Literature and the Issues of Today]. In Horupu Shuppan henshūbu, ed., *Hankaku: Bungakusha wa uttaeru,* 79–107.

————. "Kaisetsu—'kaku' o mitsumete kita me 1945–1983" [Critical Afterword—Staring at the Nuclear, 1945–1983]. *NGB,* 15:518–35.

Iwamoto Hakuzō. "Ko no shikabane o yaku" [Burning the Children's Corpses]. *GTK*, 206–17.

Iwasaki Seiichirō. "'Hachigatsu muika' o kaku dainishū kaisetsu" [Critical Afterword to vol. 2 of *Writing August Sixth*]. *NGB*, 15:330–41.

———. *Higure no machi* [The Twilight City]. Hiroshima: Keisui Sha, 1987.

———. *Hiroshima no bungei–chiteki fudo to kiseki* [Hiroshima Literature: The Intellectual Landscape and History]. Hiroshima: Hiroshima Bunka Shuppan, 1973.

Japan P.E.N. Club, ed. *The Voice of the Writer, 1984: Collected Papers of the 47th International P.E.N. Congress in Tokyo.* Tokyo: Kodansha International, 1986.

Japanese-English Buddhist Dictionary. Tokyo: Daitō Shuppansha, 1976.

Jameson, Fredric. "The Ideology of the Text." In *The Ideologies of Theory: Essays, 1971–1986,* vol. 1: *Situations of Theory,* 17–71. Theory and History of Literature, vol. 48. Minneapolis: University of Minnesota Press, 1988.

———. "Imaginary and Symbolic in Lacan: Marxism, Psychoanalytic Criticism, and the Problem of the Subject." *Yale French Studies* no. 55/56 (1977): 338–95.

———. *The Political Unconscious: Narrative as a Socially Symbolic Act.* Ithaca: Cornell University Press, 1982.

———. "On Politics and Literature." *Salmagundi* 2, no. 3 (Spring 1968): 17–26.

Jarrell, Randall. "Losses." In *The Complete Poems,* 145–46. New York: Farrar, Straus and Giroux, 1969.

Jaspers, Karl. *The Fate of Mankind.* Trans. E. B. Ashton. Chicago: University of Chicago Press, 1961.

Johnston, William. "Introduction." In Nagai Takashi, *The Bells of Nagasaki,* v–xxiii.

Kaga Otohiko. "Kaisetsu" [Critical Afterword]. In Fukunaga Takehiko, *Shi no shima,* 2:444–49.

Kahler, Erich. *The Tower and the Abyss: An Inquiry into the Transformation of the Individual.* New York: George Braziller, Inc., 1957.

Kaikō Takeshi. "Hara Tamiki 'Natsu no hana' no baai [The Case of Hara Tamiki's "Summer Flowers"]." In *Kaikō Takeshi zensakuhin,* 10:133–42. Tokyo: Shinchō Sha, 1974.

"Kaku no genjōkyō wa 'fuyukai da na'" ["I'm Not Pleased" Over the Current Nuclear Situation]. *Asahi shimbun,* Evening Edition, August 3, 1981.

"Kaku-sensō no kiken o uttaeru bungakusha no seimei" [Writers' Appeal Against the Dangers of Nuclear War]. *NGB,* 15:514.

Kamata Sadao. "Jūgonen-sensō to gembaku bungaku" [Atomic-bomb Literature and the Fifteen-year War]. Horupu Shuppan henshūbu, ed., *Hankaku: Bungakusha wa uttaeru,* 169–218.

———. "Kaisetsu (2)—Nagasaki no taiken kiroku" [Critical Afterword (2): Nagasaki Witness Accounts]. *NGB,* 14:512–17.

———, ed. *Nagasaki no shōgen* [Nagasaki Testimonies]. Nagasaki: Nagasaki no Shōgen no Kai, 1978.

Kamezawa Miyuki. "Hiroshima junrei" [Hiroshima Pilgrimage]. *NGB*, 11:417–57.

Kaminsky, Marc. *The Road From Hiroshima.* New York: Simon and Schuster, 1984.

Kanaya Masako. "Keroido o nokoshite" [Left with Keloid Scars]. *GTK*, 43–51.

Kaneko Hiroshi. *"Kuroi ame"* [*Black Rain*]. *Kokubungaku kaishaku to kanshō* 50. no. 4 (April 1985): 81–85.

Kaplan, Chaim A. *Scroll of Agony: The Warsaw Diary of Chaim A. Kaplan.* Trans. and ed. Abraham I. Katsh. New York: Macmillan, 1965.

Karatani Kōjin. "Hankaku Apīru ni tsuite" [On the Anti-Nuclear Appeal]. In *Hihyō to posuto-modan,* 235–37. Tokyo: Fukutake Shoten, 1985.

————, Kawamura Jirō and Nakagami Kenji. "Sōsaku gōhyō" [Reviews of Fiction]. *Gunzō* 37, no. 2 (February 1982): 274–94.

Kawakami Sōkun. "Seizonsha" [The Survivors]. *NGB*, 10:184–207.

Kashū Hiroshima henshū iinkai, ed. *Kashū Hiroshima* [Poetry Hiroshima]. Tokyo: Daini Shobō, 1954.

Katō, Shūichi. *A History of Japanese Literature,* vol. 3: *The Modern Years.* Trans. Don Sanderson. Tokyo: Kodansha International, 1983.

Katsuhara Sumio. "Tōge Sankichi shōron: *Gembaku shishū* seiritsu no haikei" [A Brief Essay on Tōge Sankichi: The Background of *Atomic-bomb Poems*]. *Kokubungaku kaishaku to kanshō* 50, no. 9 (August, 1985): 42–46.

Kawanishi Masaaki. "Onna-tachi ga kataru hachigatsu kokonoka" [August Ninth, As Told by Women]. In Hayashi Kyōko, *Naki ga gotoki,* 223–33.

Keene, Donald. *Dawn to the West: Japanese Literature in the Modern Era (Fiction).* New York: Henry Holt and Company, 1984.

————. *Dawn to the West: Japanese Literature of the Modern Era (Poetry, Drama, Criticism).* New York: Henry Holt and Company, 1984.

Kermode, Frank. *The Sense of an Ending: Studies in the Theory of Fiction.* New York: Oxford University Press, 1967.

Kijima Katsumi. "Kiesaranu kuyami" [Eternal Regrets]. *GTK*, 91–95.

Kitahara Takeo, Noma Hiroshi, and Saeki Shōichi. "Sōsaku gappyō" [Monthly Review of New Fiction]. *Gunzō* 21, no. 10 (October 1966): 266–80.

Kitayama Futaba. "A, rakkasan da" [Look! It's a Parachute]. *GTK*, 11–20.

Kokai Eiji. *Hara Tamiki—shijin no shi* [Hara Tamiki: The Death of a Poet]. Tokyo: Kokubun Sha, 1978.

Kokubo Hitoshi. "Futatabi 'gembaku bungaku' ni tsuite" ["Atomic-bomb Literature" Reconsidered]. *NGB*, 15:253–55.

————. "Natsu no kokuin" [The Mark of Summer]. *NGB*, 11:330–67.

Konaka Yōtarō. "Kyō no kaku-jōkyō to bungakusha no hankaku seimei" [The Nuclear Situation Today and the Writers' Anti-Nuclear Appeal]. In Horupu Shuppan henshūbu, ed., *Hankaku: Bungakusha wa uttaeru,* 33–59.

Konishi Jin'ichi. *A History of Japanese Literature,* vol. 1: *The Archaic and Ancient Ages.* Trans.

Aileen Gatten and Nicholas Teele. Ed. Earl Miner. Princeton: Princeton University Press, 1984.

—————. *A History of Japanese Literature*, vol. 2: *The Early Middle Ages*. Trans. Aileen Gatten and Nicholas Teele. Ed. Earl Miner. Princeton: Princeton University Press, 1986.

Kōno Nankei. "Haiku to gembaku" [Haiku and the Atomic Bomb]. *Kokubungaku kaishaku to kanshō* 50, no. 9 (August 1985): 154–59.

Kōuchi Nobuko. "Hayashi Kyōko ron" [Essay on Hayashi Kyōko]. *Kokubungaku kaishaku to kanshō* 50, no. 9 (August 1985): 47–52.

Koyama Yūshi. *Fuyu no hana* [A Flower in Winter]. *Teatoro*, no. 323 (April 1970): 117–88.

—————. *Taisanboku no ki no shita* [Beneath the Magnolias]. *NGB*, 12:147–211.

Kren, George M., and Leon Rappoport. *The Holocaust and the Crisis of Human Behavior*. New York: Holmes and Meier Publishers, Inc., 1980.

Kumaki Tetsu. "Chi no mure" [Crowds of the Earth]. *Kokubungaku kaishaku to kanshō* 50, no. 9 (August 1985): 72–76.

Kundera, Milan. *The Book of Laughter and Forgetting*. Trans. Michael Henry Heim. New York: Alfred A. Knopf, 1980.

Kunioka Akikazu. "Gembaku ni ikite" ["Surviving the Atomic Bomb"]. *Kokubungaku kaishaku to kanshō* 50, no. 9, (August 1985): 128–32.

Kurihara Sadako. *Dokyumento Hiroshima nijūyonen: Gendai no kyūsai* [Document Hiroshima Twenty-four Years: Salvation in Modern Times]. Tokyo: Shimpō Shinsho, 1970.

—————. "Gembaku bungaku ronsō shi (shō)—Ōta Yōko o jiku ni" [History of the Atomic-bomb Literature Debates (Selections)—Ōta Yōko]. *NGB*, 15:269–300.

—————. "Hachi—roku no imi suru mono" [What August Sixth Means]. In Oguro Kaoru, ed., *Hiroshima no imi*, 67–84.

—————. "Hiroshima no bungaku ni megutte—Aushubittsu to Hiroshima" [On Hiroshima Literature: Auschwitz and Hiroshima]. *NGB*, 15. 258–62.

—————. *Hiroshima no genfūkei o idaite* [Holding On to How Hiroshima Looked]. Tokyo: Mirai Sha, 1975.

—————. *Hiroshima o iu toki* [When One Talks of Hiroshima]. Tokyo: San'ichi Shobō, 1976.

—————. "Kaisetsu (1)—Shūmatsu e no yokaku to kokuhatsu" [Critical Afterword I: A Premonition and Warning of the End of the World]. *NGB*, 13:511–15.

—————. *Kaku—tennō—hibakusha* [Nuclear—Emperor—Bomb Victim]. Tokyo: San'ichi Shobō, 1978.

—————. *Kaku-jidai ni ikiru: Hiroshima—shi no naka no sei* [Living in the Nuclear Age: Hiroshima—Life in Death]. Tokyo: San'ichi Shobō, 1982.

—————. *Kuroi tamago* [Black Eggs]. Hiroshima: Chūgoku Bunka Hakkōjō, 1946.

—————. "Let Us Be Midwives!" "Four Poems (1941–45) by the Hiroshima Poet Kurihara Sadako." Trans. and introduced by Richard H. Minear. *Bulletin of Concerned Asian Scholars* 21, no. 1 (January-March 1989):47. "Umashimen ka na." *NGB*, 13:116.

————. *Towareru Hiroshima* [Hiroshima Interrogated]. Tokyo: San'ichi Shobō, 1992.

Kurita Tōhei. "Seidōshoku no yami" [A Bronze-colored Dark]. *NGB*, 11:276–309.

Kuroko Kazuo. "Han-hankaku no shisōteki kōsō" [The Ideological Concept of Anti-antinuclearism]. *Bungakuteki tachiba* 7 (Autumn 1982):92–100.

————. *Gembaku bungaku ron: Kaku-jidai to sōzōryoku* [Atomic-bomb Literature: The Nuclear Age and the Power of Imagination]. Tokyo: Sairyūsha, 1993.

————. "Gembaku bungaku shi nempyō" [Atomic-bomb Literary History Chronology]. *NGB*, 14:543–68.

————. "Gembaku bungaku o nokoshita hitobito" [Those Who Have Left Us Atomic-bomb Literature]. In Horupu Shuppan henshūbu, ed., *Hankaku: Bungakusha wa uttaeru*, 249–93.

————. *Gembaku to kotoba: Hara Tamiki kara Hayashi Kyōko made* [The Atomic-bomb and Language: From Hara Tamiki to Hayashi Kyōko]. Tokyo: San'ichi Shobō, 1983.

————. "'Shūmatsu' e no chōsen" [Defying the "End"]. *NGB*, 15:449–71.

Kuwahara Takeo. "Dainin geijutsu." In *Gendai Nihon bungaku taikei* [Contemporary Japanese Literature], vol 74: *Nakajima Kenzō Kawamori Yoshizō Nakano Yoshio Kuwahara Takeo shū*, 327–33. Tokyo: Chikuma Shobō, 1973. "A Second Class Art." Trans. Kano Tsutomu and Patricia Murray. In Kato Hidetoshi, ed., *Japan and Western Civilization: Essays in Comparative Culture*, 187–202. Tokyo: University of Tokyo Press, 1983.

Lammers, Wayne P., and Osamu Masuoka. *Japanese A-Bomb Literature: An Annotated Bibliography*. Wilmington: Translation Collective, Wilmington College Peace Resource Center, 1977.

Lang, Berel. *Act and Idea in the Nazi Genocide*. Chicago: University of Chicago Press, 1990.

————. "Genocide and Omnicide: Technology at the Limits." In Avner Cohen and Steven Lee, eds., *Nuclear Weapons and the Future of Humanity*, 115–30. Totowa, N.J.: Rowman and Allanheld, 1986.

————, ed. *Writing and the Holocaust*. New York and London: Holmes and Meier, 1988.

Langer, Lawrence. *The Age of Atrocity: Death in Modern Literature*. Boston: Beacon Press, 1978.

————. *The Holocaust and the Literary Imagination*. New Haven: Yale University Press, 1975.

Lapp, Ralph E. *The Voyage of the Lucky Dragon*. New York: Harper Brothers Publishers, 1957.

Levi, Primo. *The Drowned and the Saved*. Trans. Raymond Rosenthal. New York: Vintage International, 1989.

————. *Survival in Auschwitz: The Nazi Assault on Humanity*. Trans. Stuart Woolf. New York: Collier Books, 1986.

Lewis, C. Day. *The Poetic Image*. London: Jonathan Cape, 1947.

Lifton, Robert Jay. *The Broken Connection: On Death and the Continuity of Life*. New York: Simon and Schuster, 1979.

————. *Death in Life: The Survivors of Hiroshima*. New York: Simon and Schuster, 1967.

————. *History and Human Survival.* New York: Random House, 1961.

————. *The Life of the Self: Toward a New Psychology.* New York: Simon and Schuster, 1976.

Luckhurst, Roger. "Nuclear Criticism: Anachronism and Anachorism." *Diacritics* 23, no. 2 (Summer 1993): 89–97.

Lukács, Georg. *The Meaning of Contemporary Realism.* Trans. John and Necke Mander. London: Merlin Press, 1963.

Lyotard, Jean-François. *Immaterialität und Postmoderne.* Trans. Marianne Karbe. Berlin: Merve Verlag, 1985.

MacDonald, Dwight. *Memoirs of a Revolutionist: Essays in Political Criticism.* New York: Farrar, Straus, and Co., 1957.

Macherey, Pierre. *A Theory of Literary Production.* Trans. Geoffrey Wall. London: Routledge & Kegan Paul, 1978.

Madsen, Axel. *Hearts and Minds: The Common Journey of Simone de Beauvoir and Jean-Paul Sartre.* New York: Morrow Quill Paperbacks, 1977.

Maeda Masahiro. "Ani mo michigaeta kao" [A Face Even Brother Did Not Recognize]. *GTK*, 67–70.

Mainichi Shimbun Sha, ed. *Gembaku 25-nen* [Twenty-Five Years of the Atomic-bomb]. Hiroshima: Mainichi Shimbun Hiroshima Shikyoku, 1970.

Mandelbaum, Michael. *The Nuclear Revolution: International Politics before and after Hiroshima.* Cambridge: Cambridge University Press, 1981.

Mandelstam, Nadezhda. *Hope Against Hope.* Trans. Max Hayward. New York: Atheneum, 1970.

Maruya Saiichi. "Shinsensa ni kemmei" [Fresh and Impressive]. Publisher's leaflet. Iida Momo, *Amerika no eiyū,* 2–3.

Marx, Karl. *A Contribution to the Critique of Political Economy.* Trans. N. I. Stone. Chicago: Charles H. Kerr & Company, 1904.

Masuoka Toshikazu. *Gembaku shijin monogatari* [Tales of the Atomic-bomb Poets]. Osaka: Nihon Kikanshi Shuppan Sentā, 1987.

————. *Gembaku shijin Tōge Sankichi.* Tokyo: Shin Nihon Shuppan, 1985.

————. *Hachigatsu no shijin: Gembaku shijin Tōge Sankichi no shi to shōgai* [The Poet of August: The Work and Life of Atomic-bomb Poet Tōge Sankichi]. Tokyo: Tōhō Shuppansha, 1978.

————. *Hiroshima no shijin-tachi* [Poets of Hiroshima]. Tokyo: Shin Nihon Shuppansha, 1980.

Matsumoto Hiroshi. "Fumō de nai bungaku no tame ni: Kurihara Sadako-shi e no hanron" [For a Literature Which Will Not Be Barren: A Response to Kurihara Sadako]. *NGB*, 15:263–64.

————. "Genten to shite no Hiroshima" [Hiroshima as a Genesis]. *NGB*, 15:396–406.

————. "Hachi—roku, Hiroshima no imi suru mono" [August Sixth, What Hiroshima Means]. In Oguro Kaoru, ed., *Hiroshima no imi,* 133–56.

Matsumoto Ken'ichi, ed. *Ronsō no dōjidai shi* [A Contemporary History of Literary Debates]. Tokyo: Shinsen Sha, 1986.

Matsumoto Tsuruo. *Ibuse Masuji ron* [A Study of Ibuse Masuji]. Tokyo: Tōjūsha, 1978.

Matsuura Sōzo. "Senryōgun no genron dan'atsu: gembaku hōdō wa hitoku sareta" [The Supression of Speech by the Occupation: Atomic-bomb Reporting Was Concealed]. *Shisō no kagaku*, no. 22 (January 1964): 55–73.

Mayuzumi Tetsurō. "Gekisezu utawazu sambun seishin" [Prose that Neither Agitates Nor Flatters]. *Asahi shimbun*, July 11, 1993.

Merton, Thomas. *Original Child Bomb: Points for Meditation to Be Scratched on the Walls of a Cave*. New York: New Directions, 1962.

Miller, Brown. *Hiroshima Flows Through Us*. Cherry Valley: Cherry Valley Editions, 1977.

Milosz, Czeslaw. *The Captive Mind*. Trans. Jane Zielonko. New York: Vintage Books, 1981.

Minear, Richard H., trans. and ed. *Hiroshima: Three Witnesses*. Princeton: Princeton University Press, 1990.

Miyamoto Ken. *Za pairotto* [The Pilot]. Tokyo: Shōbun Sha, 1970.

Miyoshi, Masao. *Accomplices of Silence: The Modern Japanese Novel*. Berkeley: University of California Press, 1974.

Miyoshi Tatsuji. "Kennin-jikyū" [Untiring Perseverence]. *NGB*, 15:121–24.

Mizuta Kuwajirō. *Gembaku o yomu* [Reading the Atomic Bomb]. Tokyo: Kōdansha, 1982.

———. *Me o akeba shura: Gembaku kajin Shōda Shinoe no shōgai* [Hell Before One's Eyes: The Life of Atomic-bomb Poet Shōda Shinoe]. Tokyo: Mirai Sha, 1983.

Mumford, Lewis. *Technics and Civilization*. New York: Harcourt, Brace and Company, 1934.

Mutsu Katsutoshi. "Kaeranu tamashii" [A Soul Never to Come Home]. *GTK*, 104–16.

Nagai Takashi. *The Bells of Nagasaki*. Trans. William Johnston. Tokyo: Kodansha International, 1984. *Nagasaki no kane*. Tokyo: Hibiya Shuppan, 1949.

Nagaoka Hiroyoshi. "Gembaku bungaku no keifu" [The Genealogy of Atomic-bomb Literature]. In Horupu Shuppan henshūbu, ed., *Hankaku: Bungakusha wa uttaeru*, 219–48.

———. "Gembaku bungaku sakuhin mokuroku" [Atomic-bomb Literature Bibliography]. *Kokubungaku kaishaku to kanshō* 50, no. 9 (August 1985): 177–83.

———. *Gembaku bungaku shi* [History of Atomic-bomb Literature]. Nagoya: Fūbai Sha,1973.

———. "Gembaku bungaku to sengo nashonarizumu" [Atomic-bomb Literature and Postwar Nationalism]. *NGB*, 15:376–95.

———. *Gembaku bunken o yomu* [Reading Atomic-bomb Literature]. Tokyo: San'ichi Shobō, 1982.

———. *Gembaku minshūshi* [A People's History of the Atomic Bombings]. Tokyo: Mirai Sha, 1977.

————. "Kaisetsu" [Critical Afterword]. *OYS*, 2:345–55.

Nagata Hiroshi. "Kaisetsu" [Critical Afterword]. *HTZ*, 1:545–59.

Nakagami Kenji. "Karasu" [Crows]. *Gunzō*, 37, no. 3 (March 1982): 82–92.

Nakagami Kenji, et al. "Warera no bungaku tachiba—sedai ron o koete" [Our View of Literature: Transcending the Idea of a Generation Gap]. *Bungakkai* 32, no. 10 (October 1978): 98–117.

Nakagawa Kunio. "Kanōsei no gembaku bungaku o" [Towards an Atomic-bomb Literature of Possibility]. *NGB*, 15.267–68.

Nakahodo Masanori. *Hara Tamiki nōto* [Hara Tamiki Notes]. Tokyo: Keisō Shobō, 1983.

Nakajima Kenzō. "'Gembaku bungaku' no imi" [The Meaning of "Atomic-bomb Literature"]. *NGB*, 15:364–75.

Nakamura Akira. *Sakka no buntai* [Writers' Language]. Tokyo: Chikuma Shobō, 1977.

Nakamura Atsushi. "Hiroshima." In Hotta Yoshie et al., eds., *Nihon gembaku shishū*, 33–35.

Nakano Kōji. "'Bungakusha no seimei' ni tsuite" [On 'The Writers' Appeal"]. *Bungei* 21, no. 3 (March 1982): 196–99.

————. "Hankaku ni gōryū shita bungakusha no nikusei" [The Voices of Writers Come Together to Oppose Nuclear Weapons]. *Asahi jānaru* 24, no. 5 (February 5, 1982): 8–11.

————. "Tamashii no kiroku" [Records of Souls]. In Horupu Shuppan henshūbu, ed., *Hankaku: Bungakusha wa uttaeru*, 147–65.

Nakano Kōji and Nagaoka Hiroyoshi. "Gembaku bungaku o megutte" [On Atomic-bomb Literature]. *Kokubungaku kaishaku to kanshō* 50, no. 9 (August 1985): 10–23.

Nakano Shigeharu. "*Gembaku shishū* ni tsuite" [On *Atomic-bomb Poetry*]. *NGB*, 15:130–33.

Nakayama Kazuko. "Sakka annai" [Note on the Author]. In Hayashi Kyōko, *Naki ga gotoki*, 234–44.

Nakayama Shigeru. "Sekai no gembaku bungaku" [Atomic-bomb Literature in the World]. *Shisō no kagaku*, no. 90 (August 1969): 14–25.

Nakayama Shirō. "Shi no kage" [Shadows of Death]. *NGB*, 11:9–48.

Nakazato Yoshiaki. "Hyōgen katsudō ni miru Nagasaki no hibaku ishiki" [Nagasaki's Attitude Towards the Bombing as Seen in Its Literature]. *NGB*, 15:354–63.

Nakazawa Keiji. *Hadashi no Gen*. 4 vols. Tokyo: Sekibunsha, 1975. *Barefoot Gen*. Trans. Project Gen and Dadakai. 2 vols. Tokyo: Project Gen, 1978–79.

————. *Kuroi ame ni utarete* [Pelted with the Black Rain]. Tokyo: Sekibunsha, 1968.

Napier, Susan J. *Escape from the Wasteland: Romanticism and Realism in the Fiction of Mishima Yukio and Ōe Kenzaburo*. Cambridge: Council of East Asian Studies, 1991.

Nathan, John. "Introduction." In Ōe Kenzaburō, *Teach Us to Outgrow Our Madness: Four Short Novels by Kenzaburo Ōe*, ix–xxv. Trans. with an introduction by John Nathan. New York: Grove Press, 1977.

Natsubori Masamoto. "Seichi no onna" [The Woman from the Hallowed Ground]. *NGB*, 11:310–29.

Nietzsche, Friedrich. "The Birth of Tragedy." In *The Birth of Tragedy and The Genealogy of Morals*, 1–146. Trans. Francis Golffing. New York: Doubleday Anchor Press, 1956.

———. *The Will to Power*. Trans. Walter Kaufmann. New York: Vintage Books, 1968.

Nihon rekishi daijiten henshū iinkai, ed. *Nihon rekishi daijiten* [Dictionary of Japanese History]. 20 vols. Tokyo: Kawade Shobō, 1968.

Nishida Masaru, et al. "Futatabi kaku-sensō no kiki ni bungakusha wa dono yō ni tai suru ka" [How Are Writers to Face the Crisis of Nuclear War, Revisited]. *Bungakuteki tachiba* 7 (Autumn 1982): 2–48.

Nishihara Kei. "Shōdo" [Scorched Earth]. *NGB*, 11:69–107.

Noma Hiroshi. "Gembaku ni tsuite" [On the Atomic Bomb]. *NGB*, 15:145–48.

———. *Seinen no wa* [Cycle of Youth]. *Noma Hiroshi zenshū*, vols. 7–11. Tokyo: Chikuma Shobō, 1974.

———. *Zentai shōsetsu e no shikō* [Towards a Total Literature]. Tokyo: Tabata Shoten, 1969.

Norman, E. H. *Origins of the Modern Japanese State: Selected Writings of E. H. Norman*. Ed. with an introduction by John W. Dower. New York: Pantheon, 1975.

Norris, Christopher. *Deconstruction: Theory and Practice*. London: Methuen, 1982.

O'Brien, Tim. *The Nuclear Age*. New York: Alfred A. Knopf, 1985.

Ochi Michio. "Izō sareta seikatsu" [The Life Left Us]. *NGB*, 11:183–230.

Oda, Katsuzō. "Human Ashes." Trans. Burton Watson. In Ōe Kenzaburō, ed., *The Crazy Iris and Other Stories of the Atomic Aftermath*, 63–84. "Ningen no hai." *Yūsei* 18, no. 10 (October 1966): 60–69.

Oda Makoto. *Amerika* [America]. Tokyo: Kawade Shobō Shinsha, 1962.

———. *Asatte no shuki* [Notes on the Day After Tomorrow]. Tokyo: Kawade Shobō, 1951.

———. "Atarashii 'zentai shōsetsu' e no michi" [The Path to a New "Total Literature"]. In *Sengo o hiraku shisō* [Ideology That Inaugurated the Postwar], 129–38. Tokyo: Kōdansha, 1965.

———. "The Ethics of Peace." In J. Victor Koschmann, ed., *Authority and the Individual in Japan: Citizen Protest in Historical Perspective*, 154–70. Tokyo: University of Tokyo Press, 1978.

———. "Gendai bungaku wa kore de ii no ka" [Does This Suffice for Contemporary Literature?]. *Bungakuteki tachiba* 7 (Autumn 1982): 127–37.

———. "Hankaku—hansen o tsuranuku shutaisei" [The Subjectivity of the Anti-Nuclear and Antiwar Movements]. In Horupu Shuppan henshūbu, ed., *Hankaku: Bungakusha wa uttaeru*, 7–32.

———. *Hiroshima*. Tokyo: Kōdansha, 1981. *The Bomb*. Trans. D. H. Whittaker. Tokyo: Kodansha International, 1990.

———. "Katarikuchi no migotosa" [Skillful Recitation]. Publisher's leaflet. Iida Mono, *Amerika no eiyū*, 3–5.

————. "'Kochira-gawa' o dō kaku—Oda Makoto-shi ni kiku" [How Does One Write of the Close at Hand?: An Interview with Oda Makoto]. With Kuroko Kazuo. In Bungaku Jihyō Sha, ed., Igi ari! Gendai bungaku, 119–34.

————. "Kono kan no tame no kiwamete mijikai chūshaku" [Very Brief Notes for This Volume]. In Oda Makoto zenshigoto, 2:395–96. Tokyo: Kawade Shobō Shinsha, 1970.

————. Nan de mo mite yarō [I'll Give Anything A Look]. Tokyo: Kawade Shobō Shinsha, 1961.

————. "Sore kara, no koto" [To Say "And Then"]. In Shōsetsu sekai o aruku, 186–201. Tokyo: Kawade Shobō Shinsha, 1980.

————. "Yakusha atogaki" [Translator's Afterword]. In Seymour Hersh, Son Mi, 240–46.

Odagiri Hideo. "Genshiryoku mondai to bungaku" [Literature and the Issue of Nuclear Power]. NGB, 15:180–97.

Ōe Kenzaburō. "Bungaku to wa nani ka?" [What is Literature?]. In Kaku-jidai no sōzōryoku, 56–60.

————, ed. The Crazy Iris and Other Stories of the Atomic Aftermath. New York: Grove Press, Inc., 1985. Nan to mo shirenai mirai ni. Tokyo: Shūei Sha, 1984.

————. "Gembakugo no Nihonjin no jiko-kakunin" [The Self-Affirmation of Post-Atomic-bomb Japanese]. In Hiroshima no hikari: Ōe Kenzaburō dōjidai ronshū, 2:204–12.

————. "Hara Tamiki o kinen suru (kōen)" [In Memory of Hara Tamiki (A Lecture)]. In Hiroshima no hikari: Ōe Kenzaburō dōjidai ronshū, 2:175–81.

————. "Hara Tamiki to wakai hitobito to no hashi no tame ni" [For a Bridge Between Hara Tamiki and Young People]. In Hiroshima no hikari: Ōe Kenzaburō dōjidai ronshū, 2:181–86.

————. "Hibakusha no jiko-kyūsai undō" [The Hibakusha Self-Help Movement]. In Hiroshima no hikari: Ōe Kenzaburō dōjidai ronshū, 2:164–75.

————. "Hiroshima, Amerika, Yōroppa" [Hiroshima, America, Europe]. In Kaku-jidai no sōzōryoku, 179–205.

————. Hiroshima no hikari: Ōe Kenzaburō dōjidai ronshū, vol. 2 [The Light of Hiroshima: Ōe Kenzaburō Contemporary Essays, vol. 2]. Tokyo: Iwanami Shoten, 1980.

————. Hiroshima no "Inochi no ki" [The Hiroshima "Tree of Life"]. Tokyo: Nihon Hōsō Shuppan Kyōkai, 1991.

————. Hiroshima nōto. In Hiroshima no hikari: Ōe Kenzaburō dōjidai ronshū, 2:7–162. Hiroshima Notes. Trans. Toshi Yonezawa and David L. Swain. Tokyo: YMCA Press, 1981.

————. "Ikinobiru kibō to shite no bungaku" [Literature as the Hope of Survival]. In Horupu Shuppan henshūbu, ed., Hankaku: Bungakusha wa uttaeru, 19–78.

————. "Introduction: Toward the Unknowable Future." In The Crazy Iris and Other Stories of the Atomic Aftermath, 9–16.

————. "Japanese Intellectuals at Bay." Japan Times, November 24, 1986.

————. "Kaisetsu" [Critical Afterword]. NGB, 9:382–91.

————. "Kaku-jidai e no sōzōryoku" [Imagination for a Nuclear Age]. In Kaku-jidai no sōzōryoku, 98–121.

————. "Kaku-jidai no Erasumusu" [Erasmus in the Nuclear Age]. In *Hiroshima no hikari: Ōe Kenzaburō dōjidai ronshū*, 2:270–75.

————. *Kaku-jidai no sōzōryoku* [Imagination in the Nuclear Age]. Tokyo: Shinchō Sha, 1970.

————. "Kaku-kichi ni ikiru Nihonjin—Okinawa no kaku-kichi to hibakusha-tachi" [Japanese on Nuclear Military Bases: Okinawan Nuclear Military Bases and Hibakusha]. In *Hiroshima no hikari: Ōe Kenzaburō dōjidai ronshū*, 2:214–25.

————. "Kuroi ame to Nihon bundan" [*Black Rain* and Japan's Literary Establishment]. In *Gendai Nihon bungakkan* [Library of Contemporary Japanese Literature], vol. 29, *fuzoku* [Addendum], 6–7. Tokyo: Bungei Shunjū, 1967.

————. "Mirai e mukete kaisō suru—jiko-kaishaku (ni)" [Reflection on the Past While Facing the Future: A Self-Interpretation (2)]. In *Hiroshima no hikari: Ōe Kenzaburō dōjidai ronshū*, 2:277–93.

————. "Nani o kioku shi, kioku shitsuzukeru beki ka" [What Should We Remember, What Should We Continue to Remember?]. *GTK*, 247–57.

————. *A Personal Matter*. Trans. John Nathan. New York: Grove Press, 1969. *Kojinteki na taiken*. Tokyo: Shinchō Sha, 1969.

————. "Postwar Japanese Literature and the Contemporary Impasse." *The Japan Foundation Newsletter* 14, no. 3 (October 1986): 1–6.

Oguro Kaoru, ed. *Hiroshima no imi* [The Meaning of Hiroshima]. Tokyo: Nihon Hyōron Sha. 1973.

————. "Hiroshima no sei to shi" [Life and Death in Hiroshima]. In *Hiroshima no imi*, 193–215.

Ōhara Miyao. "Hiroshima—Nagasaki to gembaku shi no shihan seiki" [Hiroshima, Nagasaki, and a Quarter-Century of Atomic-bomb Poetry]. In Hotta Yoshie et al., eds., *Nihon gembaku shishū*, 259–67.

Ōhashi Kiichi. "Gembaku to watakushi ni totte no gekisaku" [The Atomic-bomb and My View of the Dramatic Text]. In Horupu Shuppan henshūbu, ed., *Hankaku: Bungakusha wa uttaeru*, 267–93.

————. *Zero no kiroku* [A Record of Zero]. *Teatoro*, no. 228 (May 1968): 102–72.

Okada Yasuo. "Gembaku-imi" [Remembering the Day of the Atomic Bomb's Dead]. In Kōno Nankei, "Haiku to gembaku," 154.

Okuno Takeo. *Nihon bungaku shi* [History of Japanese Literature]. Tokyo: Chūō Kōron Sha, 1970.

Ōoka Makoto. "Modern Japanese Poetry: Realities and Challenges." In Makoto Ōoka and Thomas Fitzsimmons, eds., *A Play of Mirrors: Eight Major Poets of Modern Japan*, 15–22. Rochester: Katydid Books, 1987.

————. *Nihongo no sekai* [The World of Japanese], vol. 2: *Shi no Nihongo* [The Japanese Language in Poetry]. Tokyo: Chūō Kōron Sha, 1980.

Ortega y Gasset, José. "The Dehumanization of Art." In *The Dehumanization of Art and Notes on the Novel*, 3–54.

————. *The Dehumanization of Art and Notes on the Novel.* Trans. Helene Weyl. New York: Peter Smith, 1951.

————. "Notes on the Novel." In *The Dehumanization of Art and Notes on the Novel,* 57–103.

Ōsato Kyōzaburō. "'Matsuri no ba'" [On "The Site of Rituals"]. *Kokubungaku kaishaku to kanshō* 50, no. 9 (August 1985): 98–102.

Ōta Yōko. "Bungaku no osoroshisa" [The Terror of Literature]. *OYS,* 2:321–23.

————. *Hachijūyonsai* [Eighty-Four Years Old]. Tokyo: Kōdansha, 1961.

————. "Han-hōrō" [Half-Vagrant]. *OYS,* 3:295–314.

————. *Han-ningen* [Half-Human]. *OYS,* 1:261–334.

————. "Hara Tamiki no shi ni tsuite" [The Death of Hara Tamiki] *HTZ,* 1:600–601

————. "Hotaru." *NGB,* 2:175–95. "Fireflies." Trans. Kōichi Nakagawa. In Ōe Kenzaburō, ed., *The Crazy Iris and Other Stories of the Atomic Aftermath,* 85–111.

————. "Ikinokori no shinri" [The Psychology of Survival]. *OYS,* 2:314–20.

————. "Kaitei no yō na hikari—genshi bakudan no kūshū ni atte" [A Light As If From the Depths: The Atomic-bomb Air Attack]. *NGB,* 15:14–17.

————. *Ningen ranru* [Human Rags]. *OYS,* 2:5–273.

————. *Ryūri no kishi* [Drifting Shores]. *OYS,* 4. 5–255.

————. "Sakka no taido" [The Stance of the Writer]. *NGB,* 15:242–45.

————. "Sanjō" [In the Hills]. *OYS,* 1:183–218.

————. *Shikabane no machi. OYS,* 1:6–156. *City of Corpses.* In Richard H. Minear, trans. and ed., *Hiroshima: Three Witnesses,* 115–273.

————. "Shikabane no machi jo" [Preface to City of Corpses]. *OYS,* 2:300–305.

————. "Yo ni mayou" [Astray in the World]. *OYS,* 3:353–401.

————. *Yūnagi no machi to hito to* [People and the City of Evening Calm]. *OYS,* 3:5–294.

Ozaki Kazuo. "Kaku-heiki: shirōto no shimpai" [Nuclear Arms: A Layman's Concerns]. *NGB,* 15:421–23.

Ozaki Shirō. "Romanteki seishin no ikitsuku tokoro" [Where the Romantic Spirit Takes Us]. *NGB,* 15:141–44.

Ozick, Cynthia. "Innovation and Redemption: What Literature Means." In *Art and Ardor,* 239–48. New York: Alfred A. Knopf, 1983.

Ozu Kunsō. "Genten kara" [From Ground Zero]. *Hiroshima,* no. 8 (September 1982): 39–47.

Pitre, Leslie Todd. "Of Patience, Faith, and Beloved Enemies." *Friends Journal* 29, no. 13 (September 1/15, 1983): 5–6.

Poe, Edgar Allan. "The Fall of the House of Usher," 231–45. In *The Complete Tales and Poems of Edgar Allan Poe.* New York: Modern Library, 1938.

Poirier, Richard. "Writing Off the Self." In Saul Friedlander et al., eds., *Visions of Apocalypse,* 216–41.

Popper, Karl R. *Quantum Theory and the Schism in Physics.* Totowa, N.J.: Rowman and Littlefield, 1982.

Powell, Irene. *Writers and Society in Modern Japan.* Tokyo: Kodansha International, 1983.

"Proposal for a Diacritics Colloquium on Nuclear Criticism." *Diacritics* 14, no. 2 (Summer 1984): 2–3.

Publishing Committee for "Children of Hiroshima," ed. *Children of Hiroshima.* Tokyo: Publishing Committee for "Children of Hiroshima," 1980.

Rimer, Thomas J. "Nationalism in the Literature of Japan." In Michael Craig Hillmann, ed. *Essays on Nationalism and Asian Literatures,* 5–17. Austin: Department of Oriental and African Languages, University of Texas, 1987.

Rosenfeld, Alvin H. *A Double Dying: Reflections on Holocaust Literature.* Bloomington: Indiana University Press, 1980.

Rousset, David. *The Other Kingdom.* Trans. with an introduction by Ramon Gunthrie. New York: Reynal and Hitchcock, 1947.

Rubenstein, Richard L. *The Cunning of History: The Holocaust and the American Future.* New York: Harper and Row, 1978.

Rubin, Jay. "From Wholesomeness to Decadence: The Censorship of Literature under the Allied Occupation." *Journal of Japanese Studies* 11, no. 1 (Winter 1985): 71–103.

———. *Injurious to Public Morals: Writers and the Meiji State.* Seattle: University of Washington Press, 1984.

Saeki Shōichi. "Shōsetsuka to kirokusha" [Novelists and Documentary Writers]. *Asahi shimbun,* Evening Edition, December 8, 1966.

Said, Edward W. *The World, the Text, and the Critic.* Cambridge: Harvard University Press, 1983.

Sakurai Mikiyoshi. "Sei to shi o mitsumete—Ibuse Masuji 'Kuroi ame' o megutte" [A Look at Life and Death: Ibuse Masuji's *Black Rain*]. *Minshū bungaku* (August 1971): 110–17.

Saotome Katsumoto. "Heiwa wa aruite kite kurenai" [Peace Does Not Saunter In]. In Horupu Shuppan henshūbu, ed., *Hankaku: Bungakusha wa uttaeru,* 295–338.

Sartre, Jean-Paul. *The Age of Reason.* Trans. Eric Sutton. New York: Alfred A. Knopf, 1952.

———. *Anti-Semite and Jew.* Trans. George J. Becker. New York: Schocken Books, 1948.

———. "The Artist and His Conscience." In *Situations,* 142–55. Trans. Benita Eisler. Greenwich: Fawcett Crest, 1966.

———. *Being and Nothingness.* Trans. Hazel E. Barnes. New York: Pocket Books, 1966.

———. *Dirty Hands.* In *No Exit, and Three Other Plays by Jean-Paul Sartre,* 129–248. Trans. Lionel Abel. New York: Vintage Books, 1949.

———. *Existentialism and Humanism.* Trans. Bernard Frechtman. New York: Philosophical Library, 1947.

———. "François Mauriac and Freedom." In *Literary Essays,* 7–23. Trans. Annette Michelson. New York: Philosophical Library, 1957.

———. *Saint Genet.* Trans. Bernard Frechtman. New York: Mentor Books, 1963.

———. "Situation of the Writer in 1947." In *What is Literature?* 161–297.

———. *Troubled Sleep.* Trans. Gerald Hopkins. New York: Alfred A. Knopf, 1950.

————. "The Wall." In *The Wall and Other Stories*, 7–37. Trans. Lloyd Alexander. New York: New Directions, 1948.

————. *What is Literature?* Trans. Bernard Frechtman. New York: Philosophical Library, 1949.

Sata Ineko. "The Colorless Paintings." Trans. Shiloh Ann Shimura. In Ōe Kenzaburō, ed., *The Crazy Iris and Other Stories of the Atomic Aftermath*, 113–25. "Iro no nai e." *NGB*, 4:37–46.

————. *Juei* [The Shade of Trees]. *NGB*, 4:47–253.

————. "Kaisetsu" [Critical Afterword]. *OYS*, 1:335–46.

————. "Kyarameru kōba kara" [From the Caramel Factory]. In *Sata Ineko sakuhinshū*, 1:5–16. Tokyo: Chikuma Shobō, 1959.

————. "Rekihō" [A Series of Visits]. *NGB*, 4:9–23.

Satō Hachirō. "Yomu made to yomioete to" [Before and After Reading]. *NGB*, 15:125–29.

Satō Haruo. "*Hara Tamiki shishū jobun*" [Preface to *The Poetry of Hara Tamiki*]. *NGB*, 1:294–95.

Satō Makoto. *Nezumi Kozō: The Rat*. In David G. Goodman, ed. and trans., *After the Apocalypse: Four Japanese Plays of Hiroshima and Nagasaki*, 269–319. *Nezumi Kozō Jirokichi*. *Atashi no bītoruzu*, 127–93. Tokyo: Shōbun Sha, 1970.

Satō Tadao. *Nihon eiga shisō shi* [An Intellectual History of the Japanese Film]. Tokyo: San'ichi Shobō, 1970.

Sawada Akiko. "*Shikabane no machi*" [Ōta Yōko's *City of Corpses*]. *Kokubungaku kaishaku to kanshō* 50, no. 9 (August 1985): 60–65.

Sawamura Mitsuhiro. "Hiroshima—waga maboroshi" [Hiroshima, My Phantasm]. In Hotta Yoshie et al, eds., *Nihon gembaku shishū*, 70.

Schell, Jonathan. *The Fate of the Earth*. New York: Alfred A. Knopf, 1982.

Scully, James. *Line Break: Poetry as Social Practice*. Seattle: Bay Press, 1988.

Seidensticker, Edward. Review of Jay Rubin, *Injurious to Public Morals: Writers and the Meiji State*. *Journal of Japanese Studies*, 11, no. 1 (Winter 1985): 218–21.

Selden, Kyoko and Mark, eds. *The Atomic Bomb: Voices from Hiroshima and Nagasaki*. Armonk: M. E. Sharpe, Inc., 1989.

Sera, Megumi. Untitled memoir. Publishing Committee for "Children of Hiroshima," ed. *Children of Hiroshima*, 255–60.

Sherwin, Martin J. *A World Destroyed: The Atomic Bomb and the Grand Alliance*. New York: Alfred A. Knopf, 1975.

Shigeoka Tōru. "'Hiroshima'" [Oda Makoto's *Hiroshima*]. *Kokubungaku kaishaku to kanshō*, 50, no. 9 (August 1985): 107–12.

Shiina Rinzō. "Sensō ron" [On War]. *NGB*, 14:53.

Shijō Miyoko. "'Gembaku bungaku' ni tsuite" [On "Atomic-bomb literature"]. *NGB*, 15:248–50.

Shimauchi Hachirō. "Heiwa no chikai—haikyo ni tachite" [A Vow of Peace from the Ruins]. In Nagaoka Hiroyoshi, *Gembaku bungaku shi*, 88.

Shimazaki Tōson. *The Broken Commandment*. Trans. Kenneth Strong. Tokyo: University of Tokyo Press, 1974. *Hakai*. Tokyo: Shinchō Sha, 1922.

Shinohara Shigeru. *Ōe Kenzaburō ron* [An Essay on Ōe Kenzaburō]. Tokyo: Tōhō Shuppansha, 1974.

Shōda Shinoe. "Ā! Genshi bakudan" [Oh! The Atomic Bomb]. In Mizuta Kuwajirō, *Me o akeba shura: Gembaku kajin Shōda Shinoe no shōgai*, 52–56.

———. *Miminari: Gembaku kajin no shuki* [A Ringing in the Ears: The Notes of an Atomic-bomb Poet]. Tokyo: Heibonsha, 1962.

———. "Minna shineba ii n da" [Let Everyone Die]. In Hotta Yoshie et al., eds., *Nihon gembaku shishū*, 256–57.

———. *Sange* [Repentance]. In Mizuta Kuwajirō, *Me o akeba shura: Gembaku kajin Shōda Shinoe no shōgai*, 205–14.

Siebers, Tobin. *The Ethics of Criticism*. Ithaca: Cornell University Press, 1988.

Sklar, Marty, ed. *Nuke Rebuke: Writers and Artists Against Nuclear Energy and Weapons*. Iowa City: The Spirit That Moves Us Press, 1984.

Sō Sakon. "Sugurete osoroshii shōsetsu" [Exceptionally Fearsome Fiction]. Publisher's Leaflet. In Iida Momo, *Amerika no eiyū*, 1–2.

Solomon, J. Fisher. *Discourse and Reference in the Nuclear Age*. Norman: University of Oklahoma Press, 1988.

Sontag, Susan. "Against Interpretation." In *Against Interpretation and Other Essays*, 3–14. New York: Octagon Books, 1982.

Spivak, Gayatri Chakravorty. "Translator's Preface." In Jacques Derrida, *Of Grammatology*, ix–lxxxvii.

Steiner, George. "'Dying as an Art.'" In *Language and Silence: Essays on Language, Literature and the Inhuman*, 295–302.

———. *Language and Silence: Essays on Language, Literature and the Inhuman*. New York: Atheneum, 1972.

———. "The Long Life of Metaphor: An Approach to the 'Shoah'." In Berel Lang, ed., *Writing and the Holocaust*, 154–71.

———. "K." In *Language and Silence: Essays on Language, Literature and the Inhuman*, 118–26.

Stephanson, Anders. "Regarding Postmodernism—A Conversation with Fredric Jameson." In Andrew Ross (for the Social Text Collective), ed., *Universal Abandon? The Politics of Postmodernism*, 3–30. Minneapolis: University of Minnesota Press, 1988.

Stevens, Wallace. *Opus Posthumous*. New York: Alfred A. Knopf, 1957.

Suga Hidemi. "'Kaku-sensō no kiken o uttaeru bungakusha no seimei' o yomu" [Reading "The Writers' Appeals Against the Dangers of Nuclear War"]. *Nihon dokusho shimbun*, no. 2143 (February 8, 1982): 2.

Sugimoto Naojirō. "Gembaku ni atta hi" [The Day of the Atomic Bomb]. *GTK*, 71–82.

Schwenger, Peter. *Letter Bomb: Nuclear Holocaust and the Exploding Word.* Baltimore: Johns Hopkins University Press, 1992.

———. "Writing the Unthinkable." *Critical Inquiry* 13 (1986): 33–48.

Taga Kōko. "Ā, Mutsuko!" [Ah, Mutsuko!]. In Masuoka Toshikazu, *Hiroshima no shijin-tachi*, 74–77.

Takahashi Hideo. "Ibuse Masuji-shi sono hito to shigoto" [Ibuse Masuji, The Man and His Work]. *Tōkyō shimbun*, Evening Edition, July 12, 1993.

Takahashi Kazumi. *Yuutsu naru toha* [The Melancholy Faction]. Tokyo: Kawade Shobō Shinsha, 1978.

Takahashi Shinji. *Hiroshima no rinri* [The Ethics of Hiroshima]. Tokyo: Hōbō Sha, 1976.

Takeda Taijun. *Daiichi no botan* [Button Number One]. In *Takeda Taijun zenshū*, 3:294–367. Tokyo: Chikuma Shobō, 1971.

Takekoshi Yoshio. "Shi to gembaku" [Poetry and Atomic-bomb Literature]. *Kokubungaku kaishaku to kanshō* 50, no. 9 (August 1985): 143–47.

Takenishi Hiroko. "Hiroshima ga iwaseru kotoba" [Words that Hiroshima Makes Us Speak]. *NGB*, 1:321–24.

———. "The Rite." Trans. Eileen Kato. In Ōe Kenzaburō, ed., *The Crazy Iris and Other Stories of the Atomic Aftermath*, 169–200. "Gishiki." *NGB*, 4:257–77.

Tanabe Kōichirō. "Gembaku no bungaku" [Atomic-bomb Literature]. *NGB*, 15:167–79.

Tanaka Chikao. *The Head of Mary.* In David G. Goodman, trans. and ed., *After Apocalypse: Four Japanese Plays of Hiroshima and Nagasaki*, 115–81. *Maria no kubi.* *NGB*, 12:85–146.

Tanuma Hajime. *Gembaku hibakusha shomondai* [Problems of the Atomic-bomb Victims]. Rev. ed. Tokyo: Shin Nihon Shuppansha, 1985.

Tayama Katai. "The Quilt." Trans. Kenneth G. Henshall. In *The Quilt and Other Stories by Tayama Katai*, 35–96. Tokyo: University of Tokyo Press, 1981. *Futon.* In *Tayama Katai zenshū*, 1:521–607. Tokyo: Bunsendō Shoten, 1973.

———. "Rokotsu naru byōsha" [Straightforward Description]. In *Gendai Nihon bungaku taikei* [Contemporary Japanese Literature], vol. 11: *Kunikida Doppo Tayama Katai*, 391–93. Tokyo: Chikuma Shobō, 1974.

Terada Tōru. "Hara Tamiki." *HTZ*, 1:604–9.

Tōge Sankichi. "August 6, 1950." In Richard H. Minear, trans. and ed., *Hiroshima: Three Witnesses*, 347–49. "1950-nen no hachigatsu muika."In *Gembaku shishū*, 99–105.

———. "August 6." In Richard H. Minear, trans. and ed., *Hiroshima: Three Witnesses*, 306–7. "Hachigatsu muika." In *Gembaku shishū*, 9–12.

———. "Chichi o kaese" [Give Me Back My Father]. In *Gembaku shishū*, 7–8. "Prelude." In Richard H. Minear, trans. and ed., *Hiroshima: Three Witnesses*, 305.

———. "Dawn." In Richard H. Minear, trans. and ed., *Hiroshima: Three Witnesses*, 344–45. "Asa." In *Gembaku shishū*, 93–95.

———. "Ehon" [Picture Book]. In Masuoka Toshikazu, *Gembaku shijin Tōge Sankichi*, 59–60.

————. "Eyes." In Richard H. Minear, trans. and ed., *Hiroshima: Three Witnesses*, 317–18. "Me." In *Gembaku shishū*, 33–36.

————. *Gembaku shishū*. Tokyo: Aoki Shoten, 1981. "Poems of the Atomic Bomb." In Richard H. Minear, trans. and ed., *Hiroshima: Three Witnesses*, 301–69.

————. "Kizuato" [The Scar]. In Masuoka Toshikazu, *Hachigatsu no shijin: Gembaku shijin Tōge Sankichi no shi to shōgai*, 356–58.

————. "Kurisumasu no kaerimichi." In Masuoka Toshikazu, *Hachigatsu no shijin: Gembaku shijin Tōge Sankichi no shi to shōgai*, 88–89.

————. "The Shadow." In Richard H. Minear, trans. and ed., *Hiroshima: Three Witnesses*, 339–40. "Kage." In *Gembaku shishū*, 83–87.

————. "When Will That Day Come?" In Richard H. Minear, trans. and ed., *Hiroshima: Three Witnesses*, 358–65. "Sono hi wa itsu ka" In *Gembaku shishū*, 124–41.

————. "Yobikake" [The Appeal]. 1950 version. In Masuoka Toshikazu, *Gembaku shijin Tōge Sankichi*, 164.

Tōge Sankichi and Yamashiro Tomoe, eds. *Genshigumo no shita yori* [From Beneath the Atomic Cloud]. Tokyo: Aoki Shoten, 1974.

Toyoda Seishi. *Gembaku bunkenshi* [A Guide to Writings on the Atomic Bomb]. Tokyo: Ron Shobō, 1971.

Toyoshima Yoshio. "Bungaku ni okeru kōsōryoku" [The Conceptual Power of Literature]. *Bungei* 2, no. 7 (September/October 1945): 25–31.

————. "'Hiroshima' e no kanshin" [Concern for "Hiroshima"]. *NGB*, 15:57–60.

Treat, John Whittier. *Pools of Water, Pillars of Fire: The Literature of Ibuse Masuji*. Seattle: University of Washington Press, 1988.

Tsukuda, Jitsuo. *Aka to kuro no moshō* [Armbands of Red and Black]. *NGB*, 10:342–415.

Tsurumi, Shunsuke. *An Intellectual History of Wartime Japan 1931–1945*. Tokyo: Kodansha International, 1986.

Tsuruta, Kin'ya. "Akutagawa Ryūnosuke and I-Novelists." *Monumenta Nipponica* 25, no. 1 (Spring 1970): 13–27.

Tucker, Anthony, and John Gleisner. *Crucible of Despair: The Effects of Nuclear War*. London: The Menard Press, 1972.

Udō Toshio. "Hara Tamiki ron" [An Essay on Hara Tamiki]. *Kokubungaku kaishaku to kanshō* 50, no. 9 (August 1985): 32–36.

The United States Strategic Bombing Survey. *The Effects of Atomic Bombs on Hiroshima and Nagasaki*. Washington, D.C.: United States Government Printing Office, 1946.

Unno Jūza. "Genshi bakudan to jikyū bōei" [The Atomic Bomb and the Defense of the Planet]. *NGB*, 15:18–25.

Uranishi Kazuhiko. "Kaisetsu" [Critical Afterword]. *OYS*, 4:341–51.

Vonnegut, Kurt. *Slaughterhouse Five, or The Children's Crusade*. New York: Delacorte Press, 1969.

Warnock, Mary. *Existentialism*. London: Oxford University Press, 1970.

Weber, Ronald. *The Literature of Fact: Literary Nonfiction in American Writing*. Athens: Ohio University Press, 1980.

White, Hayden. "Historical Employments and the Problem of 'Truth'." Lecture. April 27, 1990. University of California, Los Angeles.

———. *Tropics of Discourse: Essays in Cultural Criticism*. Baltimore: Johns Hopkins University Press, 1978.

Wiesel, Elie. *The Accident*. Trans. Anne Borchardt. New York: Hill and Wang, 1962.

———. *The Gates of the Forest*. Trans. Frances Frenaye. New York: Holt, Rinehart and Winston, 1966.

———. *One Generation After*. Trans. Marion Wiesel. New York: Pocket Books, 1970.

Williams, Raymond. "Base and Superstructure in Marxist Cultural Theory." In *Problems in Materialism and Culture: Selected Essays*, 31–49. London: Verso, 1980.

Yaguchi Hisayo. Untitled testimony. Publishing Committee for "Children of Hiroshima," ed., *Children of Hiroshima*. 202–11.

Yamada Kan. "Kaisetsu (4)—Nagasaki no gembaku shika" [Critical Afterword (4): Atomic-bomb Poetry of Nagasaki]. *NGB*, 13. 524–27.

———. "Nagasaki no gembaku kiroku o megutte" [Records of the Nagasaki Bombing]. *NGB*, 15:222–37.

Yamada Kazuko. "Dōkoku" [Wailing]. In Mizuta Kuwajirō, *Gembaku o yomu*, 243–44.

Yamamoto Kenkichi. "Chi ni tsuita heijōjin" [An Ordinary Person with his Feet on the Ground]. *Asahi shimbun*, Evening Edition, October 24, 1966.

———. "Shijin no shi no imi suru mono—Hara Tamiki no shi ni tsuite" [What the Death of a Poet Means: On the Death of Hara Tamiki]. *HTZ*, 1:581–90.

Yamamoto Yasuo. "Maboroshi" [Phantasm]. *NGB*, 14:20–24.

Yamashiro Tomoe. "Jo" [Preface to *Surviving the Bomb*]. *NGB*, 14:110–20.

Yoneda Eisaku. *Kawa yo, towa ni utsukushiku* [River, Always Be Beautiful]. Hiroshima: Shin Bummei Sha, 1951.

Yoneda Toshiaki. "Gembaku to tanka" [The Atomic Bomb and Tanka]. *Kokubungaku kaishaku to kanshō*, 50, no. 9 (August 1985): 148–53.

Yoshida, Sanroku. "An Interview with Kenzaburō Ōe." *World Literature Today* 62, no. 3 (Summer 1988): 369–74.

Yoshimitsu Yoshio. "Gembaku bungaku taibō ron o utagau" [I Doubt We Can Expect an Atomic-bomb Literature]. *NGB*, 15:265–66.

Yoshimoto Takaaki. "Hankaku" iron [Against the "Anti-Nuclear"]. Tokyo: Shin'ya Sōsho Sha, 1982.

———. "Sekai ron" [A Theory of the World]. *Kaien*, 1, no. 6 (June 1982): 22–32.

———. "Shiki' ha no honshitsu—Miyoshi Tatsuji o chūshin ni" [The Essence of the

"Four Seasons" School: Miyoshi Tatsuji]. *Yoshimoto Takaaki zenchosakushū*, 5:119–35. Tokyo: Keiso Shobō, 1970.

Young, James E. *Writing and Rewriting the Holocaust: Narrative and the Consequences of Interpretation*. Bloomington: Indiana University Press, 1988.

Zuckerman, Lord Solly. "The New Nuclear Menace." *The New York Review of Books* 40, no. 12 (June 24, 1993): 14–19.

Index

Italicized numbers denote pages containing illustrations

ABCC. *See* Atomic Bomb Casualty Commission
Abe Kōbō, 21, 429 n. 10
Abe Tomoji, 19–20, 103, 119
Adachi Yukizō, 221
Adorno, Theodor W., 58, 64, 65, 69, 74, 75, 80, 159, 160, 208, 425 n. 39
Agawa Hiroyuki, 415 n. 7; on Ōta Yōko, 216. Works: "August Sixth" (Hachigatsu muika), 76; *The Devil's Heritage* (Ma no isan), 289
Agee, James, 65, 413 n. 42
Akiya Yutaka: "Winter, the Assigned Theme" (Fuyu no shudai), 59
Alperovitz, Gar, 7, 406 n. 26
Althusser, Louis: on ideology, 261–63, 291, 292, 296, 432 n. 2. *See also* ideology
Alvarez, A., 255
America: atomic-bomb literature in, 13, 48, 52–56, 65, 264, 267, 357, 412 n. 18, 413 n. 42, 415 n. 7, 436 n. 19; in atomic-bomb literature, xii, 147, 177–78, 235, 267, 364–68, 372–89; Japanese view of, 90–91, 235, 369–

72, 373–91. *See also* atomic-bomb literature; Iida Momo; Oda Makoto
Amis, Martin, 2
Anders, Günter, 4, 17
Aono Suekichi, 99, 105
aporia, 28, 356, 391; Hiroshima and Nagasaki as, 67, 72, 361. *See also* nuclear criticism
Arendt, Hannah, 22, 367
Aristotle, 33, 61, 62, 161
Arisue Seizō, 84
Ashes of Death (Shi no hai shishū), 156
Atomic Bomb Casualty Commission (ABCC): and Ōe Kenzaburō, 243; and Shōda Shinoe, 195–96
atomic bombings: decision in favor of, 7, 406 n. 26; effects of, 48, 89; knowledge, as a new form of, 69–70, 73, 204; meaning of, 3, 15, 46, 268, 273, 296, 397–98, 400–401, 407 n. 40; responsibility for, 94, 177–78, 357, 363–68, 384–86, 406 n. 26; as a theme for literature, 39–40, 86–88, 92–120, 127, 200. *See also* atomic-

atomic bombings (*continued*)
bomb literature; Hiroshima; Hiroshima and Nagasaki; Nagasaki
atomic-bomb literature: America within, xii, 147, 177–78, 235, 255, 267, 364–68, 372–89; American (*see* America: atomic-bomb literature in); American view of, xii, 91–92; anger in, 159, 365–68; authors (*see individual entries*); and avant-garde representation, 61–62, 66, 365; and the bundan, 85, 93–94, 302–3; and the canon, 65, 86–88, 91–93, 263, 271, 274, 302, 357, 415 n. 9; censorship of, 90, 93, 97, 192, 310, 412 n. 18, 416 n. 25; as comedy, 61–62; contradiction in, 37–39, 43, 64, 69, 72, 79–81, 84, 91, 92, 159–60, 166, 171–72, 204–5, 312, 317, 318; debates over, 92–120; definition of, 3, 19; and documentary, 51–56, 99, 131–53, 205, 209–10, 217, 264, 274, 279–84, 308, 422 n. 38, 428 n. 2; difference between male and female writers of, 307, 308, 323–30, 334, 336, 347–49; difference from other thematic genres in, 25, 41–42, 96–120; and drama, 60–64, 309, 312, 413 n. 13; and fact, xv, 34–35, 51–52, 56, 69, 99, 136–38, 150, 163, 205, 282; and fiction, 40, 41, 64–69, 261–99; genre, choice of, 29, 40–41, 43, 45–81, 155–57, 167, 230–31, 307–8, 322, 429 n. 6; humor in, 311, 321; and Japanese tradition, 46–47, 96, 156–61, 176, 187, 202, 265–70, 273–74, 410 n. 21; in Nagasaki, 58, 301–49; origin of, 83–84, 134; and poetry, 56–60, 149, 155–97, 303, 307; and postwar literature, 89–103; and race, 53, 106, 184, 307, 308, 339; and the reader, 27, 42, 70–71, 152–53, 166, 168, 204, 205–7, 211–13, 218, 222–26, 322, 364, 433 n. 30; and realism, 49, 64, 66, 67–68,

73, 286, 361; and science, 11, 16, 311–12; and science fiction, 67–68, 357; and shishōsetsu, 68–69, 76, 98, 221–22; testimonial, 49–51, 155, 200, 210–14, 217, 282–83, 284, 302, 307–8; as tragedy, 61, 62–64. *See also* hibakusha; ideology; language; memory; nuclear literature
Atomic-bomb Literature in Japan (Nihon no gembaku bungaku), publication of, 357
Atomic-bomb Testimonies (Gembaku taikenki), 137
atrocity, 4–5, 72, 91, 98, 152, 313, 315, 366, 399, 400, 415 n. 7; definition of, 5–9, 288–89; and representation, 74–81, 137. *See also* atomic bombings; Holocaust
Auerbach, Erich, 48, 251–52, 314
Auschwitz. *See* Holocaust
Ayukawa Nobuo, 113, 117

Ba Jin: at 47th International P.E.N. Congress, 442 n. 18
Balzac, Honoré de, 388
Barthes, Roland, 31, 32, 42
Baudrillard, Jean, 429 n. 2
Bauman, Zygmunt, 9, 407 n. 36
Beckett, Samuel, 69
Bellow, Saul, 39
Benjamin, Walter, 18, 22, 40
Bester, John: on Ibuse Masuji, 296
Betsuyakua Minoru: *The Elephant* (Zō), 63–64
Bettelheim, Bruno, 33
Bikini atoll, hydrogen bomb test on, 3, 225
Blanchot, Maurice, 32, 234, 361
Bloom, Harold, 32
bomb victims. *See* hibakusha
Booth, Wayne, 32, 206, 207, 224
Borowski, Tadeusz, 40
Brecht, Bertolt, 4, 328
Brohl, Hans-Peter, 111–12
Brooks, Cleanth, 159

Buddhism, 288; in art, 30, 410 n. 21; in
  Black Rain, 288; as a source of metaphors, 50, 194. *See also* Maruki, Iri
  and Toshi; Shōda Shinoe
Burke, Kenneth, 43

Caldicott, Helen, 351, 439 n. 1
Camus, Albert, 27, 62, 231, 254, 257,
  430 n. 16
Canetti, Elias, 12
Celan, Paul, 159
Chernobyl, nuclear accident at, 3, 351
Christianity, 54, 348, 436 nn. 16 and 19,
  438 n. 38; and Hara Tamiki, 129–30;
  in Nagasaki, 301, 304–6, 309–15,
  325, 328, 347; prejudice in Japan
  against, 305–6; and Tōge Sankichi,
  173, 176
Chūgoku shimbun, debates on atomic-
  bomb literature in, 96–106, 107
Churchill, Winston, 348; on nuclear
  weapons, 10–11
Committee for the Compilation of Mate-
  rials on Damage Caused by the
  Atomic Bombs in Hiroshima and Na-
  gasaki: *Hiroshima and Nagasaki: The
  Physical, Medical, and Social Effects of the
  Atomic Bombings* (Hiroshima-shi
  Nagasaki-shi no gembaku saigai) 48,
  403 n. 3
Cousins, Norman, x; on Nagai Takashi,
  310–11
Culler, Jonathan, xiv

de Man, Paul, 355, 360
Derrida, Jacques, 4, 440 n. 8, 442 n. 25;
  on Hiroshima and Nagasaki, 353–54,
  356; and nuclear criticism, 353–57,
  358, 361–62, 393
Des Pres, Terrence, 35, 49, 64, 186
Doi Sadako, 49, 155–56
Dostoyevsky, F. M., 116, 388
Duras, Marguerite, 365

Eagleton, Terry, 270, 277
Eberhart, Richard: "Aesthetics after
  War," 167
Eguchi Kiyoshi, 97
Einstein, Albert, 2, 4, 364
Eliot, T. S., 170, 425 n. 37
Endo Shūsaku, 415 n. 7
Engels, Friedrich, 115
Epstein, Leslie, 96
Esashi Akiko: on Ōta Yōko, 93, 201,
  214, 428 n. 35
Etō Jun: on atomic-bomb literature, 267;
  on 47th International P.E.N. Con-
  gress, 359; on Ibuse Masuji, 266–68,
  272–73, 277–78, 288, 297–98, 299,
  417 n. 26, 433 n. 23; on Occupation
  censorship, 90; on the Writers' Ap-
  peal, 113, 116, 117
existentialism, 66. *See also* Camus, Al-
  bert; Ōe Kenzaburō; Sartre, Jean-
  Paul
Ezrahi, Sidra DeKoven, 40–41, 426 n.
  75

Farrell, Thomas F., 6
Faulkner, William, 16
47th International P.E.N. Congress,
  359–60, 442 n. 18
Foucault, Michel, 10, 31
Fowler, Alistair, 88
Frank, Anne, 4, 268
Freud, Sigmund, 195
Frye, Northrop, 72
Fukagawa Munetoshi, 103, 156
Fukuda Sumako: *I Am Still Alive* (Ware
  nao ikite ari), 308
Fukunaga Takehiko: *The Island of Death*
  (Shi no shima), 31–32, 33, 36, 66–
  67, 438 n. 38
Fumizawa Takaichi, 27, 428 n.2
Fussell, Paul, 30, 71–72

Geyer, Michael, xiii, 74, 397
Goodman, David G., 62, 413 n. 33

Gotō Minako, 29, *123*, 330–37, 347–49;
and biological survival, 334, 336–37,
347–49; Hayashi Kyōko, compared
with, 336, 337. Works: "The Town
Where It Rains Coal Dust" (Tanjin
no furu machi), 336; *Tug of Time* (Toki
o hiku), 330–37, 348–49; "The
Weight of Three Spikes" (Sambon
no kugi no omosa), 336
Groves, Leslie R., 7, 390

Hachiya Michihiko: *Hiroshima Diary* (Hiroshima nikki), 27, 52, 423 n. 46
Hamai Shinzō, 431 n. 24
Hanada Kiyoteru, 74
Haniya Yutaka: on Hayashi Kyōko, 322
Hara Mieko, 75
Hara Tamiki, 21, 29, 49, 59, *122*, 125–
53, 189, 268, 315, 365, 392, 397,
398–401; before the atomic bombing, 126–34, 167, 311; and Chō
Kōta, 127, 135; death, obsession
with, 131–32; death of, 125–26, 216;
and documentary, 126, 131–53; and
Hara [Nagai] Sadae, 132–33, 140,
144, 146, 151, 422 n. 21; and Hara
Tsuru, 126–27, 129–30; Ibuse Masuji, compared with, 262, 265, 269,
270, 271, 298, 299; Ōta Yōko, compared with, 145; and Poe, Edgar Allan 143–44, 423 n. 47; poetry of, 59,
149, 160, 167–72; reputation of, 126-
28, 432n. 11; Tōge Sankichi, compared with, 183; and Yamamoto Kenkichi, 127. Works: "Atomic-bomb
Landscapes" (Gembaku shōkei),
167–72; "The Bells of Nagasaki" (Nagasaki no kane), 136; "A Break in the
Clouds" (Kumo no sakeme), 420 n.
7; "On the Brink of a Beautiful
Death" (Utsukushiki shi no kishi ni),
132–33, 140, 145; "Death, Love and
Loneliness" (Shi to ai to kodoku),
133, 135–36; "Dreams and Life"

(Yume to jinsei), 151; "Flames"
(Honoo), 129–31, 145, 420 n. 7;
"Fog" (Kiri), 126; "Forever Verdant"
(Eien no midori), 169; "From the Ruins" (Haikyo kara), 135, 422 n. 34,
423 n. 42; "*Give Me* Water" (Mizu o
kudasai), 170–71; "The Land of My
Heart's Desire" (Shingan no kuni),
133; "Nightmare" (Akumu), 149;
"Notes on the Atomic Destruction"
(Gembaku saiji no nōto), 134–35,
141; "Prelude to Annihilation" (Hametsu no jokyoku), 135, 144, 422 n.
34; "Procession" (Gyōretsu), 131–32,
133, 141, 145; *Summer Flowers* (Natsu
no hana), 49, 85, 135, 284–85, 423
n. 42; "Summer Flowers," 90, 135–
53, 167, 267, 286, 307, 392, 423 n.
42, 440 n. 7; "*This Is A Human Being*"
(Kore ga ningen na no desu),
168–69; "A Troubled Heart" (Mune
no uzuki), 152; "Two Deaths" (Futatsu no shi), 152. *See also* Christianity
Hartman, Geoffrey, 170
Hasegawa Ken, xiv
Hashimoto Eiichi, 436 n. 16
Hashimoto Kunie, 25–26
Hayashi Kyōko, 15, 38, *123*, 315–30,
347–49, 445 n. 3; and the Akutagawa Prize, 319, 322; before the
atomic bombing, 315–16; and biological survival, 324–30, 347–49, 419 n.
68; cynicism of, 326–27; and the debates on atomic-bomb literature,
107–11, 114, 116, 327; Gotō Minako, compared with, 336; on humanism, 419 n. 68; as a kataribe,
108, 318–19, 437 n. 29; Nagai Takashi, compared with, 321, 325–26,
328; nihilism in, 326; and nuclear literature, 362–63, 384; and Shanghai,
316, 322, 436 n. 25. Works: As If Not
(Naki ga gotoki), 317–19, 321, 324,

325, 348, 362, 363, 384; *Cut Glass, Blown Glass* (Giyaman-bīdoro), 107–8, 322–25, 327; "Cut Glass, Blown Glass," 323; "Dictionaries" (Jisho), 438 n. 39; "Document" (Kiroku), 49, 323; "Echo" (Hibiki), 322; "The Empty Can" (Akikan), 323; "Friend" (Tomo yo), 26; "In the Darkness" (Mumyō), 38; "In the Fields" (No ni), 324–25, 328, 384; "Mount Kompira" (Kompirayama), 323; "Safe" (Buji), 108–9; "The Site of Rituals" (Matsuri no ba), 319–22, 326–27; "Two Grave Markers" (Futari no bohyō), 316–17, 327; "Wishing Life as It Should Be" (Shizen o kou), 110–11; "Yellow Sand" (Kōsa), 322; "Young Men" (Seinen-tachi), 322–23, 325

Hayashida, Yasumasa, 303, 306; on Tōge Sankichi, 184

Hegel, G. W. Friedrich, 40, 76, 253, 386

Heidegger, Martin, 160, 234

Hersey, John: *Hiroshima*, 48, 52–56, 264, 267, 412 n. 18

Hersh, Seymour: *My Lai 4*, 371–72

hibakusha: definition of, x–xi; Christian, 305–6, 309–15, 347; numbers of, 3, 306; reaction to atomic-bomb literature among, 165; as writers, 26, 29–39, 88, 89, 110–11, 172, 188, 209, 271–72, 397–98, 444 n. 58; uniqueness of their experience, 25–28, 33, 203–4, 207, 272, 278, 332; women, 66–67, 308, 323–30, 336, 347–49. *See also* Ōe Kenzaburō

Hirai Hiroyuki: on Oda Makoto, 388, 389

Hirakata Ryōzō: *To Speak* (Hanasu koto), 24

Hirakushi Kenjirō, 98

Hiroshima: bomb damage in, 5–6, 122, 134, 438 n. 47; Fiction Study Group (Shōsetsu Benkyō Kai) in, 97; local bundan in, 91, 93, 103–4; Hiroshima Literati Salon (Hiroshima Bunjin Konwakai) in, 104; Hiroshima Literature Society (Hiroshima Bungaku Kai) in, 103–5; Kawabata Yasunari's visit to, 429 n. 9. *See also* Hiroshima and Nagasaki; Nagasaki

Hiroshima and Nagasaki: art and photography of, xix; choice as targets, 86; meaning of, 4, 8–9, 25–27, 40, 46, 74–75. *See also* atomic bombings; Hiroshima; Nagasaki

Hiroshima bungaku (Hiroshima Literature), 94, 417 n. 35

Hirsch, E. D., 31

History: and *Black Rain*, 279–86; interpretation of the bombings and, xii, xiv–xv, 33–34, 42, 64, 111, 206, 216, 271, 273; literary genre and, 41, 47–49, 92; poetry and, 159. *See also* White, Hayden

Hochhuth, Rolf: *The Deputy*, 70

Hoffman, Frederick, 63–64, 65, 235, 242

Holleran, Andrew, 414 n. 74, 444 n. 2

Holocaust, 8, 169; atomic bombings, compared with, 9–19, 406 n. 34, 407 nn. 36 and 37, 408 n. 61, 431 n. 25; literature of, 4, 29, 30, 40–41, 85, 86, 192, 194, 309, 315. *See also* Adorno, Theodor W.; Celan, Paul; Epstein, Leslie; Ezrahi, Sidra DeKoven; Frank, Anne; Hochhuth, Rolf; Kurihara Sadako; Lang, Berel; Lyotard, Jean-François; Rosenfeld, Alvin; Rousset, David; Rubenstein, Richard; Steiner, George; Wiesel, Elie

Homer, 160

Honda Shūgo: on Hara Tamiki, 126

Hongō Shin: *Mother and Children in the Storm* (Arashi no naka no boshi), 228

Hoshino Mitsunori, 116–17, 118, 358–59

Hotta Kiyomi: *The Island* (Shima), 63–64, 309

Hotta Yoshie, 21, 86–87, 415 n. 7; on
Hara Tamiki, 152; *The Judgment* (Shimpan), 372
Howe, Irving: on the political novel,
276, 277, 278, 298–99
humanism, 68, 83, 103, 283, 312;
atomic bombings and, 17–18, 20,
114–15. *See also* Hayashi Kyōko; Ōe
Kenzaburō; Sartre, Jean-Paul

Ibuse Masuji, 21, 112, 230, 261–99,
398; ceremony in, 288–92; criticism
of, 271–72, 278, 283; death of, 298,
435 n. 58; Hara Tamiki, compared
with, 262, 265, 269, 270, 271, 298,
299; and heijōshin, 268, 272–73,
296, 298; historical fiction of, 271;
ideology in, 266–70, 271, 277–78,
283, 284, 296–99; nature in, 292–97;
Ōta Yōko, compared with, 262, 265,
269, 270, 271, 279, 283–84, 298,
299; reputation of, 263, 264–67,
270–72, 279, 298, 337, 433 n. 17,
435 n. 58; ritual in, 288–92; Tōge
Sankichi, compared with, 270; and
the Vietnam War, 274. Works: *Black
Rain* (Kuroi ame), 21, 91–92, 165,
261–99, 432 n. 11, 434 nn. 46 and
50; "The Iris" (Kakitsubata), 279;
"The Mining Town Clinic" (Tankōjitai byōin), 271; *A Record of Tea Parties
at Tomonotsu* (Tomonotsu chakaiki),
279; *Waves* (Sazanami gunki), 279;
"A Young Girl's Wartime Diary" (Aru
shōjo no senji nikki), 279
ideology, 46, 67, 88, 115–16; definition
of, 433 n. 30; and fiction, 276–78; in
Japan, 129, 266–70; of Naturalism,
128–29; of science, 311–12; in testimony, 283–86. *See also* Althusser,
Louis; Eagleton, Terry; Howe, Irving;
Ibuse Masuji; Jameson, Fredric; Oda
Makoto; Tōge Sankichi; Williams,
Raymond
Iida Momo: *An American Hero* (Amerika

no eiyū), 2, 21, 26, 83, 304, 367,
373, 443 n. 43
imagination, 31, 60–61, 171–72, 386;
drama and, 60–61; history and,
33–34; interpretation and, 150; litera-
ture and, xv, 35–38, 77, 99, 137–39,
230; in Oda Makoto, 392. *See also* Ōe
Kenzaburō
Imamura Shōhei: *Black Rain* (Kuroi ame),
260, 264, 435 n. 59
Inokuchi Motosaburō, 12, 73
Inoue Mitsuharu, 21, 302, 445 n. 3; on
Hayashi Kyōko, 322. Works: "The
House of Hands" (Te no ie), 305;
People of the Land (Chi no mure), 308,
435 n. 14
International P.E.N. Congress, 47th,
359–60, 442 n. 18
irony, 52, 69, 70–72, 152, 168–69, 171
Ishida Kōji: "Memory of a Cloud"
(Kumo no kioku), 10
Ishida Masako: *Masako Will Not Succumb:
An Account of the Nagasaki Atomic Bomb*
(Masako taorezu: Nagasaki genshi ba-
kudan ki), 307–8
Ishihara Kichirō, 10
Itō Narihiko, 117, 357
Itō Sei, 132
Iwamoto Hakuzō, 49
Iwasaki Seiichirō, 95–96, 98, 101–2

Jameson, Fredric, 76, 276–77, 278, 292,
359, 390
Japanese Atomic-bomb Poetry (Nihon gem-
baku shishū), 156
Jarrell, Randall, 17
Jaspers, Karl, 2
Johnston, William: on Nagai Takashi,
312
Joyce, James, 354

Kafka, Franz, 208, 354, 367
Kaga Otohiko, 66
Kahler, Erich, 12

Kaikō Takeshi, 428 n. 2; on Hara Ta-
miki, 139–40
Kamata Sadao, 10; on Oda Makoto,
388, 389; *Nagasaki Testimonies* (Naga-
saki no shōgen), 51
Kamezawa Miyuki: "Hiroshima Pilgrim-
age" (Hiroshima junrei), 407 n. 37
Kaminsky, Marc: *The Road From Hiro-
shima*, 264
Kanaya Masako, 49
Kaneko Hiroshi: on Ibuse Masuji, 272
Kaplan, Chaim A.: *Scroll of Agony: The
Warsaw Diary of Chaim A. Kaplan*, 151,
152–53, 286
Kanai Toshihiro, 255
Karatani Kōjin, 109–10, 115–16
Katō Shūichi, 89
Katsumoto Seiichirō, 127
Kaufmann, Walter, 232
Kawakami Sōkun: "The Survivors" (Sei-
zonsha), 6, 77
Kawamura Jirō, 109–10
Keene, Donald, 89, 94, 128, 421 n. 15
Kermode, Frank, 8, 34, 36, 37–38, 66,
72–73
Khrushchev, Nikita, 357
Kijima Katsumi, 27
Kikuchi Kan, 94
Kikuta Hitoshi, 117
Kinoshita Junji, 113
Kitayama Futaba, 50, 51, 71
Kobayashi Hideo, 108
Kokai Eiji: on Hara Tamiki, 126, 168
Kokubo Hitoshi, 20, 39, 96, 100–101,
102, 105; "The Mark of Summer"
(Natsu no kokuin), 404 n. 8
Konaka Yōtarō, 35–36
Konishi Jin'ichi, 274
Korea, 3, 178, 216; hibakusha from, 44,
235; use of nuclear weapons in, 125,
181, 219
Kozaki Kan: *The Holy Statues* (Seizō), 300
Krieger, Murray, xii
Kuboyama Aikichi, 3
Kundera, Milan, 21

Kuno Osamu: on Kurihara Sadako, 57
Kurihara Sadako, xv, 10, 19, 21, 35, 42–
43, 68, 85, 89, 98, 119, 169, 203,
367, 404 n. 14, 418 n. 53, 426 n. 67,
429 n. 10, 442 n. 16, 445 n. 3; and
Chūgoku bunka (Chūgoku Culture),
91, 156, 416 n. 25; and the debates
on atomic-bomb literature, 103–6;
on Hara Tamiki, 133; and the Holocaust, 10, 85, 103–5; on Nagai Takashi, 315; on Occupation censorship, 90; on Ōe Kenzaburō, 257; Ōe
Kenzaburō, compared with, 432 n.
32; poetry of, 161–63; on Shōda Shinoe, 189, 197; on Tōge
Sankichi, 185–86. Works: *Black Eggs*
(Kuroi tamago), 162; "Let Us Be
Midwives!" (Umashimen ka na),
162–63, 347, 424 n. 22; *When One
Says Hiroshima* (Hiroshima o iu
toki), 57
Kurihara Tadaichi, 91, 156, 416 n. 25
Kurita Tōhei: "A Bronze-colored Dark"
(Seidōshoku no yami), 26, 30
Kuroko Kazuo, xiii–xiv, 14, 18, 35, 72,
86–87, 116–17, 361, 392, 404 n. 11;
on Hara Tamiki, 138; on Hayashi
Kyōko, 436 n. 25; on Nakazawa
Keiji, 437 n. 29; on Ōta Yōko, 221
Kurosawa Akira: *Record of a Living Being*
(Ikimono no kiroku), 398
Kuwabara Takeo, 158
Kyōyū (Hometown Friend), 91, 95, 416
n. 25, 417 n. 35

Lang, Berel, xiii, 9–10, 28, 57, 61, 79,
208, 262
Langer, Lawrence, 12, 28
language: atomic bombings and, x, xiv,
84, 438 n. 39; in poetry, 158, 160–
61, 168–72, 183; post-Hiroshima literature and, 27–35, 41, 59–60, 73–
74, 137–38, 146–47, 149, 200,
202–4, 398; as rhetoric, 32, 33, 47–
50, 54, 56–57, 84, 130–31, 138–39.

language (*continued*)
  See also aporia; atomic-bomb litera-
  ture; atrocity; irony; metaphor; me-
  tonymy; synecdoche
Leahy, William D., 7
Lentricchia, Frank, 359
Levi, Primo, 27
Lévi-Strauss, Claude, 111
Lewis, C. Day, 158
Lifton, Robert Jay, 9, 16, 38, 195, 288,
  366, 406 n. 34, 423 n. 46; on Ibuse
  Masuji, 264; and Ōta Yōko, 223–24,
  225; on Tōge Sankichi, 183, 185,
  187
Lyotard, Jean-François, 75, 414 n. 65

MacDonald, Dwight, 55
Macherey, Pierre, 160, 281
Maeda Masahiro, 32
Maekawa Noritaka, 95, 416 n. 25
Mailer, Norman, 128, 231
Mallarmé, Stephané, 354
Mandelstam, Nadezhda, 17
Maruki, Iri and Toshi: *Death of the Ameri-
  can Prisoners of War* (Beihei furyo no
  shi), 350; *Water* (Mizu), 328, 329
Maruya Saiichi: on Iida Momo, 443 n.
  43
Marx, Karl, 76, 115, 262, 281, 386
Masuoka Toshikazu, 117–18, 416 n. 25,
  425 n. 43; on Hara Tamiki, 136; on
  Tōge Sankichi, 185
Matsuhara Takahisa, 103
Matsumoto Hiroshi, 105, 367, 428 n. 2;
  on Hotta Yoshie, 372
Matsumoto Ken'ichi, 117
McCarthy, Mary, 27, 55
memory, 1, 21, 42, 47, 50, 57, 74, 80,
  110, 137, 171, 187, 282. *See also*
  atomic-bomb literature: testimonial
Merton, Thomas: *The Original Child Bomb:
  Points for Meditation to Be Scratched on the
  Walls of a Cave*, 436 n. 19

metaphor, 47, 52, 64, 139, 164–67, 191,
  364, 444 n. 2
metonymy, 51, 52, 61, 137–38, 143,
  164, 191, 284–88, 336
Miller, Brown, 13
Milosz, Czeslaw, 2
Minear, Richard: on Hara Tamiki, 136
Miyamoto Ken: *The Pilot* (Za Pairotto),
  372–73
Miyoshi, Masao, 94
Miyoshi Tatsuji, 41, 157
Mizuta Kuwajirō: on Hara Tamiki and
  Occupation censorship, 90; on Inoue
  Mitsuharu, 435 n. 14; on Shōda
  Shinoe, 192
Modernism, 74–77, 159, 169–70
modernity: atrocity and, 4, 11–13, 20,
  38–39, 69, 74–77, 326, 414 n. 65; in
  Ibuse Masuji, 293; in Japan, 4, 94
Mumford, Lewis, 12
Murakami Haruki, 398, 445 n. 4
Mutsu Katsutoshi, 137

Nagai Takashi, *123*, 330, 347; death of,
  311; Hayashi Kyōko, compared
  with, 321, 325–26, 328; *The Bells of
  Nagasaki* (Nagasaki no kane), 310–
  15, 325–26, 328. *See also* Christianity
Nagaoka Hiroyoshi, 20, 53, 85, 89, 93,
  95, 96; on Hara Tamiki, 133; on Ōta
  Yōko, 214, 216
Nagasaki: bomb damage in, x, 5, *123*,
  303, 306, 438 n. 39; choice as a target, 304, 313; difference from Hiroshima, 108–9, 301–7, 308, 309, 328,
  332, 347; literature in, 58, 301–49;
  Nagasaki Literature Society (Nagasaki Bungaku Kondankai) in, 302;
  and the West, 301, 303–4. *See also*
  Christianity; Gotō Minako; Hayashi
  Kyōko; Inoue Mitsuharu; Nagai Takashi; Sata Ineko
Nagata Hiroshi, 132
Nakagami Kenji: on Hayashi Kyōko,

107–11, 114, 327, 436 n. 25; on the
Writers' Appeal, 114–16

Nakagawa Kunio, 106

Nakahodo, Masanori, 128

Nakajima Kenzō, 41, 356

Nakamura Atsushi: "Hiroshima," 169

Nakano Kōji, 7–8, 112, 114, 117; on
Hayashi Kyōko, 321–22; on Oda Makoto, 392

Nakano Shigeharu, 91

Nakayama Shigeru, 408 n. 61

Nakayama Shirō: "Shadows of Death"
(Shi no kage), 431 n. 22

Nakazawa Keiji: *Barefoot Gen* (Hadashi
no Gen), 398, 437 n. 29

Natsubori Masamoto: "The Woman
from the Hallowed Ground" (Seichi
no onna), 324, 432 n. 30

Naturalism, 98; and Freud, 131; and
Hara Tamiki, 128–33; in Japan, 128–
29, 421 nn. 15 and 16; and Shimazaki Toson's *The Broken Commandment*
(Hakai), 129, 421 n. 16; and Tayama
Katai's *The Quilt* (Futon), 129, 421 n.
16. *See also* Hara Tamiki

Never Forget the Song of Nagasaki (Nagasaki
no uta wa wasureji), 90

Nietzsche, Friedrich, 115, 151, 232,
257, 298

Noma Hiroshi, 19, 302–3, 429 n. 10; on
Ōta Yōko, 210; and total literature,
386–90

Norris, Christopher, 440 n. 8

nuclear criticism: absence of Japanese
participation in, 352–53; and *Bungakuteki tachiba*, 358–59; and deconstruction, 354–56, 361–62, 391, 440 nn. 7
and 8; and *Diacritics*, 352–53, 357,
358, 359, 392, 440 n. 8; in Japan,
357–63, 391, 393–94; in the West,
352–57, 360–62, 367, 374, 375,
393–94, 439 n. 2, 440 n. 7. *See also*
Derrida, Jacques; nuclear literature;
Oda Makoto

nuclear literature: definition of, 3; and
Hayashi Kyōko, 362–63, 384; and
Oda Makoto, 383–84. *See also*
atomic-bomb literature; nuclear criticism; O'Brien, Tim

nuclear war, 2; Derrida on, 354. *See also*
nuclear criticism; nuclear literature

O'Brien, Tim: *The Nuclear Age*, 398, 441
n. 13, 442 n. 25. 445 n. 4

Occupation, Allied, 53, 89–90, 92–93,
96, 97, 177, 178, 192, 271, 310, 416
n. 16

Ochi Michio: "The Life Left Us" (Izō sareta seikatsu), 365

Oda Katsuzō: "Human Ashes" (Ningen
no hai), 285

Odagiri Hideo, 67, 93, 102, 117, 302,
442 n. 16; on Hara Tamiki, 153

Oda Makoto, 13, 21, 117, 368–94, 429
n. 10; and America, 369–72, 373–91;
and Beheiren, 370–71, 389; and freedom, 389–91; on Hara Tamiki, 398–
401; and ideology, 389; on Iida
Momo, 443 n. 43; and totality, 374,
386–92, 399; and U.S.-Japan Security Treaty, 369; and the Vietnam
War, 370–72, 382, 384, 389. Works:
America (Amerika), 369; "The Ethics
of Peace," 375, 384; *Hiroshima*, 373–
84, 386–93, 399–400, 444 nn. 58
and 65; *I'll Give Anything a Look* (Nan
de mo mite yarō), 369; *Notes on the
Day after Tomorrow* (Asatte no shuki),
368; "The Path to a New Total Literature'" (Atarashii "zentai shōsetsu" e
no michi), 388; *Son My* (Son Mi),
371–72, 385; "To Say, 'And Then'"
(Sore kara, no koto), 398–401

Ōe Kenzaburō, 21, 112, 117, 119, 194,
229–58, 266, 279, 357, 362, 364,
403 n. 6, 428 nn. 1 and 2, 431 n. 24,
445 nn. 3 and 4; criticism of, 230,
241, 257, 266, 364, 432 n. 30; and

Ōe Kenzaburō (*continued*)
existentialism, 231–32, 234–58; and
47th International P.E.N. Congress,
359, 442 n. 18; on the Holocaust,
431 n. 25; on Hara Tamiki, 420 n. 2;
on hibakusha writers, 29, 229–30;
and humanism, 230, 247, 252, 254–
58, 432 n. 30; on Ibuse Masuji, 272–
73, 277–78, 288, 433 n. 23; Ibuse
Masuji, compared with, 267, 270,
417 n. 26; on imagination, 37, 230,
410 n. 45; Kurihara Sadako, compared with, 432 n. 32; on the meaning of the bombings, 4, 16, 19, 20;
on Miyamoto Sadao, 243–46, 249,
258; on Murato Yoshiko, 250–51; on
Oda Makoto, 369; reputation of,
229, 337, 428 n. 1, 432 n. 11; and
Sartre, Jean-Paul, 231–32, 429 n. 11;
on Shigetō Fumio, 243, 252–53, 258;
on Shōda Shinoe, 192. Works: "Erasmus in the Nuclear Age" (Kaku-jidai
no Erasumusu), 257; "Hiroshima,
America, Europe" (Hiroshima, Amerika, Yōroppa), 432 n. 30; *Hiroshima
Notes* (Hiroshima nōto), 229–32,
234–58, 266, 267, 271, 364, 430 n.
19; *A Personal Matter* (Kojinteki na
taiken), 229, 231, 430 n. 19, 431 n.
21
Ōhara Miyao, 58–59, 112
Ōhashi Kiichi, 60
Okuno Takeo, 86
Ōoka Makoto, 156–57, 158, 176
Ōoka Shōhei, 415 n. 7; 437 n. 29; on
Hayashi Kyōko, 322
Ortega y Gasset, José, 32, 47, 65,
164–66
Ōta Yōko, 21, 29, 35, 36, 95, 107, 108,
122, 199–226, 268, 279, 308, 357,
365, 392, 398, 424 n. 23, 425 n. 35,
428 n. 35, 439 n. 6, 444 n. 58; and
the atomic-bomb literature debates,
97–103, 109–10; before the atomic
bombing, 200–201; and the bundan,

93–94; death of, 225; on the difficulty of writing, 34, 42, 80, 134,
199–200, 202, 208–9, 213–14, 217,
219–21, 224, 225–26; and Hara Tamiki, 125, 216, 219; Hara Tamiki,
compared with, 145; Ibuse Masuji,
compared with, 262, 265, 269, 270,
271, 283–84, 298, 299; immediate reaction to the bombing, 201–2; on
the inadequacy of language, 160; reputation of, 120, 200–201, 214, 223–
24. Works: "Astray in the world" (Yo
ni mayou), 207; *City of Corpses* (Shikabane no machi), 34, 68, 85, 93, 100,
204, 205, 208–14, 217–19, 222, 223,
224, 225, 286, 311, 314, 320, 392;
Drifting Shores (Ryūri no kishi), 94,
201; *Eighty-four Years Old* (Hachijūyonsai), 225; "Fireflies" (Hotaru), 10,
207, 224–25; *Half-Human* (Han-
ningen), 199–200, 204, 219–23;
"Half-Vagrant" (Han-hōrō), 225; *Human Rags* (Ningen ranru), 204, 205,
208, 214–19, 223, 284; "In the Hills"
(Sanjō), 366; "A Light as if from the
Depths—The Atomic-bomb Air Attack" (Kaitei no yō na hikari—genshi-
bakudan no kūshū ni atte), 201–2;
People and the City of Evening Calm (Yūnagi no machi to hito to), 169, 225,
308; "The Psychology of the Survival" (Ikinokori no shinri), 199, 219;
"The Stance of the Writer" (Sakka no
taido), 203; "The Terror of Literature" (Bungaku no osoroshisa), 205
Ozaki Kazuo, 18–19
Ozaki Shirō, 27–28
Ozick, Cynthia, 8, 406 n. 31

P.E.N. Club, Japanese, 95–96
Plath, Sylvia, 62
Poetry Hiroshima (Kashū Hiroshima), 156
Poirer, Richard, 28
Popper, Karl, 73, 361, 443 n. 26
postmodernism, 64, 75, 406 n. 34

Press Code, 90, 192. *See also* Occupation, Allied
Proust, Marcel, 388

Reagan, Ronald, 351, 354
Realism. *See* atomic-bomb literature: and realism
Remarque, Erich Maria, 366–67
Rimer, Thomas J., 274, on Ibuse Masuji, 269, 270
Robbe-Grillet, Alain: at 47th International P.E.N. Congress, 359–60, 442 n. 18
Rosenfeld, Alvin, 75, 165–66
Rousset, David, 17–18
Rōyama Michio, 371
Rubenstein, Richard, 13–14
Rubin, Jay, 89, 90, 413 n. 49

Sachs, Nellie, 14
Saeki Shōichi: on Ibuse Masuji, 264–65, 266, 284
Said, Edward, xii-xiii, 34–35, 359, 429 n. 6
Saitō Mokichi, 302
Sakamoto Hisashi, 163, 165
Sakurai Mikiyoshi: on Ibuse Masuji, 272
Sartre, Jean-Paul, 4, 16, 241, 245–58, 266, 398; and existentialism, 231–41, 430 n. 16; on Genet, Jean, 237–38, 240, 242, 248, 251; influence on Japanese literature, 429 n. 10; on poetry, 158; on totality, 386, 387–90. *See also* Camus, Albert; existentialism; Ōe Kenzaburō
Sasaki Kiichi, 132; on Hara Tamiki, 139, 440 n. 7
Sasaki Yutaka, 288
Sata Ineko, 21, 39, 337–47, 348, 349; and biological survival, 347–49; early career of, 337–38; and Gotō Minako and Hayashi Kyōko, 347–49; and the Japan Communist Party, 338; and the Japan Proletarian Writers Federation, 338; on Ōta Yōko, 200,

221; Ōta Yōko, compared with, 338; reputation of, 338. Works: "The Colorless Painting" (Iro no nai e), 338–39; "From the Caramel Factory" (Kyarameru kōba kara), 337; "A Series of Visits" (Rekihō), 338; *The Shade of Trees* (Juei), 338–47, 348, 349, 444 n. 2
Satō Hachirō, 70–71
Satoh Makoto. *See* Satō Makoto
Satō Makoto: *Nezumi Kozō: The Rat* (Nezumi Kozō Jirokichi), 32, 61–62
Satomi Ton, 112
Satō Tadao, 90
Sawada Akiko, 213
Sawamura Mitsuhiro, 160
Schell, Jonathan, 351
Schwenger, Peter, 404 n. 15, 439 n. 6
Scully, James, 161–62, 164, 187–88
Second World War, 15, 86, 108; difference from First World War, 10, 366–67. *See also* atomic bombings; Hiroshima; Hiroshima and Nagasaki; Nagasaki
Seidensticker, Edward G.: on Hara Tamiki, Ibuse Masuji and Ōta Yōko, 432 n. 11
Sera Megumi, 49
Shiina Rinzō, 11
Shijō Miyoko, 97–98, 102, 118, 416 n. 25
Shimauchi Hachirō: "A Vow of Peace From the Ruins" (Heiwa no chikai—haikyo ni tachite), 156
Shōda Shinoe, 21, 122, 189–97, 330; before the atomic bombing, 189–90; and Buddhism, 189–90, 191–97; and *chinkon*, 195–96; Hara Tamiki and Tōge Sankichi, compared with, 189, 196–97; death of, 195–96; and Occupation censorship, 192; reputation of, 189, 192; and Sugiura Suiko, 189, 192; and Tokugawa Ieyasu, 196; and Yamazumi Mamoru, 190, 191. Works: "Let Everyone Die" (Minna

Shōda Shinoe (*continued*)
  shineba ii n da), 197; "Oh! The
  Atomic Bomb" (Ā! Genshi bakudan),
  190–91; *Repentance* (Sange), 192–96;
  *A Ringing in the Ears: The Notes of an
  Atomic-bomb Poet* (Miminari—gem-
  baku kajin no shuki), 190, 192, 195
Siebers, Tony, 88, 442 n. 19
Simile, 84, 164, 167, 191
Snow, C.P.: on Ibuse Masuji, 268–69
Solomon, J. Fisher, 440 n. 7, 442 n. 19
Songs of Hiroshima (Hiroshima no shi),
  112
Sontag, Susan, 41
Spivak, Gayatri Chakravorty, 359; on
  Derrida, 355
Steiner, George, 9, 10, 18, 62, 203
Stevens, Wallace, 36–37, 205
Stimson, Henry, 3, 348
Suga, Hidemi, 8; on the Writers' Ap-
  peal, 114–15, 116, 359
Sugimoto Naojirō, 2–3
synecdoche, 32, 151, 164, 169, 287–88,
  296, 364

Taga Kōko: "Ah, Mutsuko!" (Ā, Mut-
  suko!), 157
Takahashi Kazumi: *The Melancholy Faction*
  (Yūutsu no tōha), ix–x, 9, 79–81,
  364–65
Takahashi Shinji, 38–39
Takeda Taijun, 65, 415 n. 7; *Button Num-
  ber One* (Daiichi no botan), 67–68
Takekoshi Yoshio, 41
Takenishi Hiroko, 27, 31. Works: "The
  Rite" (Gishiki), 77–79, 289, 365–66;
  "The Words Hiroshima Makes Us
  Say" (Hiroshima ga iwaseru kotoba),
  73–74
Tanabe Kōichirō, 216
Tanaka Chikao: *The Head of Mary* (Maria
  no kubi), 309, 312
Tanaka Kishirō: "Rage" (Fundo), 159
Tanaka Yasuo, 116
Tanizaki Jun'ichirō, 65. Works: *An Ac-*

count of Brutality (Zangyakuki), 413 n.
  42; *The Makioka Sisters* (Sasameyuki),
  287, 434 n. 50
Tasaka Tomotaka, 90
Tateno Nobuyuki, 96
Teller, Edward, 351
Terada Tōru: on Hara Tamiki, 127
Terao Tomofumi: *A Flash of Light, a Clap of
  Thunder* (Senkō to bakufū), 82
Thatcher, Margaret: on nuclear weap-
  ons, 2
Three Mile Island, accident at, 351
Tōge Sankichi, 122, 134, 172–89, 194,
  398; and the Allied Occupation,
  177–78; before the atomic bombing,
  173–74; and *Chikaku* (Nucleus), 176;
  Christian influence on, 176; and the
  Culture Circle movement, 177;
  death of, 185; Hara Tamiki, com-
  pared with, 183; and the Hiroshima
  Poets Society (Hiroshima Shijin Kyōkai), 176; Ibuse Masuji, compared
  with, 270; and the Japan Communist
  Party, 177, 178, 181; and the Japan
  Steel Hiroshima Incident, 177; Marxist influence on, 173, 181–82, 188;
  and the New Japan Literature Association (Shin Nihon Bungaku Kai),
  177; and the Our Poetry Association
  (Warera no Shi no Kai), 177, 178,
  181; and politics, 176–88; reputation
  of, 173–74, 185–86, 188–89. Works:
  "The Appeal" (Yobikake), 177–78,
  181; "August 6" (Hachigatsu muika),
  178, 181; "August 6, 1950" (1950-
  nen no hachigatsu muika), 179–81;
  "Blindness" (Mōmoku), 181; "Dawn"
  (Asa), 188; "Dying" (Shi), 181; "Eyes"
  (Me), 181–82; *From Beneath the Atomic
  Cloud* (Genshigumo no shita), 156;
  "Give Me Back My Father" (Chichi o
  kaese), 172, 182–83; "Liberation of
  Aesthetics" (Bi no kaihō), 176; "Pic-
  ture Book" (Ehon), 174–75, 182;
  Poems of the Atomic Bomb (Gembaku

shishū), 172–89, 365; "The Road Home from Christmas" (Kurisumasu no kaerimichi), 175–76; "The Scar" (Kizuato), 184–85; "Season of Flames" (Honoo), 181; "The Shadow" (Kage), 186–87; "When Will That Day Come?" (Sono hi wa itsuka), 184
Tokunō Kōichi, 27, 159
Tokyo: as the center of literary production, 85, 89; as a military target, 3, 5–6, 7, 85
total literature. *See* Jameson, Fredric; Noma Hiroshi; Oda Makoto; Sartre, Jean-Paul; totality
Totality, 362. *See also* Oda Makoto
Toyoda Seishi: on Ibuse Masuji, 272
Toyoshima Yoshio, 6, 11, 20, 34, 51
Trollope, Anthony, 65
Truman, Harry, 3, 11, 181, 364, 405 n. 23
Tsukasa Osamu: *Remains* (Nokosareta katachi), 198
Tsukuda Jitsuo: "Armbands of Red and Black" (Aka to kuro no moshō), 438 n. 48
Tsurumi Shunsuke: on Iida Momo, 373

Uchimura Yoshiko, 16
Unno Jūza, 42
U.S.-Japan Security Treaty, 92, 115, 417 n. 27. *See also* Oda Makoto

Vietnam War. *See* Ibuse Masuji; Oda Makoto
Vonnegut, Kurt: at 47th International P.E.N. Congress, 442 n. 18; *Slaughterhouse Five*, 30

Warera no shi (Our Poetry), 181
White, Hayden, 145, 150, 284; on representing atrocity, 75–76
Wiesel, Elie, 10, 37, 38, 83–84, 204, 256–57
Williams, Raymond, 296–97
Wittgenstein, Ludwig, 440 n. 8
Writers' Appeal against the Dangers of Nuclear War (Kaku-sensō no kiken o uttaeru bungakusha no seimei), 112–18, 358

Yaguchi Hisayo, 38
Yamada Kan, 58–59, 302
Yamada Kazuko: "Wailing" (Dōkoku), 163–64
Yamamoto Kenkichi, 89, 95, 417 n. 35; on Ibuse Masuji, 265, 268, 269, 297–98, 299
Yamamoto Yasuo, 38
Yamashiro Tomoe, 412 n. 13; *Surviving the Bomb: Atomic-bomb Victim Memoirs* (Gembaku ni ikite—gembaku higaisha no shuki), 50–51
Yamashita Soboku: *The Blast* (Sakuretsu), 154
Yasue Ryōsuke, 240
Yoneda Eisaku: and the Hiroshima Poets Society (Hiroshima Shijin Kyōkai), 176; *River, Always Be Beautiful* (Kawa yo, towa ni utsukushiku), 156
Yoshimoto Takaaki: on Japanese poetry, 157; on the Writers' Appeal, 115–18
Yoshimoto Yoshio, 105–6

Zuckerman, Lord Solly, 405 n. 6